THE POPULATION HISTORY OF GERMAN JEWRY

——— 1815–1939 ———

Steven Mark Lowenstein

THE POPULATION HISTORY OF GERMAN JEWRY

—— 1815–1939 ——

Based on the Collections
and Preliminary Research
of Prof. Usiel Oscar Schmelz

Steven Mark Lowenstein

Edited and Introduced by David N. Myers
and Michael Berenbaum
With a Foreword by Sergio DellaPergola

Library of Congress Cataloging-in-Publication Data

Names: Lowenstein, Steven M., 1945- author. | Myers, David N., editor. | Berenbaum, Michael, 1945- editor. | Della Pergola, Sergio, 1942- writer of foreword. **Title:** The population history of German Jewry 1815-1939 : based on the collections and preliminary research of Prof. Usiel Oscar Schmelz / Steven Mark Lowenstein ; edited and introduced by David N. Myers and Michael Berenbaum ; with a foreword by Sergio DellaPergola.
Description: Boston : Academic Studies Press, 2023. | Includes bibliographical references.
Identifiers: LCCN 2022054373 (print) | LCCN 2022054374 (ebook) | ISBN 9798887191089 (hardback) | ISBN 9798887191096 (adobe pdf) | ISBN 9798887191102 (epub)
Subjects: LCSH: Jews--Germany--1800-1933. | Jews--Statistics.
Classification: LCC DS134.25 .L695 2023 (print) | LCC DS134.25 (ebook) | DDC 943/.004924009034--dc23/eng/20221115
LC record available at https://lccn.loc.gov/2022054373
LC ebook record available at https://lccn.loc.gov/2022054374

Copyright © 2023 Academic Studies Press
All rights reserved.

Book design by Lapiz Digital Services
Cover design by Ivan Grave

Published by Academic Studies Press and Leo Baeck Institute Jerusalem in 2023, Paperback 2025.
ISBN 9798897830961 (paperback)

Academic Studies Press
1577 Beacon street
Brookline, MA 02446, USA

Leo Baeck Institute Jerusalem
33 Bustenai Street
Jerusalem 9104201 P.O.B 4242, Israel

Contents

Foreword *Sergio DellaPergola, The Hebrew University of Jerusalem*   vii
Preface 1. The Life and Work of Steven M. Lowenstein *z"l* (1945–2020):
    "From Washington Heights to Skid Row—a Life of Learning and Doing"
    David N. Myers, UCLA   xi
Preface 2. Steven Lowenstein's *Demographic History*
    Michael Berenbaum, American Jewish University   xviii
Acknowledgments   xxiv
Editors' Note   xxv

Introduction   1

CHRONOLOGICAL SECTION   5
1. From the Fall of Napoleon to the Unification of Germany
   (1815–1871)   7
2. German Jewish Population Changes in Imperial Germany
   (1871–1918)   40
3. From the "Demographic Crisis" of the 1920s to the Flight to
   Escape after 1933   75

TOPICAL SECTION   97
4. Natural Growth and Changes in the German Jewish Family   99
5. Changing Age Structure   182
6. Conversion and Intermarriage   214
7. Migration—Overall Trends and Internal Migration   241
8. Immigration and Emigration   333
9. From Countryside to City: Urbanization and the Survival
   of Small-Town Jewish Communities   390
10. Jewish Residential Concentration in German Cities   450

REGIONAL SECTION	519
11. The Eastern Provinces	521
12. Central and Northwestern Germany—from Sparse Jewish Density to an Urban and Immigrant Center	552
13. Western Germany	584
14. Southern Germany	627
Conclusions	675
Bibliography	683
Geographic names in German and English (Alphabetized in German)	693
A Note on Discrepancies	695
Maps	697

Foreword

Sergio DellaPergola
The Hebrew University of Jerusalem[1]

The joy at the appearance of Steven Lowenstein's landmark study of the demography of Jews in Germany is tempered by sadness at the circumstances under which it will be published. Sadly, Professor Lowenstein did not live long enough to see the final results of his more than fifteen years of labor and scholarship; he prematurely succumbed to pancreatic cancer in 2020 when he was attending to the last details of the present volume. But the events that preceded his achievement were also sad. In fact, the involvement of Steven Lowenstein with this project began in 2003 when the then Chairman of the Jerusalem branch of the Leo Baeck Institute, Professor Robert Liberles, invited him to revive and complete the huge work of documentation that had been undertaken for decades by Prof. Usiel Oscar Schmelz at the Institute of Contemporary Jewry of the Hebrew University of Jerusalem but had not been completed due to Schmelz's death in 1995. In a sense, the present volume is twice posthumous.

Prof. Oscar Schmelz (Usiel was his adopted first name in Israel) was born in Vienna in 1918 and emigrated to Palestine in 1939. He started working at the

---

[1] Chair emeritus, The Avraham Harman Institute of Contemporary Jewry, The Hebrew University of Jerusalem, and former director of its Division of Jewish Demography and Statistics.

British Mandate's Office of Statistics, and from the time of the founding of the Israel Central Bureau of Statistics (CBS), became the head of its Division of Social Statistics and one of its leading demographers. For many years he was the closest collaborator of Professor Roberto Bachi, dean of the demographic profession in Israel, professor at the Hebrew University, founder and first director of the CBS, and cofounder of the Institute of Contemporary Jewry. With the establishment of the Division of Jewish Demography and Statistics at the Institute, Schmelz became its director and remained in the post until his formal retirement in 1986. Bachi and Schmelz envisaged the Division as the heir of the Bureau für Statistik der Juden established in Berlin in 1904 and directed by Arthur Ruppin and Jacob Segall. During his tenure at the Division and in the following years, Schmelz developed a very extensive research program on Jewish demography, which unfolded in different directions. Among them were world Jewish population estimates, the demography of the state of Israel, the urban evolution of Jerusalem, population in Ottoman Palestine, and Moses Montefiore's censuses. Schmelz was a European intellectual with an old Hapsburg style, possessed of wide cultural horizons and meticulous in his attention to the collection of detailed sources for his research. He edited a comprehensive bibliography of works on Jewish demography and statistics and also organized the physical collection and storage in Jerusalem of copies of all relevant sources of quantitative documentation on world Jewish populations.[2]

In this context, Prof. Schmelz, whose mother tongue was German, developed a particular interest in the demographic statistics of Jews in the German lands. He was able to compile a very large body of information, including a collection of original publications, copies of all original censuses, vital and social statistics, national and regional, as well as secondary sources. These documents covered decades and, sometimes, hundreds of years that captured in the most comprehensive way the demography of Jews in Germany. This documentation was intended to serve him for an ambitious project to reconstruct the demographic history of Jews in Germany. He envisaged several volumes on regional demographics and one volume of synthesis. A preliminary essay outlining the broader work to be accomplished appeared in 1982.[3] The plan was hugely ambitious, and the amount of documentation massive. During

---

2   For a complete bibliography of Schmelz's works see Judith Even, "Bibliography, Uziel O. Schmelz, 1918–1995," *Papers in Jewish Demography 1993: In Memory of U. O. Schmelz*, ed. S. DellaPergola and J. Even (Jerusalem: The Avraham Harman Institute of Contemporary Jewry, The Hebrew University of Jerusalem, 1993), 17–31.

3   U. O. Schmelz, "Die demographische Entwicklung der Juden in Deutschland von der Mitte des 19. Jahrhunderts bis 1933, *Zeitschrift für Bevölkerungswissenschaft*, 8, no. 1 (1982):, 31–72.

the 1990s Schmelz began perceiving that perhaps there would not be enough time to bring his project to full fruition, and he decided to focus on a single book devoted to the districts of Hesse, to be published under the aegis of the Leo Baeck Institute.[4] He wrote an extensive volume on the topic and followed its production until the last stages, but unfortunately he was not able to see the final product which appeared in 1996, shortly after his death from heart failure in September 1995. The volume on the Jews of Hesse remains an exemplary monograph—indeed, a prototype of what might have become a vast library of in-depth studies about one of the most interesting, influential, and central Jewish communities in Europe and globally in the modern era.

After the publication of the Hesse volume, a number of colleagues in the social sciences, modern Jewish history, and Judaic studies felt that Prof. Schmelz's legacy should not be left uncompleted—even if his grand project was not realized exactly as he had conceived it. The preferred way was to find a scholar who would be able to bring new life to the sources collected at the Hebrew University and synthesize them in a new volume. The challenge was finding a scholar who would be able to carry on his shoulders Schmelz's vast, multidisciplinary scholarship. What was needed was full command of the history of German Jews, competence in quantitative sources, and an ability to bring together an enormous volume of data. Above all, what was needed was a scholar of real stature, accomplishment, and motivation, who was also endowed with one precious resource—time.

The meeting of Steven Lowenstein, the directors of the Leo Baeck Institute in Jerusalem, and representatives of the Division of Jewish Demography and Statistics at Hebrew University—Professor Uzi Rebhun and myself—was a most fortunate one. Lowenstein agreed to take charge of the project and started his long journey through the many sources with patience. But he also brought his own independent approach as one of the leading social historians of German Jewry. The analytical choices in the present volume are Lowenstein's, not those of his predecessor. He deserves full credit for developing the structure of this volume and then filling its various parts with his own findings. The result of Steven Lowenstein's study is a remarkable piece of detailed analysis and, at the same time, a unique and brilliant synthesis of the large mass of documents he had at his disposal.

We owe a debt of gratitude to Prof. Lowenstein for bequeathing us with what will remain the definitive study of the demographic history of Jews in Germany.

---

4   Usiel Oscar Schmelz, *Die Jüdische Bevölkerung Hessens von der Mitte des 19. Jahrhunderts bis 1933* (Tübingen: Mohr Siebeck, 1996).

German Jews were among those communities whose populations anticipated later demographic transitions. Their history reveals the multiple avenues of social and geographical mobility, innovation, and assimilation, all of which contributed to the remarkable intellectual creativity of the community.

We also owe a debt of gratitude to all those who invested time and skill to bring this complex project to conclusion. At the Leo Baeck Institute in Jerusalem, the persons who were involved included Professor Robert Liberles, Shlomo Meir, Dr. Anja Siegemund, and the current director Dr. Irene Aue-Ben-David, along with Professor Guy Miron who was the head of the publications committee, Naftali M. Greenwood who did the language editing, and Liad Levy-Mousan who assisted with the tables and maps. The Institute of Contemporary Jewry of the Hebrew University of Jerusalem has been headed since 2010 by Prof. Uzi Rebhun. Their collective efforts have now been rewarded by this extraordinary piece of scholarship by our late friend and colleague, Professor Steven Lowenstein.

Preface 1.
The Life and Work of Steven M. Lowenstein z"l (1945–2020): "From Washington Heights to Skid Row—a Life of Learning and Doing"

David N. Myers
UCLA

This volume marks the crowning scholarly achievement of Steven M. Lowenstein (1945–2020). Having gained a reputation over various stages of his productive career as a master archivist, linguist, and historian, Lowenstein labored for decades on a grand project which he essentially completed before his life was prematurely taken by a fast-moving case of pancreatic cancer in 2020. What makes this monumental demographic history of German Jewry all the more remarkable is that Lowenstein worked on it after leaving his academic position as the Isadore Levin Professor of Jewish history at the American Jewish University to pursue a second career as a social worker on Skid Row, dealing with the large homeless population of Los Angeles.

This may be the most extraordinary, but by no means the only, twist in a fascinating life and career. Steven Lowenstein was born in 1945 in New York City. He grew up in the distinctive ambience of Washington Heights in upper Manhattan, which after the Second World War boasted a large population of German-Jewish refugees and survivors. It was there that he first began to develop the finely tuned sensors that he used as an historian—and later as a social worker—to discern differences within seeming uniformity. To the outside observer, the world of Washington Heights, the world of New York's *yekkes* (nickname German Jews), seemed to be a striking example of group cohesion. But from within, it teemed with variety in socio-economic, political, denominational, geographic, even linguistic terms. Lowenstein knew early on that not all German Jews were urban, educated, and assimilated. After all, his own family was of rural origins and Orthodox, two features of German Jewry that continued to fascinate him throughout his life. The resulting sense of this texture anchored his first major book *Frankfurt on the Hudson: The German-Jewish Community of Washington Heights, 1933–1983* (1989). Lowenstein would go on to study different Jewries, dialects, and customs, but he always maintained deep pride in his German-Jewish origins—to the point that when he moved to California, he got a vanity license plate for his car that read "A YEKKE."[1]

Lowenstein first exited the world of Washington Heights when he went to Bronx Science for high school. The renowned institution was filled with gifted students destined to make an impact on the world, including future Jewish studies scholars Eugene Orenstein, Rakhmiel Peltz, and Richard Steiner, journalists Joseph Berger and Clyde Haberman, and the future Black Power activist Stokely Carmichael. After graduating in 1962, Lowenstein made his way with Peltz and Orenstein to the City College of New York (CCNY). There he met a pair of students in the intellectually rich environment of the CCNY History Department who would leave a mark in the field of Jewish studies, Sara Reguer and David Ruderman. Lowenstein took a BA in history at CCNY, graduating in 1966 (three years before another future Jewish studies scholar, Deborah Lipstadt, finished there). At that point, Lowenstein decided to continue his historical studies, but not in Jewish history. He headed to Princeton, where he worked under the supervision of Theodore Rabb, the eminent European-born scholar of early modern Europe. Lowenstein chose to write a dissertation on a persecuted religious minority in Europe, not the Jews but the early modern Huguenots whom he examined in careful, almost microhistical, detail in his dissertation, "Languedoc Region: Resistance to Absolutism: Huguenot Organization in Languedoc, 1621–22" (1972). While he did not continue with the study of French history, Lowenstein did acquire and retain fluency in French, an aptitude he shared with his late wife Marilyn, who herself received a PhD in the subject. Evidence of this aptitude exists not only in the numerous French letters that he received and wrote, which are collected in his *Nachlass*, but in the curious North African-inflections that he sometimes used in liturgical Hebrew, picked up during Sabbath services at a North African synagogue in Montpelier in the course of his doctoral research there.[2]

---

1 See the *Bnai Brith Messenger*, May 27, 1983, 5.
2 Lowenstein left behind a huge archive of more than ten linear feet, including thousands of pages of memorabilia, correspondence, research notes, and scholarly drafts. Included in the

At this intriguing point in the story, Lowenstein left behind French history, where neither his deepest passions nor robust job prospects lay. When he went on the job market after receiving his PhD, and with the active encouragement of Ted Rabb, he pursued a range of employment opportunities in academia and beyond, including in the Princeton library system and at an archive in Atlanta, Georgia. He ended up receiving a job as an archivist at YIVO, the preeminent research institute for Eastern European Jewish history and Yiddish culture. It was indeed striking that this young German Jew from Washington Heights with a PhD in French history was now dwelling in the bastion of Yiddish. But he had long been interested in Yiddish, especially those traces of it preserved in rural Germany. Lowenstein now immersed himself in the world of Yiddish culture and scholarship at YIVO, where he served as assistant archivist from 1973 to 1975. He also continued to conduct research that he had begun while at CCNY in 1964 on a project devoted to creating a linguistic and cultural atlas of Ashkenazic culture that was led by two Columbia professors, Uriel Weinrich (son of YIVO's founding director Max Weinreich) and Marvin Herzog.[3]

After two years at YIVO, Lowenstein moved over to YIVO's peer and rival, the Leo Baeck Institute, where he served as archivist and assistant to director Fred Grubel from 1975 to 1979. On the face of it, this was a return home for Lowenstein, given that the LBI was the premier research institution for the study of German Jewry. But one of the distinctive features of his intellectual and scholarly personality was that Lowenstein paid no attention to the cultural chasm and mutual disdain between German and Eastern European Jews. He reveled in and attained mastery over both the German and Yiddish languages and was ceaselessly fascinated by the differences in customs and habits of each group without exhibiting any trace of condescension toward either.

Steve Lowenstein was a bridge builder. He overcame seeming opposites, taking what others cast as coarse stereotypes and crafting them into nuanced distinctions, as he did with both German and Eastern European Jewish cultures. With similar ease, he moved between east and west coasts of the United States when, in 1979, he assumed a long-sought-after academic post as an assistant professor at the University of Judaism, which in 2007 became the American Jewish University. Although he had previously taught at the college level (at

---

archive at the Leo Baeck Institute are letters and cards he received from French friends and a letter he wrote to a French colleague in French. The archive is the Steven M. Lowenstein Collection, AR 25335, Leo Baeck Institute, Center for Jewish History.
3   That work, featuring extensive interviews with Yiddish speakers and field notes, is preserved at the digital Language and Cultural Archive of Ashkenazic Jewry at the Columbia University Library, https://dlc.library.columbia.edu/lcaaj.

Columbia, Stern College, and Monmouth College), this was his first tenure-track position, and he flourished. At the UJ, as it was known then, he now had the time to publish a series of important articles and later books devoted to German-Jewish history. In doing so, Steve Lowenstein proved himself to be a bold innovator.

The field of Jewish studies has devoted a large, some would say disproportionate, amount of attention to German Jewish intellectual history.[4] This history encompasses a distinguished lineage of thinkers, beginning with Moses Mendelssohn in the eighteenth century, Samson Raphael Hirsch, Abraham Geiger, and Zacharias Frankel in the nineteenth century, and then figures such as Hermann. Cohen, Franz Rosenzweig, Gershom Scholem, and Hannah Arendt in the twentieth. These thinkers generated an exceptionally rich body of thought that deserves the abundant scholarship that envelops it.

But Steven Lowenstein pursued an entirely different path, whose roots lay in his own upbringing during which he developed sensitivity to intra-communal difference in his native Washington Heights. He did not place urban elites at the heart of his interest, but rather rural Jews (who constituted a majority of the community until 1871); nor did he concentrate on high-society German, but rather small-town German dialect. The objects of his investigations were now shopkeepers and cattle dealers (from whom his own people descended). This emphasis on normal folk added a huge degree of evidentiary difficulty, because his protagonists did not leave behind detailed written treatises on the ethics of cattle transactions.

Lowenstein had to be methodical and dogged to track down sources to reconstruct the lives of average German Jews. This, of course, is the burden of the social historian who reconstructs history from the *bottom up* rather than from the top down, focusing on material, rather than more abstract intellectual, aspects of the past. It is this careful attention to the lives of ordinary people, as well as to long-term social processes, that animated his book *The Mechanics of Change: Essays in the Social History of German Jews* from 1992. Each of the essays in this book is a condensed master class in German-Jewish social history; as a whole, they add up to a compelling look at the process by which "German Jewry was transformed from a traditional into a modern Jewish community."[5] Social historical work of this nature takes years of labor and requires a tremendous

---

4 See, for example, David Sorkin, review of *The Berlin Jewish Community: Enlightenment, Family, and Community (1770–1830)* (New York: Oxford University Press, 1994), by Steven M. Lowenstein, *Central European History* 29, no. 1 (1996): 129–133.

5 See the author's introduction to Steven M. Lowenstein, *The Mechanics of Change: Essays in the Social History of German Jews* (Atlanta: Scholars Press, 1992), 1.

attention to detail. Happily for the historian, Lowenstein evinced the same attention in preserving his own papers, thousands of pages of which are now housed in the archive of the Leo Baeck Institute.

Lowenstein brought this new methodological approach to old topics such as the Berlin Jewish community, about which he wrote a pioneering book in 1994 (*The Berlin Jewish Community: Enlightenment, Family and Crisis, 1770–1830*). Departing from previous accounts of Berlin Jewry that focused on intellectual innovation, Lowenstein set out to analyze the processes of social change of a diverse range of Jews in Berlin. He relied on a wide body of sources (including communal records, tax ledgers, and memoirs) and quantitative methods to tell a different kind of story—not the classic *histoire événementielle*, but a bottom-up glance that revealed longer-term changes affecting ordinary Berlin Jews, as well as a small handful of wealthy elites.[6] Already in this book, Lowenstein evinced a strong interest in aggregating statistics, often about important life-cycle moments (marriage, birth, conversion), to chart that change. And indeed, change was afoot in the late eighteenth century, as new fissures emerged within the community over questions of religion and class. Here Lowenstein understood, as he had intuited in his native Washington Heights, that German Jewry was not a single unified group. Beneath the surface of uniformity lay ample diversity.

Ever attentive to the dynamic tension between diversity and uniformity, Lowenstein moved away from German Jews and quantitative social history in 2000, when he published the book *The Jewish Cultural Tapestry*. This book evinced his usual interest in the quotidian experience of Jews, but used the manifold varieties of Jewish cultural production, in the form of local customs (*minhagim*), as the prism. Typical of the breadth of his cultural appetite in this book was the chapter that staged an encounter between gefilte fish and cholent, on one hand, and malawach and couscous, on the other. In recognition of its boundary-crossing quality, *The Jewish Cultural Tapestry* was awarded the National Jewish Book Award in 2002.

By this point, Steve Lowenstein had gained the acclaim of his colleagues as an historian's historian. The next year, 2003, he was approached by the Leo Baeck Institute in Jerusalem with a major request: to pick up the work of the late Usiel Oscar Schmelz, the Vienna-born Israeli demographer, who left behind massive troves of research files on German Jewry. It was this scholarly project to which Lowenstein devoted himself for the rest of his life. It was so large and exacting a project that it would take nearly two decades. And yet, in the

---

6   See David Sorkin's review of the book, referenced earlier, and the review by Jeffrey Grossman in *The Jewish Quarterly Review* 87, nos. 3/4 (1997): 396–401.

midst of it, Lowenstein made a dramatic career move that baffled many fellow academics. He left the heights of Bel Air, where the American Jewish University sat, for the flats of downtown Los Angeles, where he began a new career as a social worker after receiving his MSW. There, in his new workplace, Lowenstein met up not with nineteenth-century Jewish cattle dealers, but rather twenty-first-century unhoused people, drug addicts, the mentally ill, and those facing severe economic disadvantage. It was stunning to hear Lowenstein talk about the people he encountered in the course of his workday. As with his historical subjects, he betrayed no trace of condescension nor judgment, but rather deep appreciation for their life situation and dignity. In a certain sense, his new vocation was a continuation of his old. He was still collecting, reconstructing, and weaving together stories—rich, partial, and deeply meaningful stories.

One of the most intriguing documents in the Lowenstein archive at the Leo Baeck Institute is a National Career Services (NCS) punch-card profile from September 13, 1977, intended to highlight vocational strengths and weaknesses (see Figure 1). Unsurprisingly, one learns from the profile that Steven Lowenstein had very considerable aptitudes in public speaking and writing. It further reveals that he was not cut out for a career as a carpenter, police officer, or physical education instructor. By contrast, he rated very highly in the fields of librarianship, psychology, and social work. This assessment seems spot-on. Steve Lowenstein was a lover of libraries, as he voraciously consumed books and documents. And he betrayed a great deal of psychological insight as he entered the homes and minds of the everyday women and men who populated his social history. And unbeknownst to almost all, he was a natural social worker, sharing his great powers, empathy, and insight to offer comfort to those most in need.

It still boggles the mind to recognize that after a full day of demanding social work, Steve Lowenstein would labor into the night, poring over texts and manuals containing statistics on the births, deaths, marriages, divorces, immigrations, and conversions of German Jews. The aggregate of these thousands of data points makes for an altogether new and comprehensive picture of German Jewry, more thorough than any other account we have on record. But what, the reader may ask, links this monumental book and Lowenstein's labor as a social worker on Skid Row? While there is no explicit evidence, and in all likelihood, Steve may not even have articulated this to himself, it does not seem far-fetched to see links between his admirable work with unhoused people in Los Angeles and his obsessive quest to understand the demographic history of German Jewry. In both cases, there is an abiding quest for a stable home. The latter case of German Jewry, on which Steven Lowenstein labored until pancreatic cancer tragically sapped his strength, ended in murderous dispossesion. It is the most minimal of debts that we, his colleagues, owe him—and the victims of Nazism—to see to the publication of this book chronicling the struggle for the stable settlement of Jews in Germany.

The world of scholarship has been much diminished by Professor Lowenstein's premature death. In personal terms, I was deeply touched by Steve's extraordinary wisdom, expertise, story-telling, generosity, good cheer, humor, and array of accents, often conveyed in synagogue in the magical conversational space that lies between prayers; I, and so many others, sorely miss him. But that same world in which his absence is so conspicuous now has an enduring testament to his manifold contributions as a Jewish historian, the culmination of which comes in this extraordinary volume. May Steven Lowenstein's memory be a blessing to all who knew him. And may his remarkable scholarship continue to be an inspiration to generations of scholars and students.

Preface 2.
Steven Lowenstein's *Demographic History*

Michael Berenbaum
American Jewish University

It is a privilege to participate in bringing this volume to publication. Being asked to write this introduction allows me to participate in one of Judaism's most gracious commandments, to fulfill an obligation to do a *chesed shel emet* (an act of true grace without personal reward)—twice over. Why is it a double act of true grace? We herein honor the memory of my friend and distinguished colleague, Professor Steven Lowenstein z"l, who engaged in a true act of grace when he honored the memory of Professor Usiel Oscar Schmelz z"l, by recognizing his monumental research and his work. Lowenstein gives new life to Schmelz's demographic collections and research in this master work, *The Population History of German Jewry: Based on the Collections and Preliminary Research of Professor Usiel Oscar Schmelz*.

Characteristically, Steven Lowenstein never claimed more credit than he deserved. The subtitle of his book is testament to that: *Based on the Collection and Research of Professor Usiel Oscar Schmelz*. He would have it no other way. But we must say that his work was voluminous. One can notice his hand and his unique insights on every page of commentary.

Professor David Myers has just offered a biographical account of Steven Lowenstein's life, so I will be restrained, except to refer to an obituary I wrote on

Lowenstein for the Los Angeles Jewish community.[1] We were fortunate enough to celebrate the pending publication of this book when Professor Lowenstein was still with us and well enough to attend.

I am tempted to begin my preface by facetiously saying "I did not have time to read his work, I merely read his footnotes, along with the graphs and tables that show, in detail after detail, town after town, village after village, year after year, the demographic information of German Jews from 1815 to 1939." But I would be lying.

I read the book even as my eyes often glazed over the tables and the graphs and focused on Lowenstein's interpretations. He made certain his readers did not drown in the comprehensive, encyclopedic, overwhelming information, but could absorb the details and glean from those details the story of German Jewry during industrialization, urbanization, migration, in migration and outmigration primarily to the United States; revolution, emancipation, unification, democratization, disemancipation, escape, exile, tyranny, persecution, and ultimately deportation and annihilation. All of this occurred during those 125 years, 1815–1939, years portrayed with precise demographic detail and informed, insightful, and comprehensive interpretation of the numbers.

Lowenstein organized this book in a masterful way. He looks at the material chronologically, beginning with the period from 1815 to 1871—from Napoleon to German Unification. From 1871 to 1918, he examines the *Kaiserreich*, Imperial Germany, and from 1918 to 1939, the final pre-Holocaust chapter from the post-World War I era through the Nazi prewar period. Later chapters are arranged regionally: Eastern Provinces, Central and Northwest Germany, Western Germany, and Southern Germany. They are also arranged topically: Natural Growth and Changing Age Structure; Conversion and Intermarriage; Migration, Immigration, and Emigration; and Urbanization.

He discusses Jewish living patterns, neighborhood by neighborhood, village by village, town by town, city by city. Whatever Lowenstein touched, he illuminated. He offers comparisons to the general German population, and from time to time, to living patterns among Jews and other American ethnic groups in the United States. He suggests how this massive data can be used to understand general patterns and significant trends. He makes the demographics come to life in the lives of real German Jews, the heart and soul of his life-long research.

---

1 See Lowenstein's obituary in the *Jewish Journal*, https://jewishjournal.com/judaism/obituaries/316707/obituary-steven-lowenstein-1945-2020/.

Readers may be forgiven if they cannot fathom why Lowenstein began immediately after Napoleon. The French values of "liberty, equality, and fraternity" were imposed upon German lands by the Napoleonic conquest. For Jews, it meant Emancipation came from without, a result of invasion. It was not the internal achievement of a people committed to freedom and Jewish participation as citizens in German society. Napoleon's defeat reversed the uneven process of Emancipation in Germany and was a significant transitional moment for Jewish life in Germany.

What was the impact of German unification and Emancipation? During the *Kaiserreich*, conversion decreased, secession from the Jewish community increased. More left the community than converted to Christianity. Prior to Emancipation, the only way to avoid being discriminated against as a Jew was to convert and many of those who converted like Heinrich Heine did so for social or economic rather than religious reasons. Most who left the Jewish community during the Kasierreich declared themselves without religion, a category now familiar to students of American Jewish demography from the Pew survey. Intermarriage, then newly permissible by law, began its long and steady rise. More common in large cities than in small towns, men intermarried more than women and Jews were more likely to marry Protestants than Roman Catholics. For the Jewish community, the loss of these Jews was a defection and within families, even a betrayal. For antisemites, conversion, intermarriage, and withdrawal from the Jewish community tainted German society.

Lowenstein was a meticulous scholar. For instance, he details a small but significant difference between the 1910 census and 1925 census. In 1910, all who were in Germany were counted in the census including tourists; in 1925, only residents were counted. The difference is all the more noticeable to American readers following the Donald Trump's administration's attempt to ask the citizenship question in the 2020 US census, a request denied by the United States Supreme Court. One must pay attention to the questions being asked and to whom the questions are being asked. Dry census statistics made manifest the changes in German law. The 1939 census distinguished between Jews by religion and Jews by race, reflecting the Nuremberg laws of 1935 and their implementation later that fall by the German bureaucracy.

So, while this work seems to note "every leaf on the trees in the forest," Lowenstein never loses sight of the trees and well understands the forest—the larger picture—in context. For example, in 1871, 70 percent of the Jews in Germany lived in towns of less than 20,000. By 1910, only 32 percent lived in smaller towns. 53 percent lived in large cities, with Berlin as the most Jewishly populated. In those years, the percentage of German Jews living in Berlin more than tripled from 7 percent to 23.42 percent.

Lowenstein worked on this book for sixteen years before its completion. Knowing full well his days were numbered, he rushed to finish the work. He was aware from the onset of his last illness that this would be his final work, so different in scope from his other writings dealing with German Jews from small towns and rural communities, or those later in his career—a tapestry of diverse customs among German Jews.

This work was compiled while Lowenstein was studying full-time to become a social worker, interning and working in his new career. Lowenstein had retired from teaching at the American Jewish University to study social work and to ultimately work on Skid Row with people whose backgrounds could not be more different from his. He was able to relate to them and, often, to his own non-cynical amazement, helped them cope and occasionally heal. His last efforts at finishing this massive work came when he was fighting the cancer that was to devour his body but left his mind, his soul, and his curiosity undiminished.

Anyone who knew Lowenstein personally or read his work would notice his quick wit and keen sense of irony. At the beginning of what turned out to be a 700-page work, he apologizes for not detailing Jews by occupation and economic standing in order—and these are his words, not mine—"to reduce the project to a manageable size." (I guess 700 plus pages with maps and graphics, tables and text were manageable.)

His irony is obvious when he comments that the 1944 census measured the Jewish population of Germany on the basis of the 1939 numbers, when, with only two exceptions—the intermarried Jews and those hiding underground—the entire German Jewish population had already been deported to death camps or Theresienstadt.

Lowenstein documented the impact of urbanization on Germany and is mindful that Jews were urbanized earlier than others there. "Pioneers" in urbanization relative to the rest of the German population, German Jews were approximately one generation ahead of Germans-at-large. They were "trailblazers" in planning smaller families. They had lower infant mortality rates, lower rates of illegitimacy, married later, had fewer children than their German counterparts. It took almost half a century for the general population to catch up. Density enhanced Jewish visibility and the migration to Berlin—much like the choice of New York in the United States—enhanced the importance and the influence of the Jewish community in Germany.

Beginning in the twentieth century, this pattern of an aging population with a lower fertility rate characterized Europe as a whole. Lowenstein observed that while the Jewish birthrate was certainly linked to urbanization—urbanized residents have lower birthrates—Jews had a lower birthrate earlier than their gentile neighbors both in cities and the countryside. He even offers a correlation between birth control use and birthrates.

Lowenstein's scholarship allows us to substantiate Arthur Hertzberg's controversial claims regarding American Jewry: "The best did not come to the United States. They stayed [in Europe]." During the period of mass migration to the United States beginning in 1840, poor rural Jews left Germany. While there was a sizable German migration to the United States, Jews were disproportionately represented among those immigrants. Often, as one can witness in other immigrant groups, Jews from a town or a village tended to cluster, and a result was chain migration. As poor Jews and younger Jews left Germany, the graying German Jewish community turned into a middle-class community, which in turn served to induce Eastern European Jews to immigrate to Germany even as it set obstacles in their path, obstacles Christians did not face. Between 1840 and 1880, the peak years of German immigration to the United States, emigration of German Jews exceeded immigration. Beginning in 1880 to 1920, a period that coincided with Emancipation, immigration exceeded emigration.

Lowenstein does not miss those cities where the population composition may reflect previous restrictions on where Jews could live, even during a time of rapid assimilation where Jews were comfortable with other Jews. Core neighborhoods developed near a city center. The wealthy moved beyond it. And in a pattern recognizable for the American Jewish story, Jews in Germany moved from the core neighborhood to new neighborhoods, and as they moved, poor Jews or new immigrants moved into the "old" core neighborhoods. Lowenstein's previous studies of small towns and specific cities allowed him to interpret the demographic data clearly and precisely. Even under Nazism, without any formal ghetto, Jews were inclined to cluster. Clustering made it easy to target them but it also made life under persecution a bit more bearable as the misery could be shared and only partially alleviated by community action.

Lowenstein places the Jewish experience in its larger context. World War I resulted in a decrease in marriage yet a notable increase in German Jewish intermarriage. Intermarriage increased during the Weimar period as Jews were more integrated into German society, yet notably in the immediate postwar period when soldiers, Jews and non-Jews alike, returned home from war, intermarriage rates were the lowest of any year between 1912 and 1933. During Weimar, birthrates fell, death rates rose.

Any student of German Jewish history knows how the story ended, and Lowenstein clearly documents the beginning of the end—not through Nazi policies of boycotts and book burning, Nuremberg laws and the November pogroms, but by understanding the demographics that resulted from these policies. From 1914 onward, the deaths of German Jews exceeded birthrates, but the natural decline in population was offset by immigration. The economic turmoil of the early 1920s slowed the rate of Jewish immigration to Germany. Then the rise of the Nazi regime virtually halted Jewish immigration to Germany while, despite all the obstacles, emigration rapidly increased.

In the 1930s, while living under the Nazi regime, twice as many Jews died as were born. Men emigrated before women, mistakenly believing that the Nazis posed a greater threat to men than women. An early response to Nazism was to intermarry and convert, actions that were declined when they proved ineffective in alleviating persecution and discrimination.

The young left before the old. Non-citizens left before those who thought that their citizenship might protect them. Intermarriage virtually ceased because it was outlawed, yet, especially in the early years, marriage rates increased in anticipation and preparation for emigration—perhaps also for the need for stability in a most turbulent time. Perhaps young couples grew closer to share the ravages—economic and psychological—of persecution. Love and intimacy were a way to recommit to life in the present and to create hope for the future. Even those who stayed migrated from small towns to larger, more anonymous cities. By 1939, there were 56.2 percent fewer Jews by religion than in 1933, which may indicate who left and who stayed in the now older and disproportionately female community. It may also indicate that assimilated Jews believed they were safer.

Suffice it to say that if you give a gifted scholar who knows the history of this community the raw data gathered meticulously by a gifted demographer who did not live to interpret his findings, the result is a book that tells the fascinating yet tragic story of German Jewry. It is a tribute to Professor Lowenstein that even in his academic retirement he undertook so onerous a task. It is an even greater tribute that he brought the work to life in a manner that will only enhance the significant legacy of his distinguished scholarship and lead to a greater understanding of the German Jewish community which raised him in "Frankfurt-on-the-Hudson," New York City's Washington Heights.

Acknowledgments

When it became clear that Steve Lowenstein would not live to see the publication of this book, a community of his friends and admirers took it upon itself to see the task through to completion. We thank those colleagues of Steve's who participated in a forum devoted to the manuscript at Bnai David-Judea Congregation on October 30, 2019: Professors Lea Hochman, Paul Lerner, Elliot Dorff (on behalf of Michael Berenbaum), and Sharon Gillerman z"l, whose own untimely death widens even further the sense of loss among scholars of German Jewry. They provided Steve Lowenstein with a deeply appreciative reading of his magnum opus; the occasion also allowed scholars across the world to send in their best wishes, which brought great joy to him. Many thanks to Rav Yosef Kanefsky and Adynna Swartz of Bnai David-Judea for hosting the symposium and providing Steve with such a rich spiritual home.

A number of Steve's friends from the Bnai David community offered generous financial support to aid in the publication of this book: Albie and Debra Cohen, Shep and Rae Drazin, Jill and Gary Linder, David and Marcia Nimmer, and Howie and Barbara Wettstein. A cadre of Steve's fellow scholars also generously contributed funds toward the book's publication. They include: David Ellenson, Pinchas and Ronni Giller, Deborah Hertz, Sandy Jacoby, Marion Kaplan, Paul Lerner, Frank Mecklenburg, Rakhmiel Peltz, Michael Meyer, Ismar Schorsch, and Jack Wertheimer.

We thank Steve's admiring colleagues on the faculty of the American Jewish University, the Sady and Ludwig Kahn Chair at UCLA, and the Leo Baeck Institute in Jerusalem (and its director, Dr. Irene Aue-Ben-David) for their support of this book. We would like to express gratitude to the team at Academic Studies Press for their careful attention to this unique project; special thanks to Alessandra Anzani and the map-maker Konstantin Kuzminsky, as well as to Kira Nemirovsky for her exquisite and lightning-quick attention to detail. Penultimate thanks go to Dr. Sarah Johnson, whose mastery of German-Jewish history and careful editorial attention to matters of content and style were deeply appreciated. She has reviewed many versions of the manuscript with a keen and critical eye. A final debt of gratitude goes to Dr. Ruth and Rabbi Yaakov Glasser, Steve's daughter and son-in-law, whose enthusiastic support, commendable patience, and generosity of spirit were indispensable to completing this book.

Editors' Note

The task of bringing a colleague's work to print posthumously is a complicated one, especially for a manuscript of this size. The editors sought to respect the extraordinary labor and fine prose of Steve Lowenstein and, accordingly, edited the book with deference to the author. Only in a small number of cases did we make corrections or word changes when we felt that clarity demanded it. In some instances, the editors were unable to locate precise bibliographic details that remained unfilled in the original manuscript; we have indicated where these lacunae exist in the notes.

Introduction

This study was undertaken under the auspices of the Leo Baeck Institute in Jerusalem as a continuation of the life work of the renowned Israeli demographer Usiel Oscar Schmelz (1918–1995). As director of the Department of Jewish Demography and Statistics at the Institute for Contemporary Jewry at the Hebrew University in Jerusalem, Professor Schmelz spent many years collecting and analyzing data on the demography of modern German Jewry. In two programmatic essays published in 1982 and 1989,[1] he set forth his plans for a comprehensive demographic study of German Jewry from the middle of the nineteenth century to 1933. Professor Schmelz passed away while preparing the first regional study within the framework of the project—*Die Jüdische Bevölkerung Hessens*—for publication. The volume was published posthumously.[2] Unpublished, however, was the massive archive of five full cabinets that Schmelz left behind; a trove of information culled from official government publications, scholarly and popular articles, Jewish community reports, and other sources relating to modern German Jewish demography.

---

1 Usiel Oscar Schmelz, "Die demographische Entwicklung der Juden in Deutschland von der Mitte des 19. Jahrhunderts bis 1933," *Zeitschrift für Bevölkerungswissenschaft* 8, no. 1 (1982): 31–72; and idem, "Die demographische Entwicklung der Juden in Deutschland von der Mitte des 19. Jahrhunderts bis 1933," *Bulletin des Leo Baeck Instituts* 83 (1989): 15–62.
2 Schmelz, *Die Jüdische Bevölkerung Hessens*.

In 2003, the Leo Baeck Institute asked me to delve into the Schmelz collection and produce a publication on German-Jewish demography on the basis of Professor Schmelz's legacy. The present volume is the result. My work on Schmelz's remarkable enterprise of collection and analysis amplified the humility and respect I had already felt toward his accomplishment. As I am a social historian rather than a professional demographer, however, this study is necessarily different from Schmelz's own works. Schmelz arranged his work according to formal demographic categories—the state of the population, population change, structure of the population, and geographic distribution—but augmented his meticulous and complex statistical analyses, including regression analysis, with an enormous amount of original data. His work, which included an analysis of the Jewish occupational structure, relied heavily on official censuses and statistics of the German central, state and local governments.

I organized this volume differently. While doing my best to preserve the vast wealth of the statistical data that Schmelz gathered and to report its demographic meanings, I also sought to investigate the data's implications for major social and cultural developments in German Jewry. The demographic information indeed sheds light on changes in the German-Jewish family, Jewish health conditions, neighborhood patterns, urbanization, and intermarriage, to name only a few subjects. Interregional geographical differences are significant because they help to clarify the reasons for important cultural variances in Jewish life in different parts of Germany. The relatively heavy emphasis on rural communities in this book reflects my judgment on the significance of these often-tiny communities as backdrops for the urbanized communities that emerged in a later period.

As I worked on this book, I found myself torn between presenting as rich a selection of the original documentation as possible and crafting a coherent and readable narrative of the major demographic developments in conjunction with social conditions. In my attempt to strike the proper balance, the story that follows is heavier on description and lighter on social analysis than I had originally anticipated. It also uses a different periodization than Professor Schmelz had planned. Schmelz began his analysis in the middle of the nineteenth century primarily because that was when continuous systematic data first became available, and he ended it in 1933 as the year of the Nazi accession to power. In order to cover the whole period of the social and demographic modernization of German Jewry rather than to begin when the process was well underway, I pushed the onset of the narrative back to 1815. It was after Napoleon's defeat that German administrative boundaries stabilized, and the collection of census and other population data began in earnest. I also extended the terminus of the study to 1939 to include demographic developments in the early Nazi period and to use data from the 1939 census, which shed light on the considerable converted and intermarried population by including evidence on both Jewish ancestry and religion.

Unlike many demographic works, this book frequently parses data by individual years. In some of my earlier studies, especially my article on intermarriage,[3] I found that statistics that capture entire decades or even five-year periods often obscure important short-term developments. This is especially true for the period from World War I to 1939, when military, political, and economic developments—to which German Jews proved more sensitive than the general population—often precipitated rapid swings in demographic behavior. Thus, I summarize developments across periods of five years or longer when I find no evidence of rapid year-to-year changes and present yearly statistics where such data reveal important short-term oscillations. By proceeding in this manner, I can report a marriage and baby boom in the immediate post-World War I period, a rapid year-by-year decline in marriages and births beginning in the mid-1920s, erratic swings in the numbers of conversions, and a more gradual and steady increase in intermarriage.

This study omits census material on Jewish occupations and economic activity. I made this decision for two reasons: to reduce the project to a manageable size and to assuage my doubts about the validity of occupational reportage to the government in the first half of the nineteenth century. Given the government's ardent interest in reforming the Jewish occupational structure at that time, Jews sometimes reported what they thought the government wanted to hear about their so-called "productive" occupations. Thus, the analysis of the voluminous and valuable government statistics on Jewish occupations will have to await another chronicler.

I divided this study into three parts: a chronological summary of the major characteristics and changes in German-Jewish demographic history, an analysis of specific demographic trends, and a description and comparison of the characteristics of Germany's various regions. I also admit the possibility that there are some overlap and repetition within this taxonomy. In part 1, three chronological chapters detail the main developments in 1815–1871, 1871–1914, and 1914–1939, respectively. Part 2 examines specific major demographic themes in depth. In each of the seven chapters in this topical section, the material is organized along chronological and geographical lines. Therefore, it proceeds

---

3 Steven M. Lowenstein, "Jewish Intermarriage and Conversion in Germany and Austria," *Modern Judaism* 25, no. 1 (February 2005): 23–61.

from natural developments in the population like birth, marriage, and death and changes in family patterns, to non-biological aspects of population change such as conversion, migration, and settlement patterns. Chapter 4 centers on birth, marriage, and death, examining aspects such as illegitimacy, birth control, declines in infant mortality, and causes of death. Chapter 5 turns to changes in the age structure of the German-Jewish population, many of which were occasioned by the fertility and mortality changes discussed previously. Chapter 6 examines the interrelated topics of conversion, intermarriage, and withdrawal from the Jewish community. Chapters 7–9 document migration patterns, tracking the interrelated but distinct processes of (a) internal migration from district to district, (b) migration across international frontiers, and (c) urbanization. The final topical chapter deals with Jewish residential concentration in major cities and distinguishes among several different types of neighborhood patterns. The third section of the book, chapters 11–14, presents an in-depth discussion of regional differences in German-Jewish demography—an often neglected but nevertheless significant aspect of the broader theme. Here the narrative divides Germany into five main regions—east, central, northwest, west, and south—with the central and northwestern regions amalgamated into one chapter. Within each chapter, each region is subdivided into smaller areas for more detailed analysis. These regions are then compared and contrasted, and the changing settlement patterns of German Jews are mapped out in considerable detail. A relatively brief conclusion recapitulates some of the major themes that made the demographic history of German Jewry distinctive and offers some tentative explanations for the developments reported previously in this study.

CHRONOLOGICAL SECTION

1

From the Fall of Napoleon to the Unification of Germany (1815–1871)

Jews always accounted for a minor share of the German population and, as such, were heavily influenced by majority demographic patterns. In some parts of the country, the Jewish population was proportionally much larger than the nationwide average of about one percent; elsewhere it was much sparser. In several towns, Jews were more than one-third of the population, and in a few they even formed a majority. By the same token, a remarkable proportion of German Jewry was scattered in tiny groups of fewer than 100 individuals that nevertheless often maintained full communal (*kehilla*) structures.

While some German-Jewish demographic patterns resembled those of the majority Christian population, others were distinctive in many ways. Jewish distinctiveness was the result of both a history of legal restrictions on Jewish settlement in the various German states and an exceptional occupational structure, itself partly caused by the legal restrictions. Even after the *de jure* constraints were repealed during the first two-thirds of the nineteenth century, they continued to affect German Jews' settlement patterns. After 1840, however, German-Jewish population patterns underwent a fundamental change: German Jewry metamorphosed from a mainly small-town population with premodern demographic traits to a largely urban group whose demographic modernization preceded that of most of the non-Jewish German population.

This presentation of German-Jewish demographic history begins at the end of the Napoleonic Wars for two main reasons. First, it was at the Congress of Vienna (1815) that Germany's administrative map stabilized, as hundreds of independent principalities, duchies, city-states, and bishoprics merged into thirty-eight states of various sizes—an administrative configuration that endured in greater part until World War II. Second, and partly as a result of this territorial reorganization, demographic documentation improved radically around this time. Starting around 1815, reliable and continuous censuses became available for much of the territory that would later become united Germany.

In the immediate post-Napoleonic period, German Jewry was highly unevenly distributed among the general population. Although Jews were somewhat more likely to be city-dwellers than non-Jews, the vast majority of Jews, like other Germans, inhabited villages and small towns. Although the walled ghetto (exemplified by the Frankfurt Judengasse) was the exception by 1815, excluding some of the smallest villages, Jews were concentrated to a greater or lesser extent in particular neighborhoods within German towns and cities.

The German-Jewish population owed its distribution to historical processes from previous generations, primarily that of legal restrictions and exclusions. Between the late fourteenth and mid-sixteenth centuries, Jews were expelled from most German cities and many territorial states. Insofar as they remained, they often lived in small towns near the cities from which Jews had been evicted. Because the expulsion led to the migration of up to ninety percent of Ashkenazi Jews to Eastern Europe, the Jewish population of the German lands in the sixteenth and seventeenth centuries was far smaller than it had been in the Middle Ages.

The demographic recovery of German Jewry in the early modern period was a gradual and uneven process that unfolded in highly divergent ways in the various political territories of which Germany would later be composed. In some towns, the arrival of a court purveyor (Court Jew) or some other exceptional Jewish settler admitted for economic reasons led to the gradual arrival of additional Jewish residents. When unauthorized Jewish residents were discovered in a town that had granted residency rights to only a limited number of Jews, the community was expelled in some cases, and in others was allowed to remain in return for a hefty payment to the authorities.

The Thirty Years' War (1618–1648) devastated much of the German territory. In its aftermath, the rulers of some territories combed the larger region for people to repopulate deserted towns and to generate tax and other revenues. They often decided to admit Jews for these purposes. Thus, the late seventeenth century saw the resettlement of Jews in territories from which they had been expelled earlier, such as in Brandenburg-Prussia in 1671. The eighteenth century also witnessed net Jewish in-migration to Germany. Although few reliable statistics exist, all trends point to a considerable upturn in the Jewish population of many parts of the country. Estimates of the Jewish population in Germany all told, however, are as low as 60,000 (one-third of one percent) as late as 1750.[1] Sporadic expulsions of Jews from limited territories persisted until the late eighteenth century,[2] but many more territories accommodated Jews for the first time or saw existing communities grow vigorously during that century.[3]

Jewish Settlement Patterns after the Napoleonic Wars

The pattern of Jewish settlement in post-Napoleonic Germany reflected the political conditions of eighteenth-century Germany. In a way, one may speak of two separate Jewish populations in Germany: one in the south and west, and the other in the extreme east, which were separated by an area in the middle where very few Jews dwelled. Most of the western and, especially, southwestern parts of Germany had been split up into tiny principalities, free cities, and church territories, some of which admitted Jews. In southeastern and east-central Germany, larger political entities such as the kingdoms of Bavaria and Saxony excluded almost all Jews. East of Germany, the independent commonwealth of Poland boasted a huge Jewish population that faced relatively few residency restrictions. After the partitions of Poland beginning in 1772, vast Polish

---

1   Robert Liberles, "An der Schwelle der Moderne 1618–1780," in *Geschichte des jüdischen Alltags in Deutschland. Vom 17. Jahrhundert bis 1945*, ed. Marion Kaplan (Munich: Beck, 2003), 22, quoting Asriel Schochat, *Der Ursprung der jüdischen Aufklärung in Deutschland Ursprung* (Frankfurt: Campus Verlag, 2000), 23. Liberles quotes Jonathan Israel's estimate (*European Jewry in the Age of Mercantilism* [1985], 170) of 60,000 Jews in Germany at the end of the seventeenth century and Mordechai Breuer's estimates (*Deutsch-jüdische Geschichte in der Neuze* [1996], 147) of 25,000 in 1700 and 60,000–70,000 in 1750. All these approximations appear to exclude areas in the Kingdom of Poland that became part of Germany after the Polish partitions. Jacob Katz's estimate of 175,000 Jews in Germany at the end of the eighteenth century seems to include territories gained from the partitions. My personal impression is that most of these estimates are too low because they do not count all territories, but much more research is necessary to settle the question.
2   Places from which Jews were expelled toward the end of the eighteenth century included Kitzingen, Franconia (1789), the city of Saarbrücken (1776), and (in part) the Netze district, which Prussia annexed from Poland in 1772.
3   One particularly late foundation of a rural community was the case of Jebenhausen (later in Württemberg), where Baron Philipp von Liebenstein decided to permit a Jewish community to establish itself in 1777. By 1806, the Jewish community had grown to 244 individuals in forty-eight families, and it reached 440 individuals by 1828.

territories were incorporated into Prussia in the provinces of Posen, West Prussia, and a small portion of East Prussia.

The territories that comprised Prussia, the largest German state after 1815, had different traditions in dealing with Jews. The oldest areas of Prussian rule—Brandenburg, Pomerania, and most of East Prussia—readmitted Jews starting in 1671, but severely limited their numbers. The province of Silesia, which was captured from Austria in 1740, also restricted Jewish population, but was home to three important and growing Jewish communities: Breslau, Glogau, and Zülz. In 1812, Jews in Prussia—which at that time comprised only five provinces: East Prussia, West Prussia, Brandenburg, Pomerania, and Silesia—were granted complete freedom of movement within the country. Three years later, Prussia reacquired many of the formerly Polish provinces in the east that it had annexed between 1772 and 1795. It also took possession of former Saxon territories in central Germany and two major new provinces in the west (Westphalia and the Rhineland) that had been created out of a welter of tiny states. Each of these territories had a different legal tradition on how to treat the Jews, and each evinced markedly different patterns of Jewish settlement. Between 1815 and 1847, each Prussian area continued to follow its pre-1815 legal provisions concerning the Jews, effectively restricting Jewish freedom of movement among the various sections of the Kingdom of Prussia.

Prussia was not the only German state that saw a massive increase in its Jewish population due to territorial expansion both during and after the Napoleonic Wars. In southern Germany, both the kingdoms of Württemberg and Bavaria as well as the Grand Duchy of Baden ballooned to several times their prewar size and acquired new territories that had substantial Jewish populations. Württemberg and Bavaria, originally home to only a few Jews, acquired many new Jewish subjects who had formerly lived under the rule of tiny independent jurisdictions in Franconia and its vicinity. The Jewish population of Bavaria, for instance, grew from less than 1,500[4] in about 1800 to 53,208 by 1818. Württemberg, which had a total of 534 Jews in 1805, had 8,256 in 1817.[5] Baden(-Durlach) had 2,265 Jews in 1802 and 14,200 in 1808 after its mammoth territorial acquisitions.[6]

Throughout Germany, the distribution of the Jewish population also reflected the pre-Napoleonic rather than the post-Napoleonic boundaries, and would

---

4 Not counting the scattered Bavarian territories west of the Rhine.
5 Paul Sauer, *Die jüdischen Gemeinden in Württemberg und Hohenzollern* (Stuttgart: Kohlhammer, 1966), 2–3.
6 *Pinkas ha-Kehillot, Germania, Württemberg-Hohenzollern-Baden* (Jerusalem: Yad Vashem, 1986), 176.

remain virtually unchanged for at least another generation, until around 1840. One area of heavy concentration was in the formerly Polish areas in the extreme east; the other was in southern and western Germany, centered on the Main and Middle Rhine valleys. A much more scattered and sparse Jewish population dwelled between these two principal areas of settlement. Jewish communities in the south and west differed culturally, religiously, and in settlement patterns from those in the east.[7] While the areas of Jewish concentration in the east and south were characterized by heavy settlement in small towns or villages, much of the scanty Jewish population in central Germany lived in cities. It was only in the course of nineteenth-century migrations that the two separate Jewish settlement areas of the eighteenth century gradually merged into a single German-Jewish population. During the nineteenth and early twentieth centuries, much of the central area was inhabited by Jews who migrated to the major cities in that part of the country, especially from eastern Germany and Eastern Europe. Jewish density in small-town central Germany, however, remained meager.

The formerly Polish areas in the extreme east of Germany had the densest Jewish populations by far. Of approximately 280,000 Jews[8] in post-Napoleonic Germany, the single largest group (52,568 in 1817) inhabited the former Polish province of Posen. This represented 6.2 percent of the provincial population and almost nineteen percent of the total Jewish population of Germany. The province of West Prussia, which was also Polish before 1772 but, unlike Posen, was part of Prussia at the time of the 1812 emancipation decree, had 12,632 Jewish inhabitants (2.2 percent of the provincial population), two-thirds of whom congregated in the southern half of the province (*Regierungsbezirk* Marienwerder). Though it had been part of Prussia since 1740, another area on the eastern frontier of Germany that had a large proportion of Polish-speaking inhabitants was Upper Silesia (*Regierungsbezirk* Oppeln), with 7,608 Jews and a Jewish density of almost 1.5 percent. Together, nearly one-fourth of all German Jews lived in these regions.

---

7 The Elbe River, which ran through an area with very sparse Jewish population, was the approximate boundary between the eastern and western Ashkenazi Jewish folk traditions as manifested in liturgical traditions (the *nusah Ashkenaz* [German prayer rite] in the west versus the *nusach Polin* in the east), different dialects of Yiddish, and various aspects of Jewish folk culture such as foods and liturgical music.
8 This figure was arrived at based on the available census counts (Table 1.1).

Table 1.1. Estimated Jewish Population of Germany, by Regions, 1817

Region	1817 estimate	Actual figures for various other years	General population
Baden	16,000	1812 (or 1814?): 15,079 Jews 1825: 17,577, 1852: 23,699	1,000,740 (1812)
Württemberg	8,256	1821: 8,892, 1832: 10,670	1,447,385 (1821)
Bavaria	53,000	1818: 53,208[9] (non-Christian)	3,660,452 (1818)
		1852: 56,158 (non-Christian)	5,175,472 (1852)
Prussia: Hohenzollern (Sigmaringen)	1,000	1852: 1,038, 1858: 949	
Hesse-Darmstadt	18,500	1822: 19,530, 1828: 21,236	
Kurhessen:	13,100		
Nassau	6,000	1841: 6,404, 1842: 6,639	401,198 (1841)
Hesse-Homburg	1,000	1852–55: 1,200	
Frankfurt	4,309		
Total south	**121,175**		
Lichtenberg:	400	1834: 410	
Prussia:			
Münster	2,304		
Minden	3,930		
Arnsberg	3,489		
Düsseldorf	3,190		
Kleve	1,833		
Cologne	3,349		

---

9   *Pinkas ha-Kehillot, Germania, Bavaria* gives 52,908.

Region	1817 estimate	Actual figures for various other years	General population
Koblenz	5,791		
Trier	3,057		
Aachen	1,621		
West Prussia:	28,564		
Oldenburg: Birkenfeld	650	1843: 684	29,480 (1843)
Total west:	29,614		
Waldeck	800	1871: 834	
Schaumburg-Lippe	350	1871: 351	
Lippe	1,000	1864: 1,193, 1871: 1,035	
Hannover	10,000[10]	1848: 11,179, 1852: 11,562, 1861: 12,085	1,758,847 (1848) 1,819,253 (1852)
Oldenburg	700	1822: 746 (excluding Birkenfeld), 1855: 1,494 (including Birkenfeld)	
Braunschweig	1,000	1834: 1,124, 1861: 1,061	253,232 (1834)
Lübeck	450	1840: 478	16,187
Bremen	200	1864: 225	
Hamburg	6,300	1811: 6,429 (including Portuguese Jews)	
Schleswig-Holstein	3,500	1835: 3,674, 1845: 3,997	773,788
Total northwest	24,300		

---

10 The estimate of 6,400 in Hannover in 1816–1817 in Michael Brenner, Stefi Jersch-Wenzel, and Michael A. Meyer, *Deutsch-Jüdische Geschichte der Neuzeit*, vol. 2, *Emanzipation und Akkulturation 1780–1871* (Munich: Leo Baeck Institute Jerusalem and C. H. Beck, 1996), 59, is almost certainly a gross underestimate, perhaps because it excluded Ostfriesland.

Region	1817 estimate	Actual figures for various other years	General population
Mecklenburg-Schwerin	2,750	1815: 2,690, 1820: 2,881	
Mecklenburg-Strelitz	450		
Prussia: 1817:			
Berlin	3,700		
Potsdam	1,933		
Frankfurt/Oder	2,865		
Magdeburg	2,146		
Merseburg	189		
Erfurt	911		
Central Prussia	11,744		
Kingdom of Saxony	850	1832: 874, 1834: 850	1,558,153 [Blau] 1,595,668
Anhalt	2,000	1864: 2,302 1867: 2,108	193,046 197,041
Sachsen-Weimar	1,400	1834: 1,427 1864: 1,129	238,672 280,201
Sachsen-Meiningen	1,500	1833: 1,524 1864: 1,625	144,110 178,065
Sachsen-Coburg-Gotha	75	1864: 80	165,527
All other Thuringia	300	1864: 344	368,643
Total central	21,069		
Prussia: 1817			
Königsberg	2,098		
Gumbinnen	291		
Stettin	1,269		
Köslin	1,585		
Stralsund	122		
Breslau	6,771		
Liegnitz	1,649		
Reichenbach	448		
Total	14,233		

Region	1817 estimate	Actual figures for various other years	General population
Prussia, "Other East"			
Prussia 1817:			
Oppeln	7,608		
Danzig	3,854		
Marienwerder	8,778		
Posen	37,545		
Bromberg	15,021		
Total: Posen/West Prussia/Upper Silesia:	72,806		
Total Germany	283,197		

Sources:

Baden 1812: *Statistisches Handbuch für des Grossherzogthum Baden enthaltend den Personal-Stand der Hof- und Civil-Staats-diener nach dem Bestand vom November 1814* (Karlsruhe, 1815), 34.

Baden 1825, 1852: Blau, *Entwicklung*, 211.

Württemberg 1817: Sauer, *Die jüdischen Gemeinden*, 3; 1821, 1832; Blau, *Entwicklung*, 198, 199.

Bavaria 1818, 1852: F. B. W. von Hermann, ed., *Beiträge zur Statistik des Königreichs Bayern*, vol. 1: *Bevölkerung aus amtlichen Quellen* (Munich, 1850), 20; F. B. W. von Hermann, ed., *Beiträge zur Statistik des Königreichs Bayern*, vol. 4 (Munich, 1855), 199.

Hohenzollern 1852: Silbergleit, *Die Bevölkerungs- und Berufsverhältnisse*, 18*; 1858: Blau, *Entwicklung*, 58.

Hesse-Darmstadt 1822, 1828: Schmelz, *Hessen*, 46 (post-1866 boundaries).

Kurhessen 1817: ibid., 45.

Nassau 1841, 1842: C. D. Vogel, *Beschreibung der Herzogthums Nassau* (Wiesbaden, 1842), 428–429.

Hesse-Homburg: Jacob Toury, *Soziale und politische Geschichte der Juden in Deutschland 1847–1871* (Düsseldorf: Droste, 1977), 18.

Frankfurt 1817: Schmelz, *Hessen*, 45.

Prussian provinces 1817: Silbergleit, *Die Bevölkerungs- und Berufsverhältnisse*, 11*.

Lichtenberg 1834: Johann Gottfried Hoffmann, "Neueste Nachrichten von der Bevölkerung des preußischen Staates," *Allgemeine Preussische Staatszeitung* 229 (1838): 949.

Birkenfeld 1843: *Statistische Nachrichten* über *das Herzogthum Oldenburg*, vol. 2 (Oldenburg, 1857), 30 (Uebersicht 7).

Waldeck 1871, Schaumburg-Lippe 1871, Lippe 1871: *Statistisches Jahrbuch für das Deutsche Reich* 1 (1880): 13.

Lippe 1864: P. Steinbach, *Der Eintritt Lippes in der Industriezeitalter* (Lemgo: F. L. Wagener, 1976), 196.

Hannover 1848, 1852: "Die allgemeine Volkszählung vom 3. December 1852," *Zur Statistik des Königreichs Hannover* (Hannover, 1855), 36–39.

Oldenburg: L. Trepp, *Die Oldenburger Judenschaft* (Oldenburg: Heinz Holzberg Verlag, 1973), 266.

Braunschweig 1834: *Statistisch-topographisches Handbuch des Herzogthums Braunschweig* . . . (Braunschweig, 1851), 35–36; 1861: *Ergebniss der am 3. December 1861 im Herzogthume Braunschweig Staat gehabten Volkszählung* (Braunschweig, 1861), 3.

Lübeck 1840: "Bevölkerung des Gebietes der freien Hansestadt Lübeck im Jahre 1840" (Lübeck, 1841).

Bremen: Blau, *Entwicklung*, 251.

Hamburg: Helga Krohn, *Die Juden in Hamburg 1800–1850: Ihre soziale, kulturelle und politische Entwicklung während der Emanzipationszeit* (Frankfurt: Europäische Verlagsanstalt, 1967), 9.

Schleswig-Holstein 1835: *Tabelle über die . . . in den Herzogthümern Schleswig und Holstein am 1. Februar 1835 vorgenommene Volkszählung* (Kopenhagen, 1836), 63–64; 1845: "Recapitulation der in den Herzogthümern Schleswig, Holstein und Lauenburg am 1. Februar 1845 vorhandenen fremden Religionsverwandten" (Kopenhagen, 1846).

Mecklenburg-Schwerin 1815, 1820: M. Grünfeldt, "Die Juden in Mecklenburg-Schwerin 1810–1910," *ZSDJ* (1912): 2.

Königreich Sachsen 1834: *Statistische Mittheilungen aus dem Königreich Sachsen* (Dresden, 1851), Table 7.

Anhalt 1864, 1867: Herzoglich Anhaltisches Statistisches Bureau, *Die Ergebnisse der Volkszählung im Herzogtum Anhalt vom 3. December 1867* (Anhalt, 1867).

Sachsen-Meiningen 1833: G. Brückner, *Landeskunde des Herzogthums Meiningen* (Meiningen, 1851), 296.

Sachsen-Meiningen, Sachsen-Coburg-Gotha, Sachsen-Weimar, all other Thuringia 1864: Hildebrand, *Statistik Thüringens*, 220–221.

The 1817 data represent either the 1817 population or our estimate of the 1817 Jewish population. The other figures are census information for other dates that were used to make the estimates.

Table 1.2. Jewish Population in Prussian *Regierungsbezirke*, 1817

Regierungsbezirk	Jewish population	Jews as percent of general population
Königsberg	2,098	0.4%
Gumbinnen	291	0.1%
Danzig	3,854	1.6%
Marienwerder	8,778	2.6%
Posen	37,547	6.4%
Bromberg	15,021	5.7%
Breslau	6,771	1.3%
Liegnitz	1,649	0.3%
Reichenbach	448	0.1%
Oppeln	7,608	1.5%
Stettin	1,269	0.4%
Köslin	1,585	0.7%
Stralsund	122	0.1%
Berlin	3,700	1.9%
Potsdam	1,933	0.4%
Frankfurt/Oder	2,865	0.5%
Magdeburg	2,142	0.5%
Merseburg	189	0.04%
Erfurt	911	0.4%
Münster	2,304	0.7%
Minden	3,930	1.2%
Arnsberg	3,489	0.9%
Düsseldorf	3,190	0.8%
Kleve	1,833	0.9%
Cologne	3,349	1.0%
Aachen	1,621	0.5%
Koblenz	5,791	1.6%
Trier	3,057	1.0%
Total	127,345	1.2%

Smaller font = less than 0.5%, bold = over 2% of the general population.
Source: Silbergleit, *Die Bevölkerungs- und Berufsverhältnisse*, 11*.

Both Posen province and Marienwerder district in West Prussia shared not only heavy Jewish density but also the shtetl pattern of settlement characterized by proportionately large Jewish communities in small market towns. In all of Prussia, there were thirty-five such localities in 1817[11] with fewer than 10,000 total inhabitants but at least 500 Jewish townspeople—thirty of them in Posen province, four in Marienwerder district, and one in Oppeln district. In most of these towns, Jews made up at least one quarter of the population and in six they were the majority. Communities with such a high proportion of Jewish inhabitants such as Kempen (2,406 Jews among 4,588 inhabitants), Zempelburg (1,169 of 2,304) and Märkisch Friedland (1,151 of 2,301), were only found in these formerly Polish areas and nowhere else in Germany. Most Jews in Posen province dwelled in communities that numbered more than 500 individuals. Over 30,000 made their homes in small towns that had over 500 Jews, and 4,025 lived in the city of Posen—the only city in the province that had more than 20,000 inhabitants. The sizable Jewish presence in Posen, West Prussia, and Upper Silesia contrasted sharply with scanty Jewish settlement in the other eastern provinces of Prussia. Jews had been permitted to live in these provinces since the 1670s, but only under extremely restrictive Prussian government policies.[12] In 1817, there were only 2,389 Jews in East Prussia (0.3 percent of the population) and 2,976 in Pomerania (0.4 percent). Only formerly Austrian Lower Silesia had a larger Jewish population (8,868 or 0.6 percent of all inhabitants). In Silesia and East Prussia there were important Jewish concentrations in the largest cities, with 1,027 in Königsberg and 4,409 in Breslau, respectively. Glogau, Lower Silesia, also had a large community, with 1,238 Jews out of 10,245 inhabitants. Most of the rest of the Jewish population was scattered in smaller cities, with only a minuscule presence in rural areas.

In central Germany, between the Elbe and Oder Rivers, the Jewish population was even more sparse and scattered. In this region, unlike much of the rest of Germany, most Jews lived in the larger cities. Berlin had 3,700 Jewish residents, making it the fifth-largest Jewish community in Germany, and was by far the largest in this area. Excluding those in Berlin, the Prussian province of Brandenburg, which surrounded the city, had fewer than 5,000

---

11 Heinrich Silbergleit, *Die Bevölkerungs- und Berufsverhältnisse der Juden im Deutschen Reich*, vol. 1, *Freistaat Preussen* (Berlin: Akademie Verlag, 1930), 9. One of the towns on the list, Peisern, was ceded to the Russian Empire not long after 1817, leaving thirty-four in Prussian territory.
12 Prussian law allowed only Jewish families that met income requirements to settle in its towns. Except for the very wealthiest Jews, *Schutzjuden* (Jews with residence permits) could have only one of their children marry and start a family. In many cases, the personal residency rights of the poorest individuals could not be passed on to their children.

Jews. The Jewish presence west of Brandenburg in the Prussian province of Saxony was even weaker. Most of the 3,242 Jews in that province (0.2 percent) lived in Magdeburg district, with the old urban community of Halberstadt and a new community in Magdeburg city the largest Jewish settlements by far. In the southern part of the province (*Regierungsbezirke* Merseburg and Erfurt), most of which was acquired from the Kingdom of Saxony in 1815, there was a minute Jewish population of only 1,100 out of 742,000 inhabitants. North of Brandenburg, the Grand Duchy of Mecklenburg-Schwerin had a relatively large population of 2,690 Jews. The tiny duchies of Anhalt, which were surrounded by Saxony province, had a denser Jewish population than most of central Germany, with approximately 2,000 Jews that exceeded one percent of the population. To the south, the Jewish population of the independent Kingdom of Saxony numbered only 874 persons out of a total of a million and a half inhabitants; nearly all of these Jews lived in Dresden and Leipzig. West of Saxony were the tiny Thuringian principalities, some of which had no Jewish populations. The only substantial Jewish populations there were mainly rural and in the extreme south and west of Thuringia, in Sachsen-Meiningen-Hildburghausen (1,524 in 1833), and Sachsen-Weimar-Eisenach (1,427 in 1834).[13]

Much of northwestern Germany was as thinly populated by Jews as central Germany. Scattered across this area, however, were several important centers of Jewish population. On the lower Elbe, the great port city of Hamburg had the largest Jewish community in Germany, with 6,423 Jews in 1811.[14] Just across the border from Hamburg in Danish-ruled Schleswig-Holstein, there was a substantial Jewish community in Altona (2,014 in 1835) and a much smaller one in Wandsbek (299 in 1880). Taken together, these three communities, known in Jewish writings by their Hebrew initials *AHU*, constituted the largest agglomeration of Jews in Germany by far. The Kingdom of Hannover, covering much of northwestern Germany, had a relatively small Jewish population (about 10,000 in 1817), most of which was concentrated at the southern edge of the kingdom and in Ostfriesland on the Dutch border in the northwest. Two provinces in the northeastern part of the Kingdom of Hannover (Stade and Lüneburg) had particularly tiny Jewish populations. The tiny northwest principalities of Braunschweig, Oldenburg, Lippe, Schaumburg-Lippe, and Waldeck had Jewish populations that varied from just under half a percent

---

13 Nearly all Jews on Sachsen-Weimar-Eisenach lived in the southwestern district of Eisenach (1,378 of 1,427 in 1834), which bordered on the Hesse electorate (Kurhessen). Bruno Hildebrand, *Statistik Thüringens*, vol. 1 (Jena, 1867), 220.
14 Peter Freimark, *Juden in Preussen—Juden in Hamburg* (Hamburg: Institut für die Geschichte der deutschen Juden, 1983), 66–67.

to just slightly over one percent of the population. Schaumburg-Lippe, Lippe, and Waldeck in the southwesternmost part of northwestern Germany bordering Westphalia and Hesse had substantially larger Jewish populations than the principalities to their north. Outside the Hamburg area, most Jews in northwestern Germany lived in small, mainly rural communities. The cities of Bremen and Lübeck excluded virtually all Jews. The city of Hanover and several small cities in Ostfriesland province had the only major northwestern communities outside the Hamburg area.

In contrast to the far-flung and sparse Jewish settlements in northwestern and central Germany, there was a substantial concentration of Jews in southwestern and south-central Germany, though not nearly as dense as the Posen-West Prussian agglomeration. Unlike the mainly urban city and shtetl form of settlement in northern and eastern Germany, the Jews of the south and west were predominantly rural. The two western Prussian provinces of Rhineland and Westphalia were transitional between the thinner Jewish population of northwestern Germany and the heavier concentrations further south. In 1817, there were 28,564 Jews out of a general population of almost three million, yielding a Jewish density of just below one percent. The farther south one went in the Rhineland, the denser and more rural the Jewish population was. In Koblenz district for example, Jews accounted for more than 1.6 percent of the population.

All the major states in southern Germany had substantial but unevenly distributed Jewish populations in concentrations based on the pre-nineteenth-century political boundaries. Most German Jews in the south lived in territories that had formerly been ruled by tiny principalities or by bishops of the Catholic Church. Almost all of the more than 50,000 Jews in the Kingdom of Bavaria were concentrated in the newly acquired Rhine Palatinate, Swabia, and Franconia in the north and west. "Old Bavaria" (Upper Bavaria, Lower Bavaria, and Upper Palatinate provinces) accommodated a mere 1,485 Jews in 1818, a number that changed little before 1850. In northern Bavaria (Franconia), the 33,723 mainly rural Jews made up a substantial part of the local population, with the northwesternmost area (Lower Franconia) having the highest density of over 2.5 percent. Jews were also heavily represented west of the Rhine in the detached Bavarian province of the Rhine Palatinate, where they constituted two percent of the population. In the two large southern states immediately west of Bavaria, Jews were also heavily concentrated in the northern sections bordering on Franconia. In Baden, about half of the Jewish population of 17,000 in 1817 congregated in the northern quarter of the grand duchy in the district of the Unterrheinkreis. In Württemberg, the Jagstkreis in the northeastern quarter had almost half the Jewish population there. Between Baden and Württemberg in the Black Forest, over 1,000 Jews congregated in the northern half of the tiny territory of Hohenzollern. Directly northwest of Jewish population centers in Franconia, northern Baden, and northern Württemberg were the various states that made up Hesse. Like their neighbors, the Hessian states (Hesse-Darmstadt, Hesse-Kassel, Hesse-Homburg, Nassau, and Frankfurt am Main) had sizable concentrations of Jews—about 43,000 Jews in 1817, which constituted more than two percent of the population in many areas.

In much of southern and western Germany, Jews were excluded from most major cities. Urban localities in parts of the country that banned Jewish residence until the eighteenth century included Munich, Nuremberg, Würzburg, Augsburg, Cologne, Stuttgart, Freiburg, and Heilbronn. Sometimes Jewish communities evolved in towns or villages on the outskirts of these cities.[15] The great exception to urban exclusion was Frankfurt, where 4,310 Jews made up some ten percent of the total population. Until the end of the eighteenth century, Jews in Frankfurt were confined to the the walled ghetto of the Judengasse. Other large urban south-German communities were in Mainz, Fürth, Mannheim, and Karlsruhe. The vast majority of German Jews in the south, however, lived in villages and small towns that had fewer than 2,000 inhabitants. In the Grand Duchy Hesse-Darmstadt, for instance, 64.1 percent of Jewish inhabitants in 1828 resided in villages of under 2,000 residents, 17.0 percent in towns of 2.000–5,000, and only 10.2 percent in towns of over 20,000 (Table 1.3).[16]

Even among the largely rural South and West German Jews, there were important regional differences in the size of Jewish communities. In the extreme southwest (Bavarian Swabia, southern Baden, southern Württemberg, Hohenzollern),[17] communities were relatively large and far apart. Agglomerations of at least 200 Jews were the norm, and several small-town communities boasted at least 500 souls.[18] In several southwestern towns, Jews accounted for more than

---

15 Many such Jewish communities existed on the outskirts of larger cities. Some examples are in Fürth outside Nuremberg, in Heidingsfeld outside Würzburg, in Deutz outside Cologne, the village communities of Steppach, Pfersee, and Kriegshaber outside Augsburg, and those of Horkheim and Sontheim outside Heilbronn.
16 Schmelz, *Hessen*, 54.
17 This covers all German-speaking areas west of the River Lech and south of a line running roughly from the Danube at Donauwörth through Stuttgart to the Rhine about halfway between Colmar and Strasbourg. This approximated the area where the Alemannic dialects of German were spoken.
18 In southern Baden in 1825, for instance, there were four small-town communities with over 250 Jews (Gailingen, Breisach, Schmieheim, Randegg) and five others with 200–250 Jews. Together, these nine village communities numbered 2,888 Jews, compared to 1,269 in the other ten southern Baden small-town communities and fifteen Jews in southern Baden cities (all in Freiburg). In southern Württemberg, large Jewish communities in small towns

TABLE 1.3. Approximate Jewish Population by Region, 1817

Region	Jewish population	General population	Percent Jewish
Posen, West Prussia, Upper Silesia	72,806	1,946,389	3.7
Other eastern Germany (East Prussia, Pomerania, Lower Silesia)	14,233	3,096,316	0.5
Central Germany (Brandenburg, Prussian Saxony, Kingdom of Saxony, Mecklenburg, Anhalt, Thuringia)	21,069	c.5,685,000	0.4
Northwestern Germany (Hamburg, Schleswig-Holstein, Hannover, Braunschweig, Lübeck, Bremen, Lippe, Schaumburg-Lippe, Waldeck, Oldenburg)	24,300	c.3,600,000	0.7
Western Germany (Rhineland, Westphalia, Birkenfeld)	29,614	c. 3,015,000	1.0
Southern Germany (Bavaria, Baden, Württemberg, Hessian states, Hohenzollern)	121,175	c. 7,900,000	1.5
Total	283,197	25,242,705	1.1

Source: based on same sources as Table 1.1.

---

included Oberdorf (338 in 1812), Aufhausen (204), Buchau (345 in 1807), Buttenhausen (251 in 1807), Mühringen (354 in 1809), and Rexingen (240 in 1807)—almost 2,700 Jewish inhabitants altogether. In Hohenzollern in 1843–1844, the Haigerloch and Hechingen communities accommodated 1,191 Jews. In Bavarian Swabia, there were at least thirteen small-town communities with over 200 Jews in 1809–1812. Their combined Jewish population of over 4,900 represented more than two-thirds of the Jewish population of Bavarian Swabia. The largest Jewish communities in the small towns of southwestern Germany were Ichenhausen (893 in 1811), Gailingen (596 in 1825), and Breisach (572 in 1832).

one-third of the local population.[19] In contrast to the northern areas of Baden and Württemberg, which had few counties completely devoid of Jews and numerous relatively small Jewish communities, southern Baden and Württemberg had many counties without Jews and a small number of much larger communities (Table 1.4).[20]

Outside the far southwest, German Jewish communities in the south were more numerous but smaller. In 1816, Lower Franconia in northwestern Bavaria, for instance, had at least 117 Jewish communities in towns that had fewer than 10,000 inhabitants, of which only nine had 200 Jewish inhabitants or more.[21] The approximately 2,500 Jews in the nine large communities were less than twenty percent of the Jewish population of Lower Franconia. Somewhat farther north in Hesse-Darmstadt, all but one of the Jewish communities with over 500 people were in cities of over 10,000 inhabitants;[22] their total Jewish population of some 3,625 was less than fifteen percent of the Jewish population of the grand duchy. In 1861, 55.3 percent of Jews in Hesse-Darmstadt lived in communities of 30–200 souls and 12.6 percent inhabited communities of 200–500 (Table 1.5).[23]

Relative Stability (1815–1840) and Heavier Migration (1840–1871)

The two generations of German Jews that reached adulthood after the Napoleonic Wars and before the unification of Germany were marked by highly different demographic developments. Until the 1840s, the basic pattern of German-Jewish population distribution remained more or less unchanged

---

19 They included Rexingen, Ichenhausen (45.1 percent in 1811), Gailingen (47.6 percent in 1825) and Fellheim (61 percent in 1811).
20 In 1858, 1,468 of the 1,742 Jews in the Schwarzwaldkreis lived in one county (Horb), the other 274 inhabited six different counties, and ten counties had no Jewish inhabitants at all. Across the border in southeastern Baden, 1,615 of the 1,644 Jews in the Seekreis in 1852 lived in Radolfzell County on the western shores of Lake Constance, where they made up 9.7 percent of the county population. The other twenty-nine Jews were scattered across seven counties, and seven other counties had no Jews at all. In the northern Baden Unterrheinkreis, in contrast, there were no counties completely without Jews and only two of twenty had Jewish densities of under one percent. The overall density of Jews in the Unterrheinkreis in 1852 was 3.1 percent (as against 0.8 percent in the Seekreis), but the highest density in any one county was 6.9 percent.
21 Westheim (206), Memmelsdorf (234), Schwanfeld (230), Reckendorf (302), Unsleben (202), Niederwerrn (265), Thüngen (319), Hochberg (218), Heidingsfeld (507).
22 Schmelz, *Hessen*, 365, 380–381. Schmelz does not provide figures for the earlier period, in which very large communities may well have been even rarer.
23 Ibid., 58.

TABLE 1.4. Difference in Jewish Distribution in Northern vs. Southern Baden and Württemberg, by Number and Size of Communities, 1821-1858

Year and Counties	Number of communities	Average size per community	Total Jews	Counties with no Jews	Counties with 1–99 Jews	Counties with over 100 Jews
North						
1821						
Neckarkreis	25	81				
Jagstkreis	40	94				
1852						
Mittelrheinkeis			7084	5	3	13
Unterrrheinkreis			10873	0	2	18
1858						
Neckarkreis				5	3	9
Jagstkreis				6	0	8
South						
1821						
Donaukreis	6	274		11	1	4
Schwarzwaldkreis	10	147				
1852						
Seekreis			1644	7	7	1
Oberrheinkreis			4098	11	1	6
1858						
Schwarzwaldkreis				10	5	2
Donaukreis				7	4	5

Sources: "Vergleichende Uebersicht der Bevölkerung Württembergs in besonderer Beziehung auf die Confessions-Verhältnisse in den Jahren 1821 und 1841," *Württembergische Jahrbücher für Vaterländische Geschichte, Geographie, Statistik und Topographie* 2 (1843); "Uebersicht über die ortsangehörige Bevölkerung des Königreichs Württemberg am 3. December 1858," *Württembergische Jahrbücher für Vaterländische Geschichte, Geographie, Statistik und Topographie* 2 (1858); *Beiträge zur Statistik des inneren Verwaltung des Grossherzogthums Baden* (Karlsruhe, 1855).

Table 1.5. Size of Jewish Communities in Southern Germany

Size of community	Lower Franconia (1816)	Hesse-Darmstadt (1861)
	(towns under 10,000 inhabitants)	(towns under 10,000 inhabitants)
	Number of communities	Number of communities
Over 200 Jews	9	12
100–200	over 40	47
30–100	at least 51	185

Sources: based on *Pinkas ha-Kehillot, Germania, Bavaria*, 379–580, and Schmelz, *Hessen*, 365, 380–381.

even as German Jewry as a whole grew at a rate somewhat faster than that of the general population. Starting in the 1840s, this relative stability began to change, with some doing so earlier and some later. After 1840, German Jewry was typified by two profound demographic changes—emigration (mainly to America) and urbanization. Although neither process was completed by 1871, the changes that they caused among German Jewry were nevertheless quite advanced.

Official statistics from almost all parts of Germany show growth in the Jewish population between 1815 and 1840.[24] Although the rates of increase varied from area to area, with the exception of parts of Bavaria, no areas lost Jewish population; urban communities increased numerically but not more rapidly than non-urban ones. Prussian statistics, using the admittedly indistinct legal categories of "city" and "countryside" that were based on legal status rather than locality size, show faster growth in the "country" category than in the "cities" between 1817 and 1858. In the following generation, the "rural" population began to decline, slowly at first between 1858 and 1867 and with greater rapidity thereafter (Table 1.6).

In Prussia, every major district (*Regierungsbezirk*) substantially increased its Jewish population between 1817 and 1843, and in most cases they did so beyond numbers that can be attributed to natural increase. The strongest growth

---

24 It is possible that the growth in numbers of Jews counted was not only the result of an actual growth in population, but also the result of improved counting techniques and growing government success in bringing the Jews under bureaucratic control.

Table 1.6. Prussian Urban and Rural Jewish Population (Legal Categories), 1817–1910

Year	Stadt (urban)	Land (rural)	Total	Percent Stadt	Percent Land
1817	106,209	21,136	127,345	83.4	17.6
1849	173,199	45,574	218,773	79.2	20.8
Percent change	+63.1%	+115.6%			
1858	189,653	52,712	242,365	78.3	21.8
Percent change	+9.5%	+15.7%			
1867 (old borders)	210,904	51,822	262,726	80.3	19.7
Percent change	+11.2%	-1.7%			
1867 (new borders)	241,473	71,683	313,156	77.1	22.9
1871	256,812	68,648	325,460	78.9	21.1
Percent change	+6.4%	-4.2%			
1880	294,197	69,593	363,790	80.9	19.1
Percent change	+14.6%	+1.4%			
1895	319,991	59,721	379,712	84.3	15.7
Percent change	+8.8%	-14.2%			
1905	356,428	53,069	409,497	87.0	13.0
Percent change	+11.4%	-11.1%			
1910	363,275	52,651	415,926	87.3	12.7
Percent change	+1.9%	-0.8%			

Source: Blau, *Entwiklung*, 69.

occurred in the eastern provinces that bordered the heavily Jewish province of Posen, at rates ranging from 81.6 percent in Marienwerder to 404.1 percent in Gumbinnen district. Jews seemed to be migrating to eastern provinces that had relatively low Jewish densities, especially Pomerania and East Prussia, even though it was illegal until the introduction of freedom of movement by the Prussian law of 1847 in everywhere but Posen.[25] There may have been some immigration from the Russian-ruled Kingdom of Poland as well. In most other Prussian districts, the Jewish population increased by 40–67 percent. Even areas that lost population later on, e.g., Posen province, posted substantial increases.

---

25 The revolution of 1848 ended the restrictions on migration from Posen to the rest of Prussia.

The smallest upturn, which was in Magdeburg district, was still considerable at 21.9 percent. However, it was indicative of some out-migration because it was slower than the rate of increase occasioned by net fertility. The rate of increase in the largest city in Prussia, Berlin, exceeded the average at 125.6 percent (from 3,700 to 8,348) but fell short of the increase in East Prussia and most of Pomerania. The not-yet-industrialized Ruhr area (Düsseldorf and Arnsberg districts) showed no unusual growth in its Jewish population (Table 1.7).

Similar if somewhat slower increases were found in the Jewish populations of the overwhelmingly rural southern states. In Bavaria, the number of Jews grew from 53,208 in 1818 to 62,830 in 1844 (18.1 percent), although some sections of the kingdom showed declines after about 1830. In Hesse-Darmstadt, the Jewish population increased steadily in every census from 1822 (20,600) to 1849 (29,131) and outpaced general population growth, advancing from 3.1 percent of the total to 3.4 percent. In Württemberg between 1821 and 1846, rural areas gained Jewish population as quickly as the urban part that included the major city of Stuttgart (Table 1.8).[26]

In many parts of Germany, the Jewish population outpaced the general population in its increase. Johann Gottfried Hoffmann's analysis of the growth of the Prussian Jewish population between 1822 and 1840, which was published in 1842, attributed 42,044 to net fertility and the rest (9,567) to a favorable migration balance or improved collection of data between the two censuses. Either way, Hoffmann reports that the Prussian Jewish population increased by 34.4 percent in eighteen years compared to 27.9 percent among the population at large.[27] Hoffmann and most modern scholars attributed the greater natural increase of the Jewish population than that of non-Jews to a lower Jewish death rate rather than a higher Jewish birth rate.[28] The difference in death rates mainly resulted from much lower infant mortality among Jews than among non-Jews—a pattern that recurs in almost all known statistics.[29] One of the reasons for the lower Jewish infant mortality rate was the much lower Jewish rate of illegitimacy, since children born out of wedlock were far more likely to die than those born to a married couple.

Increases in the urban Jewish population remained relatively modest in the period between 1815 and the 1840s. In many parts of Germany, such as

---

26 After 1846, the Jewish populations of the rural areas declined and increased rapidly in the Stuttgart area (*Pinkas ha-Kehillot, Germania, Württemberg-Hohenzollern-Baden,* 5; Bruno Blau, *Die Entwicklung der jüdischen Bevölkerung in Deutschland von 1800 bis 1945,* manuscript in Leo Baeck Institute archives, New York, 202).
27 Quoted by Silbergleit, *Die Bevölkerungs- und Berufsverhältnisse,* 11*–12*.
28 For details on Hoffmann's data, see Table 4.3.
29 Schmelz, *Hessen,* 68–71, 111–113.

TABLE 1.7. Increases of Jewish Population in Prussian Districts, 1817–1843

District	1817	1843	Percent increase	Numeric increase
Königsberg	2,098	4,730	**125.5%**	2632
Gumbinnen	291	1,467	**404.1%**	1206
Danzig	3,854	5,402	40.2%	1548
Marienwerder	8,778	15,939	81.6%	7161
Posen	37,547	54,787	45.9%	17,240
Bromberg	15,021	24,788	65.0%	9767
Berlin	3,700	8,348	**125.6%**	4648
Potsdam	1,933	3,211	66.1%	1278
Frankfurt/Oder	2,865	4,642	62.0%	1777
Stettin	1,269	3,779	**198.0%**	2510
Köslin	1,585	3,781	**138.6%**	2196
Stralsund	122	156	27.9%	34
Breslau				
Liegnitz	8,868	13,046	47.1%	4178
Reichenbach				
Oppeln	7,608	15,560	**104.5%**	7952
Magdeburg	2,142	2,612	21.9%	470
Merseburg	189	458	**142.3%**	269
Erfurt	911	1,452	59.4%	541
Münster	2,304	3,215	39.5%	911
Minden	3,930	5,782	47.1%	1852
Arnsberg	3,489	5,408	55.0%	1919
Cologne	3,349	5,219	55.8%	1870
Düsseldorf	5,023	7,102	41.4%	2079
Kleve				
Koblenz	5,791	7,965	37.5%	2174
Trier	3,057	4,762	55.8%	1705
Aachen	1,621	2,522	55.8%	901

Data in bold = more than doubled.
Source: Silbergleit, *Die Bevölkerungs- und Berufsverhältnisse*, 11*, 18*–19*.

Table 1.8. Changes in Jewish Population in Districts of Württemberg

District	1821	1832	1846	Percent change 1821–1846	1858	Percent change 1846–1858	1871	Percent change 1858–1871
Neckarkreis (including Stuttgart)	2,012	2,376	2,701	+34.2%	2,809	+4.0%	4,227	+50.5%
Schwarzwaldkreis	1,466	1,691	1,953	+33.2%	1,476	-24.4%	1,328	-10.0%
Jagstkreis	3,797	4,505	5,095	+34.2%	4,230	-17.0%	4,024	-4.9%
Donaukreis	1,643	2,096	2,607	+58.7%	2,572	-1.3%	2,666	+3.7%

Sources: "Vergleichende Uebersicht der Bevölkerung Württembergs"; and Blau, *Entwicklung*, 199, 202.

Bavaria, some areas in Baden, Frankfurt, Lübeck, and Saxony, residual legal restrictions or outright prohibitions on Jewish settlement in major cities slowed Jewish migration to the cities. Even in those that imposed no restrictions, however, Jewish growth was generally relatively limited. Germany was still an overwhelmingly rural country in the early nineteenth century. In 1843, 325 towns in Prussia had more than 100 Jews and boasted a total Jewish population of 145,300—70.5 percent of all Prussian Jews. The vast majority of these Jewish communities were in small towns; only eight communities of over 500 Jews, with a combined Jewish population of fewer than 30,000, were in major cities.[30]

In 1852, there were only fifteen cities of over 50,000 inhabitants in Germany. Two of them, Bremen and Nuremberg, still excluded Jews. Other major cities that did not admit Jewish populations until the late eighteenth or early nineteenth centuries, like Munich and Cologne, now had communities of over 1,000. In Stuttgart, the community had grown to only 390, while in Saxony, where Jewish residence was still closely restricted, there were only about 675 Jews in Dresden and 390 in Leipzig. While urban Jewish communities that were already substantial in 1815, such as Berlin, Hamburg, Breslau, and Frankfurt, grew in size, only the Jewish population in Berlin doubled its population (Table 1.9). Altogether, almost twelve percent of German Jews lived in cities of over 50,000 inhabitants in 1852, and a smaller proportion inhabited towns with populations of 10,000–50,000. This brought the share of German Jewry that inhabited towns of over 10,000 to around twenty-one percent in 1852.[31] Thus, the vast majority of German Jews had not yet been affected by urbanization.

Urbanization began in earnest in the two decades after 1852. The beginning of the Industrial Revolution in Germany created new economic opportunities for Jews in urban areas and undercut the viability of some occupations that were common in rural localities. Jews were swept up in the move to the cities more rapidly and extensively than the general German population. Population

---

30 Eduard Bleich, ed., "Uebersicht sämmtlicher Städte des Preussischen Staates in welchen nach der Zählung zu Ende 1843 einhundert Juden und darüber wohnten, nach den Provinzen geordnet," in *Der erste vereinigte Landtag in Berlin 1847* (Berlin: Verlag von Karl Reimarus, 1847), vol. 1, 323–326. The towns enumerated by Bleich are Danzig (4,234), Königsberg (1,688), Posen (7,359), Berlin (8,263), Stettin (519), Breslau (6,339), Magdeburg (631), and Cologne (784), for a total of 29,817. Bleich's figure for Danzig seems to be incorrect because there were only 2,148 Jews in this city in 1817 and 2,565 in 1852. If we transpose the first two numbers in the figures for Danzig, we arrive at a Jewish population of 2,434, which fits reasonably into the trend. This would reduce the total number of Jews in the eight major cities in 1843 to 28,017.
31 For a breakdown of the distribution of Jews in towns with over 10,000 inhabitants, see Table 9.10.

TABLE 1.9. Jewish Population in German Cities over 50,000 and Their Growth, 1817, 1852–1871

City	c. 1817 Jewish population	1852 General population	1852 Jewish population	1871 General population	1871 Jewish population
Berlin	3,699	438,958	11,867 (+220.8%)	826,341	**36,015 (+203.5%)**
Hamburg (city limits)	6,300 (1811)	179,594	9,000 (+42.9)	239,107	11,954 (+32.8)
Breslau	4,409	121,052	8,000 (+81.5)	207,997	13,916 (+74.0)
Munich	451 (1814)	106,715	1,208 (+167.9)	169,693	**2,903 (+140.3)**
Dresden	683 (1834)	104,199	679 (–0.6) (1849)	177,089	1,276 (+87.9)
Cologne	124 (1806)	101,091	1,531	129,233	**3,172 (107.2)**
Königsberg	1,027	79,887	2,056 (+100.2)	112,082	3,836 (+86.6)
Magdeburg	330	76,146	880 (+166.7)	84,401	1,270 (+44.3)
Frankfurt/Main	4,309	67,332	5,730 (+33.0) (1858)	91,040	10,009 (+74.9)
Danzig	2,148	67,015	2,565 (+19.4)	88,975	2,625 (+2.3)
Leipzig	152 (1834)	66,837	324 (+112.2) (1849)	106,925	**1,739 (+436.7)**
Bremen	2 (1826)	57,055	c. 50 (+2400.0)	82,807	**321 (+542.0)**
Nuremberg	1 (1807)	53,638	87 (+8600.0)	83,214	**1,831 (+2004.6)**
Aachen	60 (1806)	52,687	363	74,146	**825 (+127)**
Stettin	81	52,252	901 (+1012.4)	76,280	**1,823 (+102.3)**
Stuttgart	130 (1832)	50,003	382 (+293.9) (1858)	91,602	**1,817 (+254.9)**
Subtotal	23906		45,623	(+90.2%)	95.332 (+109.0)

Data in bold = more than doubled.

Surpassed 50,000 after 1852:

City	1852 General population	1852 Jewish population	1871 General population	1871 Jewish population
Hannover			87,626	1,936
Strasbourg			78,130	3,088
Barmen			74,449	143
Altona			74,102	2,233
Elberfeld			71,384	626
Düsseldorf			69,365	919
Chemnitz			68,229	95
Braunschweig			57,883	394
Krefeld-Uerdingen			57,105	1,085
Posen			56,374	7,255
Mainz			53,902	2,998
Halle/Saale			52,620	464
Mulhouse			51,850	1,997
Essen			51,513	832
Augsburg			51,220	660
Total	1,621,775	44,799	3,302,205	120,057
Percent Jewish		(2.8%)		(3.6%)

Sources: Schmelz, Territorial Printout for 1852 and 1871 (except where other dates given instead of 1852); pre-1852 data from Silbergleit, *Die Bevölkerungs- und Berufsverhältnisse*, 9*; "Übersicht der Zahl der Juden in den linksrheinischen Departements in den Jahren 1806–1808," in *Zur Geschichte und Kultur der Juden im Rheinland* (Düsseldorf: Schwann, 1985), 90–97.

increase in Berlin was much greater in the twenty-eight years from 1843 to 1871 than in the previous twenty-six years. Between 1816 and 1843, the city's Jewish population rose from 3,373 to 8,348[32]—147.5 percent compared to 76.6 percent among the population of the city at large. From 1843 to 1871 however, the Jewish population more than quadrupled to 36,015 while the overall city population rose by 136.6 percent. Jews made up 1.7 percent of the Berlin population in 1816, 2.4 percent in 1843, and 4.4 percent in 1871.[33] The growth of other traditionally large urban Jewish communities was also much faster after the 1840s. The Jewish population of Frankfurt increased by only 33 percent in the forty-one years between 1817 and 1858, but by 75 percent in the thirteen ensuing years, reaching 10,009 in 1871. Similar developments occurred in Hamburg and Breslau.[34] Growth in cities where Jewish settlement had been restricted was even more spectacular from the 1850s onward (Table 1.10). Although some cities such as Nuremberg and Freiburg maintained their restrictions even into the 1860s, many others abandoned them after the 1848 revolution. By 1871, 76,653 Jews lived in the eight cities that had total populations in excess of 100,000, representing 15.0 percent of all German Jews. Meanwhile,

Table 1.10. Rapid Jewish Population Increase in Formerly Restricted Cities

City	Year: Population	Year: Population	Year: Population
Leipzig	1832: 140	1849: 320	1871: 1,768
Dresden	1832: 712	1849: 672	1871: 1,246
Stuttgart	1807: 92	1852: 390	1871: 2,074
Cologne	1806: 124	1852: 1,531	1871: 3,172
Nuremberg		1852: 87	1871: 1,831
Munich	1814: 451	1852: 1,208	1871: 2,903

Sources: Schmelz, Territorial Printout; Blau, *Entwicklung*, 184, 203; *Pinkas ha-Kehillot, Germania, Bavaria*, 105; "Übersicht der Zahl der Juden in den linksrheinischen Departementen in den Jahren 1806–1808," in *Zur Geschichte und Kultur der Juden im Rheinland*, ed. Falk Wiesemann (Düsseldorf: Schwann, 1985), 96.

---

32 8,263 according to Bleich's list (which may, however, refer to the 1842 rather than the 1843 population).
33 Silbergleit, *Die Bevölkerungs- und Berufsverhältnisse*, 25*.
34 Breslau: 1816—4,409, 1850—7,384, 1871—13,916, and Hamburg: 1811—6,429, 1852—10,000, 1871—13,796.

45,246 lived in the twenty-three towns that had populations of 50,000–100,000 (8.8 percent), and 31,022 in the forty-nine localities of 20,000–50,000 (6.1 percent). Overall, the percentage of German Jews who dwelled in cities that had populations of 20,000 or more climbed from about 17.5 percent in 1852, to nearly 30 percent in 1871, compared to only 12.7 percent of the total 1871 German population (Table 1.11).

The urbanization of German Jewry varied greatly from region to region. Official statistics for Prussia in 1871 show that 31.9 percent of Jews lived in cities of over 20,000 inhabitants, 20.9 percent in towns of 5,000–20,000, and 47.3 percent in localities that had 5,000 or fewer inhabitants. Most Prussian Jews belonged to substantial communities, only 16.3 percent inhabited communities of fewer than fifty. Jews in the western and extreme eastern parts of Prussia, however, were much less likely to live in large cities than those in the more central areas of Prussia. Jews in the western areas were also much more likely than those in the rest of Prussia to live in scattered groups of fewer than fifty (Table 1.12). In some parts of Prussia, especially in the west, more than

Table 1.11. Urbanization in Three Regions of Prussia, 1871

Number of Jews in:	Towns of over 20,000	5,000–20,000	Under 5,000	Communities with fewer than 50 Jews
West:				
Hannover, Westphalia, Hesse-Nassau, Rhineland, Hohenzollern	26,693 (25.3%)	14,719 (13.4%)	64,158 (61.3%)	28,413 (26.9%)
Extreme east:				
RBs Posen, Bromberg, Marienwerder, Oppeln	9,218 (8.8%)	32,311 (30.9%)	63,069 (60.3%)	11,374 (10.9%)
All other Prussia: **(Mainly central Prussia)**	67,794 (58.7%)	20,919 (18.1%)	26,711 (23.1%)	13,366 (11.6%)
Prussia, total	103,705 (31.9%)	67,949 (20.9%)	153,933 (47.3%)	53,153 (16.3%)

Source: "Die Ergebnisse der Volkszählung und Volksbeschreibung im Preussichen Staate vom 1. December 1871," *Preussische Statistik* 30 (1875): 83.

Table 1.12. Urbanization in Southern Germany, 1871

Region	Over 20,000	5,000–20,000	Under 5,000
Bavaria	11,449	4,780	34,419
	(28.6%)	(9.4%)	(68.0%)
Hesse-Darmstadt	19.3%	10.4%	70.3%

In communities with fewer than 50 Jews (1861): 19.0%
Sources: *Pinkas ha-Kehillot, Germania, Bavaria*, 8; Schmelz, *Hessen*, 54, 58.

three-fourths of Jews still dwelled in towns of under 5,000.[35] The percentages of Jews in towns of fewer than 5,000 and of those scattered in small communities were even larger in the South German states than in the western sections of Prussia (Table 1.13).

The 1840s and 1850s also saw the onset of large-scale migration from the traditional Jewish population centers in the south and the east. In the south, most of those who left traditional communities emigrated to the United States, while in the east some moved to America and others left for large Prussian cities like Berlin and Breslau. German emigration to the United States began slowly in the early 1830s, crested temporarily in the early 1850s, waned before and during the American Civil War, resumed afterward in two main surges between 1865 and 1874 and between 1880 and 1884, and then tailed off acutely after 1895.[36] Although no comprehensive statistics on the number of Jewish emigrants appear to exist, several estimates may illustrate the order of magnitude. Thus, it is estimated that Jews made up 2–4 percent of the emigrants to the United States, far in excess of their share in the German population but otherwise consistent with the chronological and geographic German patterns. In both population groups, emigration was greatest at first from southern and southwestern Germany and then gradually shifted northeast, especially in the second half of the nineteenth century.[37] The American Jewish population

---

35 In seven *Regierungsbezirke*, more than 75 percent of the Jewish population inhabited towns of under 5,000: Marienwerder (77.8), Stade (76.7), Münster (85.5), Minden (77.4), Kassel (82.5), Koblenz (80.4), and Trier (83.2). All of these districts except for the first-mentioned were in the western half of Prussia.
36 For exact figures, see Table 8.2.
37 Based on rather fragmentary records, Peter Marschalck, *Deutsche Überseewanderung im 19. Jahrhundert: ein Beitrag zur soziologischen Theorie der Bevölkerung* (Stuttgart: Klett, 1973), 38, estimates that 53.2 percent of German emigrants between 1835 and 1839 came from Württemberg, Baden, and Bavaria. By 1850–1854, this share had fallen to 34.9 percent while the percentage from eastern Germany (East Prussia, West Prussia, Posen, Brandenburg, Pomerania, Silesia) was about 3.4 percent. By 1865–1869, the proportions had changed to

Table 1.13. Net Annual Jewish Emigration from Prussia, 1843–1894

Year	Net Annual Jewish Emigration
1843–1846	1,069
1846–1849	934
1849–1852	974
1852–1855	1,312
1855–1858	1,420
1858–1861	1,472
1861–1864	553
1880–1884	3,213
1885–1889	1,746
1890–1894	895

Sources: a series of articles in the *Allgemeine Preussische Staatszeitung* (1838): 949–950, 953–954), in which Jewish net migration in 1822–1837 was calculated. A much more complete series of calculations was given by Silbergleit, *Die Bevölkerungs- und Berufsverhältnisse*, 14*–15*, for 1819–1864 and 1875–1910. Silbergleit's figures clash with those in the *Allgemeine Preussische Staatszeitung* due to several typographical errors in his table. Silbergleit's tables set the annual increase of Jewish population between 1831 and 1834 at 2,043, and that between 1834 and 1837 at 3,373; the correct figures are 3,043 and 2,373 respectively. When the rest of his data are recalculated accordingly, the net emigration that he identified in 1831–1834 disappears and net emigration occurs instead between 1834 and 1837.

The years 1875–1880 saw a small annual net immigration of 63. Net emigration of Jews from Prussia occurred in 1843–1846, 1849–1852, 1858–1861, and 1861–1864, whereas the general Prussian population posted net immigration. Jews exhibited a small net immigration in 1875–1880, when Prussia at large had substantial net emigration.

increased rapidly during this time—from about 15,000 in 1840 to 150,000 in 1860 and 280,000 in 1880[38]—and owed much of the growth to immigration

---

16.8 percent from Württemberg, Baden, and Bavaria and 17.2 percent from eastern Germany. Marschalck gives no figures for eastern and northeastern Germany in the period before 1845. For many emigrants, the place of origin in Germany is not given.

38 Avraham Barkai, *Branching Out: German-Jewish Immigration to the United States 1820–1914* (New York and London: Holmes & Meier, 1994), 15, 125.

from Germany. Historian Avraham Barkai estimates the total number of Jewish immigrants to the United States from Germany between 1846 and 1910 was 250,000.[39]

This growth of the American Jewish population after 1840 was matched by the beginning of Jewish population decline in the areas that yielded the most emigrants. The trend is most obvious in Bavaria, where the growth of Jewish population until the mid-1840s sharply reversed from a high of 62,830 in 1844 to 49,840 in 1867 (minus 20.7 percent), followed by a slight recovery to 53,697 in 1880.[40] In Württemberg, the Jewish population fell from 12,356 in 1846 to 11,088 in 1858.[41] In Hesse-Darmstadt, the decline was more modest: from 29,131 in 1849 to 28,249 in 1855.[42]

Migration from Prussia followed a similar but somewhat later course. Jews there showed a moderate but steady excess of immigration over emigration from 1819 to 1843, with a brief spike in emigration between 1834 and 1837. Between 1843 and 1890, Prussian Jewish emigration exceeded immigration in almost every period for which there is evidence, with net emigration highest in 1852–1861 and in 1880–1890 (Table 1.13).[43]

In eastern Germany, Jewish emigration from Posen began somewhat later than from Bavaria but lasted much longer and eventually took a much greater toll on the Jewish population. The Jewish presence in the province peaked in the mid-1840s with 81,299 in 1846, and declined steadily to 78,014 in 1849, 72,198 in 1858, and 61,982 in 1871—22.1 percent in all.[44] The share of German Jews who lived either in Posen or in Bavaria fell from about 37.8 percent in 1817 to 22.0 percent in 1871.[45] In Bavaria, one of the chief precipitants of emigration was the harsh "Matrikel-Gesetz" (registration law) of 1813, which prohibited Jews from marrying unless the death or emigration of a married head of household created a "vacancy." This restriction remained in place until 1861. In Posen, it was the repeal of restrictions that appears to have prompted out-migration.

---

39 Ibid., 126.
40 *Pinkas ha-Kehillot, Germania, Bavaria* (Jerusalem: Yad Vashem, 1973), 7, 9; and Reinhard Rürup, "The European Revolutions of 1848 and Jewish Emancipation," in *Revolution and Evolution: 1848 in German-Jewish History*, ed. Werner E. Mosse, Arnold Paucker, and Reinhold Rürup (Tübingen: Mohr Siebeck, 1981), 10, note 18.
41 Blau, *Die Entwicklung*, 199; and *Pinkas ha-Kehillot, Germania, Württemberg-Hohenzollern-Baden*, 5.
42 Schmelz, *Hessen*, 46.
43 Silbergleit, *Die Bevölkerungs- und Berufsverhältnisse*, 14*–15*.
44 Ibid., *18–*19; and Blau, *Die Entwicklung*, 69. The Jewish population of the province declined even more quickly after the unification of Germany, reaching a low of 26,512 in 1910.
45 23.9 percent excluding Alsace-Lorraine.

Until the revolution of 1848, Jewish migration from Posen to the rest of Prussia was limited. Thereafter, westward migration by Posen Jews became much easier. In both cases, out-migration seems to have been associated with pressure on the population caused by the natural increases of the early nineteenth century and tended to be greatest in areas of high Jewish population density.

The combination of urbanization and emigration set in motion both a decline in the numbers of rural Jews and a regional redistribution of German Jewry that continued well into the twentieth century. In Bavaria, the emigration-induced decrease in the Jewish population was accompanied by a strong increase in Jewish residence in major cities. In 1840, 5,438 of the 59,288 Bavarian Jews lived in the eleven largest cities. Most communities, with the exception of the largest in Fürth, with 2,535 Jews, were relatively new. The total number of Jews outside these major cities was 53,850. By 1867, when only 49,840 Jews remained in Bavaria, the Jewish population of the eleven main cities had increased to 10,122, leaving only 39,718 in the rural sector. The slight increase in the Bavarian Jewish population between 1867 and 1871 was wholly urban, with the non-urban population falling to 37,941[46] for a total decline of 29.5 percent in thirty-one years. In neighboring Württemberg, where the Jewish population recouped almost all its losses from 1846 to 1871, the rapid growth of the Stuttgart community began to drain away the rural population.[47] A highly similar process occurred in all parts of Germany.

Urbanization and emigration had an expediting effect on the redistribution of Jewish population from densely Jewish areas to less densely Jewish ones, a process which began before 1840. The aforementioned migration from heavily Jewish Posen and Bavaria was countered by increases in Jewish population density in some, although not all, regions that had low Jewish density. One area that attracted Jewish migrants was the eastern and central Prussian provinces of Pomerania, East Prussia, and Brandenburg (mainly Berlin). In 1817, the 13,741 Jews in these three provinces made up roughly 4.9 percent of the Jewish population of Germany. By 1843, the corresponding figures were 30,114 and 7.8 percent respectively. Between 1843 and 1871, these areas grew even more rapidly and by 1871 they had accumulated 74,946 Jews (almost half of them in

---

46 *Pinkas ha-Kehillot, Germania, Bavaria*, 7–8.
47 Blau, *Die Entwicklung*, 199; Usiel Oscar Schmelz, Territorial Printout (in the possession of the author, BENJAMB, GRMPR3, 90/06/06, 12.14.22), estimates in 1846: 12,356 Jews in Württemberg; in 1852: 390 in Stuttgart (leaving a rural population of 11,966); and in 1871: 12,245 Jews in Württemberg and 1,817 in Stuttgart (leaving a rural population of 10,428), with a 12.85 percent decline in the rural population.

Berlin), totaling 14.6 percent of all German Jews.[48] Among the other parts of the country, the proportions of German Jewry increased significantly in only two regions: western Germany and Silesia, and not nearly as much as East Prussia, Pomerania, and Brandenburg. The Jewish population in the western areas of Rhineland and Westphalia grew from 28,564 (10.2 percent of German Jewry) in 1817 to 41,975 (10.9 percent) in 1843 and 55,669 (11.8 percent) in 1871. The greatest upturns were in the urbanizing northern Rhineland *Regierungsbezirke* of Cologne and Düsseldorf—from 8,372 (approximately 3.0 percent of German Jewry) in 1817[49] to 19,956 (4.2 percent) in 1871. The Jewish population of industrializing Silesia increased from 16,476 (5.9 percent of German Jewry) in 1817 to 28,606 in 1843 and 46,619 (9.9 percent) in 1871. Conversely, heavily Jewish southern Germany lost share, from 44.3 percent of German Jewry in 1817 to 32.1 percent in 1871. Much of this redistribution would continue after 1871.

---

48 This proportion includes the Jews in Alsace-Lorraine, which Germany annexed in 1871 (and is not counted in the earlier figures). The exclusion of this province makes the percentage more comparable. Without Alsace-Lorraine, 15.9 percent of German Jews were domiciled in these three provinces.
49 Including Kleve district, which later merged with Düsseldorf.

2

German Jewish Population Changes in Imperial Germany (1871–1918)

It was during the Imperial period that German Jewry definitively acquired the profile of a demographically modernized community. Twentieth-century German Jewry—a population marked by urbanization, family planning, an aging population, and the predominance of immigrants over emigrants—was largely the product of developments in the four decades preceding World War I. Some of these phenomena, such as the sharp and voluntary decline in Jewish fertility, were in many ways new developments that were part of the *Kaiserreich* (Imperial) era. While Jewish urbanization, on the other hand, was already well underway before German unification, it was in the *Kaiserreich* period that the dominance of large urban communities became evident to all. The predominance of immigration over emigration was a reversal of the pre-1880 pattern but may have also been intimately connected to it. Emigration of the German-Jewish poor had been one of the factors that had helped to turn German Jewry into a middle-class community, and the resulting middle-class conditions may have given Jewish emigrants from Eastern Europe an inducement to try to settle in Germany. Middle-class conditions and values were also tied to the decline in Jewish fertility.

Overall Numbers

The Jewish population reached its numerical pinnacle during the German Empire period, even as its percentage in the total population began to decline and continued to do so rather steeply after the demise of the Empire. In 1871, newly united Germany had a Jewish population of 512,158,[1] or 1.3 percent of the total, which was substantially higher than the 280,000 and 1.1 percent of the population in around 1817. The 1910 German census provided evidence of ensuing developments, counting more Jews than before (615,021) but a smaller Jewish share of the German population (only 1 percent, see Map 2/1).

The number of German Jews reported during the *Kaiserreich* period was somewhat inflated compared to both earlier and later periods because of the German annexation of the former French districts of Alsace and Lorraine. Alsace-Lorraine was the home to a substantial, mainly rural, Jewish population that shared many characteristics with the Jews of southern Germany. In 1871, the newly acquired territory had a Jewish population of 40,928 (2.6 percent of all inhabitants of Alsace and Lorraine). Not counting Alsace-Lorraine, Germany had only 471,230 Jews in 1871 (1.2 percent of the total). The Jewish population of Alsace-Lorraine declined during the Imperial period, partly pursuant to earlier trends and partly due to Jewish emigration, mainly to France but also to the United States. By 1910, there were only 30,483 Jews in these provinces (1.6 percent).[2]

Urbanization

The move from the countryside to the cities, which began to accelerate after 1840, continued unabated after 1871. It was during the Imperial period that German Jewry changed from an overwhelmingly rural to an overwhelmingly urban population. In 1871, over 70 percent of German Jews lived in towns that had fewer than 20,000 inhabitants and only 14.6 percent dwelled in cities of

---

1 This is the figure given by the 1871 census (including troops in France) as published in *Vierteljahrshefte zur Statistik des Deutschen Reichs* 1 (1873): 188d. Several other sources give slightly different total numbers.
2 The Jewish population had already contracted in 1871 relative to its size in 1861. In 1866, Alsace and Lorraine (the *départements* of Upper Rhine, Lower Rhine, and Moselle) had 43,151 Jews. In Alsace alone, the Jewish population was 34,380 in 1861 and 35,814 in 1866. K. Brämer, "Das neue deutsche Reichsland Elsass mit Deutsch-Lothringen," *Zeitschrift des Königlich Preussischen Statistischen Bureaus* 11, nos. 1–2 (1871): 23–24. The boundaries of the German district of Alsace-Lorraine were not identical to those of the former French *départementes* of Upper Rhine, Lower Rhine, and Moselle.

over 100,000. By 1910, however, a completely different ratio prevailed: only about 32 percent still lived in towns of under 20,000 inhabitants while a full 53 percent lived in large cities with populations greater than 100,000 (Table 2.1). Jewish urbanization was not nearly as consistent after 1871 (and especially after 1880) as it was earlier, nor did it exceed the rate of non-Jewish urbanization as it had between 1840 and 1880. In 1840–1871 and until about 1880, most urban centers both large and small gained in Jewish population. After 1880, however, urbanization resulted in Jews congregating more and more in a small number of very large urban communities. As Germany as a whole urbanized, its large metropolitan or commercial cities steadily differentiated themselves from small and medium ones. Thus, whereas a city of 20,000 was still considered a relatively large place in 1871, by the eve of World War I such localities were thought of as sleepy provincial towns in comparison with the growing number of cities of either over 100,000 or even more than 500,000. The Jewish population in the smaller provincial cities often stopped growing or even declined after 1880.

The concentration of Jews in a few metropolitan centers is best exemplified by the preeminence of Berlin in this trend. In 1871, the 36,015 Jewish inhabitants of the capital represented 7.0 percent of the Jewish population of Germany, already a large increase from the 11,867 (2.8 percent) counted in 1852. After 1890, as the Jewish population in the capital continued to grow, it began to spill into cities across the city's western border, such as Charlottenburg, Schöneburg, and Wilmersdorf, which were physically already part of the metropolis, even though their legal incorporation into Greater Berlin did not occur until 1920. By 1910, the Jewish community of Berlin boasted a population of 90,013, representing 14.6 percent of German Jewry (or 144,007 and 23.4 percent with

TABLE 2.1. Urbanization of German Jewry, by Size of Municipal Population

Year	Under 20,000	20,000–99,999	100,000+
1871	360,522 (70.4%)	76,705 (15.0%)	74,811 (14.6%)
1880	347,451 (61.9%)	83,991 (15.0%)	130,181 (23.2%)
1890	292,729 (51.6%)	84,973 (15.0%)	190,188 (33.5%)
1900	240,672 (41.0%)	94,851 (16.2%)	250,683 (42.7%)
1910	195,907 (31.9%)	91,846 (14.9%)	327,268 (53.2%)
1925	117,456 (20.8%)	70,146 (12.4%)	376,782 (66.8%)

Sources: based on Schmelz's table "Juden Ortsgrössenklassen" and "Die Juden im Deutschen Reich 1816 bis 1933," *Wirtschaft und Statistik* 15, no. 4 (1935): 149.

the inclusion of the aforementioned incorporated cities). In 1871, the three next-largest Jewish communities in Breslau, Hamburg, and Frankfurt am Main had a combined population only slightly smaller than that of Berlin. By 1910, in contrast, these three communities combined were home to less than half as many Jews as Berlin. Greater Berlin now had as many Jews as the fourteen next-largest Jewish communities in Germany put together (Table 2.2).

In 1871, some of the largest Jewish communities in Germany were still in relatively small towns. The twenty largest communities at that time were located in only six of the eight German cities with over 100,000 inhabitants, and in only fourteen of the thirty-one cities that had more than 50,000. Thus, six of the twenty largest Jewish communities were in towns smaller than 50,000. By 1910, nineteen of the twenty largest Jewish communities were in cities of over 100,000, and thirteen were in cities of over 200,000 (Table 2.3). In 1871, the seventy-two Jewish communities in cities in the 20,000–100,000 class were approximately as populous as the eight communities in cities of over 100,000. By 1910, the forty-one cities that had over 100,000 inhabitants contained more than three and a half times as many Jews as the 137 towns that had populations of 20,000–100,000.

In 1871, there was still a substantial difference in size between Jewish communities in cities that had once imposed strict restrictions on Jewish settlement and those that had allowed a freer and longer-standing Jewish presence. Cities recently opened to Jews such as Leipzig, Dresden, Nuremberg, Stuttgart, Bremen, Augsburg, Chemnitz, and, to a lesser extent, Munich and Cologne, still had much smaller Jewish communities than one would expect to find in view of their large size. Cities with older Jewish communities like Berlin, Hamburg, Breslau, Königsberg, Frankfurt, Danzig, Altona, Mainz, and Fürth generally had much higher Jewish density. By 1910, the newer Jewish communities had increased by 279 percent when compared to 1871. As this increase was slightly faster than the general population, the share of Jews in the populations of these cities grew from 1.5 percent to 1.6 percent. In contrast, in the older and originally denser Jewish communities, the increase in Jewish population (140 percent) was only slightly over half that of the general population, and the Jewish proportion in the total fell from 5.3 percent to 3.5 percent. The gap between the two types of communities persisted, though in a seriously attenuated form (Table 2.4).

Unlike the pre-1871 period, the growth of the urban Jewish population in the *Kaiserreich* era, and especially after 1880, rarely outpaced the general growth of the cities. In many major cities, the percentage of Jews in the population actually declined significantly even though the numbers of Jews doubled or tripled. Two main factors precipitated this change: the vigorous growth of the German urban

Table 2.2. Concentration of German Jewry in Berlin

Largest Jewish Communities	1852		1871		1910	
	Jewish population	Percentage of German Jewry	Jewish population	Percentage of German Jewry	Jewish population	Percent of German Jewry
Berlin	11,867	2.82	36,015	7.03	90,013	14.64
Greater Berlin*					144,007	23.41
Breslau	c.22,300	5.30	35,879	7.00	65,826	10.70
Hamburg						
Frankfurt						
Fifth–tenth largest communities			23,736	4.63	53,006	8.62
Eleventh–twentieth largest communities			22,887	4.47	39,138	6.36
Total			118,517	23.13	301,977*	49.09

Percentage of Jews in Germany Living in Berlin	1871	1910
Berlin Jewish population as percent of Jewish population of twenty largest communities	30.41	29.81 (Greater Berlin: 47.69)

* Including Greater Berlin rather than Berlin within its 1910 boundaries.

Source: based on author's calculations from Schmelz, Territorial Printout.

Table 2.3. Cities with the Twenty Largest Jewish Communities in Germany, 1871 and 1910, and Their General Populations

City	1871		City	1910	
	Jewish population	General population (under 50,000 in bold)		Jewish population	General population (under 50,000 in bold)
1. Berlin	36,015	826,341	1. Berlin	90,013	2,071,257
			(Greater Berlin)	144,007	3,734,258)
2. Breslau	13,916	207,977	2. Frankfurt	26,228	414,576
3. Hamburg	11,954	239,107	3. Breslau	20,212	512,105
4. Frankfurt	10,009	91,040	4. Hamburg	19,292	931,035
5. Posen	7,255	56,374	5. Cologne	12,156	516,527
6. Königsberg	3,836	112,082	6. Munich	11,083	596,467
7. Fürth	3,250	**24,577**	7. Leipzig	9,434	589,850
8. Cologne	3,172	129,233	8. Nuremberg	7,815	333,142
9. Mannheim	3,135	**39,606**	9. Mannheim	6,402	193,902
10. Strasbourg	3,088	78,130	10. Strasbourg	5,780	178,891
11. Mainz	2,998	53,902	11. Posen	5,605	156,691
12. Munich	2,903	169,693	12. Hannover	5,155	302,375
13. Danzig	2,625	88,975	13. Königsberg	4,565	245,994
14. Kempen	2,449	**6,030**	14. Stuttgart	4,291	286,218
15. Altona	2,233	74,102	15. Düsseldorf	3,985	358,728
16. Mulhouse	1,997	51,850	16. Dresden	3,734	548,308
17. Bromberg	1,963	**27,740**	17. Karlsruhe	3,058	134,313
18. Hannover	1,936	87,626	18. Kattowitz	2,975	**43,173**
19. Gleiwitz	1,890	**12,937**	19. Mainz	2,926	110,634
20. Lissa	1,889	**10,516**	20. Wiesbaden	2,844	109,002

1871: cities of over 100,000 not on the list: Dresden, Leipzig.
1871: cities of over 50,000 not on the list: Bremen, Stuttgart, Stettin, Magdeburg, Halle, Chemnitz, Braunschweig, Düsseldorf, Krefeld, Barmen, Nuremberg, Aachen, Essen, Elberfeld, and Augsburg.
Cities of under 50,000 data in bold.
Source: Schmelz, Territorial Printout. A list of Jewish communities with over 1,000 Jews in 1905 is found in ZDSJ (1908): 92 and bears many similarities to the 1910 list here.

TABLE 2.4. Difference between Selected Formerly Restricted and Non-Restricted Cities 1871, 1910

City	1871		1910		City	1871		1910	
	Cities recently opened to Jews					Cities long opened to Jews			
	Jewish population	Percent Jewish	Jewish population	Percent Jewish		Jewish population	Percent Jewish	Jewish population	Percent Jewish
Dresden	1,276	0.72	3,734	0.68	Berlin	36,015	4.36	144,007	3.86
Munich	2,903	1.71	11,083	1.86	Hamburg	11,954	4.07	19,292	1.92
Cologne	3,172	2.45	12,156	2.35	Breslau	13,916	6.69	20,212	3.95
Leipzig	1,739	1.63	9,434	1.60	Königsberg	3,836	3.42	4,565	1.86
Stuttgart	1,817	1.98	4,291	1.50	Frankfurt/Main	10,009	10.99	26,228	6.33
Nuremberg	1,831	2.20	7,815	2.35	Danzig	2,625	2.95	2,390	1.40
Bremen	321	0.39	985	0.40	Altona	2,233	3.01	1,824	1.06
Chemnitz	95	0.14	1,605	0.56	Posen	7,255	12.87	5,605	3.58
Augsburg	660	1.29	1,217	0.99	Mainz	2,998	5.56	2,926	2.64
					Fürth	3,250	13.22	2,826	4.25
Total	13,814	1.49	52,320	1.61	Total	94,091	5.31	229,875	3.49
Percent change since 1871: +278.75					Percent change since 1871: +144.3				

Sources: Schmelz, Territorial Printout.

population between 1871 and 1910 and the spread of many large cities into formerly rural areas in which few Jews lived. Thus, whereas 1,968,467 Germans (4.8 percent of the population of Germany) inhabited the eight cities that had over 100,000 inhabitants in 1871, 14,681,080 (22.6 percent of the population of Germany) lived in the forty-four cities that had attained this size by 1910. Until about 1880, the percentage of Jews in the population of the large cities was increasing and outpacing the general urban population. After 1880, the percentage declined considerably, although, of course, the share of Jews in the smaller city and rural populations dropped even faster (Table 2.5).

The proportional decline of Jewry in the overall population was especially noticeable in several traditionally large communities. The decrease in Berlin was not particularly salient: from 4.36 percent in 1871 to 3.86 percent in Greater Berlin in 1910. In Hamburg, Breslau, and Frankfurt, the proportional contraction was greater—between one-third and one-half. In smaller urban communities where Jewish population density had been very high such as in Posen, Fürth, the percentage decrease was often much greater. In Posen, where more than one in eight inhabitants had been Jewish in 1871,[3] fewer than one in twenty-five was such by 1910 (Tables 2.6 A and B).

After 1880 there was not only a general decline in the percentage of Jews in the urban population, but the onset of a downturn of the absolute number of Jews in many cities as well. In most parts of Germany, while the absolute count of Jews continued to rise in all cities of over 100,000 inhabitants, it did not do so in all smaller cities.[4] The eastern provinces of East Prussia, West Prussia, Posen, and Pomerania were exceptions to the foregoing generalization, because Jewish numbers decreased even in their very large cities of Danzig, Stettin, Königsberg, and Posen. The industrializing eastern province of Silesia, on the other hand, showed continued growth in the number of Jews in large cities (Table 2.7). Among cities of over 100,000 elsewhere in Germany, only two saw declines in their Jewish populations: Aachen and Krefeld in the western Rhineland, which were far from the industrializing Ruhr district. Decline in cities of 50,000–100,000 inhabitants was the rule in the eastern provinces, with the exception of two cities in Upper Silesia: Beuthen and Hindenburg/Zabrze. While declining Jewish numbers were also found in three cities in central Germany (Dessau, Frankfurt an der Oder, Potsdam), in two old South German communities (Mainz, Fürth), as well as two newer southern communities (Ulm, Würzburg), none were found in the cities of the Rhineland and Westphalia. Among medium-sized towns

---

3 This, too, represents a decrease in density relative to 1817, when one in six residents in Posen was Jewish.
4 Cities over 100,000, according to the 1905 census.

TABLE 2.5. Jews as Percent of Population of Locations of Various Sizes in Germany

Cities with over 100,000 inhabitants	1817	1871	1880	1890	1900	1910 (counting all of Greater Berlin)
Number of Jews	17,424	74,811	130,170	190,182	250,689	327,268
General population	665,428	1,968,447	3,273,041	5,997,430	8,985,037	14,681,080
Percent Jewish	2.6	3.8	4.0	3.2	2.8	2.2

Locations with fewer than 100,000 inhabitants		1871	1880	1890	1900	1910
Number of Jews		437,227	431,442	377,702	336,153	287,753
General population		39,090,194	41,961,020	43,431,040	47,382,141	50,244,913
Percent Jewish		1.1	1.0	0.9	0.7	0.6

Sources: Jewish figures in Schmelz's handwritten table "Juden Ortsgrössenklassen." More approximate figures for 1871–1933 are given in 1933 census—*Statistik des deutschen Reichs* 451, no. 5 (1936): *Die Glaubensjuden im Deutschen Reich*, 5/10.

Table 2.6.

A) Jewish Population and Percent Jewish, Selected Large Cities

City	1871 Amount	1871 Percent Jewish	1880 Amount	1880 Percent Jewish	1890 Amount	1890 Percent Jewish	1900 Amount	1900 Percent Jewish	1910 Amount	1910 Percent Jewish
Berlin	36,021	4.36	53,949	4.81	79,286	**5.02**	92,206	4.88	90,013	4.35
Berlin in 1920 boundaries									[144,007]	3.86]
Breslau	13,916	**6.69**	17,543	6.43	17,754	5.30	19,743	4.67	20,212	3.95
Düsseldorf	919	**1.32**	1,006	1.06	1,401	0.97	2,131	1.00	3,985	1.11
Frankfurt/Main	10,009	**10.99**	13,881	10.15	17,426	9.68	21,974	7.60	26,228	6.33
Hamburg	11,954	5.00	12,915	4.46	17,785	**5.49**	17,797	2.52	19,386	2.08
Cologne	3,172	2.45	4,523	**3.12**	6,859	2.44	9,745	2.62	12,156	2.35
Leipzig	1,739	1.63	3,179	**2.13**	3,796	1.29	5,504	1.21	9,434	1.60
Mannheim	3,135	**7.92**	4,031	7.54	4,553	5.76	5,478	3.88	6,425	3.31
Munich	2,903	1.71	4,144	1.80	6,109	1.75	8,739	1.75	11,083	**1.86**
Nuremberg	1,831	2.20	3,032	**3.05**	4,307	3.02	5,956	2.28	7,815	2.35

Highest percentage for each city in bold.
Source: 1933 census, 5/10.

B) Jewish Population and Percent Jewish, Medium-Sized Cities with Traditionally Large Jewish Populations

City	1871		1880		1890		1900		1910	
	Amount	Percent Jewish	Amount	Percent Jewish	Amount	Percent Jewish	Amount	Percent Jewish	Amount	Percent Jewish
Fürth	3,250	**13.2**	3,330	10.6	3,175	7.4	3,017	5.5	2,826	4.3
Altona	2,233	**3.0**	1,929	2.1	2,109	1.5	2,006	1.2	1,824	1.1
Posen	7,255	**12.9**	7,063	10.8	6,126	8.8	5,988	5.1	5,605	3.6
Mainz	2,998	**5.6**	3,182	5.2	3,231	4.5	3,104	3.7	2,926	2.6

Highest percentage for each city in bold.
Sources: Schmelz, Territorial Printout.

Table 2.7. Declining Jewish Numbers in Cities in Eastern Provinces of Germany (East Prussia, West Prussia, Pomerania, and Posen)

City	General population	Jewish population				
	1905	1871	1880	1890	1900	1910
Stettin	224,078	1823	2388	2582	**3128**	2757
Königsberg	219,862	3836	**5082**	4008	3975	4565
Danzig	159,885	2625	**2736**	2535	2553	2390
Posen	137,067	**7255**	7063	6126	5988	5605
Total		15539	**17269**	15251	15644	15317
Breslau	470,904	13916	17543	17754	19743	**20212**

Peak numbers in bold.
Source: Schmelz, Territorial Printout; *Statistisches Jahrbuch für das Deutsche Reich* (1907): 16–19; "Städte in Deutschland mit mehr als 1000 jüdischen Einwohnern," *ZDJS* (1908): 92. The latter source gives slightly different general population figures.

of 30,000–50,000, absolute contraction of the Jewish population was more common. With the exception of Kattowitz in Upper Silesia, this was the rule in the eastern provinces; it was also noticeable in almost half of the communities in cities of this size in all regions of Germany except the Rhineland, Westphalia, and parts of central Germany.[5] Absolute declines were even more common in towns in the 20,000–30,000 class after 1880.[6]

---

5 In the eastern provinces, the number of Jews peaked in 1900 or earlier in Tilsit, Graudenz, Ratibor, Thorn, Stralsund, Stolp, Oppeln and Schweidnitz, and continued to grow only in Kattowitz. In central Germany, decline began in the communities of Landsberg an der Warthe, Guben, Bernburg, Mühlhausen in Thuringia, but growth continued in Gera, Kottbus, Halberstadt, Gotha, and the Berlin suburbs. In the northwest, Jewish populations began to diminish in Hildesheim and Wandsbek. In the Rhineland and in Westphalia, decline was noticeable in only one Ruhr city (Witten) and in two cities far from the Ruhr (Neuss, Trier). In the south, the Jewish populations of Bamberg, Regensburg, and Bayreuth edged downward from their peaks before 1910, while those of communities like Heidelberg, Colmar, and Pirmasens continued to grow, and those in other towns stagnated.

6 Taking a sample from Schmelz, Territorial Printout, 19 cities with a population between 30,000 and 40,000 in 1910 had a total of 6,072 Jews in 1871 and 6,911 in 1910. Twenty cities with a population between 20,000 and 30,000 in 1910 had a total of 10,759 Jews in 1871 and 9,993 in 1910. The years of highest Jewish population were

Population	1871	1880	1890	1900	1910
30–40,000	0	6	3	6	4
20–30,000	1	9	3	2	5

Regional Redistribution

The urbanization of German Jewry was accompanied by a regional redistribution of the Jewish population. Internal migration reinforced the pre-1871 migration patterns in some regions but reversed them in others. The Jewish population in the former Polish provinces continued to shrink and did so at an increased pace. The decline in Posen province, first observed in the 1840s, accelerated dramatically after 1871—from a high of about 80,000 in the 1840s to 61,892 in 1871 and then to 26,512 by 1910. After 1880, more than 20 percent of the remaining Jewish population in the province moved away in each subsequent decade. Although out-migration also occurred in the capital city of Posen, it was much more evident in the market towns. Many such towns, which had had Jewish majorities or near majorities in 1817, now had much smaller Jewish populations, which, while still very large by the standards of other parts of Germany, were no longer sizable enough to qualify the localities as *shtetlach* (Table 2.8). In neighboring West Prussia, the decline in Jewish population began only in the 1860s, but then also declined with increasing rapidity from 26,632 in 1871 to 13,954 in 1910. Upper Silesia, an industrializing area of coal mines and steel mills, was much less affected by Jewish out-migration than the other two areas that had large Polish-speaking general populations. Here, Jewish numbers continued to grow until 1880 and the decline from 1880 to 1910 was only about 25 percent (from 24,348 to 18,268).

In the pre-1871 period, the rapid growth of the Jewish populace in the neighboring provinces of East Prussia and Pomerania from only 5,365 in 1817 to 27,462 in 1871 offset most of the decline in West Prussia and Posen. Presumably, many Jews who left Posen and West Prussia moved to these adjacent areas. After

TABLE 2.8. Examples of Waning of "Shtetl" Patterns in Posen Province

Shtetl	Jewish population		General population		Percent Jewish	
	1817	1905	1817	1905	1817	1905
Lissa	3,644	995	7,934	16,021	46.0	6.2
Kempen	2,406	804	4,588	5,879	52.4	13.7
Ostrowo	718	800	3,607	13,115	19.9	6.1
Rogasen	1,173	591	3,946	5,305	29.7	11.1
Inowrazlaw	1,784	1,050	3,804	24,571	46.9	4.3

Source: Heinrich Loewe, "Die Juden Preussens im Jahre 1817," *ZDSJ* (1911), 46.

1871, the migration seems to have been completely redirected toward Berlin and, to a lesser extent, Silesia (especially Breslau). Instead of gaining Jewish inhabitants, the provinces of Pomerania and East Prussia began to lose them. By 1910, over 20 percent of Jews there had moved away, reducing the Jewish presence to 21,889. Migration was especially large and rapid out of the West Prussian district of Marienwerder and the Pomeranian district of Köslin, which lost over half of their Jewish populations between 1880 and 1910. This may have been induced, in part, by virulent antisemitism in these regions, exemplified by the burning of the synagogue in Neustettin, Pomerania in 1881 and a blood libel (ritual-murder accusation) in Konitz, West Prussia in 1900. The Silesian Jewish population, on the other hand, hardly declined at all, as Jews continued to be attracted to Breslau and the Upper Silesian industrial region.

The pre-1871 migrations tended to move Jews from more densely settled Jewish communities to less Jewish areas, somewhat smoothing the regional distribution of the Jewish population (Table 2.9). Interregional differences continued to narrow somewhat during the *Kaiserreich* era (Maps 2/2, 2/3).

A new center of Jewish concentration, however, began to appear in central Germany – the very area that had earlier had the lowest concentration of Jews.[7] The Jewish population of this region almost tripled between 1871 and 1910. Much of the increase occurred in Berlin, where 78 percent of the Jewish population of the region dwelled by 1910. The trend was also pushed by the rapid growth of the Jewish population of the Kingdom of Saxony, where almost no Jews had dwelled previously. The new Jewish population in Saxony was made up primarily of immigrants from Eastern Europe. Immigrants also figured importantly in the Jewish communities of Berlin and other central German cities. Hardly any immigrants settled in the countryside.

In northwestern Germany, the Jewish population, which had almost doubled between 1817 and 1871, increased only slightly between 1871 and 1910 and lagged far behind the overall population growth of the region. In the Rhineland and Westphalia, while Jewish numerical growth was much greater, it trailed the explosive growth of the general population. Almost all of its increase at this time occurred in the administrative district of Cologne and in the industrialized area of the Ruhr (the Düsseldorf and Arnsberg districts). Whereas the Jewish population of these three districts increased from 11,861 in 1817 to 27,850 in 1871 and then to 50,704 in 1910, the Jewish population of the rest of the Rhineland and Westphalia grew from 17,339 in 1817 to 28,458 in 1871 and then

---

7 This region roughly corresponded to the contours of the former German Democratic Republic.

TABLE 2.9. Approximate Jewish Population by Region (excluding Alsace-Lorraine)

Region	Jewish population			General population		
	1817	1871	1910	1817	1871	1910
1. Posen, West Prussia, Upper Silesia						
Absolute numbers	72,806	111,398	58,734	1,946,389	4,208,017	6,011,286
Percent Jewish	3.73	2.65	0.98			
Percent of all German Jews	25.71	23.67	10.07			
2. Other eastern Germany (East Prussia, Pomerania, Lower Silesia)						
Absolute numbers	14,233	51,314	48,606	3,096,316	5,638,020	6,799,077
Percent Jewish	0.46	0.91	0.71			
Percent of all German Jews	5.03	10.90	8.33			
3. Central Germany (Brandenburg including Berlin, Saxony [Prussian and kingdom], Mecklenburg, Anhalt, Thuringia)						
Absolute numbers	21,069	65,393	183,975	c. 5,685,000	9,512,658	16,722,693
Percent Jewish	0.37	0.69	1.10			
Percent of all German Jews	7.44	13.89	31.53			
4. Northwestern Germany (Hamburg, Schleswig-Holstein, Hannover, Braunschweig, Lübeck, Bremen, Lippe, Schaumburg-Lippe, Waldeck)						
Absolute numbers	24,300	c. 35,206	44,183	3,600,000	4,107,603	6,747,864
Percent Jewish	0.68	0.86	0.65			
Percent of all German Jews	8.58	7.48	7.57			
5. Western Germany (Rhineland, Westphalia, Birkenfeld)						
Absolute numbers	c. 29,614	56,308	c. 78,800	c. 3,015,000	5,390,650	c. 11,285,000
Percent Jewish	0.98	1.04	0.70			
Percent of all German Jews	10.46	11.96	13.50			
6. Southern Germany (Hesse-Darmstadt, Hesse-Nassau, Bavaria, Baden, Württemberg, Hohenzollern)						
Absolute numbers	121,175	151,084	169,192	c. 7,900,000	10,432,373	15,041,781
Percent Jewish	1.53	1.45	1.12			
Percent of all German Jews	42.79	32.10	29.00			

leveled off, leaving only 28,096 Jews in these less rapidly growing areas in 1910. Despite the dramatic increase in the Jewish populace of the Ruhr and Cologne District, the general population of the region grew even faster, lowering the Jews' share in the population of the Cologne, Düsseldorf, and Arnsberg districts from one percent in 1871 to only 0.7 percent in 1910.[8]

While the Jewish communities of southern Germany recouped some of their emigration-induced losses of the mid-nineteenth century, especially in Bavaria, they remained fairly stagnant overall. They were still an important portion of the German-Jewish population, but less so than a century earlier (Table 2.9). Although South German Jewry went through substantial urbanization like the rest of German Jewry, rural and small-town communities survived to a much greater extent there than elsewhere. In 1910, 54.3 percent of Jews in Germany, including Alsace-Lorraine, lived in cities of over 100,000 inhabitants. In central Germany, the share of Jews in cities of that magnitude[9] was almost 90 percent, whereas in the three large southern states of Baden, Württemberg, and Bavaria the percentage hovered close to 36 percent. In Hesse-Darmstadt, the only city that exceeded 100,000 in population was Mainz, which accommodated only 12.2 percent of the total Jewish population of the grand duchy. In neighboring Hesse-Nassau, urban Jews were 60.8 percent of the population. Large-city Jews made up an even smaller fraction of the Jewish population in the eastern provinces (30.9 percent) than in the south (Table 2.10). However, the percentage of Jews in towns of under 10,000 was much greater in the south than in the east (Table 2.11) (Map 2/4).

Fertility Decline

Just as German Jews were pioneers in urbanization relative to the rest of the German population, they were trailblazers in planning smaller families. In both their rate of urbanization and the decline of birth rates, German Jews were approximately one generation ahead of Germans at large. On a broader European scale, Central European Jews shared the characteristic of early transition to low fertility with the French, the European nobility, and the population of large

---

8   The combined population of the Düsseldorf, Arnsberg, and Cologne districts was 2,807,596 in 1871 and 7,067,777 in 1910.
9   Counting those in the suburbs of Berlin, which were subsequently incorporated into the city.

Table 2.10. Size of Jewish Communities in Cities of Over 100,000 Inhabitants by Region, 1910

City	Population	City	Population	City	Population	City	Population
Eastern Germany (four communities, total large-city Jewish population: 33,139)							
Breslau	20,212	Posen	5,605	Königsberg	4,565	Stettin	2,757
Central Germany (eight communities, total large-city Jewish population: 163,566)							
Berlin	144,007 (including suburbs incorporated later)	Leipzig	9,434				
Dresden	3,734	Magdeburg	1,843	Chemnitz	1,605	Halle	1,397
Erfurt	797	Plauen	749				
Northwest (six communities; total large-city Jewish population: 28,682)							
Hamburg	19,472	Hannover	5,155	Altona	1,824	Bremen	985
Braunschweig	720	Kiel	526				
West (fourteen communities; total large-city Jewish population 33,419)							
Cologne	12,156	Düsseldorf	3,985	Essen	2,773		
Dortmund	2,676	Elberfeld	1,919	Krefeld	1,815		
Aachen	1,565	Duisburg	1,554	Gelsenkirchen	1,251		
Saarbrücken	1,081	Bochum	992	Mülheim/Ruhr	664		
Barmen	643	Hamborn	345				
South (eleven communities; total large-city Jewish population 74,319)							
Frankfurt/Main	26,228	Munich	11,083	Nuremberg	7,815		
Mannheim	6,402	Strasbourg	5,780	Stuttgart	4,291		
Karlsruhe	3,058	Mainz	2,926	Wiesbaden	2,844		
Kassel	2,675	Augsburg	1,217				

Source: Schmelz, Territorial Printout.

Table 2.11. Distribution of Large-City Jewish Population by Region, 1910

Region	Jews in cities of over 100,000 residents	Total Jewish population	Percent in cities of over 100,000
East (East Prussia, West Prussia, Pomerania, Posen, Silesia)	33,139	107,340	30.8
Central (Berlin, Brandenburg, Prussian Saxony and Kingdom of Saxony, Thuringia, Mecklenburg, Anhalt)	163,566	183,975	88.9
Northwest (Hamburg, Schleswig-Holstein, Hannover, Bremen, Braunschweig, Lübeck, Lippe, Oldenburg, Schaumburg-Lippe, Waldeck)	28,682	45,708	62.8
West (Rhineland, Westphalia)	33,419	78,323	42.7
South (Bavaria, Baden, Württemberg, Hohenzollern, Hesse-Nassau, Alsace-Lorraine)	74,319	199,675	37.2
(South excluding Alsace-Lorraine)	68,539	169,192	40.5
(Hesse-Darmstadt and Hesse-Nassau)	34,673	76,249	45.5
(South excluding Alsace-Lorraine and Hesse)	33,866	92,943	36.4
All Germany	333,691	615,021	54.3

Source: as in Table 2.10.

cities, though the decline in French fertility rates seems to have preceded the German-Jewish decrease somewhat.[10]

The overall population of Germany showed little evidence of a decline in fertility before the 1871 unification.[11] According to sociologist John E. Knodel's calculations, the first part of Germany to experience a 10 percent decline in fertility from pre-decline levels was the city of Berlin in around 1881. Other sections of Germany experienced this magnitude of decline at various times between 1881 and 1914. The decrease in fertility in Germany at large came to ten percent in or around 1895. In general, the downturn appeared first in central Germany and parts of the south and last in the eastern provinces and some isolated areas on the western, northwestern, and southeastern borders.[12]

The Jewish crude birth rate was already lower than that of the general population throughout the nineteenth century, and the ratio between the two hardly changed until around 1875. In fact, the number of Jewish births rose gradually. After the unification of Germany, however, the Jewish and general figures begin to diverge noticeably. In the enlarged post-1866 Prussia, average annual Jewish births declined steadily from 11,349 in 1875–1880 to 10,383 in 1880–1885, 9,084 in 1885–1890, and 6,833 in 1905–1910.[13] This represented nearly a 40 percent decrease (Table 2.12), even as the number of births in the overall Prussian population increased by 18.6 percent. Thus, the share of Jews among babies born in Prussia tumbled from 1.04 percent in 1875–1880 to 0.52 percent by 1905–1910. The Jewish birth rate also

---

10 Schmelz, *Hessen*. Massimo Livi-Bacci included Jews and aristocrats among the pioneers of fertility decline; see his "Social-Group Forerunners of Fertility Control in Europe," in *The Decline of Fertility in Europe*, ed. A. J. Coale (Princeton: Princeton University Press, 1986), 182–200. On the French fertility decline, see, for example, E. A. Wrigley, "The Fall of Marital Fertility in Nineteenth Century France, Exemplar or Exception?" *European Journal of Population* 1 (1985): 31–60, 141–177; and Neil Cummins, "Marital Fertility and Wealth in Transition Era France 1750–1850," Ecole d'Economie de Paris, Working Paper no. 2009–16, accessed March 1, 2014, http://halshs.archives-ouvertes.fr/docs/00/56/68/43/PDF/wp200916.pdf.
11 John E. Knodel, *The Decline of Fertility in Germany 1871–1939* (Princeton: Princeton University Press, 1974), 52–69. Knodel uses marital fertility index (Ig, see note 184 below) as his main indicator for fertility. This index is calculated by dividing the total number of legitimate births by the number of married women of childbearing age multiplied by the fertility of Hutterite women (the highest recorded natural fertility cohort measured) of the same age. The advantage of this index over crude birth rates is, for instance, that it is not affected by the age makeup or marriage rate of the total population (ibid., 33–34).
12 Ibid., 62–65.
13 Silbergleit, *Die Bevölkerungs- und Berufsverhältnisse*, 14*–15*.

Table 2.12. Percentage Decline in Jewish Births in Prussia

1875–1880 to 1880–1885	1880–1885 to 1885–1890	1885–1890 to 1890–1895	1890–1895 to 1895–1900	1895–1900 to 1900–1905	1900–1905 to 1905–1910
8.5%	12.5%	6.9%	8.0%	6.4%	6.1%

Source: based on Silbergleit, *Die Bevölkerungs- und Berufsverhältnisse*, 14*.

slumped to less than half that of the general population during this interval.[14] There were parallel trends in the southern states of Bavaria and Hesse as well (Tables 4.16–4.18). After 1900–1905, however, the Christian birth rate in Bavaria began to fall rapidly and soon descended more precipitously than that of the Jews.

One reason for the lower birth rate among Jews than among Christians was the Jews' greater urbanization. This, however, does not fully explain the phenomenon, as fertility among Jews outside the large cities also decreased at an early stage and urban Jews generally had lower fertility than both Jews in the countryside and non-Jews in the same city. Differences in Jewish birth rates in different cities are also noticeable (Table 2.13).[15]

Changing Population Distribution within Cities—New Neighborhoods

The Jewish populations of major German cities continued to concentrate at levels that distinguished them from the cities' general populations. Whether in cities that had once had walled ghettos like Frankfurt, spatial restrictions without a ghetto as in Hamburg, or no legal restrictions like in Berlin, Jews continued to retain some of their pre-emancipation residential patterns even though their concentration waned relative to its pre-1815 level. With the development of new forms of urban transportation in the late nineteenth century, the major cities of Germany expanded geographically. City centers often began to lose residents as they slowly transformed from residential into business areas. Although the traditional Jewish population cores in city centers remained significant areas of Jewish concentration, in many cities they were also joined by newer Jewish areas in wealthier parts of town, which in some cases outweighed the old Jewish neighborhoods in both size and influence by the end of the *Kaiserreich* period.

---

14 Ibid.
15 Based on Schmelz, handwritten tables "Geburten—Städte" [Births by City].

Table 2.13. Jewish Crude Birth Rates per Thousand (Children Born to Homogeneous Jewish Couples)

Year	Prussia	Berlin	Breslau	Frankfurt/Main	Hannover	Königsberg
1880	29.45	26.02	22.00	21.87	24.93	24.20
1890	22.96	20.09	18.14	18.71	21.61	20.21
1900	18.41	16.07	14.74	16.97	12.56	15.85
1910	14.51		12.37	12.85	13.77	21.03 [!]
1925	11.85	10.17				

Source: based on Schmelz's tables "Geburten—Städte" (Birth by City) for the above-mentioned cities and "Lebengeborene for Preussen Staat"—absolute numbers of births divided by total Jewish population in that year.

In cities that had had miniscule Jewish populations before the mid-nineteenth century such as Cologne, Munich, and Leipzig, most Jews arrived long after the repeal of all legal restrictions. Nevertheless, Jewish migrants to such cities tended to concentrate in central areas and often underwent processes of neighborhood change that strongly resembled those in cities with older Jewish communities.

Rather detailed statistics exist for several of Germany's largest cities during most of the *Kaiserreich* era. The patterns and their changes seem to follow a limited number of models, and there seems to be relatively little difference between cities that had once restricted Jews to a specific quarter and those that had not. Even in cities that had not confined Jews to any particular area, Jewish concentration in the early nineteenth century was extreme. The situation in Berlin, for example, differed little from that in Frankfurt, where 89.4 percent of Jews still lived in quarters immediately bordering the old walled ghetto in 1817.[16] Jewish self-segregation in both cities was very high, with dissimilarity indices of .643 in Berlin and .652 in Frankfurt.[17]

During the half-century preceding the unification of Germany, Jewish populations in most major cities grew considerably. In the older communities, Jews' traditional concentration in the original Jewish neighborhood abated somewhat as some moved to other areas that were usually nearby. Due to the growth of the overall Jewish population, however, the absolute number of Jews in the old traditional neighborhood was often larger by 1871 than it had been around 1815. In most cities, the original Jewish neighborhood was still the main center of Jewish population at the beginning of the Imperial era. Even in Jewish communities that had been minuscule before emancipation, a perceptible pattern of concentration, usually near the center of town, developed by 1871.

In Hamburg in 1871, 60.3 percent of the Jews lived in the Neustadt section— the main area where they had been permitted to live in the eighteenth century. Since emancipation, some Jews who had left this area moved to neighboring quarters in various directions. A similar pattern was found in Berlin, with the important difference that Berlin Jewry expanded much more rapidly than had

---

16 Steven M. Lowenstein, *The Mechanics of Change: Essays in the Social History of German Jewry* (Atlanta: Scholars Press, 1992), 157, based on Jacob Jacobson, *Die Judenbürgerbücher der Stadt Berlin 1809–1851* (Berlin: de Gruyter, 1962), 55–93, and Steven M. Lowenstein, *The Berlin Jewish Community: Enlightenment, Family and Crisis 1770–1830* (New York and Oxford: Oxford University Press, 1994), 59–60, 228–229, note 37.
17 The dissimilarity index is the percentage of one population that would have to move so that said population would be identical to the distribution of another population. The index is calculated by taking the percentage of the Jewish population in each district and the percentage of the total population in the same district, adding the sum of the differences in each district, and dividing the result by two.

the Hamburg community, at more than ninefold in Berlin compared to less than double in Hamburg. Berlin's much-enlarged Jewish population required a broader area of concentration than the 1809–1812 center. Even as Jewish residents spilled into many adjacent areas in the north-central part of town, the original core in old Berlin gained in Jewish population between 1817 and 1867. By the latter year, no fewer than 68.6 percent of all Berlin Jews still lived in the now-expanded Jewish neighborhood. In Cologne, there is evidence of the concentration of Jews in the central sections of the city as early as the 1840s, rather more than in the north and south where most Jews would continue to concentrate in the twentieth century.[18] In Munich, the 1875 census showed a strong concentration of Jews in the central sections of town and very few in outlying areas. While only a little more than one-quarter of the city's overall population lived in Districts 1–4 in 1875, the four inner districts were home to five-eighths of the city's Jews.[19] In the 1870s, most urban Jewish populations that left the traditional main Jewish neighborhoods tended to scatter without concentrating much in specific new Jewish centers.[20]

The major German cities expanded greatly both in population and in area during the *Kaiserreich* period. As modern forms of mass transit such as trams, trains, and subways developed, many could live farther from work and commute into the city each day. Meanwhile, the core areas of many metropolises began to lose population as they became more and more exclusively commercial. During this time, the Jewish population also began to move out of the most central districts, though in many cities they did so less overwhelmingly than did non-Jews. Under Kaiser Wilhelm II (1888–1918), at least three main types of Jewish distribution patterns evolved in major German cities. In the first type, the main Jewish neighborhood remained in or near the city center. In the second, most Jews moved from the older Jewish neighborhood to a new Jewish center in a former suburb. In the third and perhaps most common pattern, a new Jewish population center developed outside the old area while the old Jewish neighborhood continued to house many Jews.

The last-mentioned pattern, with two main Jewish areas, was particularly marked in Berlin and Frankfurt (Tables 2.14, 2.15). In Leipzig, and to a lesser extent in Munich and Cologne, Jews continued to concentrate in the central city

---

18 Shulamit Magnus, *Jewish Emancipation in a German City, Cologne, 1798–1871* (Stanford: Stanford University Press, 1997), 173. See Table 10.14.
19 See Table 10.14.
20 In Berlin, for instance, the Luisenstadt area attracted many Jews in the late nineteenth century but failed to grow as a Jewish neighborhood in the twentieth century. The same is true of the St. Pauli district of Hamburg.

TABLE 2.14. Development of Two-Neighborhood Pattern among Berlin Jews, 1867–1910 (including suburbs)

Year	North-central*	Far western**	All other
1867	18,912 (68.6%)	1,106 (4.0%)	7,547 (27.4%)
1880	31,139		
1890	41,184 (50.5%)	14,258 (17.5%)	26,187 (32.1%)
1895	43,228 (46.5%)	21,991 (23.6%)	27,778 (29.9%)
1900	46,282 (43.4%)	31,601 (29.6%)	28,773 (27.0%)
1905	50,143 (39.4%)	44,760 (35.1%)	32,467 (25.5%)
1910	45,962 (31.9%)	61,541 (42.7%)	36,504 (25.3%)

* North-central—Alt Berlin, Alt Kölln, Spandauer Viertel, Königstadt, Stralauer Viertel West, Rosenthaler Vorstadt Süd (1910 figures also include Friedrichswerder and Dorotheenstadt but exclude Königstadt Südost).

** Far western—Schöneberger Vorstadt, Friedrichsvorstadt, Tempelhofer Vorstadt. Tiergarten (Hansaviertel), Charlottenburg, Schöneberg, Wilmersdorf (1910 figures also include Friedrichwilhelmstadt and Moabit Ost).

Sources: Hermann Schwabe, ed., *Die Resultate der Berliner Volkszählung vom. 3. December 1867* (Berlin, 1867), LVIII–LIX, 30–31; H. Schwabe, *Die Königliche Haupt- und Residenzstadt Berlin in ihren Bevölkerungs-, Berufs- und Wohnungsverhältnissen: Resultate der Volkszählung und Volksbeschreibung vom 1. December 1871* (Berlin, 1874); R. Böckh, *Die Bevölkerungs und Wohnungsaufnahme vom 1. December 1880 in der Stadt Berlin* (Berlin, 1883), vol. 2, 40–41; R. Böckh, *Die Bevölkerungs und Wohnungsaufnahme vom 1. Dezember 1890 in der Stadt Berlin* (Berlin, 1893), vol. 1, 46, and vol. 2, 46; R. Böckh, *Die Bevölkerungs- und Wohnungsaufnahme vom 2. December 1895 in der Stadt Berlin* (Berlin, 1900–1901), 1–3; *Die Grundstücks-Aufnahme Ende Oktober 1900 sowie die Wohnungs- und die Bevölkerungsaufnahme vom 1. Dezember 1900 in der Stadt Berlin* (Berlin, 1904), part 2, 1–4; *Die Grundstücks-Aufnahme Ende Oktober 1905 sowie die Wohnungs- und die Bevölkerungsaufnahme vom 1. Dezember 1905 in der Stadt Berlin und 29 benachbarten Gemeinden* (Berlin, 1910–1911), part 2, 1–5; *Statistisches Jahrbuch der Stadt Berlin* 32 (1913): 35*.

Table 2.15. Development of Two-Neighborhood Pattern of Jews in Frankfurt, 1895–1925

Year	Ostend*	Westend**	Transitional area***	All other
1895	10152 (52.1%)	3712 (19.0%)	2799 (14.4%)	2825 (14.5%)
1900	11201 (51.0%)	4228 (19.2%)	2862 (13.0%)	3690 (16.8%)
1925	12859 (43.8%)	7331 (24.9%)	4244 (14.4%)	4951 (16.8%)

* Östliche Neustadt, Östliche Aussenstadt, Nordöstliche Aussenstadt.

** Westliche Aussenstadt, Nordwestliche Aussenstadt.

*** Nördliche Neustadt, Nördliche Aussenstadt.

Sources: *Statistisches Jahrbuch der Stadt Frankfurt am Main 2: Statistik der Jahre 1906/07 bis 1926/27* (1928): 68–69.

and few gravitated to the outer suburbs that were annexed in the late nineteenth and early twentieth century (Tables 2.16, 2.17). This pattern seemed especially common in cities like Leipzig that had a large proportion of immigrant Jews. In contrast, most Jews in Hamburg moved from the old Jewish center in the Neustadt to a new Jewish area much farther north, centered in the Rotherbaum and Harvestehude neighborhoods (Table 2.18). Unlike Leipzig, Hamburg was typified by a particularly low percentage of immigrants and a high percentage of Jews born in the city itself.

In general, Jewish self-segregation did not attenuate significantly during the *Kaiserreich* period, and actually increased in some cities. Most German cities that had large Jewish populations were marked by dissimilarity indexes of 30–45 percent between the Jewish and the general population. This degree of self-segregation far exceeded that evidenced in the housing patterns of the two main Christian denominations—the Catholics and the Lutherans—whose dissimilarity indices relative to the overall city population ranged from five to seventeen percent.[21] Jewish spatial separation was more consistent with the patterns of white American ethnic groups than with those of the German religious denominations.

---

21 See Table 10.29.

Table 2.16. Leipzig: Continued Concentration in City Center

Population	1880	1890	1900	1905
Alt Leipzig				
Jewish	3,179	3796	5,502	6,736
General	149,081	179,689	192,101	188,740
Percent Jewish	2.13	2.11	2.86	3.57
Neu Leipzig				
Jewish	0	429	669	940
General	0	115,336	264,025	314,896
Percent Jewish		0.37	0.25	0.30

Sources: "Die Bewohner der Kirchspiele nach Stadtbezirken am 1. Dezember 1900," *Die Ergebnisse der Volkszählung vom 1. Dezember 1900 in der Stadt Leipzig* (Leipzig, 1901), 65–69; "Die Juden im Stadtbezirk Leipzig," *ZDSJ* (1907): 14–15.

Table 2.17. Munich: Modified City-Center Concentration

Population	1875	1880	1885	1905	1910
Altstadt (1–4)					
General	49412	48645	49588	40223	40562
Jewish	2174	2291	2289	1860	1748
Percent Jewish	4.40	4.71	4.62	4.6	4.31
Ludwigstadt (9–13)					
General	56470	71970	84042	127682	133238
Jewish	796	1269	1729	5179	5776
Percent Jewish	1.41	1.76	2.06	4.1	4.34
Maxstadt (5–8)					
General	52132	61837	71522	105277	104725
Jewish	473	550	750	1786	1700
Percent Jewish	0.91	0.89	1.05	1.7	1.62
Ostend (14–18)					
General	35010	39966	46756	114779	127601

Jewish	24	33	76	483	547
Percent Jewish	0.07	0.08	0.16	0.4	0.43
Westend (19–26)					
General	5805	11122?	10074	151022	190341
Jewish	8	1?	10	748	1312
Percent Jewish	0.14	0.01	0.10	0.5	0.69
All Munich					
General	198829	230023	261981	538983	596467
Jewish	3475	4144	4854	10056	11083
Percent Jewish	1.75	1.80	1.85	1.9	1.86

Sources: von Tyszka, "Die jüdische Bevölkerung Münchens," 91; *Mitteilungen des Statistischen Amtes des Stadt München* 24 (1912–1913): 25.

Table 2.18. Hamburg: Relocation of Jewish Community to New Center

Year	Old center Neustadt	New center Rotherbaum, Harvestehude, Eppendorf	Other areas, inner city*	Other areas, outer city
1871	8393		3555	
1880	8601 (53.8)	2264 (14.2)	4284 (26.8)	833 (5.2)
1885	7984	3649	4281	
1890	7029 (39.5)	4662 (26.2)	4418 (24.8)	1676 (9.4)
1895	5531	6206	3818	
1900	4695 (26.4)	7968 (44.8)	3223 (18.1)	1911 (10.7)
1905	3599	9660		6166
1910	2336 (12.8)	11296 (62.1)	2190 (12.0)	2361 (13.0)
1925	1334 (6.7)	12484 (62.9)	1551 (7.8)	4465 (22.5)
1933	935 (5.6)	9953 (59.1)	1091 (6.5)	4856 (28.8)

* Altstadt, St. Pauli, and St. Georg.

Sources: Helga Krohn, *Die Juden in Hamburg, 1848–1918. Die politische, soziale und kulturelle Entwicklung einer jüdischen Grossgemeinde nach der Emanzipation* (Hamburg, 1974), 127; *Statistik des Hamburgischen Staats* (1873): 32, (1880): 149, (1887): 92–99, (1894): 124–125, (1900): 51, (1902): 56–57, (1919): 56–57.

Immigration and East European Jews

Although Jewish emigration from Germany never stopped completely, and even reached a temporary peak in the 1880s, by the end of the century it was overshadowed by a major wave of immigration primarily from Eastern Europe. This new development sparked strong antisemitic reactions in German public opinion even though Jewish statisticians endeavored to prove that the perception of Jewish mass immigration was a myth.[22] German governments became increasingly reluctant to permit the naturalization of new immigrants. Since Germany based citizenship on ancestry, the ensuing policy rendered many German-born children of Jewish immigrants as foreigners in the eyes of the law.

According to Silbergleit, Jewish immigration to Prussia fell short of emigration in 1880–1895 but surpassed emigration thereafter, cresting in 1900–1905, when annual net Jewish immigration[23] reached 2,252 with 11,260 more immigrants than emigrants. The number of East European Jewish immigrants living in Germany in 1890 is estimated at 20,388, or 3.6 percent of the Jewish population. These numbers almost doubled in each of the following decades, rising to 34,360 in 1900 (5.9 percent of all Jews living in Germany) and 70,234 in 1910 (11.4 percent). The total "foreign Jewish" population in Germany was somewhat higher: 41,113 in 1900 and 79,646 in 1910.[24]

The foreign Jewish population was very heavily concentrated in the country's industrial and urban areas, foremost in Berlin, Saxony, and Munich. Foreign (mostly East European) Jews accounted for a particularly large share of the Jewish population in areas where the Jewish population had formerly been sparse. This was especially the case in the Kingdom of Saxony, where the Jewish population surged from only 3,357 of two and a half million inhabitants in 1871 to 6,518 in 1880, 9,368 in 1890, 12,416 in 1900, and 17,587 in 1910. Most of the increase took place in the international trade center of Leipzig, where the Jewish population swelled from 1,739 in 1871 to 9,434 in 1910. Most of the remaining increase in Jewish population occurred in other major cities such as Dresden (from 1,276 to 3,734) and Chemnitz (from 95 to 1,605). By 1910, Saxony had a foreign Jewish

---

22 Salomon Neumann, *Der Fabel von jüdischer Masseneinwanderung: Ein Kapitel aus der preußischen Statistik* (Berlin: Simion, 1881).
23 Net immigration is total immigration less total emigration. It is thus by definition smaller than the actual number of immigrants—often much smaller.
24 Trude Maurer, *Ostjuden in Deutschland, 1918–1933* (Hamburg: H. Christians, 1986), 72, based on Jack Wertheimer, *Unwelcome Strangers: East European Jews in Imperial Germany* (Oxford: Oxford University Press, 1991).

population of 10,293, representing 58.5 percent of the Jewish population of the kingdom and 12.9 percent of the foreign Jewish population of Germany.

In the vast state of Prussia, the absolute number of foreign Jews was much larger, with 48,166 or 60.4 percent of all foreign Jews in Germany, but their percentage in the total Jewish population was much smaller (11.6 percent) than in Saxony. In 1910, over half of Prussia's foreign Jews were concentrated in Berlin (18,694 or 20.8 percent of the Jewish population) and its suburbs (8,666 or 14.1 percent of the Jewish population of Brandenburg).[25] The 20,806 foreign Jews in the rest of Prussia made up only 7.9 percent of the Jewish population there. Outside of Brandenburg and Berlin, foreign Jews in Prussia were most numerous in the Rhineland, Hesse-Nassau, Silesia, and East Prussia. Apart from Berlin and Brandenburg, the foreign Jewish proportion was highest in the Prussian provinces of Schleswig-Holstein, East Prussia, Hannover, and Saxony; in all other Prussian provinces they were less than 10 percent of the Jewish population. Notably, except for East Prussia, there were relatively few East European immigrants in the easternmost provinces that bordered Russia and Galicia.[26]

Outside Prussia and Saxony, there were only 21,187 foreign Jews (11.7 percent of all Jews), concentrated particularly in the city-states of Bremen and Hamburg, as well as in the largest cities of southern Germany—Munich, Karlsruhe, Stuttgart, Nuremberg, Mannheim, Strasbourg, and Augsburg (Table 2.19). In the rest of Germany outside of Prussia, Saxony, and these nine cities, the foreign Jewish population was a paltry 9,014 (7.4 percent of the Jewish population).

Intermarriage and Out-Conversion

Before the unification of Germany, several states prohibited religious exogamy (intermarriage) by law; to marry in these states, one partner had to convert to the other's religion. Jews who sought a career in the government bureaucracy or in teaching, especially in universities, were under considerable pressure to embrace Christianity. Consequently, many more Jews converted to Christianity before 1871 than participated in an intermarriage. After the unification of Germany in 1871 and the introduction of civil marriage countrywide in 1875, the legal impediments to intermarriage disappeared, causing the rates of such marriages to start rising.

---

25 Wertheimer, *Unwelcome Strangers*, 185.
26 Silbergleit, *Die Bevölkerungs- und Berufsverhältnisse*, 42*–45*. See Table 8.17.

Table 2.19. Important Foreign Jewish Populations in Cities outside Prussia and Saxony, 1910

City	Foreign Jewish Population	Percent
Bremen	679	(48.2% of all Jews)
Munich	3,857	(34.9%)
Karlsruhe	654	(21.4%)
Stuttgart	836	(19.5%)
Hamburg	3,111	(16.4%)
Nuremberg	1,226	(15.7%)
Mannheim	887	(13.9%)
Strasbourg	768	(13.3%)
Augsburg	155	(12.7%)

Source: Wertheimer, *Unwelcome Strangers*, 191–192, Table IIb; *Vierteljahrshefte zur Statistik des Deutschen Reichs—Ergänzungsheft zu 1916* 4 (1918): *Die Deutschen im Ausland und die Ausländer im Deutschen Reiche*, 86.

During the *Kaiserreich* period, the number of Jews who married Jews varied relatively little,[27] while the number of intermarriages slanted upward from a low baseline. In 1876–1880, the intermarriage rate in Prussia was only 4.6 percent. The total annual number of intermarriages quadrupled between 1878 and 1912.[28] Even in the latter year, however, only 12.8 percent of Jews getting married did so out of the faith.[29] At no time did the rate spike; it merely rose steadily in the long term.[30]

Before World War I, intermarriage rates in Germany varied widely from region to region. Exogamy was disproportionately common in large cities. Between

---

27 The annual number of homogeneous Jewish marriages in Prussia between 1875 and 1900 varied in the narrow range of 2,256 (1885) to 2,675 (1875). The range in all of Germany from 1901 to 1913 was similarly narrow: 3,621 (1913) to 4,080 (1906).
28 We have statistics for all of Germany only from 1900 and for Prussia from 1876. In Prussia, there were 216 intermarriages involving Jews in 1878 and 483 in 1899. In Germany as a whole, 626 Jewish individuals intermarried in 1902 and 1,130 did so in 1912.
29 Throughout this book, intermarriage rates are calculated by dividing the number of intermarriages by the total number of Jews marrying. This means that all intramarriages are counted twice because they involve two Jews. This is the usual method in contemporary studies. Many older studies published in Germany before World War II simply divide the number of intermarriages by the number of inmarriages, yielding much higher intermarriage rates—possibly even exceeding 100 percent.
30 The year-on-year increase in the number of intermarriages exceeded 10 percent in only four of the more than thirty-five years for which we have records.

1876 and 1880, 459 (40.1 percent) of 1,144 Jewish intermarriages in Prussia were performed in Berlin, while only 12 percent of Jewish intramarriages in Prussia took place there. The proportion of Prussian intermarriages in Berlin increased to 790 of 1,545 (51.1 percent) between 1886 and 1890 and then began to decline. By 1901–1905, when 24 percent of Prussian Jewish intramarriages occurred in Berlin, the percentage of Prussian intermarriages in Berlin was 43.6 percent. In the Prussian provinces, Frankfurt and Breslau saw a disproportionate number of intermarriages in their districts but had much lower overall intermarriage rates than in Berlin. Outside Prussia, Hamburg and Munich had high intermarriage rates, with Hamburg surpassing that of Berlin[31] (Table 2.20). In mainly rural areas, in contrast, exogamy remained very uncommon. In 1904, only twelve intermarriages took place as against 196 endogamous nuptials (involving 392 Jewish individuals) in largely rural Hesse-Darmstadt, and only twenty-three intermarriages compared to 297 intramarriages in the states of Baden and Württemberg.[32] In earlier years, the intermarriage rate in Hesse-Darmstadt had been even lower, and between 1871 and 1875, only six Jews there married non-Jews compared to 840 who wed other Jews (intermarriage rate: 0.36 percent).[33] Apart from indicating a sharp discrepancy between higher intermarriage in the large cities and lower intermarriage in the countryside, the statistics also reveal important regional differences. Intermarriage rates were high in the areas of sparse Jewish population in northern and central Germany, and much lower both in the eastern provinces of Prussia and in southern Germany. In 1903 and 1904, the intermarriage rates for Berlin, eastern Germany, and southern Germany were 15.8 percent, 3.6 percent, and 4.0 percent, respectively (Tables 2.21, 2.22).

Table 2.20. Intermarriage Rates in Major German Cities, 1901–1905

Type of marriage	Berlin	Hamburg	Frankfurt	Breslau
Endogamous Jewish	3086	490	703	685
Exogamous	1138	263	176	90
Intermarriage rate	15.8%	21.2%	11.1%	6.2%

Source: Engelman, "Intermarriage," 163–165.

---

31 *Zeitschrift für Demographie und Statistik der Juden* 2 (1906): 158–159; 5 (1909): 94, 95, 157.
32 That is, intermarriage rates of 2.97 percent in Hesse-Darmstadt and 3.73 percent in Baden and Württemberg.
33 Ludwig Knöpfel, "Stand und Bewegung der jüdischen Bevölkerung im Grossherzogtum Hessen während des 19. Jahrhunderts," *ZDSJ* 1 (June 1906): 82.

Table 2.21. Intermarriage Levels in Various Parts of Germany, 1903–1904

Region	Endogamous Jewish marriages	Intermarriages	Intermarriage rate
Northern and central Germany	638	254	16.6%
Berlin	1226	461	15.8
Southern Germany	1893	141	3.6
Southern Germany plus Hesse-Nassau and Hesse-Darmstadt	2902	244	4.0
Eastern Germany	1624	122	3.6
Percent of total in southern and eastern Germany	57.8%	25.9	
Percent of total in Berlin	[15.7]	32.6	
Percent of total in other northern and central Germany	26.6	41.5	

North and central Germany: Prussian Saxony, Schleswig Holstein, Hannover, Saxon Kingdom, Braunschweig, Bremen, and Hamburg.

Southern Germany: Alsace-Lorraine, Baden, Württemberg, Bavaria, Hohenzollern.

Eastern Germany: East Prussia, West Prussia, Posen, Silesia, Pomerania.

Source: "Eheschliessungen im Jahre 1903," 8; "Eheschliessungen im Jahre 1904," 159.

Unlike the patterns that developed during the Weimar era, there was no wide gender discrepancy in Jewish intermarriage before World War I. In 1903 and 1904, 775 Jewish men married Christian women in Germany and 641 Jewish women chose Christian men as husbands. Thus, 45.3 percent of all Jews who intermarried were women. The ratios in Prussia and elsewhere were virtually the same. In the city of Berlin, however, 293 Jewish men intermarried but only 168 Jewish women did so, yielding a 63:6:36.4 ratio. In the rest of Germany, Jewish men and women intermarried in almost identical numbers at 482 vs.

Table 2.22. Provincial vs. Urban Jewish Intermarriage

Marriage Type	Frankfurt	Hesse-Nassau	Hesse-Nassau outside Frankfurt	Breslau annual average	Silesia	Silesia outside Breslau	Munich	Bavaria	Bavaria outside Munich
	1905	1904	1904	1901–1905	1904	1904	1907–1908	1907–1908	1907–1908
Endogamous Jewish marriages	164	340	176	137	324	187	86	812	726
Intermarriages	36	38	2	18	36	18	32	66	34
Intermarriage rate	9.9%	5.3%	0.6%	6.2%	5.3%	4.6%	15.7%	3.9%	2.3%

Sources: "Eheschliessungen im Jahre 1904," 159; "Die Bewegung der Juden in Frankfurt a M im Jahre 1908," *ZDSJ* 5, no. 10 (1909): 157; Engelman, "Intermarriage," 163–165.

Table 2.23. Changing Gender Ratios among Intermarrying Jews—Germany, 1901–1914

Year	Jewish husband	Jewish wife
1901	52.0%	48.0%
1902	52.1	47.9
1903	54.3	45.7
1904	55.1	44.9
1905	55.9	44.1
1906	51.5	48.5
1907	53.8	46.2
1908	55.0	45.1
1909	55.8	44.2
1910	56.3	43.7
1911	58.4	41.6
1912	57.3	42.7
1913	57.2	42.8
1914	59.1	40.9

Source: based on Stefan Behr, *Der Bevölkerungsrückgang der deutschen Juden* (Frankfurt, 1932), 111.

473.[34] There is a slow but steady increase in the percentage of male Jews who intermarried. Between 1901 and 1914, the number of Jewish men intermarrying grew by 132.2 percent, whereas that of women climbed by only 74.1 percent (Table 2.23).

Jews who intermarried were disproportionately likely to marry Protestants as opposed to Catholics. Between 1901 and 1914, the percentage of intermarrying Jews who married Catholics declined from 21.7 percent to 14.1 percent. During the entire period, 9,265 Jews married Protestants (73.6 percent) and 2,525 married Catholics (20.1 percent); 804 married persons of another or no denomination (6.4 percent),[35] as against the denominational division of the

---

34 "Eheschliessungen im Jahre 1903," *ZDSJ* 1, no. 1 (1905): 8; "Eheschliessungen im Jahre 1904," *ZDSJ* 2 (1906): 159.
35 Calculated from *Statistisches Jahrbuch für das deutsche Reich* (1903): 21; (1904): 18; (1905): 16; (1906): 18; (1907): 17; (1908): 20; (1909): 40; (1910): 22; (1911): 23; (1912): 19; (1913): 23; (1914): 23; (1915): 27.

German population in the census of 1910—61.6 percent Protestant and 36.7 percent Catholic.[36]

Jewish conversion to the Lutheran faith in Germany increased steadily in 1881–1885, at 198 persons per year, and in 1896–1900, at 459.[37] It then leveled off in the following five-year period, after which it then began to decline. By 1911–1915, the annual average number of out-conversions was only 359. It would decrease much more after World War I.[38]

---

36 *Statistik des Deutschen Reichs* 240 (1915). In 1925, after the loss of several mainly Catholic territories (Posen and Alsace-Lorraine), the percentages were 64.1 percent Protestants and 32.4 percent Catholics. Uriah Zevi Engelman, "Intermarriage among Jews in Germany, U.S.S.R., and Switzerland," *Jewish Social Studies* 2 (1940): 167.
37 Both figures are annual averages.
38 *Statistik des deutschen Reichs* 451, no. 5 (1936): *Die Glaubensjuden im Deutschen Reich*, 8.

3

From the "Demographic Crisis" of the 1920s to the Flight to Escape after 1933

The demographic changes that German Jewry experienced during the Imperial period began to alarm a number of German-Jewish sociologists and demographers in the years immediately before World War I. In 1911, when Felix Theilhaber and Arthur Ruppin published their first alarmist books,[1] warning of the threat of low birth rates, urbanization, intermarriage, and other demographic developments to the future of German Jewry, most observers thought their claims exaggerated if not totally false. Both tomes were influenced by the biological and anti-urban theories so popular in Germany at the time and saw signs of biological degeneration in all of these developments. Both were pessimistic about the future of the Jewish Diaspora at large and recommended the creation of a Jewish society in the Land of Israel as an alternative. Curiously, many developments in the 1920s and early 1930s seemed to bear out these gloomy predictions. Birth rates fell below death rates, Jewish endogamy slumped, and exogamy remained high. The average age of German Jews increased steadily. The demographic behavior of German Jews during the Weimar Republic era proved much more sensitive to political and economic crises than did that of non-Jewish Germans. East European immigration, continuing but embattled,

---

1   Especially the second edition of Ruppin's *Die Juden der Gegenwart* and Theilhaber's *Der Untergang der deutschen Juden*, both published in 1911.

could not fill the gap occasioned by negative natural increase among Germany's "native Jewry."

Hitler's accession to power in early 1933 changed the nature of the demographic challenge. Some aspects of the 1920s "crisis" such as intermarriage and the declines in Jewish endogamy and births either disappeared or became less acute. All were overshadowed by the question that all of German Jewry faced in the early years of Nazi rule—should one stand one's ground in Germany and try to preserve Jewish rights and property, or should one leave the country? Jewish emigration from Germany came in waves that spiked in early 1933, declined in subsequent years, and increased steadily thereafter, culminating in panic emigration in 1938 and 1939. The outflow slowed after 1939, as German Jews found it ever harder to find countries that would accept them.

Changes Brought about by World War I

World War I instigated numerous changes in Jewish demographic patterns, with some continuing after the war and others soon reversed. The outbreak of the war saw a sharp drop in Jewish inmarriages and a powerful increase in the intermarriage rate, to a level in 1915 of 34.2 percent of all Jews marrying that would never be equaled. The number of unmixed Jewish marriages plunged from 3,621 in 1913 to 1,098 in 1915, and from 19,021 in the five years preceding the war to only 8,580 during the four years of the conflict (1914–1918). Concurrently, intermarriage did not decline. Although the 1,143 intermarriages in 1915 were fifteen percent fewer than in 1914, total intermarriages during the war years exceeded those in the previous five years by some 5 percent (5,573 as against 5,325) at an unparalleled rate.[2]

These wartime trends turned around in the years immediately following the armistice. Making up for lost time, many young couples, both Jewish and non-Jewish, rushed to get married. The number of Jewish inmarriages in 1920 (7,497) was nearly twice the prewar annual average and exceeded the general German marriage boom in its vigor.[3] Within a few years, however, and especially after 1923, Jewish marriages went into a sharp decline.

---

2 *Statistisches Jahrbücher für das deutsche Reich* (1911), (1912): 19, (1913): 23, (1914): 23, (1915): 27, (1916): 7, (1918): 7, (1919): 44, (1920): 32, (1921–1922): 41.

3 In 1920 there were 895,000 marriages in Germany, which was about 80 percent over the prewar average.

In the settlement that accompanied its wartime defeat, Germany had to yield territory in the east comprising almost all of Posen province, most of West Prussia, and part of Upper Silesia, the west, and the north. The areas surrendered to Denmark and Belgium had very few Jews, but those ceded to Poland in the east and returned to France in the west were heavily populated by Jews. The Jewish population of Germany within the country's 1910 borders had been 615,021 in the last prewar census. Of these, 535,152 (87.0 percent) inhabited the areas that Germany retained after the war. The "lost territories" had housed 79,869 Jews—1.1 percent of the total population of 7,127,566. The territories which remained in Germany had a Jewish population of 0.9 percent (Table 3.1).

The 1925 census counted 564,379 Jews in Germany, 8.2 percent fewer than those enumerated in 1910. Excepting the "lost" territories, however, the Jewish population actually increased by 29,227 or 5.5 percent. Since natural increase among native Jews was clearly negative, this upturn must have resulted from large-scale immigration from Eastern Europe and in-migration from the territories ceded to Poland. Even with these reinforcements, however, the Jewish population could not keep pace with the general population, falling from 0.95 percent of the total in 1910 to only 0.90 percent in 1925.

Jewish Marriage and Intermarriage Trends during the Weimar Republic Era

The immediate postwar years in Germany (1919–1922) were marked by a marriage boom, in which the Jewish population participated disproportionately. In 1919, 1920, and 1921, there were 6,295, 7,497 and 5,617 Jewish inmarriages, respectively, which far surpassed the 3,800–4,100 typical of the first decades

Table 3.1. Percent of Jewish and General Population Lost in Prussian Territory Ceded by Germany after World War I

Province	General	Jewish
East Prussia	8.0%	13.1%
West Prussia	76.0	74.5
Posen	92.7	93.7
Silesia	18.5	19.2
Schleswig-Holstein	10.3	1.0

Losses in other Prussian areas were negligible.
Source: based on Silbergleit, *Die Bevölkerungs- und Berufsverhältnisse*, 23*.

of the twentieth century. The new trend was short-lived; by 1924, the Jewish marriage rate was 55 percent less than it had been in 1920.[4] Marriages were now at 87 percent of their prewar level. The general marriage rate of Germans recovered during the "good years" of the Weimar Republic and rose by one-third between 1924 and 1929—to 589,611 in the latter year—and then declined by almost 15 percent in the depression years of 1930–1932. The trends among the Jewish population were far less positive. All-Jewish marriages continued to fall to twenty percent between 1924 and 1926, and the recovery from 1926 to 1928 was a paltry twelve percent. From 1928 to 1933, the Jewish inmarriage rate declined much more sharply (27 percent) than the general rate, sinking to a new low of 2,174 marriages in 1933. In 1932, Jewish inmarriages were barely 30 percent of their 1920 levels as against a general German rate of nearly 57 percent. The share of all German marriages represented by homogeneous Jewish marriages hovered at around 0.9 percent from the beginning of the twentieth century to about 1910 and plunged in the immediate prewar and war years (to 0.4 percent in 1915). The percent of Jewish marriages then rebounded to 0.83 percent in 1920 and 1923, plummeted to 0.5 percent between 1927 and 1930, and then fell further to 0.34 percent in 1933.

The sharp decline in Jewish inmarriage was not met by a similar decrease in intermarriage. Although intermarriage did not grow in absolute numbers, its decline was much milder than the downturn in endogamy. Consequently, the intermarriage rate increased considerably during the Weimar period. In 1920, there were 2,211 Jewish-Gentile intermarriages in Germany, a record number and twice as many as in 1918. Given the extremely high rate of Jewish inmarriages in 1920, however, the actual intermarriage rate was only 12.85 percent, the lowest in any year between 1912 and 1933.

Between 1921 and 1923, annual Jewish intermarriages remained at almost the 1920 level (1,890–2,003), while inmarriages declined by about one-third. This raised the intermarriage rate from 12.85 percent in 1920 to 17.2 percent in 1923. Between 1923 and 1924, a 31.5 percent downturn in Jewish inmarriages and a 23.0 percent decline in intermarriages pushed the intermarriage rate even higher to 18.9 percent. From 1924 to 1926, endogamous Jewish marriages fell by another 19.8 percent while Jewish intermarriages slipped by only 15.0 percent. From 1926 to 1928, Jewish inmarriages increased by 12.3 percent and intermarriages by 22.0 percent. Finally, between 1928 and 1932, Jewish inmarriages dropped by 22.7 percent while intermarriages fell only 14.1

---

4 The decline was from 7,497 Jewish inmarriages in 1920 to 3,310 in 1924, as against a 50 percent decrease among the overall German population, from 894,977 to 440,039.

percent. By the latter year, the intermarriage rate was up to 23.0 percent with 2,307 Jewish inmarriages and 1,378 intermarriages.[5]

The Weimar period saw a widening gap between the intermarriage patterns of Jewish men and Jewish women. During the postwar marriage boom (1919–1921), 41.6 percent of Jews who intermarried were women. While male intermarriages soon began to increase, intermarriage by Jewish women leveled off and declined. Between 1921 and 1923, the number of Jewish men who married out of the faith increased from 1,126 to 1,306 while the number of Jewish women who did so fell from 764 to 702. In 1924–1933, only 35.6 percent of Jews who intermarried were women—5,398 as against 9,767 Jewish men. In 1932, 875 Jewish men (63.5 percent) and 503 Jewish women (36.5 percent) married out of the faith.

Conversion and Secularization

While Jewish intermarriage rates rose steadily throughout the Weimar Republic period even as the absolute number of intermarriages did not, conversions to Christianity became less and less common. Statistics on Jewish conversions to Protestantism in Germany saw a steady decline in the late German Empire from an annual average of 458.8 between 1896 and 1900 to 358.4 between 1911 and 1915 and then to 313 in 1916–1920. In the Weimar Republic era, the downward slope became even steeper, with 243.8 annually in 1921–1925 and 142 annually in 1926–1930. In 1931 and 1932, conversions rebounded slightly to 167 per year.[6]

As conversions to Christianity decreased sharply, secession from the Jewish community actually increased. Most of those who left the community in the Weimar Republic declared themselves *konfessionslos* (without religion) rather than converts to Christianity. Peter Honigmann's monograph on dissociation from the Jewish community of Berlin indicates that withdrawals from the community and baptisms were close in number between 1903 and around 1918. Thereafter, secessions increased while baptisms dropped. In 1911, there were 237 withdrawals from Judaism and twenty-eight exits from the Berlin Jewish community without leaving Judaism.[7] Between 1920 and 1923, in contrast,

---

5 *Statistische Jahrbücher für das deutsche Reich* (1924–1925): 35, (1926): 28, (1927): 29, (1928): 33, (1929): 31, (1930): 33, (1931): 30, (1932): 30, (1933): 32, (1934): 32.
6 *Statistik des deutschen Reichs* 451, no. 5 (1936): *Die Glaubensjuden im Deutschen Reich*, 8.
7 Peter Honigmann, *Die Austritte aus der jüdischen Gemeinde Berlin 1873–1941: Statistische Auswertung und Historische Interpretation* (Frankfurt, Bern, New York, and Paris: Peter Lang,

withdrawals from Judaism averaged 310 a year and those leaving the community but not Judaism averaged an additional 144 per year. In 1930, there were over 500 secessions.[8] Many more Jews left the Jewish community than converted to Christianity (Table 3.2).

The number of Germans who declared themselves members of no confession climbed rapidly during the Weimar Republic years. In the 1910 census, a mere 6,139 persons (0.01 percent of the population) were listed as "without declaration of a religious denomination" (*ohne Angabe des Religionsbekenntnisses*) in Germany. Another 2,114 declared themselves members of a non-Christian faith other than Judaism, and 205,900 (0.32 percent of the population) were listed under "other religions."[9] By 1925, the number of persons listed as *Gemeinschaftslose* (without denomination) had increased to 1,140,957 (1.7 percent of the population); in 1933, their numbers stood at 2,437,043 (3.7 percent).[10] Those without religion were particularly numerous in large North German cities such as Berlin,

TABLE 3.2. Conversions of Jews to Christianity and No Religion in Württemberg during Weimar Republic Era

Year	Conversions to Judaism	Conversions from Judaism:	
		To Christianity	Without joining other religion
1921	6	0	30
1922	3	1	7
1923	5	4	3
1924	6	2	4
1929	2	11	3
1930	2	2	4(5)

Source: "Statistik des kirchlichen Lebens der israelitischen Gemeinden Württembergs im Jahre 1930," *Gemeinde-Zeitung für die israelitischen Gemeinden Württembergs* 8, no. 9 (1931): 91.

The statistics from 1929 seem to reverse those who converted to Christianity and those who did not join another religion, but this is how they appear in the original.

1988), 150.
8 Ibid., 27, 150.
9 *Statistik des deutschen Reiches* 240 (1915): 210.
10 1933 census, 3/33.

Hamburg, Leipzig, Altona, Braunschweig, Solingen, and Harburg, and were relatively scarce in Germany's Catholic regions. Only a very small percentage of those without a denomination were of Jewish origin.[11] Since the unaffiliated tended to be young adults, they accounted for a considerable percentage among those married during the Weimar Republic era. Thus, the number of people listed as "other" in the German denominational marriage statistics rose rapidly from less than 1,000 before 1910 to 4,857 in 1919, 19,951 in 1922, 20,283 in 1925, and 41,570 in 1932. Two-thirds of those so categorized were men. The percent of intermarrying Jews who married religionless spouses also increased rapidly during the same period, although not nearly as rapidly as the total number of those without religion who married. Of those Jews who married non-Jews, the number who chose religiously unaffiliated spouses climbed from eleven in 1909 (1.1 percent of all Jews who "married out") to 126 (6.5 percent) in 1919, 176 (8.6 percent) in 1922, 140[12] (9.9 percent) in 1925, and 244 (17.7 percent) in 1932. Unlike Jews who married Christians—most of whom were men—those marrying the unaffiliated were divided almost equally between men and women.[13]

Declining Birth Rates

The sharp decline in Jewish inmarriages during the Weimar Republic period was accompanied by a downturn in Jewish births. The latter trend was milder at first; during the 1920s, the percentage decline in Jewish births was actually smaller than that in non-Jewish births in Germany. The reason for this, however, was that the Jews had already experienced a severe drop in fertility during the Imperial period and began the postwar era with a much lower birth rate than the general population. In the prewar years of 1911–1913, the number of children born to either unmixed Jewish couples or to unmarried Jewish women in Prussia was

---

11 There was little correlation between the numbers of Jews and of those without a denomination in 1933. Hamburg had 175,402 non-denominationals and 16,885 Jews; Braunschweig 24.234 and 682, respectively; Leipzig 102,413 and 11,564; and Harburg-Wilhelmsburg 15,476 and 315. In Catholic areas, there were few without religion irrespective of the size of the Jewish population. In Munich, for instance, there were 9,516 non-denominational individuals and 9,005 Jews; in Würzburg 488 and 2,145, respectively; and in Augsburg 2,270 and 1,030 (*Statistik des Deutschen Reichs* 451, no. 3 [1936]: 4–5).
12 Although the absolute number of Jews who married persons with no religion was smaller in 1925 than in 1922, it was a larger percentage of those who intermarried.
13 The statistical reason for the numerical near equality between Jewish women and men in marrying the unaffiliated was that an overwhelming percentage of the unaffiliated were men.

almost exactly 0.50 percent of the total number of children born there. Given that Jews were 1.04 percent of the population of Prussia according to the 1910 census, this indicated a birth rate far below that of the general population.[14]

World War I saw a steep falloff in childbirth relative to the prewar years among both Jews and the general population, declining from an annual average of 1,179,333 between 1911 and 1914 to 695,691 in 1915–1918 on annual average. Subsequently, average births of Jews dropped further, so that in 1917 only 0.44 percent of children born in Prussia were born to Jewish mothers.[15]

Just as the Jewish marriage boom immediately after the war was greater than that among the general population, so was the baby boom. In 1920–1924, 6,140 children were born on annual average to non-intermarried Jewish mothers in Prussia, slightly surpassing the average in 1910–1914. Average annual births in Prussia as a whole in the same years, in contrast, were 909,940, 23.4 percent less than the prewar average. In 1923, the percentage of children born in Prussia who were Jewish reached its highest point in several decades (0.77 percent). After 1924, both Jewish and general births declined. While Jewish births dropped more sharply than the general numbers, the percentage of babies born in Prussia who were Jewish in 1928 was 0.54 percent, which still exceeded the prewar average.[16] Jewish births continued to drop after 1928, presumably more quickly than among the general population. Only 2,826 Jewish children were born in Prussia in 1931 and only 2,269 in 1932—about half as many as the 4,414 births in 1926.[17]

Age Structure

As Jewish births declined and Jews continued to enjoy high life expectancy, the average age of German Jewry rose steadily. Concurrently, as more and more German Jews were above childbearing age, the rate of births per 1,000 in the Jewish population declined. In Prussia, there was a clear distinction in age spread between native Jews and Jewish non-citizens. In 1925, Prussian Jews were considerably older than the general Prussian population, but non-citizen and mainly immigrant Jews in Prussia had a younger age profile and were closer to the pattern of the general population (Tables 3.3, 5.16). Women were

---

14 Silbergleit, *Die Bevölkerungs- und Berufsverhältnisse*, 39*; *Statistik des deutschen Reiches* 240 (1915): 210.
15 These numbers exclude both Jewish mothers who intermarried as well as stillbirths.
16 Based on Silbergleit, *Die Bevölkerungs- und Berufsverhältnisse*, 39*.
17 Schmelz, handwritten table "Lebendgeborene Preussen Staat" (children of in-married plus out-of-wedlock births to Jewish mothers).

older than men on average (Table 3.4). Within Prussia, there was considerable difference in age structure from region to region in 1925. Jewish median ages ranged from 41 in the tiny South German territory of Hohenzollern to 35–36 in Pomerania and only 31–32 in the Rhineland.[18] The 1933 census showed an even

Table 3.3. Jewish vs. General Age Structure—Prussia, 1925

Age	General population	Jewish citizens	Jewish non-citizens	All Jews
0–14	9,878,230 (25.9%)	53,261 (16.3%)	17,697 (23.2%)	70,958 (17.6%)
15–64	26,070,783 (68.4%)	244,108 (74.5%)	56,390 (73.8%)	300,498 (74.4%)
65+	2,171,160 (5.7%)	30,213 (9.2%)	2,300 (3.0%)	32,513 (8.0%)

Source: Silbergleit, *Die Bevölkerungs- und Berufsverhältnisse*, 50*–51*.

Table 3.4. Native and Foreign Jewish Age Structure by Gender—Prussia, 1925

Age	Jewish citizens		Jewish non-citizens		All Jews	
	Male	Female	Male	Female	Male	Female
0–4	10109 (6.5%)	9814 (5.7%)	3718 (9.2%)	3537 (9.8%)	13827 (7.0%)	13351 (6.4%)
5–14	17058 (10.9)	16280 (9.5)	5308 (13.2)	5134 (14.2)	22366 (11.4)	21414 (10.2)
15–39	60993 (39.1)	67795 (39.5)	21256 (52.7)	17902 (49.6)	82249 (41.9)	85697 (41.3)
40–59	47845 (30.6)	50927 (29.7)	8101 (20.1)	7343 (20.4)	55946 (28.5)	58270 (28.1)
60–64	7562 (4.8)	8986 (5.2)	853 (2.1)	935 (2.6)	8415 (4.3)	9921 (4.8)
65+	12575 (8.1)	17638 (10.3)	1070 (2.7)	1230 (3.4)	13645 (7.0)	18868 (9.1)
Median age	35	37	28	27	33	35

Source: Silbergleit, *Die Bevölkerungs- und Berufsverhältnisse*, 3–7, 50*–51*.

---

18 Based on Silbergleit, *Die Bevölkerungs- und Berufsverhältnisse*, 8–65.

Table 3.5. Comparative Jewish Age Structure—Germany 1925, 1933

Age	1925	1933*
Under 5	6.7%	19,129 (3.8%)
Under 15	17.6%	82,688 (16.6%)
Over 60	12.6%	81,444 (16.3%)
Over 70	4.4%	30,832 (6.2%)

* Estimated as explained in Table 5.21. Over 70 = all born before 1862 and half of those born in 1863.
Source: 1933 census, 5/17, 42–43.

more elderly Jewish population than did the census of 1925. The median age of German Jews that year was about thirty-nine; the largest age cohort was those born in 1896. Among the general population, the median age was thirty and the largest age cohort was born in 1908 (Tables 3.5, 5.21).[19]

Rising Death Rates

As the average age of German Jewry rose, the long-term trend of falling death rates reversed. Throughout the nineteenth century, Jews had been noted for their much lower death rate than the general population and, especially, for their low infant mortality rate. Annual Jewish deaths in Prussia fell steadily until 1895–1900, at 5,719 on annual average, and increased to 6,139 in the pre-World War I years. After spiking during the war, Jewish deaths settled into a narrow annual range of 5,449–5,942 between 1920 and 1928. Among the general German population, deaths per year were much fewer in the 1920s (445,754–589,819 between 1920 and 1928) than in the prewar years (620,571–696,969).[20]

Until 1913, Jewish births always outnumbered Jewish deaths in Prussia, although the gap slowly narrowed after 1880, mainly because of the falling

---

19 Calculated from *Statistisches Jahrbuch für das Deutsche Reich* (1936): 12–13.
20 This was partly the result of improving health conditions and the loss of the provinces of Posen and Westpreussen, where death rates were higher than in the rest of Germany. In 1906–1910, for instance, the urban infant mortality rate in the districts of Danzig, Marienwerder, Posen, and Bromberg were 207, 202, 174, and 203 respectively compared to 174 for Germany as a whole. Knodel, *Decline*, 288–289.

Jewish birth rate. After 1914, however, Jewish births exceeded Jewish deaths in Prussia only in the four years of the baby boom from 1920 to 1923, and even then the disparity was substantial only in 1921 (6,510 births, 5,449 deaths). Once the excess of deaths over births began, it increased every year after 1924. By 1928, there were 3,910 Jewish births as against 5,704 Jewish deaths in Prussia[21]; in 1932, the corresponding figures were 2,269 births and no fewer than 5,677 Jewish deaths.[22] Jewish population growth not only fell below replacement rate but also showed a strongly unfavorable natural balance of births and deaths.

Urbanization

The Jewish population of Germany became slightly more urbanized during the Weimar period. Urban populations contracted slightly less than small-town Jewry did, and the regional distribution changed little. While German Jewry was highly urbanized before World War I, its tendency to concentrate in the large cities became even more evident during the Weimar era. In 1910, 54.2 percent of German Jews lived in the forty-four cities that had populations of at least 100,000. The percentage of German Jews in large cities so defined continued to rise in the censuses of 1925 and 1933. In the former year, Germany had forty-eight cities with over 100,000 inhabitants; in the latter year it had fifty-two. The total Jewish population in these fifty-two cities was 391,036 in 1925, which was 2.1 percent of the cities' total population and 69.3 percent of all German Jews. Between 1925 and the government census of June 16, 1933, the Jewish population of Germany decreased by 11.5 percent and that of the fifty-two largest cities contracted by slightly less at 9.4 percent (from 391,036 to 354,120). In 1933, Jews in the largest cities represented 70.9 percent of German Jewry but were only 1.8 percent of the total population of these cities.[23] Only three cities—two of them in the booming Ruhr district—saw slight absolute increases in their Jewish populations between 1925 and 1933.[24]

Among the urban communities, the process of concentrating in a small number of major centers continued. In Greater Berlin, where 144,007 Jews had dwelled in 1910 (23.4 percent of all German Jews), the absolute numbers grew to 172,672 in 1925 and its percentage of the total Jewish population of Germany

---

21 Silbergleit, *Die Bevölkerungs- und Berufsverhältnisse*, 14*–15*, 39*.
22 Schmelz, handwritten tables "Lebendgeborene Preussen Staat" (children of in-married couples plus out-of-wedlock births to Jewish mothers) and "Sterbefälle Preussen Staat."
23 1933 census, 3/32–33.
24 Essen, from 4,504 to 4,506; Erfurt, from 819 to 831; and Remscheid, from 261 to 273.

swelled to 31.5 percent. Between 1925 and 1933, Berlin lost over 12,000 Jewish inhabitants but increased its percentage of all of German Jewry to 32.1 percent. Most of the rest of the urban Jewish population increasingly congregated in a few cities. The combined Jewish population of Frankfurt, Hamburg, and Breslau was 65,912 in 1910 (10.7 percent of German Jewry) and 72,904 in 1925 (12.9 percent). The combined Jewish population of the cities that had the next-largest Jewish presence—Cologne, Leipzig, and Munich—was 32,673 (5.3 percent of German Jewry) in 1910 and 38,768 (6.9 percent) in 1925. In 1925, the other forty-five cities with more than 100,000 inhabitants had a combined Jewish population of only 112,787 (20.0 percent of German Jewry)—an average of only about 2,500 per community. Between 1925 and 1933, the number of Jews in Frankfurt, Breslau, and Hamburg declined to 63,245 (-12.3 percent), Jews in the three next-largest communities now numbered only 35,385 (-8.7 percent), and those in the other forty-five large cities slumped to only 94,926 (-15.8 percent).

As in earlier periods, the urbanization of the Jewish community varied greatly by region. Central Germany remained the most urbanized region and southern Germany the least. While the western and southern regions plus Hesse contained only 42.1 percent of German Jewry and 31.8 percent of German Jews in cities of over 100,000 inhabitants, they were home to no fewer than 68.0 percent of all German Jews who lived in towns of fewer than 20,000 inhabitants in 1925 (Table 3.6).

The remaining rural Jewish population was concentrated mostly in specific regions of the south and west. The 1933 census identifies a "Main-Rhein Gebiet" region where 39,794 Jews lived in towns of fewer than 10,000 inhabitants, which represented 51.6 percent of all German Jews who inhabited such small towns and 0.83 percent of the population of the area. The region includes all of Hesse(-Darmstadt) state, most of Hesse-Nassau, southeastern Westphalia, the Rhine-Mosel area, the eastern Rhine Palatinate, the northern regions of Baden and Württemberg, and most of Lower Franconia, along with a few neighboring sections of Upper and Middle Franconia (Map 9/1).

Immigration and Foreign Jews

The foreign Jewish population of Germany accounted for a larger fraction of German Jewry after World War I than it did prior to it. Much of the influx of East European Jews into Germany took place during the war years, as Jews in the east were recruited and sometimes forcibly brought to Germany for labor purposes. In the postwar years, there was much public outcry against the new arrivals, often strongly tinged with antisemitism. In some cases, foreign Jews were rounded up and interned or deported; many other foreign Jews probably

Table 3.6. Change in Level of Urbanization among German Jews, 1925–1933

Region	Total Jewish population		Over 100,000 (1933)*		Under 20,000*	
	1925	1933	1925	1933	1925	1933
Eastern Germany (East Prussia, Pomerania, Grenzmark, Silesia)	62,557	52,303	36,564 (58.5%)	31,769 (60.9%)	17,846 (28.5%)	13,164 (25.2%)
Central Germany (Berlin, Brandenburg, Prussian Saxony and State of Saxony, Thuringia, Mecklenburg, Anhalt)	218,863	200,696	198,231 (90.6%)	183,321 (91.3%)	10,143 (4.6%)	7,855 (3.9%)
Northwest (Schleswig-Holstein, Hanover, Hamburg, Oldenburg, Braunschweig, Bremen, Lippe, Lübeck, Schaumburg-Lippe)	45,326	37,747	31,872 (70.3%)	27,060 (71.7%)	9,668 (21.3%)	7,245 (19.2%)
West (Rhineland, Westphalia)	79,315	71,245	47,275 (59.6%)	43,326 (60.8%)	21,653 (27.3%)	17,307 (24.9%)
Hesse (Hesse-Darmstadt, Hesse-Nassau)	73,947	64,811	38,706 (52.3%)	33,781 (52.1%)	28,267 (38.2%)	24,421 (37.7%)
South (Hohenzollern, Baden, Württemberg, Bavaria)	84,371	72,880	38,388 (45.5%)	34,763 (47.7%)	30,260 (35.7%)	26,235 (36.0%)
Total	564,379	499,682	391,036 (69.3%)	354,010 (70.9%)	117,837 (20.9%)	96,227 (19.3%)
Percent decline, 1925–1933		11.5%		9.5%		18.3%
Percent of those within category living in south, west, or Hesse		41.8%		31.6%		70.6%

Source: 1933 census, 5/15; Schmelz, handwritten table "Juden Ortsgrössenklassen."

left Germany voluntarily. Despite this re-emigration of many of the new arrivals, the 1925 census showed a major increase in the foreign Jewish population. In Prussia alone, the number of Jewish non-citizens enumerated in 1925 (76,387) was 58.6 percent higher than the 48,166 counted in 1910. From 11.6 percent of the Prussian Jewish population in 1910, they had increased to 18.9 percent by 1925.[25] In Germany as a whole, the number of foreign Jews rose from 79,646 or 13.0 percent of the German-Jewish population in 1910 (76,387 in the territories that remained German after the war) to 107,747 (19.1 percent) in 1925. Of these foreign Jews, an estimated 80 percent were of East European origin. Between 1925 and 1933, while the Jewish population of Germany shrank by 11.5 percent, the foreign Jewish population declined by only 8.35 percent to 98,747. Given the large share of East European Jews among this populace—as much as 89.5 percent in 1933, according to some estimates—the absolute numbers of East European Jews actually increased by almost 3,000.[26]

Given Germany's illiberal citizenship laws, many of those who were counted as foreigners had in fact been born in Germany to foreign-born parents. In 1933, 41,312 (41.8 percent) of the 98,747 Jews of foreign nationality in Germany were born in the country.[27] A total of 16,258 born abroad had been granted citizenship. Thus, based on citizenship, 19.8 percent of German Jews in 1933 were foreigners but only 73,693 (14.8 percent) were foreign-born. The total number of both foreign-born and foreign-citizen Jews was 115,005—23.0 percent of all Jews in Germany[28].

As in earlier years, the foreign Jewish population was even more highly urbanized than the native Jews were. According to 1933 census categories, 354,120 (70.9 percent) of 499,682 Jews lived in cities that had populations exceeding 100,000. Among those defined as *zugewanderte* (either foreign born or a foreign citizen), no fewer than 101,374 (88.2 percent) of 115,005 lived in such cities as against 252,746 (65.7 percent) of 384,677 "native" Jews who lived there. Conversely, 28.6 percent of Jews in large cities were *zugewanderte*, while only 9.4 percent of the 145,562 German Jews who lived in other localities were

---

25 Wertheimer, *Unwelcome Strangers*, 186; Silbergleit, *Die Bevölkerungs- und Berufsverhältnisse*, 39*.
26 Maurer, *Ostjuden*, 72.
27 The Nazi statistics of 1933 created a new category of *zugewanderte* ("migrated") Jews, who were distinguished from the *einheimische* ("local") population. The *zugewanderte* category was defined to include all Jews born abroad (including those who had received citizenship) as well as all those without citizenship (including those born in Germany) to exaggerate the number of Jewish foreigners.
28 Including the 2,393 Jews with foreign citizenship who were born in the territories lost by Germany after World War I.

such. The percentage of *zugewanderte* Jews was especially small in provinces where small-town Jews were numerous, such as Grenzmark Posen-West Prussia (3.9 percent), Lower Franconia (4.7 percent), and Hesse(-Darmstadt) (8.7 percent).[29]

The Nazi Period—Patterns of Decline and Emigration

The lack of a German government census in the interval between 1925 and 1933 makes it difficult to tell how much of the aforementioned 11.5 percent decline in the country's Jewish population took place in the last eight years of the Weimar Republic and how much occurred in the first four and a half months of Nazi rule. The percentage decrease seems to have been greatest in provinces that had low Jewish density to begin with; East Prussia, Schleswig-Holstein, Thuringia, Mecklenburg, Braunschweig, Anhalt, and Lübeck all had declines of over 20 percent. Although the overall contraction was less acute in cities over 100,000 (9.4 percent) than it was in Germany as a whole, several cities saw downturns of more than 20 percent. These cities were Wuppertal, Königsberg, Oberhausen, Wiesbaden, Altona, Braunschweig, Hagen, Solingen, Lübeck, and Harburg-Wilhelmsburg. Of the numerical decline of almost 65,000, about 24,000 can be attributed to the excess of deaths over births and the remainder to net migration (Map 3/1).

In the six years that passed until the next census in 1939, the Jewish population underwent many dislocations. Although many Jews initially thought it possible to hold on in Germany, it became increasingly evident that their situation had become untenable and that emigration was the only sensible option. Emigration, however, was not the only precipitant of change in the demographic profile of German Jewry in the prewar years of Nazi rule. Jewish intermarriage declined sharply even before the 1935 Nuremberg laws made it virtually impossible. Migration from the more isolated smaller towns to the seemingly safer large cities stepped up the rate of urbanization. As emigrants were predominantly younger people and men, the percentage of women and the average age of the Jewish population increased strikingly. Finally, in the early years of Nazi rule there was a paradoxical mini-boom in Jewish marriages and births.

Despite the emigration-induced decline in Jewish population in the years after Hitler came to power in 1933, the number of Jewish homogenous marriages began to recover after 1933. Although the outlawing of intermarriage,

---

29 Source: 1933 census, 5/15, 5/16.

which forced Jews to seek Jewish marriage partners, was certainly a factor, there were other causes as well. In part, the rebound reflected a general increase in German marriages during those years and, in part, young Jews' desire to marry in preparation for emigration (Table 4.46).

In 1939, there were 166,001 Jews in cities of over 100,000 in the *Altreich* (Germany proper, excluding annexed territories), which was 74.9 percent of all *Altreich* Jews,[30] as against 354,120 (70.9 percent) in 1933. The ten largest Jewish communities had 278,121 Jewish inhabitants in 1933 (55.7 percent of all German Jews). By 1939, the absolute numbers in the largest ten communities had decreased to 135,134, but the percentage of German Jewry concentrated there had increased to 61.0 percent.

The 1939 census, which was based on Nazi racial categories, surprised many observers who had expected far higher numbers of "half-Jews" and "quarter-Jews" as well as "full Jews" who had converted from the Jewish religion. Although antisemites often claimed that these categories were larger than the official tallies of Jews by religion and that there were "millions" of people of disguised Jewish origin in Germany, the census results showed otherwise. There are many reasons to believe that the census figures were not the results of massive concealment by partially Jewish inhabitants, but were instead a rather accurate reflection of the actual size of the partly Jewish population.[31] In Greater Germany, the 1939 census found 330,539 "full Jews" by race, of whom 297,407 (90.0 percent) were Jews by religion, 71,126 "half-Jews," of whom 6,660 (9.4 percent) were Jews by religion, and 41,456 "quarter-Jews," of whom only 490 were Jews by religion. Of 443,121 persons with Jewish ancestry who were enumerated in the census, 74.6 percent were "full Jews" and 68.7 percent were Jews by religion. In Germany within its 1933 boundaries[32] there were 233,095 "full Jews," 51,756 "half-Jews," and 32,478 "quarter-Jews" (Table 3.7). Although conversion and intermarriage had certainly affected the German-Jewish population, the mixed and convert populations were still much smaller than the unmixed population that belonged to the Jewish community.

---

30 Counting only cities that had more than 100,000 inhabitants in 1933.
31 For a detailed argument for the relative accuracy of the 1939 census, see Lowenstein, "Jewish Intermarriage and Conversion," 51–53. Part of the argument made there is that a comparison of the 1939 data with data on Jewish marriages between 1921 and 1929 shows that a slightly larger percentage of intermarried couples counted in the 1920s were counted in the 1939 census than were unmixed Jewish couples. This would contradict any argument of massive hiding of origins by people of mixed origin.
32 That is, excluding Saarland, Austria, and the Sudetenland.

Table 3.7. Percent of Persons of Jewish Origin in Various Nazi Racial Categories—1939

Area	"Full Jews"	"Half-Jews"	"Quarter-Jews"	Total
Greater Germany	330,539 (74.6%)	71,126 (16.1%)	41,456 (9.4%)	443,121
Altreich	233,095 (73.5%)	51,756 (16.3%)	32,478 (10.2%)	317,329

Source: 1939 census (*Statistik des Deutschen Reichs* 552, no. 4 (1944): 6–9.

In many ways, the geographic distribution of the "mixed" and converted population reflected patterns of assimilation and tradition that belonged to the earlier part of the twentieth century. The so-called *Mischling* (mixed Jewish-Gentile ancestry) population outnumbered "full Jews" in only a few provinces that had sparse Jewish populations such as Schleswig-Holstein, Mecklenburg, and Oldenburg. It was less than 25 percent of the number of "full Jews" in such areas of heavy (and heavily rural) Jewish population like Hesse-Nassau, Hohenzollern, Baden, Hesse(-Darmstadt), and Schaumburg-Lippe. The percentage of "half-Jews" who belonged to the Jewish community was highest in Berlin, while that of "full Jews" who converted was especially high in Hamburg, Schleswig-Holstein, and Schaumburg-Lippe (Table 3.8). In general, converts and "mixed-race" individuals were especially common in central and northwestern Germany and particularly uncommon in southern Germany (Table 3.9).

German Jewry's age and gender patterns underwent much displacement due to skewed patterns of emigration. In 1933, women were 52.2 percent of the Jewish population of Germany; by 1939, among Jews by religion, their share had increased to 57.6 percent, far from a natural gender balance.[33] The share of women was almost exactly 58.0 percent among "full Jews by race," 53.8 percent among half Jews, and only 51.9 percent among quarter Jews. Among "full Jews" who had left the Jewish religion, 60.4 percent were women and among those

---

[33] Counting all *Glaubensjuden* (Jews by religion), whether they were "full Jews," "half-Jews," or "quarter-Jews" by race. In the *Altreich* alone, the percentage of females among *Glaubensjuden* was 57.4 percent. Excluding the Saarland, annexed in 1935, it was 57.39 percent. There seems to have been little regional differences in gender ratios.

Table 3.8. Percent of Persons of Jewish Origin in Various "Racial" and Religious Categories, 1939, by Region (from Highest to Lowest Percent of Full Jews following the Jewish Religion)

Region	"Full Jews"		"Half-Jews"		"Quarter-Jews"		Total
	Jewish religion	Not Jewish religion	Jewish religion	Not Jewish religion	Jewish religion	Not Jewish religion	
Hohenzollern	87.6	2.4	0	2.4	0	7.6	210
Baden	79.2	5.3	1.2	8.9	0.3	5.1	11012
Hesse-Nassau	78.4	4.2	1.1	10.1	0.1	6.2	25845
Hesse (-Darmstadt)	77.2	4.8	1.0	10.1	0.1	6.8	7402
Schaumburg-Lippe	73.7	12.8	0.6	6.4	0	6.4	156
Bavaria	73.1	5.1	1.1	12.7	0.1	7.9	21825
Württemberg	71.8	5.5	1.0	12.9	0.2	8.7	6096
Silesia	71.7	4.9	2.2	12.3	0.1	8.9	22090
Lippe	69.3	1.6	0.9	15.1	0	13.2	319
Berlin	68.8	6.5	2.2	14.4	0.1	8.1	109573
Rhine Province	68.4	5.6	1.3	14.1	0.2	10.4	33779
Westphalia	66.0	5.2	1.2	14.8	0.1	12.7	11197
East Prussia	65.5	5.8	1.9	15.0	0.2	11.7	4448
Pommern	64.6	5.5	1.8	14.9	0.3	13.0	4877
Hannover	63.2	5.4	0.8	16.6	0.1	13.9	8436
Thuringia	61.6	9.0	0.5	15.6	0.1	13.2	2758
Saxony	57.2	8.6	2.0	18.7	0.2	13.3	11653
Oldenburg	51.7	5.3	0.6	22.3	0	27.2	731
Braunschweig	50.3	7.3	1.7	18.0	2.4	20.4	752
Brandenburg	49.9	8.0	1.6	21.8	0.1	18.6	6946
Hamburg	47.3	10.2	1.0	23.3	0.1	18.1	17273
Bremen	45.6	7.7	0.8	25.2	0.4	20.3	1355
(Pr.) Saxony	45.4	7.7	1.7	24.6	0.04	20.5	5129
Anhalt	44.9	7.9	0.8	24.9	0	21.5	758
Schleswig-Holstein	33.0	10.3	0.6	26.6	0.1	29.5	1742
Mecklenburg	27.3	10.0	0.7	30.6	0	31.5	965
All Germany (Greater Germany)	67.1	7.5	1.5	14.6	0.1	9.2	443121

Source: 1939 census, 4/6–9.

Table 3.9. Regional Variations among Converted and "Mixed-Race" Jews, 1939

Region	"Full Jews"		"Half-Jews"		"Quarter-Jews"		Total
	Jewish religion	Not Jewish religion	Jewish religion	Not Jewish religion	Jewish religion	Not Jewish religion	
East (East Prussia, Pommern, Silesia)	21902 (69.7%)	1605 (5.1%)	648 (2.1%)	4097 (13.0%)	44 (0.1%)	3119 (9.9%)	31415
Central (Berlin, Brandenburg, Mecklenburg, Province of Saxony, Free State of Saxony, Anhalt, Thuringia)	90107 (65.4%)	9462 (7.0%)	2857 (2.1%)	21617 (15.7%)	142 (0.1%)	13597 (9.9%)	137782
Northwest (Schleswig-Holstein, Hannover, Hamburg, Braunschweig, Oldenburg, Bremen, Lippe, Schaumburg-Lippe)	15741 (51.2%)	2627 (8.5%)	274 (0.9%)	6579 (21.4%)	57 (0.2%)	5486 (17.8%)	30764
West (Rhine Province, Westphalia)	30492 (67.8%)	2470 (5.5%)	591 (1.3%)	6411 (14.3%)	62 (0.1%)	4950 (11.0%)	44976
South (Bavaria, Baden, Württemberg, Hesse-Nassau, Hesse, Hohenzollern)	55215 (76.3%)	3474 (4.8%)	801 (1.1%)	7881 (10.9%)	87 (0.1%)	4934 (6.8%)	72392
Total	213457 (67.3%)	19638 (6.2%)	5171 (1.6%)	46585 (14.7%)	392 (0.1%)	32086 (10.1%)	317329

Source: based on 1939 census, 4/6–9.

who had joined a Christian denomination, the gender ratio was 61.9 percent women to 38.1 percent men.

Since young adults were the most likely to emigrate, German Jewry became progressively older on average (Table 3.10). In 1939, the median age of German Jews[34] was fifty-one, much older than the average of thirty-nine in 1933. A more direct insight into the degree to which emigration affected the age and gender makeup of German Jewry may be obtained by comparing the same birth cohort in the censuses of 1933 and 1939.[35] Approximately 65 percent of those born between 1923 and 1932 had emigrated by 1939. This percentage was even higher for those born between 1904 and 1923, especially among men. The proportion of emigrants was largest among men born in 1916, only 14 percent of whom remained in Germany in 1939. The share of women who emigrated was lower in these age groups and was highest among those born in 1914 (78 percent). Most women born before 1898 remained in Germany, and the share of emigrants was lowest (under 34 percent) in the 1874–1878 cohort. Among men, those who emigrated outnumbered those who stayed in all age groups born after 1883.[36]

The 1939 census was essentially the last systematic enumeration of German Jewry before its destruction. After a few preliminary deportations to Poland and southern France in 1940, the massive deportations to the east began in late 1941. By 1943, almost all German Jews who were not living in "privileged intermarriages" had been deported to ghettos or camps and most had been murdered. It is a bizarre fact that in 1944 the German government published a detailed report on the demographic makeup of German Jews according to the census of May 1939 at a time when most of those enumerated were either dead or no longer living in Germany.

---

34 "Full Jews" in Greater Germany by race who were also Jews by religion.
35 Since the 1939 census covers all of "Greater Germany" including the large Viennese community, our calculations are reached by subtracting a percentage of the figures for each year, counted in 1939, by a percentage equivalent to the percentage of Viennese Jews of the total in that age group (within five years).
36 For more comprehensive data on the percentages of each age cohort that left Germany between 1933 and 1939, see Table 8.33.

Table 3.10. Aging of German Jewry, 1925–1939

Age	1925					1933				1939				
	Total	Percent of all German Jews	Male	Female	Total	Percent of all German Jews	Male	Female	Total	Percent of all German Jews	Male	Female	Total	Percent female	Pecent of all German Jews
0–4	38827	6.9				(3.8)				2541	2552	5093	50.1	1.7
5–9	23723	4.2				(6.1)				3516	3353	6869	48.8	2.3
10–14	38651	6.9	54188	52778	106966	(11.9)				6092	6000	12092	49.6	4.1
15–19	43808	7.8								7216	7574	14790	51.2	5.0
20–24	95244	16.9	16811	17502	34313	14.2				2125	3224	5349	60.3	1.8
25–29			17410	19329	36739					3789	5824	9613	60.6	3.2
30–34	92117	16.3				16.5				5610	8155	13765	59.2	4.6
35–39			39622	43356	82978					7683	11239	18922	59.4	6.4
40–44	90035	16.0	19016	21477	40493	16.1				9696	15205	24901	61.1	8.4
45–49			19191	21029	40220					10829	16812	27641	60.8	9.3
50–54	69987	12.4				15.3				13026	17758	30784	57.7	10.4
55–59			37175	39354	76529					14273	17856	32129	55.6	10.8
60–64	46307	8.2	13403	15394	28797	16.3				14553	18022	32575	55.3	11.0
65–69			21931	30716	52647					11029	14311	25340	56.5	8.5
70–75	25698	4.6								7544	10977	18521	59.3	6.2
75–80										4523	7293	11816	61.7	4.0
80+										2891	5446	8337	65.3	1.0
Total			238747	260935	499682					125707	171400	297407	57.6	

Sources:
1925: according to Schmelz's tables; exact source unknown.
1933: 1933 census, 5/17, 44.
1939 (full Jews who were *Glaubensjuden*, Greater Germany): 1939 census, 4/48–57.

TOPICAL SECTION

4

Natural Growth and Changes in the German Jewish Family

Premodern families were marked by high levels of both fertility and mortality, as well as a relatively short lifespan. They had many children, a large proportion of whom did not survive to adulthood and many households were non-nuclear. By the twentieth century, households characterized by birth control, small numbers of children, much longer life spans, and lower mortality rates replaced these older patterns. Other changes also occurred in rates of illegitimacy, marriage age, and interreligious marriage. Among European populations, German Jews were in the vanguard in making this transition from premodern to modern family patterns.

German Jewish Family Patterns in the First Half of the Nineteenth Century

Although the German-Jewish family underwent a thorough transformation between 1815 and 1939, it was already quite different from medieval European Jewish families by the time that this period began. As early as the eighteenth century, Jews in the western sections of Germany displayed patterns of late marriage that were consonant with their Christian neighbors' "European" marriage pattern.¹ In many areas, Jews in early nineteenth-century western Germany married even later than non-Jews did. This may be one reason why Jewish birth rates were lower than Christian birth rates, although they were very high by later standards. All of this stood in contrast to the patterns of very early marriage that are documented among medieval German Jews and among East European Jews until the end of the nineteenth century.² At least at first glance, late marriage appears to be a deviation from the Jewish religious tradition. Another distinctive and modern feature of German Jewry was its pattern of much lower infant mortality than that found among its neighbors.

Despite anecdotal evidence of very early marriage in earlier periods (such as the memoirist Gluckel of Hameln's marriage before age fourteen in c. 1660), delayed marriage had become the rule in German Jewry by the late eighteenth century. At least two main factors precipitated the adoption of late marriage patterns: the example of the Christian population of Germany, which married quite late, and the influence of widespread restrictive legislation, which made it hard for Jews to establish new families. In highly restricted Berlin between 1759 and 1813, the median age at first marriage was 26 for Jewish grooms and 22.5 for brides. Only twenty-one of 519 grooms and 117 of 523 brides married before the age of twenty and only forty-seven of the brides were under age eighteen.³ Wealthier Jews and Jews with more favorable legal status married much earlier than the poor and those under the strongest legal restrictions; men in the most restricted class married at age thirty-six on average (Tables 4.1, 4.2). All this indicates that late marriage was influenced by governmental restrictions.

Jews in early nineteenth-century western Germany married even later than eighteenth-century Berlin Jews did. In Darmstadt (Hesse), the median age

---

1 The classic description of the pattern of late marriage in Western Europe since the seventeenth century is John Hajnal's "The European Marriage Pattern in Historical Perspective," in *Population in History*, ed. D. V. Glass and D. E. C. Eversley (Chicago: Aldine, 1965), 101–143.

2 See, for example, David Biale, *Eros and the Jews. From Biblical Israel to Contemporary America* (Berkeley and Los Angeles: University of California Press, 1997), 64, 127–128, 153, 278, note 13; and Abraham Grossman, "Nisuei Boser be-Hevrah ha-Yehudit bi-Yemei ha-Benayim ad ha-Meah ha-Shlosh-Esre" [Very early marriage in Jewish society from the Middle Ages to the thirteenth century], *Peamim* 45 (1990): 108–125.

3 These figures are based mainly on Jacob Jacobson, *Jüdische Trauungen in Berlin 1759–1813* (Berlin: de Gruyter, 1968). The average age at marriage was a little higher than the median: at thirty among men and twenty-four among women. Decade by decade, the median age of marriage slowly increased. From 1759 to 1770, the median age of Jewish grooms was twenty-seven, and of Jewish brides, twenty-two. This includes all marriages, not only first ones. Although the age of brides remained unchanged, that of grooms rose to twenty-nine in both the 1770s and the 1780s. See Steven M. Lowenstein, "Ashkenazic Jewry and the European Marriage Pattern: A Preliminary Survey of Jewish Marriage Age," *Jewish History* 8, nos. 1–2 (1994): 155–175.

Table 4.1. Relation between Level of Taxpaying and Marriage Age in Late Eighteenth-Century Berlin

Amount Taxed	Median age at marriage	Mean age at marriage
Taxed at over 4 Taler	23	26 (N = 52)
2–4 Taler	24	26 (N = 47)
1–2 Taler	26	28 (N = 107)
Taxed at less than 1 Taler	32	33 (N = 100)

Source: Jacobson, *Jüdische Trauungen in Berlin 1759–1813*.

Table 4.2. Relation between Legal Status of Groom's Family and Marriage Age in Late Eighteenth-Century Berlin

Legal status	Mean age at marriage	
	Grooms	Brides
General Privilege (virtually no marital restrictions)	27 (N = 70)	22 (N = 58)
Ordinarii (entitled to marry off one or two children)	30 (N = 329)	24 (N = 325)
Publique Bediente (employees of the Jewish community)	33 (N = 32)	26 (N = 33)
Extraordinarii (right to marry for themselves only, not inherited by their children)	36 (N = 47)	27 (N = 29)

Source: Jacobson, *Jüdische Trauungen in Berlin 1759–1813*.

of Jews' first marriage between 1840 and 1875 was twenty-nine among men and twenty-three among women. In Altdorf, Baden, Jewish grooms married at 29 and brides at 27.4 in mid-century. Jews in nearby Nonnenweier married several years later than their Catholic neighbors between 1800 and 1849. Jewish grooms averaged 32.1 as against 27.9 among Catholic men, and Jewish brides averaged 26.6 as against 24.3 for non-Jewish brides. Jewish marriage ages were highest of all in Bavaria, where the marriage laws were by far the strictest.[4] In a

---

4 Ibid., 157–158; Alice Goldstein, "Village Jews in Germany: Nonnenweier 1800–1931," in *Modern Jewish Fertility*, ed. Paul Ritterband (Leiden: Brill, 1981), 112–143; and Alice Goldstein, "Aspects of Change in a Nineteenth Century German Village," *Journal of Family*

sample of communities in the Bavarian province of Middle Franconia, Jewish men's ages at first marriage were found to average 31.6–34.3 and those of Jewish brides 25.7–28.1. In the Bavarian village of Harburg from 1817 to 1861, Jewish grooms averaged 31.4 years of age and brides averaged 25.2.[5] In the French district of Alsace-Lorraine, where the demographic patterns resembled those of southern Germany, the estimated Jewish median age at marriage (brides and grooms combined) was 21.9 in 1808, 25.2 in 1846, and 25.7 in 1851.[6] Since nineteenth-century France had no legal restrictions on Jewish marriage, the steadily rising age of marriage there seems to indicate cultural rather than legal reasons for the pattern.

In the eastern provinces of Germany, Jews did not marry as late as they did in the western areas, although they married much later than Jews just across the eastern border in Russian Poland. In Fordon, Posen province, the median ages of Jews at first marriage between 1820 and 1846 were twenty-six among men and twenty-four among women. In Zülz, Upper Silesia, between 1815 and 1839, grooms' median age at first marriage was also twenty-six, but brides at first marriage were younger at twenty-two. These patterns, while much younger than marriage ages in western Germany, were still different from the median age of twenty among both brides and grooms in Russian Poland.[7]

While the marriage ages of German Jews conformed more or less to those of Christian Germans, their mortality rates, especially in infant mortality, were quite distinctive. Two calculations of stillbirths and deaths before the age of one in early nineteenth-century Prussia show Jewish rates more than 25 percent lower than those of Christians (Table 4.3). There is evidence that the stillbirth rate among Prussian Jews, which much lower than that of the general population to begin with, began to drop significantly after 1840. There is no evidence of a similar decline in non-Jewish stillbirths[8] (Tables 4.4, 4.5). In all of Baden between 1852 and 1863, 25.3 percent of Protestants, 27.8 percent

---

    History 9 (Summer 1984): 151, note 2—both quoted in note 18 of Lowenstein, "European Marriage Pattern."

5 Lowenstein, "Voluntary and Involuntary Restriction of Fertility in 19th-Century Bavarian Jewry," in *Modern Jewish Fertility*, ed. Paul Ritterband (Leiden: Brill, 1981), 94–111; and Reinhard Jakob, *Die jüdische Gemeinde von Harburg (1671–1871)* (Nördlingen: Steinmeier, 1988), 61.

6 Lowenstein, "European Marriage Pattern," table in note 22, based on Paula Hyman, "Jewish Fertility in 19th-Century France," in *Modern Jewish Fertility*, ed. Paul Ritterband (Leiden: Brill, 1981), 83.

7 Lowenstein, "European Marriage Pattern," 159.

8 Stillbirth rates in official statistics must be used with caution because possible cultural differences in reporting stillbirths may mask differences (see Table 4.5).

Table 4.3. Infant Mortality and Stillbirth Rates, of Jews and General Population, Prussia, 1822–1840

Year	Number of births	Birth rate per 1,000	Death rate per 1,000	Stillbirths	Stillbirths per 100 births	Live born, died by age 1	Percent died by age 1	Stillborn and died by age 1
Jews								
1822–1837	87,249	35.37	21.97	2,153	2.47	11,347	13.01	15.47
1822–1840		35.46	21.61		2.52		12.94	15.46
General population								
1822–1837	7,744,587	40.08	29.78	271,904	3.51	1,341,117	17.32	20.83
1822–1840		40.01	29.61		3.57		17.41	20.98

Increase in population, 1822–1840: Jews 34.4 percent; general population 27.9 percent.

Sources: Johann Gottfried Hoffmann, "Neueste Nachrichten von der Bevölkerung des preußischen Staates," *Allgemeine Staatszeitung* 229 (1838); and Johann Gottfried Hoffmann, "Uebersicht der Anzahl und Vertheilung der Juden im Preußischen Staate nach einer Vergleichung der Zählungen zu Ende der Jahre 1840 und 1822," *Allgemeine Staatszeitung* 141 (1841, 1842), quoted in Silbergleit, *Die Bevölkerungs- und Berufsverhältnisse*, 11*–12*.

Table 4.4. Stillbirths per 1,000 Births—Prussia

Year	General population	Jews
1820–1828	30.39	22.96
1829–1840	36.53	26.09
1841–1855	38.95	19.92
1856–1864	41.54	14.88

Source: Goldscheider, "Entwicklung," 73.

of Catholics, but only 17.5 percent of Jews born alive died before their first birthday.[9] In Nonnenweier before 1820, 93.6 percent of Jewish children born survived to age thirteen, but only 74.0 percent of Christian children did so; in 1820–1839, however, the Jewish rate of child and infant mortality was slightly higher than that of Christians (Table 4.6).[10] In Hamburg, where Gentile deaths exceeded births in most years between 1816 and 1848, Jewish births exceeded deaths (Table 4.7) but Jewish stillbirth rates were substantially higher than those reported in Prussia.[11] Jews were more likely than non-Jews to reach the age of seventy (Table 4.8). Despite the Jews' relatively good showing in the infant-mortality statistics, infant mortality overall was appalling. In Prussia between 1850 and 1854, 49.3 percent of Jews who died had not reached their fifteenth birthday.[12] The median age at death of Jews in Hamburg between 1816 and 1848 was around thirty. This figure, however, is misleading, as very few Jews there died in early adulthood: 35.7 percent of Jewish deaths occurred before the age of five, 32.3 percent occurred after sixty, and only 32.0 percent took place between the ages of five and sixty (Table 4.9).

In general, Jewish women had much lower rates of out-of-wedlock birth than did their Christian compatriots. The differences were especially great in Bavaria,

---

9 Goldstein, "Nonnenweier," 138.
10 Ibid., 137. Goldstein speculates that the reason that Jewish infant mortality in Nonnenweier was only marginally lower than that of Christians was because the statistics excluded illegitimate children, who were more common among Christians and more likely to die in infancy than children born in wedlock.
11 Between 1816 and 1848, there were 484 reported Jewish stillbirths out of 6,854 births reported—a stillbirth rate of 7.06 percent, far above the 2–3 percent rate among Prussian Jews reported in notes 8 and 9.
12 Schmelz's handwritten table 13A, this does not look like the codes in the bibliography, "Sterbefälle Preussen Staat." The mortality figures for 1852 were unusually high especially for children at 3,084 under 15 as against 1,822 in 1851 and 1,976 in 1853. They seem to be related to a cholera epidemic. See, for instance, S. L. Kotar and J. E. Gessler, *Cholera: A Worldwide History* (Jefferson: McFarland & Company, Inc., 2014), 183.

Table 4.5. Infant Mortality as Percent of Jewish Births—Hamburg

Year	Stillborn	Died before age 1	Subtotal	Died age 1–5	Total
1816–1820	8.83	11.56	20.39	13.64	34.03
1821–1825	7.59	12.24	19.83	10.65	30.48
1826–1830	5.41	15.35	20.76	11.39	32.15
1831–1835	5.96	14.22	20.18	13.76	33.94
1836–1840	8.15	12.40	20.55	11.73	32.28
1841–1845	7.14	14.60	21.74	9.60	31.34
1846–1848	6.66	15.00	21.66	14.03	35.69

Source: Calculated from "Uebersicht der Gebornen in den Jahren 1816 bis 1848" and "Mortalitäts-Tabelle nach dem Lebensalter," in *Bericht über die finanziellen Verhältnissen der deutsch-israelitischen Gemeinde in Hamburg* (Hamburg, 1849), 100, 102.

Table 4.6. Childhood Survival among Jews and Christians in Nonnenweier, Baden

Year	Jews			Christians		
	Infant death	Child death	Survived to age 13	Infant death	Child death	Survived to age 13
Before 1820	4.8%	1.6%	**93.6%** (N = 63)	16.7%	9.3%	74.0% (N = 54)
1820–1839	19.8%	5.5%	74.7 (N = 91)	10.6%	9.6%	**79.8%** (N = 104)
1840–1859	12.3%	8.0%	**79.7** (N = 163)	13.5%	12.3%	74.2% (N = 89)
1860–1879	17.7%	7.0%	**75.3** (N = 158)	20.9%	11.6%	67.5% (N = 129)
1880–1899	12.6%	1.7%	**85.7** (N = 119)	18.9%	4.9%	76.2% (N = 143)

Source: Goldstein, "Nonnenweier," 137.

where Christian illegitimacy rates were traditionally higher than in most of the rest of Germany. Jews in early nineteenth-century Bavaria, on the other hand, had very low rates of out-of-wedlock births. In the all-Christian village of Anhausen, Bavaria, for instance, 21 percent of all births between 1834 and 1849 were out of wedlock. The percentage of out-of-wedlock children born to Jewish

TABLE 4.7. Jewish and General Births and Deaths—Hamburg, 1816–1848

Year	Jewish births	Jewish deaths	General births	General deaths
1816	145	127	3266	3243
1817	170	130	3145	3234
1818	144	134	3576	3118
1819	148	171	4553	3487
1820	163	158	3547	3583
1821	152	147	3524	3698
1822	149	139	3719	3338
1823	167	183	5589 [?]	3554
1824	177	162	3779	3859
1825	172	131	3876	3509
1826	221	173	4005	4385
1827	184	210	3967	3792
1828	204	177	4036	4275
1829	222	190	4128	4771
1830	205	193	4167	4926
1831	205	236	4156	4918
1832	204	213	3411	5647
1833	219	183	4545	4846
1834	231	208	4783	5101
1835	231	172	4529	4327
1836	233	197	4734	4315
1837	225	208	4632	5450
1838	240	218	4723	5415
1839	258	218	4866	4740
1840	246	205	4716	4866
1841	249	210	4806	5293
1842	243	200	4939	5658
1843	235	231	4879	5235
1844	235	216	5236	5213
1845	257	195	5387	5196
1846	245	208	5435	5375

1847	238	246	5030	5575
1848	237	286	5036	6779
Total	6854	6275	142529	150921
Balance		+579		-8392

Jewish percent of total:	Births	Deaths
	4.81%	4.16%

Source: *Bericht über die finanziellen Verhältnissen der Deutsch-Israelitischen Gemeinde in Hamburg* (Hamburg, 1849), 100–102. The anomalous figure for general births in 1823 appears in the original and is probably a typographical error.

Table 4.8. Longevity of Jews and General Population—Prussia, 1822–1837

Population	Deaths	Died over age 70	Percent
General	5,754,161	673,582	11.7
Jewish	54,195	8,347	15.4

Source: Hoffmann, "Neueste Nachrichten von der Bevölkerung des preußischen Staates," 949.

women in sample towns in the Bavarian province of Middle Franconia between 1813 and 1876, by contrast, was a mere 3–4 percent.[13] In Nonnenweier, Baden, between 1800 and 1849, only 14.3 percent of first Jewish children were born nine months or less after their parents' weddings as against 52.5 percent of Christian first children.[14]

The Jews of Berlin between about 1780 and 1815 did not share the pattern of low Jewish illegitimacy rates that was common elsewhere in Germany.[15] Until 1806, many children were born out of wedlock to mixed Jewish-Christian couples, including both children with Jewish fathers and those who had Jewish mothers, with the former in the majority. After 1806, mixed couples had fewer

---

13 Lowenstein, *Mechanics*, 68, 83. Only thirty-five of the 946 children in the sample were born out of wedlock
14 Goldstein, "Nonnenweier," 134.
15 The exceptions outside of Germany, especially in Galicia, are more apparent than real. Because most Jews did not report their (religious) marriages to the government in Galicia, the Austrian government did not accept such marriages and registered children born to such couples as illegitimate. This bureaucratic practice yielded an incredibly high official illegitimacy rate among Galician Jews that do not reflect actual births out of wedlock.

Table 4.9. Age at Death of Jews in Hamburg, 1816–1848

Years	Total Jewish deaths	Stillbirths	Under 1	1–5	6–10	11–20	21–30	31–40	41–50	51–60	61–70	71+
1816–1820	720	68	89	105	25	34	51	55	44	60	69	120
		9.4%	12.4	14.6	3.5	4.7	7.1	7.6	6.1	8.3	9.6	16.7
1821–1825	762	62	100	87	21	39	55	42	47	64	76	169
		8.1%	13.1	11.4	2.8	5.1	7.2	5.5	6.2	8.4	10.0	22.2
1826–1830	943	56	159	118	21	29	58	54	62	93	113	180
		5.9%	16.9	12.5	2.2	3.1	6.2	5.7	6.6	9.9	12.0	19.1
1831–1835	1012	65	155	150	26	32	60	53	52	83	137	209
		6.4%	15.2	14.7	2.5	3.1	5.9	5.2	5.1	8.1	13.4	20.5
1836–1840	1046	98	149	141	21	40	72	46	55	80	136	208
		9.4%	14.2	13.5	2.0	3.8	6.9	4.4	5.3	7.7	13.0	19.9
1841–1845	1042	87	178	117	28	27	66	48	67	54	114	256
		8.4%	17.1	11.2	2.7	2.6	6.3	4.6	6.4	5.2	10.9	24.6
1846–1848	740	48	108	101	25	20	44	43	48	62	89	152
		6.5%	14.6	13.7	3.4	2.7	6.0	5.8	6.5	8.4	12.0	20.5
1816–1848	6275	484	938	819	167	221	406	341	375	496	740	1288
		7.7%	15.0	13.1	2.7	3.5	6.5	5.4	6.0	7.9	11.8	20.5

Total burials in Hamburg, 1816–1848: 150,921

Source: *Bericht über die finanziellen Verhältnissen der Deutsch-Israelitischen Gemeinde in Hamburg*, 102.

children but the percentage of out-of-wedlock children born to purely Jewish couples remained high until 1815. Jewish illegitimacy seems to have been close to the general rate in Berlin at the time (about 20 percent). After 1815, the Jewish out-of-wedlock rate in Berlin dropped precipitously—from 14 percent in 1813–1815 to 1–4 percent in 1819–1840.[16] Until the present study, I was convinced that Berlin was an exceptional outlier within German Jewry, and that its high rates of illegitimacy were symptomatic of the especially acute "crisis of modernity" that swept Berlin Jewry in the years after the death of Moses Mendelssohn. It turns out, however, that equally high out-of-wedlock birth rates were found at the same time in Frankfurt am Main, with 22.0 percent of Jewish children born in 1809 and 1810 and 18.0 percent of those born between 1811 and 1820, dropping to only 1.7 percent of those born between 1821 and 1856. In this case, the very high Jewish illegitimacy rates in the first years of the nineteenth century may reflect a more widespread urban pattern in more of Germany than previously recognized.[17]

In most other demographic characteristics, German Jewry in the early nineteenth century still bore the markers of a premodern community—high fertility, high mortality, large families, and a relatively short lifespan—although somewhat less so than their Christian neighbors. In most places in Germany, the Jewish birth rate was not quite as high as that of the Christians, in part because Jews usually married later than non-Jews and in part because Jews had a lower rate of out-of-wedlock births[18] (Table 4.10). Whether the intentional practice of birth control was another reason for the lower Jewish birth rate before 1850 is not clear from the available evidence. In general, such a practice would have manifested itself in the lowering of mother's age at last birth rather than wider

---

16 Lowenstein, *The Berlin Jewish Community*, 112–119, 164–165, 239–244. According to William H. Hubbard, *Familiengeschichte: Materialen zur deutschen Familie seit dem Ende des 18. Jahrhunderts* (Munich: Beck, 1983), 109, Table 3.29, the overall out-of-wedlock birth rate in Berlin between 1816 and 1820 was 18.3 percent, though other scholars offer lower estimates. Between 1780 and 1805, ninety children in Berlin were born out of wedlock to Jewish fathers and Christian mothers and fifty-three to Jewish mothers and Christian fathers. Many of the Jewish fathers had multiple out-of-wedlock children with the same woman.
17 In the birth registers of the Frankfurt Jewish community, which do not necessarily include all Jews living in the city, we find fifty-four out-of-wedlock children as against 192 born in wedlock in 1809–1810 (an illegitimacy rate of 22.0 percent), 147 children born out of wedlock in 1811–1820 (18.0 percent), and then only forty-one in the thirty-six years from 1821 to 1856 (1.7 percent). Josef Unna, "Statistik der Frankfurter Juden bis zum Jahre 1866, Ein Versuch historischer Bevölkerungsstatistik," *ZDSJ* 3, nos. 1–3 (1926): 32.
18 In Prussia between 1822 and 1840, the Jewish birth rate averaged 35.46 per 1,000, while the Christian rate was 40.01 per 1,000. The Jewish birth rate was 88.63 percent of the Christian rate. During the first half of the nineteenth century, there is no clear trend of change in the Jewish and general birth rates in Prussia.

Table 4.10. Jewish and General Birth Rates—Prussia, 1819–1851

Year	Jewish birth rate per 1,000, including stillbirths	General birth rate per 1,000, including stillbirths	Jewish birth rate as percent of general birth rate
1819–1821	39.11	43.91	89.1
1822–1824	36.49	42.58	85.7
1825–1827	35.78	40.45	88.5
1828–1830	33.82	38.38	88.1
1831–1833	34.84	39.58	88.0
1834–1836	35.94	39.64	90.7
1837–1839	36.04	39.70	90.8
1840–1842	36.98	39.91	92.7
1843–1845	37.56	40.04	93.8
1846–1848	34.19	38.05	89.9
1849–1851	36.09	40.72	88.6

Source: Silbergleit, *Die Bevölkerungs- und Berufsverhältnisse*, 14*–15*.

spacing between children. In the sparse local studies of German-Jewish fertility based on family reconstruction, only one community—that of the small city of Ansbach, Bavaria—showed a clear drop in fertility among Jewish women over age thirty-five that far exceeded what can be explained "naturally" (Table 4.11).

Compared with its counterparts later in the nineteenth century, German Jewry before 1850 placed few limits on its fertility. Nevertheless, family size on average was not as large as one might imagine, in part because many families were not "completed" (that is, did not remain married beyond the wife's forty-fifth year due to the premature death of one spouse) and in part due to patterns of late marriage. In Middle Franconia, Jewish couples that married between 1813 and 1830 had an average of 4.2 children (4.4 in completed families). In Nonnenweier, Baden, where legal marriage restrictions were less extreme, the number of children was considerably higher—6.2 for completed marriages between Jews in 1800–1849.[19] The actual number of children in the household was, of course, much smaller because some children died and others moved out of the home to work, train for employment, or marry.

---

19 Lowenstein, "Voluntary and Involuntary Limitation," 96; Goldstein, "Nonnenweier," 129.

Table 4.11. Jewish Age-Specific Fertility in Bavaria as Percent of "Natural" (Hutterite) Fertility[20]

Urban couples marrying in Ansbach by age, 1813–1850						
20–24	25–29	30–34	35–39	40–44	45–49	
94.9% ($Ig = 0.672$)	101.8%	64.4%	58.9%	35.6%	11.5%	

Village Jews marrying by age, 1813–1850						
20–24	25–29	30–34	35–39	40–44	45–49	
112.4% ($Ig = 0.889$)	101.6%	103.8%	79.6%	64.9%	29.5%	

Source: Lowenstein, "Voluntary and Involuntary Limitation," 100–103.

Changes in the German Jewish Family, 1850–1914

Marriage Age

With the removal of government restrictions in the 1850s and 1860s, Jewish marriage ages declined somewhat but still remained relatively late. This was especially noticeable in Bavaria where the restrictions had been the strongest. In the Middle Franconia sample, the extremely elevated Jewish marriage age in 1836–1845 (first marriages of men at 34.8 and of women at 31.1) fell off quite rapidly in the 1860s and 1870s after the repeal of the Bavarian Matrikel laws in 1861. Even in the 1870s, however, Jews followed the general late marriage pattern of Western Europe, with husbands first marrying at an average age of 26.3 and wives at 23.1 (Table 4.12). In Nonnenweier, the decrease in marriage age was less striking and was reversed after 1880, perhaps as a correlate of the decline in village Jewry (Table 4.13). The downturn in Jewish marriage age and the rise in the percentage of persons who married paralleled a similar rise in nuptiality among the German population at large, although the magnitude of

---

20 There seems to be clear evidence of restriction of births in Ansbach in couples over the age of thirty. Such restriction was absent (or at least much less clear) among couples marrying during the same years in villages in the same Middle Franconia province of Bavaria. In France, on the other hand, a steady drop in Jewish mothers' age at birth of their last child was in evidence among women born after 1795 (that is, having their last child around 1835). Hyman, "Jewish Fertility in 19th-century France," 83.

Table 4.12. Marriage Age of Jews at First Marriage in Middle Franconia

Year	Grooms	Brides
1836–1845	34.8	31.1
1846–1855	32.6	26.7
1855–1865	33.3	25.5
1866–1875	30.4	24.4
(1871–1880	26.3	23.1)

Source: Lowenstein, "Voluntary and Involuntary Limitation," 98.

Table 4.13. Marriage Age of Jews and Christians in Nonnenweier, Baden

Year	Jews		Non-Jews	
	Grooms	Brides	Grooms	Brides
1800–1849	32.1	26.6	27.9	24.3
1850–1879	30.8	25.7	29.9	25.1
1880–1931	31.8	26.1	28.7	24.4

Source: Goldstein, "Nonnenweier," 123.

the Jewish increase in marriage relative to the general German trend has not yet been calculated.[21]

Declines in Fertility and Mortality and Their Relationship—the First Demographic Transition

After 1875, German Jewish demographic patterns rapidly began to show signs of passage through what has been called the "first demographic transition of modernity," which involved sharp and seemingly interrelated declines in both fertility and mortality, especially infant and child mortality. German Jews made the demographic transition before the rest of the German population did, often by a difference of one to three decades. As the transition proceeded, initial

---

21 Knodel, *Decline*, 68–75. According to Knodel, men's age at first marriage dropped from 28.8 in 1871 to 27.8 in 1900 and 27.5 in 1925 (single census estimate) while women's age at first marriage declined from 26.3 in 1871 to 25.3 in 1910 and then rebounded to 26.1 in 1925 (ibid., 70). The share of German men who had never married by age 50–54 declined from 9.3 percent in 1871 to 6.4 percent in 1925. Among women, the fraction declined from 11.9 percent in 1871 to 10.1 percent in 1900, after which it fluctuated within a narrow range.

sharp rises in population were replaced by stagnating and sometimes decreasing numbers of inhabitants. In many places, especially in Europe, the demographic transition correlated closely with rising living standards, although the nature of the causal relation between demographic and socioeconomic developments, if any, is a matter of much debate. Scholars continue to disagree both about the causes of the transition as well as the temporal and causal connection between falling mortality and falling fertility. It seems clear, however, that both aspects of the transition were part of a growing modern tendency to place aspects of nature under rational human control.[22]

Both Jews and the general German population showed notable and parallel declines in fertility and mortality—especially infant mortality—at the end of the nineteenth and beginning of the twentieth centuries. For Prussia, we have statistics on Jewish births for more than 100 years from 1819 to 1932. As both the Jewish and the general population of Prussia increased from 1819 to 1861, the number of births also increased in both groups. Jewish births multiplied more quickly than those of the general population until 1843–1845, when 1.25 percent of all babies born in Prussia were Jewish, and then multiplied less rapidly thereafter. By 1861–1863 (before the territorial expansion of Prussia in 1866), the Jewish proportion of Prussian births reverted to its 1820s level (1.11 percent). Jewish birth rates show a similar pattern of change.[23] Before the onset of the "demographic transition," both the general German and the German-Jewish populations posted increases in both fertility and mortality after 1850.

---

22 For example, see Oded Gabor, "The Demographic Transition and the Emergence of Sustained Economic Growth," *Journal of the European Economic Association* 3 (2005): 494–504; Matthias Doepke, "Child Mortality and Fertility Decline: Does the Barro-Becker Model Fit the Facts?," *Journal of Population Economics* 18 (2005): 337–366, Patrick R. Galloway, E. A. Hammel, R. D. Lee, "Final Report on the Project: Economic and Cultural Factors in Demographic Behavior," R01 HD25841, unpublished manuscript.

23 The Jewish crude birth rate in Prussia fluctuated between 34.02 per 1,000 and 39.11 per 1,000 between 1819 and 1860. The trend was slightly downward during the whole period but there were times of upturn as well. Jewish birth rates often tracked general ones, remaining within the very narrow range of 85.7–93.8 percent of the overall rates between 1819 and 1857. Jews came closest to the rate for the rest of the population in 1843–1845 (Table 4.10).

According to Ruppin's analysis (Arthur Ruppin, *Die Soziologie der Juden* [Berlin: Jüdischer Verlag, 1930], vol. 1, 172–173), the Jewish birth rate declined only slightly between 1822–1840 and 1841–1866 in Prussia (from 35.5 per 1,000 to 34.7—a decline of less than 2.5 percent). Between the latter period and 1878–1882, however, it showed a considerable decline (to 30.0 for a decline of 13.5 percent). In Berlin the same source shows a decline from 26.1 per 1,000 in 1876–1880 to 18.0 in 1891–1900 (down 31 percent) and 16.0 by 1901–1905 (down another 11 percent). By leaving out some of the time period between 1841–1866 and 1878–1882, Ruppin seems to exaggerate the sharpness of the decline between the 1860s and late 1870s.

Generally, then, the decline period is clearly marked off from the pre-decline period.[24]

Declines in fertility and infant mortality can be measured in various ways.[25] All such methods show that the behavior of the Jewish population preceded that of most of the German population by many years. The exact priority and interrelation of fertility and mortality decline is complex. In some parts of Germany, infant mortality declined before marital fertility; in other areas, the reverse was true. Total infant mortality rates for Germany as a whole were generally stable between 1876 and 1895 and then dropped increasingly faster until the 1930s. Masking the overall stability in infant mortality that prevailed until 1895, the timing of the decline varied widely between various parts of Germany. The middle of the nineteenth century saw large differences in rates of infant mortality, with especially high levels in rural Catholic parts of Bavaria and much lower rates in more urbanized and Protestant districts. Among the German population at large, infant mortality declined earliest (in the late 1860s) in areas where it had originally been high. On the other hand, many areas of originally low infant mortality showed scanty decreases before around 1905. In the mainly rural and Catholic district of Lower Franconia where infant mortality was originally high, the infant mortality decrease preceded the decline in fertility by almost two decades and was much stronger. In urban and Protestant Bremen,

---

24 John C. Brown and Timothy W. Guinnane, "The Fertility Transition in Bavaria," Economic Growth Center Discussion Paper 821, April 2001, 10–12 and Figure 1. The increase in fertility in Bavaria seems to have lasted from about 1850 to the late 1870s. According to Silbergleit, the crude birth rate of the general population was 37.61 per 1,000 in 1852–1855 and 40.48 between 1858 and 1864. Between 1871 and 1875, it reached a high of 41.63. Silbergleit does not show a parallel rise in Jewish birth rate except between 1852–1855 (34.53) and 1855–1858 (34.73) and then records a slight decline to 32.97 in 1861–1864. During the same period, mortality rates in Prussia declined from 30.71 (1852–1855) to 26.72 (1858–1861) among the general population and from 18.17 to 16.39 in the same period for Jews. Both populations experienced a slight uptick in mortality in the early 1860s (to 27.35 and 16.82, respectively) (Silbergleit, Die Bevölkerungs- und Berufsverhältnisse, 14*–15*). Goldscheider gives an even higher figure of 17.3 for Jews in Prussia in 1863–1865 (Anton Goldscheider, "Die Entwicklung der jüdischen Bevölkerung in Preussen im 19. Jahrhundert mit besonderer Berücksichtigung der Zeit von 1816 bis 1875," ZDSJ 3 [1907]: 73). In Hesse, the crude birth rate of the general population increased from 37.36 in 1866–1870 to 38.88 in 1871–1875 while that of Jews rose from 31.75 to 32.76 in the same period. Total births in Hesse overall increased from an annual average of 31,175 in 1866–1870 to 34,068 in 1876–1880. Among Jews, the number of births climbed from an annual average of 805 in 1866–1870 to 835 in 1871–1875 ("Geburten und Sterbefälle im Grossherzogtum Hessen im Jahre 1910 mit Rückblick," ZDSJ 8, nos. 7–8 [1912]: 113).

25 For a detailed discussion of the various measurements, see the Appendix to this chapter.

on the other hand, where infant mortality was originally low, fertility declined much earlier than infant mortality did.[26]

Among German Jews, the originally low infant-mortality rate did not delay the decline as it did among the general population, that is, Jewish infant mortality began to drop at a relatively early point in time. The decrease in Jewish fertility, in contrast, usually preceded the sharp downturn in infant mortality, as it did among non-Jews with relatively low original infant mortality. Jewish fertility tended to fall more sharply than mortality. Between 1876–1880 and 1881–1890, Jewish crude birth rates (for live births) sank by 17 percent, 20 percent, and 20.3 percent in Prussia, Bavaria, and Hesse, respectively, even as Jewish crude death rates (excluding stillbirths) dropped by only 6.2 percent, 8.6 percent, and 12.5 percent, respectively. Jewish death and birth rates fell much earlier than corresponding rates among non-Jews. In the Grand Duchy of Hesse, the Christian crude live birth rate in 1906–1910 was closest to the Jewish rate in 1876–1880, while the Christian crude infant mortality rate of 1906–1910 matched the Jewish rate in 1881–1885.[27] In Bavaria, the Christian crude birth and mortality rates in 1900 exceeded the Jewish rates in 1876.[28]

Birth Rates and Birth Control

No matter what measures we use, Jewish fertility showed a clearly delineated period of decline that began in the late 1870s and lasted until the first years of the twentieth century (see Appendix). In Prussia, a gap in the records in the 1860s leaves uncertainty about whether the trend began before 1876; after that year, however, a continuous decline is evident.[29] In Hesse-Darmstadt, however, where Jewish birth data are available uninterrupted from 1866 on, the highest number of Jewish births (855) was recorded in 1878, followed by a steady decline to an annual average of 439 between 1901 and 1904. This confirms the late 1870s as

---

26 Knodel, *Decline*, 148–171, especially 181.
27 Ludwig Knöpfel, "Der Geburtenrückgang und die Sterblichkeit bei der jüdischen Bevölkerung," *ZDSJ* 9 (1913): 7.
28 J. Thon, "Die Bewegung der jüdischen Bevölkerung in Bayern seit dem Jahre 1876," *ZDSJ* 1, no. 8 (August 1905): 8.
29 Differences in calculating Jewish births introduce complexity into the statistics on both the number of Jewish births and the Jewish crude birth rate. Some statistics record only live births while others include stillbirths. Some include only the offspring of homogeneous Jewish marriages while others include illegitimate births to Jewish mothers and/or children born to intermarried parents (usually but not always limiting this to Jewish mothers).

the beginning of the decline in Jewish births.[30] In all but five years, Jewish births in Prussia decreased year-on-year. By 1914, there were only half as many Jewish births as there had been in 1876 (Tables 4.14, 4.15). Among the overall Prussian population, in contrast, births increased steadily until 1905–1909 to a level 18.6

Table 4.14. Jewish Births as Percent of All Births in Prussia (annual averages, including stillbirths)

Year	Jewish (in-married plus out of wedlock)	General births	Percent Jewish
1819–1821	5462	497173	1.10
1822–1824	5445	509226	1.07
1825–1827	5629	505268	1.11
1828–1830	5551	494429	1.12
1831–1833	5988	525363	1.14
1834–1836	6470	547243	1.18
1837–1839	6814	576216	1.18
1840–1842	7416	606560	1.22
1843–1845	7915	632328	1.25
1846–1848	7416	617282	1.20
1849–1851	8044	677303	1.19
1852–1854	7961	641863	1.24
1855–1857	8278	686501	1.21
1858–1860	8457	733431	1.15
1861–1863	8518	764050	1.11
Expanded territory of Prussia			
1875–1879	11349	1088389	1.04
1880–1884	10383	1081678	0.96
1885–1889	9084	1129812	0.80
1890–1894	8453	1181750	0.72
1895–1899	7774	1252616	0.62
1900–1904	7275	1291272	0.56
1905–1910	6833	1291826	0.53

Source: Silbergleit, *Die Bevölkerungs- und Berufsverhältnisse*, 14*–15*.

---

30 Knöpfel, "Stand und Bewegung," 83.

Table 4.15. Jewish Births in Prussia by Year, 1876–1913

Year	1 To in-married Jews	2 Out of wedlock to Jewish mother	3 Total	4 Change	5 Five-year change	6 Born to intermarried Jews	7 General population	8 Percent Jewish births (column 3 divided by column 7)
1876	10866	288	11,154			331	[1,056,876]	1.08
1877	10822	301	11,123	-0.28%			[1,046,795]	1.06
1878	10741	289	11,030	-0.84%		402	[1,028,660]	1.07
1879	10547	292	10,839	-1.73%			[1,041,523]	1.04
1880	10389	310	10,699	-1.29%			[1,022,794]	1.05
1881	10078	282	10,360	-3.17%	-7.12%	484	[1,014,336]	1.02
1882	10027	277	10,304	-0.54%		455	[1,026,516]	1.00
1883	9637	277	9,914	-3.78%		470	[1,015,270]	0.98
1884	9632	254	9,886	-0.28%		441	[1,040,527]	0.95
1885	9470	244	9,714	-1.74%		470	[1,044,876]	0.93
1886	8689	237	8,926	-8.11%	-13.84%	500	[1,054,664]	0.85
1887	8729	240	8,969	+0.48%		498	[1,061,276]	0.85
1888	8555	239	8,794	-1.95%		546	[1,063,890]	0.83
1889	8410	239	8,649	-1.65%		533	[1,070,632]	0.81
1890	8318	227	8,545	-1.20%		580	[1,062,033]	0.80

The Population History of German Jewry 1815–1939

Year	1 To in-married Jews	2 Out of wedlock to Jewish mother	3 Total	4 Change	5 Five-year change	6 Born to intermarried Jews	7 General population	8 Percent Jewish births (column 3 divided by column 7)
1891	8391	221	8,612	+0.78%	-3.52%	554	[1,115,144]	0.77
1892	7992	227	8,219	-4.56%		548	[1,088,358]	0.76
1893	7988	221	8,209	-0.12%		558	[1,130,623]	0.73
1894	7852	265	8,117	-1.12%		549	[1,115,770]	0.73
1895	7573	250	7,823	-3.62%		575	[1,137,630]	0.69
1896	7512	261	7,773	-0.64%	-9.74%	587	[1,160,338]	0.67
1897	7397	240	7,637	-1.75%		595	[1,167,574]	0.65
1898	7270	266	7,536	-1.32%		609	[1,190,627]	0.63
1899	7265	279	7,544	+0.11%		636	[1,200,064]	0.63
1900	7057	250	7,307	-3.14%		672	[1,221,635]	0.60
1901	6979	252	7,231	-1.04%	-6.97%	706	[1,243,776]	0.58
1902	7072	294	7,366	+1.87%		671	[1,239,139]	0.59
1903	6660	250	6,910	-6.19%		617	[1,213,644]	0.57
1904	6720	259	6,979	+1.00%		721	[1,239,818]	0.56

Year	1 To in-married Jews	2 Out of wedlock to Jewish mother	3 Total	4 Change	5 Five-year change	6 Born to intermarried Jews	7 General population	8 Percent Jewish births (column 3 divided by column 7)
1905	6559	260	6,819			742	[1,216,173]	0.56
1906	6845	306	7,151	-2.29%		781	[1,237,756]	0.58
1907	6437	303	6,740	+4.87%		750	[1,223,959]	0.55
1908	6407	312	6,719	-5.75%		790	[1,233,212]	0.54
1909	6083	266	6,349	-0.31%		750	[1,210,706]	0.52
1910	5864	284	6,148	-5.51%	-1.11	768	[1,191,438]	0.52
1911	5735	320	6,055	-3.17%		759	1,189,452	0.51
1912	5549	347	5,896	-1.51%		803	1,186,450	0.50
1913	5497	365	5,862	-2.63%	-15.22%	776	1,173,605	0.50
				-0.58%				

Sources: Schmelz, handwritten table "Lebendgeborene Preussen Staat"; Silbergleit, *Die Bevölkerungs- und Berufsverhältnisse*, 39*; *Statistisches Jahrbuch für den Freistaat Preussen* (1933), 26. Pre-1911 general figures are estimated by taking the figures for total live births in Germany from G. Hohorst, J. Kocka, and G. A. Ritter, *Sozialgeschichtliches Arbeitsbuch*, vol. 2: *Materialen zur Statistik des Kaiserreichs 1870–1914* (Munich: Beck, 1978), 27–28, and adjusting them for the percent of the German population that lived in Prussia (60% for 1876–1879, 60.3% for 1880–1884, 60.4% for 1885–1889, 60.6% for 1890–1899, 61.2% for 1900–1909, and 61.9% for 1910).

percent higher than that in 1875–1879. The percent of Jews among births in Prussia fell from 1.04 percent in 1875–1879 to only 0.48 percent in 1914.

Crude birth rates (births per 1,000 of population) parallel the chronology of the decline in absolute numbers. In Prussia, Bavaria, and Hesse-Darmstadt, the Jewish crude birth rate fell by just under fifty percent between the mid-1870s and around 1900 (Tables 4.16, 4.17). Between 1875 and 1909, the Jewish birth rate in Prussia slipped by about 10 percentage points every five years, sinking to barely half its 1875–1879 level by 1905–1909. During the same period, the birth rate of the general population fell slightly from 41.05 per 1,000 to 33.35—19 percent in all, most of it after 1900 (Table 4.18).[31]

In the twentieth century, when data on the age makeup of the Jewish community became widely available, it became possible to determine that the decline in births until 1933 was more than the result of an aging Jewish population; it also reflected a real change in childbearing behavior (that is, some form of birth control). Only in the 1939 census was the skewed structure of the German-Jewish age pyramid the main reason for the falling number of births. (See Appendix for detailed data confirming this pattern.)

Both general fertility and marital fertility rates among the general German population exceeded those among the Jews almost everywhere, although they began to converge toward levels approximating those of the Jews during the

Table 4.16. Decline in Jewish Crude Birth Rate (per 1,000) in Various Sections of Germany

Prussia		Bavaria		Hesse-Darmstadt		Hamburg	
1875–1880	32.26	1877	34.5	1871–1875	32.76	1885	29.5
1905–1910	16.55	1900	18.1	1901–1905	18.66	1910	15.2

Sources: Silbergleit, *Die Bevölkerungs- und Berufsverhältnisse*, 14*; Thon, "Bewegung seit dem Jahre 1876," 8; "Geburten und Sterbefälle im Grossherzogtum Hessen im Jahre 1910 mit Rückblicke," 113, Dora Weingert, "Die jüdische Bevölkerung in Hamburg," *ZDSJ* 15, nos. 5–7 (1919): 82.

---

31 Goldscheider, "Entwicklung," 71, uses a somewhat different periodization from Silbergleit's. His figures show a continual drop in Jewish birth rates up to 1865.

Year	Jewish crude birth rate	General crude birth rate	Jews as percent of general
1860–1862	33.8	39.7	85.14%
1863–1865	33.1	41.4	79.95%

Table 4.17. Crude Birth Rates in Hesse-Darmstadt, 1866–1904 (including stillbirths)

Year	Jewish crude birth rate	Christian crude birth rate	Jews as percent of Christians
1866–1870	31.7	37.3	85.0
1871–1875	32.6	39.1	83.4
1876–1880	31.6	37.6	84.0
1881–1885	26.8	33.7	79.5
1886–1890	24.0	32.6	73.6
1891–1895	22.6	33.2	68.1
1896–1900	19.8	34.2	57.9
1901–1904	19.0	34.0	55.9

Source: Knöpfel, "Stand und Bewegung," 84.

Table 4.18. Jewish and General Crude Birth Rates in Prussia (including stillbirths)

Year	Jewish births per 1,000	Total births per 1,000	Jewish rates as percent of general
1816–1818		44.09	
1819–1821	39.11	43.91	89.1
1822–1824	36.49	42.58	85.7
1825–1827	35.78	40.45	88.5
1828–1830	33.82	38.38	88.2
1831–1833	34.84	39.58	88.0
1834–1836	35.94	39.64	90.7
1837–1839	36.04	39.70	90.8
1840–1842	36.98	39.91	92.7
1843–1845	37.56	40.04	93.8
1846–1848	34.19	38.05	89.9
1849–1851	36.09	40.72	88.6
1852–1854	34.53	37.61	91.8
1855–1857	34.73	39.29	88.4
1858–1860	34.02	40.48	84.0
1861–1863	32.97	40.48	81.5

Year	Jewish births per 1,000	Total births per 1,000	Jewish rates as percent of general
1867–1870		38.37	
1871–1874		41.63	
1875–1879	32.26	41.05	78.6
1880–1884	28.43	38.91	73.1
1885–1889	24.60	38.78	63.4
1890–1894	22.49	38.24	58.8
1895–1899	20.14	37.77	53.3
1900–1904	18.15	35.98	50.4
1905–1909	16.55	33.35	49.6

Source: Silbergleit, *Die Bevölkerungs- und Berufsverhältnisse*, 14*–15*.

Weimar period. In most areas, Jewish fertility remained noticeably lower than that of the general population. In a few districts, most notably in Berlin, where non-Jewish fertility had fallen to extremely low rates, the fertility of Jews in 1925 was actually somewhat higher than that of the general population (Tables 4.19, 4.20).

One of the conspicuous characteristics of the decline in fertility among the general population of Germany was wide regional differences in the chronology of the transformation. The fertility decline among German Jews, in contrast, was much more regionally consistent.[32] Before the demographic transition, fertility of both the Jewish and the general population of Germany varied considerably by region, and on a similar order of magnitude. Among both populations, birth rates tended to be highest in the eastern provinces as well as in the Rhineland, Westphalia, and Bavaria, and lowest in Berlin. There were a few exceptions: Jews in Silesia had a relatively low birth rate while the general population there tended to high fertility, whereas in Hesse-Darmstadt, Jewish fertility was high by the standards of Jews in other regions while general fertility tended to be relatively low. Once the transition began, however, Jews in most regions of Germany acted similarly to each other. All regions for which evidence exists, except Prussian Saxony, show a ten percent drop in Jewish crude birth rates between 1878–1882 and either 1883–1887 or 1888–1892, irrespective of the early or belated onset of

---

[32] This parallels the much lower regional variance in illegitimacy among German Jews than among Christians.

Table 4.19. Jewish Marital Fertility in Various Regions, 1910–1939

Grand Duchy of Hesse (Knöpfel, "Stand und Bewegung," 103)		
All Jews in Hesse-Darmstadt, 1910	Jews in six largest cities, 1910	Jews in Hesse-Darmstadt outside 6 largest cities, 1910
Marital fertility = 114 Index of marital fertility (Ig) = 321	Marital fertility = 114 Ig = 308	Marital fertility = 114 Ig = 332

Jewish/general comparison 1910—Index of marital fertility (Ig), Hesse-Darmstadt		
General (Knodel, *Decline*)	Jewish	Jewish as percent of general
477	321	67.3%

Berlin, 1910
Marital fertility = 100 (live births), 111 (including stillbirths)

Berlin, 1925		
All Jewish women	Foreign Jewish women	Native Jewish women
Marital fertility = 72 Ig= 210	Marital fertility = 94 Ig = 255	Marital fertility = 63 Ig = 191

Prussian fertility, 1925 (Silbergleit, *Die Bevölkerungs- und Berufsverhältnisse*)		
All Jews	Foreign Jewish women	Jewish women citizens
Marital fertility = 80 Ig = 235	Marital fertility = 112 Ig = 298	Marital fertility = 76 Ig = 230

Prussian provinces, 1925 (1924–1926)

Province	Jewish women, marital fertility	Jewish Ig	General Ig	Jewish Ig as percent of general
Schleswig-Holstein	124	338	297	113.9
Westphalia	107	321	415	77.4
Upper Silesia	107	312	568	54.8
Brandenburg	102	299	284	105.2

Grenzmark	97	298		
Hannover	97	286	346	82.5
Hesse-Nassau	89	273	322	84.8
Rhine Province	92	271	357	75.9
Saxony	94	266	299	89.1
East Prussia		264	476	55.6
Pomerania	83	248	373	66.4
Lower Silesia	77	227		
Berlin		210	147	142.9

1933, Germany, Jewish marital fertility = 42; Ig = 133.

1939, Greater Germany (Jews by religion, all "races"):

Jewish marital fertility		Ig
(age 0–1)	29	109
(age 1–2)	35	131

Source unknown.

Table 4.20. Jewish Age-Specific Fertility Rates in Berlin, 1923

	Children born 1923		Women in Berlin Jewish population, 1925		Married women in Berlin Jewish population, 1925	
Mother's age	Number	Percent of total	Number	Age-specific general fertility	Number	Age-specific marital fertility
15–20	26	1.28	6090	0.004	90	0.289
20–25	449	22.17	7065	0.064	1656	0.271
25–30	784	38.72	8244	0.095	4593	0.171
30–35	516	25.48	7798	0.066	5239	0.099
35–40	193	9.53	7882	0.025	5582	0.035
40–45	37	1.83	7280	0.005	5197	0.007
45–50	4	0.20	7357	0.001	4922	0.001

General fertility rate	0.039
Marital fertility rate	0.074

Source: Felix Theilhaber, "Bevölkerungsvorgänge bei der Berliner Juden," *ZDSJ* 3, nos. 4–6 (1926): 52; Silbergleit, *Die Bevölkerungs- und Berufsverhältnisse*, 16–20.

the decrease in Christian fertility. Jews in the eastern provinces of East Prussia, West Prussia, and Posen saw sharply declining fertility by 1890 even though it took until 1908–1912, if not later, for overall marital fertility in their provinces to fall by 10 percent. The percentage decline in Jewish birth rates from 1878–1882 to 1908–1910 ranged from 42.0 percent in Westphalia to 58.6 percent in Pomerania. The decline in general fertility among the various provinces in the same period spanned a much broader range, from 2.5 percent in Posen to 49.0 percent in Berlin. Unlike their non-Jewish compatriots, whose fertility decline showed strong interregional variance, Jews throughout Germany experienced the trend in much the same way. Thus, while Jewish birth rates in various provinces varied from about 25 percent in 1878–1882 to 36.8 percent in 1908–1912, the range among the general population went from 29.4 percent to 61.3 percent in the respective five-year brackets (Table 4.21 and Figures 4.1 and 4.2).

Death Rates

As was common in most premodern societies, both Jewish and general death rates fluctuated sharply from year to year until the mid-1850s, with steep spikes in years of crisis such as famine and disease.[33] In the second half of the century, such sharp fluctuations became much rarer and both Jewish and general death rates began to decline fairly steadily.

The mortality part of the demographic transition among German Jews found much stronger expression in a decline in infant and child mortality than in a steeper overall fall in Jewish death rate relative to that among Gentiles. The Jewish decline in crude death rates (deaths per 1,000 of population) tended to precede that of non-Jews, but was overtaken by general death-rate decline. Since the Jewish death rate started out lower than the general rate, it remained lower throughout the pre-World War I period. After about 1890, however, the Gentile rate fell more rapidly than the Jewish rate. Consequently, the Jewish crude death rate as a percentage of the general crude death rate bottomed out at 59.2 percent in Prussia in 1852–1854 and then began to rise, slowly at first to 73.1 percent in 1901–1905, and then more rapidly to 81.2 percent in 1906–1910 (Table 4.22).

Nearly all of the decline in mortality took place among the young. In 1880 in Prussia, 42.8 percent of Prussian Jews who died had not yet reached their

---

33 Especially high death rates for both the general and the Jewish populations were observed between 1829 and 1831 and between 1847 and 1849. Silbergleit, *Die Bevölkerungs- und Berufsverhältnisse*, 14*.

Table 4.21. Decline in Jewish Birth Rates and General Marital Fertility, by District

Year	East Prussia		West Prussia		Westphalia		Hesse(-Darmstadt)		Posen	
	Jews	General	Jews	General	Jews	General	Jews	General	Jews	General
1878–1882	36.76	.794	34.14	.823	32.06	.811	31.68*	.663	31.56	.802
1883–1887	34.94	.800	31.23	.845	27.29	.819	26.35	.646	28.57	.821
1888–1892	28.60	.794	26.90	.829	25.12	.811	24.05	.629	24.35	.810
1893–1897	25.03	.800	25.18	.844	22.91	.817	22.65	.623	21.15	.834
1898–1902	22.50	.781	22.56	.844	22.66	.793	19.88	.602	18.94	.841
1903–1907	20.91	.739	20.25	.812	20.14	.758	18.66	.550	16.56	.821
1908–1912	20.47	.692	17.44	.770	18.60	.677	17.69	.477	15.20	.782

Percent decline between 1878–1882 and 1908–1912

	Jews	General	Jews	General	Jews	General	Jews	General	Jews	General
	44.31	12.85	48.92	6.44	41.98	16.52	44.16	28.05	51.84	2.49

Year	Pomerania		Hesse-Nassau		Hannover		Silesia		Pr. Saxony	
	Jews	General	Jews	General	Jews	General	Jews	General	Jews	General
1878–1882	31.23	.736	30*	.674	29.03	.655	28.91	.738	28.60	.693
1883–1887	28.11	.741	27	.652	26.25	.655	25.14	.747	27.24	.691

1888–1892	24.35	.722	24	.636	23.58	.639	22.40	.745	27.48	.666
1893–1897	21.44	.711	21	.624	22.50	.640	21.03	.751	22.73	.635
1898–1902	17.17	.679	19	.598	19.67	.610	19.58	.735	19.73	.597
1903–1907	14.45	.621	18	.548	18.95	.566	17.10	.697	16.84	.540
1908–1912	12.93	.556	17	.478	16.38	.512	15.33	.656	14.55	.474

Percent decline between 1878–1882 and 1909–1912

Jews	General	Jews	General	Jews	General	Jews	General	Jews	General
58.60	24.47	43.33	29.08	43.58	21.83	46.97	11.11	49.13	31.60

Year	Bavaria		Berlin		Rhineland		Hamburg	
	Jews	General	Jews	General	Jews	General	Jews	General
1878–1882	31.4	.786	*27.51	.594	31.43	.841		
1883–1887	27.2	.771	22.75	.534	27.87	.831	29.5	.594
1888–1892	22.2	.750	21.01	.494	25.96	.811	23.2	.584
1893–1897	19.1		19.05	.448	23.68	.800	23.6	.561
1898–1902	18.1	.725	17.46	.394	21.99	.768	19.1	.474
1903–1907	17.93		15.86	.356	20.65	.705	18.4	.406
1908–1912	14.94	.605	14.62	.303	18.12	.604	15.2	.396

Percent decline between 1878–1882 and 1909–1912

Jews	General	Jews	General	Jews	General	Jews	General
52.42	23.03	46.86	48.99	42.35	28.18	48.47	33.33

Data in bold = first drop of at least 10 percent below original figure.

Underlined = never declined 10 percent.

General fertility is measured by the percentage of age-specific Hutterite fertility achieved by married couples (Ig) as calculated by Knodel, *Decline*, 34.

Jewish figures are measured by crude birth rates per 1,000 Jews for births either to homogeneous Jewish couples or to Jewish women out of wedlock.

Sources: general population: Knodel, *Decline*, 272; Jewish figures: Schmelz, handwritten table, "Geburten—Provinzen" (Birth by Province). The absolute annual average number of Jewish births in each province was divided by the total Jewish population of the province in the year ending in zero or five included in each time span.

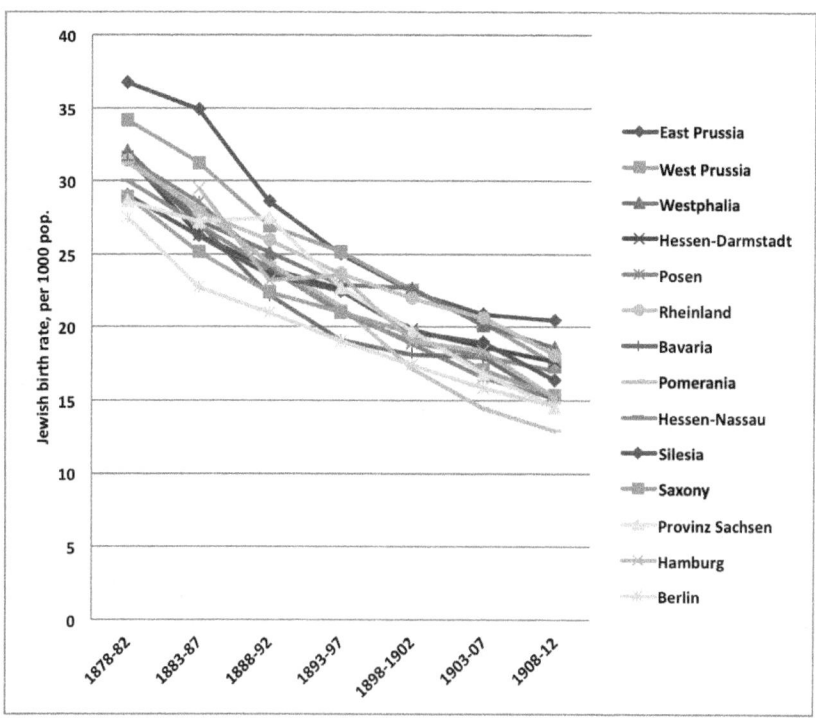

Fig. 4.1. Jewish Birth Rate by Province, 1878–1912

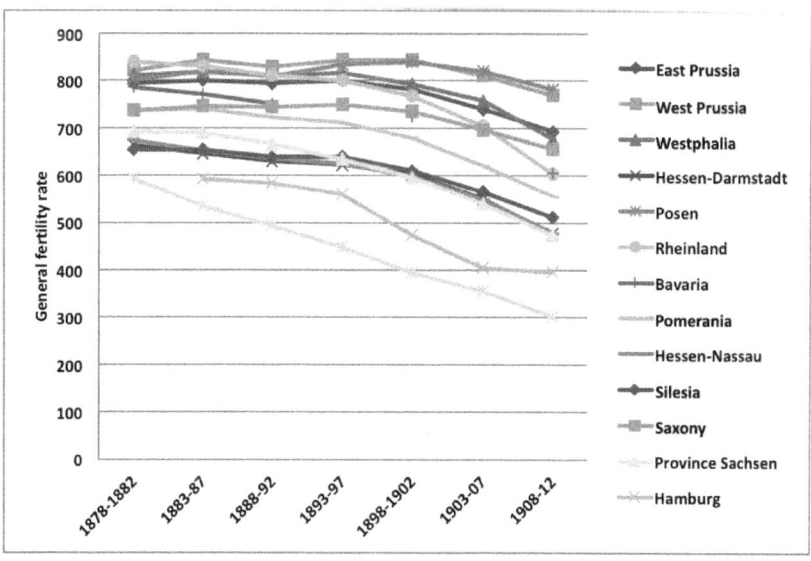

Fig. 4.2. General Fertility by Province, 1878–1912

Table 4.22. Death Rates of Jews and General Population in Prussia, Annual Averages (including stillbirths until 1910)

1 = Average general population during period
2 = Average Jewish population
3 = Deaths per year, general population
4 = Deaths per year, Jewish population
5 = Deaths per 1,000, general population
6 = Deaths per 1,000, Jewish population
7 = Jewish deaths as percent of all deaths
8 = Jewish death rate per 1,000 as percent of general death rate per 1,000

Year	1	2	3	4	5	6	7	8
1816–1818	10,655,483	129,271	318,500		29.86			
1819–1821	11,323,032	139,670	299,669	2,856	26.47	20.45	0.95	77.3
1822–1824	11,960,429	149,213	321,591	3,001	26.89	20.11	0.93	74.8
1825–1827	12,491,418	157,333	364,532	3,600	29.18	22.88	0.99	78.4
1828–1830	12,882,535	164,154	413,874	4,023	32.13	24.51	0.97	76.3
1831–1833	13,273,480	171,895	419,678	3,738	31.62	21.75	0.89	68.8
1834–1836	13,803,062	180,020	398,378	3,703	28.86	20.57	0.93	71.3
1837–1839	14,513,313	189,069	413,904	3,817	28.52	20.19	0.92	70.5
1840–1842	15,199,793	200,543	431,670	3,958	28.40	19.74	0.92	69.5
1843–1845	15,792,011	210,692	436,685	4,069	27.65	19.31	0.93	69.8

Year	1	2	3	4	5	6	7	8
1846–1848	16,222,063	216,928	517,613	5,102	31.91	23.52	0.99	73.7
1849–1851	16,633,304	222,933	487,098	4,447	29.28	19.95	0.91	68.1
1852–1854	17,069,126	230,558	524,131	4,189	30.71	18.17	0.80	59.1
1855–1857	17,471,372	238,332	506,581	4,135	28.99	17.35	0.82	59.8
1858–1860	18,115,567	248,600	484,069	4,075	26.72	16.39	0.84	61.3
1861–1863	18,873,180	258,393	516,210	4,346	27.35	16.82	0.85	61.5
In expanded Prussia								
1867–1870	24,305,522	319,372	704,346		28.98			
1871–1874	25,191,055	332,689	731,058		29.02			
1875–1879	26,510,758	351,790	720,160	6,612	27.16	18.80	0.92	69.2
1880–1884	27,798,791	365,183	748,634	6,613	26.93	18.11	0.88	67.2
1885–1889	29,136,876	369,317	741,088	6,241	25.43	16.90	0.84	66.4
1890–1894	30,905,202	375,887	743,270	6,029	24.05	16.04	0.81	66.7
1895–1899	33,163,816	386,019	736,737	5,719	22.22	14.82	0.78	66.7
1900–1904	35,882,917	400,912	745,335	6,091	20.77	15.19	0.82	73.1
1905–1909	38,729,272	412,714	709,220	6,139	18.31	14.87	0.87	81.2
1910	39,925,889	415,926	638,078		16.0			
1911	40,500,280		696,969	5,877	17.2		0.84	
1912	41,074,671		636,401	5,753	15.5		0.90	
1913	41,649,062		620,571	5,741	14.9		0.93	

Sources: Silbergleit, *Die Bevölkerungs- und Berufsverhältnisse*, 14*–15*, 39*; *Statistisches Jahrbuch für den Freistaat Preussen* (1933): 26.

fifteenth birthday. In the early 1880s, the percentages of Jewish deaths under age fifteen were higher in eastern provinces of Prussia than in western Prussia, with the unexplained exceptions of Posen and the Rhineland (Table 4.23). Thereafter, the percentage of Jewish dead who were age fifteen or younger plummeted to 32.7 percent in 1890, 23.3 percent in 1900, and 13.0 percent in 1910 (Table 4.24). In absolute numbers, there were 2,696 deaths of Jewish children under age fifteen in Prussia in 1880 but only 1,365 in 1900 and 743 in 1910. This was precipitated by an improvement in the treatment of childhood diseases, which made a rapid impact on German Jewry before it became highly

Table 4.23. Percent of Jewish Deaths under Age Fifteen, by Prussian Province and Region, 1880–1921

Region: Eastern

Year	Province:				
	East Prussia	West Prussia	Posen	Pomerania	Silesia
1880–1884	51.3	48.9	39.9	50.9	40.6
1885–1889	44.2	44.4	36.5	44.9	33.7
1890–1894	39.3	36.5	28.1	33.3	28.4
1895–1899	28.9	31.1	23.9	26.5	21.8
1900–1904	27.7	27.8	20.9	17.0	20.6
1905–1909	20.2	20.0	15.2	12.9	16.3
1910–1914	15.6	13.5	10.5	9.5	11.8
1920–1921	12.8			13.6	11.0

Region: Central

Year	Province:		
	Berlin	Brandenburg	Saxony
1880–1884	45.2	36.9	43.0
1885–1889	37.8	33.6	35.6
1890–1894	32.0	23.9	33.8
1895–1899	25.4	17.6	28.8
1900–1904	21.5	16.3	18.3
1905–1909	18.7	11.5	14.4
1910–1914	12.8	8.3	14.4
1920–1921	10.5	5.9	9.1

Region: Western

Year	Province:				
	Schleswig-Holstein	Hannover	Westphalia	Rhineland	Hohenzollern
1880–1884	25.2	34.0	35.7	40.8	28.4
1885–1889	33.2	31.7	32.8	35.5	23.0
1890–1894	22.7	27.6	29.4	32.7	29.9
1895–1899	23.5	21.1	26.1	29.9	28.9
1900–1904	16.5	19.3	24.5	27.6	29.1
1905–1909	10.0	16.6	20.4	22.1	7.7
1910–1914	15.3	13.6	16.8	15.0	3.7
1920–1921	15.3	12.3	14.3	11.7	9.1

Sources: Calculated from absolute figures on numbers of death in Schmelz, handwritten table "Sterbefälle Preussen Staat" (five-year figures by province) divided by Jewish population in the census year within the range ending in zero or five.

noticeable in the overall population. This was possibly due to greater affluence and better secular education among German Jews. Concurrently, however, the number of Jewish adults dying annually in Prussia increased steadily, from 3,599 to 4,503 and 4,966 in the respective years.

The absolute numbers of Jewish children dying annually did not necessarily reflect a drop in the infant mortality rate. The falling Jewish birth rate, which seems to have begun somewhat earlier than the decline in infant mortality, would have diminished the total number of Jewish children who died even without a decrease in the death rate. The actual rate of Jewish infant and child mortality (deaths per 1,000 births), which is not affected by changes in fertility, began to fall clearly only after 1886 but then proceeded rapidly. By the end of the first decade of the twentieth century, Jewish mortality rates before age fifteen had dropped by about 50 percent, fluctuating between 233 and 266 per 1,000 live births between 1877 and 1886 and then slumping to 175 in 1896, 148 in 1906, and 116 in 1914 (Table 4.25).

In Hesse, the Jewish infant mortality rate declined from 1876–1880 onward. In contrast, there is little evidence of a downturn in child mortality among the general population of Germany until about 1900. In Prussia, for instance, 50.8 percent of Christian deaths but only 23.3 percent of Jewish deaths in 1900 occurred among those under fifteen years of age. For the German population as

Table 4.24. Percent of Jewish Deaths above and below Age Fifteen—Prussia, 1850–1921

Year	Males				Females				All		
	0–14	%	15+	%	0–14	%	15+	%	0–14	15+	Total
1850	1,008	51.7	941	48.3	831	45.4	1,001	54.6	48.6	51.4	3,781
1851	1,000	50.6	977	49.4	822	46.8	936	53.2	48.8	51.2	3,735
1852	1,657	55.1	1,296	44.9	1,427	49.7	1,444	50.3	53.0	47.1	5,824
1853	1,065	49.4	1,090	50.6	911	45.6	1,087	54.4	47.6	52.4	4,153
1854	961	47.4	1,066	52.6	841	46.1	983	53.9	46.8	53.2	3,851
1855	1,046	45.1	1,273	54.9	920	41.0	1,323	59.0	43.1	56.9	4,562
Annual average 1850–1856											
	1,123	50.4	1,107	49.6	959	45.9	1,129	54.1	48.2	51.8	4,318
Annual average 1877–1880											
	1,461	44.8	1,803	55.2	1,262	42.5	1,706	57.5	43.7	56.3	6,231
Annual average 1881–1885											
	1,349	41.3	1,918	58.7	1,155	38.5	1,844	61.5	40.0	60.0	6,266
Annual average 1886–1890											
	1,104	35.6	2,001	64.4	959	33.9	1,869	66.1	34.8	65.2	5,933
Annual average 1891–1895											
	895	29.9	2,097	70.1	782	28.1	1,998	71.9	29.1	71.0	5,771
Annual average 1896–1900											
	729	24.8	2,212	75.2	584	22.8	1,980	77.2	23.9	76.2	5,504

Year	Males				Females				All		Total
	0–14	%	15+	%	0–14	%	15+	%	0–14	15+	
Annual average 1901–1905											
	638	21.6	2,317	78.4	534	19.7	2,173	80.3	20.7	79.3	5,663
Annual average 1906–1910											
	493	16.4	2,519	83.6	404	15.0	2,292	85.0	15.7	84.2	5,715
Annual average 1911–1913											
	383	12.8	2,621	87.3	328	11.8	2,457	88.2	12.3	87.2	5,790
1914	356	9.5	**3,394**	90.5	292	10.5	2,493	89.5	9.9	90.1	**6,535**
Annual average 1920–1921											
	330	11.0	2,674	89.0	255	9.5	2,426	90.5	10.3	89.7	5,685

Numbers in bold = particularly high mortality.

Sources: Calculated from Schmelz's table "Sterbefälle Preussen Staat." Cf. Arthur Ruppin, "Die Bewegung der jüdischen Bevölkerung in Preussen im Jahre 1905," *ZDSJ* 3, no. 3 (1907): 44; Arthur Ruppin, "Das Wachstum der jüdischen Bevölkerung in Preussen," *ZDSJ* 1, no. 6 (June 1905): 7; Jacob Segall, "Die Bewegung der jüdischen Bevölkerung in Preussen, Bayern und Hessen," *ZDSJ* 12, nos. 4–6 (1916): 29.

Table 4.25. Jewish Deaths before Age Fifteen in Prussia Divided by 1,000 Live Births (In-Married and Illegitimate) vs. Overall Infant Mortality of the General Prussian Population (Deaths under Age 1)

Year	Jewish births	Jews who died by age 15	Jewish deaths before age 15 per 1,000 live births	General German infant mortality rate below 1 (estimated below 15)	
1877–1880	43871	10891	248	1875–1880: 228	351*
1881–1885	50178	12516	249	226	348*
1886–1890	44883	10316	230	224	345*
1891–1895	40980	8382	205	221	340*
1896–1900	37797	6562	174	213	328*
1901–1905	35305	5863	166	199	306*
1906–1910	33111	4485	135	174	268*
1911–1914	23402	2783	119	164	252*
1920–1921	12501	1170	94	1924–1926: 102	157*

* Estimated general rate of deaths under 15 (assuming deaths by age 1 are 65% of deaths by age 15), as per general deaths in Hamburg, 1923–1927.

Sources: Christian rates for deaths before age 1 are from Knodel, *Decline*, 288–289. Jewish figures are based on Schmelz, handwritten tables "Lebendgeborene Preussen Staat" and "Sterbefälle Preussen Staat," adding individual years. Birth figures include children of Jewish in-married couples plus illegitimate children of Jewish mothers.

a whole, 21.3 percent of births ended in death before one year of age between 1896 and 1900. The share fell to 17.4 percent between 1906 and 1910, 10.2 percent between 1924 and 1926, and 7.5 percent between 1932 and 1934.[34]

The age-specific death rate of Jews was consistently lower than that of the general population among those under the age of one, and even more so among those in the 1–15 age bracket. In the over-50 age groups, Jewish mortality rates were only slightly less than those of Christians (Tables 4.26 A and B). Although Jewish mortality among the young remained distinctively low, the rise in average age of the Jewish population, itself occasioned by greater longevity, eventually stopped the decline in overall Jewish death rates not corrected for age.

Table 4.26. Age-Specific Death Rates of Jews and Christians

A) Average Annual Deaths per 1,000 Living in Age Category, Grand Duchy of Hesse

Age	Christians 1906–1910		Jews 1903–1910		Age-specific Jewish death rate as percent of Christian rate	
	Males	Females	Males	Females	Males	Females
Under 1	140.21	117.42	76.73	66.52	54.73	56.65
1–4	13.69	13.76	4.99	6.83	36.45	49.64
5–9	2.72	2.84	1.39	2.44	51.10	85.92
10–14	1.80	2.22	0.84	1.29	46.67	58.11
15–19	3.31	3.40	2.20	1.84	66.47	54.12
20–29	4.49	5.05	3.65	3.18	81.29	62.97
30–39	6.21	6.65	3.71	5.13	59.74	77.14
40–49	10.39	8.64	6.72	7.39	64.68	85.53
50–59	20.78	16.47	19.33	15.56	93.02	94.47
60–69	45.32	41.25	44.32	36.59	97.79	88.70
70–79	100.32	96.69	95.26	89.18	94.96	92.23
80+	226.52	215.35	214.29	209.91	94.60	97.47
Overall	15.84	15.19	14.17	13.59	89.46	89.47

Sources: Knöpfel, "Geburtenrückgang und Sterblichkeit," 4.

---

34 Knodel, *Decline*, 289. Converting from Knodel's figures, which are calculated per thousand.

B) Number of Deaths and Age-Specific Deaths per 1,000, Hamburg, 1923–1927

Age	General population			Jews			Age-specific Jewish death rate as percent of Christian rate
	No. in group	No. of deaths	Age-specific annual death rate	No. in group	No. of deaths	Age-specific annual death rate	
Under 1	77393	6740	87.5	1316	51	40.5	46.3
1–2		905	13.4		7	5.0	37.3
2–5		1031	4.3		11	2.8	65.1
5–10	58096	653	2.3	800	1	0.2	8.7
10–20	193722	2064	2.1	2625	17	1.3	61.9
20–30	217503	4834	4.4	3315	61	3.7	84.1
30–40	201722	4929	4.9	3177	66	4.2	85.7
40–50	174322	6560	7.5	3131	113	7.2	96.0
50–60	122181	9190	15.0	2782	185	13.3	88.7
60–70	71864	12101	33.7	1764	374	42.4	125.8
70–80	29418	12347	83.9	793	382	96.3	116.0
80+	6180	5519	187.3	201	196	188.6	100.7
Total	1152378	66873	11.6	19984	1466	14.7	126.7

Source: "Die Gestaltung der jüdischen Sterblichkeit im Staate Hamburg 1923/27," ZDSJ 5, no. 3 (1930): 45–46.

Causes of Death

The Jews' lower rates of infant and child mortality and their greater longevity were also reflected in differences in causes of death among Jews and non-Jews. A comparison of Jewish and general causes of death in Hesse in the first decade of the twentieth century shows that Jews were much less likely to die of childhood maladies, which included congenital weakness, scarlet fever, measles, diphtheria, and whooping cough, as well as *Magen- und Darmkatarrh* (stomach and intestinal infections). Jews were overrepresented in deaths from diseases of later life such as old age (*Altersschwäche*), circulatory diseases, stroke, cancer, and genitourinary diseases. Their rates were near the average in respiratory diseases, suicide, homicide, and death in childbirth. The lower Jewish death rates from tuberculosis probably related to the lower instance of poverty among Jews (Tables 4.27 A and B).

Social Differences in Fertility and Mortality Decline

Studies of the German fertility transition have often noted that urban and more middle-class populations were affected earlier and more powerfully than rural and poorer groups. In Prussia, urban areas in virtually every district began the decline in fertility earlier than did rural areas in the same district.[35] In general, the Jews of Germany fit into both categories affected earliest—the more urban and the more middle-class (and better educated). Although it seems evident that the Jews' urbanization and higher economic status correlated with their more rapid mortality and fertility declines, it is not always clear whether this was the sole reason for the distinction or whether there were other specifically Jewish cultural reasons as well. German Jews were less diverse in their demographic patterns than the German population as a whole. The degree to which fertility was lower in urban areas than in rural ones was much narrower among Jews than among the general population. Moreover, while the gap between rural and urban fertility often increased in the general population, especially in the early stages of the demographic transition, it tended to narrow among Jews.[36] By the 1920s, Jewish marital fertility was actually lower in small towns than in large cities, at least in Bavaria (Table 4.28).

---

35 Ibid., 98–101, 280–282.
36 Ibid., 89–110; Schmelz, *Hessen*, 65–66, 109–110; Ruppin, *Soziologie*, vol. 1, 176–177.

Table 4.27. Causes of Death among Jews and Christians

A) Hesse(-Darmstadt)

Disease	Jews, 1901–1912			Christians, 1906–1910		
	Male	Percent of Christian deaths	Female	Percent of Christian deaths	Male	Female
Scarlet fever, measles, diphtheria, whooping cough (Ch)	21	1.22	23	1.24	1720	1854
Stomach and intestinal catarrh (Ch)	62	1.45	46	1.27	4286	3629
Tuberculosis (M)	117	1.75	136	1.94	6696	7000
Accidents (*)	28	1.89	15	3.92	1479	383
Other illnesses of the nervous system	73	2.22	69	2.80	3294	2460
Congenital weakness (Ch)	61	2.40	37	1.97	2541	1875
Murder, manslaughter, fatal wounds (*)	3	3.95	3	6.12	76	49
Sicknesses of the respiratory organs	298	3.92	257	3.73	7610	6897
Childbed fever and complications of giving birth (M)	—		22	4.11	—	535
Suicide (*)	54	4.69	14	3.84	1151	365

Disease	Jews, 1901–1912			Christians, 1906–1910	
	Male	Percent of Christian deaths	Female	Male	Female
Other illnesses of the digestive organs (*)	77	5.42	91	1420	1392
Old age (O)	263	6.05	332	4346	5310
Cancer and neoplasms (O)	168	6.25	267	2689	3553
Urinary and reproductive organs (*)	91	8.10	53	1124	959
Stroke (O)	172	8.12	162	2117	2068
Illnesses of the circulatory system (*)	351	9.69	319	3621	4219
Other causes	125	6.07	130	2059	1772
Unknown causes	23	1.09	27	2109	2002
All Causes	1987	4.11	2003	48338	46322

Ch = Most deaths in category before age 15.

M = Most deaths in category at ages 15–59.

O = Most deaths in category at ages over 60.

* No clear age distribution.

Source: Ludwig Knöpfel, "Die gegenwärtige Sterblichkeit der jüdischen und christlichen Bevölkerung der Grossherzogtums Hessen nach Geschlecht, Alter und Todesursache," ZDSJ 10, no. 4 (1914): 67–68.

B) Causes of Death in the Berlin Population, by Religion, 1911–1914 (percent of all deaths due to each cause)

Disease by Year	Protestants	Catholics	Jews	Total
Tuberculosis				
1911	10.67	13.74	4.58	10.77
1912	11.35	15.97	7.15	17.06 (?)
1913	11.25	15.97	6.27	11.58
1914	11.09	14.79	7.04	11.33
Cancer				
1911	7.20	6.55	13.99	7.43
1912	7.83	7.01	10.09	7.86
1913	8.45	7.86	12.46	8.03
1914	8.26	7.01	12.55	8.37
Intestinal infection, diarrhea, stomach and intestinal inflammation				
1911	8.08	9.28	2.41	8.00
1912	5.29	8.45	11.45(?)	5.17
1913	5.05	6.48	1.09	5.07
1914	5.25	6.44	1.78	5.49

Source: Wilhelm Hanauer, "Zur Mortalitätsstatistik der Juden," ZDSJ 15, nos. 1–3 (1919): 16–17, quoting a study by H. Guradze.

Table 4.28. Marital Fertility Rates in Bavaria, 1924–1926 (legitimate births per married women aged 16–45)

City	General population	Jews
Munich, Nuremberg, Augsburg, Ludwigshafen	0.088 (15,710 births)	0.128 (255 births)
Regensburg, Bamberg, Fürth, Würzburg	0.142 (5,049 births)	0.152 (88 births)
Smaller towns	0.194 (120,380 births)	0.101 (226 births)
All Bavaria	0.169 (141,139 births)	0.118 (569 births)

Although Jewish marital fertility was higher than that of Christians in the cities, their overall fertility was lower because a large percentage of the non-Jewish population lived in small towns.

Source: Ph. Schwarz, "Nachwuchsverhältnisse der jüdischen Familien in Bayern," *Bayerische Israelitische Gemeindezeitung* (April 1, 1930): 104–105.

Even in large cities, however, Jewish fertility rates were generally lower than those of the population at large, indicating that urbanization alone does not fully explain the difference. In Frankfurt am Main, for instance, the Christian crude birth rate between 1905 and 1908 varied from 27.18 to 29.32 per 1,000 while the Jewish rate ranged from 14.85 to 17.14. In Hamburg, the Jewish crude birth rate was much lower than the general crude birth rate in every measurement between 1885 and 1910 (Table 4.29).[37] In Munich, the index of marital fertility was considerably lower for Jews than for Protestants or Catholics between 1875 and 1892. A similar if less extreme difference was found in Berlin between 1893 and 1902 (Table 4.30). In most cities, the Jewish birth rate remained lower than that of the general population. The main exception was Berlin, where the general birth rate fell even further than the Jewish rate, and which Felix Theilhaber called *das sterile Berlin*—"the sterile Berlin." In 1925, the index of marital fertility (Ig) in Berlin was 210 for Jews and only 147 for the general population, and the respective crude birth rates were 11.9 and 11.7 per 1,000.

---

37 "Die Bewegung der jüdischen Bevölkerung in Frankfurt am Main," *ZDSJ* 5, no. 10 (October 1909): 157.

Table 4.29. Crude Birth Rates (per 1,000) of Jews and General Population in Hamburg

Year	Jews	General population	Jewish as percent of general birth rate
1885	29.5	34.5	85.5
1890	23.2	35.1	66.1
1895	23.6	33.6	70.2
1900	19.1	28.8	66.3
1905	18.4	25.6	71.9
1910	15.2	22.8	66.7

Source: Weigert, "Bevölkerung," 82.

Table 4.30. Decline in Marital Fertility Index (I_g), by Religion

Year	Munich Marital Fertility Index Decline		
	Catholic	Protestant	Jewish
1875	.660	.534	.522
1878–1882	.607	.497	.414
1883–1887	.564	.459	.335
1888–1892	.532	.384	.299
Percent decline	19.4	28.1	42.7

Year	Berlin Marital Fertility Index Decline		
	Catholic	Protestant	Jewish
1893–1897	.499	.448	.367
1898–1902	.446	.393	.337
Percent decline	10.6	12.5	8.2

Source: Knodel, *Decline*, 136.

In Breslau, in contrast, the Jewish birth rate in 1925 was far below that among non-Jews: 11.2 compared to 17.9 per 1,000 (Table 4.31).

There is strong evidence that fertility was higher in the lower socioeconomic classes than in the higher classes among the general population of Germany. In Hamburg in 1901 and 1902, for example, the overall crude birth rates of the Lutheran and Jewish populations were 24.1 per 1,000 and 16.2 per 1,000,

Table 4.31. Jewish and Christian Crude Birth Rates per 1000 in Large Cities, 1926

City	Jewish	Christian
Frankfurt am Main	13.4	14.0
Cologne	14.8	18.1
Breslau	11.1	17.9

Source: Ruppin, *Soziologie*, vol. 1, 175, 177.

respectively.[38] Among Lutherans, the crude birth rate was 41.9 per 1,000 in the Inner City as against 13.8 in the wealthy Harvestehude section. The Christian birth rate in the latter affluent neighborhood, which was 13.9 percent Jewish in 1900, was lower than the city's overall Jewish birth rate.[39] Jews' generally higher socioeconomic status is often offered as a partial explanation for the change. For Berlin in the 1920s, the higher classes within the Jewish community do appear to have had lower fertility than the lower classes. In Berlin in 1922–1923, the share of Jewish newborns who were third, fourth, or later children was much higher in the poor Mitte district (22.9 percent) than in the wealthy Jewish neighborhoods of western Berlin (6.9 percent) (Table 4.32). Jewish birth rates were much lower in the wealthy western suburbs of Charlottenburg, Schöneberg, and Wilmersdorf than in Berlin proper, and the relatively poor suburb of Rixdorf (later Neukölln) seems to have had a much higher Jewish birth rate than the central city (Table 4.33).

Illegitimacy

Rates of illegitimacy (out-of-wedlock births) in Germany varied widely by region. In certain areas, such births seemed to be an accepted part of traditional mores in both urban and rural communities. While illegitimacy rates were relatively low in northwestern Germany, they were very high in the south and southeast, especially in Bavaria and Saxony (Table 4.34). Illegitimacy rates in parts of southern Germany were higher in the early nineteenth century than later; rates in Bavaria (east of the Rhine) exceeded twenty percent between the 1830s and about 1870 and then dropped to slightly below fifteen percent

---

38 Marital crude birth rates were 21.0 and 15.3, respectively.
39 Dora Weigert, "Die jüdische Bevölkerung in Hamburg," *ZDSJ* 15, nos. 5–7 (May 1919): 84.

Table 4.32. Birth Order of Jewish Children Born in Berlin, 1922–1923

District	First	Second	Third	Fourth and higher
Western districts (Charlottenburg, Wilmersdorf, Schöneberg, Steglitz, Zehlendorf, Tiergarten—mainly wealthy and heavily Jewish)				
	1225	574	99	34
	(63.4%)	(29.7%)	(5.1%)	(1.8%)
Other sections of Inner Berlin (Wedding, Prenzlauer Berg, Friedrichshain, Kreuzberg, Neukölln—poorer districts)				
	541	298	86	65
	(54.7%)	(30.1%)	(8.7%)	(6.6%)
Mitte (poor and heavily immigrant-Jewish)	458	295	106	118
	(46.9%)	(30.2%)	(10.9%)	(12.1%)

Source: Theilhaber, "Bevölkerungsvorgänge bei den Berliner Juden," 53.

Table 4.33. Jewish Crude Birth Rates in Berlin and Suburbs per 1,000 of Population

Year	Wealthy suburbs				Poor suburb
	Berlin	Charlottenburg	Schöneberg	Wilmersdorf	Rixdorf
1878–1882	27.51	[21.60]			
1883–1887	22.75	[20.08]			
1888–1892	21.01	19.66	20.73*		[55.93]
1893–1897	19.05	17.41	17.03		[34.55]
1898–1902	17.46	16.08	16.83	14.16**	[29.78]
1903–1907	15.86	12.69	13.28		21.77
1908–1912	14.62	10.36	12.01	10.74	18.56

[ ] = total Jewish population under 500.
* 1890–1892.
** 1900.

Sources: comparing the absolute number of Jewish births in Schmelz, handwritten tables "Geburten—Städte" for the above-mentioned five cities with the known Jewish population of the city in the year ending in a zero or five within those years.

Table 4.34. Percent of Out-of-Wedlock Births in Various Parts of Germany—General Population, 1878–1887

Region	Frequency	Ranking*
1. Berlin	13.52	2
2. East Prussia, West Prussia	9.59	7
3. Pomerania, Schleswig-Holstein, Mecklenburg, Lübeck, and Hamburg	10.70	5
4. Brandenburg (not including Berlin)	10.48	6
5. Posen	6.77	11
6. Upper Silesia	6.60	12
7. Lower Silesia	13.21	3
8. Kingdom of Saxony and Thuringia	12.36	4
9. Prussian Saxony, Hildesheim, Braunschweig, and Anhalt	9.41	8
10. Hannover (not including Hildesheim), Münster, Oldenburg, and Bremen	5.47	13
11. Rhine Province, Arnsberg, and Birkenfeld	3.32	15
12. Hesse-Nassau, Minden, Hesse, Waldeck, Lippe, and Schaumburg-Lippe	5.98	14
13. Bavaria east of the Rhine	14.61	1
14. Württemberg, Baden, and Hohenzollern	8.58	9
15. Rhine Palatinate and Alsace-Lorraine	6.99	10

* Highest = 1.
Source: "Die Eheschliessungen, Geburten und Sterbefälle im Deutschen Reich im Jahre 1888," *Monatshefte zur Statistik des Deutschen Reichs* (December 1888): XII, 3.

around 1880. In Württemberg, illegitimacy crested at more than fifteen percent in the 1860s and then fell to below ten percent by the late 1870s.[40] In Hesse-Darmstadt, it dropped from 12.7 percent in 1866–1870 to 7.8 percent in 1871–1875. In Baden, it fell from sixteen percent to about eight percent between 1850 and 1909.[41] Some attribute the decline in illegitimacy in the 1870s to the

---

40 Brown and Guinanne, *Pre-Marital and Extra-Marital Fertility in Munich 1825–1910*, Figure 1.
41 "Geburten und Sterbefälle im Grossherzogthum Hessen im Jahre 1910 mit Rückblicken," 113; Baden: Auguste Lange, *Die unehelichen Geburten in Baden. Eine Untersuchung über ihrer Bedingungen und ihre Entwicklung* (Karlsruhe, 1912), 99*.

introduction of civil marriage in 1875. In Prussia, however, where illegitimacy rates were never as high as in southern Germany, out-of-wedlock births rose gradually from the 1840s until the 1880s and then remained more or less steady until World War I (Table 4.35).

Between 1872 and 1911, the out-of-wedlock birth rate in Germany as a whole ranged from 8.2 percent to 9.4 percent with no clear pattern of change over time. Thereafter, larger and clearer fluctuations became evident. There was an increase to 13.0 percent during World War I (1918), a reversion to just over ten percent in the early 1920s, a new peak of 12.4 percent in 1926, slow decline to 10.7 percent in 1933, and then an abrupt downturn under Nazi rule to 7.6 percent by 1938. The regional rankings in illegitimacy changed little during the *Kaiserreich* period.[42]

In virtually all parts of Germany throughout the nineteenth century and into the early twentieth, Jewish rates of out-of-wedlock births were much lower than those of the general population. This was despite the fact that such births were more common among urban than among rural populations in Germany for both Jews and non-Jews, as well as that Jews were much more urbanized than Germans at large. Furthermore, regional variations in illegitimacy rates were much less marked among Jews than among Christians. Where Christian out-of-wedlock rates were particularly low, such as in the Rhineland, Westphalia, and Hannover, Jewish illegitimacy rates were only slightly lower, but in the high illegitimacy areas of southern Germany—especially in Bavaria and Württemberg—they were much lower. Even in the large cities of Hamburg and Berlin, where both Jewish and general non-marital birth rates were relatively high, Jewish rates were still considerably lower than general rates (Table 4.36).

The percent of Jewish births out of wedlock tended to rise over time, at least in Prussia. This was, however, more the result of a decrease in the number of legitimate births than an increase in the population of Jewish women who bore children outside of wedlock. The low rate of out-of-wedlock births among Jews held steady until the early 1890s. In Prussia between 1876 and 1893, the annual share of Jewish births that were out of wedlock[43] fluctuated in the very narrow range of 2.5–2.9 percent. During this time of very rapid decline in the numbers

---

42 According to Knodel, *Decline*, 76, regional differences in the index of illegitimate fertility (Ih) between 1880 and 1933 correlate at the 0.83 level. The indexes of 1900 correlate with those of 1880 at 0.96, and with those of 1933, at 0.86.

43 This number was calculated by dividing the number of live out-of-wedlock births by the sum of such births and the number of live births to homogeneous Jewish marriage couples. If we had included births to intermarried couples, the illegitimacy rate would have been somewhat lower and would have climbed less rapidly.

Table 4.35. Jewish and General Annual Average Illegitimacy Rates, Prussia (percent recalculated)

Year	All births	Out of wedlock	Percent out of wedlock	Jewish births	Out of wedlock	Percent out of wedlock
1821–1823	501,936	24,257	4.83	5,337	88	1.65
1824–1826	518,204	24,766	4.78	5,678	107	1.88
1827–1829	495,221	22,586	4.56	5,498	85	1.55
1830–1832	489,993	23,172	4.73	5,595	100	1.79
1833–1835	541,990	26,639	4.92	6,222	123	1.98
1836–1838	558,305	27,332	4.90	6,563	137	2.09
1839–1841	584,584	21,494	3.76	7,010	149	2.13
1842–1844	617,122	30,277	4.91	7,685	161	2.09
1845–1847	619,045	31,156	5.03	7,745	120	1.55
1848–1850	648,494	33,349	5.14	7,540	167	2.21
1851–1853	670,366	34,981	5.22	8,012	212	2.65
1854–1856	630,752	32,200	5.11	7,990	216	2.70
1857–1859	726,914	42,041	5.78	8,428	302	3.58
1860–1862	725,263	42,542	5.87	8,401	309	3.86
1863–1865	787,942	47,699	6.05	8,546	303	3.55

	All births including stillbirths				
1876–1880	1,086,717	82,936	7.63	11,545	315	2.73
1881–1885	1,081,103	87,670	8.11	10,625	283	2.66
1886–1890	1,129,498	90,591	8.02	9,159	249	2.72
1891–1895	1,181,491	91,593	7.75	8,738	248	2.84
1896–1900	1,252,440	96,213	7.68	8,093	270	3.34
1901–1905	1,291,503	92,035	7.13	7,632	274	3.59
1906–1910	1,292,002	98,129	7.60	7,204	310	4.30
1911	1,225,091	97,705	8.00	6,642	335	5.04
1912	1,222,168	101,379	8.30	6,475	365	5.64
1913	1,209,385	102,345	8.46	6,433	374	5.81
1914	1,402,528	103,808	7.40	6,128	322	5.25
1915	918,821	92,843	10.10	5,005	292	5.83
1916	697,658	71,028	10.18	3,623	231	6.38
1917	623,201	66,046	10.60	3,026	185	6.11
1918	630,524	76,617	12.15	3,171	191	6.02
1919	827,335	85,338	10.31	4,426	219	4.95
1920	1,005,525	108,873	10.83	6,638	372	5.60

Alternate calculation of Jewish out-of-wedlock birth rates—Prussia, 1911–1928

Year	1 In-married Jewish parents plus out-of-wedlock	2 Jewish mother, including intermarried Jews	3 Out-of-wedlock Jewish mother	Percent of 1	Percent of 2
1911	6055	6424	320	5.28	4.98
1912	5896	6250	347	5.89	5.55
1913	5862	6217	365	6.23	5.87
1914	5589	5952	308	5.51	5.17
1915	4471	4789	276	6.17	5.76
1916	3223	3477	223	6.92	6.42
1917	2680	2906	175	6.53	6.02
1918	2775	3017	180	6.49	5.97
1919	3960	4273	214	5.40	5.01
1920	5991	6396	351	5.86	5.49
1921	6510	6888	386	5.93	5.60
1922	5952	6306	380	6.38	6.03
1923	6106	6451	401	6.57	6.22
1924	5547	5846	326	5.88	5.58
1925	5025	5361	345	6.87	6.44
1926	4414	4653	279	6.32	6.00
1927	4020	4280	291	7.24	6.80
1928	3910	4158	235	6.01	5.65

Source: Anton Goldscheider, "Entwicklung," 71; "Geburten und Sterbefälle in Preussen von 1876–1920," ZDSJ 1, no. 1 (1924): 26; Silbergleit, Die Bevölkerungs- und Berufsverhältnisse, 39*.

Table 4.36. Jewish and General Illegitimacy Rates, 1901, Selected Provinces

Province	General illegitimacy rate (1901)	Jewish illegitimacy rate* (1900–1904)	Ratio
Berlin	15.1%	5.9%	2.6
Bavaria east of Rhine	14.0		
All Bavaria	12.9	2.2	5.8 (1900)
Saxony (kingdom)	12.6		
Hamburg	12.0	5.5	2.2
Prussian Saxony	10.4	2.9	3.6
Pomerania	10.0	2.7	3.7
Brandenburg	9.9	3.1	3.2
Württemberg	9.6	c. 1.5 (1900–1905)	6.5
East Prussia	9.5	2.6	3.6
Silesia	8.9	3.5	2.5
Schleswig-Holstein	8.6	5.8	1.5
Baden	7.7		
Hesse	7.1	3.2 (1901–1904)	2.2
Hannover	6.7	4.1	1.6
West Prussia	6.5	0.9	7.1
Rhineland	6.4	4.0	1.6
Hohenzollern	6.4	0	
Bavaria west of Rhine	6.2		
Posen	5.5	2.4	2.3
Westphalia	2.6	2.1	1.3

* Excluding intermarried.

Sources: *Statistisches Jahrbuch für das deutsche Reich* 24 (1903): 21; Schmelz's tables; Thon, "Bewegung seit dem Jahre 1876," 8; Weigert, "Bevölkerung," 82, 84; Knöpfel, "Stand und Bewegung," 84; Hugo Nathanson, "Die unehelichen Geburten bei den Juden," *ZDSJ* 6, no. 7 (1910): 104–105.

of Jewish births, the number of out-of-wedlock births dropped in tandem with the overall decrease—from 310 in 1880 to 229 in 1893. Thereafter, the Jewish rate of out-of-wedlock births increased steadily and quite rapidly to 3.8 percent by 1905 and 6.2 percent by 1913. The number of Jewish children born out of wedlock began to rise despite the continued drop in births to in-married Jewish couples. By 1913, there were 365 illegitimate Jewish births in Prussia. During the five years before World War I (1910–1914), Jewish out-of-wedlock rates in the various Prussian provinces ranged from 2.5 percent in Posen to 11.1 percent in Berlin, growing relative to 1880–1884 by anywhere from 24 percent in Posen province to 174 percent in Westphalia (Table 4.37). During World War I, out-of-wedlock births to Jewish women did not decrease nearly as much as the number of births within Jewish marriages, allowing the Jewish illegitimacy rate to climb to 6.9 percent in 1916. During the postwar baby boom, the rate of Jewish births out of wedlock dropped slightly to 5.4 percent in 1919, but the absolute numbers surged from a mere 175 in 1917 to a high of 401 in 1923. As Jewish legitimate births plunged in the late 1920s and early 1930s, out-of-wedlock births declined less rapidly, and the Prussian-Jewish out-of-wedlock rate reached an all-time high of 7.2 percent in 1927.

While Jewish illegitimacy rates were rising, those of the general population showed a murkier trend. In some cases, this was caused by traditional patterns of high illegitimacy that began to fade with modernity[44] (Table 4.38). Although the overall general rate of illegitimacy also rose in the first decades of the twentieth century, it did so less sharply than the Jewish rate. Thus, between 1901 and 1927, illegitimacy climbed by 50.7 percent among the general Prussian population (from 7.2 percent to 10.9 percent) and by 108.1 percent among Prussian Jews (from 3.5 percent to 7.2 percent).[45]

In South German states, evidence of growing illegitimacy among Jews is scantier even though the general rate of out-of-wedlock births remained high. Nowhere was the difference in illegitimacy between Jews and the general population greater than in Bavaria. In 1878, the general illegitimacy rate in Bavaria east of the Rhine was 13.8 percent—higher than in any other region

---

[44] In Hesse, for instance, the overall share of births out of wedlock in the general population dropped sharply from 12.3 percent in the 1860s to 6.4 percent in the 1870s, it then leveled off until the beginning of World War I, and then increased during and after the war. The percentage of illegitimacy among Jews was always far below that of the general population but trended upward overall. Schmelz, *Die jüdische Bevölkerung Hessens*, 111.
[45] Ruppin, *Soziologie*, vol. 1, 185–186 and Schmelz, handwritten table "Lebendgeborene Preussen Staat" (individual years).

Table 4.37. Percent of Jewish Out-of-Wedlock Births in Various Prussian Provinces

Province	1875–1879	1880–1884	1885–1889	1890–1894	1895–1899	1900–1904	1905–1909	1910–1914	Range	Change, 1880–1914
Schleswig-Holstein		9.8	5.6	7.1	9.0	5.8	9.4	11.1	5.6–11.1	+13.5%
Berlin		6.1	5.1	4.9	5.7	5.9	7.7	11.1	4.9–11.1	+84.1%
Hannover	3.5	4.3	2.7	3.3	3.8	4.1	5.7	7.3	2.7–7.3	+69.4%
Rhineland	2.6	2.9	2.9	2.7	3.7	4.0	3.9	3.9	2.6–3.9	+35.4%
Silesia	2.9	2.4	3.0	2.7	3.1	3.5	4.1	5.0	2.4–5.0	+107.4%
Prussian Saxony	3.0	3.0	2.4	2.3	3.0	2.9	4.5	6.9	2.3–6.9	+132.4%
Brandenburg		2.2	2.6	2.8	3.4	3.1	3.3	3.7	2.2–3.7	+63.0%
Pomerania	1.7	2.1	2.6	1.9	2.7	2.7	2.0	2.9	1.7–2.9	+34.0%
Posen	2.4	2.0	1.8	1.6	2.1	2.4	2.3	2.5	1.6–2.5	+23.8%
Westphalia	1.6	1.2	1.5	1.8	1.6	2.1	2.3	3.3	1.2–3.3	+174.2%
East Prussia	1.3	2.1	1.1	2.4	2.7	2.6	2.0	3.6	1.1–3.6	+74.4%
West Prussia	2.3	1.9	1.9	2.0	1.1	0.9	2.0	3.2	0.9–3.2	+73.0%

Source: calculated from Schmelz, handwritten table "Geburten—Provinzen."

Table 4.38. Percent of Children Born Out of Wedlock in Hesse

Year	All Hessian areas		Hesse-Darmstadt		Hesse-Nassau	
	Jews	General population	Jews	General population	Jews	General population
1861–1870		12.3	2.9	14.9		10.6
1871–1879		6.4	2.0	7.4		5.8
1880–1889	1.8	6.6	2.0	7.6	1.6	6.0
1890–1899	2.2	6.9	2.3	7.9	2.2	6.3
1900–1913	4.0	6.8	4.0	7.5	4.1	6.4
1914–1919	4.6	9.0	2.8	9.6	5.3	8.7
1920–1929	4.2	8.0	2.1	9.0	4.9	7.5
1930–1932			4.5	8.8		

Source: Schmelz, *Hessen*, 111.

of Germany including Berlin.[46] The overall illegitimacy rate in 1924–1926 in Bavaria was 14.4 percent, little changed from what it had been forty years earlier. The rate was only slightly lower in the countryside (12.8 percent) and considerably higher in the largest cities (23.6 percent overall and 30.7 percent in Munich). In contrast, the Jewish out-of-wedlock rate was only 2.1 percent of all Jewish births. It also varied between countryside and the cities, but even in the large cities only 2.7 percent of all Jewish children were born out of wedlock. Of 23,829 live births out of wedlock in Bavaria between 1924 and 1926, only twelve were Jewish[47] (Table 4.39). Very low Jewish illegitimacy rates also occurred in Württemberg and Hesse (Table 4.40). In the former kingdom of Saxony, which was an area of generally high illegitimacy, Jewish out-of-wedlock birth rates were much higher than in southern Germany, at least before World War I[48] (Table 4.41).

---

46 "Die Eheschliessungen, Geburten und Sterbefälle im Deutschen Reich im Jahre 1888," *Monatshefte zur Statistik des Deutschen Reichs* 12, no. 2 (December 1888), Table 3.

47 Ph. Schwarz, "Nachwuchsverhältnisse der jüdischen Familien in Bayern," *Bayerische Israelitische Gemeindezeitung* (April 1, 1930): 104–105; Thon, "Bewegung," 6, 9; "Die Bewegung der Geburten im Königreich Bayern 1908 und 1909 mit Rückblick bis 1875," *ZDSJ* 7, no. 10 (1911): 152.

48 The statistics on Jews in Saxony may be skewed by the large numbers of migrants to Saxony from Galicia who married in religious ceremonies that were not registered by the state. Therefore, children of these marriages were often registered as illegitimate.

Table 4.39. Jewish and Christian Out-of-Wedlock Births in Bavaria, 1876–1909

Yearly Average	Christian births	Christian out of wedlock	Percent out of wedlock	Jewish births	Jewish out of wedlock	Percent out of wedlock
Annual average 1876–1880	215,236	27,905	12.96	1,703	23	1.36
Annual average 1881–1885	206,921	28,182	13.62	1,532	24	1.58
Annual average 1886–1890	203,512	28,687	14.10	1,284	23	1.76
Annual average 1891–1895	212,404	30,080	14.16	1,133	20	1.80
Annual average 1896–1900	226,340	31,085	13.73	1,028	25	2.43
Annual average 1902–1903	234,741	29,198	12.44	994	25	2.46
Annual average 1908–1909	227,880	28,224	12.39	869	30	3.45

Source: Thon, "Bewegung seit dem Jahre 1876," 6, 9; "Die Bewegung der Geburten im Königreich Bayern 1908 und 1909 mit Rückblicken bis 1875," *ZSDJ* (October 1911): 152.

Table 4.40. Out-of-Wedlock Rates in Various German States, 1898–1908

Year	Prussia		Württemberg		Hesse		Bavaria	
	General	Jewish	General	Jewish	General	Jewish	General	Jewish
1898	7.34%		10.03%	2.92%	8.04%	3.01%	13.61%	2.71%
1899	7.03%							
1900	7.08%	3.90%	9.72%	0.53%	7.94%	4.48%	13.17%	2.21%
1901	7.20%	8.46% [??]						
1902	7.24%	3.56%	9.26%	3.14%	7.36%	3.98%	12.76%	2.39%
1903	7.49%	3.63%	8.49%	1.19%	7.28%	1.57%	12.62%	2.23%
1904	7.61%	4.01%	8.56%	1.02%	6.96%	2.10%	12.37%	1.82%
1905		4.21%			7.08%	1.70%		
1906		4.48%					12.28%	3.39%

Source: Hugo Nathansohn, "Die unehelichen Geburten bei den Juden," ZDSJ 6, no. 7 (1910): 104–105.

Table 4.41. Jewish Out-of-Wedlock Birth Rates in Various German States, 1910–1922

Year	Total Jewish births*			Born out of wedlock to Jewish mothers			Percent illegitimate		
	Hesse	Baden	Saxony	Hesse	Baden	Saxony	Hesse	Baden	Saxony
1910–1914	2054	2343	1696 (1911–1914)	52	67	114	2.5	2.9	6.7
1915–1919	1198	1284	1432	17	75	86	1.4	5.8	6.0
1920–1922		1307	1627		36	62		2.8	3.8

* Total born to Jewish women in homogeneous marriages, intermarriages, or out of wedlock.
Sources: Herbert Philippsthal, "Die Bewegung der Juden in Deutschland," ZDSJ 1, nos. 3–4 (1924): 76.

One fascinating study of Jewish illegitimacy in Berlin points to a much higher rate of out-of-wedlock births in areas with many poor and immigrant Jews compared to that of wealthy "West Berlin" Jews, in contrast to the much lower rate of intermarriage of the former than the latter. The author speculates that the two phenomena were interrelated: whereas wealthy and "assimilated" Jews in out-of-wedlock mixed relationships married their partners, poorer Jewish women in similar relationships preferred not to marry out of the faith and instead raised their children out of wedlock (Table 4.42).

Crisis Characteristics of Jewish Population Behavior: World War I, the Weimar Years, and the Nazi Period

Marriages and Births

From the outbreak of World War I onward, Jewish fertility and marital behavior proved highly susceptible to the influence of the various political and economic crises that the German Jewish population faced. In many ways, the oscillations in births and marriages were more extreme among the Jews than among the general population. The gradual but thoroughgoing changes seen in the Imperial period were replaced by sudden short-term fluctuations in Jewish demographic behavior.

Jewish births fell rather steadily during most of the *Kaiserreich* era. Births among the general population began to decrease much later than Jewish births did, but showed clear signs of decline by 1910. Before the outbreak of World War I, Jewish marital behavior was reasonably stable, with little change in the number of homogeneous Jewish marriages and a gradual increase in the formation of exogamous unions.

The onset of World War I and the military induction of most able-bodied men induced a sharp decrease in both marriages and births in the German population. Between 1913 and 1915, marriages in Germany declined by almost 46 percent and homogeneous Jewish marriages plummeted by almost 70 percent.[49] In Prussia, total births fell by more than 48 percent, from 1,167,823

---

49 Overall, there were 513,283 marriages in Germany in 1913 and 278,076 in 1915. The number of homogeneous Jewish marriages fell from 3,621 to 1,098 during this time (*Statistisches Jahrbuch für das deutsche Reich* [1915]: 27, [1918]: 7).

Table 4.42. Intermarriage vs. Out-of-Wedlock Birth among Jewish Women in Different Parts of Berlin

District	1921	1922	1923	1921	1922	1923	1921	1922	1923
	Births to homogeneous Jewish married couples			Births to intermarried couples			Out-of-wedlock births to Jewish women		
Western Berlin	1017	1071	978	196	150	176	17	15	21
Inner Berlin plus suburbs	1149	938	1057	158	161	147	155	158	167
Percent of total births to Jews									
Western Berlin	82.7	86.7	83.2	15.9	12.1	15.0	1.4	1.2	1.8
Other Berlin	78.6	74.6	77.1	10.8	12.8	10.7	10.6	12.6	12.2

Source: Theilhaber, "Bevölkerungsvorgänge bei den Berliner Juden," 54–55. Unfortunately, there are slight discrepancies in Theilhaber's figures. In addition, he does not clearly define what areas are included in "im Westen Berlins" and what in "eigentlichen Alt-Berlin und Vororte," although in other tables he includes the Berlin districts of Charlottenburg, Wilmersdorf, Schöneberg, Steglitz, Zehlendorf, and Tiergarten in "Verwaltungsbezirke des Westens." Theilhaber states that Jewish illegitimacy reached a high of 18 percent in the poorest district but was less than one percent in Steglitz and Zehlendorf. Infant mortality was even higher among out-of-wedlock Jewish babies in Berlin than among illegitimate children of non-Jewish mothers.

in 1914⁵⁰ to 604,631 in 1917, and births to Prussian Jewish mothers dropped by nearly 51 percent, from 5,922 to 2,906.

In the immediate postwar years, Germany experienced a short-lived baby and marriage boom. Again, it was more prominent among Jews than among the general population. Among the latter, births in the peak birth year, 1920 (989,996), were more than 15 percent fewer than in 1914. Among Prussian Jews, on the other hand, births in the peak birth year (1921 for Jews) were 6,888, a full 16 percent higher than the 1914 figure. In the 1920s, the prewar process of fertility decline, which German Jews had essentially completed before the war, continued among the general population. More than twice as many Jews married other Jews in 1920 than had done so in 1913. Among the overall German population, marriages in 1920 were only 74.4 percent higher than in 1913. Until 1923, Jewish births declined much less than did births in the general population. The share of children born in Prussia who were Jewish climbed to 0.77 percent in 1923, its highest level since the late 1880s (Table 4.43).

These relatively favorable postwar demographic developments among Jews were succeeded in the later Weimar Republic years by a much sharper decline in Jewish births and marriages than among the rest of the population. The sharper drop in marriage among Jews than among non-Jews was caused in part by the 1923 inflation, which wiped out many of the dowry funds available to Jewish brides.⁵¹ It also reflected a much sharper reaction to economic downturns among Jews than among the rest of the population. Finally, it seems to have been a response to the growing antisemitism in German society, which made young Jews more hesitant to marry and have children. Thus, fewer Jewish children were born in 1932 than in the lowest birth year of World War I. While the declines in births among the general population were a part of a long-term demographic transition, those among Jews were more sudden and crisis-like,⁵² possibly indicating a sense of despair about the future.

During World War I and up to the mid-1920s, Jewish births were less volatile year-on-year than Jewish marriages. In 1915, there were 70 percent fewer homogeneous Jewish marriages than before the war; in their lowest year

---

50 Births in 1914 were unaffected by the war because all children born that year had been conceived before the war began in August 1914.
51 Dowries played a much larger role in early twentieth century in German-Jewish matches than among the Christian population.
52 By 1930, even as detached an observer as Heinrich Silbergleit (*Die Bevölkerungs- und Berufsverhältnisse*, 38*) stated (emphasis in original), "*Das alles ist nicht mehr krisenhaft, das ist vollständiger Zusammenbruch der jüdischen Bevölkerung von innen heraus!*" ("This is no longer a crisis. This is the complete collapse of the Jewish population from within!").

Table 4.43. Jewish and General Births, Prussia, 1913–1932

Year	1 To in-married Jews	2 Out of wedlock	3 Total Jewish	4 Change	5 Five-year change	6 To Jewish intermarried population	7 To general population	8 Percent Jewish births in all births (column 3 divided by column 7)
1913	5497	365	5,862	−0.58%		776	1173605	0.50
1914	5281	308	5,589	−4.66%		786	1167823	0.48
1915	4195	276	4,471			722	891012	0.50
1916	3000	223	3,223			613	676127	0.48
1917	2505	175	2,680			519	604631	0.44
1918	2595	180	2,775			569	610993	0.45
1919	3746	214	3,960			720	802251	0.49
1920	5640	351	5,991	+51.29%		877	989996	0.61
1921	6124	386	6,510	+8.66%		872	968844	0.67
1922	5572	380	5,951	−8.59%		799	864059	0.69
1923	5705	401	6,106	+2.60%		763	792862	0.77
1924	5221	326	5,547	−9.15%		747	784713	0.71
1925	4680	345	5,025	−9.41%	−17.02%	760	796879	0.63
1926	4135	279	4,414	−12.16%		585	754041	0.59
1927	3729	291	4,020	−8.93%		674	714266	0.56
1928	3675	235	3,910	−2.74%		645	725244	0.54
1929	3283	221	3,504	−10.38%		579	701966	0.50
1930	3004	209	3,213	−8.30%	−35.81%	622	690331	0.47
1931	2640	186	2,826	−12.04%		508	634712	0.45
1932	2096	173	2,269	−19.71%		441		

Sources: Schmelz, handwritten table "Lebendgeborene Preussen Staat"; Silbergleit, *Die Bevölkerungs- und Berufsverhältnisse*, 39*; *Statistisches Jahrbuch für den Freistaat Preussen* (1933): 26.

during the war, Jewish births fell by only 54.3 percent. In the postwar marriage boom, when Jewish marriages in 1920 doubled relative to their prewar level, Jewish births rose to only slightly above their 1913 level. After 1925 or so, the trend reversed, and Jewish births declined much more vigorously than Jewish marriages. Thus, between 1924 and 1932, Jewish inmarriage fell by just over 30 percent and births to in-married Jewish couples plunged by almost 60 percent. The Jewish crude birth rate in 1932 was approximately 6 per 1,000, far lower than any other population group in its time and even lower than the extremely low birth rates that Europe attained in the late twentieth- and early twenty-first centuries in the "second demographic transition."[53] Jewish out-of-wedlock births dropped almost as much as did births to homogeneous Jewish couples. While homogeneous marriages became much rarer, intermarriages between Jews and non-Jews declined only moderately from their peak in 1920–1923 and remained clearly higher than they had been before World War I. Even though the number of intermarrying couples grew, the number of children that they produced waned moderately, although less so than the numbers of children of homogeneous Jewish couples (Table 4.44, Figure 4.3).

Paradoxically, Jewish marriage and birth statistics rebounded slightly during the first few years of Nazi rule. Part of this may have been a reflection of the increasing prosperity among the general German population and of the Nazis' pro-natalist policies, which may have had an indirect effect on the Jews. Likely a more important factor was the formation of matches in anticipation of emigration from Germany. Jewish homogeneous marriages increased in the early Nazi years, in part, because Jews were forbidden to marry "Aryans." Even including mixed marriages, which, of course, declined rapidly, Jewish marriages actually increased in the 1933–1935 period (Table 4.45).

Although Germany-wide statistics are hard to come by, various sets of local statistics show that Jewish births also recovered to some extent during the early years of the Nazi regime as more Jewish couples married ahead of emigration. This is especially remarkable because of the steady decline in the overall

---

53 This would yield a crude birth rate of 5.92 per 1,000 based on the 1933 census, which counted 2,960 Jews born in 1932 out of a total of 499,682 Jews in Germany. The actual number of Jews born in Germany in 1932 was probably slightly larger because some may have died and others may have emigrated with their parents before the census was taken in June 1933. The overall Jewish population in Germany, however, undoubtedly reduced even more between 1933 and the time of the census by emigration. Thus, the 5.92 figure may actually be a slight overestimate. The crude birth rate in Germany between 2004 and 2006 was 8.2–8.4 per 1,000, down from 11.4 in 1990 ("Crude Birth and Death Rates for Selected Countries," www.infoplease.com/ipa/A0004395.html).

Table 4.44. Changes in Jewish Marriages and Births (index: 1913 = 100)

Year	Marriages in Germany						Live births in Prussia						All Jewish women	
	Homogeneous marriages	Index	Intermarriages	Index	Total Jews marrying	Index	To inmarried Jewish women	Index	Out of wedlock	Index	To intermarried couples	Index		Index
1913	3621	100	1122	100	8364	100	5497	100	365	100	776	100	6638	100
1914	2617	72.27	1344	119.79	6578	78.65	5281	96.07	308	84.38	782	100.77	6535	98.45
1915	1098	30.23	1143	101.87	3339	39.92	4195	79.44	276	75.62	722	93.04	5193	78.23
1916	1292	35.68	967	86.19	3551	42.46	3000	54.58	223	61.10	613	78.99	3836	57.79
1917	1402	38.72	1035	92.25	3839	45.90	2505	45.70	175	47.95	519	66.88	3199	48.19
1918	2171	59.96	1084	96.61	5426	64.87	2595	47.21	180	49.32	569	73.32	3344	50.38
1919	6295	**173.85**	1926	**171.66**	14519	**173.59**	3746	68.15	214	58.63	720	92.78	4680	70.50
1920	7497	**207.04**	2211	**197.06**	17205	**205.70**	5640	102.60	351	96.16	877	113.02	6868	103.46
1921	5617	**155.12**	1893	**168.72**	13124	**156.91**	6124	111.41	386	105.75	872	112.37	7382	111.21
1922	5025	**138.77**	2038	**181.64**	12088	**144.52**	5572	101.36	380	104.11	829	106.83	6781	102.15
1923	4833	**133.47**	2008	**178.97**	11674	**139.57**	5705	103.78	401	109.86	763	98.32	6869	103.48
1924	3310	91.41	1547	**137.88**	8167	97.64	5221	94.98	326	89.32	747	96.26	6294	94.82

Year														
1925	2904	80.20	1413	**125.94**	7221	86.33	4680	85.14	345	94.52	760	97.94	5785	87.15
1926	2656	73.34	1315	117.20	6627	79.23	4135	75.22	279	76.44	585	75.39	4999	75.31
1927	2789	77.02	1505	**134.14**	7083	84.68	3729	67.84	291	79.73	674	86.86	4694	70.71
1928	2983	82.38	1604	**142.96**	7570	90.51	3675	66.85	235	64.38	645	83.12	4555	68.62
1929	2817	77.80	1664	**148.31**	7298	87.25	3283	59.72	221	60.55	579	74.61	4083	61.51
1930	2851	78.74	1642	**146.35**	7344	87.80	3004	54.65	209	57.26	622	80.15	3835	57.77
1931	2484	68.60	1405	**125.22**	6373	76.20	2640	48.03	186	50.96	508	65.46	3334	50.23
1932	2307	63.71	1378	**122.82**	5992	71.64	2096	38.13	173	47.40	441	56.83	2710	40.83

Data in bold—index over 120

Red—index below 80

Sources: births until 1928: Silbergleit, *Die Bevölkerungs- und Berufsverhältnisse*, 39*; births after 1928: Schmelz, handwritten table "Lebensgeborene Staat Preussen"; marriages: *Statistisches Jahrbuch für das Deutsche Reich* (1915): 27, (1916): 27, (1918): 7, (1919): 44, (1920): 32, (1921–1922): 41, (1923): 31, (1924–1925): 35, (1926): 28, (1927): 29, (1928): 33, (1929): 31, (1930): 33, (1931): 30, (1932): 30, (1933): 32, (1934): 32.

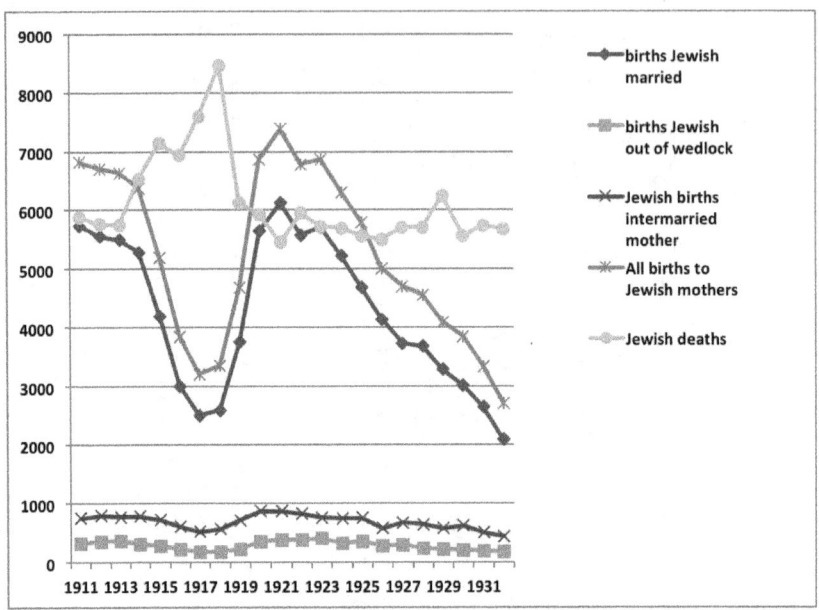

FIG. 4.3. Jewish Births by Marital Status of Mothers, 1911–1932

Table 4.45. Indications of Increasing Homogeneous Jewish Marriage—Germany after 1933

Year	Homogeneous Jewish marriages	Intermarriages between Jews and non-Jews (religious definition)	Total number of Jews marrying
1933	2,174	1,693	6,041
1934	2,522	792	5,836
1935	2,751	503	6,005
1936	2,665	90	5,420
1938 (*Altreich*)	2,851	93	5,795

Sources: *Statistisches Jahrbuch für das Deutsche Reich* (1935): 41, (1936): 41, (1937): 43, (1938): 46, (1939–1940): 52.

Jewish population—especially those of childbearing age—during those years (Table 4.46).

As economic, social, and political developments made Jews ever more reluctant to marry, the average age of Jews at marriage showed a marked increase during the late Weimar and early Nazi period. In 1925, half[54] of the male Jewish population was married by age thirty, as was half of the female Jewish population at age twenty-six. These figures indicate later marriage ages among Jews than among the general population, especially for men.[55] The 1933 census shows a further delay in Jewish marriages, with half of Jewish men marrying by age thirty-three and half of Jewish women by twenty-eight. The 1939 statistics are skewed by the mass emigration of German Jews, especially those in the younger age groups. In 1939, the ages at which the "never married" category ceases to be the majority for racially "full Jews" who were also Jews by religion[56] were twenty-nine for women and thirty-four for men. Although this may be a mere reflection of emigration patterns, it also seems to indicate continued difficulties for Jews in finding marriage partners (Table 4.47).

Death Rates

As the average age of the Jewish population increased steadily, the Jewish advantage over the general population in crude death rates decreased and finally turned around. Since Jewish infant mortality had already fallen off vigorously before World War I, it had little further decline left to accomplish. The annual number of Jewish deaths remained fairly constant throughout the Weimar era, even as Jewish births plummeted. By the 1920s, the overall Jewish death rates per 1,000 exceeded those of the non-Jewish population and were increasing while the non-Jewish rates were decreasing.

---

54 For the purposes of these statistics we count all persons not listed as single (*ledig*) as married, even if their status in the statistics was widowed or divorced because all of these had been married at some previous time.

55 The average age of first marriages in Germany as a whole in 1925 was 27.5 for men and 25.3 for women. In 1933, the figures were unchanged for men and 25.4 for women. Statistisches Bundesamt, *Bevölkerung und Wirtschaft 1872–1972* (Stuttgart and Mainz, 1972), 105.

56 For "half-Jews" of all religions the figures were only slightly less extreme. "Never married" ceased to be the majority category at age 29 for "half-Jewish" women and at 32 for "half-Jewish" men. For "quarter-Jews" the comparative figures were 26 for women and 28 for men, an indication that "quarter-Jews" experienced relatively little difficulty finding a mate compared to "half-Jews" and "full Jews."

Table 4.46. Local Statistics Indicating Recovery in Jewish Births after 1933

Year	Frankfurt	Berlin	Königsberg, births to:	
			In-married Jewish couples	All of Jewish ancestry
1924	431		103	113
1925	416		50	61
1926	350		64	76
1927	326		62	73
1928	328		46	52
1929	282 [257]		46	51
1930	277 [236]	1215	42	55
1931	247 [190]	1055	32	38
1932	169 [127]	865	20	27
1933	135 [107]	775	20	25
1934	100 [67]	545	14	18
1935	127 [103]	695	17	21
1936	[83]		17	21

Sources:

Frankfurt: *Beiträge zur Statistik der Stadt Frankfurt am Main* (1924); "Die Schrumpfung einer jüdischen Grossgemeinde—Die Bevölkerungsbewegung der Israelitischen Gemeinde—Eine vorbildliche Statistik," *Bayerische Israelitische Gemeindezeitung* (March 15, 1934): 107; and *Gemeindeblatt der Israelitischen Gemeinde Frankfurt am Main* for 1929–1938. Figures in brackets reflect presumably only those registered with the Jewish community, while the other figures are those registered with the government.

Berlin: "Über die Abnahme der jüdischen Bevölkerung in Deutschland. Die natürliche Bevölkerungsbewegung der Berliner Juden 1930–1935, *Bayerische Israelitische Gemeindezeitung* (April 15, 1936): 172.

Königsberg: *Königsberger Jüdische Gemeindeblatt* (June 1, 1927; October 1, 1928; February 1932; February 1933; February 1934; February 1, 1935; February 1937).

From 1914 onward, not including children of intermarriages, Jewish deaths outnumbered Jewish births every year except the baby-boom period (1920–1923). By the mid-1920s, the death rate of German Jews exceeded their birth rate (Table 4.48). Even including children of intermarriages, there were more Jewish deaths than births every year starting in 1926. The excess seemed to increase from year to year. By the early 1930s, more than twice as many Jews

Table 4.47. Evidence of Rising Jewish Marriage Age, 1925–1933

Age	Changing marriage patterns in 20–39 age group: Percent never married			
	1925 (Prussia)		1933 (Germany)	
	Males	Females	Males	Females
20	3072 (99.5%)	3021 (92.5%)	3301 (99.8%)	3203 (97.0%)
21	3061 (98.9%)	2773 (85.4%)	3335 (99.4%)	3286 (94.1%)
22	3576 (96.9%)	2709 (78.0%)	3268 (99.4%)	3027 (88.9%)
23	3182 (92.9%)	2348 (68.4%)	3304 (97.4%)	2902 (83.3%)
24	3075 (88.4%)	2008 (59.9%)	3226 (95.3%)	2793 (76.9%)
25	3011 (80.4%)	1889 (51.8%)	3324 (92.9%)	2513 (68.1%)
26	2602 (73.9%)	**1665 (45.6%)**	3013 (87.5%)	2308 (60.8%)
27	2327 (67.5%)	1528 (40.4%)	2888 (83.2%)	2041 (53.5%)
28	2093 (60.5%)	1259 (35.0%)	2649 (78.4%)	**1848 (47.8%)**
29	1864 (55.2%)	1299 (34.1%)	2485 (70.9%)	1731 (42.8%)
30	**1691 (49.1%)**	1129 (30.6%)	2329 (66.3%)	1446 (37.4%)
31	1461 (44.8%)	1027 (28.8%)	2244 (57.2%)	1448 (34.6%)
32	1298 (40.4%)	1004 (28.2%)	2007 (51.7%)	1244 (30.9%)
33	1128 (36.4%)	833 (24.6%)	**1852 (45.8%)**	1141 (26.9%)
34	979 (31.7%)	829 (24.0%)	1667 (40.8%)	1101 (25.6%)
35	996 (30.8%)	828 (23.0%)	1447 (35.6%)	1135 (24.9%)
36	872 (27.1%)	719 (20.9%)	1277 (31.2%)	983 (22.1%)
37	841 (25.8%)	744 (21.5%)	1176 (29.0%)	988 (21.5%)
38	714 (22.8%)	659 (19.5%)	1033 (26.0%)	911 (20.3%)
39	690 (21.4%)	671 (19.3%)	902 (22.7%)	892 (20.3%)
		Born 1893:	863 (22.7%)	879 (20.1%)

Data in bold: earliest age at which never-married people were no longer a majority of the age group.

Sources: Silbergleit, *Die Bevölkerungs- und Berufsverhältnisse*, 3–7; 1933 census, 5/42–43.

died every year than were born, which was almost as negative a ratio as in the worst years of the First World War (Table 4.49, Figure 4.3).

Jewish communal leaders found this development frightening because it meant that the Jewish population of Germany was bound to decrease absent substantial immigration. It was, however, not a sign of a medically unhealthy Jewish population. The rise in the crude death rate was the natural result of the German Jews' rising average age. In terms of age-specific death rates or life expectancy, the Jewish community continued to compare favorably with the rest of the German population.

Hamburg was one of the places where demographers noted the rising Jewish crude death rate. Arthur Ruppin viewed the fact that the crude death rate of Hamburg Jews had increased from 11.4 per 1,000 in 1910 to 15.4 in 1921–1925 while the Christian rate fell from 14.7 to 10.8 with some alarm.[57] An analysis of the age-specific death rate shows that despite the higher crude birth rate, the death rate in the younger age groups remained lower for Jews than for non-Jews, while in the oldest age groups Jewish death rates were slightly higher than the average (Table 4.50 A and B).

---

57 Ruppin, *Soziologie*, vol. 1, 238–239.

Table 4.48. Death Rates of Jews and General Population in Prussia

Year	Average, general population	Annual deaths, general population	Annual deaths, Jewish population	Jewish deaths as percent of total deaths
1913	41,649,062	620,571	5,741	0.93
1914	42,233,453	805,669	6,535	0.81
1915	42,364,107	864,551	7,140	0.83
1916	42,244,353	804,555	6,931	0.86
1917	42,042,359	864,551	7,591	0.88
1918	41,768,120	1,052,535	8,459	0.80
1919	39,536,126	628,130	6,128	0.98
1920	38,410,549	589,819	5,921	1.00
1921	38,887,722	530,066	5,449	1.03
1922	37,189,158	539,426	5,942	1.10
1923	37,486,493	522,826	5,717	1.09
1924	37,779,915	459,046	5,685	1.24
1925	38,130,052	450,973	5,554	1.23
1926	38,446,761	445,754	5,504	1.23
1927	38,727,068	461,938	5,697	1.23
1928	38,991,000	449,709	5,704	1.27
1929	39,289,880	494,042	6,235	1.39
1930	39,523,260	431,525	5,559	1.29
1931	39,749,614	440,810	5,728	1.30
1932			5,677	

Sources: Silbergleit, *Die Bevölkerungs- und Berufsverhältnisse*, 39*; *Statistisches Jahrbuch für den Freistaat Preussen* (1933): 26; Schmelz, handwritten table "Sterbefälle Preussen Staat."

Table 4.49. Jewish Births and Deaths in Prussia, 1911–1932 (Excluding Stillbirths)

Year	Births to homogeneous Jewish couples	Out-of-wedlock births to Jewish mothers	Subtotal	Children of intermarriage	Total births to parents of Jewish origin	Jewish deaths	Deaths as percent of births (including intermarried)
1911	5735	320	6055	759	6814	5877	86.3
1912	5549	347	5896	803	6699	5753	85.9
1913	5497	365	5862	776	6638	5741	86.5
1914	5281	308	5589	782	6371	6535	102.6
1915	4195	276	4471	722	5193	7140	137.5
1916	3000	223	3223	613	3836	6931	180.7
1917	2505	175	2680	519	3199	7591	227.0
1918	2595	180	2775	569	3344	8459	253.0
1919	3746	214	3960	720	4680	6128	130.9
1920	5640	351	5991	877	6868	5921	86.2
1921	6124	386	6510	872	7382	5449	73.8
1922	5572	380	5952	829	6781	5942	87.6
1923	5705	401	6106	763	6869	5717	83.2
1924	5221	326	5547	747	6294	5685	90.3

Year	Births to homogeneous Jewish couples	Out-of-wedlock births to Jewish mothers	Subtotal	Children of intermarriage	Total births to parents of Jewish origin	Jewish deaths	Deaths as percent of births (including intermarried)
1925	4680	345	5025	760	5785	5554	96.0
1926	4135	279	4414	585	4999	5504	110.1
1927	3729	291	4020	674	4694	5697	121.4
1928	3675	235	3910	645	4555	5704	125.2
1929	3283	221	3504	579	4083	6235	152.7
1930	3004	209	3213	622	3835	5559	145.0
1931	2640	186	2826	508	3334	5728	171.8
1932	2096	173	2269	441	2710	5677	209.5

Sources: Silbergleit, *Die Bevölkerungs- und Berufsverhältnisse*, 39* (up to 1928); Schmelz, handwritten tables "Lebendgeborene Preussen Staat" and "Sterbefälle Preussen Staat."

Table 4.50. Age at Death in Jewish Communities in Various Parts of Germany, 1920s and 1930s

A) Age at Death in General and Jewish Populations—Saxony, 1927–1936

Population	0–14	15–19	20–29	30–39	40–49	50–59	60–69	70–79	80+	Percent of deaths after age 60
Jewish	92	6	40	69	135	245	354	360	131	
Percent of all	6.4	0.4	2.8	4.8	9.4	17.1	24.7	25.1	9.2	59.0
General	47990	4755	17449	18840	24677	42416	69082	80992	39581	
Percent of all	13.9	1.4	5.1	5.5	7.1	12.3	20.0	23.4	11.5	54.9
Percent Jewish in each age group	0.19	0.13	0.23	0.37	0.55	0.58	0.51	0.44	0.33	

B) Jewish Deaths in Frankfurt (68.71 Statistische Übersicht, in *Gemeindeblatt der Israelitischen Gemeinde Frankfurt am Main*, Leo Baeck Institute Jerusalem, Special Collection Schmelz)

Year	0–1	1–5	6–14	15–29	20–29	30–39	40–49	50–59	60–69	70+
1929–1936	38	26	26	20	75	98	166	390	639	966
Percent of all	1.6	1.1	1.1	0.8	3.1	4.0	6.8	16.0	26.2	39.5
1929–1932	26	21	18	11	45	61	101	231	380	567
1933–1934, 1936	12	5	8	9	30	37	65	159	259	399

For age-specific death rates in Hamburg, see Table 4.26 B.

Conclusion

Even at the beginning of the nineteenth century, German Jewry had some typically Western or modern demographic features, including late marriage and low infant mortality. In the course of the late nineteenth and early twentieth centuries, Jews in Germany made the demographic transition to low fertility and low mortality considerably earlier than did the general population and did so in a geographically more uniform and temporally less drawn-out manner. While the rest of the population eventually caught up and developed very similar patterns, these trends gave German Jewry a very distinctive appearance in the early twentieth century. Jewish patterns during the late Weimar Republic era demonstrated greater sensitivity to economic and political upturns and downturns than those of the general population. In the last pre-Hitler years, Jews exhibited the symptoms of extremely low birth rates, general aging, and subreplacement behavior that did not become common among the general European population until more than half a century later. At the time, these trends seemed indicative of a specifically Jewish demographic crisis; in the longer term, however, they may be seen as further indications that German Jewry's patterns were chronologically earlier but not qualitatively very different than patterns in the general German population.

Appendix

Various Measures of Fertility and Infant Mortality Decline

Many different measures of fertility and fertility decline are available to researchers. Because Jewish data have been subject to less thorough analysis than the general statistics for Germany, some of the more complex and more accurate measuring tools are not available for the German-Jewish population. Sometimes, too, the statistics available for the two populations are not the same. The classical study of German fertility decline—John E. Knodel's *The Decline of Fertility in Germany, 1871–1939*—used the index of marital fertility (Ig) in most of its statistics. These data, which require knowledge of the size of the overall population by age and marital status, are rarely available for the Jewish population before 1925. Thus, where a uniform index of fertility is unavailable for both populations, I tried to compare at least the rate of decline in the same period as a proxy for comparison.[58]

---

58 The measures of fertility that may be used as indicators of a decline in fertility in order from crudest to most sophisticated are total births, birth rate per 1,000 of population, general fertility rate, marital fertility rate, and index of general or marital fertility (Knodel's If and Ig, described below). The general fertility rate (births per woman of childbearing age) and the marital fertility rate (legitimate births per married women of childbearing age) filter out distortions caused by changes in age structure. John Knodel and other participants in the Office of Population Research at Princeton University used mainly indexes that compared the fertility rates of various populations with the number of children who would have been born had the population had the same fertility as the Hutterites of Canada, who had the highest rate

The disadvantage of using crude birth rates is that they do not take into account the age structure of the population. To ascertain whether a decline in birth rates was caused by a change in fertility behavior or merely reflected a changing age structure, it is necessary to use the more precise general fertility and marital fertility rates. The demographers of the Princeton Fertility Project used a series of indexes that compared the age-specific birth rates of the studied population to the schedule of Hutterites' age-specific fertility. Given the scarcity of accurate age, gender, and marital status information for Jews, especially in the nineteenth century, we can calculate only approximate general and marital fertility rates and the Princeton project indexes, but with no semblance of chronological continuity.[59]

---

of natural fertility known to demographers. The indexes used by Knodel et al. are If (index of general fertility—children born divided by children born had the female population had the same age-specific fertility as Hutterite women), Ig (index of marital fertility—the number of children born to married women divided by the number of children born had the married female population had the same age-specific fertility as Hutterite women), and Ih (index of non-marital fertility, children born to unmarried women divided by children who would have been born to unmarried women if they had the same age-specific fertility as Hutterite women).

59 We often have to readjust the existing figures to make them comparable. Many demographers calculate the childbearing population as comprising women aged 15–44; others use 15–49 or 16–50. In the case of Prussian figures from the mid-nineteenth century, the age structure is given only for persons aged 14–59 and require readjustment. For the purpose of this analysis, all age distribution figures were adjusted approximately to equal the female population aged 15–44. The adjustments of the raw figures are explained in the footnotes. I used known age distributions from as close to the period of the original figures as possible. Another complication relates to the data on births. Some of the data include actual births (either live or including stillbirths). Other data, however, specify only the number of babies under the age of one. This figure almost always underestimates actual births because it excludes children who died before their first birthday and does not take into account in- or out-migration by families with infants. The discrepancy is greater in the nineteenth century, when infant mortality exceeded twentieth-century levels.

Table 4.51. Changes in General Fertility Rate and Percent of Childbearing Women in the Population as Components of Declining Birth Rates

Year	Place	Childbearing women as percent of population	General fertility rate	Crude birth rate, per 1,000
(Figures are for Jews unless otherwise stated)				
1855	Prussia	24.2%[60]	0.142	34.39
1861	Prussia	24.1%[61]	0.140	33.69
1880	Frankfurt	26.1%[62]	0.090[63]	23.31
1905	Berlin	25.8%	0.057[64]	14.61
			0.065[65]	16.81
1905	Hesse-Darmstadt	22.1%[66]	0.080[67]	17.54
			0.062[68]	
1910	Hesse-Darmstadt	24.2%[69]	0.069[70]	16.66
			0.061	
			0.06[71]	

[60] Women 14–59 as a percentage of total population (29.45 percent) multiplied by 82.03 percent (percent of Berlin Jewish women 16–45 in 1871 divided by percent of Berlin Jewish women aged 16–60 in 1871).

[61] Women 14–59 as a percentage of total population (29.38 percent) multiplied by 82.03 percent (percent of Berlin Jewish women 16–45 in 1871 divided by percent of Berlin Jewish women aged 16–60 in 1871).

[62] Women 14–49 (28.23 percent) multiplied by 92.29 percent (percent of Berlin Jewish women 16–45 in 1871 divided by Berlin Jewish women 16–49 in 1871).

[63] Including all children of Jewish mothers (including those born out of wedlock and to intermarried Jews).

[64] Jewish population below the age of one year (13 percent less than number of births to Jewish mothers in 1904).

[65] Total births to Jewish women in 1904 (1905 data missing in Schmelz's table).

[66] Women 15–49 multiplied by 88.44 percent (percent of Berlin Jewish women 16–45 in 1905 divided by Jewish women 16–50 in 1905).

[67] Jewish population below one year of age (13 percent fewer than births to Jewish mothers in 1904).

[68] Dividing the 415 Jewish births in 1905 by the 6677 Jewish women between the ages of 15 and 50.

[69] Women 15–49 (27.34 percent) multiplied by 88.44 percent (percent of Berlin Jewish women 16–45 in 1905 divided by Jewish women 16–50 in 1905).

[70] Jewish population below one year of age (13 percent fewer than births to Jewish mothers in 1904).

[71] Based on children born to the 6,580 Jewish women between the ages of 15 and 50. The lower figure is calculated from the 401 Jewish children under one year of age in 1910 and the higher figure from the 414 actually born in 1910.

Year	Place	Childbearing women as percent of population	General fertility rate	Crude birth rate, per 1,000
	Hesse-Darmstadt		**0.098**	
			0.113[72]	
1925	Prussia	25.2%	0.053	13.27
		25.8%	**0.081**	
1924–1926	Bavaria	22.3%	0.053	11.82
1933	Germany	22.4%	0.026	5.83
1939	"Greater Germany"	15.7%	0.021[73]	3.30

Sources: *Tabellen und amtliche Nachrichten über den Preussischen Staat für das Jahr 1855* (Berlin, 1858), 114; *Preussicher Statistik* 5 (1864): 5; *Beiträge zur Statistik der Stadt Frankfurt*, alte Folge 4 (1882): 18, 70; Arthur Ruppin, "Zur Statistik der Juden im Grossherzogtum Hessen," *ZDSJ* 3, no. 11 (1907): 168; Ludwig Knöpfel, "Die jüdische Bevölkerung vom Grossherzogtum Hessen nach den Ergebnissen der Volkszählung vom 1. Dezember 1910," *ZDSJ* 8, nos. 7–8 (1912): 97–103; Silbergleit, *Die Bevölkerungs- und Berufsverhältnisse*, 39*, 56*–57*, 62*, 70*–71*; Ph. Schwartz, "Nachwuchsverhältnisse der jüdischen Familien in Bayern," *Bayerische Israelitische Gemeindezeitung* (April 1, 1930): 105; data for Germany 1933 is from the 1933 census, 5/17, 42; Germany 1939: *Statistik des deutschen Reichs* 552 (1944): 4/48–51, 56–57.

---

72 Based on the 31,6701 Christian women between the ages of 15 and 50 in Hesse in 1910. The lower figure counts the 31,009 children under one year of age; the higher figure counts all Christian children born in 1910.
73 Based on children under the age of one.

Table 4.52. Changes in Marital Fertility Rate and Percent of Childbearing Married Women in Population, 1910–1939

	Married Jewish women aged 15–49	Births to Jewish women	Marital fertility rate*
Grand Duchy of Hesse, 1910	3530	401 (under 1)	0.113
	2988 (15–44)	401	0.134
		402 (legitimate births for 1910)	0.114
	Married women aged 15–44	**Births to married women**	**Marital fertility rate**
Prussia, 1925			
Jews	51060	4680 (legitimate births only)	0.092
		5025 (including illegitimate births)	0.098
Christians	4,810,441	796,879 (including illegitimate births)	0.166
	Married women aged 16–45	**Legitimate live births**	**Marital fertility rate**
Bavaria, 1924–1926			
Jews	4804	569	0.118
Christians	835115	141139	0.169
Germany, 1933	**Married Jewish women aged 15–44 (born 1888–1917)**	**Births to Jewish women (including illegitimate births)**	**Marital fertility rate**

	Married Jewish women aged 15–49	Births to Jewish women	Marital fertility rate*
Grand Duchy of Hesse, 1910	58503	2908[74]	c. 0.050
	Married Jewish women aged 16–44 (*Glaubensjuden*)	Births to Jewish women (*Glaubensjuden* under age 1)	Marital fertility rate
Greater Germany, 1939	24209	1008	0.042

* Marital fertility rate = births divided by number of married women in age group 15–44.

Sources:

Hesse 1910: Knöpfel, "Die jüdische Bevölkerung vom Grossherzogtum Hessen," 101–102;

Prussia 1925: Silbergleit, *Die Bevölkerungs- und Berufsverhältnisse*, 39*, 70*–71*;

Bavaria 1924–1926: Schwartz, "Nachwuchsverhältnisse," 105;

Germany 1933: 1933 census, 5/42;

Germany 1939: *Statistik des deutschen Reichs* 552 (1944), 4/48–51, 56–57.

Since only a portion of the childbearing population was married, the marital fertility rate was always considerably higher than the general fertility rate. This was especially true in the German Jewish population, which had comparatively lower rates both of marriage and of out-of-wedlock births than the general population (Table 4.19).

Only the 1925 census and, in a few respects, that of 1910, yield sufficient data on the marital status of Jews by age to calculate the index of marital fertility (Ig) used in Knodel's study of fertility decline in Germany. In this manner, we can compare it with figures for the overall population in the major geographic regions of Germany.

---

[74] The number of Jewish births was estimated by taking two-thirds of the sum of those born in 1932 and in 1933 before the census (June 15). It is assumed that fewer Jewish children were born in 1933 than in 1932.

5

Changing Age Structure

As in all populations, the age distribution within German Jewry was a function of changing birth, death, and migration patterns. Rising birth rates and falling infant mortality rates tended to raise the percentage of the population that was very young. In-migration tended to boost the proportion of the population in young adulthood, while out-migration tended to lower the share of those age groups. Falling birth rates and increasing longevity tended to induce population aging. Sometimes the trends reinforced each other; such was the case when falling birth rates raised the average age, reducing the percentage of women of childbearing years, and in turn pushing birth rates even lower. The trend in European populations since the late nineteenth century has been toward steady aging. Although Jewish demographers of the early twentieth century viewed this development with alarm, it seems integral to the general demographic transition in developed countries. As with many other demographic phenomena, the transition from a youthful to an aging population was more extreme and earlier among Jews than among non-Jews in Germany.

The relatively fragmentary early documentation of the German-Jewish age distribution shows a relatively youthful population, sometimes even younger than the German population at large. In Prussia in the middle of the nineteenth century, the relative youth of the Jewish population gave way to a slowly rising average age (Table 5.1). Unlike later periods in which women were known

Table 5.1. Age Distribution of Jews in Prussia, 1852–1861

Age	1852	1855	1861
0–14	37.0	36.9	36.6
14–59	57.05	57.0	56.8
60+	5.9	6.1	6.6

Source: *Tabellen und amtliche Nachrichten über den Preussischen Staat für das Jahr 1852* (Berlin, 1855), 118; *Tabellen und amtliche Nachrichten über den Preussischen Staat für das Jahr 1855* (Berlin, 1858), 114; *Preussicher Statistik* 5 (1864): 5.

to have greater longevity, men outnumbered women in the older age group. Death in childbirth probably explains this only in part (Table 5.2). Jews in the countryside (*Plattes Land*) were slightly younger than urban Jews, again the reverse of later patterns (Table 5.3). Those in the densely Jewish provinces in the east were somewhat younger than those living in the western parts of Prussia or in sparsely Jewish provinces of central Germany. Particularly high percentages of persons of middle age (14–59) were found in areas of heavy in-migration, especially the central districts of Prussia (such as Stralsund, Berlin, Breslau, and

Table 5.2. Gender Distribution of Jews over Sixty in Prussia

Gender	1852	1855	1861
Male	7076 (52.8%)	7392 (51.8%)	8653 (51.9%)
Female	6324 (47.2%)	6878 (48.2%)	8021 (48.1%)

Sources: as in Table 5.1.

Table 5.3. Difference in Jewish Age Distribution between Cities and Countryside, Prussia

Area	1852			1855		
	0–14	14–59	60+	0–14	14–59	60+
Städte (cities)	64,950 (36.5%)	102,559 (57.6%)	10,627 (6.0%)	66,515 (36.3%)	105,249 (57.5%)	11,375 (6.2%)
Plattes Land (countryside)	18,826 (39.1%)	26,506 (55.2%)	2,773 (5.8%)	19,555 (38.9%)	27,872 (54.8%)	2,895 (5.8%)

Since Jews were more likely to live outside the cities in the western parts of Prussia where Jews were older on average than in the eastern areas, these data may understate the difference between cities and countryside.
Sources: as in Table 5.1.

Merseburg). High percentages of persons over sixty were found in most of the western districts. The share of the 60+ bracket was extraordinarily high in the isolated, rural South German district of Hohenzollern (Table 5.4).

Records from the Hesse area and, especially, from the city of Frankfurt, also show a Jewish population that was somewhat younger than the population at large. According to Schmelz's explanation, reasonably high Jewish fertility coupled with relatively low infant mortality led to an overrepresentation of children among Jews. Thus, in 1828, some 40 percent of Jews in the city of Darmstadt were under fourteen years of age, and in 1808 33 percent of Jews in Frankfurt were under fifteen—a somewhat lower percentage than in Darmstadt.[1] The 1858 Frankfurt census showed Jews overrepresented among persons in both the under-21 and the over-48 cohorts, leaving non-Jews more concentrated in the middle brackets. This may have been the result of legal restrictions that held migration to the city smaller in percentage terms among Jews than among Christians (Table 5.5). Overall, the Jewish population was somewhat younger than the overall population of the city.

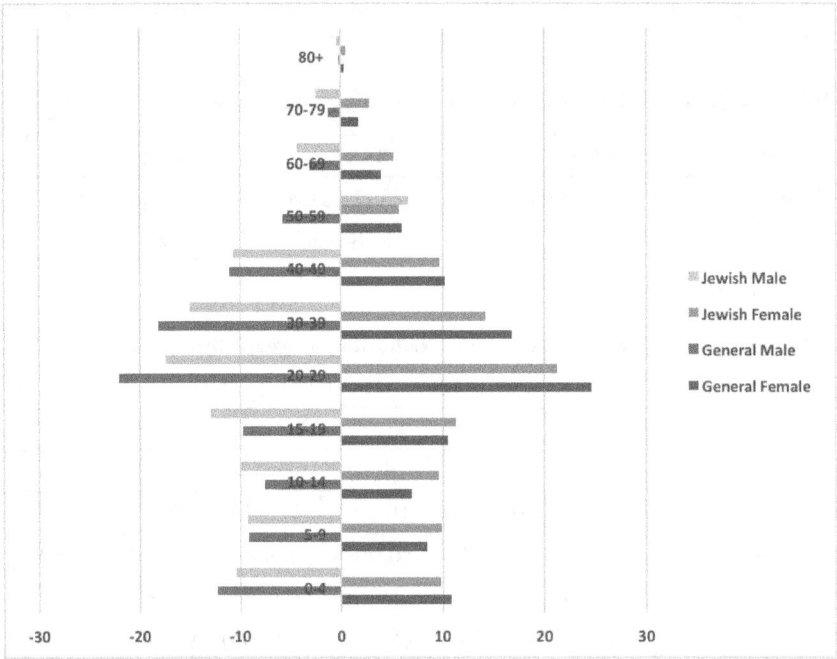

Fig. 5.1. Frankfurt Age Distribution, 1880

---

1 Schmelz, *Hessen*, 124, 125

Table 5.4. Jewish Age Distribution by Prussian Government District (RB) and Province (percentages)

District and Province	1852			1855		
	Under 14	14–59	60+	Under 14	14–59	60+
RB Königsberg	36.8	58.4	4.8	37.5	58.5	4.05
RB Gumbinnen	38.7	58.4	2.9	37.8	59.1	3.1
RB Danzig	37.9	56.3	5.9	38.3	56.0	5.7
RB Marienwerder	41.7	53.0	5.3	42.2	52.6	5.2
Province: East and West Prussia	39.9	54.9	5.2	40.25	54.7	5.0
RB Stettin	37.8	57.1	5.8	39.4	55.6	5.0
RB Köslin	41.6	52.7	5.7	41.0	53.8	5.2
RB Stralsund	22.4	69.0	8.6	28.6	64.5	6.9
Province: Pomerania	39.2	55.3	5.5	39.9	55.0	5.1
RB Posen	36.8	57.4	5.8	36.2	57.9	5.9
RB Bromberg	40.2	54.0	5.8	39.0	53.3	7.7
Province: Posen	37.9	56.3	5.8	37.1	56.4	6.5
RB Breslau	32.3	63.1	4.5	32.9	62.9	4.25
RB Oppeln	39.7	55.5	4.8	39.4	55.85	4.7
RB Liegnitz	34.5	59.2	6.3	34.4	58.9	6.7
Province: Silesia	36.3	58.8	4.9	36.4	58.8	4.8

The Population History of German Jewry 1815–1939

RB Berlin	31.3	63.7	5.0	30.3	64.6	5.1
Province: Brandenburg	34.3	60.0	5.7	34.1	60.1	5.7
RB Magdeburg	35.1	58.1	6.8	35.8	57.4	6.8
RB Merseburg	35.7	59.0	5.3	38.2	56.75	5.0
RB Erfurt	34.6	58.6	6.8	34.5	58.9	6.6
Province: Saxony	35.0	58.4	6.6	35.6	57.9	6.5
RB Münster	32.1	58.9	9.0	31.7	59.3	9.0
RB Minden	34.5	57.6	7.9	36.6	55.8	7.6
RB Arnsberg	36.4	56.3	7.3	35.9	57.0	7.1
Province: Westphalia	34.7	57.4	7.9	35.25	57.05	7.7
RB Cologne	34.5	58.5	7.0	34.9	58.4	6.7
RB Düsseldorf	33.5	58.8	7.7	34.35	57.7	7.95
RB Koblenz	36.8	56.3	6.9	36.1	56.8	7.1
RB Trier	38.9	53.9	7.2	37.6	55.7	6.75
RB Aachen	32.7	59.0	8.3	32.6	58.6	8.7
Province: Rhineland	35.4	57.3	7.3	35.3	57.4	7.3
RB Hohenzollern	35.1	54.2	10.7	34.2	51.4	14.4

Sources: as in Table 5.1.

Table 5.5. Age Distributions in Frankfurt, 1858 (*Staatsgebiet*)

Age	General population	Percent of general population (excluding unknown)	Jews	Percent of Jews (excluding unknown)	Jews as percent of total age group
0–6	6767	9.1	580	10.3	8.6
6–15	10015	13.5	878	15.5	8.8
15–21	11543	15.6	1027	18.2	8.9
21–24	5738	7.7	374	6.6	6.5
24–36	17330	23.4	950	16.8	5.5
36–48	10679	14.4	725	12.8	6.8
48–60	7525	10.1	670	11.9	8.9
60+	4562	6.2	449	7.9	9.8
Unknown	1055		80		
Percent under 24:		45.9		50.6	

Source: *Beiträge zur Statistik der freien Stadt Frankfurt*, 1, no. 3 (1861): 21 (percentages recalculated to exclude unknown).

The 1880 Frankfurt census shows only moderate change relative to 1858; Jewish birth rates were at the very beginning of their decline while Jewish migration to the city now exceeded the overall average (Table 5.6, Figure 5.1). Again, the Jewish percentage was greater among those under twenty and those over fifty. The median age of both Jews and Gentiles hovered in the mid-twenties.

Migration was an important factor in determining the age structure of the population (Table 5.7). Indeed, wherever comparative data on native-born and migrant Jews are available, the two populations diverge noticeably. In 1880, approximately sixty percent of both the general and the Jewish population of Frankfurt had migrated to the city. Those born there were much younger in median terms than in-migrants were. Most of those under the age of fifteen were born in Frankfurt; most of those between fifteen and eighty had migrated to the city. In the 15–69 age cohorts among the Jewish population and those in the 15–49 range among the general population, migrants were over 65 percent of the total. The fact that Jews were less represented in the 0–4 age group despite being otherwise overrepresented among the young may be the first sign of the decline in Jewish fertility that would soon become overwhelming. The higher percentage of migrants among Jews in the 10–19 and, especially, the 10–14 age bracket may have been caused by the greater tendency of Jews from outside Frankfurt to send their children to the city for schooling.[2]

Most of our information about the age distribution of the Jewish population during the Imperial period comes from major cities. The patterns in smaller towns and villages may have been quite different from those discussed below, but we lack the evidence necessary to be certain. In the period from 1871 to 1910, the urban Jewish population became noticeably older while the age structure of the general population of the same cities changed little. This is a reflection of the earlier and more thoroughgoing onset of fertility limitation among the Jewish population as well as differences in migration patterns between Jews and non-Jews.

---

2 This may also explain the predominance of males in these age groups among Jews but not among the general population. Another reason may be the higher percentage of young female domestic servants among the general population.

Percent Male—Frankfurt, 1880		
Age	Jewish population	General population
10–14	50.7%	49.6%
15–19	53.2%	44.0%

Table 5.6. Age Distributions in Frankfurt, 1880

Age	Jews			General Population			Jews as percent of age group
	Male	Female	Total	Male	Female	Total	
(Percent of total in column is given in parentheses)							
0–4	720 (10.4)	682 (9.8)	1402 (10.1)	7915 (12.3)	7816 (10.8)	15731 (11.5)	8.9
5–9	646 (9.3)	684 (9.9)	1330 (9.6)	5907 (9.2)	6051 (8.4)	11958 (8.7)	11.1
10–14	685 (9.9)	665 (9.6)	1350 (9.7)	4909 (7.6)	4983 (6.9)	9892 (7.2)	13.6
15–19	890 (12.9)	782 (11.3)	1672 (12.1)	5966 (9.7)	7605 (10.5)	13571 (9.9)	12.3
20–29	1200 (17.4)	1472 (21.2)	2672 (19.3)	14216 (22.0)	17774 (24.6)	31990 (23.4)	8.4
30–39	1038 (15.0)	987 (14.2)	2025 (14.6)	11706 (18.1)	12137 (16.8)	23843 (17.4)	8.5
40–49	737 (10.7)	670 (9.7)	1407 (10.2)	7107 (11.0)	7383 (10.2)	14490 (10.6)	9.7
50–59	462 (6.6)	409 (5.7)	871 (6.3)	3772 (5.8)	4305 (6.0)	8077 (5.9)	10.8
60–70	337 (4.4)	361 (5.2)	698 (5.0)	2080 (3.2)	2749 (3.9)	4829 (3.2)	14.5
70–80	170 (2.5)	191 (2.8)	361 (2.6)	821 (1.3)	1200 (1.7)	2021 (1.5)	17.9
80+	25 (0.4)	36 (0.5)	61 (0.4)	140 (0.2)	202 (0.3)	342 (0.3)	17.9
Unknown	4	3	22	61	32	93	
Percent under 20	42.5	40.5	41.5	38.7	36.6	37.4	
Percent under 30	59.9	61.7	60.8	60.7	61.2	60.8	

Source: *Beiträge zur Statistik der Stadt Frankfurt*, alte Folge 4 (1882): 18, 70.

Table 5.7. Difference in Age Distribution of Frankfurt Residents (Stadtsbezirk) Born in and outside the City, 1880

Age	Born in Frankfurt				Born elsewhere				Percent of age group born in Frankfurt	
	Jews	Percent	General population	Percent	Jews	Percent	General population	Percent	Jews	General
0–4	1293	22.9	13901	24.9	109	1.3	1830	2.3	92.2	88.3
5–9	1072	19.0	9110	16.3	258	3.1	2848	3.5	80.6	76.2
10–14	791	14.0	6527	11.7	559	6.8	3365	4.2	58.6	66.0
15–19	544	9.6	4708	8.4	1128	13.7	8865	11.0	32.5	34.7
20–29	560	9.9	6012	10.3	2112	25.7	25978	32.1	21.0	18.8
30–39	392	7.0	5147	9.2	1633	19.9	18696	23.1	19.4	21.6
40–49	372	6.6	4196	7.5	1035	12.6	10288	12.7	26.4	29.0
50–59	240	4.3	3075	5.5	631	7.7	5002	6.2	27.55	38.1
60–69	208	3.7	2067	3.7	490	6.0	2762	3.4	29.8	42.8
70–79	131	2.3	981	1.7	230	2.8	1040	1.3	36.3	48.5
80+	32	0.6	188	0.3	29	0.4	154	0.2	52.5	55.0
Unknown	3		14		4		79			
Totals and median ages	5638	c. 12	58626	c. 15	8218	c. 30	80907	c. 28	40.7	42.0

Source: as in Table 5.6.

Table 5.8. Changing Age Structure in Munich, 1875–1910 (percentages)

Ages	1875	1880	1885	1890	1895	1900	1905	1910
0–15								
Jews	35.1	31.6	29.2	25.5	23.45	21.7	22.1	20.8
General	22.0	24.7	25.0	24.7	24.5	24.5	26.5	
16–30								
Jews	29.6	28.9	29.6	31.9	34.9	34.25	31.55	30.7
General	32.6	30.0	29.9	32.3	32.9	33.4	29.5	
31–50								
Jews	22.3	25.45	27.3	28.4	27.3	28.95	30.2	31.0
General	29.1	28.9	28.8	28.15	28.1	28.1	29.5	
51–70								
Jews	10.9	11.6	10.9	11.2	11.6	12.5	14.0	15.0
General	13.9	13.8	13.6	12.6	12.3	11.8	12.2	
70+								
Jews	2.1	2.5	3.2	2.9	2.7	2.6	2.1	2.5
General	2.4	2.5	2.7	2.3	2.3	2.2	2.3[3]	

Sources: Segall, *Entwicklung der jüdischen Bevölkerung München 1875–1905*, 13, 18, 25; and Cohen, "Die jüdische Bevölkerung in München im Jahre 1910," 123–124.

As a city with a high rate of Jewish in-migration, Munich yields a particularly rich dataset.[4] The decline in the percentage of Jews in the 0–15 age group is striking; equally perceptible is the lack of such a decline among the general population (Table 5.8, Figure 5.2). In 1875, the Jewish population of Munich was noticeably younger than the general population. By 1910, the opposite was true. The steady drop in the share of Jews under age fifteen between 1875 and 1900 must be related to the increased practice of birth control in Jewish families.

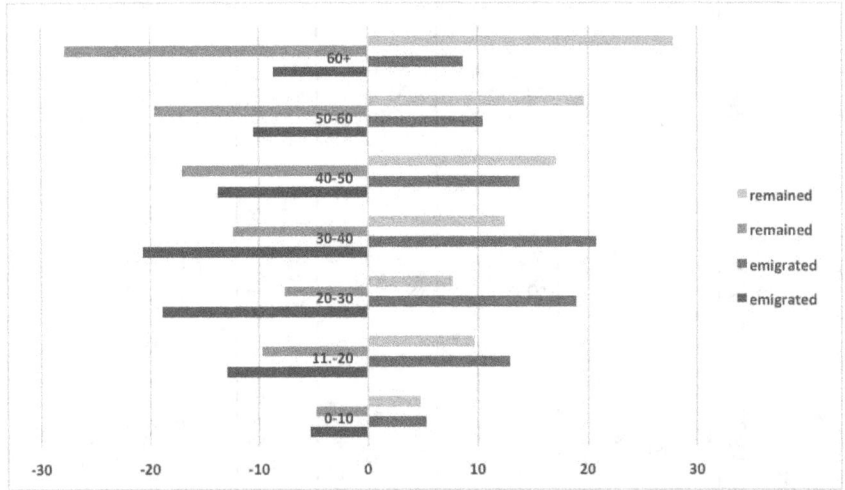

Fig. 5.2. Munich Emigrants vs. Non-Emigrants, 1938[5]

Munich Jews had a much higher rate of in-migration than Frankfurt Jewry, partly because Jewish residence in the former had been so restricted before 1861 that relatively few Jews native to the city had been born before that year. After 1880, the percentage of Jews in Munich who had been born elsewhere far exceeded the fraction of the general population that was not native to the city.[6] Migrants to Munich may be divided into three groups by place of birth, each of

---

4 Jakob Segall, *Die Entwicklung der jüdischen Bevölkerung in München 1875–1905: Ein Beitrag zur Kommunalstatistik* (Berlin: Bureau für Statistik der Juden, 1910), 13, 15, 18, 25; Carl von Tyszka, "Die jüdischen Bevölkerung von München nach dem Stande vom 1. Dezember 1905," *ZDSJ* (1907): 88; Arthur Cohen, "Die jüdischen Bevölkerung von München im Jahre 1910 mit besonderer Berücksichtigung der Gebürtigkeit," *ZDSJ* (1919): 123–124, 125, 129.
5 Editors' note: The data listed in Figure 5.2. are referred to in the following order from top to bottom: Jews, Total population.
6 For data on the birthplaces of Munich residents as percentages of the total municipal population in 1880–1905, see Table 7.39.

which had a distinctive age pattern. Compared with the general population of the city, Jews had a much lower percentage of migrants from elsewhere in Bavaria, a higher share from places in Germany outside of Bavaria, and the highest rate of all of persons born abroad. In general, Jews from elsewhere in Bavaria (mainly Franconian and Swabian villages) arrived first, those from elsewhere in Germany came later, and foreign-born Jews were among the most recent arrivals. In the censuses of 1905 and 1910, foreign-born Jews were noticeably younger and Bavarian-born Jews were perceptibly older than those who had migrated from non-Bavarian parts of Germany (Table 5.9). In the 16–30 age group, male Jewish inhabitants far outnumbered females, as most Jews who came to Munich in search of work appear to have been men. The gender imbalance was most noticeable among migrants from German locations outside Bavaria, who constituted the most recent group of migrants that came primarily for economic reasons. Among immigrants from Eastern Europe, whose immigration more frequently involved families, the imbalance was less extreme (Table 5.10).

Jews in most other major cities for which data are available displayed changing age patterns similar to those in Munich. Berlin, for instance, saw parallel developments (Table 5.11). By the early twentieth century, the youngest age groups had also shrunk among Jews in Hamburg and Berlin. Even in the largely rural state of Hesse-Darmstadt, the Jewish population was noticeably older than the non-Jewish population by 1910 (Table 5.12). Developments in Leipzig, however, ran contrary to changes elsewhere. The average age and the age patterns of Jews in Leipzig hardly changed between 1885 and 1905, evidently because an increasing proportion of Leipzig Jewry had been born in Eastern Europe. By the early twentieth century these immigrants were the majority of the city's Jewish population. The immigrant influx brought more people in young adulthood as well as, apparently, a population less affected by the fertility decline than native German Jews (Table 5.13). Leipzig Jewry remained relatively young well into the early twentieth century, boasting an age distribution that was almost identical to that of the general population of the city.

A salient difference in age distribution among subgroups of the Jewish population was found in some cities. In Greater Berlin, there were conspicuous differences between Jews born abroad and those born in Germany, as well as between those in richer districts as opposed to poorer ones. The foreign-born Jewish population was more heavily represented in the 15–50 age group than were native-born Jews, and was somewhat underrepresented among those over fifty (Table 5.14). In Berlin's wealthy western suburbs of Charlottenburg, Schöneberg, and Wilmersdorf, the Jewish population was older than in Berlin proper; they were younger in the poorer and more heavily immigrant suburbs of Neukölln and Lichtenberg (Table 5.15).

Table 5.9. Age Distribution of Munich Jews

Age	Born in Munich	Born elsewhere in Bavaria	Born elsewhere in Germany	Born abroad	All Munich Jews
1905					
0–15	1497 (51.9%)	123 (4.9%)	151 (7.3%)	369 (**14.3%**)	2225 (22.1%)
16–30	761 (26.4%)	679 (27.1%)	772 (**37.1%**)	961 (**37.1%**)	3173 (31.5%)
31–50	473 (16.4%)	904 (36.1%)	752 (**36.2%**)	905 (35.0%)	3034 (30.2%)
51–70	133 (4.6%)	671 (**26.8%**)	361 (17.4%)	244 (9.4%)	1409 (14.0%)
70+	18 (0.6%)	130 (**5.2%**)	43 (2.1%)	24 (0.9%)	215 (2.1%)
Total	2882	2507	2079	2503	10056
1910					
0–15	1629 (51.5%)	114 (4.4%)	138 (5.9%)	419 (**13.8%**)	2300 (20.8%)
16–30	784 (24.8%)	571 (22.2%)	816 (35.1%)	1237 (**40.8%**)	3408 (30.7%)
31–50	572 (18.1%)	966 (**37.6%**)	873 (**37.6%**)	1023 (33.8%)	3434 (31.0%)
51–70	149 (4.7%)	770 (30.0%)	428 (18.4%)	316 (10.4%)	1663 (15.0%)
70+	27 (0.9%)	147 (**5.7%**)	69 (3.0%)	35 (1.2%)	278 (2.5%)
Total	3161	2568	2324	3030	11083

Data in bold: highest row percentage among migrants.

Sources: von Tyszka, "Die jüdische Bevölkerung Münchens," 89; Cohen, "Die jüdische Bevölkerung in München im Jahre 1910," 123.

Table 5.10. Gender Balance among Munich Jews by Age and Place of Birth, 1905 (percentages)

Age	Born in Munich		Born elsewhere in Bavaria		Born elsewhere in Germany		Born abroad		All Munich Jews	
	Male	Female	Male	Female	Male	Female	Male	Female	Male	Female
0–15	50.0	50.0	54.5	45.5	49.7	50.3	45.8	54.2	49.35	50.65
16–30	48.0	52.0	61.1	38.9	67.4	32.6	62.1	37.9	59.8	40.2
31–50	49.7	50.3	54.0	46.0	57.85	42.15	55.25	44.75	54.65	45.35
51–70	46.6	53.4	53.1	46.9	52.35	47.65	56.6	43.4	52.9	47.1
70+	(38.9)	(61.1)	53.85	46.15	(51.2)	(48.8)	(33.3)	(66.7)	49.8	50.2
All age groups	49.2	50.8	55.7	44.3	59.7	40.3	56.1	43.9	54.7	45.3

In parentheses: N < 50.

Sources: calculated from von Tyszka, "Die jüdische Bevölkerung Münchens," 89.

Table 5.11. Changing Jewish Age Distribution in Berlin, 1871–1910 (amount and percentages)

Age	1871		1905*		1910	
0–5	3732	10.4%	7154	7.2%	7079	7.9%
6–10	3489	9.7	7070	7.2	5018	5.6
11–15	3315	9.2	7321	7.4	6627	7.4
Subtotal 0–15	10536	29.3	21545	21.8	18724	20.8
16–20	4205	11.7	8699	8.8	7791	8.7
21–25	4314	12.0	10182	10.3	8871	9.9
26–30	3771	10.5	10651	10.8	8588	9.5
Subtotal 16–30	12290	34.1	29532	29.9	25250	28.1
31–35	2954	8.2	9224	9.3	8814	9.8
36–40	2409	6.7	8161	8.3	7552	8.4
41–45	1837	5.1	7073	7.2	6869	7.6
46–50	1641	4.6	6365	6.4	5837	6.5
Subtotal 31–50	8841	24.5	30823	31.2	29072	32.3
51–55	1487	4.1	4988	5.0	5160	5.7
56–60	1048	2.9	4073	4.1	3924	4.4
61–65	762	2.1	3154	3.2	3041	3.4
66–70	493	1.4	2174	2.2	2202	2.4
Subtotal 51–70	3790	10.5	14389	14.6	14327	15.9
70+	558	1.5	2562	2.6	2600	2.9
Unknown			42	0.04	40	0.04

Sources: Statistisches Amt Berlin, *Volkszählung 1871* (Berlin, 1873), Table 44; Jacob Segall, "Die Juden in Gross-Berlin," *ZDSJ* (1914): 128–129.

Table 5.12. Age Group Distribution in Various Cities and Districts, 1905–1910 (percentages)

Age	Jews											Christians	
	Hamburg 1905		Berlin 1905		Hesse 1905		Hesse 1910					Hesse 1910	
	Male	Female	Male	Female	Male	Female	Male	Female				Male	Female
0–4	7.6	7.0	7.2	7.3	8.2	8.2	9.2	7.5				12.2	11.8
5–9	8.4	7.9	7.1	7.2	8.7	8.0	8.3	8.3					
10–14	8.1	7.8	7.2	7.6	9.4	9.2	8.7	8.2?				22.2	21.7
15–19	8.65	8.5	9.4	8.2	8.4	8.1	8.5	8.3				9.4	9.3
20–29	17.8	17.6	22.0	20.05	18.6	17.4	16.1	16.1				16.8	15.8
30–39	16.5	16.5	17.7	17.5	14.6	14.9	15.5	15.9				14.5	14.5
40–49	13.0	13.2	13.2	14.0	11.7	12.1	12.2	12.7				10.4	10.6
50–59	10.2	9.9	11.2	11.8	9.9	10.5	10.0	10.55				7.1	7.6
60–69	6.05	6.9	5.0	5.8	7.25	7.5	7.3	7.9				4.8	5.6
70+	3.7	4.8	2.2	3.0	4.1	4.0	4.2	4.5				2.6	3.1

Sources: *Statistik des Hamburger Staates* 24 (year): 25; Knöpfel, "Die jüdische Bevölkerung vom Grossherzogtum Hessen," 10; *Die Grundstücksaufname vom Ende Oktober 1905 sowie die Wohnungs- und Bevölkerungs Aufnahme vom 1. Dezember 1905 in der Stadt Berlin* ... (Berlin, 1911), part 2, 18–21.

Table 5.13. Jewish Age Distribution in Leipzig, 1885–1910 (percentages)

Age	1885	1890	1895	1900	1905	1910, Jews*	1910, general population*
0–9	20.4	19.0	20.5	19.6	20.05	20.2	18.8
10–19	19.1	19.5	19.0	20.6	20.1	19.4	19.4
20–29	21.4	19.7	18.5	19.7	20.1	20.8	20.7
30–39	15.2	17.4	17.6	15.3	14.75	15.3	16.4
40–49	11.3	11.9	11.1	12.4	12.8	11.5	11.5
50–59	6.3	6.45	7.45	6.0	6.4	7.8	7.6
60–69	4.45	4.4	3.8	4.2	3.55	3.25	3.9
70+	1.8	1.7	2.0	2.15	1.7	1.7	1.6

* 1910 percentages recalculated from absolute numbers.

Sources: Segall, "Die Juden im Königreich Sachsen," 41; Herbert Philippsthal, "Die jüdische Bevölkerung in Leipzig," *Gemeindeblatt der Israelitischen Religionsgemeinde zu Leipzig* 7, nos. 2–3 (1931).

Table 5.14. Age Distribution of General Population and Native-Born and Foreign-Born Jews, Berlin, 1910 (percentages)

Age	General population	Native-born Jews	East-European-born Jews
0–15	23.96	22.63	11.22
15–30	30.64	26.04	37.22
30–50	30.09	31.38	36.71
50–70	13.07	16.70	13.36
70+	2.21	3.25	1.20
Unknown	0.02	0	0.05
15–50	60.73	57.42	73.93

Source: Klara Eschelbacher, "Die ostjüdische Einwanderungsbevölkerung der Stadt Berlin," *ZDSJ* (1920): 8 (recalculated from absolute numbers to combine both genders).

The aging of German Jewry became much more extreme after World War I. During the Weimar Republic era, it was induced mainly by a continued drop in Jewish births coupled with high longevity. From 1933 on, however, it was acutely exacerbated by mass emigration, which younger Jews underwent far more than older ones did.

Table 5.15. Jewish Age Distributions, Greater Berlin, 1910 (percentages)

Age	Berlin proper	Western suburbs	Neukölln and Lichtenberg
0–10	13.4	11.95	20.0
10–20	16.0	13.9	13.5
20–30	19.4	18.1	19.7
Under 30	48.8	44.0	53.2
30–40	18.2	18.4	23.5
40–50	14.1	15.4	12.1
50–60	10.1	12.1	7.0
60–70	5.8	7.1	2.8
70+	2.9	3.1	1.45

Source: Segall, "Die Juden in Gross-Berlin," 128–129 (percentages recalculated from absolute numbers).

In the 1925 census, the Jewish population was proportionately smaller in age groups below twenty-five than the non-Jewish population of the same age because the Jews' birth rates fell earlier. Nevertheless, although Jewish demographers bemoaned the aging of the Jewish population, the census of 1925 showed a substantial Jewish population below the age of five due to the baby boom of the first postwar years (Table 5.16). Although the proportion of Jews under five years of age was smaller than that of non-Jews on a national scale, in most major cities the reverse was the case (Table 5.17).

The large cities to which many young adults migrated had a considerably higher percentage of their Jewish population in the 20–54 age groups than did the smaller towns. Smaller Jewish communities had larger proportions of residents under twenty than did the largest cities (Table 5.18). The age profile of non-citizen Jews differed considerably from that of Jewish citizens and was actually closer to that of the general population.[7] Jewish non-citizens[8] were more

---

7 Index of differentiation:
   general population—all Prussian Jews: 14.82;
   all Prussian Jews—foreign Jews: 15.26;
   general population—foreign Jews: 8.22.
8 The collected statistics count Jews who held foreign citizenship. This group is not identical to the foreign-born because the German-born children of non-citizens were also non-citizens while some of the foreign-born were able to acquire citizenship.

Table 5.16. Age Distribution of Jewish and General Populations in Prussia, 1925 (amount and percentages)

Age	General population		Jewish population		Jewish citizens		Jewish non-citizens	
1–4	3,602,542	9.45%	27,178	6.73%	19,923	6.08%	7,255	9.50%
5–9	2,457,794	6.45	16,739	4.14	12,512	3.82	4,227	5.53
10–14	3,817,894	10.02	27,041	6.69	20,826	6.36	6,215	8.14
15–19	4,003,552	10.50	31,163	7.71	24,377	7.44	6,786	8.88
20–24	3,763,266	9.87	33,548	8.30	25,711	7.85	7,837	10.26
25–29	3,255,735	8.54	36,038	8.92	25,928	7.91	10,110	13.24
30–34	2,820,402	7.40	33,767	8.36	25,933	7.92	7,834	10.26
35–39	2,644,141	6.94	33,430	8.28	26,839	8.19	6,591	8.63
40–44	2,373,896	6.23	31,958	7.91	26,679	8.14	5,279	6.91
45–49	2,323,275	6.09	32,250	7.98	27,806	8.49	4,444	5.82
50–54	1,933,365	5.07	26,787	6.63	23,581	7.20	3,206	4.20
55–59	1,313,957	3.45	22,921	5.67	20,406	6.23	2,515	3.29
60–64	981,169	2.57	18,336	4.54	16,548	5.05	1,788	2.34
65–69	637,748	1.67	14,562	3.60	13,362	4.08	1,200	1.57
70+	552,223	1.45	17,951	4.44	16,854	5.14	1,097	1.44
Total	38,120,173		403,969		327,582		76,387	

Sources: Silbergleit, *Die Bevölkerungs- und Berufsverhältnisse*, 62*, 1–7.

Table 5.17. Comparative Jewish and General Age Distribution, 1910 and 1925—Selected Cities (percentages)

Age	Berlin 1910		Berlin 1925		Hamburg (city) 1925		Frankfurt/Main 1925		Wiesbaden 1925	
	Jews	General population	Jews	General population	Jews	General population	Jews	General population	Jews	General population
0–4	7.9	8.3	5.8	5.0	6.6	6.6	7.4		7.3	6.3
5–9	5.6	7.85	3.9	4.4	4.0	4.95	4.1	11.2	3.2	4.4
10–14	7.4	7.8	6.0	7.2	6.05	7.9	6.4	7.6	5.7	7.0
15–19	8.65	8.9	7.0	8.8	7.1	8.75	8.6	9.7	8.7	9.4
20–29	19.4	20.7	17.7	18.8	16.7	18.9	18.3	20.1	17.9	18.3
30–39	18.2	17.0	17.7	18.5	15.4	17.7	16.5	17.0	15.9	15.2
40–49	14.1	12.7	16.9	16.5	15.7	15.3	15.5	16.1	15.4	16.1
50–59	10.1	9.0	12.8	11.3	14.0	10.7	12.3	10.8	13.0	12.5
60–69	5.8	5.5	8.2	6.4	8.9	6.2	7.05	5.2	8.0	7.1
70+	2.9	2.22	4.05	3.0	4.95	3.0	3.85	2.3	4.9	3.7

Sources: based on Silbergleit, *Die Bevölkerungs- und Berufsverhältnisse*, 16–20, 86–87, 114–116; Segall, "Die Juden in Gross-Berlin," 128; *Statistisches Jahrbuch für die freie- und Hansestadt Hamburg* (1929–1930): 27.

heavily weighted towards the under-forty age groups than were Jewish citizens. The 20–39 age groups were more heavily represented among Jewish non-citizens than among the general population of Germany. The Jewish population in the eastern provinces of Prussia tended to be older than the Jews of western and central Prussia. Jews tended to be younger in provinces that eitherhad many Jewish immigrants like Schleswig-Holstein or that were heavily industrialized such as Upper Silesia, Westphalia, Prussian Saxony, and the Rhineland.

The age profiles of Jews in different large cities differed considerably. Berlin had the smallest proportion of Jews under age five; this age group was also low in the eastern cities of Stettin, Königsberg, and Breslau. These three cities also had the highest proportions of Jews over age fifty. There were relatively high rates of young children in the industrial cities of the Ruhr and Upper Silesia (Essen, Dortmund, Beuthen). Berlin, Düsseldorf, and Essen had the highest proportions of Jews in their peak working ages of 20–49 (Table 5.19).

In the eight years between the 1925 and the 1933 censuses, the German-Jewish population continued to age. This was caused mainly by the sharp drop in Jewish births during the last years of the Weimar Republic but was also abetted by emigration during the four and a half months from Hitler's appointment as chancellor on January 30 to the census date of June 16. A direct comparison with the 1925 data is difficult because the age categories used in the 1933 (and 1939) census were different than those employed earlier (Table 5.20). An estimate based on year of birth, however, shows how steep the drop in the youngest age groups really was. There were far fewer Jewish children under age five in all of Germany in 1933 than there had been in Prussia alone in 1925. The decline among those under fifteen was gentler due to the after-effect of the early 1920s baby boom (Table 5.21). There was relatively little variance in the age structures of Jews in various German states, with the notable exception of Saxony, where the mainly immigrant Jewish population was much younger than the Jewish population in other states (Table 5.22). Within Prussia, however, there was much variation among provinces, with high median ages in tiny Southwest German Hohenzollern and eastern provinces such as Pomerania and somewhat lower median ages in the Rhineland and in Westphalia.

As in 1925, Jewish communities outside large cities had higher percentages of both children and elderly than did the Jews in cities with over 100,000 inhabitants in 1933 (Table 5.23). Again, Berlin had both a disproportionately small share of persons under fifteen and a disproportionately large percentage of persons aged 25–50. Despite journalistic accounts of village Jewry as an aged population with many widows, data from various small-town communities show a wide range of age structures during the 1930s (Tables 5.24 and 5.24.1).

Table 5.18. Jewish Age Distribution in Prussia by Town Size, 1925 (amount and percentages)

Age	Prussia, total		Berlin		Other cities over 100,000		Towns under 100,000	
0–4	27178	6.7	9989	5.8	9324	7.7	7865	7.2
5–9	16739	4.1	6770	3.9	5233	4.3	4736	4.3
10–14	27041	6.7	10402	6.0	8231	6.8	8408	7.7
15–19	31163	7.7	12137	7.0	9885	8.1	9141	8.3
20–24	33548	8.3	14360	8.3	10544	8.7	8644	7.9
25–29	36038	8.9	16157	9.4	11290	9.3	8591	7.8
30–34	33767	8.4	15169	8.8	10303	8.5	8205	7.5
35–40	33430	8.3	15385	8.9	9874	8.1	8171	7.4
41–45	31958	7.9	14432	8.4	9353	7.7	8173	7.4
46–50	32550	8.1	14692	8.5	9312	7.7	8546	7.8
50–55	26787	6.6	11880	6.9	7868	6.5	7139	6.5
56–59	22921	5.7	10212	5.9	6490	5.3	6219	5.7
60–64	18336	4.5	8008	4.6	5003	4.1	5335	4.9
65–69	14562	3.6	6094	3.5	4049	3.3	4419	4.0
70+	17951	4.4	6985	4.0	5236	4.3	6202	5.7
Total	403969		172672		121558		109739	

Source: calculated from Silbergleit, *Die Bevölkerungs- und Berufsverhältnisse*, 3–7, 16–20, 116–120.

Table 5.19. Age Proportions in Prussian Cities with the Largest Jewish Populations, 1925 (from lowest percent under five to highest)

Age	Berlin	Stettin	Königsberg	Breslau	Wiesbaden	Kassel	Düsseldorf
0–4	5.8	5.9	6.4	6.7	7.3	7.3	7.4
5–19	17.0	16.0	19.1	17.6	17.65	22.1	17.3
20–49	52.2	47.5	48.3	47.9	49.1	45.8	50.3
50–69	21.0	22.8	21.3	22.8	21.0	19.5	19.3
70+	4.0	6.1	4.8	5.1	4.95	5.3	3.9

Age	Frankfurt/Main	Hannover	Cologne	Dortmund	Essen	Beuthen
0–4	7.4	7.9	7.9	9.3	9.3	9.3
5–19	19.1	19.9	18.0	21.2	22.3	19.3
20–49	50.3	51.6	54.8	51.1	51.9	50.7
50–69	19.4	17.5	17.5	16.3	13.8	17.1
70+	3.9	3.1	3.1	2.1	2.6	3.6

Source: calculated from Silbergleit, *Die Bevölkerungs- und Berufsverhältnisse*, 16–20, 73–78, 84–87, 93–96, 98–102, 113–116, 343–344.

Table 5.20. Age Distribution of Jews in Germany, 1933 Census

Age	Number of Jews	Percentage
0–5	24,318	4.9
6–15	61,901	12.4
16–20	20,747	4.2
20–24	34,313	6.9
25–29	36,739	7.4
30–39	82,978	16.6
40–44	40,493	8.1
45–49	40,220	8.1
50–59	76,529	15.3
60–64	28,797	5.8
65+	52,647	10.5

Source: 1933 census, 5/44.

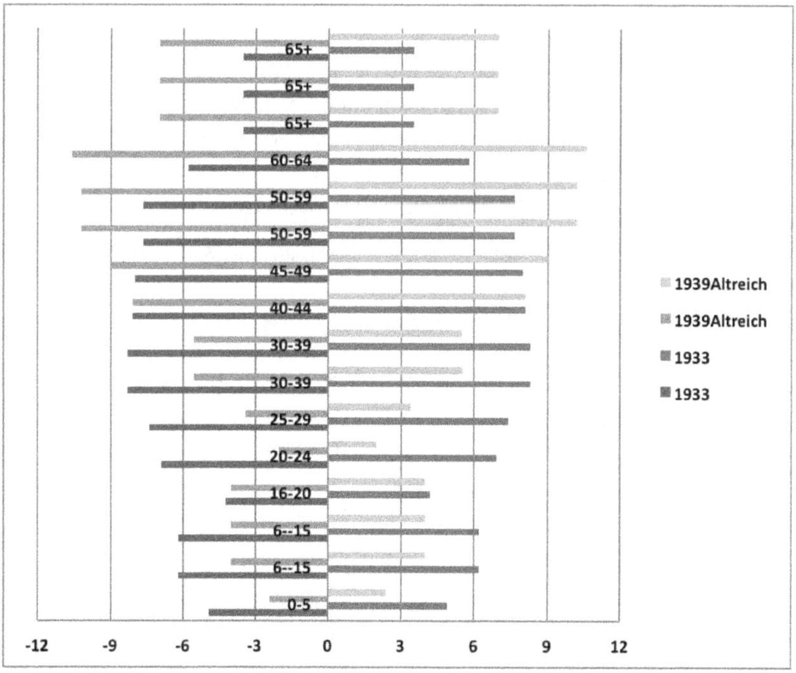

Figure. 5.3. CHANGES IN JEWISH AGE DISTRIBUTION, 1933–1939[9]

---

9 Editors' note: The data listed in Figure 5.3. are referred to in the following order from top to bottom: Jews, Total population.

Table 5.21. Jewish Age Distributions, 1925–1933

Age	Prussia 1925	Percent	Germany 1933 (estimated)	Percent
0–4	27178	6.7%	19129	3.8%
5–9	16739	4.1	30378	6.1
10–14	27041	6.7	33181	6.6
0–14	70958	17.6	82688	16.6
15–19	31163	7.7	24075	4.8
20–24	33548	8.3	34313	6.9
25–29	36038	8.9	36379	7.3
30–39	67197	16.6	82978	16.6
40–44	31958	7.9	40493	8.1
45–49	32550	8.1	40220	8.1
50–59	49708	12.3	76529	15.3
60–64	18336	4.5	28797	5.8
65+	32513	8.1	52647	10.5

The figures for 1933 (below age 20) are estimates based on data on year of birth. The group listed under 0–4 (that is, up to but not including the fifth birthday) is estimated by taking those born in 1933 (up to June 15) and one-half of those born in 1928 and adding them to those born between 1929 and 1932. This is approximately correct because the date of the census, June 16, 1933, was almost halfway through the year.

Sources: Silbergleit, *Die Bevölkerungs- und Berufsverhältnisse*, 3–7; 1933 census, 5/17, 42–43.

The mass emigration that began with the Nazi accession did even more to skew the Jewish age distribution than had earlier decreases in births and increases in longevity. Young adults were much more likely to emigrate than the elderly, and men, who felt they were in more danger than women, were more predisposed to leaving. The inevitable result was an ever-aging and female-dominated Jewish population that remained behind.

A special census undertaken by the Munich Jewish community in May 1938 showed sharp differences in age and gender between emigrants and those who stayed behind. The former outnumbered the latter only in the 21–30 cohort. Among those over fifty, only about 18.5 percent of the Jewish residents in 1933 had left by 1938. Males were 55.8 percent of emigrants as against 45.2 percent of those who remained behind (Table 5.25, Figure 5.2).

Table 5.22. Age Distributions of Jews by Major Territories, 1933 (amount and percentages)

Age	Prussia		Bavaria		Saxony		Württemberg and Hohenzollern		Baden		Hesse	
0–5	17623	4.9	1899	4.5	1206	5.9	476	4.6	962	4.7	923	5.2
6–13	38949	10.8	4474	10.7	2962	14.4	1176	11.4	2248	10.9	2005	11.2
14–15	5079	1.4	554	1.3	422	2.0	149	1.4	285	1.4	224	1.3
16–17	5682	1.6	681	1.6	436	2.1	162	1.6	308	1.5	261	1.5
18–19	9205	2.5	1035	2.5	643	3.1	267	2.6	526	2.6	465	2.6
20–24	24603	6.8	2846	6.8	1646	8.0	721	7.0	1533	7.4	1241	6.9
25–29	27021	7.5	2774	6.6	1616	7.89	732	7.0	1449	7.0	1240	6.9
30–39	61914	17.1	5991	14.8	3722	18.1	1519	14.7	2955	14.3	2607	14.6
40–44	29986	8.3	3194	7.6	1742	8.5	732	7.0	1495	7.3	1280	7.2
45–49	29264	8.1	3404	8.1	1572	7.7	818	7.9	1653	8.0	1418	8.0
50–59	54667	15.1	7195	17.2	2471	12.0	1719	16.7	3545	17.2	2889	16.3
60–64	20484	5.7	2803	6.7	817	4.0	693	6.7	1271	6.2	1128	6.3
65+	37349	10.3	5089	12.1	1329	6.5	1160	11.2	2387	11.6	2207	12.3
Percent under 20		21.5		20.6		27.5		22.0		21.0		21.7
Percent under 40		52.5		48.8		61.5		50.8		49.8		52.8
Percent over 60		16.0		18.8		10.4		18.0		17.7		18.6
Percent 20–59		62.9		60.6		62.0		60.0		61.3		59.7

Source: 1933 census, 5/46–48.

Table 5.23. Jewish Age Distribution in Cities of Various Sizes—Germany, 1933 (amount and percentages)

Age	Berlin		Other cities of over 100,000		Towns of under 100,000	
0–5	6654	4.1	10096	**5.2**	7568	5.2
6–13	15122	9.4	23038	**11.9**	16626	11.4
14–15	2104	1.3	3039	**1.6**	1972	1.3
16–17	2379	1.5	3275	**1.7**	2277	1.6
18–19	3785	2.4	5292	**2.7**	3739	2.6
20–24	10709	6.7	13786	**7.1**	9818	6.7
25–29	12474	**7.8**	13965	7.2	10300	7.1
30–39	29145	**18.2**	32413	16.8	21240	14.6
40–44	13939	**8.7**	15674	8.1	10880	7.5
45–49	13659	**8.5**	15184	7.8	11377	7.8
50–59	25118	**15.6**	28767	14.9	22644	15.6
60–64	9368	5.8	10449	5.4	8980	**6.8**
65+	16108	10.0	18578	9.6	17961	**12.3**
Percent under 20		18.7		23.1		22.1
Percent over 40		48.5		45.8		49.4
Percent over 60		15.9		15.0		18.5

Source: based on 1933 census, 5/44–45.

By the time of the German census in May 1939, emigration had progressed even further and had produced an even more aged Jewish population. The change relative to 1933 was quite dramatic. The share of Jews under twenty years of age dropped from 21.4 percent of the total to 14.4 percent while those over 60 increased from 16.3 percent to 31.5 percent. The median age of Jews by religion in Greater Germany in 1939 was fifty-one as against thirty-nine among German Jews in 1933. The steepest decreases in Jewish population occurred among those in their twenties (Table 5.26, Table 3.11, Figure 5.3).

An overview of developments in the post-World War I period shows a process of steady aging that changed radically in 1933 (Table 5.27). Until the Nazis came to power, the greatest decline was among children and adolescents, caused mainly by the decrease in Jewish fertility and the decrease among young adults was much milder. After 1933, however, it was precisely the young-adult cohort (19–39) that was most likely to emigrate, contracting even more sharply

Table 5.24. Variations in Jewish Age Structure in Small Towns, 1930s

Age	Neustadt am Rübenberge (Hannover)	Bad Mergentheim (Württemberg)	Ermershausen (Lower Franconia)	Schenklengsfeld (Hesse-Nassau)	Rimbach (Hesse)
0–9	2 (6.1%)	19 (7.8%)	7 (13.0%)	18 (12.4%)	11 (14.3%)
10–19	3 (9.1)	21 (8.6)	9 (16.7)	20 (19?) (13.8)	6 (7.8)
20–29	4 (12.1)	44 (18.0)	5 (9.3)	33 (22.8)	10 (13.0)
30–39	3 (9.1)	36 (14.8)	3 (5.6)	17 (16?) (11.7)	9 (11.7)
40–49	5 (15.2)	34 (13.9)	13 (24.1)	20 (21?) (13.8)	16 (20.8)
50–59	10 (30.3)	42 (17.2)	9 (16.7)	19 (13.1)	11 (14.3)
60–69	3 (9.1)	30 (12.3)	1 (1.9)	6 (4.1)	6 (7.8)
70+	3 (9.1)	18 (7.4)	7 (13.0)	12 (8.3)	8 (10.4)
Percent under 20	15.2	16.4	29.6	26.2	22.1
Percent over 60	18.2	19.7	14.8	12.4	18.2
Amount	33	244	54	145	77

Age	Buchau (Württemberg) 1933	Ludwigsburg (Württemberg) 1933
Under 20	21 (12.7%)	46 (24.6%)
Percent over 60	45 (27.3%)	26 (13.9%)
Amount	165	187

Sources: List of Jews in Neustadt a/Rbge. (October 10, 1935), in Friedel Homeyer, *Gestern und Heute: Juden im Landkreis Hannover* (Hannover, 1984), 147–150; Hermann Fechenbach, *Die letzten Mergentheimer Juden* (Stuttgart, 1972), 180–188; List of Jews in Schenklengsfeld (February 1, 1933), in *Geschichte der jüdischen Gemeinde in Schenklengsfeld*, ed. Karl Honikel (Schenklengsfeld, 1988); Wolfgang Gebhard, *Geschichte der Rimbacher Juden* (Rimbach, 1987); *Pinkas ha-Kehillot, Germania, Württemberg-Hohenzollern-Baden*, 57, 106.

Table 5.24.1. Variations in Jewish Age Structure in Small Towns, 1925

Rural Lower Franconia
Rabbinat Burgpreppach

Age	1925	Percent
0–5	32	4.8
6–10	33	4.9
11–14	45	6.7
15–20	50	7.5
21–30	69	10.3
31–40	102	15.3
41–50	93	13.9
51–60	84	12.6
61–70	87	13.0
71+	73	10.9

Sources: "Alterbau der israelitischen Bevölkerung des Rabbinatsbezirk Burgpreppach nach der Volkszählung von 1925," *Bayerische Israelitische Gemeindezeitung* (July 15, 1927): 228; Police list of Jews in Ermershausen (1935, in author's possession).

than did the youngest groups. Because few Jews over age sixty emigrated, their percentage in the Jewish population skyrocketed after 1933. The post-1933 developments were not a general continuation of the aging process of the earlier twentieth century but were instead a by-product of the dissolution of German Jewry through emigration—a process that, unfortunately, the Nazis did not allow to run its natural course.

Table 5.25. Difference in Age Structure of Munich Jews Leaving or Staying, 1933–1938

Age	Munich 1938		Jews emigrating from Munich, 1933–1938		Combined (approximate Jewish population 1933)		Percent of age group that emigrated
0–10	305	4.8%	190	5.3	495		38.4
11–20	622	9.7	459	12.9	1081		42.5
21–30	494	7.7	677	18.9	1171		57.8
31–40	796	12.4	742	20.7	1538		48.2
41–50	1093	17.1	492	13.8	1585		31.0
51–60	1251	19.6	377	10.5	1628		23.2
61+	1780	27.8	310	8.7	2090		14.8
Unknown	51	0.9	327	9.3	378		86.5
Total	6392		3574		9966		
Median age	just under 50		just over 35		c. 45		

Source: Werner J. Cahnman, "The Decline of the Munich Jewish Community, 1933–38," *Jewish Social Studies* 3 (1941): 286–287, 296.

Table 5.26. Age Distribution of Jews in Germany, 1933–1939

Age	Greater Germany 1939 (*Glaubensjuden* of all "races")		Percent male	Altreich 1939 (Greater Germany minus Vienna)		Germany 1933		Altreich 1939 as percent of Germany 1933
0–5	6,825	2.2	50.2	5,370	2.4	24,318	4.9%	22.1%
6–15	23,325	7.7	50.2	17,930	8.0	61,901	12.4	29.0
16–20	11,272	3.7	43.2	8,904	4.0	20,747	4.2	42.9
20–24	5,755	1.9	40.2	4,507	2.0	34,313	6.9	13.1
25–29	10,003	3.3	39.7	7,670	3.4	36,739	7.4	20.9
30–39	33,397	11.0	40.7	24,720	11.1	82,978	16.6	29.8
40–44	25,239	8.3	38.9	18,087	8.1	40,493	8.1	44.7
45–49	27,983	9.2	39.2	20,096	9.0	40,220	8.0	50.0
50–59	63,504	20.8	43.4	45,573	20.4	76,529	15.3	59.5
60–64	32,846	10.8	44.6	23,641	10.6	28,797	5.8	82.1
65+	64,422	21.1	40.6	46,702	20.9	52,647	10.5	88.7
All	304,571		42.4	223,200		499,682		44.7

Source: based on 1933 census, 5/44; 1939 census, *Statistik des Deutschen Reichs* 552 (1944): 4/56–59. The slash is part of the page number in the cited volume.

Table 5.27. Stages in the Aging of German Jewry, 1910–1939

Age	Prussia, 1910		Prussia, 1925		Prussia, 1933		Germany, 1933		Greater Germany, 1939 (Jewish religion, all "races")	
Under 18	117,175	28.2%	89,614	22.2%	67,333	18.6%	94,150	18.8%	36,407	12.0%
18–39			149,290	37.0%	122,743	33.9%	166,846	33.4%	54,110	17.8%
40–59			114,216	28.3%	113,917	31.5%	157,242	31.5%	116,726	38.3%
60+			50,849	12.6%	57,833	16.0%	81,444	16.3%	97,268	31.9%
Over 18	297,621	71.8%	314,355	77.82%	294,493	81.39%	405,532	81.16%	268,104	88.0%

Sources: based on Statistisches Jahrbuch für den Preussischen Staat 10 (1912): 12; Silbergleit, Die Bevölkerungs- und Berufsverhältnisse, 4–7, 70*–71*; 1933 census, 5/17, 19, 46; Statistik des Deutschen Reichs 552 (1944): 4/48–55.

6

Conversion and Intermarriage

Losses in Jewish numbers caused by conversion to Christianity and intermarriage with non-Jews have concerned many observers of German Jewry since the late eighteenth century. Of the two phenomena, out-conversion has had a much longer history and has occurred at various levels throughout much of German-Jewish history. Intermarriage (marriage between unconverted Jews and non-Jews) was generally illegal before the emancipation of the Jews. Various German states legalized intermarriage without conversion by either spouse at different dates in the middle of the nineteenth century.

While the Jews were a persecuted minority in Germany, there was always at least a trickle of Jews who converted to Christianity either to improve their legal and economic position or for genuine religious motives.[1] Statistics on their numbers are extremely fragmentary and reliable statistics are unlikely ever to come to light. In an attempt to count Jewish conversions to Protestantism in Germany in the seventeenth century, Martin Friedrich arrived at an undoubtedly incomplete tally of 388 (266 of them after 1671).[2] This suggests that the

---

1 For a discussion of the role and dilemmas of Jewish converts to Christianity in the early modern period, see Elisheva Carlebach, *Divided Souls: Converts from Judaism in Germany, 1500–1750* (New Haven and London: Yale University Press, 2001).
2 Martin Friedrich, *Zwischen Abwehr und Bekehrung: Die Stellung der deutschen evangelischen Theologie zum Judentum im 17. Jahrhundert* (Tübingen: Mohr, 1988), 150–163.

conversion of Jews to Christianity, although much talked about by missionaries in the early modern era, was rarely accomplished.

While the beginnings of discussions on improving the status of the Jews and the inroads of the Enlightenment in the Jewish community in the second half of the eighteenth century did not put an end to conversions from Judaism to Christianity, they did transform the phenomenon. In Berlin, the capital of Prussia and of the German Enlightenment, both Jewish and non-Jewish, the period from about 1780 to 1830 was marked by a remarkable increase in conversion that particularly affected the Jewish elite and not merely the downtrodden as had previously been the case. Contemporary observers and later historians alike viewed this movement of conversion in the wake of Enlightenment as a crisis, which they titled the *Taufepidemie* ("epidemic of baptisms"). Some observers saw the very survival of Judaism as endangered. Quantitative twentieth-century historians who investigated the Berlin *Taufepidemie* in some depth, however, generally concluded that its dimensions were much more modest than imagined.

Based on the *Judenkartei* compiled by the Nazis of Jewish conversions to Protestantism in Berlin, we can construct a picture of the dimensions of conversion in the city[3] (Table 6.1). The statistics show three overlapping waves of conversion. In the first phase from 1770 to 1805, illegitimate children of mixed Christian-Jewish liaisons predominate conversions. In the second wave, from about 1800 to 1820, many of the converts belonged to the Berlin Jewish elite and were balanced in gender terms; several entire families converted as well. In the third wave from 1820–1830, most converts were young adult males migrating to Berlin who converted for career reasons. After 1830, the *Taufepidemie* seems to subside, partly because of increasing numbers of traditional Jews from the eastern provinces of Prussia who migrated to Berlin. Although the actual number of baptisms did not drop by much, the percentage of Jews in Berlin who underwent baptism declined greatly as the Jewish community grew rapidly.

According to Abraham Menes's research, baptisms of Jews in the early nineteenth century were disproportionately common in Berlin and a few other major cities, especially Königsberg and Breslau, between 1816 and 1846 (Table 6.2). The three provinces that included Berlin (Brandenburg), Königsberg (East Prussia), and Breslau (Silesia) together accounted for about 70 percent of

---

3 Inclusion in the *Judenkartei* was based on Nazi racial characteristics. Therefore, the statistics include persons who were not technically converts: infants baptized at birth, children of converted Jews, and children of Jewish fathers and non-Jewish mothers.

Table 6.1. Changing Dimensions of Conversion of Jews to Protestantism in Berlin, 1770–1830

Year	Total number	Baptized infants (under age 2)	Infants born out of wedlock (above age 2 months)	Males	Females
1770–1774	19	4	3		
1775–1779	20	10	6		
1780–1784	39	20	15		
1785–1789	38	21	18		
1790–1794	52	30	29		
1795–1799	85	60	52		
1800–1804	96	65	48		
Total	349	210	171	63	108
1805–1809	144	68	45		
1810–1814	179	69	31		
1815–1819	218	74	25		
Total	541	211	101	188	152
1820–1824	234	71	19		
1825–1829	381	93	22		
1830	67	26	9		
Total	682	190	50	340	165
Total, 1770–1830	1572	611	322	591	425

Source: Lowenstein, *Berlin Jewish Community*, 116, 246, 267, based on *Judenkartei*.

Table 6.2. Conversion of Jews to Protestantism in Various Prussian Provinces

Province	1816–1821	1822–1831	1832–1841	1842–1846
East Prussia	53 (8.8)	114 (11.4)	208 (20.8)	120 (24.0)
West Prussia	21 (3.5)	21 (2.1)		
Posen	67 (11.2)	94 (9.4)	59 (5.9)	22 (4.4)
Brandenburg	323 (53.8)	441 (44.1)	442 (44.2)	228 (45.6)
Pomerania	29 (4.8)	53 (5.3)	50 (5.0)	14 (2.8)
Silesia	169* (22.0)	290 (29.0)	223 (22.3)	92 (18.4)
Pr. Saxony	37 (6.2)	85 (8.5)	48 (4.8)	38 (7.6)
Westphalia	28 (4.7)	50 (5.0)	32 (3.2)	27 (5.4)
Rhineland	36 (6.0)	126 (12.6)	91 (9.1)	40 (8.0)
Total	763 (127.2)	1274 (127.4)	1153 (115.3)	581 (116.2)

(Annual averages in parentheses)

* Menes lists the number of converts in Silesia in 1816–1821 in one place as 169 and in another as 69. He gives the total number of conversions in Prussia as 763 and 663.

Conversions between 1816 and 1842 as Percent of 1821 Jewish Population of Each Province

Province	Conversions
East Prussia	3.14
West Prussia	
Posen	0.5
Brandenburg	15.6
Silesia	4.2
Pr. Saxony	6.0
Rhineland	1.5
Westphalia	1.3

Source: Menes, "The Conversion Movement in Prussia," 192, 195.

converts in Prussia during the period, although they only had some 22 percent of the total Jewish population of Prussia.[4]

---

4   Abraham Menes, "The Conversion Movement in Prussia during the First Half of the 19th Century," *YIVO Annual of Social Science* 6 (1951): 192, 195.

All indications seem to show a drop in Jewish conversions to Christianity between 1847 and 1871 and then a sharp jump with the rise of political antisemitism in the 1880s. Arthur Ruppin stated that the fifty converts[5] in Prussia in 1876 represented the lowest figure in the entire nineteenth century. According to Deborah Hertz, the annual number of converts to Protestantism in Berlin held steady between seventy-five and eighty[6] between 1830 and 1875, even though the city's Jewish population increased more than six-fold (Table 6.3). In de le Roi's estimation, 17,500 Jews in Germany (13,128 in Prussia) converted to Protestantism and 5,000 to Catholicism in the nineteenth century.[7] Parsed by periods, the estimates show a clear drop in 1847–1874, followed by a sharp rise (Tables 6.4–6.6).

Religious intermarriage, previously allowed only in a few states, became legal everywhere in Germany in 1875 with the introduction of civil marriage. It was in that year that statistics on the number of Jews who intermarried began in most states. In several states, however, we have statistics that go back further. In the Grand Duchy of Hesse, statistics beginning in 1866 show a very small number of intermarriages. From then to 1873, no Jewish man married a non-Jewish woman and only seven Jewish women married non-Jewish men.[8] Intermarriages in Hesse and several other southern states remained low for quite a while afterward as well (Table 6.7).

It is remarkable that intermarriages outnumbered conversions by a wide margin as soon as they were legalized. In 1875, there were fifty-four recorded conversions of Jews to Protestantism in Prussia and 277 recorded marriages

---

5 Ruppin's source appears to have been Nathan Samter, *Judentaufen im neunzehnten Jahrhundert mit besonderer Berücksichtigung Preussens* (Berlin, 1906), 145. The figures refer only to the eight provinces of Prussia within its pre-1866 borders.
6 Hertz's figures, based on the Nazi *Judenkartei*, far exceed those quoted by de le Roi and Samter (and those used in Table 6.4) for two chief reasons. First, the Nazis used racial criteria for their list and thus included the children of converted Jews as well as the children of Jewish fathers and Christian mothers, neither of which group would have been counted as converts in the official statistics that the others used. Second, the official conversion statistics often omitted baptized children of intermarried or Jewish couples, whom the *Judenkartei* would include. The use of Hertz's figures for conversions at age six or above yields a better approximation of the actual conversion numbers.
7 Johannes Friedrich Alexander de le Roi, *Judentaufen im 19. Jahrhundert: Ein statistischer Versuch* (Leipzig, 1899).
8 In the Grand Duchy of Baden in 1871, there were 4,185 homogeneous Jewish married couples, six Jewish men married to Christians, and ten Jewish women married to non-Jews. Of married Jews, only 0.19 percent lived in an intermarried family. In-married Jewish families had two married Jews; intermarried couples had only one. "Beiträge zur Statistik der inneren Verwaltung des Grossherzogthums Baden," *Die Volkszählung vom 1. December 1871* (Carlsruhe, 1874), xxxii.

Table 6.3. Changes in Numbers of Conversions to Protestantism, Berlin, 1800–1874 (based on *Judenkartei*)

Year	Male	Female	Total per-year conversions	Percent aged 0–5	Converts aged 6 and above (annual average in parentheses)	Approx. Jewish population of Berlin	Approximate annual conversions as percent of Berlin Jewry
1800–1809	192	165	35.7	87	46 (4.6)	3,400	1.1%
1810–1819	225	237	46.2	59	189 (18.9)	3,400	1.4
1820–1829	405	252	65.7	41	388 (38.8)	4,200	1.6
1830–1839	456	321	77.7	53	365 (36.5)	5,600	1.4
1840–1849	393	360	75.3	62	286 (28.6)	8,600	0.9
1850–1859	423	342	76.5	62	291 (29.1)	12,300	0.6
1860–1869	462	402	76.4	74	225 (22.5)	19,400	0.4
1870–1874			76.8	73	104 (20.8)	36,500	0.2

Source: Deborah Hertz, "The Troubling Dialectic between Reform and Conversion in Biedermeier Berlin," in *Towards Normality? Acculturation and Modern German Jewry*, ed. Rainer Liedtke and David Rechter (Tübingen: Mohr, 2003), 103–126, especially 119, 121–122.

Table 6.4. Estimated Number of Jewish Conversions to Protestantism in Prussia

Year	Conversions	Conversions per year
1800–1811	640	(58 per year)
1811–1846	3771	(121.7 per year)
1847–1874	2683	(95.8 per year)
1875–1900	6034	(232.1 per year)
Total	13128	

The figures for 1847–1874 are calculated by taking de le Roi's figure of 13,128 conversions in Prussia in the nineteenth century (de Le Roi, *Judentaufen*, 16) and subtracting the known figures for conversions in the periods 1800–1811, 1811–1846 and 1875–1900 given in Samter, *Judentaufen*, 145–146.

Table 6.5. Annual Number of Conversions to Protestantism, 1875–1933

Year	Germany	Germany outside Prussia	Prussia Old Provinces	Prussia All	Berlin	Protestant conversions to Judaism (Germany)
1875			54		17	
1876			50		19	
1877			57		27	
1878			74		35	
1879			76		28	
1880	172	40	120	132	43	
1881	235	103	127	132	43	
1882	193	44	136	149	51	
1883	198	35	157	163	54	
1884	178	31	134	147	59	
1885	247	60	163	187	67	
1886	243	51	170	192	88	
1887	326	68	240	258	103	
1888*	457	89?	348	368	145	
1889	396	91	283	305	162	
1890	389	84	262	305	146	
1891	447	135	289	312	116	
1892	361	108	219	253	103	

Year	Germany	Germany outside Prussia	Prussia Old Provinces	Prussia All	Berlin	Protestant conversions to Judaism (Germany)
1893	500	119	340	381	184	
1894	391	74	277	317	140	
1895	489	148	290	341	106	
1896	465	102	312	363	103	
1897	486 [482]	131	299	351	138	
1898	478	134	301	344	140	18
1899	480 [488]	132 [140]	331	348	155	25
1900	486	111	346	375	160	
1901	483 [485 Z]	106 [108Z]	324	377	154	24
1902	541 [545Z]	132 [128K, 142Z]	343	413	132	46
1903	491 [498Z]	138 [145Z]	300	353	165	52
1904	501 [503Z]	97 [99Z]		404	153	52
1905	458 [463Z]	112 [117Z]		346	135	81
1906	434 [440Z]	136 [142Z]		298	127	124
1907	478 [492Z]	135 [149Z]		343	151	47
1908	494	110		384	163	94
1909	420 [423Z]	106 [109Z]		314	134	49
1910	465 [469Z]	105 [109Z]		360	156	77
1911	464 [466Z]	101 [103Z]		363	164	59
1912	408 [411Z]	120 [123Z]		288	131	77
1913	456 [462Z]	131 [137Z]		325	146	58
1914	432 [439]	127 [134Z]		305	143	64
1915	327 [335Z]	83 [91Z]		244	112	63
1916	358 [362Z]	90 [94Z]		268	122	80
1917	365	75		290	113	70
1918	389	127		262	101	106
1919	473 [472Z]	120 [119Z]		353		138
1920	452 [447]	128		324	119	82
1921	375 [361Z]	123 [109Z]		252	92	67

Year	Germany	Germany outside Prussia	Prussia Old Provinces	Prussia All	Berlin	Protestant conversions to Judaism (Germany)
1922	328 [317R]	111 [110Z]		207	78	74
1923	453 [423R]	121		332 [302RZ]	94	95
1924	244 [243R]	66		178 [177RZ	54	86
1925	221 [226R]	71 [77R]		150 [149R]	34	43
1926	218	69		149		44
1927	180	47		133		57 [58]
1928	166	55		111		45
1929						
1930	212	59		153		55
1931	173	61		112		45
1932	241	63		178		35
1933	993	366		627		36

Data in bold = years of sharp increase (more than 20 percent above the previous year) in conversions.

Sources: Samter, *Judentaufen*, 145–150; "Uebertritte der Juden zur evangelisch. Landeskirche von 1901 bis 1918," *ZDSJ* (1924): 27; "Uebertritte von Juden zur evangelischen Landeskirche 1919–1924," *ZDSJ* (1927): 85; Arthur Ruppin, "Der Verlust des Judentums durch Taufe und Austritt," *ZDSJ* (1930): 22; *Allgemeines Kirchenblatt für das evangelische Deutschland (1900–1933)*. Unless otherwise marked, data from 1875 to 1903 come from Samter, *Judentaufen*, and thereafter come from the annual figures in *Allgemeines Kirchenblatt*.

* The 1888 figures in Samter, *Judentaufen*, are erroneously labelled 1897.

Discrepant figures from other sources besides Samter, *Judentaufen*, are given in square brackets. They come from: Z = "Uebertritte von Juden from ZDSJ 1924 and 1927"; or R = Ruppin, "Die Verlust."

The totals given in the 1927 *ZDSJ* for Germany are incorrect because the figures for Berlin were double counted. The incorrect figures are not used here.

Table 6.6. Net Conversion Rate of Jews in Germany to Protestantism (out-conversions minus in-conversions)

Year	Overall	Annual average
1881–1885	991	198.2
1886–1890	1750	350.0
1891–1895	2127	425.4
1896–1900	2294	**458.8**
1901–1905	2234	446.8
1906–1910	1913	382.6
1911–1915	1792	358.4
1916–1920	1565	313.0
1921–1925	1219	243.8
1926–1930	710	142.0
1931–1932	334	167.0

Source: 1933 census, 5/8.

Table 6.7. Jewish Inmarriages and Intermarriages in Hesse-Darmstadt (annual averages)

Year	Jewish inmarriages	Jewish man–non-Jewish woman	Jewish woman–non-Jewish man
1866–1870	164	0	0.8
1871–1875	168	0.4	0.8
1876–1880	171	2.6	5.4
1881–1885	172	2.4	4.4
1886–1890	168	3.0	5.2
1891–1895	165	2.8	4.2
1896–1900	161	3.4	5.8

Source: Knöpfel, "Stand und Bewegung," 82.

between Jews and non-Jews. In the last quarter of the nineteenth century, both conversions and intermarriages increased considerably in Prussia. Intermarriages grew slowly and steadily from the 1870s through the turn of the century, doubling during that time. Conversions, in contrast, seem to have been affected much more by political upturns and downturns. A 50 percent increase between 1877 and 1878 was followed by an additional 60 percent upturn in

1880, and then more than doubled during the 1880s. The upward tendency continued until the turn of the century with occasional spikes, such as in 1893 and 1902. Overall, the increase in conversions was much steeper than the rise in intermarriages in the late nineteenth century. In Prussia, there were 1.73 intermarriages for every conversion to Protestantism in 1880, but by 1900 the ratio had fallen to 1.26.

In the southern state of Bavaria, between 1875 and 1889, annual intermarriages varied between ten and eighteen per year while homogeneous marriages were in the 332–385 range. Just over one-half of the intermarriages were with Catholic partners. During these years, 1.32–2.52 percent of Jews who married did so with a non-Jewish spouse. Beginning around 1890, intermarriages in Bavaria started increasing steadily, especially among Jewish men. Between 1895 and 1900, annual intermarriages ranged between 27 and 39 while inmarriages increased only slightly from 358 to 418 (Table 6.8).

The extent both of conversion to Protestantism and intermarriage varied widely on a regional basis and generally followed a similar pattern. Systematic data on the regional variation in conversions and intermarriages are hard to find until the first decade of the twentieth century. Still, both phenomena were more common in large cities and in northern and central Germany than they were in the south (Table 6.9).

At approximately the same time as the legalization of interreligious intermarriage, various states permitted the withdrawal from a religious denomination without conversion. In addition, special laws in Prussia and Hesse, passed in 1876 and 1878 respectively, permitted Jews to declare their withdrawal from the Jewish community without withdrawing from Judaism. This second type of *Austritt* (secession or resignation) was intended at least in part for the benefit of Orthodox Jews who wished to withdraw from

Table 6.8. Jewish Inmarriages and Intermarriages in Bavaria, 1876–1900 (annual averages)

Year	Jewish inmarriages	Jewish man–non-Jewish woman	Jewish woman–non-Jewish man
1876–1880	356.6	6.0	7.8
1881–1885	357.0	6.6	5.2
1886–1890	357.4	9.6	6.6
1891–1895	363.8	12.4	12.4 (sic)
1896–1900	391.6	23.0	11.6

Source: Thon, "Bewegung seit dem Jahre 1876," 7.

Table 6.9. Conversions from and to Judaism and Protestantism and Intermarriages, by Province

Province	1900 Jewish population	Conversions to Protestantism		Conversions 1900 and 1904 as percent of Jewish population	Conversions to Judaism		Inmarriages	Intermarriages
		1900	1904		1903	1904	1904	1904
East Prussia	13877	21	9	0.2	1	2	70	8 (5.4%)
West Prussia	18226	3	11	0.1	0	1	94	4 (2.1)
Berlin	92206	161	153	0.3	?	34	628	248 (16.5)
Brandenburg	25766	36	32	0.3	0	2	193	72 (15.7)
Pomerania	10880	14	15	0.3	0	0	53	6 (5.4)
Posen	35327	5	1	0.0	0	1	253	5 (1.0)
Silesia	47586	60	66	0.3	1	2	324	36 (5.3)
Pr. Saxony	8047	16	17	0.4	0	0	44	12 (12.0)
Westphalia	20640	5	9	0.1	1	0	148	22 (6.9)
Rhineland	52251	25	36	0.1	3	0	357	82 (10.3)
Schleswig-Holstein	3486	5	5	0.3	0	0	16	15 (31.9)
Hannover	15393	2	14	0.1	0	0	95	34 (15.2)
Hesse-Nassau	48105	22	36	0.1	1	6	340	38 (5.3)

Hohenzollern							5	0
Prussia	392322	375	404	0.2	7	48	2602	582 (10.1)
Bavaria	54928	25	9	0.1	4	0	445	36 (3.9)
Saxony	12416	33	26	0.5	1	1	52	15 (12.6)
Württemberg	11916	10	4	0.1	3	0	92	5 (2.6)
Baden	26132	14	10	0.1	1	1	205	18 (4.2)
Hesse	24486	0	0	0	0	0	196	12 (3.0)
Hamburg	17949	?	29			0	102	51 (20.0)
Alsace-Lorraine		2	2		2	0	226	12 (2.6)
All other		27	13		2	2	81	17 (9.5)
All Germany	586833	486	497	0.2	20	52	4001	748 (8.5)

Percentage of all Jews married in 1904 who intermarried is given in parentheses.

Sources: "Austritt vom und Uebertritte zum Judentum im Jahre 1904," *ZDSJ* (1906): 176; 1900 census by Kaiserliches Statistisches Amt, in *Die Volkszählung am 1. Dezember 1900 im Deutschen Reich*, vol. 1 (Berlin: Puttkammer & Mühbrecht, 1903), 116*; "Eheschliessungen im Jahre 1904," *ZDSJ* (1906): 159.

Reform-dominated local Jewish community organizations and pay dues only to their separate Orthodox ones.[9] Before World War I, there was a sharp difference between those who withdrew from Judaism (converts and secularists) and those who withdrew from the Jewish community (separatist Orthodox). After World War I, this was no longer the case because withdrawal from the Jewish community without withdrawal from Judaism no longer required a declaration by the withdrawer that he or she was motivated by a matter of conscience. In general, before World War I, the number of recorded conversions was not far below the number of recorded withdrawals from Judaism; after World War I, this ceased to be the case (Table 6.10).

World War I saw a sharp break in the patterns of conversion, intermarriage, and withdrawal from Jewish communities. After cresting around the year 1900, conversions to Christianity began to decline. The downturn became especially

Table 6.10. Withdrawals (*Austritte*) from Judaism or the Jewish Community in Berlin

Year	Withdrawals from Judaism	Withdrawals from Jewish community	Total	Eintritte (admissions to Judaism)
1910	230			
1911	238			
1912	197	23	220	92
1913	170	32	202	104
1914	124	16	140	56
1927			559	
1928			555	
1929			579	
1930			586	
1931			722	

Sources: *Mitteilungen über die Verwaltung der jüdischen Gemeinde zu Berlin* (1916); *Wochenblatt für den Synagogenbezirk Erfurt* (October 14, 1932).

---

9 C. Zander, *Handbuch enthaltend die sämmtlichen Bestimmungen* über *die Verhältnisse der Juden im Preussischen Staate* (Leipzig, 1881), 59–64, gives the text of the Prussian secession law. The law in Hesse-Darmstadt is described in Renate Penssel, *Jüdische Religionsgemeinschaften als Körperschaften des öffentlichen Rechts von 1800 bis 1919* (Cologne and Weimar: Böhlau, 2014), 297.

sharp during the 1920s, when conversions to Protestantism dropped by over 50 percent. Concurrently, withdrawals from Jewish communities were often more than twice the prewar level. Instead of converting to Christian denominations, however, those who withdrew now declared themselves konfessionslos (without religion) in ever-larger numbers. As conversion declined, secularization more than took its place in depleting the Jewish population.

Intermarriage after World War I also differed sharply from its prewar manifestation in terms of its patterns. Before World War I, intermarriages increased gradually but steadily while homogeneous Jewish marriages held steady or declined very slightly. In this gradual way, intermarriages almost tripled in number between 1875 and 1912.[10] During and after World War I, there were sharp upward and downward swings in homogeneous Jewish marriages but much less fluctuation in intermarriages. The concurrence of a slight upward trend in Jewish intermarriages and a sharp downturn in inmarriages resulted in a noticeable increase in the intermarriage rate during most of the Weimar Republic period. Although disguised somewhat by the sharp fluctuation in yearly figures, the absolute number of intermarriages actually increased less sharply between 1912 and 1932 than it had in the years before 1912, even though intermarriage rates climbed more rapidly in the latter period (Table 6.11). There were 10,436 Jewish intermarriages in Germany between 1901 and 1912 (870 on annual average), 14,763 between 1913 and 1922 (1,476 on annual average), and 15,481 between 1923 and 1932 (1,548 on annual average).

Jewish patterns of intermarriage and conversion were by no means random. Jews were much more inclined to marry Protestants and convert to Protestantism than to marry Catholics and convert to Catholicism. In contrast to the German denominational makeup of 64 percent Protestants and 32 percent Catholics, 77 percent of Jewish intermarriages in the first three decades of the twentieth century were with Protestants and only 23 percent were with Catholics. These tendencies remained stable throughout the period. The 1939 German census, which enumerated Jews by "race" who had converted to Christianity, yielded very similar figures (Table 6.12).[11]

During the Weimar period, the percentage of Germans who declared themselves without religion increased greatly; so did the percentage of intermarrying Jews who married persons without a religion. In 1919 only 116

---

10 Intermarriages in Prussia increased from 277 in 1875 to 474 in 1900. In 1901, the total number of intermarriages in all of Germany was 658 (1.45 times those in Prussia). By 1912 the number of intermarriages in Germany was 1,122. Ruppin, "Wachstum," 7; *Statistisches Jahrbuch für das Deutsche Reich* (1903): 21, (1914): 23.
11 Lowenstein, "Jewish Intermarriage and Conversion," 40–41.

Table 6.11. Jewish Religious Intermarriage Patterns in Germany, 1901–1935

Year	Homogeneous Jewish marriages	Intermarriages	Intermarriage rate*
1901	3878	658	7.82%
1902	3925	626	7.39
1903	3831	668	8.02
1904	4001	748	8.55
1905	3905	819	9.49
1906	4080	855	9.48
1907	4052	920	10.20
1908	3907	939	10.73
1909	3873	982	11.25
1910	3880	1003	11.45
1911	3814	1088	12.48
1912	3833	1130	12.85
1913	3621	1122	13.41
1914	2617	1344	20.43
1915	1098	1143	32.66
1916	1292	967	27.23
1917	1402	1035	26.96
1918	2171	1084	19.98
1919	6295	1929	13.29
1920	7487	2211	12.85
1921	5617	1890	14.40
1922	5025	2038	16.86
1923	4833	2008	17.20
1924	3310	1547	18.94
1925	2904	1413	19.57
1926	2656	1315	19.84
1927	2789	1505	21.25
1928	2983	1604	21.19
1929	2817	1664	22.80
1930	2851	1642	22.36
1931	2484	1405	22.05

1932	2307	1378	23.00
1933	2174	1693	28.03
1934	2522	792	13.57
1935	2751	503	8.38

* Intermarrying Jews divided by total number of Jews marrying.

1912 figures divided by 1901 figures	1.0	1.7	1.6
1932 figures divided by 1912 figures	0.6	1.2	1.8

Sources: *Statistisches Jahrbuch für das deutsche Reich* (1903): 21, (1904): 18, (1905): 16, (1906): 18, (1907): 17, (1908): 20, (1909): 40, (1910): 22, (1911): 23, (1912): 19, (1913): 23, (1914): 23, (1915): 27, (1916): 7, (1918): 7, (1919): 44, (1920): 32, (1921–1922): 41, (1923): 31, (1924–1925): 35, (1926): 28, (1927): 29, (1928): 33, (1929): 31, (1930): 33, (1931): 30, (1932): 30, (1933): 32, (1934): 32, (1935): 41, (1936): 41, (1937): 43.

Table 6.12. Discrepancy between Catholic–Protestant Balance in Population and Percent of Jewish Converts to Catholicism, 1939

Region	Overall population		Jewish converts to Christianity	
	Protestant	Catholic	Protestant	Catholic
Prussia	61.8%	31.8	75.6%	22.7
Bavaria	28.2	69.8	51.5	43.2
Baden	38.1	58.3	57.5	29.0
Württemberg	63.6	32.3	78.7	17.6
Hesse	64.1	31.0	69.1	26.0
Hamburg	79.3	5.9	92.7	5.9

Sources: Calculated from *Statistisches Jahrbuch für das Deutsche Reich* (1941–1942): 26; 1939 census, 4/6–9.

of the 14,519 Jews who married did so with persons without a religion. By the early 1930s, the annual number of Jews marrying persons without religion averaged about 240, more than one in every eight intermarriages. Meanwhile, the increasing numbers of Jews who left the Jewish community did not join a Christian denomination but the ranks of the unchurched instead.

The gender pattern of intermarriage also changed sharply over time. In most places, the earliest data show that Jewish women were the majority of those intermarrying. In some areas of relatively low intermarriage and low urbanization, the proportion of Jewish women among the intermarried remained high until the end of the nineteenth century. In Prussia, however, the Jewish male intermarriage rate began to exceed the female rate at a relatively early point in time. In the years immediately before World War I, women made up 40–45 percent of intermarrying Jews. During the Weimar years, the number of Jewish men intermarrying exceeded that of Jewish women by a large measure—5,517 between 1919 and 1933. In the latter year, which was marked by a rush to intermarry before intermarriage was forbidden by law, marriages between Jewish men and Gentile women increased immensely; intermarriages of Jewish women, in contrast, did not grow at all (Table 6.13).

The Nazis' rise to power had a large effect on conversion, *Austritt*, and intermarriage. Jews reacted to the crisis of 1933 in several different ways. One was a short-term jump in both intermarriages and conversions to Christianity; there were 1,378 Jewish intermarriages in Germany in 1932 and 1,693 in 1933. Conversions to Protestantism jumped even more, from 241 in 1932 to 993 in 1933. Evidently, in the first year of Nazi rule, many Jews felt that conversion or intermarriage would assure them better treatment, or at least should be undertaken while still legal. In 1934, with intermarriage still technically legal although discouraged by informal pressures, Jewish intermarriages in Germany fell to 792. In 1935, before the passage of the Nuremberg laws, they declined

Table 6.13. Changing Gender Distribution of Jewish Intermarriages, Germany (Annual Average in Parentheses)

Year	Jewish men–non-Jewish women		Jewish women–non-Jewish men		Percent Jewish men–non-Jewish women
1901–1905	1,906	(381.2)	1,613	(322.6)	54.2%
1906–1910	2,564	(512.8)	2,135	(427.0)	54.6
1911–1915	3,462	(692.4)	2,365	(473.0)	59.4
1916–1920	4,276	(855.2)	2,950	(590.0)	59.2
1921–1925	5,644	(1128.8)	3,252	(650.4)	63.4
1926–1930	4,871	(974.2)	2,859	(571.8)	63.0
1931–1932	1,775	(887.5)	1,008	(504.0)	63.8
1933	1,194	(1194.0)	499	(499.0)	70.5

Source: *Statistisches Jahrbuch für das Deutsche Reich*, as in Table 6.11.

again to 503. Meanwhile, homogeneous Jewish marriages increased from 2,174 in 1933 to 2,522 in 1934 and to 2,751 in 1935. The Nuremberg laws outlawed so-called "interracial" Jewish-Aryan marriages but did not totally end religious intermarriages between people of the same racial status. The 1939 census counts various categories of "racial" intermarriages and also analyzes their relationship to religious intermarriages. Marriages of racial "full Jews" and "Aryans" fell off from 1933 on, with a sharp drop between 1935 and 1936. The passage of the Nuremberg laws in 1935 actually increased the number of marriages between "full Jews" and "half-Jews" as well as between "half-Jews" and other "half-Jews." It also slashed the number of "half-Jews" who married "Aryans," and had little effect on the marriage of "quarter-Jews" with "Aryans" or other "quarter Jews" (Table 6.14). For the *Altreich* (Greater Germany minus Vienna), the 1939 census also showed an interesting correlation between "racial" and religious status in intermarriages. Among the 39,368 marriages in which both partners were classified "racially" as "full Jews," a mere 267 were religious intermarriages and, in 680 cases, both partners had left the Jewish community. When "full Jews" married "pure Aryans," sharp differences appeared between Jewish husbands and Jewish wives. When Jewish men married "Aryan" women, in almost eight percent of the marriages, the wife converted to Judaism and in 27.6 percent of cases the Jewish husband withdrew from the Jewish community. About 64.4 percent of the unions (5,544) were still true intermarriages, composed of unconverted Jewish and "Aryan" partners. When "Aryan" men married Jewish women, however, only twenty-four of them (0.4 percent) converted to Judaism and in 3,310 cases (54.6 percent) the wife withdrew from the Jewish community. Only 45 percent of the unions remained intermarriages in the religious sense (Table 6.15).

Of the 19,624 persons of fully Jewish "racial" background in the *Altreich* who had left the Jewish community in 1939, 13,764 (70.1 percent) joined a Christian denomination and 5,860 (29.9 percent) opted for one of the non-denominational categories. Jewish men were slightly more likely than Jewish women to remain in the Jewish community or declare themselves to be without religion, and women were somewhat more likely than men to convert to a Christian denomination. The percentage of Jews who left the Jewish community was lowest in the South German states of Bavaria, Württemberg, and Baden and in the Prussian provinces of Rhineland, Westphalia, and Hesse-Nassau. Withdrawal from the Jewish community and conversion were most common in Hamburg, the Free State of Saxony, and the Prussian provinces of Saxony and Schleswig-Holstein (Table 6.16). The percentage of persons of "mixed blood"

Table 6.14. Marriage Patterns of Persons of Jewish "Racial" Origin, Altreich*, 1933–1938 (Nazi categories in 1939 census)

Year	Both Jews	Jew and "German"	Jew and "Half-Jew"	Jew and "Quarter-Jew"	Both "Half-Jews"	"Half-Jew" and "Quarter-Jew"	"Half-Jew" and "German"	Both "Quarter-Jews"	"Quarter-Jew" and "German"	Total
1938	969	39	62	2	91	4	111	28	245	1551
1937	767	40	47	1	59	7	87	17	199	1224
1936	658	46	32	4	45	5	73	11	208	1082
1935	589	248	25	7	25	12	291	17	218	1432
1934	541	364	25	11	44	15	403	22	234	1659
1933	447	683	15	3	47	11	481	12	228	1927
Total	3971	1420	206	28	311	54	1446	107	1332	8875

Influence of Nuremberg laws (1935) on changing marriage patterns

1933–1935	1577	2394	125	21	141	195	1175	56	652	3857
1936–1938	2394	125								
Percent before 1936	39.7%	91.1	31.6	75.0	37.3	81.3	47.7	51.1	56.5	

"German" = "Aryan"

* Greater Germany minus Vienna = Altreich.

Source: 1939 census, 4/62–63, 68–69.

Table 6.15. "Racial" and Religious Intermarriages and Homogeneous Marriages according to 1939 Census (*Altreich*)

"Racial" status of woman:	"Full Jew"		"Half-Jew"		"Quarter-Jew"		"Aryan"	
Religious status of woman:	Jewish (*Glaubensjuden*)	Not Jewish	Jewish	Not Jewish	Jewish	Not Jewish	Jewish	Not Jewish
"Racial" and religious status of man:								
"Full Jew"								
Jewish religion	38,421	124	227	116	15	54	684	5,544
Not Jewish religion	143	680	4	67	0	20	3	2,378
"Half-Jew"								
Jewish religion	205	1	47	5	0	3	16	125
Not Jewish religion	73	62	2	1,079	0	91	0	3,921
"Quarter-Jew"								
Jewish religion	5	0	6	1	18	0	2	35

"Racial" status of woman:	"Full Jew"		"Half-Jew"		"Quarter-Jew"		"Aryan"	
Religious status of woman:	Jewish (*Glaubensjuden*)	Not Jewish	Jewish	Not Jewish	Jewish	Not Jewish	Jewish	Not Jewish
Not Jewish religion	53	35	7	140	2	367	0	2178
"Aryan"								
Jewish religion	24	5	4	0	4	0	13	8
Not Jewish religion	2,723	3,310	81	3,666	20	2,159	5	?

Altreich = total Germany minus Vienna.

Data in bold = "racial" intermarriage. Normal lettering = same "racial" category.

Dotted underlining = religious intermarriage. Solid underlining = religious inmarriage.

Source: 1939 census, 4/60–61.

Table 6.16. "Racially" Jewish Converts (*Volljuden*) to Other Religious Categories, 1939 Census

A) By Territory

Region	Un-converted Jews (*Glaubensjuden*)		Protestant		Catholic		Other Christian		Gottglaeubig ("believers," no specified religion)		Glaubenslos ("non-believers")		No indication of religion	
	M	F	M	F	M	F	M	F	M	F	M	F	M	F
Prussia	67592	92286	2828	4550	722	1491	60	111	744	1267	831	1032	102	130
	92.7%	91.5	3.9	4.5	1.0	1.5	0.1	0.1	1.0	1.3	1.1	1.0	0.1	0.1
Bavaria	6857	9105	141	279	126	226	18	25	47	76	71	81	0	14
	94.4%	92.9	1.9	2.8	1.7	2.3	0.2	0.3	0.6	0.8	1.0	0.8	0	0.1
Saxony	3006	3659	236	407	27	40	3	5	65	74	53	37	4	7
	88.3%	85.9	6.9	9.6	0.8	0.9	0.1	0.1	1.9	1.7	1.6	0.9	0.1	0.2
Württemberg	1822	2555	49	139	17	25	1	8	22	39	13	20	1	2
	94.6%	91.6	2.6	5.0	0.9	0.9	0.1	0.3	1.1	1.4	0.7	0.7	0.1	0.1
Baden	3505	5222	102	142	40	83	25	32	30	67	20	38	2	3
	94.1%	93.5	2.7	2.5	1.1	1.5	0.7	0.6	0.8	1.2	0.5	0.7	0.1	0.1
Hesse	2351	3364	65	118	20	49	7	6	16	26	23	19	3	1
	94.6%	93.9	2.6	3.3	0.8	1.4	0.3	0.2	0.6	0.7	0.9	0.5	0.1	0.04

Region	Un-converted Jews (*Glaubensjuden*)		Protestant		Catholic		Other Christian		*Gottglaeubig* ("believers," no specified religion)		*Glaubenslos* ("non-believers")		No indication of religion	
	M	F	M	F	M	F	M	F	M	F	M	F	M	F
Hamburg	3401	4774	373	605	23	39	2	13	107	202	146	199	26	33
	83.4%	81.4	9.1	10.3	0.6	0.7	0.05	0.2	2.6	3.4	3.6	3.4	0.6	0.6
All other *Altreich* (Thuringia, Mecklenburg, Braunschweig, Oldenburg, Bremen, Anhalt, Lippe, Schaumburg-Lippe)	2105	1855	162	241	37	49	2	2	24	49	58	27	3	6
	88.0%	84.5	6.8	11.0	1.55	2.2	0.1	0.1	1.0	2.2	2.4	1.2	0.1	0.3
Total *Altreich* amount	90639	122820	3956	6481	1012	2002	116	197	1055	1800	1215	1453	141	196
	92.4%	91.1	4.0	4.8	1.0	1.5	0.1	0.1	1.1	1.3	1.2	1.1	0.1	0.1
Percent of non-*Glaubensjuden* in each category			52.8	53.4	13.5	16.5	1.5	1.6	14.1	14.8	16.2	12.0	1.9	1.6

Data in bold = territory with highest percent of the religious category.

B) By Major Provinces of Prussia, 1939

Province	Unconverted Jews (Glaubensjuden)		Protestant		Catholic		Other Christian		Gottglaeubig ("believers," no specified religion)		Glaubenslos ("non-believers")		No indication of religion	
	M	F	M	F	M	F	M	F	M	F	M	F	M	F
Berlin	31325	44019	1491	2348	213	395	32	50	516	728	548	665	65	62
	91.6%	91.2	4.4	4.9	0.6	0.8	0.1	0.1	1.5	1.5	1.6	1.4	0.2	0.1
Silesia	6544	9296	216	323	137	244	1	3	30	38	34	38	4	13
	93.9%	93.4	3.1	3.2	2.0	2.5	0.01	0.03	0.4	0.4	0.5	0.4	0.1	0.1
Westphalia	3214	4170	102	171	50	126	4	9	22	47	20	26	3	0
	94.1%	91.7	3.0	3.8	1.5	2.8	0.1	0.2	0.6	1.0	0.4	0.6	0.1	0
Rhine Province	9900	13208	253	482	210	501	3	8	64	168	61	117	7	16
	94.3%	91.1	2.4	3.3	2.0	3.5	0.03	0.1	0.6	1.2	0.6	0.8	0.1	0.1
Hesse-Nassau	8295	11957	181	373	47	125	8	29	42	129	49	78	9	22
	96.1%	94.1	2.1	2.9	0.5	1.0	0.1	0.2	0.5	1.1	0.6	0.6	0.1	0.2
All other Prussia:														

Province	Unconverted Jews (*Glaubensjuden*)		Protestant		Catholic		Other Christian		*Gottglaeubig* ("believers," no specified religion)		*Glaubenslos* ("non-believers")		No indication of religion	
	M	F	M	F	M	F	M	F	M	F	M	F	M	F
East (East Prussia, Brandenburg, Pomerania)	4515	5013	310	433	42	53	9	4	36	77	54	46	4	9
	90.8%	89.0	6.2	7.7	0.8	0.9	**0.2**	0.1	0.7	1.4	1.1	0.8	0.1	0.2
Center (Saxony, Schleswig-Holstein)	1229	1676	171	223	9	22	2	3	20	48	30	37	4	5
	83.9%	83.2	**11.7**	**11.1**	0.6	1.1	0.1	0.1	1.4	**2.4**	**2.0**	**1.8**	0.3	0.3
West (Hannover, Hohenzollern)	2570	2947	104	197	14	25	1	5	14	32	35	25	6	3
	93.7%	91.1	3.8	6.1	0.5	0.8	0.04	0.2	0.5	1.0	1.3	0.8	0.2	0.1

Source: calculated from 1939 census, 4/6–9.

(a sign of earlier intermarriage) was generally highest in areas where conversion out of Judaism was high, especially in northwestern Germany.[12]

The 1939 census confirms some of the impressions gained from earlier data on Jewish conversion and intermarriage. The regional differences in intermarriage and conversion seem to have held steady for many decades. On the other hand, the 1939 census places our impressions of massive intermarriage and conversion in perspective; despite the expectations of many Nazis (and probably of many Jews), the number of converts to Christianity and persons of partial Jewish ancestry was far smaller than the number of unconverted "full Jews."[13] Intermarriage rates had indeed increased—partly due to declines in homogeneous Jewish marriages—but conversions actually passed their peak in the twentieth century and began to fall. During the years of the Weimar Republic, the perceived threat of secularization and abandonment of all religion was becoming a stronger phenomenon than conversion itself. Conversion and intermarriage in particular affected a substantial minority of German Jewry. Notwithstanding racist antisemitic fears, however, only a tiny proportion of the "Aryan" population of Germany was ever involved in an intermarriage with a person of Jewish origin.[14]

---

12 See chapter 3, note 36.
13 According the 1939 census, there were 318,320 persons of Jewish ancestry in Germany within its 1937 boundaries. Among them, 213,930 (67.21 percent) were both members of the Jewish community and persons classified by the Nazis as "full Jews."
14 Looking at some of the chief years of intermarriage in the 1920s, we find the following: among 731,157 marriages in Germany in 1921 (involving 1,432, 314 individuals), including 13,124 that involved Jewish individuals, only 1,890 were composed of a Jew and a non-Jew. In 1927, among 538,463 marriages in Germany, only 1,505 were intermarriages between Jews and non-Jews. In the latter year approximately 0.15 percent of people in Germany who married were involved in a Jewish–Gentile marriage (*Statistisches Jahrbuch des Deutschen Reichs* [1923]: 31, [1929]: 31).

7

Migration—Overall Trends and Internal Migration

This section analyzes migration to and from German Jewish communities in three separate chapters (7–9). Each chapter is devoted to one of three aspects of the phenomenon—1) internal migration, 2) immigration and emigration, and 3) urbanization in the sense of countryside-to-city relocation—even though the distinctions are not always as clear as the analysis may imply.

Migration was an important factor in the demographic history of nineteenth- and twentieth-century Germany. Jews shared many of the geographical and chronological patterns of migration that the rest of the population exhibited regarding overseas emigration, urbanization, and migration from province to province, although distinctively Jewish patterns also existed at times. For various reasons, Jews were even more prone than the rest of the German population to change their domicile. One precipitant of this was occupational: Jews lacked the tie to landownership that bound many Gentile farmers to their home villages. Many Jewish occupations were itinerant—especially in commerce, such as peddling, cattle dealing, or selling at fairs outside one's hometown. This often gave Jews a broader geographical horizon than their agrarian neighbors. Legal restrictions on parents' ability to settle children in their own places of residence and the need to find marriage partners for offspring outside often tiny Jewish communities created a network of family relationships in various localities that paralleled business networks. In the premodern world, religious persecution, expulsions, and violence often forced Jews to move from one area to another. Given the difficulty in procuring legal residency rights in the eighteenth century, much of the Jewish population (estimates are elusive, but the proportion may have been as high as twenty percent) traveled from town to town as beggars. The *Betteljuden*, as they were known, received food and shelter from the Jewish communities through which they passed. During the first half of the nineteenth century, these roving populations reduced in number, though *Wanderbettelei* remained an issue even in the second half of the century. Whether most settled down in Germany or emigrated to America is not yet known in detail. In the first half of the nineteenth century, the uneven pace of political emancipation in different German territories also often induced Jews to leave more restrictive areas and move to less restrictive ones or to immigrate to America. Religious worldviews, both Jewish and non-Jewish, that saw the Jews as a nation in exile may have been yet another factor in making the Jewish population more geographically mobile than the Christian population, which thought of itself as rooted in the soil of its native land.

There were, however, many traits that German Jews and German Gentiles shared. Religious factors affected not only Jews, but also the residential patterns of Protestants and Catholics, who frequently lived in mono-confessional towns and sometimes had to leave territories that came under the rule of a prince of the opposite faith. Christian artisans often had to serve for several years as journeymen, learning their trades before finding a place to settle as masters. In early nineteenth-century Germany, when legislation, especially in southern Germany, encouraged Jews to switch from commerce to crafts, many young Jewish men also took to the road, sometimes using this as a path towards emigration.

Both German Christians and German Jews participated in mass migrations to Eastern Europe during the medieval and early modern periods, although the end results were different. Many of the territories east of the Elbe were Germanized as German colonists either replaced or Germanized Slavic natives. Farther east, there were islands of German-speaking colonies in Hungary, the Baltic region, Poland, and Russia. As late as the eighteenth century, rather large numbers of German colonists settled in the Volga region of Russia. An even larger percentage of German Jews moved to Eastern Europe in the medieval and early modern eras, leaving only a tenth of the Ashkenazi communities in German-speaking territories. Jews lived as a mainly urban minority throughout the sprawling Polish Commonwealth. By the eighteenth century, however, the direction of Jewish migration seems to have reversed, with Jews beginning to move from east to west.

The social makeup of Jewish migration was often quite distinct from Christian migration, especially from the countryside to the cities. Among Christians, those who migrated were often unmarried women in search of domestic work or landless young men seeking industrial jobs. Although the migration of Jewish female domestics had long been a factor, it virtually ceased to be so after 1850. Jewish migrants to cities were by then more likely to be young men looking for education or occupational training or businessmen whose enterprises had outgrown their rural confines.[1] Jews were often more attracted to centers of commerce, culture, and administration than to the industrial centers that Christians found more alluring.[2]

Jewish migration patterns changed several times during the lengthy period from 1815 to 1939. Various provinces experienced Jewish out-migration in some periods and in-migration in others. The percent of Jews who participated in migration waves also changed from decade to decade. While both the general population and the Jews had similar chronological patterns of emigration and immigration and often migrated in the same direction from one German area to another, the proportional magnitude of Jewish migration was often greater. Even at times of massive urbanization or mass migration from certain provinces, actual declines in the general population of an entire province were extremely rare. Jewish populations in some areas of Germany, however, declined steeply—by more than fifty percent in a few cases. As Jews participated in the mass migration from Germany to America in the nineteenth century, their share among the emigrants was often more than twice their proportion of the population of their territory of origin.

In the period from about 1815 to 1840, official population records were less reliable and detailed than at later times. During this period, the recorded Jewish populations of virtually all areas of Germany for which records exist increased markedly. Although we have a general idea of Jewish natural increase, which, when separated from the overall increase, should indicate the migration balance, some of the upturn may also be attributed to the government's growing success in registering the entire population. While most regions showed moderately positive migration balances, there were two exceptions. In Bavaria, especially in Franconia and Swabia, there were rather large negative migration balances in the Jewish population by the 1830s. On the other side of Germany, especially in

---

1 See Steven M. Lowenstein, "The Rural Community and the Urbanization of German Jewry," *Central European History* 13, no. 3 (1980): 218–236.
2 One need only think of the much heavier Jewish migration to commercial centers like Cologne and Frankfurt am Main than to the Ruhr industrial cities of Dortmund and Essen.

East Prussia and Pomerania, the percentage increase in Jewish population was overwhelming. Most of the excess out-migration from Bavaria seems to have gone overseas whereas most migration to East Prussia and Pomerania came from other parts of Prussia. In both cases, the Jews' migration rate far exceeded that of non-Jews.

Between 1840 and the unification of Germany in 1871, emigration from Bavaria continued and spread to other areas in southern Germany. It tapered off after unification, allowing some areas to recover some of their population losses. The migration of Jews from the East German province of Posen, which began in the 1840s, gathered momentum and became overwhelming; by 1910, over two-thirds of the Jewish population of the province had left. Jews also began to leave some of the smaller central German states in considerable numbers, most notably Anhalt and Mecklenburg. Migration from small towns to large cities in Germany, not very marked before 1840, attained its greatest rapidity between 1840 and the 1880s. Thereafter, migration to the largest cities, especially Berlin, continued to grow in absolute numbers but no longer kept up with the overall growth of urban populations. In many smaller and middle-sized cities, Jewish populations began to decline in absolute as well as relative terms after cresting in the late nineteenth century. Nevertheless, the proportion of Jews living in large cities increased greatly during the Imperial period, with Jews in cities of over 100,000 inhabitants climbing from 14.6 percent of all of German Jewry in 1871 to 53.2 percent in 1910.

After the unification of Germany, while Jewish immigrants began to outnumber emigrants, emigration never totally ceased. Most immigrants came from Galicia or the Russian Empire. After the expulsion of many foreign Jews and Poles from the eastern provinces of Prussia in the 1880s, immigrants avoided these regions and congregated mainly in Berlin, the Kingdom of Saxony, and major cities in various parts of Germany. Migration from the eastern provinces of Prussia, no longer limited to Posen province but also very noticeable in West Prussia and Pomerania, was directed mainly toward Berlin and, to a lesser extent, Breslau as well. The regional balance of Germany's Jewish population underwent a particularly powerful change during the *Kaiserreich* era. The greatest influx of Jewish population occurred in central Germany, especially in Berlin and the Kingdom (later the Free State) of Saxony. Most of the migrants came from abroad and from the eastern provinces of Prussia. Migration to the Ruhr District and the city of Cologne in western Germany also occurred in appreciable numbers, although the Jewish population in the Ruhr district grew more slowly than the general population. The relative decline of Jewish population in the southern regions continued after 1871 but at a slower pace than before. There was relatively little migration between northwestern and other parts of Germany. Within each of the larger regions, considerable redistributions of population often occurred, probably through relatively short-distance migration. In central Germany, the Jewish populations of the small states of Mecklenburg and Anhalt declined sharply in contrast to nearby Berlin and Saxony. In southern Germany, the Jewish population migrated toward more urbanized regions such as the Frankfurt area and away from more rural regions in parts of Baden, Württemberg, and Bavarian Franconia and Swabia. Less industrialized areas in northwestern and western Germany also tended to see marked Jewish out-migration to more urbanized parts of their region such as Hamburg, Hannover, Cologne, and the Ruhr.

After World War I, most Jews who still lived in the now-forfeited Polish-speaking regions migrated to Berlin or Breslau. Between 1910 and 1925, the concentration of Jews in Berlin and in other parts of the central region continued to increase and some migration to the Ruhr and Cologne districts continued as well. Immigration from Eastern Europe seems to have peaked during and immediately after World War I and then began to decline. The exact magnitudes of these developments are difficult to determine because the German-born children of non-naturalized immigrants (the majority of recent Jewish immigrants) were also counted as foreign Jews. Between 1925 and 1933, the decline in the German-Jewish population traced at least partly to emigration. How much of this emigration took place between Hitler's accession to the chancellorship in January 1933 and the census in June cannot be determined. Either way, Jewish emigration accelerated after 1933, especially in 1938 and 1939. Among the Jews who remained in Germany, the tendency to move from small towns to larger cities, which for a time seemed safer, continued.

Internal Migration

In most cases, we have no direct information on how many Jewish individuals moved from one place to another within Germany. To estimate their number, we usually need to make inferences based on calculations of net migration balances (in-migration minus out-migration).[3]

---

3 The net migration balance is calculated by subtracting the natural balance (births less deaths) from the change in population over a particular period. In some cases, other non-migratory phenomena such as religious conversion or improved governmental collection of statistics may be excluded as well. At least some of the Jewish population increase in the early decades of the nineteenth century may be the result of improved governmental record-keeping. The

Most German states restricted the entry of "foreign" Jews, including Jews from other German states, in the early nineteenth century and, in some cases, until 1871. Although this did not prevent all Jews from migrating from state to state or from other countries, it meant that Jewish migration within states was often greater in scope than immigration across political frontiers until the unification of Germany.

Census enumerations of Jewish residents in almost all areas in Germany showed a considerable increase between about 1815 and 1840 (Tables 7.1 A–E, Map 7/1). In Prussia we know that Jewish increase outstripped the growth of the general population at the time.[4] In Prussia as a whole, the increase of over 44 percent exceeded the estimated 1.34 percent annual natural growth of the Jewish population, leaving a moderate net excess of immigration over emigration of 13.7 percent.[5] In the South German states—the Grand Duchy of Hesse, Württemberg, Bavaria, and Baden—the annual increases in Jewish population were smaller. In Baden, Württemberg, and Hesse-Darmstadt,

---

migration balance thus calculated is always less than the actual number of migrants because it measures the difference between in-migration and out-migration rather than the total number of migrants. As the Jewish birth rate declined during the *Kaiserreich* period, the migration balance increasingly approximated the actual change in regional populations.

Even after establishing the migration balance, it is not an easy task to separate internal migration from migration across boundaries. Statistics on the places of origin of residents of a particular location (where available) can help distinguish immigrants from migrants arriving from elsewhere in Germany. Also, some data are available on emigrants' destinations for certain places and periods. In most cases, we have much less information on the destinations of people who left a particular area without crossing a frontier. In addition, before 1871, data on some of the smaller independent states of Germany are missing.

The interpretation of negative migration balances is difficult. Especially in the preunification period, such balances can usually be attributed to emigration (especially overseas) except in cases that offer clear evidence of the specific domestic destination of out-migrants. Until the 1880s or so, a large proportion of the increase in Jewish population can be attributed to the excess of births over deaths. Thereafter, as systematic birth control spread among German Jewry, this positive "natural" population balance fades and, by the twentieth century, increases in Jewish population are almost always attributable to in-migration.

4 Johann Gottfried Hoffmann, "Neueste Nachrichten von der Bevölkerung des preußischen Staates," part 5, *Allgemeine Preußische Staatszeitung* 229 (1838): 949.

5 These figures are considerably higher than those given by the Prussian statistician Johann Gottfried Hoffmann in 1838, who reckoned that between 1822 and 1837, 33,054 more Jews were born in Prussia than died, 1,888 Jews converted to Christianity, and 410 lived in an area that had been annexed in 1834. This leaves 7,266 Jews unaccounted for in the increase in the Jewish population; most of this increment can be attributed to an excess of immigration over emigration. This resulted in a relatively modest net immigration of 5.02 percent of the total Prussian Jewish population of 1822 for Prussia as a whole. Hoffmann's calculations exclude the 1817–1822 period, when the reported Jewish population of Prussia increased from 127,345 to 144,737 (13.7 percent). Presumably, Hoffmann attributed much of this increase to improved census accuracy rather than to actual population growth.

immigration and emigration almost balanced each other out, leaving nearly all of the Jewish population increase attributable to natural growth. In Bavaria, there was a substantial excess of emigration over immigration, which was larger on a percentage basis than Prussia's positive migration balance.

The moderately positive migration balance in the huge Kingdom of Prussia masked substantial regional differences. The eastern provinces of East Prussia and Pomerania as well as the Upper Silesia district of Oppeln showed very large upturns in both percentage and in absolute terms with arrivals exceeding departures by more than 7,000 between 1817 and 1837. Even the provinces of Posen and West Prussia showed moderately positive migration balances on a percentage basis and over 7,500 more arrivals in absolute terms. Most parts of the western provinces of Rhineland and Westphalia, in contrast, showed below-average growth or even small negative migration balances. Among *Regierungsbezirke* (administrative districts or RBs) that posted above-average percentage growth, eight were in the eastern sections of Prussia, four were in central areas, and none were in the west (Table 7.1). Almost 90 percent of the favorable migration balance for all of Prussia occurred in the eastern provinces. Since all major eastern provinces showed substantial positive migration balances, at least some of the migration must have come from outside Prussia, especially from former Polish Commonwealth territories that came under Russian and Austrian control. There must have been substantial gaps in the enforcement of Prussia's laws against Jewish emigration across the eastern frontier.

In the eastern provinces, Jewish migration was very heavy into East Prussia and Pomerania and, especially, the Pomeranian Stettin and East Prussian Gumbinnen districts on a percentage basis. Although East Prussia and Pomerania also experienced somewhat above-average growth in general population at the same time, the percentage increase in the Jewish population was almost three times as great. The Jewish percentage of the population of the two provinces increased from 0.34 percent to 0.55 percent between 1817 and 1840 (Table 7.2).[6] Until the Prussian Emancipation decree in 1812, both East Prussia and Pomerania, which bordered the heavily Jewish formerly Polish provinces of West Prussia and Posen, had sparse Jewish populations. The 1812 edict granted Jews free movement within Prussia but the government did not extend this entitlement, let alone citizenship, to Jews who dwelled in areas acquired by Prussia after

---

6 Based on Silbergleit, *Die Bevölkerungs- und Berufsverhältnisse*, 7*, 18*–19*; and Salomon Neumann, *Zur Statistik der Juden in Preussen von 1816 bis 1880*, 2nd ed. (Berlin, 1884), Table Ib.

Table 7.1. Changes in Jewish Population and Estimated Migration Balances—Early Nineteenth Century (areas with fewer than 1,000 Jews in smaller font)

A) Prussia by *Regierungsbezirk*

Regierungsbezirk	1817	1837	Percent change	Expected population based on natural growth[1]	Estimated migration balance	
					Number	Percent
Königsberg	2098	3943	+87.9	2869	+1074	+37.4
Gumbinnen	291	1102	+278.7	397	+705	+177.6
East Prussia					+1779	+54.5
Danzig	3854	5056	+31.2	5258	-202	-3.8
Marienwerder	8778	13777	+57.0	11977	+1800	+15.0
West Prussia					+1598	+9.3
Posen	37545	52017	+38.6	51226	+791	+1.5
Bromberg	15021	22179	+47.7	20494	+1645	+8.1
Posen					+2436	+3.4

1 Natural growth may be estimated in various ways with somewhat different results. I chose to use the natural growth percentages for Prussian Jews as calculated by Silbergleit, *Die Bevölkerungs- und Berufsverhältnisse*, 14*–15*, for the years 1819–1849, and assumed that these rates were uniform for all districts, which is not likely. For 1817–1819, I assumed the same rate as in 1819–1822. The annual rates for Jewish natural growth given by Silbergleit are: 1819–1822—1.866 percent, 1822–1825—1.638 percent, 1825–1828—1.290 percent, 1828–1831—1.309 percent, 1831–1834—1.537 percent, 1834–1837—1.537 percent, 1837–1840—1.585 percent, 1840–1843—1.724 percent, 1843–1846—1.825 percent, 1846–1849—1.067 percent. Since there are no comparable figures for non-Prussian areas, I had to use these percentages for all parts of Germany.

Migration—Overall Trends and Internal Migration | 249

Regierungsbezirk	1817	1837	Percent change	Expected population based on natural growth[1]	Estimated migration balance	
					Number	Percent
Stettin	1269	2953	+132.7	1731	+1222	+70.6
Köslin	1585	3006	+89.7	2163	+843	+39.0
Stralsund	122	184	+50.8	166	+18	+10.8
Pomerania					+2083	+51.3
Breslau						
Liegnitz	8868	11396	+28.5	12099	-703	-5.8
Reichenbach*						
Oppeln	7608	13179	+73.2	10380	+2799	+27.0
Silesia					+2096	+9.3
East					**+9992**	**+8.4**
Berlin	3700	5645	+52.6	5048	+597	+11.8
Potsdam	1933	2576	+33.3	2523	+53	+2.8
Brandenburg					+1003	+8.7
Magdeburg	2142	2334	+8.0	2922	-588	-20.1
Merseburg	192	416	+117.8	155	+292	+81.1
Erfurt	911	1339	+47.0	1243	+96	+7.7
Saxony					-337	-7.6

Regierungsbezirk	1817	1837	Percent change	Expected population based on natural growth[1]	Estimated migration balance	
					Number	Percent
Central					**+552**	**+3.4**
Münster	2304	2985	+29.6	3144	-159	-5.0
Minden	3930	5273	+34.2	5362	-89	-1.7
Arnsberg	3489	4792	+37.4	4760	+32	+0.7
Westphalia					**-216**	**-2.6**
Düsseldorf	5023	6622	+31.8	6853	-231	-3.4
Kleve*						
Cologne	3349	4629	+38.2	4569	+60	+1.3
Aachen	1621	2229	+37.5	2212	+17	+0.8
Trier	3057	4377	+43.2	4171	+206	+4.9
Koblenz	5791	7308	+26.2	7901	-593	-4.3
Rhineland					**-541**	**-2.1**
West					**-757**	**-2.3**
All Prussia	**127345**	**183579**	**+44.2**	**173752**	**+9787**	**+5.6**

* RBs Kleve and Reichenbach existed in 1817 but not in later census periods. Therefore, their data is combined with the RBs with which they were merged.

Sources: Loewe, "Die Juden Preussens im Jahre 1817," 45; Allgemeine Zeitung des Judenthums 2, no. 109 (September 11, 1838): 439–442.

B) Bavaria by Region

Region	1818	1840	Percent change	Expected population based on natural growth	Estimated migration balance	
					Number	Percent
Upper Franconia	6286	6568	+4.5	8664	-2096	-24.2
Middle Franconia	11816	11377	-3.7	16286	-4909	-30.1
Lower Franconia	16637	16451	-1.1	22931	-6480	-28.3
All Franconia	34739	34396	-1.2	47881	-13485	-28.2
Swabia	6514	6891	+5.8	8978	-2087	-23.2
Rhine Palatinate	10470	15396	+47.1	14431	+965	+6.7
Upper Palatinate	991	1062	+7.2	1366	-304	-22.2
Upper Bavaria	489	1528	+212.5	674	+854	+126.7
Lower Bavaria	5	15	+200.0	7	+8	+114.3
All Bavaria	53208	59288	+11.4	73337	-14049	-19.2

Source: F. B. W. von Hermann, *Beiträge zur Statistik des Königreichs, Bayern* (Munich, 1850), 20.

C) Württemberg

District	1821	1841	Percent change	Expected population based on natural growth	Estimated migration balance	
					Number	Percent
Jagstkreis	3761	4827	+28.3	4989	-162	-3.2
Neckarkreis	2023	2609	+29.0	2683	-74	-2.8
Schwarzwaldkreis	1466	1849	+26.1	1945	-96	-4.9
Donaukreis	1643	2299	+39.9	2179	+120	+5.5
All Württemberg	8893	11584	+30.3	11796	-212	-1.8

Source: *Württembergische Jahrbücher für vaterländische Geschichte, Geographie, Statistik und Topographie* 2 (1843), Anhang.

D) Baden

District	1812	1845	Percent change	Expected population based on natural growth	Estimated migration balance	
					Number	Percent
Seekreis	1483					
Oberrheinkreis	4007					
Mittelrheinkreis	6725					
Unterrheinkreis	11043					
All Baden	15079	23258	+54.2	25406	−2148	−8.5

Sources: *Statistisches Handbuch für das Grossherzogthum Baden . . .* (Karlsruhe, 1815), 34; *Die politischen- Kirchen- und Schulgemeinden des Grossherzogthums Baden mit der Seelen und Bürgerzahl vom Jahr 1845* (Karlsruhe, 1847), 94–97.

E) Hesse-Darmstadt

Hesse-Darmstadt	1822	1840	Percent change	Expected population based on natural growth	Estimated migration balance	
					Number	Percent
	20600	26721	+29.7	26370	+351	+1.3

Source: Schmelz, *Hessen*, 46.

Table 7.2. Changes in General and Jewish Population of East Prussia and Pomerania, 1817–1843

Regierungsbezirk	Jewish		General	
	1817	1843	1817	1843
Königsberg	2098	4730	533,101	821,946
Gumbinnen	291	1467	366,479	619,553
Stettin	1269	3779	327,002	517,552
Köslin	1585	3781	244,515	413,106
Stralsund	122	156	129,239	177,722
Total	5365	13913 +159.3%	1,600,336	2,548,879 +62.4%

Source: Silbergleit, *Die Bevölkerungs- und Berufsverhältnisse*, 11*, 18*; W. Dieterici, *Die Statistischen Tabellen des Preussischen Staats nach der amtlichen Aufnahme des Jahres 1843* (Berlin, 1845), 17.

1812.[7] The large majority of migrants to East Prussia and Pomerania came from within Prussia, especially from those parts of West Prussia where Jews had been granted citizenship in 1812. Until the Prussian Emancipation decree, some of these Jews were legal residents in other provinces but spent many months at a time doing business in East Prussia. Many of the new migrants to East Prussia had formerly lived in towns in West Prussia and northern Posen province. After the 1812 decree, many of them became legalized residents of towns where they had previously done business. As a result, many new Jewish communities developed in the small towns and cities of East Prussia.[8]

---

7 When the Prussian state expanded after the Napoleonic Wars, its Jewish inhabitants were kept under the original legal status given to them by the territories that had previously controlled them. In some Prussian provinces, Jews had citizenship, while in others, especially formerly Polish Posen, as well as formerly Saxon or Swedish territories, they were denied citizenship. In general, when Jews migrated to a new area, they retained the legal status they had had in their old residence. During the period from 1816 to 1843 this situation did not change in principle, though many individual Jews (especially in Posen) received naturalization.

8 Jacob Adam, *Zeit zur Abreise: Lebensbericht eines judischen Handlers aus der Emanzipationszeit; bearbeitet und herausgegeben von Jorg H. Fehrs und Margret Heitmann* (Hildesheim and New York: Olms, 1993); Trude Maurer, "Migration von Juden—Eine Problemskizze," in *Probleme der Migration und Integration im Preussenland vom Mittelalter bis zum Anfang des 20. Jahrhunderts*, ed. Klaus Militzer (Marburg: Elwert, 2005), 217–247. Maurer showed that Jews were especially likely to migrate from the heavily Jewish region in the southwestern section of West Prussia. The direction of migration differed from town to town. Whereas a large percentage of migrants from Märkisch Friedland gravitated to Berlin, migrants from nearby Flatow, Tütz, and Krojanke often moved to East Prussia, including locations as far to the east as Tilsit, Memel, Gumbinnen, and Heydekrug.

The bulk of newly arrived Jewish residents in Pomerania and East Prussia between 1816 and 1843 were Prussian citizens; only a few were immigrants or came from Prussian areas where Jews did not have citizenship (Table 7.3). In contrast, there were noticeable increases in Jewish non-citizens in the West Prussian district of Marienwerder, Berlin, Merseburg District in Saxony, and Arnsberg District in Westphalia. These figures seem to indicate migration from areas where Jews did not have citizenship, such as from Posen to Marienwerder and to Berlin, and from formerly non-Prussian Saxon areas to Merseburg; they do not necessarily point to immigration from outside Prussia.

Jews who moved to Pomerania and East Prussia in the early nineteenth century migrated either to the countryside or to relatively small cities. After the middle of that century, large-scale Jewish migration to rural and small-town communities was virtually unheard of anywhere in Germany. While the number of Jews living in places designated as "countryside" (*Land*) doubled in Prussia overall between 1817 and 1849, the increase in Pomerania and East Prussia was more than twenty-fold. Steep increases in Jewish rural population were also found in several other east Prussian districts, such as West Prussia. In the western and central sections of Prussia, which traditionally had much larger rural Jewish populations than the east, the upturn in rural population was much more modest (Table 7.4).[9]

Except in cities that had formerly totally excluded Jews, the rate of Jewish migration to major German cities before 1840 was no greater than the increase in Jewish population in more rural areas (Table 7.5). Berlin showed only slightly above-average growth, similar to that in other established Prussian communities like Posen and Königsberg, while Breslau had a slightly negative migration balance and Danzig a more substantial one. Negative migration balances also occurred in the old Jewish communities of Mannheim, Karlsruhe, and Frankfurt. The newly opened southern cities of Munich, Würzburg, and Stuttgart showed considerable growth, probably from migration from rural parts of their states. The losses in some cities were probably caused by migration overseas or to larger cities rather than to migration back into the countryside.

The birthplaces of all new Jewish citizens of Berlin between 1809 and 1851 are well documented[10] (Table 7.6). Until about 1827, about 30 percent of all Jewish migrants came from the province of Brandenburg, which surrounded

---

9 The share of rural Jews in the eastern sections of Prussia (excluding RBs Posen and Oppeln) climbed from 9.4 percent of Jews living in areas considered "Land" in 1817 to 24.8 percent by 1858.
10 Jacobson, *Die Judenbürgerbücher der Stadt Berlin*. Only a few of the entries in the volume occurred after 1850.

Table 7.3. Changes in Citizen and Non-Citizen Jewish Population in Prussian Districts, 1816–1843

District	1816		1843		Change 1816–1843			
	Citizens	Non-citizens	Citizens	Non-citizens	Citizens		Non-citizens	
					Number	Percent	Number	Percent
Königsberg	1790	113	4641	89	+2851	+159.3	-24	-21.2
Gumbinnen	246	18	1434	33	+1188	+4829.0	+15	+83.3
Danzig	3791	5	5229	173	+1438	+37.9	+168	+33600
Marienwerder	7300	1553	10629	5310	+3329	+45.6	+3757	+246.4
Posen	5	37763	12921	41866	+12916		+4103	
Bromberg	5	14184	1621	23167	+1616		+8983	
Berlin	3322	28	7417	931	+4095	+123.3	+903	+3225.0
Potsdam	1763	86	3088	123	+1325	+75.2	+37	+43.0
Frankfurt/Oder	2406	445	4116	526	+1719	+83.5	+81	+18.2
Stettin	1142	76	3739	40	+2597	+227.4	-36	-47.4
Köslin	1439	29	3757	24	+2321	+161.1	-5	-17.2
Stralsund	0	123	0	156			+33	
Breslau	6549	98	10182	194	+3633	+55.5	+96	+97.6
Liegnitz	1641	96	2548	122	+907	+55.3	+26	+27.1
Oppeln	7690	5	15515	45	+7825	+101.8	+40	+800.0

District	1816		1843		Change 1816–1843			
					Citizens		Non-citizens	
	Citizens	Non-citizens	Citizens	Non-citizens	Number	Percent	Number	Percent
Magdeburg	1868	211	2452	160	+584	+31.3	-51	-24.2
Merseburg	150	19	210	248	+60	+40.0	+229	+1205.3
Erfurt	454	387	700	752	+246	+54.2	+365	+94.3
Münster	1896	288	3179	36	+1283	+67.7	-252	-87.5
Minden	3762	168	5757	25	+1995	+53.0	-143	-85.1
Arnsberg	2281	1087	2603	2805	+321	+14.1	+1718	+158.1
Cologne	2822	0	5157	62	+2335		+62	
Düsseldorf	4693	203	7102	0	+2409		-203	
Koblenz	4095	1299	6221	1744	+2126	+51.9	+445	+34.3
Trier	2583	231	4761	1	+2178		-230	
Aachen	1632	1	2519	3	+887		+2	
Total	65438	58500	206133	78635	+140695	+215.0%	+20135	+34.4

Changes in citizenship in Posen are the result of naturalization of non-citizens rather than migration.

Source: Silbergleit, *Die Bevölkerungs- und Berufsverhältnisse*, 7*, 18*.

Table 7.4. Rise and Decline in Rural Jewish Population in Selected Prussian Areas, 1817–1880 (Jewish population in areas considered *Land* rather than *Stadt*)

Region	1817	1849	1858	1867	1871	1880
Königsberg	29 (1.4)	768 (13.7)	1084 (**14.8**)	1279 (13.1)	1389 (13.1)	**1757** (14.1)
Gumbinnen	22 (7.6)	602 (31.7)	871 (32.5)	1100 (35.9)	1569 (40.9)	**3126** (**54.0**)
East Prussia	51	1370	1955	2379	2958	**4883**
Danzig	41 (1.1)	554 (10.0)	865 (13.6)	963 (15.2)	984 (14.5)	**1026** (**15.6**)
Marienwerder	279 (3.2)	2809 (16.1)	4188 (**21.5**)	4151 (20.4)	4095 (20.6)	3881 (19.4)
West Prussia	320	3363	5053	**5114**	5079	4907
RB Posen	1209 (3.2)	2209 (4.2)	**2212** (4.6)	2193 (5.2)	1985 (4.9)	1944 (**5.3**)
Bromberg	592 (3.9)	1958 (8.0)	**2312** (9.5)	2165 (9.4)	2082 (**9.6**)	1710 (8.6)
Prov. Posen	1801	4167	**4524**	4358	4067	3654
Stettin	50 (3.9)	728 (15.0)	**1091** (**17.2**)	929 (14.3)	899 (13.8)	972 (13.9)
Köslin	26 (1.6)	767 (16.7)	**1087** (**19.8**)	1076 (17.5)	1007 (16.3)	1007 (15.6)
Stralsund	0	19 (4.2)	24 (**10.5**)	34 (8.5)	30 (8.7)	17 (4.2)
Pomerania	76	1514	**2202**	2039	1936	1996
Liegnitz	8 (0.5)	392 (10.8)	**584** (**13.9**)	501 (11.0)	453 (9.7)	331 (6.4)
Reichenbach	33 (7.4)					
Breslau	948 (**14.0**)	**1075** (8.9)	961 (6.5)	984 (5.4)	805 (4.2)	940 (4.1)
Oppeln	3161 (**41.6**)	6115 (36.7)	7859 (39.2)	7368 (33.3)	7069 (31.1)	7506 (30.8)

Region	1817	1849	1858	1867	1871	1880
Silesia	4150	7582	9404	8853	8327	8777
Total East Prussia	6365 (7.1)	17996 (12.0)	23138 (**14.5**)	22743 (14.0)	22367 (13.7)	**24217** (14.4)
Central Prussia (Brandenburg and Prussian Saxony)	478 (4.1)	3230 (**13.1**)	**3611** (11.0)	2970 (6.6)	2644 (4.9)	2674 (3.7)
Western Prussia (Rhineland and Westphalia)	14260 (49.9)	24428 (**55.3**)	25835 (52.2)	**25992** (48.2)	25039 (45.0)	25132 (40.2)
All Prussia (including Hohenzollern, not listed above)	21136 (16.6)	45574 (20.8)	**52712** (**21.7**)	51822 (19.7)	50182 (18.4)	52125 (17.1)

In parentheses: percent of the total Jewish population living in countryside.

Percent increase 1817–1849: East Prussia +182.7 percent, East Prussia and Pomerania +2170.9 percent, central Prussia +575.7 percent, West Prussia +71.3 percent.

Sources: Silbergleit, *Die Bevölkerungs- und Berufsverhältnisse*, 11*; Neumann, *Zur Statistik der Juden in Preussen*, 30–31.

Table 7.5. Increase in Jewish Population of Some Major German Cities, c. 1815–c. 1840

Cities	Number of Jews		Percent change	Expected population based on natural growth[1]	Estimated net migration	
					Number	Percent
Berlin	3699 (1817)	5645 (1837)	+52.6	5048	+597	+11.8
Königsberg	1027 (1817)	1454 (1837)	+41.6	1404	+50	+3.6
Posen	4025 (1817)	6828 (1837)	+69.6	5492	+1336	+24.3
Danzig	2148 (1817)	2367 (1837)	+10.2	2931	-564	-19.2
Breslau	4409 (1817)	5413 (1837)	+28.0	6016	-371	-6.2
Frankfurt	4530 (1823)	5730 (1858)	+26.7	7460	-1722	-23.1
Karlsruhe	893 (1825)	1163 (1845)	+30.2	1191	-28	-2.4
Mannheim	1456 (1825)	1578 (1845)	+8.5	1942	-364	-18.7
Cologne	354 (1823)	454 (1837)	+28.3	426	+28	+6.6
Stuttgart	124 (1832)	350 (1845)	+182.3	154	+196	+127.3
Munich	451 (1814)	1423 (1840)	+215.5	669	+754	+112.7
Würzburg	138 (1816)	425 (1840)	+208.7	197	+229	+116.2

Cities that had formerly excluded Jews are in bold.

Sources: Silbergleit, *Die Bevölkerungs- und Berufsverhältnisse*, 9*; Blau, *Entwicklung*, 33; *Allgemeine Zeitung des Judenthums* 2, no. 109 (September 11, 1838): 439–441; *Pinkas ha-Kehillot, Germania, Bavaria*, 8, 105, 474; Schmelz, *Hessen*, 45, 51; *Pinkas ha-Kehillot, Germania, Württemberg-Hohenzollern-Baden*, 141, 373, 444; *Die politischen, Kirchen- und Schul-gemeinden des Grossherzogthums Baden 1845* (Karlsruhe, 1847), 96–97.

1 Calculated as in Table 7.1.

Table 7.6. Place of Birth of New Jewish Citizens of Berlin, 1809–1851

City	Number	Percent of 1843 Jewish population of home district	Year of citizenship acquisition				Percent of migrants, 1809–1851	Percent of migrants, 1841–1851
			1809–1820	1821–1830	1831–1840	1841–1852		
Berlin	730	8.7	314	105	126	185		
Posen	612	0.8	89	76	139	314	25.7	30.5
Other Brandenburg	532	6.8	131	82	128	189	22.3	18.3
West Prussia	359	1.7	33	43	108	175	15.1	17.0
Silesia	330	1.2	34	44	97	155	13.8	15.0
Pomerania	128	1.7	30	15	28	45	5.4	4.4
Prussian Saxony	92	2.0	14	6	21	51	3.9	5.0
Anhalt	68	c3.4	10	6	13	38	2.9	3.7
East Prussia	49	0.8	10	7	6	22	2.1	2.1
Mecklenburg-Strelitz	35		12	8	5	10	1.5	1.0
Bavaria	18		7	2	6	4	0.8	0.4
Mecklenburg-Schwerin	14	3	3	3	5	0.6	0.5	

Rhineland	13		0	2	9	0.6	0.9
Hamburg	13	0.1	9	1	3	0.6	0.3
Hanover	13		5	1	4	0.6	0.4
Saxony (Kingdom)	9				0.4		
Westphalia	6	0.04			0.3		
Baden	5				0.2		
Schleswig-Holstein	3						
All other Germany	26				1.1		
Austria-Hungary	15		6	2	5	0.6	0.5
Russia	38		13	2	15	1.6	1.5
Holland	5					0.2	
Denmark	3						
Alsace	2						
Sweden	1						
Total outside Germany	64						
Total	3114						

Source: Calculated from Jacobson, *Jüdische Bürgerbücher*.

Berlin, and a slightly larger percent originated in the provinces immediately to the east—especially the heavily Jewish provinces of Posen, West Prussia, and Silesia). Relatively few came from areas west of Berlin or from the distant eastern East Prussian area. Over time, the percentage of migrants from surrounding Brandenburg declined while the numbers from West Prussia and Posen increased. Most migrants from Brandenburg came from towns and villages in the northeastern part of the province (Neumark) near the Pomeranian, West Prussian, and Posen borders. Most Jewish migrants from West Prussia originated in the southwest corner of the province that bordered Pomerania and Brandenburg, especially from the town of Märkisch Friedland, which sent more migrants to Berlin than any other town.[11]

Patterns of migration within South German states may be inferred from differences in the growth rates of their subdistricts. In Württemberg (Table 7.1), the pattern in which the Neckarkreis (containing the major city of Stuttgart) grew more than other sections of the country, was not in evidence before 1845. Bavarian law imposed severe restrictions on Jewish marriage and settlement in all provinces except the Rhine Palatinate. Migration patterns within Bavaria therefore fell into three groups. The traditional centers of Jewish population in Bavaria east of the Rhine (Franconia and Swabia) showed substantial emigration between 1818 and 1840 (mostly after 1832), ranging from 28.2 percent to 37.7 percent of the population. Concurrently, Munich (Upper Bavaria) tripled its Jewish population, mainly due to migration from Swabia and Middle Franconia.[12] In the Rhine Palatinate, where Jewish settlement was less restricted, there seems to have been substantial in-migration during the same years, although its origins are not clear. In most non-Bavarian states in southern Germany, out- and in-migration were almost entirely balanced.

---

11 Towns that sent at least fifty migrants to Berlin were Märkisch Friedland, West Prussia (133); Breslau, Silesia (89); Glogau, Silesia (84), Lissa, Posen (74); Posen, Posen (74); Danzig, West Prussia (56); and Frankfurt an der Oder, Brandenburg (50).
12 According to Hendrikje Kilian, *Die jüdische Gemeinde in München, 1813–1871: eine Grosstadtgemeinde im Zeitalter der Emanzipation* (Munich: Utz, 1989), 346, new citizens in Munich's places of origin between 1813 and 1870 were as follows: Bavarian Swabia 151; Middle Franconia 129; Upper Bavaria (mainly Munich) 104; Lower Franconia 33; Upper Franconia 10; Rhine Palatinate 5 (total: 333). James F. Harris, *The People Speak! Anti-Semitism and Emancipation in Nineteenth-Century Bavaria* (Ann Arbor: University of Michigan Press, 1994), 31, gives some data on Jewish population in the various Bavarian provinces in 1822, 1826, 1829, and 1832 based on districts with different boundaries than those used for the 1818 and 1840 data in Table 7.1. According to these figures, the Swabian and Franconian districts had negative annual migration balances of 169 in 1822–1826, 202 in 1826–1829, and 407 in 1829–1832. This seems to indicate escalating out-migration, most of which came from Middle Franconia.

Outside Bavaria, few Jewish communities, rural or urban, lost population during the 1815–1840 period. One of the exceptions was Märkisch Friedland, from which many migrants went to Berlin. The town was in a corner of the West Prussian province, almost completely surrounded by Pomerania and only a few miles from the Brandenburg border. Its Jewish inhabitants became Prussian citizens in 1812 and therefore received total freedom of movement within Prussia. Although Märkisch Friedland was the home of the famous rabbi Akiba Eger until 1815, its Jewish population began to decline rapidly even as most other German-Jewish communities grew. A similar case was the Upper Silesian town of Zülz, one of the few towns in Silesia where Jews had been permitted to live in the eighteenth century. Elsewhere in Germany, exceptional cases of declining communities before 1840 were found on the outskirts of cities that had formerly excluded Jews, such as Heidingsfeld just outside Würzburg. In Posen province, only a small minority of Jewish communities, most of them on the edges of the province, lost population between 1823 and 1840.[13]

Migration Patterns 1840–1880

Jewish migration patterns show much more regional variance in 1840–1880 than in the previous period (Map 7/2). The departure of many Jews from Bavaria was joined by migration from most other South German states, as well as movement from Posen province. In central Germany, there was migration from the small states of Anhalt and Mecklenburg and the beginning of the massive growth of Berlin Jewry. In the west and northwest, there were smaller waves of migration from rural areas to more urbanized ones (Table 7.7).

Within Prussia, the most substantial change was the onset of mass migration from Posen province (Table 7.19). Between 1817 and 1825, this province still showed a positive Jewish migration balance. Although the balance turned somewhat negative after 1825 (especially in RB Posen), the absolute number of Jews in the province continued to rise until 1846. Afterward, there was a steady outflow of Jewish migrants from the province. Unlike RB Posen, out-migration from the northern half of the province (RB Bromberg) did not exceed natural

---

13 Obersitzko: from 716 to 606; Tirschtiegel: from 349 to 305; Graetz: from 1706 to 1620; Fraustadt: from 629 to 558; Schlichtingheim: from 165 to 110; Lissa: from 3710 to 3466; Storchnest: from 259 to 248; Reisen: from 81 to 54; Bojanowo: from 321 to 311; Sarne: from 84 to 50; Zduny: from 227 to 210; Kempen: from 3830 (1831) to 3577; Schoenlanke: from 830 to 791; Margonin: from 456 to 438; Fordon from 1430 to 1057 (1849); Schubin: from 454 to 412; Schocken: from 445 to 340.

growth by much until around 1864. By 1880, however, RB Posen had lost about one-third of its Jewish population.[14] Some of those who left the province emigrated overseas; others migrated within Germany, especially to Berlin and Silesia.

In eastern Germany, massive out-migration was restricted to Posen province at first, but after mid-century began to be noticeable, although smaller in scale, in West Prussia, which, like Posen, had a majority Polish-speaking population. In Pomerania, an area of massive in-migration until the late 1850s, migration turned increasingly negative after about 1858, especially in RB Stettin. In East Prussia, the robust excess of in-migration over out-migration continued unabated and the rural Jewish population continued to grow even as the non-urban Jewish population elsewhere declined[15] (Table 7.7). In contrast to earlier periods, a considerable number of the migrants to East Prussia now came from across the Russian frontier.[16] The Silesian district of Breslau, and especially its eponymous capital, attracted a steady stream of migrants in contrast to the pre-1840 period. Other sections of Silesia showed little evidence of a clear pattern.

In central Germany, the meteoric growth of Berlin's Jewish community contrasted with steady out-migration from the small states of Anhalt and Mecklenburg. While the industrial areas of Saxony and Thuringia began to show some in-migration, it remained inconsiderable compared with later migration patterns after 1880. The increase in the Jewish population of Berlin was fastest between 1840 and 1871. In percentage, this growth far exceeded both the Jewish population increase in the city before 1840 and the overall city population's rate of increase between 1840 and 1871 (Table 7.8). By 1880, Berlin had almost six times as many Jews than in 1849 and had become home to almost 15 percent of all Prussian Jews. Afterward, the rate of growth, although not the raw numbers, began to slow. After 1885, the percentage of Jews in the Berlin population leveled off or declined. Compared with other central German localities, Berlin

---

14 The Jewish population of Posen province reached an all-time high of 81,299 in 1846 (Blau, *Entwicklung*, 37, Table 3).
15 In Königsberg District, the percentage of the Jewish population living in the city of Königsberg went from 35.7 percent in 1843 to 40.9 percent in 1880. In the district of Breslau, the percentage in the city of Breslau went from 61.1 percent in 1843 to 75.7 percent in 1880. In the district of Stettin, the percentage in the city of Stettin went from 13.7 percent in 1843 to 34.1 percent in 1880, a sharper degree of urbanization than in the other two districts, and the result of the former exclusion of Jews from the city.
16 This was especially noticeable in the border city of Memel, where the majority of Jews in 1871 were foreigners—a situation unheard of almost anywhere else in Germany at the time (Table 8.13).

Table 7.7.

A) Growth and Decline of Jewish Population in Prussia, 1843–1880 (numbers under 1,000 are in smaller font)

Regierungsbezirk	1843	1849	1858	1871	1880	Change 1843–1880	Change 1843–1858	Change 1858–1880
Königsberg	4730	5613	7310	10579	**12427**	+162.7%	+54.6%	+70.0%
Gumbinnen	1467	1999	2679	3837	**5791**	+294.8	+82.6	+116.2
Danzig	5402	5566	6386	6782	6567	+21.6	+18.2	+2.8
Marienwerder	12928	17409	19513	19850	**19980**	+54.6	+50.9	+2.4
Posen	**54787**	52486	47907	40224	36570	-33.3	-12.6	-23.7
Bromberg	**24788**	24528	24291	21758	20039	-19.2	-2.0	-17.5
Stettin	3779	4846	6332	6501	**7014**	+85.6	+67.6	+10.8
Köslin	3781	4584	5496	6188	**6465**	+71.0	+45.4	+17.6
Stralsund	156	216	229	347	**407**	+160.9	+46.8	+77.7
Breslau	10376	12059	14814	19189	23176	+123.4	+42.8	+56.5
Oppeln	15560	16662	20029	22766	24348	+56.5	+28.7	+21.6
Liegnitz	2670	3618	4202	4664	**5158**	+93.2	+57.4	+22.8
Berlin	8348	9604	15491	36015	53949	+546.3	+85.6	+248.3
Potsdam	3211	4013	4841	4548	**5423**	+68.9	+50.8	+12.0
Frankfurt/Oder	4642	4846	6915	6921	6873	+48.1	+49.0	-0.1
Magdeburg	2612	2833	3150	3372	**3568**	+36.6	+20.6	+13.3

Regierungsbezirk	1843	1849	1858	1871	1880	Change 1843–1880	Change 1843–1858	Change 1858–1880
Merseburg	458	649	886	1049	**1332**	+190.8	+93.5	+50.3
Erfurt	1452	1457	1478	1537	**1800**	+24.0	+1.8	+21.8
Münster	3215	3265	3452	3403	**3466**	+7.8	+7.4	+0.4
Minden	5782	5894	**6149**	5949	5849	+1.2	+6.4	−4.9
Arnsberg	5408	5834	6498	7893	**9495**	+75.6	+20.2	+46.1
Cologne	5219	5866	6963	8538	**10370**	+98.7	+33.4	+48.9
Düsseldorf	7102	7658	9297	11419	**13211**	+86.0	+30.9	+42.1
Koblenz	7965	8475	8718	8713	**9312**	+16.9	+9.5	+6.8
Trier	4762	4990	5069	5985	**6566**	+37.9	+6.5	+29.5
Aachen	2522	2685	3052	3769	**4235**	+67.9	+21.0	+38.8

Highest number is in bold.

Sources: Silbergleit, *Die Bevölkerungs- und Berufsverhältnisse*, 18*–19*; Blau, *Entwicklung*, 69. For 1871, Silbergleit gives 10,588 for Königsberg and 6,189 for Köslin.

B) Estimated Net Jewish Migration in Various Prussian Districts, 1843–1880 (annual averages in parentheses)[1]

District	1843–1849	1849–1858	1858–1871	1871–1880	Total 1843–1880
Königsberg	+458 (76)	+799 (89)	+1248 (96)	+338 (38)	+2843
Gumbinnen	+400 (67)	+360 (40)	+418 (30)	+1407 (156)	+2585
Danzig	-322 (54)	-70 (8)	-1069 (82)	-1226 (136)	-2687
Marienwerder	+3319 (553)	-681 (76)	-4139 (318)	-2828 (314)	-4329
Posen	-7227 (1204)	-12969 (1410)	-14587 (1122)	-7975 (886)	-43028
Bromberg	-2489 (415)	-4161 (462)	-6034 (464)	-4056 (451)	-16740
Stettin	+727 (121)	+711 (55)	-1425 (110)	-404 (45)	-391
Köslin	+463 (77)	+179 (14)	-692 (53)	-596 (66)	-646
Stralsund	+46 (8)	-22 (2)	+60 (5)	+11 (1)	+95
Breslau	+750 (125)	+828 (92)	+297 (23)	+1082 (120)	+2957
Oppeln	-297 (50)	+701 (78)	-2776 (214)	-1865 (207)	-4237
Liegnitz	+708 (118)	+5 (1)	-695 (53)	-212 (24)	-195
Berlin	+505 (84)	+4350 (483)	+17036 (1310)	+11590 (1288)	+33481
Potsdam	+513 (86)	+186 (21)	-1286 (99)	+347 (39)	-240
Frankfurt/Oder	-213 (36)	+1294 (144)	-1412 (109)	-851 (95)	-1182
Magdeburg	-14 (2)	-136 (15)	-200 (15)?	-225 (25)	-575?
Merseburg	+150 (25)	+133 (15)	+152 (17)	+493?(55)	+345?
Erfurt	-126 (21)	-212 (24)	-139 (11)?	+71 (8)	-369?
Münster	-239 (40)	-522 (58)	-669 (51)	-355 (39)	-1785

District	1843–1849	1849–1858	1858–1871	1871–1880	Total 1843–1880
Minden	-408 (68)	-943 (105)	-1304 (100)	-830 (92)	-3485
Arnsberg	-60 (10)	-269 (30)	+228 (18)	+633 (70)	+532
Cologne	+178 (30)	+159 (18)	+325 (25)	+761 (85)	+1423
Düsseldorf	-83 (14)	+414 (45)	+452 (35)	+359 (40)	+1142
Koblenz	-206 (34)	-1113 (124)	-1571 (121)	-494 (55)	-3384
Trier	-200 (33)	-719 (80)	+6 (1)	-170 (19)	-1083
Aachen	-64 (11)	-63 (7)	+169 (13)	-7 (1)	+35
All Prussia	-3731 (622)	-5566 (618)	-1686 (130)	+194 (22)	-10367

1 Data for 1843–1855 are calculated as in Table 7.1. Data after 1855 are based on Schmelz's data, which, in turn, are based on actual birth and death figures for individual provinces of Prussia. I calculated the migration balances for each RB by assuming that the birth and death rates for the whole province were uniform.

Table 7.8. Absolute and Relative Growth of Berlin Jewish Population

Year	Jewish population	Percent of total city population	Change from previous census	Index of growth (1816 = 100)
1811	3202	1.9		94.9
1813	2825	1.7	-11.8	83.8
1816	3373	1.7	+19.4	100
1819	3610	1.8	+7.0	107.0
1822	3795	1.8	+5.1	112.5
1825	4079	1.8	+7.5	120.9
1828	4427	1.9	+8.5	131.3
1831	4959	2.0	+12.0	147.0
1834	5426	2.1	+9.4	160.9
1837	5648	2.0	+4.1	167.5
1840	6456	2.0	+14.3	191.4
1843	8348	2.4	+29.3	247.5
1846	8243	2.1	-1.3	244.4
1849	9595	2.3	+16.4	284.5
1852	11835	2.8	+23.4	350.9
1855	12675	2.9	+7.1	375.8
1858	15491	3.4	+22.2	459.3
1861	18859	3.4	+21.7	559.1
1864	24280	3.8	+28.7	719.8
1867	27607	3.9	+13.7	818.5
1871	36015	4.4	+30.5	1067.7
1875	45464	4.7	+26.2	1347.9
1880	53949	4.8	+18.7	1599.4
1885	64355	4.9	+19.3	1908.0
1890	79286	5.0	+23.2	2350.6
1895	86152	**5.1**	+8.7	2554.2
1900	92206	4.9	+7.0	2733.7
1905	98893	4.9	+7.3	2931.9
1910 (old boundaries)	90013	4.4	-9.0	2668.6
1925 (Greater Berlin)	172672	4.3	+91.8	5119.2

Sources: based on Silbergleit, *Die Bevölkerungs- und Berufsverhältnisse*, 25*.

was by far the greatest magnet for migrants in 1840–1880; its share of the Jewish population in the region increased from 22.4 percent in the former year to 61.3 percent in the latter.

In Brandenburg province, which surrounded Berlin, the Jewish population initially grew fairly rapidly, exceeding natural growth. Its increase was fastest in the 1830s and 1840s. The Jewish population of provincial Brandenburg, however, was rapidly overshadowed by the growth of Jewry in Berlin, and the increase in the surrounding provincial area slowed considerably until 1880. Thus, the proportion of Jews in Berlin relative to those in Brandenburg climbed from only 51.5 percent in 1843 to 81.4 percent in 1880. The Jewish population of the eastern half of the province (RB Frankfurt an der Oder) began to decline after 1861 while that in the more westerly Potsdam District grew, albeit slowly. For the time being, this growth in RB Potsdam had nothing to do with the increase in Jewish population in the suburbs of Berlin.

In contrast, the Jewish populations of the small and mainly agrarian independent states of Mecklenburg and Anhalt declined substantially as Jews migrated to more urban areas such as Hamburg, Berlin, and Saxony from areas in which their receipt of legal rights lagged behind that of Prussia. In Mecklenburg-Schwerin, rising absolute numbers of Jews until 1845 were succeeded by a steady decline from which Mecklenburg Jewry never recovered. Thus, the number of Jews declined by over 40 percent, from 3,318 in 1845 to 1,945 in 1871. Later on, the downturn was even more rapid (Table 7.9). In Anhalt, which was divided into three separate duchies until 1863, a substantial Jewish population in the eighteenth century contracted thereafter. In Dessau, the capital of one of the three Anhalt duchies, a Jewish community that was very important in the eighteenth century, declined noticeably in population. It is remarkable how many leaders in German Jewish intellectual life had once lived in tiny Anhalt;[17] Moses Mendelssohn, for one, was born there (Table 7.10). The duchy of Anhalt-Dessau showed little change in Jewish numbers between 1818 and 1838, probably because out-migration offset all natural growth.[18] By 1864, when Anhalt was united into a single duchy, the Jewish population had already declined relative to 1838 and saw an additional sharp decrease in the following seven years. Many Jews who migrated from Anhalt settled either in

---

17 Among them were the Neo-Kantian philosopher Hermann Cohen, the newspaper editor and Reform Jewish leader Ludwig Philippson, the cofounder of "Völkerpsychologie" Heymann Steinthal, the composer Kurt Weill, and, as mentioned above, Moses Mendelssohn himself.

18 *Allgemeine Zeitung des Judenthums* 2/97 (August 14, 1838). The newspaper specifically attributes emigration from the duchy in previous years to the harsh anti-Jewish laws that had been in effect there.

Table 7.9. Jewish Population of Mecklenburg, 1815–1933

Year	Mecklenburg-Schwerin			Mecklenburg-Strelitz		
	Number	Percent change	Change per year	Number	Percent change	Change per year
1810	2494					
1815	2690	+7.9	1.6%			
1820	2881	+7.1	1.4			
1825	3050	+5.9	1.2			
1830	3126	+2.5	0.5			
1835	3117	-0.3	-0.1			
1840	3211	+3.0	0.6			
1845	3318	+3.3	0.7			
1850	3216	-3.1	-0.6			
1855	3105	-3.5	-0.7			
1860	3190	+2.7	0.6			
1865	3042	-4.6	-0.9			
1871	2945	-3.2	-0.6	485		
1875	2786	-5.4	-1.1			
1880	2580	-7.4	-1.5	458	-5.6	-0.6
1885	2347	-9.0	-1.8	497	+8.5	1.7
1890	2182	-7.0	-1.4	489	-1.6	-0.3
1900	1763	-19.2	-1.9	331	-32.2	-3.2
1905	1482	-15.9	-3.2			
1910	1413	-4.7	-0.9	254	-23.3	-2.3
1925	1225	-13.3	-0.9	182	-28.4	-1.9
1933	1003*	-28.1	-3.6			

* Mecklenburg-Schwerin plus Mecklenburg-Strelitz.

Sources: Max Grünfeldt, "Die Juden in Mecklenburg-Schwerin, 1810–1910," *ZDSJ* (January 1912): 2; *Vierteljahrshefte zur Statistik des Deutschen Reichs* (1873): 188d, (1892): III, 31; *Statistik des Deutschen Reichs* 67 (1883): 250; neue Folge 32 (1888): 26* and 243; 150 (1903): 108* and 185; 240 (1915): 210 and 401; 2 (1925): 618–619; 1933 census, 5/11.

Table 7.10. Declining Jewish Population in Anhalt

Year	Number	Percent change	Annual change from last census	Number
	Duchy of Anhalt-Dessau			City of Dessau
1787				705
1807				763
1818				807
1830				763
1838	1602 (2.6% of total)			743
Year	United Duchy of Anhalt			City of Dessau
1864	2302			
1867	2108	-8.4	-2.8	466
1871	1896	-10.1	-2.5	
1880	1752	-7.6	-0.8	420
1885	1601	-8.6	-1.7	
1890	1580	-1.3	-0.3	
1900	1605	+1.6	+0.2	
1910	1383	-13.8	-1.4	
1925	1140	-17.6	-1.2	399
1933	901	-21.0	-2.6	360

Sources: *Die Ergebnisse der Volkszählung im Herzogtum Anhalt vom 3. December 1867* (Dessau, 1868), 2, 8, 10; Blau, *Entwicklung*, 251; Simone Laessig, *Jüdische Wege ins Bürgertum. Kulturelles Kapital und sozialer Aufstieg im 19. Jahrhundert* (Göttingen: Vandenhoeck & Ruprecht, 2004), 118, note 26; *AZJ* 2, no. 97 (August 14, 1838): 391.

the neighboring Prussian province of Saxony or in the independent Kingdom of Saxony. In 1900, the city of Leipzig alone was home to no fewer than 117 Jews born in Anhalt. Some Jews from Anhalt also settled in Berlin.[19] For Anhalt Jews,

---

19 "Die Zahl der Juden in Leipzig," *ZDSJ* 2 (1906): 111. Of Berlin's general population in 1900, only 17,558 were born in Mecklenburg (c. 0.93 percent of all Berliners) and 7,466 in Anhalt (0.40 percent). Of all German residents in 1900 who had been born in Anhalt, 73.68 percent still lived in the duchy and 13.08 percent had moved to the adjacent Prussian province of

emigration from Germany seems to have been less common than migration within Germany.

Prussian Saxony, the area surrounding Anhalt, was more industrialized than Anhalt but, except for RB Magdeburg, had a very sparse Jewish population until 1815 (Table 7.11). RB Magdeburg experienced a slight but steady negative migration balance and its overall Jewish numbers increased only very slowly. Until 1871, the same was true of Erfurt District despite its low original Jewish density. Although the Prussian Saxon district of Merseburg never had a substantial Jewish population, it did experience a relatively significant influx of Jews, causing the numbers of Jews to increase more than tenfold between 1817 and 1925.

Thuringia, composed of eight small principalities south of the Prussian province of Saxony, had few Jews outside its southwestern section (Table 7.12). In 1864, five of every six Jews in Thuringia lived in the two southernmost and westernmost principalities—Sachsen-Meiningen-Hildburghausen and Sachsen-Weimar-Eisenach—and mainly in the southern and western districts of these principalities. The Jews in these two principalities resembled those in Hesse and Bavaria further south and west in that they lived mainly in village communities. Small groups of Jews dwelled in the two Schwarzburg principalities, but Jews were virtually excluded from the other Thuringian states, some of which were early areas of industrialization. The Jewish population of the two southwestern principalities was more or less steady since the 1830s, which is probably evidence of rather vigorous out-migration. Between 1864 and 1880, there was a modest Jewish migration into the states that had once excluded Jews, while the Jewish populations of the southwestern principalities remained stagnant.

Developments in the Kingdom of Saxony resembled those in the formerly exclusionary Thuringian principalities on a much larger scale. Before 1871, Saxony had one of the most restrictive anti-Jewish policies in Germany. Its tiny Jewish population was confined almost completely to the two largest cities, Dresden and Leipzig. The Jewish community of the capital, Dresden, was well established at the beginning of the nineteenth century and comprised about 700 souls. Leipzig, in contrast, had only 140 permanent Jewish residents in 1832, although its thrice-annual fairs attracted masses of Jewish businessmen

---

Saxony, 2.56 percent to the Kingdom of Saxony, 2.42 percent to Berlin, and 1.84 percent to other locations in Brandenburg province. As early as 1838, Ludwig Philippson, editor of the *Allgemeine Zeitung des Judentums*, noted that at least twenty-one former residents of Anhalt-Dessau were then living in Magdeburg.

Table 7.11. Changes in Jewish Population of Prussian Saxony, by District (Regierungsbezirk)

Year	RB Magdeburg			RB Merseburg			RB Erfurt			Total	Percent of total living in Magdeburg District
	Number	Percent change	Annual change since last census	Number	Percent change	Annual change since last census	Number	Percent change	Annual change since last census	Number	
1817	2142			189			911			3273	66.1%
1825	2287	+5.8	0.7	192	+1.6	0.2	1093	+20.0	2.5	3572	64.0
1834	2314	+1.1	0.1	303	+57.8	6.4	1282	+18.2	2.0	3899	59.4
1843	2612	+12.9	1.4	458	+51.2	5.7	1452	+13.3	1.5	4522	57.8
1849	2833	+8.5	1.4	649	+41.7	7.0	1457	+0.3	0.1	4939	57.4
1852	2946	+4.0	1.3	735	+13.3	4.4	1429	-1.7	-0.1	5110	57.7
1858	3150	+6.9	1.2	886	+20.5	3.4	1478	+3.4	0.6	5514	57.1
1861	3279	+4.1	1.4	1008	+13.8	4.6	1488	+0.7	0.2	5775	56.8
1867	3441	+4.9	0.8	1062	+5.4	0.9	1464	-1.6	0.3	6007	57.3
1871	3372	-2.0	-0.5	1049	-1.2	-0.3	1537	+5.0	1.3	5958	56.6
1880	3568	+5.8	0.7	1332	+27.0	3.0	1800	+17.1	1.9	6700	53.3
1890	4214	+18.1	1.8	1743	+30.9	3.1	1992	+10.7	1.1	7949	53.0
1895	4066	-3.5	-0.7	1808	+3.7	0.8	1976	-0.8	-0.2	7850	51.8
1900	3999	-1.7	-0.3	2070	+14.5	2.9	1978	+0.1	0.02	8047	49.7
1905	3924	-1.9	-0.4	2205	+6.5	1.3	1921	-2.9	-0.6	8050	48.8
1910	3670	-6.5	-1.3	2208	+0.1	0.03	1955	+1.77	0.4	7833	46.9
1925	4255	+15.9	1.1	2236	+1.3	0.1	1850	-5.4	-0.4	8341	51.0
1933	3449	-18.9	-2.4	1882	-15.8	-2.0	1815	-1.9	-0.2	7146	48.3

Sources: Silbergleit, *Die Bevölkerungs- und Berufsverhältnisse*, 11, 18*–19*; Blau, *Entwicklung*, 69; Schmelz, Territorial Printout.

Table 7.12. Changes in Jewish Population of Thuringian Principalities

Principality	1833–1834	1837	1840	1843	1858	1861	1864	1871	1880
1) Sachsen-Weimar-Eisenach	1427	1387	1406	1448		1088	1129[a]	1120	1248
2) Sachsen-Meiningen-Hildburghausen	1524	1523	1511	1508	1530	1547	1625	1625	1627
Southwestern Thuringian principalities	2981	2910	2917	2956		2635	2754	2745	2875
3) Sachsen-Altenburg							1	10	33
4) Sachsen-Coburg-Gotha							80[b]	210	490
5) Schwarzberg-Rudolstadt							153	119	45
6) Schwarzberg-Sonderhausen							174	186	212
7) Reuss jüngere Linie							16	20	69
8) Reuss ältere Linie								19	60
Thuringia outside southwest							424	564	909
Total Thuringia							3178	3309	3784

Sources: G. Brückner, *Landeskunde des Herzogthums Meiningen* (Meiningen, 1851), 296; Hildebrand, *Statistik Thüringens*, 220, 221; *Statistisches Jahrbuch für das Deutsche Reich* 1 (1880), 13; Bosse, *Die Verbreitung der Juden*, 114, 119, 120, 121, 123, 125.

[a] 1059 in Eisenach *Kreis*.
[b] Sachsen-Gotha 32, Sachsen-Coburg 48.

from Germany and Eastern Europe.[20] The Jewish population of Leipzig began to increase substantially in the 1840s, while that of Dresden held steady. The Jewish community that developed in Leipzig, however, was very peculiar; it had few families and, in 1849, comprised 236 men and only 88 women. Were most Jews in Leipzig men who had recently settled there without families, or were they businessmen who happened to be in the city at the time of the census? Since most censuses of the time counted those present (Ortsanwesende) rather than permanent or legal residents (Wohnbevölkerung or Ortszugehörige), the latter is a distinct possibility.

Jewish population growth in Saxony remained modest until the 1860s and then accelerated powerfully, nearly doubling between 1858 and 1871 and almost doing so again from 1871 to 1880 (Table 7.13). Most of the growth occurred in Leipzig, where the Jewish numbers soon surpassed those of Dresden. After the unification of Germany, Jews continued to migrate into Saxony at a rapid pace.

Northwestern Germany was divided into entities that ranged in size from the Kingdom of Hannover to tiny principalities and city-states. Population statistics for parts of the region are spotty until the 1860s. The Jewish population was highly unevenly distributed in this part of Germany and extremely sparse in some areas. Most Jews in northwestern Germany either lived in or around Hamburg or in the Kingdom of Hannover, which was incorporated into Prussia in 1866. Although the Jewish population of Hamburg almost kept pace with the overall growth of the city until 1890, it grew less rapidly than the Jewish population in other large cities. Thus, Hamburg had the largest Jewish community in Germany in 1811 but only the third-largest in 1871. The Jewish population in the neighboring towns of Altona, Wandsbek, and Harburg stagnated or even declined during the period. With the exceptions of Altona and Wandsbek, the Jewish population of Schleswig-Holstein was sparse; in 1835, there were only 1,560 Jews among 747,394 inhabitants in Schleswig-Holstein outside of Altona. This changed little between 1835 and 1880 and seems to indicate some out-migration rather than in-migration.

In 1848, 8,506 of the 11,179 Jews in the Kingdom of Hannover lived either in the two southern Landdrostreien (later RBs) of Hannover and Hildesheim or in the northwestern district of Ostfriesland. In these three districts, Jews ranged from 0.9 to 1.3 percent of the total population. The 2,673 Jews in the

---

20 In the 1830s, 6,348 Jews attended the Leipzig Easter fair. About one in four of the fairgoers in 1837 was Jewish and Jews sent away two-thirds of the textiles shipped from the fair. Fred Grubel and Frank Mecklenburg, "Leipzig: Portrait of a Jewish Community during the First Years of Nazi Germany," *YLBI* 42 (1997): 158–159.

Table 7.13 Jewish Population of Kingdom (later Free State) of Saxony

Year	Total	Dresden	Leipzig	Other
1832	874	712	140	22
1834	850	683 682^	152	15
1837	848	652@ 647^	172	24
1840	868	645@ 644^	198	25
1843	882	627@ 626^	239	16
1846	988^@ 980*	663@ 660^	309	16
1849	1022	679@ 672^*	324@ 320^*	19
1858	1419	679	713	27
1861	1555	719	786	50
1864	1964	859	1027	78
1867	2103	870	1148	85
1871	3357# 3346*^	1276*# 1246^*	1739*# 1768^*	342
1875	5360	1956	2616^* 2551	788
1880	6518# 6516^*	2228	3265*^ 3179#	1025
1885	7755	2315^* 2353*	3749^* 3664	1691
1890	9368	2616# 2595^	4225# 4136^	2524
1895	9905 9902*^	2547* 2558^	4872* 4844^	2486
1900	12416# 12378*^	3029# 3096^ 2131*	6171	3216
1905	14697	3514	7676	3507
1910	17587	3734	9434*# 9874^	4419
1925	23252	5120	12594# 12549*	5538
1933	20584	4397	11564	4623

Sources: *Statistische Mitteilungen aus dem Königreich Sachsen* (Dresden, 1851), Table 7; Segall, "Die Juden im Königreich Sachsen," 33–46; Blau, *Entwicklung*, 181, 183, 184; Schmelz, Territorial Printout.

Where all sources agree, the numbers are unmarked. Where there are discrepancies, they are marked by the symbols below:

Segall: ^   Blau: *   Schmelz, Territorial Printout: #   *Statistische Mitteilungen*: @.

other three Landdrostreien varied from only 0.2 to 0.4 percent of the district population (Table 7.14). The largely rural Hildesheim District showed considerable out-migration, losing ten percent of its Jewish population between 1848 and 1880 and had almost 1,900 more out-migrants than in-migrants.

Sparsely populated RB Stade saw little change during the period, while heavily Jewish Aurich (Ostfriesland) and sparingly Jewish RB Lüneburg gained just short of 20 percent in absolute terms but generated a rather strong net outflow of migrants—though less than in Hildesheim. The greatest gains were in the districts of Hannover and Osnabrück and, especially, their chief cities, although the rural Jewish population also increased in Osnabrück District. In RB Hannover, the Jewish population outside the largest city actually declined. After excluding Jews during most of the nineteenth century, Bremen received in-migration that raised the Jewish population of the state to 465 in 1871 and 766 in 1880.[21] The duchy of Braunschweig had a very slight positive migration balance. Beginning in 1871, much of the increase in its Jewish population was in the capital city (Table 7.15). Lübeck Jewry changed little in numbers between 1845 and 1880, even though during this period almost all Jews in the city-state moved from the village ghetto of Moisling to the city of Lübeck itself.[22]

The various districts in the Rhineland and Westphalia saw different trends in their Jewish populations from 1840 to 1880. With a rapidly growing Jewish population in its eponymous capital, only Cologne District showed consistent in-migration throughout the period. The districts of Arnsberg and Düsseldorf, within which the later industrialized area of the Ruhr was positioned, began to show consistent in-migration somewhat later, after 1849 for Düsseldorf and 1858 for Arnsberg. Contrarily, the mainly rural northern Westphalian districts of Minden and Münster, like the bordering RB Hildesheim in Hannover, and the equally rural southern Rhineland area of Koblenz saw considerable out-migration during this period. The patterns in the Trier and Aachen districts are murkier. Out-migration in the various West German regions was not as extreme as migration from Posen province. Out-migration from the more rural areas in the northern and southern extremes of Rhine province and Westphalia was slightly larger numerically than net immigration to the Cologne, Düsseldorf, and Arnsberg districts. This suggests that some migrants from the former areas settled in the urbanizing sections of western Germany (Tables 7.7 A and B).

The period from 1840 to 1880 witnessed major out-migration from southern Germany, partly to cities elsewhere in the country, but mainly overseas to America. Before 1840, only parts of the Kingdom of Bavaria experienced a

---

21 The Jewish population of the city of Bremen was 321 in 1871 and 570 in 1880.
22 Jewish population of Lübeck State:

1840	1871	1880
478	565	560

Table 7.14. Jewish Population in Various Districts of Hannover

Year	Hannover	Hildesheim*	Lüneburg	Stade	Osnabrück	Aurich
1848	3099	**3153**	918	1130	625	2254
(Percent Jewish)	(0.9)	(0.9)	(0.3)	(0.4)	(0.2)	(1.3)
1852	3360	3031	981	1140	684	2366
1871	4221	2765	1065	**1165**	1060	2511
1880	**5656**	2847	**1092**	1137	**1387**	**2671**
Percent change	+2557 (82.5)	-306 (-9.7)	+174 (19.0)	+7 (0.7)	+762 (121.9)	+417 (18.5)

* Including Clausthal.

Sources: *Zur Statistik des Königreichs Hannover* (Hannover, 1855), 38–39; *Vierteljahrshefte zur Statistik des Deutschen Reichs* 1 (1873), 188b; Bosse, *Die Verbreitung der Juden*, 6–15.

Table 7.15. Jewish Population of the Duchy of Braunschweig

Area	1834	1861	1871	1880
Duchy	1124	1061	1171	1388
City of Braunschweig		308	394	506
Rest of Duchy		753	777	882

Sources: *Statistisch-topographisches Handbuch des Herzogthums Braunschweig* (Braunschweig, 1851); *Ergebnisse der am 3. December 1861 im Herzogthum Braunschweig stattgehabten Volkszählung* (Braunschweig, 1861); *Statistik des deutschen Reichs* (1880): 13; Bosse, *Die Verbreitung der Juden*, 118; Schmelz, Territorial Printout.

substantial decrease in Jewish population; soon thereafter, however, the other southern states also showed evidence of considerable out-migration. In areas where slight population increases occurred during the period, they lagged far behind the rate of Jewish natural increase. These patterns were not merely the continuation and spreading of earlier patterns of migration from the south. Migration occurred not only from the region but within it as well, especially from older rural areas to new urban centers.

Several traditional centers of rural Jewry showed very high rates of out-migration (Table 7.16). In Bavaria, the greatest declines were in the Swabia and Upper Franconia provinces on the southwestern and northeastern edges of the heavily Jewish sections of Bavaria, each of which lost about one-third of their Jewish population between 1840 and 1871. Almost an equally high percentage of Jews left the Prussian enclave of Hohenzollern in the Black Forest. Only slightly lower declines were registered in the neighboring Schwarzwaldkreis just across the border in Württemberg, and in the Württemberg district of Jagstkreis, bordering on Bavarian Lower and Middle Franconia. The latter two Franconian districts as well as the Bavarian Rhine Palatinate also experienced considerable out-migration, albeit somewhat less than in the other districts mentioned above. As the absolute upturns were smaller than the expected natural growth, most areas within Baden and Hesse-Darmstadt showed increases in absolute numbers but also more out-migration than in-migration. In contrast, three areas with important urban centers received large-scale migration. In both Bavaria and Württemberg, these districts and their capitals (Munich and Stuttgart, respectively) had previously accommodated scanty Jewish populations. In the case of Frankfurt am Main, an old Jewish urban center drew many migrants, especially after 1858.

In Bavaria, the Jewish population posted an absolute decline of 8,640—14.6 percent—between 1840 and 1871. Baden, Hesse-Darmstadt, and Württemberg saw either only moderate or no decreases in Jewish population after 1855. Even without an actual loss in numerical terms, however, these states had some excess of out-migration over in-migration. Whether the lesser out-migration in Baden and Hesse was the result of better economic or political conditions cannot be determined at present. The Jewish population of southern Germany recovered somewhat after the mid-1860s. The American Civil War (1861–1865) led to a temporary sharp decline in emigration. In Bavaria, the Jewish population bottomed out in 1867 and then rebounded slightly (Table 7.16). In most parts of southern Germany, the Jewish population increased somewhat between 1871 and 1880. Although migration from southern Germany certainly did not end in 1871, it fell well below the peak years of the 1850s and 1860s.

There is much evidence of migration within southern Germany and within each state to the major cities, especially Mannheim, Karlsruhe, Frankfurt, Stuttgart, and Munich (Table 7.17). Migration from southern Germany to other parts of Germany was most likely not a widespread phenomenon in this period.

In all, migration from various parts of Germany was heaviest in the 1840–1880 period and was strongest in the Franconian and Swabian parts of Bavaria and in Posen province where net negative migration balances of nearly 40,000 and more than 55,000, respectively, were observed. It seems that out-migrants from Posen split their destinations between other Prussian provinces and other countries, while the latter predominated among Bavarian Jews. There is another difference between migration patterns in the two areas: in Swabian and Franconian Bavaria, out-migration was much greater before 1867 than after,[23] whereas in Posen, the rate of migration from the province did not slow at all. The Jewish population in Posen province declined by 7,377 between 1843 and 1858, compared to 15,589 between 1858 and 1880. The greatest in-migration by far occurred in Berlin, with a positive migration balance of over 37,000.

Migration 1880–1910

Migration in the 1880–1910 period, which encompassed most of the *Kaiserreich* (1871–1918), had three definitive characteristics: Jewish migration from many outlying regions of Germany, continued urbanization, and large-scale

---

23 The Jewish population of the Swabian and Franconian territories decreased by 7,734 between 1840 and 1867 and increased by 1,966 between 1867 and 1880.

Table 7.16. Jewish Population in South German States and Subregions, 1840–1880

Bavaria	1840	1852	1867	1871	1880*	Change 1840–1880		Population with	
						Number	Percent	Expected natural growth	Calculated migration balance
Upper Bavaria	1528	1252	2154	3033	4343	+2815	+184.2%	2635	+1708
Lower Bavaria	15	15	36	111	134	+119	+793.3	27	+107
Upper Palatinate	1061	916	1054	1221	1522	+461	+43.5	1884	-362
Upper Franconia	6568	5438	4129	4045	4148	-2420	-36.8	11666	-7518
Middle Franconia	11377	10674	10522	10830	11689	+312	+2.7	20207	-8518
Lower Franconia	16451	15848	14400	14573	15256	-1195	-7.3	29219	-13963
Swabia	6891	6379	4512	4369	4436	-2455	-35.6	11764	-7328
Rhenish Palatinate	15396	15636	13042	12466	11998	-3398	-22.1	27345	-15347
Total Bavaria	59288	56158	49840	50648	53526	-5762	-9.7	104747	-51221

Württemberg	1841	1852	1858	1871	1880	Change 1840–1880		Population with	
						Number	Percent	Expected natural growth	Calculated migration balance
Neckarkreis	2609	c. 2750	2820	4227	5288	+2679	+102.7	4665	+627
Schwarzwaldkreis	1849	c. 1710	1742	1328	1505	-344	-18.6	3362	-1857
Jagstkreis	4827	c. 4650	4838	4024	3911	-916	-19.0	8779	-4868
Donaukreis	2299	c. 2590	2806	2666	2627	+328	+14.3	4182	-1555
Total Württemberg	11,584		12,206	12,245	13,331	+1747	+15.1	20895	-7653

Baden	1845	1852		1871	1880*	Change 1840–1880		Population with	
						Number	Percent	Expected natural growth	Calculated migration balance
Seekreis	1483	1644			1751	+268	+18.1	2467	-716
Oberrheinkreis	4007	4098			5027	+1020	+25.5	6667	-1640
Mittelrheinkreis	6725	7084			c. 8338	+1613	+24.0	11190	-2852
Unterrheinkreis	11043	10873			c. 12162	+1119	+10.1	18103	-5941
Total Baden	23,258	23,699		25,703	27,278	+4020	+17.3	40306	-11149

Migration—Overall Trends and Internal Migration

Upper Hesse	1828	1852	1871	1880	Change 1840–1880 Number	Percent	Population with Expected natural growth	Calculated migration balance
Rhenish Hesse	7639	c. 9500	9138	9452	+1813	+23.7	16414	-6962
Starkenberg	7502	c. 9900	9207	9700	+2198	+29.3	16119	-6419
Upper Hesse	6095	c. 8300	7028	7594	+1499	+24.6	11785	-4191

Hesse-Darmstadt	1840	1855	1871	1880	Change 1840–1880 Number	Percent	Population with Expected natural growth	Calculated migration balance
Hesse-Darmstadt (post-1866 boundaries)	25,651	27,179	25,373	26,746	+1095	+4.3	28734	-17572

Hohenzollern	1852	1858	1861	1871	1880	Change 1852–1880 Number	Percent	Population with Expected natural growth	Calculated migration balance
Hohenzollern	1038	949	958	721	771	-267	-25.7	1578	-807

	1827	1842	1855	1858	1864	Change 1827–1864		Population with	
						Number	Percent	Expected natural growth	Calculated migration balance
Hesse-Kassel	14422		18117	18164	17934	+3512	+24.4	25219	−7285
Nassau		6639							
Hesse-Homburg		c. 1000							

	1823	1858	1864	1871	1880	Change 1823–1880		Population with	
						Number	Percent	Expected natural growth	Calculated migration balance
Frankfurt am Main	4530	5730	7620	10009	13856	+9326	+205.9	c. 10360	+3496

	1871	1880	Change 1871–1880		Population with	
			Number	Percent	Expected natural growth	Calculated migration balance
Hesse-Nassau	36390	41316	+4926	+13.5		(+364)

Sources: Harris, *The People Speak*, 13, 31; Schmelz, *Hessen*, 45,46, 48, 346; Silbergleit, *Die Bevölkerungs- und Berufsverhältnisse*, 18*–19*; von Hermann, *Beiträge zur Statistik des Königreichs Bayern*, vol. 2, 198–199; *Politische Gemeinden [Baden] (publication data)*, 94–98; *Württembergische Jahrbücher für Vaterländische Geschichte, Geographie, Statistik und Topographie* (1845): Table 1, (1860): Table II/3; *Württembergische Jahrbücher für Statistik und Landeskunde* (1886): 20–24; *Beiträge zur Statistik der inneren Verwaltung des Grossherzogthums Baden 1855* (1874): 214.

Table 7.17. Growth of Jewish Population in Major South German Cities

City	1840	1845	1852	1858	1871	1880
Mannheim		1578	1670		3135	4031
Karlsruhe		1163	1073		1329	1689
Frankfurt				5730	10009	13843
Stuttgart			c390	512	1817	2485
Munich	1423		1208		2903	4144
Nuremberg	6		87		1831	3032

Sources: *Beiträge zur Statistik der inneren Verwaltung des Grossherzogthums Baden* (1855): 210–211; *Die politischen, Kirchen- und Schul-gemeinden des Grossherzogthums Baden 1845* (1847): 96–97; *Württembergische Jahrbücher für vaterländische Geschichte, Geographie, Statistik und Topographie* (1860): Table II/3; Bosse, *Die Verbreitung der Juden*, 20, 67, 76, 90, 103, 104; 1933 census, 5/10.

immigration from Eastern Europe. These three characteristics partly reinforced each other and partly worked in opposite directions. While emigration never totally stopped, it was outweighed by immigration during this time (Map 7/3).

Out-migration in Posen province continued unabated during the Imperial period, depleting the Jewish population by more than 50 percent in thirty years. Growth in other parts of eastern Germany was reversed, with the Jewish population dropping by almost 50 percent in West Prussia, over 35 percent in Pomerania, and nearly 30 percent in East Prussia between 1880 and 1910. Only in Silesia did the decline remain within bounds at about 15 percent. Many migrants from the eastern provinces ended up in Berlin. Elsewhere, steep declines were found mainly in areas where most Jews remained rural. Chief among them were Mecklenburg and Anhalt in the center, Lippe, Schaumburg-Lippe, and Waldeck in the northwest, and Alsace-Lorraine and Hohenzollern in the south.

Conversely, there were large increases in Jewish population in highly industrialized areas, notably Berlin and environs, the Kingdom of Saxony, Bremen, and to a lesser degree Hamburg, Braunschweig, the Rhineland, and Hesse-Nassau as well. Foreign Jews accounted for most migrants in some areas such as the Kingdom of Saxony, but in others, like the Rhineland and Hesse-Nassau, the overwhelming majority of migrants came from elsewhere in Germany (Table 7.18).

In Eastern Germany, each district exhibited a slightly different pattern. The wave of migration from Posen province continued unabated after 1880, eventually draining the bulk of the province's Jewish population. The periods that

Table 7.18. Migration Balances, 1880–1910, and Foreign Immigration in Various German Districts (*Länder* and Prussian Provinces), 1910 (under 1000 in smaller font)

District	1880	1910	Percent difference	Absolute difference	Migration balance[1]	Foreign Jews in 1910	
Brandenburg outside Berlin	12296	61343	+398.9	+49047	+47,699	8666	(14.1%)
Kingdom of Saxony	6518	17587	+169.8	+11069	+9286	10293	(58.5)
Bremen	766	1843	+140.6	+1077	+865	745	(40.4)
Berlin	53949	90013	+66.9	+36064	+23332	18694	(20.8)
Rhineland	43694	57287	+31.1	+13593	+1223	4843	(8.5)
Braunschweig	1388	1757	+26.6	+369	+73	251	(14.3)
Hesse-Nassau	41316	51781	+25.3	+10465	+2253	4835	(9.3)
Total with positive migration balance	159927	281611	+76.1	+121684	+84731	48327	(17.2%)
Hamburg	16024	19472	+21.5	+3448	-727	3136	(16.1)
Prussian Saxony	6700	7833	+16.9	+1133	-757	2554	(32.6)
Westphalia	18810	21036	+11.2	+2226	-3374	1674	(8.0)
Lübeck	560	623	+11.1	+63	-143	135	(21.7)
Thuringia (combined)	3784	4149	+9.7	+365	-332	737	(17.8)
Hannover	14790	15545	+5.1	+755	-1565	1820	(11.7)

District	1880	1910	Percent difference	Absolute difference	Migration balance[1]	Foreign Jews in 1910	
Bavaria	53526	55065	+2.9	+1539	-5859	7320	(13.3)
Total with positive population balance but negative migration balance	114194	123723	+8.3	+9529	-12757	17376	(14.0%)
Baden	27278	25896	-5.1	-1382	-5784	2620	(10.1)
Schleswig-Holstein	3522	3343	-5.1	-179	-793	913	(27.3)
Oldenburg	1654	1525	-7.8	-129	-407	199	(13.0)
Hesse-Darmstadt	26746	24063	-10.0	-2683	-7125	2494	(10.4)
Württemberg	13331	11982	-10.1	-1349	-3431	1156	(9.6)
Silesia	52682	44985	-14.6	-7697	-14416	2554	(5.7)
Anhalt	1752	1383	-21.1	-369	-657	218	(15.8)
Schaumburg-Lippe	295	230	-22.0	-65	-?	3	(1.3)
Alsace-Lorraine	39278	30483	-22.4	-8795	-15096	1971	(6.5)
Lippe	1030	780	-24.3	-250	-481	19	(2.4)
East Prussia	18218	13027	-28.5	-5191	-8123	2108	(16.2)
Waldeck	854	590	-30.9	-264	-366	6	(1.0)
Pomerania	13886	8862	-36.2	-5024	-6815	242	(2.7)

District	1880	1910	Percent difference	Absolute difference	Migration balance[1]	Foreign Jews in 1910	
Mecklenburg-Strelitz	458	254	-44.5	-204		45	(17.8)
Mecklenburg-Schwerin	2580	1413	-45.2	-1167	-1829	142	(10.0)
West Prussia	26547	13954	-47.4	-12593	-16949	412	(3.0)
Hohenzollern	771	405	-47.5	-366	-364	5	(1.2)
Posen	56609	26512	-53.2	-30097	-34065	324	(1.2)
Total with negative population balance	287491	209687	-27.1	-77804	-116701	15431	(7.4%)

Source: *Statistik des Deutschen Reichs* 57 (1883): 249–250; 240 (1915): 210; *Vierteljahrshefte zur Statistik des Deutschen Reichs—Ergänzungsheft zu 1916* 4 (1918): *Die Deutschen im Ausland und die Ausländer im Deutschen Reiche*, 53.

1 Schmelz's data, calculated by subtracting deaths from births.

showed the highest annual percentage rates of out-migration were 1885–1890 and 1900–1905. Between 1880 and 1910, well over half of the remaining Jewish population in the province left (Table 7.19). While RB Bromberg showed slower out-migration until around 1864, thereafter the differences between the Bromberg and Posen subdistricts nearly disappeared. The decline in Jewish population was much less extreme in towns with over 10,000 inhabitants and was especially small in the two cities of Posen and Bromberg. Especially after 1880, the percentage of Jews in the province who lived in the larger cities increased as the villages and, particularly, the former *shtetlakh* (population 5,000–10,000) rapidly lost Jewish inhabitants (Table 7.20). The migration of Jews from small towns to larger cities in Posen made up for some of the losses caused by the relocation of urbanites in Posen province to Berlin and Breslau.

After 1880, the decline of Jewish population spread throughout much of eastern Germany, especially East Prussia, West Prussia, and Pomerania (Table 7.21). In Pomerania and East Prussia, the Jewish population fell less than it had grown in the previous decades, while West Prussia lost more Jewish inhabitants after 1880 than it had gained in 1843–1880. In the eastern provinces, only Breslau District retained much of its Jewish population, mainly because of the Jewish community's growth in the city of Breslau. In West Prussia, RB Marienwerder most resembled the neighboring province of Posen with a steady if slightly accelerating decline throughout the 1880–1910 period. To the north, the less densely Jewish RB Danzig showed less of a decline due to the staying power of the Jewish community in the port city of Danzig. In Pomerania, too, the RB closest to Posen (Köslin) showed the greatest drop, particularly between 1895–1905, while RB Stettin saw a smaller decline due to the durability of the Jewish presence in its own port city of Stettin. In East Prussia, unlike the other eastern provinces, an initial sharp decline in the 1880s, perhaps occasioned by expulsions of foreign Jews, later tapered off. Outside eastern Germany, the principal areas of out-migration were small states or enclaves with mainly small-town Jewish populations like Mecklenburg, Anhalt, Lippe, Waldeck, Hohenzollern, and Alsace-Lorraine.

Annexed by Germany in 1871, Alsace-Lorraine had a steady outflow of emigrants throughout the Imperial period. Although this continued a longstanding trend of migration, it was accentuated by many Alsatian and Lorraine Jews's resentment of the German takeover of the territory. Many Jewish migrants opted for French citizenship or later emigrated to France;[24]

---

24 Vicki Caron, "The Social and Religious Transformation of Alsace-Lorraine Jewry, 1871–1914," *YLBI* 30 (1985): 323–326. In 1871–1872, 517 Jews opted for France and left Alsace-Lorraine. Of 309 Jews who left Haguenau county between 1873 and 1898, 30.7 percent went to France,

TABLE 7.19. Decline of Jewish Population in Posen, 1843–1910

Year	RB Posen		RB Bromberg		Entire province			
	Number	Change from last census	Number	Change from last census	Number	Change from last census		
						Number	Percent	(Annual)
1843	54787		24788		79575			
1846	52486	-2301			81299	+1724	+2.2	(+575 +0.7)
1849	50155	-2331	24548	-240	77014	-4285	-5.3	(-1428 -1.8)
1852	47907	-2248	24098	-450	74253	-2761	-3.6	(-920 -1.2)
1858	49949	+1974	24291	+193	72198	-2055	-2.8	(-343 -0.5)
1861	45706	-4243*	24223	-68	74172	+1974	+2.7	(+658 +0.9)
1864	42453	-3253	24306	±83	70012	-4160*	-5.6	(-1387 -1.9)
1867	40224	-2229	23055	-1251	65508	-4504	-6.4	(-1501 -2.1)
1871	40479	+255	21758	-1297	61982	-3526	-5.4	(-882 -1.4)
1875	36570	-3909	21959	+201	62438	+456	+0.7	(+114 +0.2)
1880	32891	-3679	20039	-1920	56609	-5829	-9.4	(**-1706** -1.9)
1885	28431	**-4460**	17975	**-2064**	50866	-5743	-10.2	(-1149 -2.0)
1890	25379	-3052	15915	-2060	44346	**-6520**	-12.8	(-1304 -2.5)
1895	22303	-3076	14640	-1275	40019	-4327	-9.8	(-866 -2.0)
1900	19392	-2911	13024	-1616	35327	-4692	-11.7	(-938 -2.3)
1905	16964	-2428	11041	-1983	30433	-4894	**-13.9**	(-979 **-2.8**)
1910			9548	-1493	26512	-3921	-12.9	(-784 -2.6)
Decline 1849–1910:	67.7%		61.1%		65.6%			

Sources: Silbergleit, *Die Bevölkerungs- und Berufsverhältnisse*, 18*–19*; Blau, *Entwicklung*, 37, 69; Aron Heppner and Isak Herzberg, *Aus Vergangenheit und Gegenwart der Juden und der jüdischen Gemeinden in den Posener Landen* (Koschmin-Bromberg, 1909), 267 (some figures before 1875 are slightly different in this source).

Table 7.20. Number of Jews in Communities of Various Sizes in Posen Province with Percent of All Jews in Posen (by 1880 population of cities)

Distribution	1861	1871	1880	1885	1895	1905	Decline, 1861–1905
Cities of Posen and Bromberg	9157	9218	8952	8330	7298	7274	-20.6%
	(12.5)	(14.9)	(15.8)	(16.4)	(18.2)	(23.9)	
Other cities over 10,000	8343	6866	6919	6519	5373	4223	-49.4
	(11.3)	(11.1)	(12.2)	(12.8)	(13.5)	(**13.9**)	
Other cities 5,000–10,000	13325	11427	10205	8943	6200	4305	-67.7
	(18.0)	(**18.4**)	(18.0)	(17.6)	(15.5)	(14.2)	
Other cities under 5,000	43347	34471	30533	27074	21138	14631	-66.3
	(**58.0**)	(55.6)	(53.9)	(53.2)	(52.8)	(48.1)	

Sources: Bosse, *Die Verbreitung der Juden*, 24–29; Silbergleit, *Die Bevölkerungs- und Berufsverhältnisse*, 18*–19*; Bernard Breslauer, *Die Abwanderung der Juden aus dem Provinz Posen* (Berlin, 1909), Table A. Figures for towns under 5,000 were calculated by subtracting known populations in towns over 5,000 from the total Jewish population of the province of Posen.

Table 7.21. Jewish Population Decline in Eastern Germany after 1880

Regierungsbezirk	1880	1885	1890	1895	1900	1905	1910	Change 1880–1910	Change 1843–1880	Migration balance
Königsberg	12427	10586	9780	9646	9178	7293	7138			
Change		-14.8	-7.6	-1.4	-4.9				+162.7%	
Gumbinnen	5791	5081	4631	4718	4690	6260	3155			
Change		-12.3	-8.9	+2.5	-1.2				+294.7%	
[Allenstein]							2734			
East Prussia	18218	15667	14411	14364	13877	13553	13027			
Change		-14.0	-8.0	-0.3	-3.4	-2.3	-3.9	-28.5%	+194.0%	-2917
Danzig	6567	6526	5928	5615	5504	5247	4653			
Change		-0.6	-9.2	-5.3	-2.0	-4.7	-11.3	-29.2%	+21.6%	-13732
Marienwerder	19980	18128	15822	14623	12722	10892	9301			
Change		-9.3	-12.7	-7.6	-13.0	-14.4	-14.6	-53.5%	+54.6%	-16949
West Prussia	26547	24654	21750	20238	18226	16139	13954			
Change		-7.1	-11.8	-7.0	-9.9	-11.5	-13.5	-47.4%	+44.8%	-22169
Posen	36570	32891	28431	25379	22303	19392	16964			
Change		-10.1	-13.6	-10.7	-12.1	-13.1	-12.5	-53.6%	-33.3%	-11896
Bromberg	20039	17975	15915	14640	13024	11041	9548			
Change		-10.3	-11.5	-8.0	-11.0	-15.2	-13.5	-52.4%	-19.2%	
Posen	56609	50866	44346	40079?	35327	30433	26512			-34065

Regierungsbezirk	1880	1885	1890	1895	1900	1905	1910	Change 1880–1910	Change 1843–1880	Migration balance
Change		-10.2						-53.2%	-28.9%	
Stettin	7014	6832	6527	6416	6292	5752	5217			-2702]
Change		-2.6	-4.5	-1.7	-1.9	-8.6	-9.3	-25.6%	+85.6%	
Köslin	6465	6048	5343	4923	4300	3641	3374			-3925]
Change		-6.5	-11.7	-7.9	-12.7	-15.3	-7.3	-47.8%	+71.0%	
Stralsund	407	411	376	322	288	267	271			-189]
Change		+1.0	-8.5	-14.4	-10.6	-7.3	+1.5	-33.4%	+160.9%	
Pomerania	13886	13291	12246	11661	10880	9660	8862	-36.2%	+80.0%	-6815
Liegnitz	5158	5080	4624	4291	4031	3860	3556			-2251]
Change		-1.5	-9.0	-7.2	-12.8	-4.2	-7.9	-31.1%	+93.2%	
Breslau	23176	23010	22232	22507	23285	23546	23161			-2971]
Change		-0.7	-3.4	+1.2	+3.5	+1.1	-1.6	-33.4%	+123.4%	
Oppeln	24348	23391	21147	20795	20270	19439	18268			-9186]
Change		-3.9	-9.6	-1.7	-2.5	-4.1	-6.0	-25.0%	+56.5%	
Silesia	52682	51481	48003	47593	47586	46845	44985	-14.6%	+84.2%	-14416
Total Eastern provinces	164942	155959	140756	133935	125896	116627	107340	-34.9%		-80368
Decline from previous census				5.5%	9.8%	4.9%	6.0%	7.4%	8.0%	

Sources: Silbergleit, *Die Bevölkerungs- und Berufsverhältnisse, 18*–19**; *Statistik des Deutschen Reichs*, neue Folge 32 (1888): 240–241; Blau, *Entwicklung*, 69.

many others emigrated to America and some moved to Switzerland. The decline was greatest in the Haut Rhin (Oberelsass) district, which was closest to Switzerland. The excess of emigration over immigration among the Jews of Alsace-Lorraine should not obscure the fact that there was also a wave of Jewish migration into Alsace-Lorraine as well, both among *Reichsdeutsche* (residents of Germany proper) and from Eastern Europe.[25] Among the cities of the province, the Jewish community of Strasbourg grew considerably while Jewish populations in Colmar, Mulhouse, and Metz expanded somewhat more slowly (Tables 7.22 A and B). Nevertheless, rural Jewry remained strong in Alsace and Lorraine, much as it did in southern Germany.

Compared with mass migration from the eastern provinces of Germany—a striking aspect of the out-migration pattern between 1880 and 1910 – migration from the southern regions of Germany was relatively moderate. Within each state, a rather strong urbanizing trend was evident. In Bavaria, acute differences among provinces persisted between 1880 and 1910; Upper Bavaria continued attracting sizable numbers of Jewish in-migrants and the Jewish population in Middle Franconia began growing as more Jews moved to Nuremberg. All the other traditional rural centers of Jewish population in Swabia, Franconia, and the Rhine Palatinate saw perceptible declines. In Lower Franconia, relatively slow declines before 1900 yielded to sharper out-migration thereafter (Table 7.23). In Württemberg, too, the Neckarkreis, which was the region of the growing urban communities of Stuttgart and Heilbronn, gained in Jewish population while the three more rural *Kreise* recorded steep losses (Table 7.24). The decline in the Jagstkreis was especially great while the Donaukreis and its main urban community, Ulm, shifted from an increase in Jewish population to a decrease. The Jewish population of rural Hohenzollern continued to decline steeply. Overall, Jewish numbers in Württemberg outside Stuttgart fell by almost thirty percent. In Baden, similarly, the Jewish communities in the three largest cities increased sharply between 1880 and 1910 while the Jewish population in the rest of the state declined (Table 7.25).

---

56 percent to the United States or Canada, and 6.5 percent each to South America or elsewhere in Europe.

25 Ibid., 319–356. In 1910, 1,970 Jews in Alsace-Lorraine totaling 6.47 percent of the Jewish population of the province held foreign citizenship. Of them, 768 lived in Strasbourg. The number of migrants from Germany seems to have been much higher, at least in the large cities. In 1895, 1,052 of the 4,012 Jews in Strasbourg were "Old Germans." Concurrently, the total number of Russian and Austro-Hungarian Jews in the city was 86. In 1885 it was claimed that one in every four Jews in Metz was also from Germany. In Thionville (Diedenhofen) in 1904, twenty of the sixty-six Jewish families came from Germany. Most Jewish students at the University of Strasbourg in 1898 were also "Old Germans."

Table 7.22.

A) Jewish Population of Alsace-Lorraine, 1871–1910

District	1871	1880	1890	1900	1910	Change	Migration balance
Bas Rhin (Unterelsass)	20179	19848	17810	16453	15779	-21.8%	-9820]
Haut Rhin (Oberelsass)	12103	11313	9760	8961	7689	-36.5	-7665]
Lorraine (Lothringen)	8646	8117	7075	6850	7015	-18.9	-3953]
Total	40928	39278	34645	32264	30483	-25.5	-21438

These figures are based on the official census data (Schmelz, Territorial Printout). Caron, "The Social and Religious Transformation," 333, gives slightly lower numbers for 1871 because she counts the civilian population only.

B) Jewish Population of Main Cities in Alsace-Lorraine, 1871–1910

City	1871	1880	1890	1900	1910	Change, 1871–1910
Strasbourg	3088	3521	4023	4605	5780	+87.2%
Colmar	1139	1135	1079	1187	1202	+5.5
Mulhouse	1997	2183	2132	2466	2287	+14.5
Metz	1496	1592	1434	1451	1911	+27.7
Total	7720	8431	8668	9709	11180	+44.8
Jewish population outside the four cities	33208	30847	25977	22555	19303	-41.9

Schmelz, Territorial Printout, gives 723 as the Jewish population of Colmar in 1871. Blau, *Entwicklung*, 270, 284, and Caron, "The Social and Religious Transformation," 332, give 1,139. Blau gives the following data that deviate from Schmelz: Colmar, 1900: 1,204; Mulhouse, 1900: 2,271; and Metz, 1900: 1,385.

Table 7.23. Change in Jewish Population in Bavarian Provinces, 1880–1910

Province	1880	1885	1890	1895	1900	1910	Change 1880–1900	Change 1900–1910	Change 1880–1910
Lower Bavaria	134	183	182	240	294	468	+160	+174	+334
Change		+36.6%	-0.5%	+31.9%	+22.5%	+59.2%			
Upper Bavaria	4343	5090	6291	7411	9076	11652	+4733	2576	+7309
Change		+17.2	+23.6	+17.8	+22.5	+28.4	+109.0	+28.4	+168.3
Middle Franconia	11689	12138	12294	12291	13111	14219	+1422	+1108	+2530
Change		+3.8	+1.3	-0.02	+6.7	+8.5	+12.2	+8.5	+21.6
Increasing areas	16166	17411	18767	19942	22481	26339	+6315	+3858	+10173
Change							+39.1	+17.2	+62.9
Upper Palatinate	1522	1435	1487	1486	1472	1395	-50	-77	-127
Change		-5.7	+3.6	-0.1	-0.9	-5.2%	-3.3	-5.2	-8.3%
Lower Franconia	15256	14939	14646	14157	13641	11925	-1615	-1716	-3331
Change		-2.1	-2.0	-3.3	-3.6	12.6	-10.6	-12.6	-21.8
Swabia	4436	4362	4323	4226	3904	3462	-532	-442	-974
Change		-1.7	-0.9	-2.2	-7.6	-11.3	-12.0	-11.3	-22.0
Rhenish Palatinate	11998	11526	10998	10423	10273	8998	-1725	-1275	-3000
Change		-3.9	-4.6	-5.2	-1.4	-12.4	-14.4	-12.4	-25.0%
Upper Franconia	4148	4024	3664	3516	3322	2946	-826	-376	-1202
Change		-3.0	-9.0	-4.0	-5.5	-11.3	-19.9	-11.3	-29.0
Decreasing areas	37360	36286	35118	33808	32612	28726	-4748	-3886	-8634
All Bavaria	53526	53697	53885	53750	55093	55065	+1567	-28	+1539

Sources: *Pinkas ha-Kehillot, Germania, Bavaria*, 9, 13 (in this source the 1885 figures are mistakenly listed under 1880); Bosse, *Die Verbreitung der Juden*, 67–82; *Statistik des Deutschen Reichs*, neue Folge 32 (1888): 242–243; *Vierteljahreshefte zur Statistik des Deutschen Reichs* 1 (1892): III, 30–31.

Table 7.24. Changing Jewish Population in Württemberg Districts and Hohenzollern, 1880–1910

District	1880	1885	1890	1900	1910	Change, 1880–1910	Migration balance
Neckarkreis	5288	5515	5463	5544	6276	+18.7%	+162]
(Stuttgart	2485		2758	3015	4291		+1418]
Heilbronn	871		838	815	867		-140]
All other Neckarkreis)	1932		1867	1714	1118		-1116]
Schwarzwaldkreis	1505	1466	1432	1237	1287	-14.5	-453]
Donaukreis	2627	2422	2250	2086	1935	-26.3	-1102]
(Ulm	694		664	609	588		-214]
All other Donaukreis)	1933		1586	1480	1347		-888]
Jagstkreis	3911	3768	3494	2990	2412	-38.3	-2110]
All Württemberg	13331	13171	12639	11857	11910	-10.7	-3431
Hohenzollern	771		661	532	405	-47.5	-364
Württemberg minus Stuttgart	10846		9881	8842	7619	-29.8	-4849

Sources: Bosse, *Die Verbreitung der Juden*, 65, 89–97; *Statistik des Deutschen Reichs*, neue Folge 32 (1888): 242–243; *Vierteljahrshefte zur Statistik des Deutschen Reichs* 1 (1892): III, 30–31; Schmelz, Territorial Printout.

Table 7.25. Jewish Population of Baden, 1880–1910

City	1880	1890	1900	1910	Migration balance	
Mannheim	4031	4553	5478	6402		+1720]
Karlsruhe	1689	2056	2576	3058		+1096]
Freiburg	725	999	1013	1320		+478]
Major cities	6445	7608	9067	10780	+67.3%	+3295]
Other Baden	20833	19127	17065	15116	−27.4	−9079]
Baden total	27278	26735	26132	25896	−5.1	−5784

Sources: Bosse, *Die Verbreitung der Juden*, 98–106; *Statistik des Deutschen Reichs*, neue Folge 32 (1888): 242–243; *Vierteljahrshefte zur Statistik des Deutschen Reichs* 1 (1892): III, 30–31; Blau, *Entwicklung*, 284; Schmelz, Territorial Printout.

In Thuringia and Hannover, a small overall increase in Jewish population masked important internal differences as well. Most of the Thuringian states, which had excluded Jews before 1871, witnessed sharp percentage gains in Jewish population, although the overall numbers remained small. The traditional Jewish centers in the rural southwest, however, lost population. This cannot be traced to migration within Thuringia because a large proportion of Jews in principalities that boasted "new" Jewish populations came from abroad (Table 7.26). In Hannover province, most of the increase in Jewish population took place in the city of Hannover (Table 7.27).

While Hesse-Nassau and the Rhineland both showed considerable increases in Jewish population from 1880 to 1910, each was part of a larger region that had wide discrepancies and considerable internal migration. The Prussian province of Hesse-Nassau and the Grand Duchy of Hesse(-Darmstadt) formed a single rather densely Jewish region. During the *Kaiserreich* era, there was much migration from the Grand Duchy to the Prussian province and, within Hesse-Nassau, toward the larger cities and Frankfurt in particular (Table 7.28). Although all major districts except RB Wiesbaden lost Jewish population, none of the rural districts in Hesse declined nearly as much as most of the declining districts in Württemberg and Bavaria. The percentage of Hessian Jews who lived in Frankfurt am Main increased from about 20 percent to about 35 percent during this period.

Like Hesse, the Rhineland and Westphalia area formed a region that gained Jewish population overall between 1880 and 1910 but with wide internal differences (Table 7.29). In-migration was strongest in RB Cologne, where much of the influx was directed to the city of Cologne itself, as well as in RBs Düsseldorf and Arnsberg, within which lay the industrial center of the Ruhr basin (Table 7.30). These areas were home to 53.1 percent of all Jews in the Rhineland and Westphalia in 1880 and 65.0 percent in 1910. RB Cologne showed the greatest relative inflow, and the growth of its Jewish population almost kept pace with the rapid growth of the general population. By 1890, most Jews in the Cologne district lived in Cologne city. The other two rapidly growing districts lacked a single dominant Jewish community comparable to Cologne. Within them, Ruhr District proper saw much faster general population growth from 1880 to 1925 at 231.4 percent (from 1,153,676 to 3,823,212)[26] while the

---

26 The categories differ from census to census due to changes in *Kreis* boundaries and the growth and merger of many cities. Counted as part of the Ruhr in the censuses of 1871, 1880, and 1925 are the counties of Rees, Mülheim an der Ruhr, Essen, and Mörs, the cities of Duisburg, Mülheim an der Ruhr, and Essen in Düsseldorf District, the counties of Hamm, Dortmund, Bochum, and Hagen as well as the cities of Dormund and Bochum in Arnsberg District, and

Table 7.26. Redistribution of Jewish Population in Thuringia, 1880–1910

	1880	1890	1900	1910	Change	Percent foreign, 1910	Migration balance
Sachsen-Meiningen	1627	1560	1351	1137	−30.1%	5.45%	−790]
Sachsen-Weimar	1248	1252	1188	1323	+6.0	9.75	−155]
Traditional centers of Jewish population	2875	2712	2539	2460	−14.4	7.76	−945]
Schwarzburg-Sondershausen	212	228	166	215	+1.4	11.16	−36]
Schwarzburg-Rudolstadt	45	71	48	78	+73.3	23.08	+25]
Schwarzburg combined	257	299	212	293	+14.0	14.33	−11]
Reuss Elder Line	60	62	48	44	−26.7	63.64	−27]
Sachsen-Coburg-Gotha	490	549	608	783	+59.8	21.46	+203]
Reuss Junior Line	69	147	178	375	+443.5	52.80	+293]
Sachsen-Altenburg	33	45	99	194	+487.9	51.55	+155]
Former exclusionary areas	652	803	933	1396	+114.1	35.39	+624]
Total Thuringia	3784	3814	3684	4149	+9.7		−332

Sources: Bosse, *Die Verbreitung der Juden*, 113–114, 119–121, 123, 125; *Statistik des Deutschen Reichs* 150 (1903): 108*; 240 (1915): 210; *Vierteljahrshefte zur Statistik des Deutschen Reichs* 1 (1892): III, 30–31; *Vierteljahrshefte zur Statistik des Deutschen Reichs—Ergänzungsheft zu 1916* 4 (1918): *Die Deutschen im Ausland und die Ausländer im Deutschen Reiche*, 53.

Table 7.27. Jewish Population of Hannover Province, 1880–1910

District	1880	1890	1900	1910	Change Percent	Change Number	Migration balance
City of Hannover	3450	3933	4540	5155	+49.4	+1705	+884]
Rest of RB Hannover	2206	2117	2035	1887	−14.5	−319	−844]
RB Aurich (Ostfriesland)	2671	2713	2755	2787	+4.3	+116	−520]
RB Osnabrück	1387	1495	1438	1430	+3.1	+43	−287]
RB Hildesheim	2847	2761	2697	2541	−10.8	−306	−984]
RB Lüneburg	1092	1081	992	959	−12.2	−133	−393]
RB Stade	1137	1012	936	786	−30.9	−351	−622]
Total	14790	15112	15393	15545	+5.1	+755	−2765

Sources: *Statistik des Deutschen Reichs* 57 (1883): 248; 150 (1903): 108*; 240 (1915): 210; *Vierteljahrshefte zur Statistik des Deutschen Reichs* 1 (1892): III, 30–31; Bosse, *Die Verbreitung der Juden*, 8; Blau, *Entwicklung*, 284; Schmelz, Territorial Printout.

Table 7.28. Jewish Population in Hessian Area, 1880–1910

District	1880	1890	1900	1910	Change	Migration balance
Rhenish Hesse	9452	8963	8601	7769	-17.8%	-3253]
Starkenburg	9700	9166	9070	9740	+0.4	-1571]
Upper Hesse	7594	7402	6815	6554	-13.7	-2301]
Hesse-Darmstadt	26746	25531	24486	24063	-10.0	-7125
RB Kassel	19142	18468	17483	17072	-10.8	-5875]
RB Wiesbaden	22174	26075	30622	34709	+56.5	+8128]
Hesse-Nassau	41316	44543	48105	51781	+25.3	+2253
Cities:						
Frankfurt	13856	17426	21974	26228	+89.3	+9618]
Wiesbaden	1202	1537	2109	2844	+136.6	+1403]
Kassel	1756	2017	2445	2675	+52.3	+570]
Mainz	3182	3231	3104	2926	-8.1	-784]
All Hesse outside the four cities	48066	45863	42959	41172	-14.3	-15679]
All Hessian area	68062	70074	72591	75844	+11.4	-4872]

Source: Schmelz, *Hessen*, 48–49.

Table 7.29. Changes in Jewish Population of Western Germany, 1880–1910

Regierungsbezirk	Province	1880	1885	1890	1900	1910	Change	Migration balance
Cologne	Rhineland	10370	11082	12043	14950	17041	+64.3	+3497]
Düsseldorf	Rhineland	13211	14092	15151	17664	21276	+61.1	+4021]
Arnsberg	Westphalia	9495	9825	10177	11802	12387	+30.5	+65]
Total		33076	34999	37371	44416	50704	+53.3	+8169]
Münster	Westphalia	3466	3462	3593	3743	4040	+16.6	-458]
Aachen	Rhineland	4235	4429	4387	4325	4211	-0.6	-1320]
Trier	Rhineland	6566	6534	6562	6773	6489	-1.2	-2087]
Koblenz	Rhineland	9312	9268	9091	8539	7910	-15.1	-4252]
Minden	Westphalia	5849	5648	5402	5095	4609	-21.2	-2981]
Total		29428	29341	29035	28475	27259	-7.4	-11098]
Rhineland-Westphalia		62504	64340	66406	72891	77963	+24.7	-3095
Hildesheim	Hannover	2847	2887	2761	2697	2541	-10.8	-984]
Schaumburg-Lippe		295	303	366	257	230	-22.0	
Lippe		1030	1024	989	879	780	-24.3	-541
Birkenfeld	Oldenburg	677	678	583	524		(-22.6)	
Total		67353	69232	71105	77248			

Source: Silbergleit, *Die Bevölkerungs- und Berufsverhältnisse*, 18*–19*; Bosse, *Die Verbreitung der Juden*, 116–117, 126; *Vierteljahreshefte zur Statistik des Deutschen Reichs*, neue Folge 1 (1892): III, 30–31; *Statistik des Deutschen Reichs* 57 (1883): 250; neue Folge 32 (1888): 240–243; 150 (1903): 108*; 240 (1915): 240.

Table 7.30.

A) Breakdown of Increase in Population in Cologne and Ruhr District

District		Population	1880	1890	1900	1910	1925	Change
RB	Cologne	Jewish	10370	12043	14950	17041	20361	+96.4%
		General	702934	827074	1021878	1249540	1434827	+104.1
		Percent Jewish	1.5	1.5	1.5	1.4	1.4	
City of Cologne		Jewish	4523	6859	9745	12156	16093	+255.8
		General	144772	281681	372529	516527	700222	+383.7
		Percent Jewish	3.1	2.4	2.6	2.4	2.3	
RB Cologne outside the city		Jewish	5847	5184	5205	4885	4268	−27.0
		General	558162	545393	649349	733013	734605	+31.6
		Percent Jewish	1.0	1.0	0.8	0.7	0.6	
RB	Düsseldorf	Jewish	13211	15151	17664	21276	24494	+85.4
		General	1591369	1973115	2599806	3418388	3866119	+142.9
		Percent Jewish	0.8	0.8	0.7	0.6	0.6	
Sections of RB Düsseldorf in Ruhr District* (cities only)		Jewish	1859	2304	3661	5739	8246	+345.7
		General	137012	191143	324617	828409	975376	+611.9
		Percent Jewish	1.4	1.2	1.1	0.7	0.8	

District	Population	1880	1890	1900	1910	1925	Change
RB Düsseldorf outside Ruhr cities	Jewish	11352	12847	14003	15537	16248	+43.1
	General	1454357	1781972	2275189	2589979	2890743	+98.8
	Percent Jewish	0.8	0.72	0.62	0.60	0.56	
RB Arnsberg	Jewish	9495	10177	11802	12387	13390***	+41.1
	General	1068141	1342711	1851319	2399849	2721367***	+154.8
	Percent Jewish	0.9	0.8	0.6	0.5	0.5	
Sections of RB Arnsberg in Ruhr District** (cities only)	Jewish	1936	2631	3737	4919	6383	+229.7
	General	114599	165321	245219	520670	741504	+547.0
	Percent Jewish	1.7	1.6	1.5	0.9	0.9	
RB Arnsberg outside Ruhr cities	Jewish	7559	7546	8065	7468	7007	-7.3
	General	953542	1177390	1606100	1879179	1979863	+107.6
	Percent Jewish	0.8	0.6	0.5	0.4	0.3	

* Ruhr sections of RB Düsseldorf include the cities of Duisburg (counted together with Hamborn), Essen, Mülheim/Ruhr, and Oberhausen.
** Ruhr sections of RB Arnsberg include the cities of Bochum, Dortmund, and Gelsenkirchen.
*** Including Gelsenkirchen, although it was transferred to RB Münster in 1928.

B) Breakdown for all of the Ruhr

Area		Population	1880	1925	
(All Ruhr Counties and cities—RB Düsseldorf)		Jewish	3916	9605	+145.3%
		General	476159	1577120	+231.2
		Percent Jewish	0.8	0.6	
Other parts of RB Düsseldorf outside Ruhr		Jewish	9295	14889	+60.2
		General	1115213	2288999	+105.3
		Percent Jewish	0.8	0.7	
All Ruhr cities and counties RB Arnsberg		Jewish	5462	11574	+111.9
		General	677520	2246092	+231.5
		Percent Jewish	0.8	0.5	
Other parts of RB Arnsberg not in Ruhr District		Jewish	4033	1816	-55.0
		General	390621	475275	+21.7
		Percent Jewish	1.0	0.4	

Sources: Bosse, *Die Verbreitung der Juden*, 38–40, 63–65; Silbergleit, *Die Bevölkerungs- und Berufsverhältnisse*, 31*–33*; Schmelz, Territorial Printout.

other sections of RBs Düsseldorf and Arnsberg increased by only 83.6 percent (from 1,505,834 to 2,764,274). The Jewish population of the Ruhr portion of the two RBs increased by 125.8 percent (from 9,378 to 21,179), as against only 25.3 percent (from 13,328 to 16,705) in the non-Ruhr sections.

In western Germany, the greatest losses in Jewish population were in the rural districts of Minden in the northeast and Koblenz in the southeast. In Trier District in the southwest, there was a difference between the industrializing Saar basin and the rest of the RB. In the Saar region, the Jewish population rose from some 2,600 in 1871 to 3,472 in 1910 (+33.5 percent); in the rest of RB Trier, it declined after 1890 from 3,862 to 3,377 (-12.6 percent). The number of migrants to the Saar basin from elsewhere in RB Trier cannot be determined directly.

Three areas—Bremen, the Kingdom of Saxony, and the city and environs of Berlin—had particularly large inflows of Jewish migrants during the *Kaiserreich* years. In the city-state of Bremen, the Jewish population nearly quadrupled between 1871 and 1910 (Table 7.31).[27] Some Jews also settled just outside the city-state of Bremen in the territory of Hannover and Oldenburg.[28]

The Kingdom of Saxony saw massive Jewish in-migration (about 11,600 net) during the Imperial period, almost all of which was to the largest cities. Until 1890, over 80 percent of Saxon Jews lived in Leipzig or Dresden. After that year, additional large communities developed in Chemnitz, Plauen, and Zwickau. Only a little over ten percent of the Jewish population of Saxony lived outside these five cities (Table 7.32). Although Saxony became famous for the large percentage of foreigners among its Jewish population, this was not the case in the early years of the *Kaiserreich*.[29]

Recklinghausen county in Münster District. To these were added several additional cities that grew between 1871 and 1925. These cities were Hamborn, Oberhausen, and Sterkade in Düsseldorf District, Hamm, Hagen, Herne, Hörde, Wanne-Eickel, Wattenscheid, and Witten in Arnsberg District, and Bottrop, Buer, Gladbeck, and Osterfeld.

27 It cannot be ruled out that some foreign Jews counted in Bremen in 1910 were temporary residents en route to America. Outside the city of Bremen, the largest Jewish community was in Bremerhaven, a growing port far north of the main part of the state of Bremen.

28 In the province of Hannover there was a sizable Jewish population in the port cities of Geestemünde (seventy-six Jews in 1910) and Lehe (141 in 1910), which eventually merged into a single city that took the name Wesermünde. In 1939 this city merged with Bremerhaven in the state of Bremen. In Delmenhorst, in the Grand Duchy of Oldenburg just across the Weser from the city of Bremen, there were 124 Jews (or 102 according to Schmelz [exact source unknown]) in 1910.

29 At first, the majority of migrants to Saxony were mainly German Jews from Prussia, but, especially after 1885, the vast majority of new residents came from Eastern Europe. Large cities in Saxony other than Leipzig and Dresden gained considerable Jewish populations after 1871 but rural areas and small towns had hardly any Jewish residents.

Table 7.31. Jewish Population Growth in *Land* of Bremen, Imperial Period

1871	1880	1890	1900	1910	Change	Foreign Jews, 1910	Percent foreign 1910	Migration balance
465	766	1031	1409	1843	+296.3%	745	40.4	+1094

Sources: *Vierteljahreshefte zur Statistik des Deutschen Reichs* 1 (1873): 188 d; neue Folge 1 (1892): III, 30–31; *Statistik des Deutschen Reichs* 57 (1883): 250; 150 (1903): 108*; 240 (1915): 240; *Vierteljahrshefte zur Statistik des Deutschen Reichs—Ergänzungsheft zu 1916* 4 (1918): *Die Deutschen im Ausland und die Ausländer im Deutschen Reiche*, 53.

Table 7.32. Jewish Population Growth in Kingdom of Saxony, 1871–1910

City	1871	1880	1890	1900	1910	Change 1871–1910	Foreign Jews, 1910	Percent foreign Jews, 1910	Migration balance
City of Leipzig	1739	3179	4225	6171	9434	+425.0%	6401	67.9	+6353]
City of Dresden	1276	2228	2616	3029	3734	+192.6	1948	52.2	+1473]
City of Chemnitz	95	294	953	1137	1605	+1589	642	40.0	+1437]
City of Plauen	10	34	180	208	749	+7390	432	57.7	+731]
City of Zwickau	10	34	50	102	159	+1490			+141]
All other Saxony	227	749	1344	1769	1906	+491.9	870	45.7	+1335]
Entire kingdom	3357	6518	9368	12416	17587	+423.9	10293	58.5	+11639

Sources: Blau, *Entwicklung*, 284; Bosse, *Die Verbreitung der Juden*, 83–88; Schmelz, Territorial Printout.

No area gained more Jewish migrants from elsewhere in Germany than the Berlin region, with a positive migration balance of some 71,000 between 1880 and 1910. By 1890, Jewish migration to the suburbs of Berlin took on ever-growing magnitude, eventually outstripping migration to the city itself (Table 7.33).

Migrants' Places of Origin

Detailed information on in-migrants' places of origin is available mainly in regard to communities of considerable in-migration (especially large cities). Several urban communities like Berlin, Hamburg, Leipzig, and Munich did not have large Jewish populations in their immediate vicinity. As a corollary, their Jewish migrants tended to come from farther away than non-Jewish migrants did. Other cities such as Cologne, Mannheim, and Frankfurt am Main had hinterlands of dense Jewish settlement in small towns and villages and were therefore more likely to have Jewish migrants from nearby.

The most detailed information available pertains to Berlin and its suburbs. Most Jewish migrants to the Berlin area were from Eastern Europe and the eastern provinces of Prussia. Among Jewish inhabitants in the area in 1910, 21,687 were foreign-born and no fewer than 49,043 came from the five east Prussian provinces of East Prussia, West Prussia, Posen, Pomerania, and Silesia—far outnumbering the 14,264 Jews who migrated to this area from elsewhere in Germany outside Brandenburg province. A substantial proportion—probably more than half—of those who left the eastern Prussian provinces ended up in Berlin (Table 7.34). Of those originating in Prussia's eastern provinces, the most common place of birth was Posen province, followed by Silesia, West Prussia, Pomerania, and faraway East Prussia.

Compared with the general population, Jewish migration patterns yielded fewer short-distance migrants (those coming from elsewhere in the same province) than non-Jews and a much higher percentage of migrants from abroad. Among those who migrated from outside Brandenburg but inside Germany, 69.6 percent of migrants in general and 81.1 percent of Jewish migrants to Berlin proper came from the five east Prussian provinces (Table 7.35). Migrants to Berlin who had been born in the provinces of Posen, West Prussia, and Pomerania tended to reach the capital earlier than those from Silesia and the provinces west of Berlin (Table 7.36).

Newcomers to the western suburbs tended to be higher in social class than those who settled within the pre-1920s boundaries of Berlin (Table 7.37).

Table 7.33. Jewish Population in Berlin Area

Area	1871	1880	1890	1900	1910	
City of Berlin	36015	53949	79286	92206	90013	+149.9%
RB Potsdam	4548	5423	7831	20780	57289	+1258.7
Later suburbs of Berlin	291	802	3878	15834	49744	+17093.2
Total Berlin plus later suburbs	36306	54751	83164	108040	139757	+284.9
RB Potsdam minus later suburbs	4257	4621	3953	4946	7545	+77.2

Sources: Silbergleit, *Die Bevölkerungs- und Berufsverhältnisse*, 18*–19*.

Table 7.34. Percent of Net Out-Migration from Eastern Prussian Provinces Settling in Berlin Area by 1910

Province	Negative migration balance 1880–1910	Jews from province (in 1910)			New inhabitants of Berlin area as percent of migration balance
		Berlin city	Berlin suburbs	Berlin area	
Pomerania	6815	3855	1891	5746	84.3%
Silesia	14416	6549	4780	11329	78.6
West Prussia	16949	7023	2725	9748	57.5
Posen	34065	12792	5616	18408	54.3
East Prussia	8123	2456	1360	3816	47.0
Total	80368	32675	16372	49047	61.0

The actual number of persons who left the eastern provinces exceeded the negative migration balance because it subtracted the (unknown) number of migrants to the provinces from the actual number of migrants from the provinces.

Source: based on Blau, *Entwicklung*, 109.

Table 7.35. Jewish Migrants and Total Migrants to Berlin

Birthplace of residents of Berlin (within 1910 city limits)

Birthplace	General population 1900		Jewish population 1910	
Berlin	772,784	40.9%	29,394	32.6%
Brandenburg	334,637	17.7	4,808	5.3
Sum native or short-distance migrants	1,107,421		34,202	
Posen	95,366	5.1	12,792	14.2
West Prussia	72,612	3.8	7,023	7.8
Silesia	137,961	7.3	6,549	7.3
Pomerania	118,779	6.3	3,855	4.3
East Prussia	91,898	4.9	2,456	2.7
Sum eastern provinces	516,616	27.4	32,675	36.3
Prussian Saxony	80,015	4.2		
Hesse-Nassau	8,014		690	0.8
Rhineland	15,956		854	1.0
Other Prussia	28,697		2,343	
Kingdom of Saxony	21,897	1.2		
Mecklenburg states	17,558			
Anhalt	7,466			
Hamburg	3,896			
South German states (Bavaria, Baden, Württemberg, Hesse, Alsace-Lorraine)	20,440			
Other German	3,675			
Foreign	38,745	2.1	15,524	17.3

Unfortunately, the Jewish and general data are not directly comparable because the general data stem from 1900 and the Jewish data from 1910 (*SJDR* [1903]: 11–14; Blau, *Entwicklung*, 107, 109).

Table 7.36. Year of Arrival of Jewish Migrants to Berlin and Three Western Suburbs from Various Areas, 1910

Year	Brandenburg*	West Prussia	Pomerania	Posen	East Prussia	Silesia	Other Prussia
After 1906	1940 (33.0)	3238 (33.8)	1853 (33.1)	6101 (34.0)	1441 (38.6)	4685 (42.5)	3768 (52.3)
1901–1905	964 (16.4)	1709 (17.8)	1029 (18.4)	3111 (17.3)	633 (17.0)	1995 (18.1)	1282 (17.8)
1896–1900	685 (11.7)	1282 (13.4)	743 (13.3)	2304 (12.8)	383 (10.3)	1150 (10.4)	778 (10.8)
1886–1895	984 (16.7)	1680 (17.5)	953 (17.0)	3173 (17.7)	661 (17.7)	1728 (15.7)	800 (11.1)
Before 1885	1305 (22.2)	1673 (17.5)	1029 (18.4)	3274 (18.2)	611 (16.4)	1470 (13.3)	579 (8.0)
Total known	5878	9582	5607	17963	3729	11028	7207
Unknown	13	19	17	47	8	31	49
Percent after 1900	49.6	51.6	51.4	51.3	55.6	60.6	70.1

Data in bold = highest column percent within row; italic = lowest column percent within row.

*Not including Berlin suburbs.

Source: Blau, *Entwicklung*, 111–113.

Table 7.37. Birthplaces of Jews in Berlin and Five Major Suburbs, 1910

Birthplace	Berlin	Charlottenburg	Schöneburg	Wilmersdorf	3 western suburbs	Neukölln	Lichtenberg	2 eastern suburbs	Total
Berlin	29394	5918	2907	2449		405	221		41294
A Berlin suburb	779	1790	857	796		253	126		4601
Other town in Brandenburg province	4029	1007	485	364		64	53		6002
Brandenburg	34202	8715	4249	3609	16573(31.9)	722	400	1122(2.2)	51897
Other Prussia	3887	1601	1025	744	3370(45.4)	101	63	164(2.2)	7421
Other Germany	3675	1447	865	714	3026(44.2)	119	23	142(2.1)	6843
Silesia	6549	2221	1320	969	4510(39.8)	193	77	270(2.4)	11329
East Prussia	2456	676	307	278	1261(33.1)	62	37	99(2.6)	3816
Pomerania	3855	878	504	388	1770(30.8)	63	58	121(2.1)	5746
Posen	12792	2663	1435	1120	5218(28.3)	248	150	398(2.2)	18408
West Prussia	7023	1311	676	498	2485(25.5)	168	72	240(2.5)	9748
Foreign-born	15524	2996	1260	1278	5534(25.5)	408	221	629(2.9)	21687
Total	89963	22508	11641	9598	43747	2084	1101	3185	136895

The 84,800 Jewish migrants born outside Berlin or the rest of Brandenburg were distributed as follows:

East Prussia	4.5%	Silesia	13.4%
West Prussia	11.5	Other Prussia	8.8
Pomerania	6.8	Other Germany	8.1
Posen	21.7	Outside Germany	25.6

Source: Blau, *Entwicklung*, 107, 109.

Migrants from western Prussian provinces and Silesia were the most likely to settle in the western suburbs; Jews from Posen and West Prussia were the least likely. Some 69.5 percent of Posen-born Jews lived within the pre-1920 Berlin city limits and accounted for 14.2 percent of the Jewish population. The percentages of Jews from Posen and West Prussia in Greater Berlin who lived within the old city limits were almost as high as the percentage of the foreign born.

Somewhat similar information comes to us from Hamburg. Given the slow growth of the Hamburg Jewish community, a larger percentage of Jews than of non-Jews were born in the city. However, only one in every seven Jews as against almost one in three of the general population came from the areas closest to the city. Jews were also underrepresented among migrants from the wider vicinity (northwestern and central Germany) but overrepresented among migrants from southern Germany and abroad (Table 7.38).

Table 7.38. Birthplace of Residents of Hamburg City, 1910

Birthplace	General population		Jews	
Hamburg city	363,737	39.1%	9384	48.6%
Other Hamburg state	39,175	4.2	151	0.8
Schleswig-Holstein	197,468	21.2	1862	9.7
RB Hannover, Stade, Lüneburg	61,443	6.6	745	3.9
Nearby	298.086	32.0	2758	14.2
RB Hildesheim, Osnabrück, Aurich	7,482	0.8	241	1.3
Berlin	16,203	1.7	884	4.6
Brandenburg	14,200	1.5	134	0.7
Prov. Saxony	15,881	1.7	192	1.0
Lübeck	11,265	1.2	267	1.4
Bremen	7,476	0.8	130	0.7
Oldenburg	6,693	0.7	6	0.3
Mecklenburg states	54,391	5.8	317	1.6
Lippe, Schaumburg-Lippe, Waldeck	879	0.1	48	0.3
Thuringia	4,739	0.5	36	0.2
Kingdom Saxony	12,834	1.4	156	0.8

Other northwestern or central Germany	152,043	16.3	2,471	12.8
Posen	4,220	0.5	220	1.1
Silesia	8,694	0.9	320	1.7
Pomerania	12,754	1.4	127	0.7
East and West Prussia	16,600	1.8	226	1.2
Eastern Germany	42,268	4.5	893	4.6
Hesse-Nassau	6,580	0.7	492	2.6
Westphalia, Rhineland, Hohenzollern	16,964	1.8	513	2.7
Hesse-Darmstadt	1,730	0.2	117	0.6
Baden	2,898	0.3	139	0.7
Württemberg	2,172	0.2	59	0.3
Bavaria	6,208	0.7	210	1.1
Alsace-Lorraine	2,211	0.2	30	0.2
Southern and western Germany	38,763	4.2	1,560	8.1
Outside Germany or unknown	30,248	3.3	2,146	11.1
Total	931,035		19,292	

Source: Weigert, "Bevölkerung," 79–80.

For Munich, there is ongoing information for much of the *Kaiserreich* period. Since almost no Jews lived in Upper Bavaria province, which surrounded the city, almost no Jewish migrants came from there. Between 1813 and 1871, most Jewish migrants to Munich originated in the Bavarian provinces that bordered Upper Bavaria on the immediate west and north, both of which had substantial Jewish populations. From 1875 to 1910, there was an ever-widening circle of Jewish migration to Munich. The earliest wave of migration was mainly from elsewhere in Bavaria, followed by areas of Germany outside Bavaria, and finally by a strong increase in Jewish migration from Eastern Europe. As in Berlin and Hamburg, Jews who migrated to Munich came from farther away than did non-Jewish migrants. The differences between the sources of Jewish and Christian migration increased over time (Table 7.39).

In Leipzig, too, the tendency for Jews to arrive from far away increased over time. Even more than in Munich, Jewish migrants in Leipzig came from Eastern

Table 7.39. Place of Birth of Residents of Munich, 1880–1910

Birthplace	Jews												
	1880	Percent	1885	1890	1895	1900	1905	1910	Percent				
Born in Munich	1483	35.8	1729	1989	2308	2573	2882	3161	28.5				
Born elsewhere in Bavaria	1552	37.5	1736	2024	2186	2433	2507	2568	23.2				
Born in Germany outside Bavaria	742	17.9	918	1301	1602	1828	2079	2324	21.0				
Born outside Germany	367	8.9	471	794	1076	1905	2588	3030	27.3				
Total	4144		4854	6108	7172	8739	10056	11083					

Birthplace	Percent of Christians				Percent of Jews				
	1880	1890	1900	1905	1880	1890	1900	1905	
Born in Munich	35.2	36.0	36.2	39.7	35.8	32.5	29.4	28.7	
Born elsewhere in Bavaria	56.2	54.2	52.6	49.4	37.4	30.2	28.7	24.9	
Born in Germany outside Bavaria	5.2	6.2	6.6	6.6	17.9	21.3	20.9	20.7	
Born outside Germany	4.4	3.6	4.5	4.3	8.9	13.0	21.8	25.7	

Sources: Cohen, "Die jüdische Bevölkerung in München im Jahre 1910," 122, and von Tyszka, "Die jüdische Bevölkerung Münchens," 90.

Europe. The percent of Leipzig Jews born in Saxony was far lower than that of the general Saxon population born in the kingdom (Table 7.40). The percentage of foreign-born increased rapidly; in 1885, only 25.6 percent of the Jewish population of Leipzig had been born abroad whereas 24.5 percent were born in the city. Migrants from within Germany, who then made up about half of Leipzig Jewry, came mainly from Prussia and very few came from other parts of Saxony. Between 1885 and 1900, the number born in Germany outside Leipzig hardly increased, but the foreign-born Jewish population grew by 1,717—an indication that the vast majority of German-born Jews who migrated to Leipzig by 1900 had arrived before 1885 (Table 7.41). Of the 1,924 Jewish migrants to Leipzig from within Germany who were enumerated in 1900, almost 18 percent came from Posen province, which far exceeded the percentage of non-Jewish German migrants to Saxony from Posen (2.4 percent) at the same time. The Prussian provinces of Saxony and Silesia, which bordered the Kingdom of Saxony on the east and the northwest, accounted for 52.5 percent of non-Jewish German-born migrants to Leipzig as against 22.3 percent of Jewish German-born migrants to this city. Most of the remaining German-born non-Jewish migrants to Saxony (85,571) came from the Thuringian states, an area unlikely to have sent more than a few Jewish migrants to Saxony.

Unlike the previously mentioned cities, Frankfurt am Main was situated in an area that had many nearby Jewish communities. The Jews in this city, at least in 1885, most likely did not come from much farther away than non-Jews. Most Jewish migrants to Frankfurt came from the Hessian region, and the rest came mainly from areas immediately bordering on Hesse. Among the general population, there was a larger proportion of migrants from more distant parts of Germany, and among Jewish migrants, there was a larger percentage of foreign-born; neither group, however, represented a substantial proportion of the migrants (Table 7.42). Unfortunately, we do not have comparable figures for Frankfurt for later periods, when migration from more distant regions became more common. Partial data for Hesse and Frankfurt, however, seem to indicate that long-distance migration to these destinations remained less common than in Berlin, Hamburg, or Leipzig. For the *Kaiserreich* period, the only other information we have on the source of migrants are figures from 1910, which show that the number of foreign Jews[30] in Frankfurt had grown from 904 in 1885 to 3,538 in 1910. During those twenty-five years, the overall Jewish population of Frankfurt increased by 10,691 and the foreign Jewish population by 2,634, implying that the vast majority of migrants to Frankfurt during the interim came

---

30 The data for 1885 refer to birthplace; those for 1910 refer to citizenship.

TABLE 7.40. Birthplaces and Citizenships of Leipzig Jews

Birthplace	1885	Percent	1890	Percent	1900	Percent	Citizenship	1905	Percent	1910
Leipzig	893	24.5	1059	25.6	1599	25.9	Saxony	1214	15.8%	1180 12.4%
Other Saxony	52	1.4	50	1.2	75	1.2				
Prussia	1364	37.5	1331	32.2	1446	23.4	Other Germany	1619	21.1	1878 19.8
Other Germany	399	11.0	399	9.6	403	6.5				
Outside Germany	931	25.6	1296	31.3	2648	42.9	Foreign	4843	62.1	6426 67.8
Total	3640		4136		6176			7676		9484

Birthplaces of Leipzig Jews, 1900			Birthplaces of general population, Kingdom of Saxony, 1900		
Leipzig	1594	25.8			
Other Kingdom of Saxony	80	1.3	Kingdom of Saxony	3,604,388	**83.9**
Prussian Saxony	233	3.8	Prussian Saxony	138,558	3.2
Berlin	143	**2.3**	Berlin	8,221	0.2
Anhalt	117	**1.9**	Anhalt	7,920	0.2
			Thuringian states	85,571	2.00
			Brandenburg	24,512	0.6
			Mecklenburg states	2,704	0.1
Nearby areas (Central Germany)	573	**9.3**	Nearby areas (Central Germany)	267,486	6.2
Posen	345	**5.6**	Posen	11,487	0.3
Silesia	196	3.2	Silesia	117,476	2.7
			Other eastern Germany	16,531	0.4
Eastern Germany	541	**8.8**	Eastern Germany	145,494	3.4

Birthplaces of Leipzig Jews, 1900			Birthplaces of general population, Kingdom of Saxony, 1900		
Other Prussia (besides provinces listed)	427	6.9			
Hesse-Nassau	102	1.7	Hesse-Nassau	5,678	0.1
Bavaria	70	1.1	Bavaria	32,507	0.8
Hamburg	51	0.8	Hamburg	2,146	0.1
Other Germany	165	2.7	Other Germany	34,823	0.8
Western and Southern Germany	388	6.3	Western and Southern Germany	75,154	0.8
Abroad (including 1774 Austria-Hungary)	2648	42.9	Abroad	109,694	2.6
Total	6171		Total	4,292,216	

Sources: "Die Zahl der Juden in Leipzig," *ZDSJ* (1906): 111; Segall, "Die Juden im Königreich Sachsen von 1832 bis 1910," 42–43.

Table 7.41. Citizenship of Jews in Saxony and Dresden

Citizenship of Jews in Saxony	1905	1910	Increase	Citizenship of Jews in Dresden	1895	1905	1910
Saxony	2549	2739	+190				
Other Germany	4369	4470	+101	Germany	1792	1799	1749
Austria-Hungary	4918	6450	+1532	Austria-Hungary	512	1087	1278
Other foreign	2860	3910	+1050	Other foreign	254	628	705
Unknown	1	18	+17				
	14697	17587			2558	3514	3732
							[3734]

Sources: Segall, "Die Juden im Königreich Sachsen von 1832 bis 1910," 33–46; "Die Zahl der Juden in Leipzig," *ZDSJ* (1906): 111; *Statistisches Jahrbuch für das Deutsche Reich* (1903): 10–14.

Table 7.42. Birthplaces of Jews and General Population of Frankfurt, 1885

Birthplace	Jews		General population	
Frankfurt	6017	38.7%	60,945	39.5%
Other Hesse-Nassau	2132*	13.7	30,760*	19.9
Hesse-Darmstadt	2675*	17.2	21,878*	14.2
Nearby	4807*	30.9	52,638*	33.1
Rhineland	724*	4.7	4,675*	3.0
Bavaria	1171*	7.5	11,407*	7.4
Baden	714*	4.6	4,862*	3.2
Middle distance	2609*	16.8	20,944*	13.6
Other Germany	1200*	7.7	15,801*	10.2
Outside Germany	904*	5.8	4,114*	2.7
Total	15537		154,441	

* Reconstructed from data on percentages of migrants to the city.

Source: Schmelz, *Hessen*, 185.

from inside Germany. Partial data for Hesse and Frankfurt after World War I indicate that long-distance migration to these locations remained less common than in Berlin, Hamburg, or Leipzig (Table 7.43).

Migration after World War I

After World War I, the most salient migration patterns involved the crossing of frontiers, with immigration dominating between 1910 and the 1920s and emigration in the 1930s. However, some notable trends in migration within Germany still persisted during this time. After World War I, some of the territories that Germany lost in the east, north, and west (especially Posen, West Prussia, Upper Silesia, and Alsace-Lorraine) had considerable Jewish populations. Though few Jews appear to have migrated from Alsace-Lorraine to Germany after the war—unlike the many non-Jewish migrants from Alsace-Lorraine— most Jews in the areas assigned to Poland left for locations in Germany.

The 1925 census enumerated 806,777 migrants of all religions in Germany who had originated in the so-called "lost territories." Of them, almost three-fourths came from lands ceded to Poland—468,481 from Posen and West Prussia, 90,107 from Upper Silesia, and 44,047 from Danzig. Another 15,545

Table 7.43. Places of Origin of Migrants to Hesse Area, 1925, 1933

Residence at outbreak of World War I of Jews living in Hesse-Darmstadt in 1925		
In same town as in 1925	14,797	82.8%
Elsewhere in Hesse-Darmstadt	885	5.0
Elsewhere in Germany (postwar boundaries)	1,497	8.4
In territories lost by Germany in World War I	169	0.9
Outside Germany	525	2.9
Birthplace of Jewish residents of Frankfurt am Main in 1933		
Frankfurt	10,680	40.8
Elsewhere in Germany (postwar boundaries)	11,324	43.3
Territories lost by Germany in World War I	665	2.5
Outside Germany	3,475	13.3
Unknown	14	0.1

Sources: Schmelz, *Hessen*, 146; 1933 census, 5/50.

came from the Memel district, which had been ceded to Lithuania, while 132,045 migrated from Alsace and Lorraine. Those from Posen and West Prussia settled mainly in central and eastern Germany, especially in the Berlin area and in Lower Silesia and Pomerania (Table 7.44). Those from Upper Silesia settled chiefly in those parts of Upper Silesia and Lower Silesia that remained German. Danzig residents migrated mainly to East Prussia, Berlin, Pomerania, and Westphalia, while a large number of Memel residents who left moved to neighboring East Prussia. In contrast to the general population of Memel migrants, Jews from Memel settled mainly in Berlin (Table 7.45).

Although the 1925 census did not distinguish between Jews and non-Jews who came from the lost territories, the 1933 census did count Jews from these territories but did not specify from which area they came. A total of 46,550 such Jews were counted, of whom 25,524 (54.8 percent) lived in the city of Berlin, where they made up 15.9 percent of the Jewish population. Another 9,352 (20.1 percent) of Jews born in the lost territories lived in Silesia, where they made up an even larger proportion of the total Jewish population (27.2 percent). Jews from these territories made up 26.5 percent of those in Breslau, 30.0 percent of those in Beuthen, and 31.8 percent of those in the other large cities of Upper Silesia.[31]

---

31 1933 census, 5/50.

Table 7.44. Residence in 1925 of Migrants from Territories Lost to Poland (General Population)

Migrants from Posen and West Prussia			Migrants from Polish Upper Silesia		
Berlin	84,253	(18.0%)	Upper Silesia	51,034	(56.6%)
Brandenburg	68,915	(14.7)	Lower Silesia	16,265	(18.1)
Lower Silesia	53,918	(11.5)	Berlin	4,984	(5.5)
Pomerania	49,836	(10.6)	Other Germany	28,874	(32.0)
Westphalia	38,940	(8.3)			
East Prussia	38,452	(8.2)			
Other Prussia	105,601	(22.5)			
Other Germany	28,566	(6.1)			

Source: *Statistik des deutschen Reichs* 401 (1930): *Die Bevölkerung des Deutschen Reichs nach den Ergebnissen der Volkszählung 1925*, part 2: *Textliche Darstellung der Ergebnisse*, 539.

The 1925 census also indicated other types of domestic migration that had taken place since the prewar census of 1910 (Table 7.46). Most of the southern, more rural states[32] showed losses of Jewish population in the range of 7–17 percent. Only a small fraction of the total was made up by an increase in Hesse-Nassau (mainly in Frankfurt). Most of the rest must have either migrated to other sections of Germany or emigrated outright. With the exception of Bavaria, where there was heavy migration from antisemitic Munich, migration from more rural to more urban areas continued within each of the southern states. Rural losses seem to have been greater and the urban gains less than in the prewar decades. Rural losses were generally smaller in the Hessian area than farther south (Table 7.47). Elsewhere in Germany, the internal migration patterns of the prewar period continued (Map 7/4).

Between the 1925 and 1933 censuses, the Jewish population of almost every German region declined mainly due to emigration in early 1933. There was little correlation between the degree of the decline after 1925 and the growth

---

[32] Baden (7.07 percent), Württemberg (9.64 percent), Bavaria (10.84 percent), Hesse(-Darmstadt) (15.22 percent), and the Prussian province of Hohenzollern (17.28 percent). The total decline in Jewish population in these five territories was 12,675.

Table 7.45. Destinations of Migrants from Memel and Danzig

Danzig and Memel citizens in Prussia 1925

Destinatin	Danzig citizens					Memel citizens			
	General	Percent of migrants	Jews	Percent of migrants	General	Percent of migrants	Jews	Percent of migrants
East Prussia	1319	24.6	22	7.5	301	42.4	11	20.4
Berlin	1069	19.9	193	66.1	121	17.0	31	57.4
Pomerania	654	12.2	5	1.7	24	3.4	1	1.9
Westphalia	225	4.2	2	0.7	19	2.7	0	0
Rhineland	215	4.0	1	0.3	63	8.9	3	5.6
All other	1887	35.1	69	23.6	182	25.6	8	14.8
Total	5369	100	292	100	710	100	54	100
Memel residents in 1914 (general population)					Danzig residents in 1914 (general population)			
East Prussia	7,348 (47.3%)				East Prussia	8,102 (18.4%)			
Berlin	1,936 (12.5%)				Berlin	7,746 (17.6%)			
Rhineland	1,393 (9.0%)				Pomerania	4,798 (10.9%)			
Westphalia	1,295 (8.3%)				Westphalia	4,755 (10.8%)			
All other	3,573 (23.0%)				Rhineland	3,223 (7.3%)			
					All other	15,423 (35.0%)			
Total	15,545				Total	44,047			

Sources: Silbergleit, *Die Bevölkerungs- und Berufsverhältnisse*, 42*–45*; *Statistik des deutschen Reichs* 401 (1930): *Die Bevölkerung des Deutschen Reichs nach den Ergebnissen der Volkszählung 1925*, part 2: *Textliche Darstellung der Ergebnisse*, 539–540.

Table 7.46. Change in Jewish Population of Various Districts, 1910–1933

District	1910	1925	Change, 1910–1925 according to postwar boundaries	Migration balance	1933	Change, 1925–1933	Migration balance	Change, 1910–1933
Saxony (Free State)	17587	23252	+32.2%	+3299	20584	-11.5%	-2946	+17.0%
Berlin (1920 boundaries)	144007	172672	+19.9	+40142	160564	-7.0	-2462	+11.5
Brandenburg	7349	8442	+14.9		7616	-9.8	-177	+3.6
Rhineland	53266	58223	+8.4	+3762	52426	-9.2	-4547	-1.6
Upper Silesia	9700	10069	+3.8	+7114	9228	-8.4	-3365	-4.9
Lower Silesia	26654	29953	+12.4	+1629	25145	-5.9	-921	-5.9
Schleswig-Holstein	3311	4152	+25.4	+232	3117	-14.3	-990	-8.8
Prussian Saxony	7833	8341	+6.5	+166	7146	-12.9	-2471	-10.1
Westphalia	20939	21595	+3.1	+2372	18819	-12.7	-4504	-11.4
Hesse-Nassau	51781	52757	+1.9	+1663	46923	-14.7	-2081	-12.8
Hamburg	19472	19904	+2.2	-732	16973	-7.4	-289	-16.4
Württemberg	11982	10827	-9.6	+56	10023	-18.0	-209	-18.7
Oldenburg	1525	1513	-0.8		1240			

District	1910	1925	Change, 1910–1925 according to postwar boundaries	Migration balance	1933	Change, 1925–1933	Migration balance	Change, 1910–1933
Schaumburg-Lippe	230	180	-21.7	?	187	+3.9	?	-18.7
Hannover	15596	14895	-4.5	-515	12611	-15.3	-1751	-19.1
Lübeck	623	629	+1.0	+33	497	-21.0	-105	-20.2
Baden	25896	24064	-7.1	-775	20617	-14.3	-2239	-20.4
Bremen	1843	1508	-18.2	-253	1438	-4.6	-6	-22.0
Bavaria	55117	49145	-10.8	-3252	41939	-14.7	-4989	-23.9
Thuringia	3820	3603	-5.7	-361	2882	-26.3	-340	-24.6
Hesse(-Darmstadt)	24063	20401	-15.2	-3335	17888	-12.3	-1547	-25.7
Hohenzollern	405	335	-17.3	-7	301	-10.2	-8	-25.7
Grenzmark	3835	3437	-10.4	-17	2775	-19.3	-441	-27.6
Pomerania	8862	7761	-12.4	-348	6317	-18.6	-953	-28.7
East Prussia	12715	11337	-10.8	-595	8838	-22.0	-1956	-30.5
Braunschweig	1757	1753	-0.2	+73	1174	-33.0	-505	-33.2
Lippe	780	607	-22.2	-177	510	-16.0	-57	-34.6
Anhalt	1383	1140	-17.6	-181	901	-21.0	-191	-34.9
Mecklenburg (both states)	1669	1407	-15.6	-186	1003	-28.7	-344	-39.8

Sources: *Statistik des deutschen Reichs* 401 (1930): *Die Bevölkerung des Deutschen Reichs nach den Ergebnissen der Volkszählung 1925*, part 2: *Textliche Darstellung der Ergebnisse*, 603–615, 618–619; 1933 census, 5/11.

Table 7.47. Changes in Urban and Rural Sections of Southern Germany, 1910–1925

Urban City		1910	1925	Change	
Frankfurt am Main		26228	29385	+3157	+12.0%
Nuremberg		7815	8603	+788	+10.1
Mannheim		6402	6972	+570	+8.9
Stuttgart		4291	4548	+257	+6.0
Munich		11083	10068	-1015	-9.2
Total Urban		55819	59576	+3757	+6.7
Rural District (Land)		1910	1925	Change	
Karlsruhe	Baden	6858	6904	+46	+0.7
RB Wiesbaden (excluding Frankfurt)	Hesse-Nassau	9104	8854	-250	-2.8
Neckarkreis (excluding Stuttgart)	Württemberg	1985	1830	-155	-7.8
Rhine Palatinate (excluding Saar)	Bavaria	8721	7850	-871	-10.0
RB Kassel	Hesse-Nassau	17603	15498	-2105	-12.0
Donaukreis	Württemberg	1935	1694	-241	-12.5
Upper Hesse	Hesse-Darmstadt	6554	5732	-822	-12.5
Rhenish Hesse	Hesse-Darmstadt	7769	6675	-1094	-14.1
Freiburg	Baden	5063	4341	-722	-14.3
Upper Palatinate	Bavaria	1395	1181	-214	-15.3
Lower Franconia	Bavaria	11925	9879	-2046	-17.2
Hohenzollern	Prussia	405	335	-70	-17.3
Starkenburg	Hesse-Darmstadt	9740	7994	-1746	-17.9
Swabia	Bavaria	3462	2834	-628	-18.1
Middle Franconia (excluding Nuremberg)	Bavaria	6404	5116	-1288	-20.1
Upper Franconia	Bavaria	3279	2544	-735	-22.4
Mannheim (without city)	Baden	5904	4566	-1338	-22.7
Konstanz	Baden	1669	1281	-388	-23.3
Schwarzwaldkreis	Württemberg	1359	1010	-249	-25.7
Jagstkreis	Württemberg	2412	1745	-667	-27.7
Total non-urban		113546	97863	-15683	-13.8

Source: Schmelz, Territorial Printout.

or contraction of the Jewish population of the regions before 1925. The above-average declines in Braunschweig, Thuringia, and Schleswig-Holstein may be attributable to either the Nazis' early rise to power and influence there or to a high percent of particularly vulnerable foreign Jews. The almost universal drop in Jewish population masked the continuation of migration patterns from rural areas to the largest cities in both the late Weimar period and the early years of Nazi rule. Between 1933 and 1939, the German-Jewish population fell by more than 50 percent due almost entirely to emigration. Regional variance in the steepness of the decline was linked to factors such as varying degrees of pressure to leave a particular area because of antisemitism and the extent of rural-to-urban migration. We know that many German Jews moved from their hometowns to other parts of Germany during the 1930s. Some then left their new domiciles for destinations outside Germany while others remained in their new places of residence from which they were deported to their deaths in the early 1940s.

Stable Geographic Patterns despite Migration before 1933

Despite many changes over a period of more than a century, many early nineteenth-century geographical patterns remained noticeable into the 1920s and 1930s, especially in rural areas. Although many Jews migrated to cities where few Jews had formerly lived, very small numbers moved to rural areas where Jews had not traditionally dwelled. Exceptions occurred mainly in the eastern areas of East Prussia, Pomerania, and Upper Silesia in the early nineteenth century. When comparing the geographic pattern of Jewish settlement in the countryside in 1871 and 1925, we find remarkable stability.

Data on the Jewish and general population of every county (*Kreis*) in Prussia are available for 1871, 1880, and 1925.[33] During this time, great changes took place both in German society and in Jewish residence patterns. The percentage of Jews living in urban areas increased while the rural Jewish population decreased and the overall percentage of the Prussian population that was Jewish decreased as well. Nevertheless, at the county level, areas that had had low percentages of Jews remained low and those with proportionately dense Jewish populations retained them—with certain notable exceptions. Within each larger district (*Regierungsbezirk*), the relative distribution of Jews by county remained

---

33 In Friedrich Bosse, *Die Verbreitung der Juden im deutschen Reiche auf Grundlage der Volkszählung vom 1. Dezember 1880* (Berlin, 1885); and Silbergleit, *Die Bevölkerungs- und Berufsverhältnisse*, 28*–33*.

remarkably stable except in districts that had growing cities. Statistically, the correlation among the percentages of Jews by counties was very high: 0.987, in 1871–1880, 0.911 in 1880–1925, and 0.883 in the entire 1871–1925 period. There are often explanations for those counties that strayed far from the norm of change. Areas where the Jewish percentage in 1925 exceeded the prediction included several large or medium cities,[34] several districts that had originally had much lower Jewish densities than nearby counties,[35] and some outlying districts in the general vicinity of Berlin.[36] Areas where the Jewish percentage was much lower than the expected norm in 1925 include the rump districts on the eastern frontier, especially Upper Silesia, that had lost most of their territory to Poland after World War I,[37] as well as several rural counties that surrounded substantial cities.[38]

This stability in the relative Jewish density of most rural counties, especially within each region, coexisted with the massive shift of Jewish population from region to region, which, except in its earliest stages, was associated with the process of urbanization. Small-town exodus from Posen and later from most East German areas left the remaining Jewish population there severely depleted. Rural southern Germany experienced a substantial migration in the early nineteenth century but more moderate one thereafter. The main beneficiaries of this internal migration were the city of Berlin, the Kingdom (later Freistaat) of Saxony, and the Ruhr and Cologne districts in the west. No German city experienced greater growth in Jewish population than Berlin, which far outstripped all other Jewish communities in Germany in the twentieth century.

---

34 Berlin, Wiesbaden, Cologne, Elberfeld, Barmen, Halberstadt, and Fulda. The latter two cities are interesting because they were relatively small and were regional centers of Orthodoxy. In the case of Fulda, much of the migration probably came from the surrounding countryside.
35 Daun, Bitburg, Hersfeld, Dillkreis, and Frankenberg.
36 Zauch-Belzig, Niederbarnim, and Teltow.
37 Falkenberg, Rybnik, Lublinitz, Tarnowitz, Tost-Gleiwitz, Bomst, and Fraustadt.
38 Hildesheim (*Land*), Halberstadt (*Land*), and Hannover (*Land*). Breslau (*Land*), however, had a higher than predicted Jewish percentage in 1925.

8

Immigration and Emigration

As governments frequently collect statistics about both emigration and immigration, Jewish migration is generally easier to trace when it crosses frontiers than when it is internal. In some cases, the exact number of Jews who left or entered Germany is known, while in other instances we know only the migration balance (in-migration minus out-migration). In all periods, at least before 1933, there were always Jews among both immigrants to and emigrants from Germany, even when the migration balance tilted strongly in one direction or the other.

Chronologically, a period of small positive Jewish migration balances before 1840 with slightly more immigration than emigration was succeeded by a heavily negative balance between about 1840 and 1880. Thereafter, immigration exceeded emigration until the mid-1920s with some interruptions. The largest wave of Jewish migration across Germany's borders began in 1933; this was the emigration of ever-increasing numbers of Jews trying to escape worsening persecution by leaving the country.

That there was a slight excess of Jewish immigration over emigration before 1840, especially in Prussia is identified mainly through the indirect medium of migration balances, in which natural increase (births less deaths) is subtracted from the growth in the number of Jews. The net migration data, of course, do not tell us exactly how many Jews entered Germany and how many left, it merely yields the difference between the two. What is more, actual emigration always exceeded net emigration.

The estimated net migration of Jews in Prussia was moderately but steadily positive from 1819 to 1834. After a brief interlude of greater emigration between 1834 and 1837, net immigration persisted until 1843. Then, between 1843 and 1890, Prussian-Jewish emigration exceeded immigration in every period for which evidence exists; the largest net emigration surpluses appeared in 1852–1861 and again in 1880–1890[1] (Table 8.1[2]; see also Table 7.18).

Emigration to America

For the wave of emigration from Germany that arrived mainly in the United States, we do not need to rely solely on migration balances, because we also have direct evidence from both the German and the American records. In American Jewish history, the 1820–1880 years are known as the "German period." During that time, American Jewry grew from approximately 3,000 to about 280,000. The total number of Jews in the United States reached about 15,000 in 1840 and then increased rapidly to 150,000 by 1860.[3] A large majority of Jewish immigrants to the United States during these years came from territories that would be incorporated into Germany at later times. Estimates of the total number of Jewish emigrants from German lands to the United States range from about

---

1 A series of articles in the *Allgemeine Preussische Staatszeitung* (1838): 949–950, 953–954 calculated Jewish net migration for 1822–1837. Silbergleit gives a much more complete series of calculations (*Die Bevölkerungs- und Berufsverhältnisse*, 14*–15*), 1819–1864 and 1875–1910. Silbergleit's data clash with those in the *Allgemeine Preussische Staatszeitung* due to several typographical errors in Silbergleit's table. Silbergleit's tables give the annual increases in Jewish population as 2,043 between 1831 and 1834 and as 3,373 between 1834 and 1837. The correct figures are 3,043 and 2,373. A recalculation of the rest of his data leads to the disappearance of the net emigration that he reported for 1831–1834 and instead shows net emigration between 1834 and 1837. Jews also evinced net emigration from Prussia in 1843–1846, 1849–1852, 1858–1861, and 1861–1864, even as the general Prussian population showed net immigration, and showed small net immigration in 1875–1880 as Prussia overall had substantial net emigration.
2 Between 1843–1864 and 1880–1894, the Jewish migration balance in Prussia was 52,457 more emigrants than immigrants, as against 1,282,287 among the general population in the same years. The Jewish emigration balance was 4.1 percent of the figure for all Prussian emigration (Silbergleit, *Die Bevölkerungs- und Berufsverhältnisse*, 14*–15*).
3 Barkai, *Branching Out*, 15, 125. Estimates for the four communities of Boston, Chicago, Charleston, and Philadelphia show an increase in Jewish population from 5,191 in 1850 to 13,327 in 1860 (ibid., 79, quoting Kenneth Roseman, "The Jewish Population of America 1860–1870: A Demographic Study of Four Cities" [PhD diss., HUC-JIR, Cincinnati, 1971], 163–164).

Table 8.1. Estimated Net Cross-Border Migration Balances, 1816–1933

Year	Prussia				All Germany
	General population		Jews		Jews
	Annual	Whole period	Annual	Whole period	Whole period
1816–1818	+59,147	+177,441	?		+2316
1819–1821	+29,896	+89,688	+772	+1620	
1822–1824	+9,896	+29,688	+540	+1203	
1825–1827	+15,726	+47,178	+401	+1767	
1828–1830	+23,728	+71,184	+589	–18621	
1831–1833	+50,661	+151,983	–207	+1818	
1834–1836	+47,844	+143,532	+606	+1989	
1837–1839	+114,480	+343,440	+663	+1596	
1840–1842	+5,971	+17,913	+532	–3207	
1843–1845	+18,308	+54,924	–1069	–2802	
1846–1848	–26,919	–80,757	–934	–2922	
1849–1851	+11,206	+33,618	–974	–3936	
1852–1854	–28,595	–85,785	–1312	–4260	
1855–1857	–893	–2,679	–1420	–4416	
1858–1860	+1074	+3,222	–1472	–1659	
1861–1863	+6800	+20,400	–553	?	
1867–1871	–61,189	–244,756	?		

Year	Prussia						All Germany	
	General population		Jews				Jews	
	Annual	Whole period	Annual	Whole period				
1871-1874	-42,029	-168,116	?	?				
1875-1879	-60,888	-304,440	+63	+315				
1880-1885	-125,172	-625,860	-3213	-16,065	(1880-1884)		-15,775	
1885-1889	-61,362	-306,810	-1746	-88,730	(1886-1890)		-27,247	
1890-1894	-58,512	-292,560	-892	-84,460	(1891-1895)		-16,257	
1895-1899	+7598	+37,990	+466	+2,330	(1896-1900)		-15,290	
1900-1904	+18,226	+91,130	+2252	+11,260	(1901-1905)		+1,234	
1905-1909	-8,227	-41,135	+591	+2,955	(1906-1910)		+10,125	
1910-1925 (within 1925 borders)							+475	
1925-1933							+49,713	
							-40,710	

Sources:

Prussia: Silbergleit, *Die Bevölkerungs- und Berufsverhältnisse,* 14*-15*.

All Germany: Schmelz, Territorial Printout.

150,000 to 250,000.[4] Although the "German-Jewish wave" of immigration to America is generally periodized as ending in 1881, the evidence shows that it continued with considerable strength in 1881–1914 as well.[5]

Jewish emigration to America was part of a much larger wave of German migration. In its timing and the migrants' shifting geographic origins, it resembled the general German wave, albeit with several peculiar characteristics of its own. Overall, German emigration to the United States increased rapidly from a very low baseline—from an annual count of about 8,000 in the early 1830s to more than 130,000 by the early 1850s. After cresting at that time, it waned before and during the American Civil War but resumed in two main surges between 1865 and 1874 and again between 1880 and 1884. After 1895, emigration from Germany to the United States slumped dramatically (Table 8.2). It is estimated that Jews comprised 2–4 percent of the emigrants, far in excess of their share in the German population.

Precise figures on total overseas emigration from Germany—not merely net emigration—are available for the post-unification period of 1871 and thereafter (Table 8.3).[6] Earlier figures from some of the constituent states are available as well. Most of these statistics do not distinguish among groups of emigrants by religion. The main exceptions in this respect are data for Bavaria and Württemberg from mid-century. The most extensive records of this kind, which came from Württemberg and pertained to the 1856–1871 period (Table 8.4), count a total of 1,595 Jewish emigrants.[7] Although Jews were only 0.7

---

4 Barkai, *Branching Out*, 236, note 17, quotes the following estimates of German-Jewish emigration to America: 150,000 during the nineteenth century (Jacob Lestschinsky, "Jewish Migration 1840-1956," in *The Jews: Their History, Culture, and Religion*, vol 2 [New York: Harper, 1960]), 50,000 from 1830 to 1870 (Liebman Hersch, "Jewish Migrations During the Last Hundred Years," in *The Jewish People, Past and Present*, vol 1 [New York: Jewish Encyclopedic Handbooks, 1946]), 250,000 from 1830 to 1930 (Blau, *Entwicklung*), and almost 200,000 Jews from German-speaking countries by 1881 (Joseph Jacobs, "Statitics of Jews," *The American Jewish Yearbook* 16 [5675]). Barkai (*Branching Out*, 126) estimates the total number of German-Jewish immigrants to the United States from Germany between 1846 and 1910 at 250,000.
5 Barkai (*Branching Out*, 125–127) argues for a figure of at least 70,000 German-Jewish migrants to the United States between 1865 and 1914.
6 *Statistisches Jahrbuch für den Preussischen Staat* (1905): 26.
7 Between 1859 and 1871, 1,392 Jews left Württemberg and 530 immigrated to the kingdom from elsewhere. In 1856 and 1857, apart from the 126 Jewish emigrants from Württemberg to America, there were twenty to Baden, eighteen to Bavaria, three to Switzerland, three to Prussia, three to other German states, and three to France. Concurrently, fourteen Jews from Baden, twenty-two from Bavaria, four from Hohenzollern, three from other German states, two from Switzerland, one from France, and two from North America immigrated to Württemberg (Jacob Segall, "Die Entwicklung der jüdischen Bevölkerung in Württemberg von 1820 bis 1910," *ZDSJ* [1913]: 52, 67).

Table 8.2. General German Immigration to America

Year	Immigrants
1820–1824	1,900
1825–1829	3,800
1830–1834	39,300
1835–1839	85,500
1840–1844	100,500
1845–1849	284,900
1850–1854	654,300
1855–1859	321,800
1860–1864	204,100
1865–1869	519,600
1870–1874	450,500
1875–1879	120,000
1880–1884	797,900
1885–1889	452,600
1890–1894	428,800
1895–1899	120,200
1900–1904	128,600
1905–1909	123,500
1910–1914	84,100

Source: Marschalck, *Deutsche Überseewanderung*, 48.

Table 8.3. Total Emigrants from Prussia, 1871–1900

Year	Overseas emigrants	Migration balance from Table 8.1	Calculated overland migration balance
1871–1875	239,533	-168,116	+71,417
1876–1880	140,401	-304,440	-164,039
1881–1885	542,506	-625,860	-83,354
1886–1890	294,259	-306,810	-12,551
1891–1895	252,575	-292,560	-40,185
1896–1900	71,335	+37,990	+109,325

The number of emigrants from Prussia to European locations, although unknown, may explain why the emigration balance sometimes exceeded the number of known overseas emigrants.

Source: *Statistisches Jahrbuch für den Preußischen Staat* (1905): 26.

Table 8.4. Emigration from Württemberg, 1856–1871

Year	Total	Jews:		
		All	Overseas	Europe
1856	4791	78	55	23
1857	6192	98	71	27
1858	2989	27		
1859	3480	60		
1860	3613	83		
1861	3334	85		
1862	3165	109		
1863	3657	82		
1864	4731	79		
1865	5777	114		
1866	6995	204		
1867	7182	126		
1868	5444	111		
1869	6359	146		
1870	4370	108		
1871	2256	85		
Total	74335	1595 (2.14%)		

Source: Segall, "Die Entwicklung der jüdischen Bevölkerung in Württemberg von 1820 bis 1910," 53, 67.

percent of the Württemberg population in 1852, they were about 2 percent of all emigrants from the kingdom, which was almost three times the share that would have been expected. A list for Bavaria in 1856–1858 shows 757 Jewish emigrants to destinations overseas and 170 to European locations, yielding a ratio of about three Bavarian Jewish immigrants for every Jewish emigrant from Württemberg in those three years. Jews accounted for 4.3 percent of all emigrants from Bavaria in those years, even though their proportion of the Bavarian population was only slightly over one percent.[8] The extant data shed light on only a small section of the entire picture of German-Jewish emigration, making

---

8 Avraham Barkai, "German Jewish Migrations in the Nineteenth Century, 1830–1910," *YLBI* 30 (1985): 307–309.

it difficult to tell how representative the years covered were of larger patterns. Stefan Rohrbacher's study of the emigration of 314 Jews from the Württemberg village of Jebenhausen between 1825 and 1870 demonstrated that almost 80 percent of emigrants left before 1856–1871, which was the period addressed by the confessional statistics in Table 8.4 (Table 8.5).

It is also difficult to assess the changing geographical origins of German-Jewish emigrants. There are copious data on the geographical origins of German emigrants in general, but, except for the Bavarian and Württemberg data quoted above, there was rarely any breakdown for Jews (Tables 8.6, 8.7).[9] Much emigration to America in and before the 1840s originated in southwestern Germany; in the second half of the century, however, the geographic balance shifted more and more toward the north and the east (Tables 8.8 A and B). There seems to have been a parallel shift among Jewish migrants in Germany, but data on their exact origin are skimpy and often inaccurate.[10] Most accounts

Table 8.5. Jewish Emigration from Jebenhausen, Württemberg, 1825–1870

Year	Immigrants	Percent
1825–1829	9	2.9%
1830–1834	8	2.5
1835–1839	53	16.9
1840–1844	19	6.1
1845–1849	91	29.0
1850–1854	73	23.2
1855–1859	19	6.1
1860–1864	16	5.1
1865–1870	26	8.3
Total	314	
Total 1855–1870	61	19.4
Total emigrated in 1854 or earlier	253	80.6

Source: Barkai, *Branching Out*, 18, quoting Stefan Rohrbacher, "From Württemberg to America," *American Jewish Archives* 41 (1989): 148.

---

9 *Statistisches Jahrbuch für das Deutsche Reich* 1 (1880): 20.
10 The definition of Germany in the pre-1871 period was rather loose, often including such German-speaking areas as Bohemia and parts of Hungary. Jews from the provinces of Posen and West Prussia were sometimes considered German, sometimes "Prussian," and at other times "Polish." Most German statistics on emigration do not distinguish between Jewish emigrants and others. Most American data, in turn, are vague about places of origin, sometimes

Table 8.6. Places of Origin of Overseas Emigrants from Germany 1872–1875 (general population, by German states and Prussian provinces)

Place of Origin	Number	Percent of total
East and West Prussia	39,448	12.9%
Pomerania	37,462	12.3
Posen	30,665	10.1
Hannover	23,376	7.7
Schleswig-Holstein	18,209	6.0
Brandenburg	11,841	3.9
Hesse-Nassau	11,034	3.6
All other Prussia	26,566	8.7
All Prussia	198,601	65.2
Bavaria	27,686	9.1
Mecklenburg-Schwerin	17,629	5.8
Baden	13,514	4.4
Württemberg	13,443	4.4
Hesse(-Darmstadt)	7,223	2.4
Saxony (Kingdom)	6,998	2.3
All other	19,748	6.5
All Germany	304,842	100

By this time, the predominance of southern Germans among the emigrants was long over.

Source: "Bilanz der Bevölkerung," *Statistisches Jahrbuch für das deutsche Reich* 1 (1880): 20.

of nineteenth-century American Jewry distinguish loosely between the Jews of southwestern Germany (sometimes referred to as "Bayers," that is, Bavarians) and those of northeastern Germany (sometimes called "Pollacks" but also, more politely, "Prussians" or "Poseners"). In general, the Bavarian and other south German Jews tended to arrive earlier than Jews from northeastern Germany.

While some local studies of nineteenth-century American Jewish communities indicate the earliest Jewish settlers' place of origin, the patterns

---

mentioning exact birthplaces (towns), sometimes German states (Bavaria, Prussia), and on other occasions merely referring to Germany or Poland. Often German place names are garbled, sometimes to the point of unrecognizability.

Table 8.7. Percent Distribution of Emigrants from Various Prussian Provinces, 1871–1900

Province	1871–1875	1876–1880	1881–1885	1886–1890	1891–1895	1896–1900
East Prussia		7.6	1.8	3.3	3.3	3.5
West Prussia	18.8	10.4	14.5	19.2	15.6	9.5
Brandenburg and Berlin	6.2	7.9	8.4	7.39	9.7	14.6
Pomerania	18.0	15.0	17.5	12.7	11.7	6.5
Posen	15.1	13.3	13.5	17.0	18.2	14.9
Silesia	4.0	5.1	4.4	4.2	4.2	4.7
Subtotal east	62.2	59.3	60.0	63.8	62.7	53.8
Sachsen	2.6	2.9	2.9	2.5	3.6	4.2
Schleswig-Holstein	9.0	9.1	9.0	7.2	6.1	8.9
Hannover	12.9	12.4	11.6	10.6	11.1	15.5
Subtotal north-central	24.5	24.4	23.6	20.3	20.9	28.6
Westphalia	3.2	4.5	4.3	3.6	3.9	4.1
Hesse-Nassau	5.9	5.4	5.9	5.3	4.6	5.4
Rhineland	3.9	5.5	6.0	6.8	7.4	8.8
Hohenzollern	0.1	0.2	0.1	0.1	0.1	0.1
Subtotal west and south	13.2	15.6	16.3	15.8	15.9	17.9

Source: Calculated from *Statistisches Jahrbuch für den Preussischen Staat* (1905): 26.

Table 8.8.

A) Percent of German Emigrants from Various Regions, 1839–1869 (geographical origins of only about half of known migrants are calculated)

Region	1835–1839	1840–1844	1845–1849	1850–1854	1855–1859	1860–1864	1865–1869
Southwestern Germany	36.8	33.9	28.8	28.1	21.8	16.6	13.8
Bavaria east of the Rhine	16.4	15.7	11.1	6.8	5.9	6.3	3.0
Western Germany			12.5	6.8	11.5	12.0	7.9
Mecklenburg				3.9	5.1	4.9	4.3
Northeastern Germany			0.7	0.5	3.0	6.2	5.9
Eastern Germany			2.9	2.9	11.6	14.8	11.3

Definition of regions before 1871: southwestern Germany = Württemberg, Baden, and Rhine Palatinate, western Germany = Rhineland and Westphalia, northeastern Germany = East Prussia, West Prussia, and Posen, and eastern Germany = Brandenburg, Pomerania, and Silesia.

B) Percent of German Emigrants from Various Regions, 1871–1910 (based on 100% of migration)

Region	1871–1875	1876–1880	1881–1885	1886–1890	1891–1895	1896–1900	1901–1906	1906–1910
Northeastern Germany	39.3	35.4	38.2	37.7	34.8	28.6	30.7	27.5
Northwestern Germany	15.4	15.2	14.4	12.0	13.3	14.8	13.8	13.3
Southwestern Germany	25.6	25.3	24.1	28.9	25.3	26.1	23.6	23.4
Central Germany	3.8	4.2	3.8	3.2	4.4	4.8	5.0	5.2
Southeastern Germany	5.2	7.2	6.3	5.1	7.1	6.9	7.8	8.7
Western Germany	8.3	9.8	10.6	10.1	10.7	10.8	14.1	15.7
Hanseatic cities	2.1	3.1	2.6	3.0	4.4	8.0	5.0	6.2

Definition of regions after 1871: northeastern Germany = East Prussia, West Prussia, Pomerania, Posen, Brandenburg, and Mecklenburg; northwestern Germany = Schleswig-Holstein, Hanover, and Oldenburg, southwestern Germany = Bavaria, Baden, Württemberg, Hesse(-Darmstadt), Alsace-Lorraine, and Hohenzollern, central Germany = Thuringia, Prussian Saxony, Braunschweig, and Anhalt, southeastern Germany = Silesia and Kingdom of Saxony, and western Germany = Rhineland, Westphalia, Hesse-Nassau, Waldeck, and Lippe.

Source for Tables 8.8. A and B: Marschalck, *Deutsche Überseewanderung*, 38–39, 45.

of geographic origin as well as the specificity of the data vary from place to place. While Bavarians predominated among the first Jews in Cincinnati and Columbus, Ohio, many early Chicago Jews came from the border zone between the Rhine Palatinate and Rhine Hesse. In contrast to these predominantly south German settlers, the early Jews of Boston arrived overwhelmingly from northeastern Germany (Tables 8.9 A and B).[11] The early settlers in many of these communities often exemplify the widespread phenomenon of chain migration, by which emigrants moved to places where they already had relatives and former neighbors. A remarkably large number of the first Jews in Cincinnati came from Demmelsdorf, in the Oberfranken province of Bavaria. Similar connections are found between the village of Mittelsinn in Lower Franconia, Bavaria, and Columbus, Ohio, between Unsleben in the same Bavarian province and Cleveland, and between Chicago and Eppelsheim, in Rhine Hesse[12] (Table 8.10).

Table 8.9.

A) Origins of Jewish Inhabitants of American Cities, 1845–1861

Region of Origin	Boston	New York City	Milwaukee
	1845–1861	1856, 1858	1844–1855
Eastern and Northeastern Germany	44%	37	4
Southwestern Germany and Bavaria	19	less than 1%	32
Bohemia and Austria	less than 1%	4	43
Unspecified Germany	29	51	15
Other	8	8	6

Source: Stephen G. Mostov, "A Sociological Portrait of German Jewish Immigrants in Boston: 1845–1861," *AJS Review* 3 (1978): 150.

---

11 Stephen G. Mostov, "A 'Jerusalem on the Ohio': The Social and Economic History of Cincinnati's Jewish Community" (PhD diss., Brandeis University, Waltham, 1981), 77–78. Marc Lee Raphael, *Jews and Judaism in a Midwestern Community: Columbus, Ohio, 1840–1875* (Columbus, OH: Ohio Historical Society, 1979), 14, states that twenty-five of the first twenty-seven Jewish families in Columbus were from southern or southwestern Germany. See also Tobias Brinkmann, *Von der Gemeinde zur "Community". Jüdische Einwanderer in Chicago 1840–1900* (Osnabrück: Rasch, 2002), 65–70, 132, 140.
12 Mostov, A 'Jerusalem on the Ohio,'" 78–80; Raphael, *Jews and Judaism*, 16–17; Brinkmann, *Von der Gemeinde zur "Community,"* 65–70.

B) Origins of Foreign-Born Jews in American Cities, 1870 (percentages)

Place of Origin	Baltimore	Atlanta	Los Angeles	Milwaukee	Nashville	Portland
Germany	80	72	69	42	43	78
Bohemia, Austria	0	3	2	36	*	6
Russia	2	4	1	12	8	1
France	2	0	10	7	*	4
England	1	2	3	3	6	0
Hungary	2	19	1	0	8	1
Poland	1	0	12		30	9
Europe not specified	9					
Other	2	1	0	5	1	
(Amount)	(308)	(119)	(147)	(1204)	(384)	(215)

* Included among "other."

Source: Ira Rosenwaike, "Characteristics of Baltimore's Jewish Population in a Nineteenth-Century Census," *American Jewish History* 82 (1994): 129. Rosenwaike states (ibid., 129–130) that in Los Angeles, sixty-two persons were listed as being from Prussia and only eight from Bavaria, whereas in Baltimore thirty-nine are listed from Bavaria and twenty-five from Prussia.

Table 8.10. Birthplaces of Early Jewish Settlers in Two Ohio Cities

Birthplace	Columbus	Cincinnati (1817–1865)	
Upper Franconia		73	
Lower Franconia		23	
Middle Franconia		7	
Palatinate		32	
Other Bavaria		10	
Bavaria	35 (almost all from Mittelsinn)	145	(25%)
Baden	5		
Württemberg	3		9%
Hesse-Darmstadt	1		
Hesse and Nassau			7%
Prussia	2		14%
Saxony	2		
Austria (*sic*)			1%
Germany not specified		143	(24%)
Other Germany			3%
Germany		481	(82%)
Poland and Russia		26	(4%)
England		38	(7%)
France		31	(5%)
Austria-Hungary		4	(1%)
Total	48	c.588	

No fewer than eighty Jews in Cincinnati came from twelve villages on the Upper Main in Bavaria, including thirty from Demmelsdorf, eighteen from Burgkunstadt, ten from Mitwitz, and seven from Altenkunstadt, but only six from Fürth and three from Bayreuth.

Sources: Raphael, *Jews and Judaism*, 17; Mostov, *A Jerusalem on the Ohio*, 79; Table 3.4.

Emigration from Germany to America had a huge effect not only on the growth of American Jewry between 1820 and 1880, but also on the Jewish population in Germany itself as well. Although later overshadowed by the much larger wave of East European emigration to America, German-Jewish emigration never totally ended, but instead continued at least until World War I. Even during the period of net Jewish immigration to Germany, which was an offshoot of the same wave of migration from Eastern Europe, German-Jewish emigration to America remained substantial. It is estimated that as many as one-third of the total German Jewish population eventually emigrated to America. Many analysts attribute the gradual disappearance of widespread poverty among nineteenth-century German Jewry to the emigration of many of the poor. By the late nineteenth century, many German Jews had relatives in America; during the Nazi era, descendants of these relatives saved many Jewish lives in Germany by sponsoring distant cousins who had remained behind in Europe.

Immigration Patterns after 1880

In the late nineteenth century, massive Jewish net emigration from Germany switched to net immigration. By the 1870s, Jewish immigration, especially from Eastern Europe, had become an important political issue in Germany.[13] According to antisemites, Germany was being "invaded ... by assiduous pants-selling youths from the inexhaustible cradle of Poland."[14] Jewish writers and demographers tried to refute these claims, most notably in Salomon Neumann's *Der Fabel von der jüdischen Masseneinwanderung*. Scholars still disagree about who was right about the magnitude of East European immigration in the 1870s, but it is clear that Jewish immigration after the 1880s was both much greater in size and different in settlement pattern than that of the 1870s.

---

13 Statistics on Jewish immigration and foreign Jews are highly complicated and sometimes confusing by the enumeration of foreign Jews in at least three different ways. Some statistics counted Jews born outside of Germany as foreign, while others assigned this designation to persons who lacked German citizenship. In 1933, the Nazis combined both groups into a new category called *zugewanderte* ("in-migrated") as opposed to "at-home" (*einheimische*) in order to exaggerate the number of foreign Jews as much as possible. German citizenship laws were generally predicated on ancestry rather than place of birth. Therefore, "foreign Jews" could include any of the following groups of individuals: foreign-born with foreign citizenship, foreign-born with German citizenship (naturalized), or German-born with foreign citizenship (either German-born children of non-citizens or German-born spouses who had lost their German citizenship). The size of the second and third groups depended more on the relative liberality with which the various German governments granted citizenship at various times than on the actual magnitudes of immigration. Sometimes when we use citizenship categories, we may mistakenly assume immigration rather than the birth of a second generation of non-citizens. Generally, earlier figures show more foreign-born than foreign citizens, a sign of a relatively liberal naturalization program. Later figures show the reverse, signifying growing reluctance to grant citizenship to Jewish immigrants or their children.

14 Heinrich von Treitschke, "Unsere Aussichten," *Preussiche Jahrbücher* 44 (1879): 572–573.

The total population of foreigners in Germany, which was rather small at the time of the German unification, rose slowly and steadily to just over 1.25 million non-citizens by 1910 (Table 8.11). A study of Jewish immigration based on the 1871 census[15] gave some scattered samples of Jewish immigrant populations in selected Prussian cities and counties. By far the highest percentage of foreigners in the Jewish population was in Memel on the Russian border, where 631 (60.5 percent) of 1,043 Jews had been born outside of Germany. The next-highest fraction was in Wiesbaden (8.7 percent). Most other areas studied had much smaller foreign Jewish populations (Table 8.13).

According to data for the 1870s, a large proportion of foreign Jews lived in the eastern provinces of Prussia, not far from the border. This changed overwhelmingly after the Prussian expulsions of Poles and Jews from the eastern provinces in the 1880s, and especially after 1885–1886. The 1880 census found 11,611 Jews who had been born outside of Germany (9,350 of them in the Russian Empire and 1,659 in the Austro-Hungarian Empire) and now lived in the four eastern Prussian provinces of East Prussia, West Prussia, Posen, and Silesia. These foreign Jews far outnumbered the 3,586 foreign-born Jews who dwelled in Berlin at the time.[16] Later figures did not always distinguish between

Table 8.11. Foreigners in Germany, 1871–1910

Status	1871 (foreign citizens)	1875 (foreign citizens)	1900 (foreign-born)	1910 (foreign citizens)
Foreign	206,934	290,799	837,979	1,259,880
Unknown	16,823	1,679		
Total	223,757	292,478		
Percent of total German population	0.54	0.68	1.49	1.94

Sources: *Statistisches Jahrbuch des Deutschen Reichs* (1880): 14; (1903): 14; *Vierteljahrshefte zur Statistik des Deutschen Reichs—Ergänzungsheft zu 1916* 4 (1918): *Die Deutschen im Ausland und die Ausländer im Deutschen Reiche*, 53.

---

15 "Die Fremdbürtigen im preussischen Staate," *Zeitschrift des Königlichen Preussischen Statistischen Bureaus* 20 (1880): 387–398.
16 Helmut Neubach, *Die Ausweisungen von Polen und Juden aus Preussen 1885/86* (Wiesbaden: Harrassowitz, 1967), 11. According to Wertheimer, *Unwelcome Strangers*, 187, the number of foreign-born Jews in Berlin was 3,662.

Table 8.12. Foreigners as Percent of General Population by State and Prussian Province

State or Province	1875 (foreign citizens)		1900 (foreign-born)		1910 (foreign citizens)	
East Prussia			15,505	0.9%	15,004	0.7%
West Prussia			11,394	0.7	7,087	0.4
Berlin			39,745	2.1	54,046	2.6
Brandenburg			26,625	0.9	70,984	1.7
Pomerania			6,963	0.4	16,140	0.9
Posen			14,120	0.8	10,166	0.5
Silesia			73,436	1.6	105,962	2.0
Saxony			17,027	0.6	29,112	0.9
Schleswig-Holstein			26,059	1.9	32,661	2.0
Hannover			20,810	0.8	30,015	1.0
Westphalia			50,546	1.6	86,019	2.0
Hesse-Nassau			21,034	1.1	26,271	1.2
Rhineland			122,042	2.1	205,037	2.9
Hohenzollern			745	1.1	284	0.4
All Prussia	120,993	0.5%	446,051	1.3	688,788	1.7
Bavaria	53,190	1.0	100,179	1.6	134,124	1.9
Saxony	35,230	1.3	109,964	2.6	188,443	3.9
Württemberg	11,737	0.6	20,007	0.9	25,491	1.0
Baden	13,083	0.9	36,978	2.0	41,912	1.9
Hesse	2,961	0.3	8,575	0.8	11,328	0.9
Mecklenburg-Schwerin	1,744	0.3	3,717	0.6	12,972	2.0
Lübeck	1,236	2.2	2,061	2.1	2,272	2.0
Bremen	1,588	1.1	5,874	2.6	10,908	3.6
Hamburg	9,236	2.4	18,735	2.4	28,149	2.8
Alsace-Lorraine	34,581	2.3	64,560	3.8	76,456	
All other states	5,220	0.2	21,278		38,677	
All Germany	290,799	0.7	837,979	1.5	1,259,880	1.9

Sources: *Statistisches Jahrbuch des Deutschen Reichs* (1880): 14, (1903): 14; *Vierteljahrshefte zur Statistik des Deutschen Reichs—Ergänzungsheft zu 1916* 4 (1918): *Die Deutschen im Ausland und die Ausländer im Deutschen Reiche*, 53.

Table 8.13. Foreign Jews in Selected Areas of Prussia, 1871

Location	Total Jewish population	Number born in Germany	Number born abroad	Percent born abroad
Towns				
Memel	1043	412	631	60.5
Harburg (Hannover)	213	207	6	2.8
Oberhausen	90	86	4	4.4
Stollberg	38	36	2	5.3
Bonn	524	503	21	4.0
Wiesbaden	873	797	76	8.7
Ruhrort	132	131	1	0.8
Munich-Gladbach	348	340	8	2.3
Counties				
Haigerloch (Hohenzollern)	386	386	0	
Marienburg/Nogat (West Prussia)	230	228	2	0.9
Schubin (Posen)	2296	2248	48	2.1
Steinau	181	180	1	0.6
Ahaus	309	295	14	4.5
Zell	290	289	1	0.3

Source: "Die Fremdbürtigen im Preussischen Staate," *Zeitschrift des königlich Preussischen statistischen Bureaus* 20 (1880): 387–398.

Jews from Russia or Galicia and other natives of those areas. A total of 43,943 "illegal" Russian and Austrian subjects (Überläufer) were counted in the eastern Prussian provinces in October 1884. Of these, 30,705 were listed as having been expelled by the end of 1887. The largest number of foreigners was in the Marienwerder district of West Prussia. Of the 8,027 in the eastern provinces who had not yet been expelled, 3,045 were listed as still liable to expulsion, most of them in East Prussia and West Prussia (Table 8.14). Estimates of the share of Jews among the "illegals" varied from province to province—40 percent in East Prussia, 10 percent in West Prussia, 25 percent in Posen, and 15–20 percent in Silesia (among Russians only).[17]

17 Neubach, *Ausweisungen*, 55–59.

After the expulsions, the enforcement of anti-foreigner laws seems to have been strictest in the eastern Prussian provinces; accordingly, Jewish emigrants turned their sights to Berlin and the non-Prussian states, especially Saxony. In the largest Saxon city of Leipzig, there were only 931 foreign-born Jews (25.6 percent of all Leipzig Jews) in 1885. A modest increase in the late 1880s and then a huge jump between 1890 and 1900 boosted their numbers from 1,296 in 1890 (31.3 percent of the total), to 2,658 in 1900 (43.0 percent).[18] A similar strong upturn in the population of foreign Jews began in the Bavarian city of Munich at around the same time. In 1880, only 367 Jews in Munich (8.9 percent of the total) had been born outside of Germany. By 1890, there were twice as many (794—13.0 percent), and their numbers then jumped to 1,905 in 1900 (21.8 percent) and 3,030 in 1910 (27.3 percent).[19] Although the percentage of Jews in Berlin who were foreign-born never reached the levels of Saxony or Munich, the absolute numbers of foreign-born Jews in the capital increased the most of all: from 3,662 in 1880 to 15,524 in 1910 (21,683 if one includes the suburbs incorporated into Berlin in 1920) (Table 8.15). This made Berlin's foreign Jews by far the largest "colony" of foreign Jews in Germany.

Outside the three areas where the foreign Jewish concentration was heaviest—Berlin, Saxony, and Munich—smaller numbers of foreign Jews lived in many parts of Germany, mainly the largest cities. This population group increased steadily after 1880, although it never attained the huge numbers projected by those who feared that Germany was being "invaded" by Ostjuden (Table 8.16).

The census of December 1, 1910, documented the distribution of foreign Jews in Germany in detail and allows us to compare their distribution and numbers with those of other foreigners.[20] According to the census, there were 1,259,880 resident non-citizens (1.94 percent of the population of Germany)

---

18 Segall, "Die Juden im Königreich Sachsen," 42. For a table of birthplaces and citizenship of Leipzig Jews in 1885–1910, see chapter 7, note 80.

19 Cohen, "Die jüdische Bevölkerung in Munich im Jahre 1910," 122, 90. For birthplaces of Munich Jews in 1880–1910, see Table 7.39. Because of illiberal citizenship laws, there were 827 more Jewish non-citizens than foreign-born Jews in Munich. Most were women, perhaps the native-born wives of immigrants. Foreign birth and foreign citizenship, Munich, 1910:

Citizenship	Male	Female
Foreign-born	1740	1290
Non-citizens	2101	1756
Difference	361	466

20 *Vierteljahrshefte zur Statistik des Deutschen Reichs—Ergänzungsheft zu 1916* 4 (1918): *Die Deutschen im Ausland und die Ausländer im Deutschen Reiche*, 53, 86.

Table 8.14. Status of Illegal Foreign Residents (*Überläufer*) in Eastern Prussian Provinces as of January 1, 1888

Regierungsbezirk	Total *Überläufer* as of October 1, 1884	Expelled by December 31, 1887	Still present on January 1, 1888	Not to be expelled	Temporary residence permit granted	Still to be expelled
Gumbinnen	c. 5800	?	1715	131	1194	390
Königsberg	c. 6100	?	1764	63	1301	400
East Prussia	11,935	8,456	3,479	1942	495	790
Danzig	496	247	249	141	87	21
Marienwerder	15,673	10,130	5,543	282	1744	1978
West Prussia	16,169	10,377	5,792	2961	831	1999
Bromberg	4,142	3,230	912	245	502	165
Posen	2,640	2,009	631	132	412	87
Posen	6,782	5,239	1,543	377	914	252
Liegnitz	142	96	46	20	21	5
Breslau	1,152	770	382	213	160	9
Oppeln	7,763	5,758	2,005	66	1,909	30
Silesia	9,057	6,624	2,433	299	2,090	44
Total	43,943	30,696	13,247	3,831	6,330	3,085

Source: Neubach, *Ausweisungen*, 126–128.

Table 8.15. Foreign Jews in Berlin

Year	Total Jewish population	Foreign-born Number	Foreign-born Percent	Foreign citizens Number	Foreign citizens Percent	Percent of foreign Jews in Germany By birth	Percent of foreign Jews in Germany By citizenship
1880	53,916	3,662	6.8				
1890	79,286	6,141	7.7	5,036	6.4	30.1	24.7
1900	92,206	11,651	12.6			28.3	
1905	98,893			18,316	18.5		
1910	90,013	15,524	17.3	18,694	20.8		23.5
1910 (Greater Berlin)	137,043	21,683	15.8	25,241	18.4		31.7
1925	172,672			43,818	25.4		
1933	160,564	32,687	20.4	41,122	25.6	44.4	41.9

Sources: Wertheimer, *Unwelcome Strangers*, 187; 1933 census, vol. 5, 49.

Table 8.16. Foreign Jewish Population of Germany

Year	Foreign-born	Foreign citizens
1880	17–18,000?	
1890	20,388 ("Eastern Jews")	
1900	41,113	
1910		79,646
1925		107,747
1933	73,206	98,747

Sources: Wertheimer, *Unwelcome Strangers*, 185; 1933 census, 5/50, 52; Felix Theilhaber, "Deutsche Juden im Ausland und ausländische Juden im Deutschen Reich," *ZDSJ* (December 1905): 6.

and 79,646 foreign Jews, who represented 6.32 percent of all foreigners in Germany and 12.95 percent of all Jews in Germany. The gender distribution of the foreign Jews (55.1 percent male) resembled that of foreigners in Germany as a whole. Although the majority of Germans were Protestant, the foreign population of Germany was overwhelmingly Catholic.[21] All three countries that "contributed" the largest numbers of foreigners in Germany in 1925—Poland, Czechoslovakia, and Austria—were predominantly Catholic.[22]

Foreigners in Germany were generally more likely than citizens to settle in large cities. Foreign Jews were even more urbanized than non-Jewish ones. Thus, 27.65 percent of non-Jewish foreigners and 77.90 percent of all foreign Jews lived in cities of over 100,000 inhabitants in 1910 and over one-third of all foreigners in Berlin were Jewish. Foreign Jews were markedly overrepresented among foreigners in several other very large cities as well. Outside cities of over 100,000 inhabitants, Jews were only 2.04 percent (17,574 of 860,580) of all foreigners.

The geographical distribution of Jewish and non-Jewish foreigners also varied widely. In only a few regions like Saxony, Upper Bavaria, Bremen, the Rhineland, and Mecklenburg-Strelitz did non-Jewish foreigners make up more than 2.5 percent of the population.[23] The share of foreigners was especially

---

21 850,688 (67.52 percent) of 1,259,880 foreigners were Catholic. Only 309,329 (24.55 percent) were Lutheran. Lutheran foreigners outnumbered Catholics only in West Prussia, Schleswig-Holstein, Lippe, and Hamburg.
22 In 1925 there were 259,004 Polish citizens, 222,521 Czechoslovaks, and 128,859 Austrians living in Germany—collectively 60.64 percent of all foreigners in Germany.
23 Excluding foreign Jews, the percentage of foreigners in the local population was highest in Saxony (3.71 percent), Upper Bavaria (3.62 percent), Bremen (3.39 percent), the Rhineland

low in the eastern provinces of Prussia as well as in some of the less urbanized sections of western Germany. Except along the eastern border, provinces near the frontier tended to have high percentages of foreigners.[24]

The distribution of Jewish non-citizens in Germany in 1910 seems to have been related in part to the overall distribution of foreigners in the country and in part to the distribution of native Jews. Sometimes, however, it was independent of both (Map 8/1). As mentioned above, the concentration of Jewish non-citizens was heaviest in the Kingdom of Saxony and the cities of Berlin and Munich. No region had a higher percent of foreigners among its Jewish inhabitants than the Kingdom of Saxony, where 58.5 percent of the Jews lacked German citizenship.[25] Foreign Jews were especially numerous in the trading center of Leipzig, where they numbered 6,406 (64.8 percent) of 9,874 Jews in 1910. The foreign-born were also strongly represented in the mass migration of Jews to the German capital. By 1910, one in every four foreign Jews in Germany lived in Berlin as against one in seven of all Jews in Germany and one in seventy-four non-Jewish foreigners. Foreign Jews found Berlin much more alluring than foreign Christians did.

Other areas in which substantial numbers of foreign Jews settled were Hesse-Nassau, the Rhineland, Upper Bavaria, Hamburg, Baden, Silesia, Hesse-Darmstadt, and East Prussia. All but two of these regions were in western rather than eastern Germany. Except for Silesia and East Prussia, the eastern parts of Prussia attracted negligible numbers of foreign Jews (Table 8.17). Although most major cities had substantial numbers of foreign Jews, in the more rural parts of the same regions foreign Jews were much less common. In Hesse-Nassau, for instance, most foreign Jews lived in Frankfurt am Main, a city with a very

---

(2.81 percent), Mecklenburg-Strelitz (2.71 percent) and Hamburg (2.46 percent).

24 Percentage of foreigners in eastern provinces: East Prussia 0.73, West Prussia 0.42, Pomerania 0.94, Posen 0.48. The only eastern province that had a high percentage of foreigners was Silesia (2.03 percent). Among provinces farther to the west, the percentage of foreigners was low in Hohenzollern (0.40), Lower Franconia (0.42), Sachsen-Meiningen (0.38), Sachsen-Coburg-Gotha (0.54), Schaumburg-Lippe (0.23), Lippe (0.32), and Alsace-Lorraine (0.41).

Frontier areas outside the east with high percentages of foreigners were Schleswig-Holstein (2.01), Upper Bavaria (3.87), Lower Bavaria (2.01) Upper Palatinate (2.44), Bavarian Swabia (2.02), and Baden (1.96). In contrast, the borderland Alsace-Lorraine area had very few foreigners (0.41 percent)—a great change since 1871.

25 This is not to say that all non-citizens were foreign-born. The Saxon census of 1905 showed that 6,918 (47.1 percent) of the 14,697 Jews in the kingdom had been born in Germany (males 46.9 percent, females 47.3 percent). Of the foreign-born, at least 56.2 percent had been born in the Austrian half of the Austro-Hungarian Empire and another 2,795 in Hungary. The highest percentage of foreign-born was in the city of Leipzig (63.1 percent), far exceeding the other major cities of Saxony (Chemnitz: 30.8 percent, Dresden: 48.8 percent, Plauen: 47.9 percent).

Table 8.17. Geographic Distribution of Jewish and Non-Jewish Foreigners in Germany, 1910 (administrative regions by absolute number of Jewish foreigners in decreasing order)

Region	All non-citizens	Foreign Jews	Percent of Jewish population	Non-Jewish foreigners
Berlin	**54,046**	**18,694**	**20.8**	**35,352**
Saxony (Kingdom)	**188,443**	**10,293**	**58.2**	**178,150**
Brandenburg	70,984	8,666	14.1	62,318
Rhineland	205,037	4,843	8.5	200,194
Hesse-Nassau	26,271	4,835	9.3	21,436
Upper Bavaria	**59,360**	**3,966**	**34.0**	**55,394**
Hamburg	28,149	3,136	16.1	25,013
Baden	41,912	2,620	10.1	39,292
Silesia	105,962	2,554	5.7	103,408
Hesse(-Darmstadt)	11,328	2,494	10.4	8,834
East Prussia	15,004	2,108	16.9	12,896
Alsace-Lorraine	76,456	1,971	6.5	74,485
Hannover	30,015	1,820	11.7	28,195
Middle Franconia (Bavaria)	12,870	1,803	12.7	11,067
Westphalia	86,019	1,674	8.0	84,345

Region	All non-citizens	Foreign Jews	Percent of Jewish population	Non-Jewish foreigners
Württemberg	25,491	1,156	9.7	24,335
Saxony (Pruss. province)	29,112	1,070	13.7	28,042
Schleswig-Holstein	**32,661**	**913**	**27.3**	**31,748**
Bremen	**10,908**	**745**	**40.4**	**10,163**
All other	149,852	4,285	4.7	145,567

Bold = foreigners over 20% of Jewish population.

Areas in Eastern Prussia with Low Numbers of Foreign Jews, 1910

Area	Total Population	Jewish Population	Percent	Non-Jewish Population
West Prussia	7,087	412	3.0%	6,675
Posen	10,166	319	1.2	9,847
Pomerania	16,140	248	2.7	15,898
Total	**33,393**	**979**		**32,420**

Sources: *Vierteljahrshefte zur Statistik des Deutschen Reichs—Ergänzungsheft zu 191 64* (1918): *Die Deutschen im Ausland und die Ausländer im Deutschen Reiche*, 53, Table 17. Total Jewish population from *Statistik des Deutschen Reichs* 240 (1915): 210.

dense Jewish presence. The 3,538 foreign Jews in Frankfurt were 13.5 percent of the city's Jewish population. Outside Frankfurt, there were 257 foreign Jews in Kassel (10.3 percent of Jews in Kassel), 750 (26.4 percent) in Wiesbaden, and only 290 (1.4 percent) in all the rest of the province. In the Rhineland, which, unlike Hesse-Nassau, was an important magnet for non-Jewish immigration, foreign Jews, like foreign Christians, were attracted mainly to industrial cities, especially in the Ruhr basin. Foreign Jews were especially numerous in Cologne (1,672 or 13.5 percent of all Cologne Jews), but made up an even larger proportion of the Jewish population in Düsseldorf (569 or 14.3 percent), Essen (445 or 16.0 percent), Duisburg (309 or 19.9 percent), and Elberfeld (289 or 15.1 percent). In the rest of the Rhineland, there were only 1,559 foreign Jews, 4.5 percent of the total Jewish population. Whereas most foreign Jews in the Rhineland were of East European origin, a substantial proportion of non-Jewish foreigners, especially outside the Ruhr area, were of Dutch background.[26] In Upper Bavaria, almost all foreign Jews (3,857 of 3,966) but only 56 percent (33,232 of 59,360) of all foreigners lived in Munich, which was also home to nearly all native Jews in the province. While the vast majority of foreign Jews in Bavaria were from Eastern Europe, many non-Jewish foreigners came from neighboring German-speaking Austria.[27]

In the port city of Hamburg, the 1910 census counted a substantial number of foreign Jews. This was a matter of some surprise as Hamburg had the reputation of having a limited foreign Jewish population. The mystery is at least partly resolved when we realize that in the 1905 census, 809 Jews were counted in the Veddel area in the port, of whom 804 were transmigrants preparing to sail to America. One difference between the Jewish communities of Hamburg and neighboring Altona was that the latter was much more attractive to East European immigrants than the former, perhaps because the city-state of Hamburg had more restrictive policies (Table 8.18). By 1910, the province of Schleswig-Holstein and, especially, the cities of Altona and Kiel had some of

---

26 The figures for total number of foreigners and foreign Jews in the province and selected cities come from 1910 (*Vierteljahrshefte zur Statistik des Deutschen Reichs—Ergänzungsheft zu 1916* 4 (1918): *Die Deutschen im Ausland und die Ausländer im Deutschen Reiche*, 53, 86). The information on the countries of origin of Jewish and overall foreigners come from 1925 (Silbergleit, *Die Bevölkerungs- und Berufsverhältnisse*, 45*; and *Statistik des deutschen Reichs* 401 (1930): *Die Bevölkerung des Deutschen Reichs nach den Ergebnissen der Volkszählung 1925*, part 2: *Textliche Darstellung der Ergebnisse*, 627).
27 As in previous footnotes, the overall figures for foreigners and foreign Jews come from 1910 and the information on countries of origin for the general population comes from *Statistik des deutschen Reichs* 401 (1930): *Die Bevölkerung des Deutschen Reichs nach den Ergebnissen der Volkszählung 1925*, part 2: *Textliche Darstellung der Ergebnisse*, 628.

Table 8.18. Foreign Percent of Jewish Populations of Hamburg and Altona

City	1910	1933 (zugewanderte)	Foreign-born
Hamburg	16.4%	18.4	13.2
Altona	35.3	56.3	33.8 (large cities of Schleswig-Holstein)

Sources: Wertheimer, *Unwelcome Strangers*, 191–192; 1933 census, 5/15, 50–51.

the highest percentages of foreign Jews in Germany.[28] This fraction increased further in 1925 and remained high in 1933 (Table 8.19). Evidently, many of the original Jewish inhabitants of Schleswig-Holstein moved away, probably to Hamburg, and were replaced by recent immigrants from Eastern Europe. The Jewish community of the port city of Bremen, which, like Kiel, had had a small Jewish population, also grew mainly because of foreign immigration. This was not surprising since the city was a major port of embarkation for East European Jews who were emigrating to America. The Jewish population of the city-state of Bremen more than tripled between 1871 and 1910, mostly due to growth in the city proper. In 1910, the Jewish community of Bremen had a proportionately larger foreign element than Schleswig-Holstein. After World War I, the total number of Jews in Bremen declined, as did the proportion of foreign Jews (Table 8.20).[29] Except for the rapidly growing Jewish community of the city of Hannover, relatively few foreign Jews settled in Hannover province.[30]

---

28 One sign of Hamburg's weakness in attracting migrants was its share of Jews born within the city in 1933—50.8 percent, the highest of any city in Germany. In neighboring Altona, it was only 29.3 percent, one of the lowest rates in the country.

29 One possible reason for the decline of Bremen Jewry was that the pre-World War I census counted *Ortsanwesende Bevölkerung* (inhabitants present on the day of the census) while the 1925 and 1933 censuses counted *Wohnbevölkerung* (resident population). The former method may have enumerated migrants in the harbor area who were waiting to embark for America, while the latter method did not. This may also explain the strange discrepancy in our figures for the Jewish population of Bremen city in 1910 (985 vs. 1,609).

30 In 1910, there were 1,820 foreign Jews in the entire province of Hannover (11.7 percent of the total Jewish population), of whom 1,091 lived in the city of Hannover (21.2 percent of the city's Jewish population). Outside the city, only 7.02 percent of the Jewish population of the province lacked German citizenship. In the 1925 census, the province of Hannover had 1,921 Jewish residents who lacked German citizenship (14.8 percent), of whom 1,311 lived in the city of Hannover, where they were 23.75 percent of the Jewish population (Silbergleit, *Die Bevölkerungs- und Berufsverhältnisse*, 50*–51*, 58*–59*). The 1933 census counted 1,547

Table 8.19. Foreign Jewish Population in Schleswig-Holstein, 1910–1933

City	Total Jewish population			Foreign Jews			Percent of foreign Jews in total		
	1910	1925	1933	1910	1925	1933	1910	1925	1933
Altona	1824	2409	2006	643	1128	1130	35.3	46.8	56.3
Kiel	526	605	522	100	236	298	19.0	39.0	57.0
Other	993	1138	589	170	162	102	17.1	14.2	17.3
Schleswig-Holstein	3343	4152	3117	913	1526	1530	27.3	36.8	49.1

Sources:

1910: *Vierteljahrshefte zur Statistik des Deutschen Reichs—Ergänzungsheft zu 1916* 4 (1918): *Die Deutschen im Ausland und die Ausländer im Deutschen Reiche*, 53, 86, Tables 17 and 26.

1925: Silbergleit, *Die Bevölkerungs- und Berufsverhältnisse*, 56*–59*.

1933: 1933 census, 5/15, 16 (for 1933 all foreign Jews are included in the *zugewanderte* category).

Table 8.20. Jewish Population Changes in Bremen

Location and Nationality	1871	1880	1885	1890	1900	1910	1925	1933
Bremen State—all Jews	465	766	840	1031	1409	1843	1508	1438
Bremen State—foreign Jews						745		357 (*zugewanderte*)
Bremen city—all Jews	321	602	734	836	985	1609	1328	1314
Bremen city—foreign Jews						679		337 (*zugewanderte*)

Sources: *Vierteljahrshefte zur Statistik des Deutschen Reichs* 1 (1873): 188d, 1 (1892): III, 31; *Statistik des Deutschen Reichs, neue Folge* 31 (1888): 242–243, 150 (1903): 108*, 240 (1915): 210; Bosse, *Die Verbreitung der Juden*, 127; *Statistik des deutschen Reichs* 401 (1930): *Die Bevölkerung des Deutschen Reichs nach den Ergebnissen der Volkszählung 1925*, part 2: *Textliche Darstellung der Ergebnisse*, 620–621; 1933 census, 5/15–16; Schmelz, Territorial Printout (1885 figure mistakenly under 1890, 1880 figure = 570); *Vierteljahrshefte zur Statistik des Deutschen Reichs—Ergänzungsheft zu 1916* 4 (1918): *Die Deutschen im Ausland und die Ausländer im Deutschen Reiche*, 53, 86.

Foreign Jews in Hesse-Darmstadt were highly unevenly distributed in the duchy. Across the Main River from Frankfurt, Foreign Jews were very common in Offenbach (1,131 in 1910 or 47.9 percent of the Jewish population), coming mostly from Russia and working in the leather and cigarette industries. Between 1905 and 1910, the number of foreign Jews in Offenbach increased by over 450, probably because of expulsions of foreigners from Frankfurt. In Darmstadt, in contrast, 147 of the 512 foreign Jews were students at the city's Technische Hochschule. In 1910 there were 380 foreign Jews in Mainz and only 479 Jews without German citizenship in all the rest of the grand duchy.[31] In Baden, where a substantial minority of the general foreign population consisted of Swiss citizens living in the southern half of the state, foreign Jews were mainly East Europeans who concentrated heavily in the two largest cities of Mannheim and Karlsruhe.[32]

Silesia and East Prussia were the only eastern provinces that accommodated substantial numbers of foreign Jews in 1910. In Silesia, 56.7 percent of the foreign Jews (1,455 of 2,554) but only 6.6 percent of all foreigners lived in Breslau, which was also the home of most Jews in the province. In East Prussia, foreigners made up a relatively small proportion of the overall population but a large percentage of the Jews. Some 14.05 percent of all foreigners in the province were Jews, but the 1,169 foreign Jews in the capital of Königsberg accounted for 54.5 percent of all foreigners in the city and 25.6 percent of the local Jewish population.

Statistics on foreigners in Germany sometimes mislead because they are often based on the number of non-citizens and thus may include persons born in Germany. Some of the foreign-born eventually received citizenship. The percentage of Jews naturalized varied from state to state according to the degree of anti-Jewish prejudice among legislators and naturalization officials. Since German citizenship was acquired by ancestry rather than birth, foreigners' German-born children did not receive it automatically. The number of Jews defined both as foreign and born in Germany increased over time and far exceeded the number of naturalized foreign-born Jews in most places (Table 8.21).

Most, but certainly not all, foreign Jews in Germany came from Eastern Europe, with substantial differences in the mix of nationalities at different

---

zugewanderte Jews in the city of Hannover (32.0 percent of all Jews there) and 2,401 in the entire province (19.0 percent).

31 Knöpfel, "Die jüdische Bevölkerung vom Grossherzogtum Hessen," 97–108, esp. 105; and n.a., "Die ausländischen Juden in Hessen," *ZDSJ* (1912): 77.

32 Of 41,912 foreigners in Baden in 1910, 8,862 (21.1 percent) lived in Mannheim or Karlsruhe. Among foreign Jews, 1,539 of 2,620 (58.7 percent) lived in these two cities.

Table 8.21. Foreign-Born vs. Foreign Citizenship for Jews by Date and Region

Year	Region and City	Foreign-born	Foreign citizens	Ratio of foreign citizens to foreign-born
1890	Berlin	6141 (7.75%)	5036 (6.89%)	0.8
1910	Berlin	15524 (17.2%) [incl. 1926 citizenship]	18694	1.2
	Munich	3030 (27%)	3957	1.3
	Hamburg (city)	2146	3111	1.4
	East Prussia	893	[821 born in Germany] 601	0.7
1933	Berlin	32,687	41122	1.3
	Brandenburg and Grenzmark	866	1027	1.2
	Lower Silesia	1997	2384	1.2
	Upper Silesia	935	1377	1.5
	Saxony (Prussia) and Anhalt	1407	1929	1.4
	Schleswig-Holstein	924	1420	1.5
	Hannover, Braunschweig, and Schaumburg-Lippe	1561	2352	1.5
	Westphalia and Lippe	2394	3611	1.5
	Hesse-Nassau	4512	6920	1.5
	Rhine Province	6779	10149	1.5

Prussia	**55002**	73034	**1.3**
Bavaria	3467	4640	1.3
Leipzig	4610 [incl. 369 cit]	8088 [3847 b in Ger]	1.7
Dresden	1759	2384	1.4
Saxony	**7985**	**12804**	**1.6**
Württemberg and Hohenzollern	745	957	1.3
Baden	1801	2205	1.2
Hesse	969	1194	1.2
Hamburg	2301	2105	0.9
Bremen	222	292	1.3
Total Germany	73693 (14.8%)	98747 (19.8%)	1.3

Sources: 1933 census, 5/50–51.

points in time and among different areas. The vast majority of Jews who moved westward from Eastern Europe between 1880 and 1914 came from the Russian Empire;[33] only a minority left the Austro-Hungarian Empire, especially Galicia. Russian subjects also made up the majority of Jewish immigrants to Germany until about the mid-1880s. Thereafter, government hostility toward Jews from Czarist Russia resulted both in the deportation of Russian subjects already in Germany and in stronger efforts to keep out those who wished to come as well. This effort was complicated by Germany's strong encouragement of Jews' transmigration from Russia to America via German ports, which was a very lucrative line of activity for German shipping. Since the Austro-Hungarian Empire was an ally of Germany during most of the 1880–1914 period, Germany was much more reluctant to restrict the entrance of Austrian subjects than it was to restrict Russian nationals. Therefore, Galician Jews, as Austrian citizens, tended to make up the majority of foreign Jews in Germany from the late 1880s (Table 8.22).

After 1914

World War I created much upheaval in migration patterns. During the war, a large number of inhabitants of German-occupied Eastern Europe (including Jews) were brought to Germany as workers, both voluntarily and involuntarily. After the war, there was much political agitation against immigrants, especially Jews from Eastern Europe. This hostility, as well as difficult economic conditions, induced many East European Jews to leave Germany in the early years of the Weimar Republic. This combination of factors brought about changes in the distribution of foreigners in Germany as counted by the 1925 census.

The world war affected Jews and non-Jews in notably different ways. Overall, the foreign population of Germany as defined by citizenship decreased 24.0 percent from 1,259,880 to 957,096. This was partly the result of a change in counting methods between the 1910 and 1925 censuses. The 1910 census counted everyone who was in the country on the census day, including tourists and visiting merchants. The 1925 census enumerated only residents, and excluded persons who were simply traveling through Germany—although

---

33 Most Russian nationals who immigrated to Germany were probably from "Congress Poland" rather than Lithuania, Belarus, or Ukraine. After World War I, most of the same people were listed as Polish rather than Soviet citizens. East Prussia was the only Prussian province in 1925 in which Jewish citizens of the USSR and Lithuania combined outnumbered Jewish citizens of Poland (Silbergleit, *Die Bevölkerungs- und Berufsverhältnisse*, 42*–45*).

Table 8.22. Changing Balance of Russian and Austro-Hungarian Jews in Germany

Year and Location		Russia	Austria	Hungary	Austria-Hungary	Romania	Ratio Russia to Austria-Hungary (percent)	
1880	Berlin	2048	957					
1890	Germany	9897	8803	1688	10,491		(48.5)	(51.5)
	Prussia	8264	5514	978	6492	220	(56.0)	(44.0)
1900	Germany	12752	17410	3340	20,750	858	(38.1)	(61.9)
By birthplace								
1905	Prussia	13185	16665	3386	20,051	854	(39.7)	(60.3)
	Saxony	2271	4701	217	4,918		(31.6)	(68.4)
	Leipzig	1401	3010	117	3127		(30.9)	(69.1)
	Dresden	513			1087		(32.1)	(67.9)
By citizenship								
1905	Berlin	6730	7900	1911	9811	520	(40.5)	(59.3)
	Hesse-Darmstadt	886	690	74	764	10	(53.7)	(46.3)
1910	Germany	21644	41512	5475	46987	1509	(31.5)	(68.5)
	Berlin	3606			6098	555		
	Saxony	3192	6129	321	6450		(33.1)	(66.9)
	Leipzig	2005	3851	148	3999		(33.4)	(66.6)
	Dresden	555			1278		(30.3)	(69.7)
	Hesse-Darmstadt	1606	689	71	760	3	(67.9)	(32.1)

Sources: Wertheimer, *Unwelcome Strangers*, 185–189; Felix Theilhaber, "Deutsche Juden im Auslande und ausländische Juden im Deutschen Reich," *ZDSJ* (December 1905): 6; Königlichen Statistischen Landesamt, *Statistisches Jahrbuch für den Preussischen Staat* 4 (1906): 17; Jacob Segall, "Die Juden im Königreich Sachsen von 1832 bis 1910," *ZDSJ* 10, 3 (March 1914).

migrant farm workers appear to have been counted as well. Despite these procedural changes, the number of Jews holding foreign nationality in Germany increased considerably. Instead of 79,646, they now numbered 107,747, with an increase of 35.3 percent compared to 1910; their share among all foreign nationals climbed from 6.32 to 11.26 percent in the respective years while their fraction among all Jews in Germany rose from 14.3 to 19.1 percent.[34] This increase in foreign Jews and decrease in non-Jewish foreigners, however, did not necessarily mean that more Jews immigrated to Germany between 1910 and 1925. It may also simply be the result of a much less generous naturalization policy toward foreign-born Jews relative to foreign-born Christians. The majority of all migrants to Germany between 1914 and 1925 acquired German citizenship by the latter year (Table 8.23). Migrants from eastern and southeastern Europe were much less likely to receive citizenship than migrants from other countries. All the evidence, especially the detailed data from the 1933 census, indicates that relatively few Jewish immigrants acquired citizenship and a large share of their German-born children failed to acquire it as well. If so, the "foreign" Jewish numbers are overstated due to divergent political policies that left many German-born Jewish children in the rubric of "foreigners" because of their parentage.[35]

The concentration of foreign Jews in Berlin was even greater in 1925 than it had been in 1910. The 43,838 foreign Jews in the capital in 1925 were 40.7 percent of all foreign Jews in Germany, almost double the 27,360 foreign Jews in Berlin and surrounding Brandenburg fifteen years earlier. In contrast, the number of non-Jewish foreigners in the same region increased only from 97,670 in 1910 to 106,592 in 1925. In 1925, only 7.4 percent of non-Jewish foreigners lived in Berlin. The number and percentage of foreign Jews in Germany who lived in the huge state of Prussia increased from 48,166 and 60.5 percent in 1910 to 76,387 and 70.9 percent in 1925. The numbers of foreign Jews in the rest of Germany remained essentially unchanged (31,480 in 1910, 31,360 in 1925), with declines in Bavaria and increases in Saxony. Presumably, Prussia gave foreign Jews somewhat better legal treatment and less popular hostility than did the rest of Germany. Within Prussia but outside of Berlin, the numbers of foreign Jews increased most steeply in the Rhineland, Westphalia, Pomerania, Prussian Saxony, and Schleswig-Holstein (Table 8.24), while changed little in Hannover,

---

34 Wertheimer, *Unwelcome Strangers*, 193 and Maurer, *Ostjuden*, 72–73.
35 See below for a discussion on the differing rates of naturalization and the differing percentages of German-born foreign Jews in various parts of Germany.

Table 8.23. Naturalization of Migrants to Germany from Abroad between August 1, 1914, and June 16, 1925

Residence in 1914	Number of migrants	Still foreigners in 1925	
German territories lost in World War I	769,733	20,818	2.7%
Eastern Europe (Poland, Russia, Lithuania, Latvia, Estonia, Finland)	253,069	118,228	58.6
Southeastern Europe (Czechoslovakia, Austria, Hungary, Romania, Yugoslavia, Bulgaria)	115,472	72,267	62.6
Southern Europe (Italy, Spain, Greece, Portugal, Albania)	12,844	5,246	40.8
Western Europe (Switzerland, France, Great Britain, Belgium, Netherlands, Luxemburg)	134,065	23,618	17.6
Northern Europe (Denmark, Iceland, Sweden, Norway)	9,260	3,543	38.3
Non-European	35,866	9,036	25.2
Former German colonies	9,102	142	1.6
Total from outside Germany	561,241	262,080	46.7
Percent from Eastern and Southeastern Europe	65.7	72.7	

Source: *Statistik des deutschen Reichs* 401 (1930): *Die Bevölkerung des Deutschen Reichs nach den Ergebnissen der Volkszählung 1925*, part 2: *Textliche Darstellung der Ergebnisse*, 538, 540.

and declined considerably in East Prussia.[36] In 1925 as in 1910, foreign Jews were disproportionately resident in cities of over 100,000 inhabitants. In 1910, these cities were home to 82.9 percent of foreign Jews in Prussia but to only 30.7 percent of the total foreign population of Prussia. In 1925, 88.7 percent of

---

[36] The sharp drop in the number of foreign Jews in East Prussia may not have meant that East European Jews left the province. Instead, it may reflect a more generous naturalization policy than elsewhere in Germany. In 1933, there were 543 Jewish citizens of Germany born abroad and only 347 foreign-born Jews without citizenship. There were also 254 Jewish non-citizens born in Germany. In contrast, in Germany as a whole there were only 15,988 naturalized Jews born abroad as against 57,218 foreign-born Jews without citizenship and 41,312 Jews born in Germany without German citizenship.

Table 8.24. Number of Foreign Jews (by Citizenship) in Prussia

Region	1910 Number	1910 Percent of all Jews	1925 Number	1925 Percent of all Jews	1910–1925 Absolute change	1910–1925 Percent change
Westphalia	1674	(8.0)	3439	(15.9)	+1765	+105.4%
Rhineland	4843	(9.0)	9700	(16.7)	+4857	+100.3
Pomerania	248	(2.7)	472	(6.1)	+124	+95.0
Prussian Saxony	1070	(13.7)	1849	(22.2)	+779	+72.8
Schleswig-Holstein	913	(27.3)	1526	(36.8)	+613	+67.1
Berlin	18694	(20.8)	43838	(25.4)	+17491	+64.0
Brandenburg	8666	(14.1)	1013	(12.0)		
Hesse-Nassau	4835	(9.3)	7855	(14.9)	+3020	+62.5
Silesia	2554	(5.7)	3847	(9.6)	+1293	+50.6
Hannover	1820	(14.4)	1921	(12.9)	+101	+5.6
Hohenzollern	5	(1.2)	5	(1.5)	0	0
East Prussia	2108	(16.2)	825	(7.3)	-1283	-60.9
West Prussia	412	(3.0)			Grenzmark Posen-	
Posen	324	(1.2)	97	(2.8)	West Prussia	

Due to the incorporation of suburban areas in Brandenburg province that had large Jewish populations into Berlin in 1920, a comparison between the 1910 and 1925 populations makes sense only by combining the city and the province. In 1925 there were 2,629 foreign Jews in Lower Silesia (8.8 percent of all Jews there), and 1,218 in Upper Silesia (12.1 percent).

Sources: *Vierteljahrshefte zur Statistik des Deutschen Reichs—Ergänzungsheft zu 1916* 4 (1918): *Die Deutschen im Ausland und die Ausländer im Deutschen Reiche*, 35; Silbergleit, *Die Bevölkerungs- und Berufsverhältnisse*, 42*–45*.

foreign Jews but only 72.8 percent of the overall Jewish population of Prussia lived in cities of over 100,000.

Outside Prussia, foreign Jews remained numerous in Saxony but much less so in Bavaria, especially in Munich. This seems to have been a direct result of the hostile political climate in Bavaria and, especially, the Nazi agitation in Munich in 1923. The decline in Munich is very well documented; there were only half as many foreign-born Jews in the city in 1933 as there had been in 1910 (Table 8.25).

The percentage of all foreigners in Germany who made their homes in Prussia rose somewhat between 1910 and 1925, although not as much as among Jews.[37] The declines in the foreign presence were greatest in Baden, the Rhineland, Schleswig-Holstein, Saxony, southern Bavaria, Württemberg, Hesse, Hamburg, and Waldeck, all of which saw downturns of over 25 percent.[38] The few provinces that saw substantial increases in their foreign populations were Mecklenburg-Schwerin, Mecklenburg-Strelitz, Pomerania, and East Prussia. Several areas that underwent the largest Jewish gains, such as the Rhineland, now had the greatest general losses, while areas of Jewish loss like East Prussia had very appreciable general gains.[39]

---

37 Percentages of non-citizens in Germany who settled in Prussia:

Jews		Non-Jews	
1910 (within 1925 boundaries)	1925	1910 (within 1925 boundaries)	1925
60.48	70.89	56.16	62.88

38 *Statistik des deutschen Reichs* 401 (1930): *Die Bevölkerung des Deutschen Reichs nach den Ergebnissen der Volkszählung 1925*, part 2: *Textliche Darstellung der Ergebnisse*, 624–628.
39 Ibid. One of the reasons for the decline in foreign Jews may have been the loss of the city of Memel in East Prussia to Lithuania after World War I. According to several encyclopedias, the Jewish population of Memel in 1905 was 488, a huge drop from 1880 when it stood at 1214 before the expulsions of the mid 1880s. In 1880, most Memel Jews were born in Russia. East Prussia, however, also had a more generous policy toward naturalizing Jews than did other areas (see note 293).

In Prussia in 1925, almost half of the foreign Jews (46.3 percent) held Polish citizenship, as did only 31.1 percent of all foreigners. Most Polish citizens in Berlin were Jewish, but fewer than 10 percent of Polish citizens were so in the provinces of East Prussia, Pomerania, Grenzmark, Lower Silesia, Prussian Saxony, and Hanover, where there were large numbers of Polish migrant workers. Jews were the majority of foreigners from Romania and Turkey and over 20 percent of foreigners from Hungary, Latvia, Lithuania, and the Soviet Union. Berlin was home to 76.8 percent of Jewish Hungarians in Prussia, 81.9 percent of Jewish Latvians, 64.3 percent of Jewish Lithuanians, and 74.2 percent of Jews who held Soviet citizenship. Citizens of the Netherlands made up 12.9 percent of all foreigners in Prussia but only 2.3 percent of those who were Jewish. Fewer than 5 percent of Czech, Yugoslav, Greek, Italian, French, Swiss, Danish, and Swedish citizens living in Germany were Jews. (Silbergleit, *Die Bevölkerungs- und Berufsverhältnisse*, 42*–45*).

Table 8.25. Birthplaces of Jews in Munich

Birthplace	1910	1933	1938	Emigrants from Munich, 1933–1938
Munich	3161 (28.5%)	3400 (37.8%)	2169 (33.9%)	1479 (41.4)
Other Bavaria	2568 (23.2)		1599 (25.0)	521 (14.6)
Other Germany	2324 (21.0)		1625 (25.4)	685 (19.2)
Outside Germany	3030 (27.3)	1506 (16.7)	999 (15.6)	889* (24.9)
Total	11083	9005	6392	3574

* Including 339 born in "other countries and unknown."

Sources: Cohen, "Die jüdische Bevölkerung in München im Jahre 1910," 122; Cahnman, "The Decline of the Munich Jewish Community, 1933–38"; 1933 census, 5/51.

The only data on when the foreign-born came to Germany was on the pre-World War I places of residence of those counted in the 1925 census. They help us differentiate between longstanding immigrants to Germany and relatively recent arrivals.[40] In 1925, there were 957,096 non-citizens in Germany as well as an unknown number of foreign-born persons who had been naturalized. In the same count there were only 570,343 who had moved from a foreign location or former colony to Germany between August 1914 and June 1925, of whom 262,222 had not acquired German citizenship. Some 368,541 of these new arrivals came from Eastern or Southeastern Europe, of whom 190,545 were still non-citizens.[41] In general, the published data do not differentiate between Jewish and non-Jewish residents. In Hesse-Darmstadt, for which such differentiated information does exist, the number of Jewish residents who had

---

40 By its nature, however, the material excludes all those born between 1914 and 1925 and thus anyone who arrived in Germany as a child.
41 *Statistik des deutschen Reichs* 401 (1930): *Die Bevölkerung des Deutschen Reichs nach den Ergebnissen der Volkszählung 1925*, part 2: *Textliche Darstellung der Ergebnisse*, 538, 624. It is notable how much larger a percentage of immigrants from these lands were not naturalized compared to those of other national origins.

immigrated since 1914 was extremely small, at less than one-third of all Jewish non-citizens in the state.[42]

During the years from 1910 to 1933, the number of foreign Jews increased greatly in some regions and cities and declined greatly in others (Table 8.26). Naturalization policies varied from region to region. Some areas like Hamburg and East Prussia appeared to have more liberal policies on naturalizing Jews, while other areas such as Saxony, Schleswig-Holstein, and Thuringia had much lower percentages of naturalized foreign-born Jews, and much more restrictive attitudes (Table 8.27). The percentage of non-citizens who were actually born in Germany displayed less variation; it was somewhat higher in western and southern Germany than elsewhere, perhaps indicating that immigrants there had lived in Germany longer than those who had settled elsewhere (Table 8.28). The areas with the highest percentage of foreign-born or foreign-citizen Jews in 1933 tended to be the same as in earlier periods, especially Saxony, Schleswig-Holstein, and Berlin (Table 8.29, Map 8/2). The data on those actually born abroad show how exaggerated the usual statistics on foreign Jews based on citizenship were, not to speak of the Nazi category of *zugewanderte* (Maps 8/3, 8/4).

The Emigration of 1933–1939

From the time the Nazis rose to power, all demographic characteristics of German Jewry were affected by the escalating wave of Jewish emigration. Although the census of June 16, 1933, held after four and a half months of Nazi rule, already reflected the beginnings of this outflow, most of the emigration may be traced by observing differences between the 1933 and 1939 censuses. Whereas the census of 1933 counted 499,682 *Glaubensjuden* ("Jews by religion") in Germany, the 1939 enumeration counted Jews both by religion and by "race." In the *Altreich* (Germany within its 1933 boundaries), the 1939 census identified 233,095 "full Jews by race" and 219,020 *Glaubensjuden*—56.2 percent fewer than the number of Jews by religion in Germany within its 1933 boundaries (Table 8.30).[43]

---

42 Schmelz, *Hessen*, 145–146, 181. In 1925, only 525 Jews living in Hesse-Darmstadt had resided abroad before World War I as against 1,762 "foreign Jews" (without German citizenship) in the state. In 1933, by which time many foreign Jews had left Hesse, there were only 1,194 foreign Jews (by citizenship), of whom 542 to 614 were born abroad, depending on whether we count persons of unknown birthplace (ibid., 186).

43 In a few cases, seemingly small decreases in Jewish population were documented in 1939 because Jews imprisoned in concentration camps were listed as residents there. Thus,

Table 8.26. Changes in Number of Foreign Jews in Selected Cities, 1910–1933

City	1910 foreign citizens		1925 foreign citizens		1933 foreign citizens		1933 (zugewanderte)		1933 foreign-born*	
Decline in population of foreign Jews										
Bremen	679	48.2			276	26.6	337	25.6	213	16.2
Plauen	432	45.3							279	53.8
Munich	3857	34.9			2041	22.7	2408	26.7	1506	16.7
Königsberg	1169	25.6	440	10.9	271	8.6	565	17.8	451	14.2
Stuttgart	836	19.5			680	15.1	819	18.2	520	11.6
Hamburg	3111	16.4	2851	14.3	2098	12.4	3113	18.4	2293	13.6
Nuremberg	1226	15.7			850	11.3	1044	13.9	624	8.3
Mainz	373	12.8			298	11.4	435	16.7	302	11.6
Augsburg	155	12.7					84	8.2		
Total	11838				6535+ (<6898)		9084			
Increase in population of foreign Jews										
Altona	643	35.3	1,128	46.8			1130	56.3		
Kiel	100	20.9	236	39.0			298	57.1		
Duisburg	309368	19.9	807	38.81283			1184	46.2		
Hamborn	59	16.6	476	58.2						

Immigration and Emigration

City										
Wiesbaden	750	30.7	1,098	35.6			823	30.3		
Magdeburg	295	16.0	820	34.8			748	37.9		
Dortmund	391	13.8	1,200	31.4	1412	34.4	1489	36.2	884	21.5
Essen	445	15.1	1,173	27.9	1459	32.4	1615	35.8	1031	22.9
Berlin	18694	20.8								
Berlin and suburbs	25241	+	43,838	25.4	41,122	25.6	48,075	29.9	32687	20.4
Cologne	1672	13.5	3,908	24.3	4319	29.1	4664	31.5	2615	17.7
Bochum	81	8.1	268	23.9			289	27.0		
Hannover	1091	20.3	1,311	23.8	1400	28.9	1547	32.0	898	18.6
Gelsenkirchen	229	18.2	326	22.6			612	37.9		
Düsseldorf	569	14.3	1,054	20.6	1207	23.9	1371	27.1	905	17.9
Frankfurt/Main	3538	13.5	5,753	19.6	5277	20.2	5981	22.9	3489	13.3
Elberfeld	289	15.1	387	16.6						
Barmen	69358	10.3	120507	16.6	Wuppertal					
Stettin	108	3.9	162	6.2	268	11.3	531	21.5	208	8.8
Breslau	1455	7.2	2,006	8.6	1995	9.9	321	13.6	1654	8.2
Erfurt	103	12.8	128	15.6			2581	12.8		
Kassel	257	9.6	355	12.9			197	23.7		
Leipzig	6401	64.8			8088	69.9	459	19.9	4610	39.9
Dresden	1948	52.2			2384	54.2	8457	73.1	1759	40.0
Chemnitz	642	33.6					2671	60.7		
							1443	60.5		

	1910		1925		1933			
Braunschweig	160	9.0			249	36.5		
Number of foreign Jews stable								
Karlsruhe	654	21.4	689	22.1	772	24.8	456	14.6
Halle/Salle	263	18.8	248	20.1	270	24.9		
Mannheim	887	13.9	895	14.0	1107	17.3	706	11.0
Aachen	131	8.4	139	9.8	176	13.1		
Krefeld	97	5.3	80	4.9	112	7.6		
Mülheim/Ruhr	54	8.1	86	13.7	86	16.6		

* Including birthplace unknown.

Not specified for 1910: Remscheid, Ludwigshafen, Harburg-Wilhelmsburg, Hagen, Beuthen, Oberhausen, Solingen, Hindenburg, Gleiwitz, Munich-Gladbach, Würzburg, Münster, and Bielefeld.

No longer part of Germany or no longer independent cities in 1933: Danzig, Posen, Saarbrucken, Strasbourg, Charlottenburg, Neukölln, Schöneberg, and Wilmersdorf.

Sources: *Vierteljahrshefte zur Statistik des Deutschen Reichs—Ergänzungsheft zu 1916 4* (1918): *Die Deutschen im Ausland und die Ausländer im Deutschen Reiche*, 86; Silbergleit, *Die Bevölkerungs- und Berufsverhältnisse*, 57*–61*; Wertheimer, *Unwelcome Strangers*, 91–92; 1933 census, 5/15, 5/50–53, "Die jüdischen Ausländer im hamburgischen Staat 1925," *ZDSJ* (February 1931): 32.

Table 8.27. Foreign-Born Jews Naturalized, 1933 (percentages from highest to lowest)

Region	Jews born abroad	Jewish citizens born abroad	Percent naturalized
East Prussia	890	543	61.0
Oldenburg	132	60	45.5
Hamburg	2236	954	42.7
Lower Silesia	1996	688	34.5
Baden	1797	614	34.2
Hesse(-Darmstadt)	823	281	34.1
Brandenburg and Grenzmark	864	280	32.4
Lübeck	92	29	31.5
Württemberg and Hohenzollern	745	224	30.1
Bremen	222	65	29.3
Bavaria (all)	3429	950	27.7
Pomerania	399	104	26.1
Hannover, Braunschweig, and Schaumburg-Lippe	1560	341	21.9
Germany	73206	15988	21.8
Prussia	54978	11767	21.4
Berlin	32683	6953	21.3
Mecklenburg	156	33	21.2
Upper Silesia	935	194	20.8
Prussian Saxony and Anhalt	1405	282	20.1
Hesse-Nassau	4498	878	19.5
Rhineland	6779	1139	16.8
Westphalia and Lippe	2393	367	15.3
Thuringia	463	62	13.4
Schleswig-Holstein	924	110	11.9
Rhine Palatinate	413	49	11.9
Saxony (Free State)	7785	837	10.8

Source: based on 1933 census, 5/50–53.

Table 8.28. Percent of Jewish Non-Citizens Born in Germany, 1933

Region	Jewish non-citizens	Jewish non-citizens born in Germany	Percent born in Germany
Lübeck	124	60	48.4
Oldenburg	149	72	48.3
Rhine Palatinate	719	336	46.7
Hesse(-Darmstadt)	1194	554	46.4
Hannover, Braunschweig, and Schaumburg-Lippe	2352	1091	46.4
Hesse-Nassau	6909	3182	46.1
Bavaria (all)	4640	2094	45.1
Bremen	292	131	44.9
Württemberg and Hohenzollern	957	429	44.8
Saxony (Free State)	12804	5612	43.8
Baden	2205	962	43.6
Rhineland	10149	4381	43.2
Mecklenburg	216	92	42.6
Westphalia and Lippe	3611	1534	42.5
Schleswig-Holstein	1420	594	41.8
Germany	98747	38919	39.4
Prussian Saxony and Anhalt	1929	743	38.5
Thuringia	658	253	38.5
Prussia	73025	27726	38.0
Hamburg	2105	797	37.9
Pomerania	511	193	37.8
Lower Silesia	2384	871	36.5
Upper Silesia	1377	494	35.9
Brandenburg and Grenzmark	1027	367	35.7
Berlin	41122	14212	34.6
East Prussia	601	201	33.4

Source: based on 1933 census, 5/50–53.

Table 8.29. Birthplaces of Jewish Population, 1933 (in Order of Percent of *Zugewanderte*)

Region	Born within postwar German boundaries	Born in lost territories	Born abroad	*Zugewanderte* (non-citizens and born abroad)
Saxony	11,783 (57.8)	816 (4.0)	7,785 (38.2)	13,716 (67.3)
Schleswig-Holstein	2,071 (66.4)	122 (3.9)	924 (29.6)	1,530 (49.1)
Lübeck	375 (75.5)	30 (6.0)	92 (18.5)	153 (30.8)
Berlin	102,353 (63.8)	25,524 (15.9)	32,683 (20.4)	48,075 (29.9)
Prussian Saxony and Anhalt	5,626 (69.9)	1,014 (12.6)	1,405 (17.5)	2,213 (27.5)
Thuringia	2,323 (80.7)	93 (3.2)	463 (16.1)	722 (25.1)
Mecklenburg	791 (78.9)	55 (5.5)	156 (15.6)	250 (25.0)
Bremen	1,157 (80.5)	59 (4.1)	222 (15.4)	357 (24.8)
Prussia	263,294 (72.8)	43,530 (12.0)	54,978 (15.2)	84,801 (23.4)
Germany	379,439 (76.0)	46,550 (9.3)	73,206 (14.7)	115,005 (23.0)
Rhineland	44,633 (85.1)	1,014 (1.9)	6,779 (12.9)	11,288 (21.5)
Westphalia and Lippe	16,474 (85.2)	461 (2.4)	2,393 (12.4)	3,979 (20.6)
Hamburg	14,117 (83.5)	555 (3.3)	2,236 (13.2)	3,124 (18.5)
Oldenburg	1,074 (86.8)	32 (2.6)	132 (10.7)	211 (17.0)
Upper Silesia	5,651 (61.2)	2,642 (28.6)	935 (10.1)	1,571 (17.0)
Hesse-Nassau	41,498 (88.5)	913 (2.0)	4,498 (9.6)	7,801 (16.6)

Region	Born within postwar German boundaries	Born in lost territories	Born abroad	Zugewanderte (non-citizens and born abroad)
Hannover, Braunschweig, and Schaumburg-Lippe	11,990 (72.0)	421 (2.5)	1,560 (9.4)	2,693 (16.2)
Baden	18,373 (89.1)	443 (2.2)	1,797 (8.7)	2,823 (13.7)
Bavaria (all)	37,994 (90.7)	478 (1.1)	3,429 (8.2)	5,625 (13.4)
East Prussia	6,428 (72.8)	1,517 (17.2)	890 (10.1)	1,147 (13.0)
Brandenburg and Grenzmark	7,247 (69.8)	2,278 (21.9)	864 (8.3)	1,309 (12.6)
Lower Silesia	16,438 (65.4)	6,710 (26.7)	1,996 (7.9)	3,073 (12.2)
Rhine Palatinate	5,993 (92.4)	80 (1.2)	413 (6.4)	768 (11.8)
Württemberg and Hohenzollern	9,433 (89.6)	146 (1.4)	745 (9.0)	1,181 (11.2)
Pomerania	4,840 (76.6)	1,078 (17.1)	399 (6.3)	615 (9.7)
Hesse(-Darmstadt)	16,770 (94.5)	149 (0.8)	823 (4.6)	1,549 (8.7)

Source: 1933 census, 5/16, 50–53.

Table 8.30. Decline in Jewish Population by District, 1933–1939

Region	1933	1939 by religion (all "races")	Percent decline	1939 by "race" ("full Jews")
Oldenburg	1,240	330	73.4	365
Mecklenburg	1,003	270	73.1	359
Hesse(-Darmstadt)	17,888	5,801	67.6	6,068
Saxony (Free State)	20,584	6,920	66.4	7,663
East Prussia	8,838	3,004	66.0	3,169
Braunschweig	1,174	409	65.2	433
Pomerania	6,317		(48.5)	
		3,254	64.2	3,417
Grenzmark[44]	2,775			
Anhalt	901	346	61.6	400
Bavaria	41,939	16,231	61.3	17,066
Westphalia	18,819	7,534	60.0	7,964
Hannover	12,611	5,413	57.1	5,789
Baden	20,617	8,886	56.9	9,309
Schleswig-Holstein[45]	3,117	586	(81.2)	755

there were 221 Jews by religion in Oranienburg (Sachsenhausen) in the Prussian district of Brandenburg, 184 in Dachau (Bavaria), and 621 in Weimar (Buchenwald). In the last-mentioned case, this number represented 36.2 percent of all Jews resident in Thuringia. It is relatively easy to tell that most Jews in these localities were prisoners because the vast majority of them (200 in Oranienburg, 184 in Dachau, and 607 in Weimar) were male.

44 In 1939, the former Grenzmark was incorporated into Pomerania. Pomerania and Grenzmark combined showed the following developments:

1933	1939 by religion	Percent decline	1939 by "race"
9092	3254	-64.2	3417

45 The seemingly much steeper decline in Jewish population in Schleswig-Holstein was due not to emigration but to the annexation of the largest Jewish community in the province—Altona—to Greater Hamburg in 1937. On the other hand, Lübeck was annexed by Schleswig-Holstein between 1933 and 1939. If we combine the areas of Schleswig-Holstein, Lübeck, and Hamburg, we come up with the following information:

1933	1939 by religion	Percent decline	1939 by "race"
20,587	8,945	56.6	10,698

Region	1933	1939 by religion (all "races")	Percent decline	1939 by "race" ("full Jews")
Hamburg*	16,973	8,359	(50.8) 56.6	9,943
Lübeck*	497			
Hesse-Nassau	46,923	20,554	56.2	21,344
[Total *Altreich*	499,682	219,020	56.2	233,095]
Lippe	510	224	56.1	226
Bremen	1,438	635	55.8	722
Württemberg	10,023	4,447	55.6	4,713
Rhine Province	52,426	23,611	55.0	24,998
[All Prussia	361,826	164,332	54.6	173,746]
Brandenburg	7,616	3,586	52.9	4,019
Silesia	34,373	16,336	52.5	16,921
Saxony (Prussian province)	7,146	2,420	52.1	2,724
Berlin	160,564	77,850	51.5	82,457
Thuringia	2,882	1,714	40.5	1,947
Hohenzollern	301	184	38.9	189
Schaumburg-Lippe	187	116	38.0	135

* See note 303.

Sources: 1933 census, 5/11; *Statistik des deutschen Reichs* 552, no. 4 (1944): 6–9.

Unlike the period after the outbreak of World War II, when Jews were often forcibly ghettoized in *Judenhäuser* or deported from particular regions, in the period between 1933 and the census of 1939, most migration was still largely voluntary. The only exception before 1939 seems to have been in the Bavarian province of Middle Franconia, where Jews living in the countryside were expelled after the November 1938 pogrom.

Jews were strongly inclined to move out of small towns, where they felt in greater danger, to large cities where they could live in relative anonymity. Those who left large urban communities were replaced in part by recent migrants from the countryside, resulting in a smaller decline in the urban than the rural population. The decline in Jewish population was greater proportionately in small towns than in cities of over 100,000 inhabitants (Tables 8.31 A and B).

Table 8.31.

A) Decline in Jewish Population by Town Size, 1933–1939

Size	1933	1939 (*Glaubensjuden, Altreich*)[46]	Percent decline
Towns with over 100,000 inhabitants	354,120 (70.9%)	168,479 (75.5%)	52.4
10,000–99,999	68,394 (13.7%)	28,000 (12.6%)	59.1
Under 10,000	77,168 (15.4%)	26,707 (12.0%)	65.4

B) Major German Cities and the Decline in Their Jewish Populations, 1933–1939

City	1933 *Glaubensjuden*	1939 *Glaubensjuden*	Percent decline
Chemnitz	2,387	623	73.9
Duisburg	2,560	803	68.6
Dresden	4,397	1,459	66.8
Nuremberg	7,502*	2,589	65.5
Dortmund	4,108	1,423	65.4
Düsseldorf	5,053	1,813	64.1
Essen	4,506	1,620	64.1
Leipzig	11,564*	4,237	63.4
Outside main cities (*Altreich*)	168,197	62,414	62.9
Communities 11–26	53,334	21,911	58.9
Wuppertal	2,471	1,059	57.1
Beuthen	3,148	1,358	56.9
Karlsruhe	3,119	1,368	56.1

---

46 Greater Germany minus Vienna (including Saarland).

City	1933 Glaubensjuden	1939 Glaubensjuden	Percent decline
Hamburg	16,885*	8,359	50.5 55.8[47]
Altona	2,006	Part of Hamburg—	combined
Wiesbaden	2,713	1,225	54.9
Mannheim	6,402*	2,962	53.7
Stettin	2,365	1,102	53.4
Hanover	4,839*	2,256	53.4
10 largest communities	278,151	134,695	51.6
Berlin	160,564*	77,850	51.5
Stuttgart	4,490	2,198	51.1
Königsberg	3,170	1,566	50.6
Munich	9,005*	4,500	50.0
Würzburg	2,145	1,094	49.0
Frankfurt	26,158*	13,751	47.4
Breslau	20,202*	10,659	47.2
Cologne	14,816*	7,975	46.2
Mainz	2,609	1,453	44.3
Kassel	2,301	1,304	43.3

* 10 largest communities.

Sources: 1933 census, 5/11, 15; *Statistik des Deutschen Reichs* 552 (1944): 4/10–35.

Among cities that saw disproportionate depletion of Jewish population were those that had a large presence of foreign Jews like Leipzig, Dresden, and Chemnitz, those with particularly viciously antisemitic local leaderships such as Nuremberg, and several towns in the Ruhr region like Düsseldorf, Essen, Dortmund, and Duisburg. Towns with particularly small declines in Jewish numbers, such as Frankfurt, Cologne, Kassel, Mainz, and Würzburg, often had hinterlands with large rural Jewish populations that migrated to the city.

Not surprisingly, Jews who did not hold German citizenship left the country in greater proportions than did those with German nationality. Many who held

---

47 Including Altona.

Polish nationality were expelled in October 1938, although some returned after the Polish authorities refused to admit them (Table 8.32). The probable reason for the relatively small decline in stateless Jews was less the greater difficulty that stateless persons had in finding a country willing to take them than the increasing number of Jews residing in Germany who had lost their original foreign citizenship.

The pattern of emigration from Germany was far from random. Young adults and men were much more likely to leave than women and older people. Over 80 percent of male Jews aged 20–29 in 1933 left Germany by 1939, but only 72–78 percent of the female Jewish population in this age group did so. More than half of all Jewish men born in 1887 or earlier and Jewish women born in 1895 or earlier who had been counted in 1933 were still counted as living in Germany in 1939. The smallest declines were among those born in 1874–1878 (aged 61–65 in 1939). The greater declines among those over 65 were due to natural mortality rather than emigration (Table 8.33). The percentage of men who left Germany far exceeded that of women who did so (Table 8.34).

In most cases, our evidence for the emigrants from Germany's makeup can only be extrapolated from changes in the structure of the Jewish population that remained behind. In the case of Munich, however, where the Jewish community conducted an internal census in May 1938, direct data on those who left may be compared with data on those who remained. Like most German-Jewish communities, Munich Jewry experienced a marked increase in average age and a growing predominance of women in the first years of Nazi rule. The data[48] show clearly that this was caused mainly by more emigration of both male and younger Jews than of female and older ones during those years[49] (Table 8.35).

The emigration of German Jews between 1933 and 1939 created the greatest and fastest population change in the history of German Jewry. It not only left German Jewry severely reduced in numbers, but also shifted the makeup of the remaining community by steeply increasing the percentage of women and older people. Emigration also continued after the 1939 census until it was finally forbidden in 1941. Nearly all Jews who remained in Germany after 1941 were murdered, as were many who had emigrated to European countries that the Nazis conquered during World War II.

---

48 Not counting 171 "youths almost all under 20" who were in town for vocational retraining.
49 Werner J. Cahnman, "The Decline of the Munich Jewish Community, 1933–38," *Jewish Social Studies* 3 (1941): 285–300. For the age distributions of emigrants from Munich and those who stayed behind, see Table 5.25.

Table 8.32. Foreign Jews in Germany

Origin	1933 citizenship	1933 Birth	1939 (citizenship)[50]	Percent decrease
Germany and lost territories	400,935	425,989	c. 208,223	48.1
Foreign	98,747	73,206	30,606	69.0
Poland	56,480	47,159	12,624	77.7
USSR	1,650	4,742	181	89.0
(Austria)	4,647	3,237	No longer considered foreign	
(Czechoslovakia)	4,275	3,882	1,213[51]	71.6
Romania	2,210	3,138	482	78.2
Hungary	2,280	2,295	879	61.5
Netherlands	1,604	1,099	202	87.4
Stateless	19,746		12,566	36.4
Unknown	214		871	+307.0
Other countries	5,641	7,654	1,588	71.8

Sources: 1933 census, 5/49; *Statistik des deutschen Reichs* 552, no. 4 (1944): 70–73.

50 Greater Germany minus Vienna, "full Jews by race."
51 Protectorate plus Slovakia.

Table 8.33. Decline in Jewish Population, 1933–1939 (*Altreich*), by Birth Years

In this table, persons aged 17–29 in 1939 are counted by individual years due to significant differences within each group. Those under age ten in 1933 or over thirty in 1939 are counted in five-year groups.

Birth year	1933		1939 (*Glaubensjuden*)			
	Male	Female	Male[52]	Percent decline	Female[53]	Percent decline
1928–1932	10277	9940	3358	67.3%	3193	68.9%
1923–1927	15989	15506	5405	66.2	5371	65.5
1922	3718	3656	954	74.3	1287	64.8
1921	4006	3789	956	76.1	1295	65.8
1920	3902	3689	822	78.9	1048	71.7
1919	2542	2450	488	80.8	654	73.3
1918	1805	1776	301	83.3	417	76.5
1917	1697	1650	280	83.5	367	77.8
1916	1996	1948	278	86.1	441	77.4
1915	2537	2584	362	85.7	597	76.9
1914	3251	3316	495	84.8	722	78.2
1913	3307	3301	524	84.2	771	76.6
1912	3355	3494	563	83.2	843	75.9
1911	3289	3407	533	83.8	871	74.4
1910	3393	3486	663	80.5	956	72.6
1909	3385	3632	682	79.9	989	72.8
1904–1908	17380	19170	4239	75.6	6149	67.9
1899–1903	19452	20628	5838	70.0	8419	59.2
1894–1898	20049	22498	7153	64.3	11207	50.2
1889–1893	18948	21517	8027	57.6	12254	43.1
1884–1888	19292	21195	9624	50.1	12860	39.3
1879–1883	19228	20168	10463	45.6	12957	35.8
1874–1878	18183	19472	10458	42.5	12877	33.9

52 Total *Glaubensjuden* multiplied by 72.30 percent (percent of all male Jews in Greater Germany who lived in the *Altreich*).
53 Total *Glaubensjuden* multiplied by 71.65 percent (percent of all female Jews in Greater Germany who lived in the *Altreich*).

Birth year	1933		1939 (*Glaubensjuden*)			
	Male	Female	Male[52]	Percent decline	Female[53]	Percent decline
1869–1873	13924	15670	7835	43.7	10141	35.3
1864–1868	10035	12611	5315	47.0	7726	38.7
1859–1863	6848	9459	3129	54.3	5036	46.8
1858 and earlier	6270	10184	1929	69.2	3611	64.5

Sources: 1933 census, 5/42–43; *Statistik des Deutschen Reichs* 552 (1944): 4/40–47.

Table 8.34. Decline in German-Jewish Population by Gender, 1933–1939

Gender	1933	1939 (*Glaubensjuden, Altreich*)	Percent decline
Male	238,747	93,514	60.8
Female	260,935	125,985	51.7

Sources: 1933 census, 5/17; *Statistik des Deutschen Reichs* 552 (1944): 4/6–9.

German Jewry went through several major waves of cross-frontier migration between 1815 and 1939. The first wave, between 1840 and 1880, consisted mainly of emigration to overseas destinations, especially the United States while the second saw immigration from Eastern Europe between 1880 and 1930. Although this wave involved fewer migrants than the previous wave of emigration, it aroused much more anxiety in the German public and was often exploited by antisemites. The final wave of emigration, which took place from 1933 onward, was the largest and quickest of all; it managed to save perhaps half of the German-Jewish community that existed before 1933.

Table 8.35. Decline in Munich Jewish Population by Gender, 1933–1938

Gender	Munich 1938		Jews emigrating from Munich, 1933–1938		Combined (approximate) Jewish population, 1933		Percent emigrated
	Number	Percent	Gender distribution		Number	Percent	
Male	2891	45.2	1983	55.5	4874	48.9	40.7
Female	3501	54.8	1591	44.5	5092	51.1	31.3

Source: Werner J. Cahnman, "The Decline of the Munich Jewish Community 1933–38," *Jewish Social Studies* 3 (1941): 286, 296.

9

From Countryside to City: Urbanization and the Survival of Small-Town Jewish Communities

---

In the 125 years from the fall of Napoleon to the outbreak of World War II, German Jewry underwent an uneven but thoroughgoing process of urbanization, which was parallel to but tended to precede, the urbanization of the German population at large. Both urbanization processes were largely the result of the migration of individuals and families from smaller to larger towns. Some of it, however, took place without migration, as towns or cities where people lived either grew rapidly and entered a new size category[1] or as a city's physical expansion led to the absorption of a small-town community nearby.

---

1 As Germany became more urban, the definitions of large city and small town tended to shift. Whereas a town of 20,000 was quite large in the early or middle nineteenth century, it was rather small by the standards of the early twentieth century. Many nineteenth-century statistics divide broadly between towns of under 5,000, of 5,000–20,000, and of over 20,000, but in the twentieth century the categories "under 20,000," "20,000–100,000" and "over 100,000" are more common. This shift in categories sometimes makes comparison difficult. Where necessary and possible, this study converts such data into comparable categories.

Patterns of Settlement and Urbanization in the Early Nineteenth Century

Jewish urbanization and settlement patterns differed regionally in accordance with different settlement histories and legal restrictions on Jews. Whereas in southern and western Germany Jews were often excluded from large cities, in eastern Germany Jews were sometimes barred from villages and forced to live in towns.[2] In Prussia in 1817, almost 97 percent of Jews in the two former Polish provinces of West Prussia and Posen lived in places that were legally considered cities (*Stadt*) as against 44 percent of Jews in the western provinces of Rhineland and Westphalia and 86 percent in the central Prussian provinces (Table 9.1). South German Jewry was even more rural than the Jewish population in the western provinces of Prussia. In Württemberg in 1832, for instance, 93 percent of Jews lived in villages rather than in cities (Table 9.2).[3]

In terms of actual size rather than legal status, many Jews in the eastern provinces lived in towns, that is, settlements with populations between those of cities (more than 10,000 inhabitants) and villages (2,000 or fewer). In Posen province, where a classic East European "shtetl" pattern was evident, the categories of 2,000–5,000 and 5,000–10,000 were typical of towns with Jewish communities until 1871, with slow growth in the largest cities. In this province, Jews made up over 30 percent of all residents of towns in the 5,000–10,000 class

Table 9.1. Distribution of Jews between City and Countryside in Various Parts of Prussia 1817 (by legal category)

Location	West Prussia and Posen	Between Elbe and West Prussia and Posen	Rhineland and Westphalia
City	63,079 (96.7%)	28,826 (85.8%)	12,909 (47.5%)
Countryside	2,121 (3.3%)	4,755 (14.2%)	14,260 (52.5%)

Based on Silbergleit, *Die Bevölkerungs- und Berufsverhältnisse*, 11*.

---

2 Statistical sources often distinguished between cities and villages on the basis of historical and legal categories. Due to uneven patterns of growth, the legal status of a town did not always correspond to its size. Some relatively large towns remained villages *de jure* while some towns that enjoyed the legal status of cities remained very small.

3 The percentage of those in cities rather than "in the countryside" changed during the nineteenth century but only after mid-century did the percentage in towns categorized as *Land* clearly decrease relative to the city category.

Table 9.2. Changing Percentages of Jewish Population in Cities and the Countryside

Location	1817	1828	1846	1849	1858	1860	1861	1864	1867 (old borders)
Percent in cities									
Prussia (total)	83.4%			79.2	78.3				81.9
Posen and West Prussia	**96.7**			92.5	90.2	94.1*			89.7
Rhineland and Westphalia	47.5			45.3	47.8				**51.8**
Württemberg		7	18.8				33.7	**40.2**	
Percent in villages									
Prussia (total)	16.6			20.8	**21.8**				18.1
Posen and West Prussia	3.3			7.5	**9.8**	5.9*			10.3
Rhineland and Westphalia	52.5			**54.7**	52.2				48.3
Württemberg		**93**	81.2				66.3	59.8	

The highest figure for each category is in bold.

Sources: Blau, *Entwicklung*, 69, 199; "Uebersicht über die jüdische Bevölkerung in Württembergs Städten mit mehr als 2000 Einwohner," *Württemberger Jahrbücher für Statistik und Landeskunde* (1864): 124–125; Utz Jeggle, *Judendörfer in Württemberg* (Tübingen: Tübinger Vereinigung f. Volkskunde e. V., 1969), 7.

(Table 9.3). By comparison, the vast majority of non-Jews in the area lived in villages of fewer than 2,000 residents.

The rather scattered Jewish population of central Germany was more likely to live in larger cities. In the Kingdom of Saxony, virtually all Jews lived in Dresden and Leipzig. In the Prussian province of Brandenburg, the growing Berlin community accommodated a large and increasing percentage of the total Jewish population. In the Prussian province of Saxony and the Duchy of Anhalt, the percentage of urban Jews was slightly lower but still substantial. The Jewish populations in Mecklenburg and the various Thuringian principalities were, in contrast, overwhelmingly rural (Table 9.4). While Jews in Posen concentrated primarily in towns of 2,000–10,000 inhabitants and those in central Germany did so in cities of over 20,000, south German Jews settled primarily in village communities of under 2,000 (Table 9.5).

These patterns persisted until German unification. Prussian statistics from 1871 onward (using the categories of below 5,000, 5,000–20,000, and over 20,000) continued to show central Prussia as having a much higher percentage of Jews in major cities than elsewhere. Both the former Polish territories and western Germany had large percentages in towns under 5,000. In the intermediate category, eastern Prussia had by far the greatest representation. The former Polish districts resembled central Prussia in the percentage of Jews who dwelled in medium-sized localities, which far exceeded the proportion in the western Prussian provinces (Table 1.9). In the below-5,000 category, Jews in the eastern areas of Prussia were much more numerous in "shtetl" settlements of over 2,000 than in villages of fewer than 2,000 inhabitants, while in southern and western Germany, villagers outnumbered those in the 2,000–5,000 class (Table 9.6).

Table 9.3. Percent of Inhabitants in Posen Area in Towns of Various Sizes

Town size	1817 Posen province*		1840 (RB Posen only) All communities				1871 (RB Posen only) All communities	
	Jews	Percent of all Jews	General	Jews	Percent of all Jews	Percent Jewish	Jews	Percent of all Jews
Over 10,000	4025	11.5	31822	6763	12.8	21.3	10309	25.6
5,000–9,999	5608	16.1	41131	13152	25.0	32.0	7018	17.5
2,000–4,999	17073	48.9	80090	20061	38.1	25.1	15454	38.4
Under 2,000	8225	23.3		12733	24.2		7443	18.5
Total	34931			52657			40224	

* Information for towns with over 500 Jews only. The 34,931 Jews in communities that had over 500 Jews in 1817 accounted for about two-thirds of all the Jews in the province. If data were available for smaller communities, the percent in the under-2,000 category would probably be larger. For large communities, the 2,000–5,000 category was clearly the most typical.

Sources: Silbergleit, *Die Bevölkerungs- und Berufsverhältnisse, 9*; Heppner and Herzberg, *Aus Vergangenheit und Gegenwart*, 273–279.

Table 9.4. Urban and Rural Jewish Populations in Central Germany, 1880

City size	Brandenburg	Prussian Saxony	Kingdom of Saxony	Anhalt	Thuringia	Mecklenburg Schwerin	Strelitz
Over 20,000	57133	3865	5879	420	314	588	—
10,000–19,999	1524	647	146	**695**	1152	232	—
5,000–9,999	2524	885	124	22	335	474	198
2,000–4,999	2046	556	56	516	99	**1107**	**217**
All others	972	927	311	99	**1795**	179	43

Source: based on Bosse, *Die Verbreitung der Juden*, 1–6, 44–50, 83–88, 111–112, 115, 119–123, 125.

Table 9.5. South German Jewish Population by Town Size

Town size	Hesse-Darmstadt (1828)	Lower Franconia (1816)
Over 10,000 inhabitants	2176 (10.2%)	311 (2.8%)
2000–9999	5443 (25.6)	1361 (12.3)
1000–1999	13617 (64.1)	2426 (22.0)
Under 1000		6680 (60.5)
Total	21236	10778[4]

Sources: *Pinkas ha-Kehillot, Germania, Bavaria*, 379–580; Blau, *Entwicklung*, 231; Schmelz, *Hessen*, 54.

Table 9.6. Regional Differences in Sizes of Towns Inhabited by Jews

Town size	East[5]			West and South[6]		
	RB Posen			Hessian region	Württemberg	
	1871			1861	1861	
	Jews		General	Jews	Jews	
Over 20000	7255	18.0%	5.5%	20.3%	1174	10.3%
10000–20000	3054	7.6	2.4	4.4	396	3.5
5000–10000	7018	17.5	3.8	4.5	292	2.6
2000–5000	15454*	38.4	9.7	16.2	1967	17.3
Under 2000**	7443	18.5	78.6	54.6	7544	66.3

---

4 These figures, based on *Pinkas ha-Kehillot, Germania, Bavaria*, add up to 10,778. The total Jewish population of Lower Franconia in 1818 was 16,637. The towns for which we have figures thus cover almost two-thirds of all the Jews of the province. It stands to reason that most of the "missing" Jewish population was found in villages rather than large cities.

5 The Posen figures are based on the table in Heppner and Herzberg, *Aus Vergangenheit und Gegenwart*, 273–279 (Table E), figures for 1871. Of the eighty-five places listed in the table we have excluded only *Kreis* Bomst [number 49] because it is a county rather than a town.

    * This follows ibid., 278, which lists Ostrowo's overall population as 4,964 and its Jewish population as 1,611. The statistical yearbook counts Ostrowo in the 5,000–20,000 category.

    ** The below-2,000 category is calculated by subtracting the categories over 2,000 from the known total Jewish and general populations. The numbers actually included in the eighty-four cities was lower, especially for the general population, which was much more heavily concentrated in villages than were the Jews.

6 The figure for towns under 2,000 was taken by subtracting the number of Jews in towns over 2,000 from the known Jewish population of Württemberg in 1861. Of the 1,967 Jews in Württemberg in towns of 2,000 to 5,000, all but 198 were in the four towns of Laupheim, Mergentheim, Crailsheim, and Buchau.

Sources: Heppner and Herzberg, *Aus Vergangenheit und Gegenwart*, 273–279 (Table E); Schmelz, *Hessen*, 387, "Uebersicht über die jüdische Bevölkerung in Württembergs Städten mit mehr als 2000 Einwohner nach der Aufnahme vom 3. Dez. 1864," *Württembergische Jahrbücher für Statistik und Landeskunde* (1864).

Regional Variation in the Size of Jewish Communities

In 1815, most Jewish communities in former Polish areas resembled East European shtetls not only due to the size of the towns (2,000–10,000 inhabitants), but also because they were much larger than small-town Jewish communities farther west. Thirty of the forty[7] Prussian communities that had at least 500 Jewish inhabitants in 1817 were in Posen province, four were in the West Prussian district of Marienwerder, and four were elsewhere in West Prussia or Silesia. Berlin had the only Prussian-Jewish community of over 500 west of the present western boundary of Poland (the Oder-Neisse line). The 23,264 Jews in communities of over 1,000 Jews accounted for 44.3 percent of Jews in Posen province and the 34,931 who belonged to communities of at least 500 Jews were 66.5 percent of all Posen Jews.

The "village communities" of southern and western Germany were much smaller on average. It was quite remarkable how small a Jewish community could be in those regions and still be viable. Although many South German village communities had 100 Jews if not more, even communities of thirty or forty individuals often maintained a functioning set of Jewish institutions and a sense of community with its own traditions and sense of pride. In 1828, only four of 395 localities with Jewish populations in the west-central duchy of Hesse-Darmstadt had 500 or more Jews and only 3,797 Jews lived in these four towns (17.0 percent of the 22,306 Jews in Hesse-Darmstadt).[8] In the neighboring northwest Bavarian province of Lower Franconia, only one Jewish community had more than 500 members in 1816, and only two had 300–500 individuals among a Jewish population of well over 10,000.

In southwestern Germany, large communities were somewhat more numerous, although not nearly as common as in the Posen area. In the southwest

---

7 Both Blau and Silbergleit list Cologne and Deutz as having 535 Jewish inhabitants, but most of these inhabitants were in Deutz, not Cologne and neither community totaled 500 Jews. Also included in the list is Peisern, which was then part of the province of Posen, but soon thereafter was returned to the Russian-ruled Kingdom of Poland.

8 Schmelz, *Hessen*, 46, 50–51, 324. The four communities were Darmstadt, Offenbach, Mainz, and Worms, all of them urban.

Bavarian province of Swabia between 1809 and 1812, 893 Jews lived in the town of Ichenhausen and communities of 300–499 dwelled in eight other towns, for a total Jewish population of 2,955. At least four localities had 200–300 Jewish inhabitants as well. Together, these thirteen large communities made up the great majority of the province's Jewish population. In Württemberg, there was a considerable difference between the northern and southern halves of the kingdom. In northern Württemberg (Jagst and Neckarkreis) in 1828, 1,111 (16.1 percent) of 6,883 Jews lived in communities of 300 or more members, while in southern Württemberg (Schwarzwaldkreis and Donaukreis), 2,252 (59.5 percent) of 3,787 Jews inhabited communities of that size[9] (Table 9.7).

A list of communities in Prussia with at least 100 Jews in 1843 illustrated the regional variance in community size. In the eastern provinces, especially those in the former Polish areas, large communities were the rule; in the west, they were the exception. Most Jews in the western provinces of Prussia lived scattered in very small communities (Table 9.8).

Jewish Urbanization in the Late Nineteenth and Early Twentieth Centuries

Until the middle of the nineteenth century, urban Jewish communities experienced relatively moderate growth rates that hardly exceeded those of German Jewry at large. Many small towns and villages in various parts of Germany had much higher Jewish populations in mid-century than in 1815. Of the eighteen communities in towns of fewer than 10,000 inhabitants that had more than 500 Jews in *Regierungsbezirk* Posen (easternmost Germany) in 1817, fifteen gained Jewish population by 1840. In southwestern Germany, too, many of the large rural Jewish communities were considerably larger in the mid-nineteenth century than they had been a quarter of a century earlier (Table 9.9). Despite restrictive laws that induced village Jews to emigrate early on, the same was true even in Bavaria between 1812 and 1837. In most of these small-town communities, the increase in Jewish population began to reverse itself sometime around mid-century, and the new trend spread to most regions before the unification of Germany.[10]

---

9 The data for Jewish communities of over 300 are from 1828 while the total numbers in each *Kreis* come from 1832.

10 Of the sixteen Jewish communities over 500 in 1816 in *Regierungsbezirk* Posen that grew between 1817 and 1840, only two gained additional population between 1840 and 1871— Posen city and Ostrowo. Some of the other communities declined precipitously. The nineteen

Table 9.7. Differences in Jewish Community Size in Various Parts of Southern Germany

Size of Jewish community	Main River area				Extreme southwest			
	Lower Franconia (1816)		North Württemberg (1824)		Bavarian Swabia (1809–1812)		South Württemberg (1824)	
	Amount of Jews	Percent of total in province	Amount of Jews	Percent of total in province	Amount of Jews	Percent of total in province	Amount of Jews	Percent of total in province
over 500	507	3.1			893	13.7	504	21.4
400–500			414	8.8	910	14.0	464	19.7
300–400	610	3.7			2,045	31.4	317	13.5
Under 300	15,520	93.3	4,291	91.2	2,666	40.9	1,072	45.5
Total	16,637 (1818)		4,705		6,514 (1818)		2,357	

Sources: Based on *Pinkas ha-Kehillot, Germania, Bavaria*, 379–580, 583–640; Jeggle, *Judendörfer in Württemberg*, 327–329 (excluding Stuttgart and Hohenzollern towns).

Table 9.8. Differences in Jewish Community Size in Various Parts of Prussia, 1843

Province	Over 500			100–499 Jews			Percent of Jews in all communities over 100
	Number of communities	Jews in community	Percent of total[1]	Number of communities	Jews in community	Percent of total	
Former Polish areas:							
West Prussia	12	11762	55.1	36	8365	39.2	94.3
Posen	43	57259	72.0	66	17057	21.4	93.4
Other Eastern:							
Silesia	7	10889	38.1	41	8637	30.2	68.3
Pomerania	1	519	6.7	26	4677	60.6	67.3
East Prussia	1	1688	27.2	11	1343	21.7	48.9
Central:							
Brandenburg	2	8905	55.0	12	2188	13.5	68.5
Prussian Saxony	1	631	14.0	7	1304	28.8	42.8
Western:							
Rhineland	1	794	2.9	29	6353	23.0	25.9
Westphalia	0	—	0.0	29	4269	29.6	29.6

Sources: "Übersicht sämmtlicher Städte des Preussischen Staates in welchen nach der Zählung zu Ende 1843 einhundert Juden und darüber wohnten, nach Provinzen geordnet," in *Die erste vereinigte Landtag in Berlin 1847*, ed. Edward Bleich (Berlin: Verlag von Karl Reimarus, 1847), 322–326. (Towns in East Prussia and West Prussia are combined in the original table; I separated them).

1 Total Jewish population based on Silbergleit, *Die Bevölkerungs- und Berufsverhältnisse*, 11*, 18*–19*.

Table 9.9. Growth of Selected South German Village Jewish Communities in Early Nineteenth Century

Württemberg

Mühringen	354 (1809)	512 (1854)
Buchau	345 (1807)	724 (1854)
Oberdorf	338 (1812)	548 (1854)
Rexingen	317 (1824)	427 (1854)
Freudenthal	324 (1833)	364 (1851)
Laupheim	270 (1807)	796 (1856)
Buttenhausen	251 (1827)	334 (1847)
Aufhausen	204 (1812)	578 (1854)
Pflaumloch	187 (1824)	255 (1854)
Nordstetten	176 (1807)	352 (1854)
Hochberg	172 (1828)	305 (1852)
Braunsbach	165 (1807)	293 (1843)

Sources: *Pinkas ha-Kehillot, Germania, Württemberg-Hohenzollern-Baden*, 31, 33, 55, 60, 66, 76, 78, 100, 110, 116, 117, 130.

Lower Franconia

Location	Jewish population 1814–1816	Change 1814–1837	Jewish population 1837	Change 1837–1867	Jewish population 1867
Villages	5692	+1054	6746	-1211	5535
Cities	310	+120	430	+873	1303
Towns with Jewish population increase		45		19	
Towns with Jewish population decrease		13		39	
No change				1	

The two cities counted are Würzburg and Aschaffenburg. The table includes only towns for which 1837 figures are available.

Source: based on *Pinkas ha-Kehillot, Germania, Bavaria*, 379–580.

Until the middle of the nineteenth century, urbanization was not much in evidence among German Jews. With a few exceptions, the size of urban Jewish communities depended far less on the size of the city than on traditional patterns of settlement. Except in cities that had formerly excluded Jews, Jewish communities in cities of over 50,000 inhabitants underwent only relatively moderate changes between 1837 and 1852, although most experienced a much greater increase between 1852 and 1871 (Table 1.7).

Among cities that had not excluded Jews, only Berlin had an urban Jewish community that grew rapidly at an early date. In fact, Berlin became home to Germany's largest Jewish community by the late 1840s. The percent of German Jews who lived in Berlin increased from about one and one-third percent in 1817 to just above two percent in 1843 and to 2.82 percent in 1852. The Jewish population more than tripled from 1817 to 1852 and did so again by 1871. By the latter date, this Jewish community was almost three times as populous as its nearest competitor.

Substantial differences in every category of locality size between towns that had large Jewish communities in the eighteenth century and those that had lacked them were still evident in 1852. Besides Berlin, the two cities of over 100,000 inhabitants in 1852 that had also had Germany's largest Jewish communities before the Napoleonic Wars (Breslau and Hamburg) far overshadowed the three other German cities of over 100,000 (Dresden, Cologne, and Munich), which had traditionally restrictive policies toward Jewish settlement. In the 50,000–100,000 class, three cities—Königsberg, Danzig, and Frankfurt am Main—had over five times as many Jewish residents as the six urban centers that had traditionally restricted their Jewish populations. More than half of the 23,972 Jews in the thirty-three German cities of 20,000–50,000 lived in the three longstanding traditional communities of Posen, Mainz, and Altona. Mannheim and Karlsruhe were the only other cities in this category that had over 1,000 Jews and only five others harbored communities of more than 500. Only 5,491 Jews dwelled in the other twenty-three German cities in this size category. Of the 16,863 German Jews who lived in the forty-one towns that had Jewish populations and belonged to the 10,000–20,000 size category[11] in 1852, 8,886 lived in eight communities that were larger

---

communities that accommodated over 500 Jews in 1817 had a total of 25,127 Jews in 1817, 33,757 in 1840, and 24,414 in 1871. Excluding the one large-city community (Posen city) in the region, the figures are 21,102 in 1816, 26,994 in 1840, and 17,159 in 1871.

11 Calculated from Schmelz, Territorial Printout.

than 500.[12] Thirteen of the other towns in this category had fewer than 200 Jewish inhabitants. Most of the very small urban Jewish communities were in regions that were traditionally sparse in Jewish settlement[13] (Table 9.10).

Characteristic of the pre-urbanization pattern of German Jewry was the lack of correlation between the size of Jewish communities and the size of the cities in which they were. As the nineteenth century proceeded, such a correlation took shape and gathered strength, with ever-growing communities in the largest cities and fewer large communities remaining in small towns. In 1817, thirty-four of forty communities in Prussia that had over 500 Jews were in towns of under 10,000. By 1852 in Germany as a whole, twenty-eight communities of over 500 Jews were located in cities of more than 10,000 inhabitants and sixteen remained in towns smaller than 10,000. By 1871, only ten large communities remained in the smaller towns whereas sixty-eight were in larger cities. These changes were powered both by migration out of large communities in small towns and by migration to the largest cities, creating new large urban centers (Table 9.11).

Even with the redistribution of the largest communities, Prussian statistics from 1871 showed continued geographical differences in the distribution of small and medium-sized communities, with a much larger proportion of Jews in the western areas living in small communities than was the case in the eastern provinces (Table 9.12). As late as 1900, more than half of the 3,451 localities in Germany that had Jewish inhabitants still had fewer than fifty, even though only 40,976 Jews (7.0 percent of the total) lived in such scattered groups.[14] Very small communities were most common in the Grand Duchy of Hesse, where 18.9 percent of Jews lived in communities of fewer than fifty and 43.4

---

12 Four of these eight towns were important Jewish centers in the eighteenth century; the other four were in densely Jewish provinces to which small-town Jews migrated in the early nineteenth century.
13 Of eighty-nine Jewish communities in cities of over 10,000 inhabitants, twenty-three had fewer than 200 Jewish members. Two of them (Bremen and Nuremberg) were in substantial cities (over 50,000 inhabitants) that had traditionally excluded Jews. Almost all of the others in this category—Stralsund, Goerlitz, Erfurt, Chemnitz, Luebeck, Barmen, Elberfeld, Regensburg, Augsburg, Ulm, Memel, Insterburg, Brieg, Kiel, Flensburg, Bielefeld, Herford, Iserlohn, Duisburg, Remscheid, Kaiserslautern, Heilbronn and Freiburg—were also in cities that had legally excluded Jews. By region, they were in formerly Swedish Pomerania (1), Lower Silesia (2), the Prussian province of Saxony (1), the Kingdom of Saxony (1), Northwest German city-states (2), the later industrial cities of the Ruhr (5), Bavaria (2), Württemberg (2), East Prussia (2), Schleswig-Holstein (2), Westphalia (outside the Ruhr) (1), the Rhine Palatinate (1), and Baden (1).
14 These statistics include only Jewish groupings of known size. We do not know the size of the communities in which 26,477 Jews lived, but many of them were also probably small.

Table 9.10. Urban Jewish Communities in Germany, 1852 (community size by city size and formerly restricted status)

Major Communities		Entire category	Percent of German Jewry
Over 100,000 (6 cities)			
Berlin (11867)			
50,000–100,000 (9 cities)			
Hamburg and Breslau c. 17000	Formerly restricted cities 3414 (3 cities)	c. 32281	7.9
Königsberg, Danzig, and Frankfurt/Main 13335	Formerly restricted cities c. 2600 (6 cities)	c. 15935	3.8
20000–50000 (33 cities)			
Posen, Mainz, and Altona c. 12106	Communities of 500–999 c. 3632 (5 cities)		
Mannheim and Karlsruhe 2743	Communities of fewer than 500 c. 5491 (23)	c. 23972	5.7
10000–20000 (41 cities)			
Glogau, Offenbach, Fürth, and -Rawitsch	Communities of 200–500 c. 6696 (20 cities)		
	Communities of fewer than 200[1] c. 1281 (13 cities)	c. 16863	4.0
Total			
Established communities c. 69569 (24 towns)	New or tiny communities c. 19482 (65 towns)	c. 89051	21.4
Average size: 2900	Average size: 300		

Source: Schmelz, Territorial Printout.

[1] Twenty communities with 200–500: Tilsit, Stargard, Schweidnitz, Neisse, Prenzlau, Schwerin, Nordhausen, Minden, Paderborn, Dortmund, Essen, Mülheim/Ruhr, Wesel, Bonn, Trier, Hanau, Wiesbaden, Speyer, Heidelberg, and Graudenz. Thirteen communities under 200: Memel, Insterburg, Brieg, Kiel, Flensburg, Bielefeld, Herford, Iserlohn, Duisburg, Remscheid, Kaiserslautern, Heilbronn, and Freiburg.

Table 9.11. Correlation of Jewish Community Size and Overall Population—Communities of over 500 Jews

Town size	1817 (Prussia)		1852 (Germany)		1871 (Germany)[1]	
	Number of communities	Number of Jews	Number of communities	Number of Jews	Number of communities	Number of Jews
Over 100000	1	3699	6	32381	8	74811
50000–100000	3	7584	5	11601	18	43829
20000–50000	1	4025	9	17581	18	18898
10000–20000	1	1238	8	8886	14	15420
Under 10000	34	35277	16	23577	10	13713

Sources: Silbergleit, *Die Bevölkerungs- und Berufsverhältnisse*, 9*; Schmelz, Territorial Printout (some large communities in villages may be omitted from the 1852 and 1871 counts).

[1] Including Alsace-Lorraine.

Table 9.12. Jews in Various Prussian Jewish Communities by Size and District, 1871

Regierungsbezirk	Under 50 Jews	50–100	101–200	201–500	501–1,000	Over 1,000
Former Polish areas:						
Danzig	837	98	372	989	1861	2625
Marienwerder	3562	468	1731	6886	6028	1175
Posen	1733	1052	3307	7733	7065	19334
Bromberg	1900	790	1815	3762	8513	4878
Subtotal	8032	2408	7225	19370	23467	28012
Other Eastern Germany						
Königsberg	1774	931	2107	900	—	4876
Gumbinnen	1394	424	594	910	515	—
Stettin	1132	890	1162	1494	—	1823
Köslin	1025	250	1301	2734	879	—
Stralsund	111	—	236	—	—	—
Breslau	1152	641	1651	1829	—	13916
Liegnitz	699	350	814	1011	1790	—
Oppeln	4279	1740	2447	5778	3599	4923
Subtotal	11566	5226	10312	14656	6783	25538
Central Germany						
Berlin	—	—	—	—	—	36015

Regierungsbezirk	Under 50 Jews	50–100	101–200	201–500	501–1,000	Over 1,000
Potsdam	1631	854	774	1289	—	—
Frankfurt	1899	1173	1927	425	1497	—
Magdeburg	708	757	167	470	—	1270
Merseburg	380	67	138	464	—	—
Erfurt	87	399	278	773	—	—
Subtotal	4705	3250	3284	3421	1497	37285
Northwestern Germany						
Schleswig	329	296	871	—	—	2233
Hannover	1105	821	359	—	—	1936
Hildesheim	1059	633	355	718	—	—
Lüneburg	378	130	356	201	—	—
Stade	897	145	123	—	—	—
Osnabrück	544	378	138	—	—	—
Aurich	249	150	305	1129	681	—
Subtotal	4561	2553	2507	2048	681	4169
Western Germany						
Münster	1222	1288	527	366	—	—
Minden	2002	768	1843	1336	—	—
Arnsberg	2438	1188	1710	1880	677	—

Regierungsbezirk	Under 50 Jews	50–100	101–200	201–500	501–1,000	Over 1,000
Koblenz	3825	2137	1189	1562	—	—
Düsseldorf	1831	2253	2242	1631	2377	1085
Cologne	2060	1144	1136	490	536	3172
Trier	1951	1243	1945	846	—	—
Aachen	1491	800	653	825	—	—
Sigmaringen	25	—	111	585	—	—
Kassel	4230	4787	4848	2334	509	1322
Wiesbaden	3561	1647	1410	255	1478	10009
Subtotal	24636	17255	17614	12110	5577	15588
All Prussia	53500	30692	40942	51605	38005	110592
Percent divisions						
Formerly Polish areas	(9.1)	(2.7)	(8.2)	(21.9)	(26.5)	(31.6)
Other Eastern Germany	(15.6)	(7.1)	(13.9)	(19.8)	(9.2)	(34.5)
Central Germany	(8.8)	(6.1)	(6.1)	(6.4)	(2.8)	(69.8)
Northwestern Germany	(27.6)	(15.5)	(15.2)	(12.4)	(4.1)	(25.2)
Western Germany	(26.6)	(18.6)	(19.0)	(13.1)	(6.0)	(16.8)
All Prussia	(16.4)	(9.4)	(12.6)	(15.9)	(11.7)	(34.0)

Source: Neumann, *Zur Statistik der Juden in Preussen*, Table 5.

Table 9.13. Percentages of Jews in Communities of Various Sizes, 1900

Region	1–50	51–100	101–250	Over 250
Prussia	6.4	7.2	12.0	74.4
Bavaria	9.6	16.3	15.1	59.0
Württemberg	6.9	12.2	21.1	59.8
Baden	7.4	10.2	24.9	57.5
Hesse	18.9	24.5	16.5	40.1

Source: *Die jüdischen Gemeinden und Vereine in Deutschland* (Berlin and Halensee: Verlag des Bureaus für Statistik der Juden, 1906), 69.

percent in communities smaller than 100. In other south German states, small communities were less prevalent than in Hesse but more common than in Prussia (Table 9.13). In 1900, the 120 communities of over 500, which were now found overwhelmingly in urban areas, were home to 57.6 percent of German Jewry. Seventy-eight of these communities, with 244,312 Jewish inhabitants in all, were in Prussia. The five South German areas of Bavaria, Württemberg, Baden, Hesse, and Alsace-Lorraine had only thirty-five communities of this size, with 62,793 Jewish inhabitants. In the southern areas, 41.9 percent of Jews lived in communities of over 500, as against 65.8 percent in Prussia.

The Pace of Urbanization

Since the Jewish migration from countryside to city typically preceded that of the general population by approximately one generation, the growth rate of Jewish communities in most cities exceeded that of the larger population until around 1880. Thereafter, while Jewish urbanization continued, it no longer kept pace with the more rapid overall growth of German cities. Important regional differences remained, as did differences between cities that started out with very high Jewish densities and those that began with few Jews.

Although statistics predating the middle of the nineteenth century are rather spotty, they provide enough evidence to trace the outlines of the urbanization process from the end of the Napoleonic Wars. Two of the eight cities that had over 100,000 inhabitants in 1871 (Hamburg and Breslau) had Jewish populations of five percent or more at the end of the Napoleonic Wars and two others (Königsberg and Berlin) had Jewish populations of 1–2 percent of the total. The other four (Dresden, Leipzig, Munich, and Cologne) began that period with very small numbers of Jews. Except for Dresden, Jewish numbers in the latter four cities grew much more rapidly than in the others. The combined absolute number of Jews in the eight largest cities crested in 1925 while the percentage of Jews did so in 1880.

The share of Jews in the largest cities grew consistently (Table 9.14)[15] while the share declined slowly but very unsteadily in medium-sized cities of 20,000–100,000. Many towns entered or left their population categories as they grew in size. At no time after 1871 did more than one-sixth of German Jewry live in medium-sized cities.

Only some of the growth of Jewish presence in the large-city category was caused by migration; it also traced to the growth of medium cities and their entry into the over-100,000 category. From eight cities in Germany that had more than 100,000 inhabitants in 1871, there were fifty-two by 1933. In 1910, the Jewish population of the original eight communities was 58.0 percent of all Jews in the forty cities of over 100,000 inhabitants in Germany.[16] With the exception of Königsberg, all eight cities had populations of over 500,000 by 1910 and more than 600,000 by 1933. Each decade, several cities joined the 100,000-plus class. In a few cases, these cities were absorbed into even larger cities at a later date while several others were in territory that Germany surrendered after World War I.[17] Except for the greater number of Jews in cities already over 100,000 by 1871, there was relatively little significant difference among cities

---

15 Based on Schmelz's tables from Large Folder 6.

16 These eight cities accounted for the following percentage of all German Jews in cities of over 100,000 (1871: 100 percent, 1880: 79.6 percent, 1890: 72.9 percent, 1900: 64.2 percent, 1910: 58.0 percent, 1925: 70.0 percent, 1933: 63.9 percent). The reason for the sharp increase after World War I was that several cities of over 100,000, but none of the original eight, were in territory that Germany lost after the war. Another factor was the incorporation of several large cities into Greater Berlin in 1920.

17 The following cities joined this category between 1871 and 1880: Hanover, Bremen, Frankfurt am Main, Stuttgart, Danzig, and Strasbourg (6), between 1880 and 1890: Stettin, Magdeburg, Halle an der Saale, Chemnitz, Altona, Braunschweig, Düsseldorf, Krefeld, Barmen, Elberfeld, Nuremberg, and Aachen (12), between 1890 and 1900: Charlottenburg, Kiel, Dortmund, Essen, Kassel, Posen and Mannheim (7), between 1900 and 1910: Neukölln-Rixdorf, Schöneberg, Wilmersdorf, Erfurt, Plauen, Gelsenkirchen, Bochum, Duisburg, Mülheim an der Ruhr, Hamborn, Saarbrücken, Wiesbaden, Mainz, Augsburg, and Karlsruhe (15), between 1910 and 1925: Lübeck, Münster, Munich-Gladbach, Oberhausen and Ludwigshafen (5), and between 1925 and 1933: Beuthen, Gleiwitz, Hindenburg, Harburg-Wilhelmsburg, Hagen, Remscheid, Solingen, Würzburg (8).

Charlottenburg, Neukölln-Rixdorf, Schöneberg, and Wilmersdorf became part of Greater Berlin in 1920, Hamborn became part of Duisburg between 1925 and 1933, and Barmen and Elberfeld were combined during the same period to form the new city of Wuppertal.

Large cities in territories lost by Germany after World War I were Danzig, Strasbourg, Posen, and Saarbrücken.

Table 9.14. Changing Jewish Population and Density in Major German Cities, 1817–1933

City	1817	1837	1843	1852	1861	1871	1880	1890	1900	1910	1925	1933
Königsberg	1027	1454	1688	2056	2586	3836	**5082**	4008	3975	4565	4049	3170
	1.62%						**3.61**	2.48	2.10	1.86	1.45	1.00
Breslau	4409	5413	6339	8000	10483	13916	17543	17754	19743	20212	**23240**	20202
	5.74%			6.61	**7.20**	6.69	6.43	5.30	4.67	3.95	4.17	3.23
Berlin	3699	5645	8263	11867	18953	36021	53949	79286	92206	90013	**172672**	160564
	1.96%			2.70	3.46	4.36	4.81	**5.02**	4.88	4.35	4.29	3.78
Dresden		652	645	675	719	1276	2228	2616	3029	3734	**5120**	4397
				0.65%	0.56	0.72	**1.01**	0.95	0.76	0.68	0.83	0.68
Leipzig		172	239	390	786	1739	3179	4225	6174	9434	**12594**	11564
				0.58%	1.00	1.63	**2.13**	1.43	1.35	1.60	1.85	1.62
Hamburg	6423*			9000	10000	11954	12915	17785	17797	19292	**19904**	16973
	6.00%			5.01	5.00	5.00	4.46	5.49	2.52	2.07	1.83	1.50
Cologne	124*	454	784	1531	2322	3172	4523	6859	9745	12156	**16093**	14816
				1.51%	1.93	2.45	**3.12**	2.44	2.62	2.35	2.30	1.96
Munich	451*	1423**		1208	1400	2903	4144	6109	8739	11083	10068	9005
				1.13%	1.08	1.71	1.80	1.74	1.75	**1.86**	1.48	1.22
Total				34727	47249	74811	103563	138642	161408	189961	**263630**	240603
				2.90	3.27	3.80	**4.03**	3.85	3.27	3.16	3.06	2.63

Data in bold = highest number or percent.

Sources: Bleich, *Die erste vereinigte Landtag*, 322–326; *Allgemeine Zeitung des Judentums* 2, no. 109 (September 11, 1838); 1933 census, 5/10; Blau, *Entwicklung*, 284; Bosse, *Die Verbreitung der Juden*, 29, 83, 85; Schmelz, Territorial Printout.

Table 9.15. Number and Percent of Jews in Germany in Towns of Various Sizes, 1852–1933

Town Size	1852	1861	1871	1880	1890	1900	1910	1925	1933
Over 100000	c. 32281	c. 43877	74811	130170	190201	251310	327268	**376,782**	354,120
	7.7%	9.9%	14.6	23.2	33.5	42.8	53.2	66.8	**70.9**
50000–100000	c. 12518	c. 27026	**45246**	44006	36279	[46615]	42974	36,199	25,510
	3.0%	6.1	**8.8**	7.8	6.4	[7.9]	7.0	6.4	5.1
20000–50000	c. 23162	c. 24549	31549	39985	48695	**52045**	48872	34,010	25,642
	5.5%	5.5	6.2	7.1	8.6	**8.9**	8.0	6.0	5.1
Under 20000	c. 352432	c. 349,683	**360522**	347451	292729	238683	195907	117,388	94,610
	83.8%	78.6	70.4	61.9	52.1	40.7	31.9	20.8	18.9
Decline in under-20000 category since previous census				13071	55172	54046	42776	78519	22778
Percent decline since previous census				3.6	15.9	18.5	17.9	40.1	19.4

Data in bold = highest figure.

Source: Schmelz's table "Juden Ortsgrössenklassen."

that entered the over-100,000 category in terms of the growth patterns of Jewish communities in various decades.

German-Jewish urban growth differed significantly from region to region. In all periods, the central and northwestern regions had a much more urbanized population than the rest of the country. Large-city populations increased the most in the western region, especially in the Ruhr Valley industrial district. The Jewish population was much more urbanized than the general population everywhere in Germany except for the western region, where it was only very slightly more urbanized than the population at large. Despite the rapid urbanization of most parts of Germany, regional differences remained remarkably stable.[18] Both the eastern and the southern regions started out with a relatively low rate of city dwellers, but only the southern Jewish population remained much less urban than counterparts elsewhere in Germany after World War I (Table 9.16).

Paradoxically, although it was during the Imperial period that most German Jews moved to large cities, it was no longer true at that time that every urban Jewish community grew in size. In some provincial centers that had seen rapid growth earlier, the Jewish population began to decline precipitously after 1880. In others, growth continued steadily throughout the period and even continued after World War I. In the eastern provinces of West and East Prussia, Pomerania, and Posen, Jewish populations in several cities showed signs of decline while many Silesian communities, especially in industrialized Upper Silesia, continued to grow steadily. Important declines occurred in four large East German cities: Posen, Danzig, Stettin, and Königsberg (Table 9.17). In Silesia, the Oppeln and Ratibor communities reached their peak in 1890, as did Gleiwitz in 1900, but Beuthen continued to grow steadily until 1925. Growth also continued in the Kingdom of Saxony, where a steady stream of East European immigrants moved into formerly restricted cities. Another area of steady increase in the Jewish urban population was the industrialized Ruhr Valley, where most communities grew rapidly, although not as much as the general population. Except for the cities of the Kingdom of Saxony and the metropolis of Berlin, however, the population of most central German communities, especially those in medium sized cities, declined from the peak that they had attained in the late nineteenth century.

In southern and western Germany, the pattern of rise and fall was evident in many longstanding middle-sized communities, notably those of Bamberg,

---

18 The sudden jump in Jewish urbanization in the eastern region after World War I was caused by Germany's loss of most of the Posen-West Prussia area, where most Jewish communities were of the small-town kind.

Table 9.16. Percent of Population Living in Cities That Had Over 100,000 Inhabitants in 1933, by Region

Region	Population	1871	1880	1890	1900	1910	1925	1933
East	General	5.8	6.9	8.1	10.1	11.9	14.6	16.8
	Jewish	20.4	23.4	26.7	32.4	38.1	57.7	60.9
Central	General	14.8	17.4	23.0	26.9	30.0	36.1	36.9
	Jewish	63.2	71.0	78.6	82.9	84.5	90.6	91.3
Northwest	General	14.6	16.8	19.3	26.5	30.5	34.0	32.9
	Jewish	50.4	50.7	62.2	62.5	64.5	72.9	71.7
West	General	14.3	16.1	19.3	26.5	30.5	34.0	52.6
	Jewish	18.8	23.4	26.4	37.1	44.9	57.4	59.7
Hesse	General	11.8	12.3	14.7	18.7	22.5	22.0	25.8
	Jewish	24.7	29.4	34.6	40.8	45.7	51.2	52.1
South*	General	6.4	7.6	11.5	13.6	15.7	17.5	18.6
	Jewish	15.0	19.9	25.2	32.1	39.8	45.3	47.7[1]

* Not including Alsace-Lorraine.

[1] The cities in the various regions included in this table are: east—Königsberg, Breslau, Stettin, Beuthen, Gleiwitz, Hindenburg, and, before World War I, Danzig and Posen; central—Berlin, Dresden, Leipzig, Halle an der Saale, Magdeburg, Erfurt, and Plauen (before World War I the suburbs of Berlin are also included); northwest—Hamburg, Hanover, Bremen, Altona, Braunschweig, Kiel, Lübeck, and Harburg-Wilhelmsburg; west—Cologne, Düsseldorf, Krefeld, Barmen, Elberfeld, Dortmund, Essen, Oberhausen, Aachen, Gelsenkirchen, Bochum, Duisburg, Mülheim an der Ruhr, Hamborn, Münster, Munich-Gladbach, Hagen, Remscheid, and Solingen (and Saarbrücken before World War I); Hesse—Frankfurt am Main, Kassel, Wiesbaden and Mainz; south—Munich, Stuttgart, Nuremberg, Mannheim, Augsburg, Karlsruhe, Ludwigshafen, and Würzburg.

Table 9.17. Rise and Decline of Several Major East German Jewish Communities

City	1817	Highest point and date	1910
Posen	4025	7356 (1852)	5605
Danzig	2148	2975 (1861)	2390
** Stettin	81	3128 (1900)	2757
** Königsberg	1027	5082 (1880)	4565 (3975 in 1900)

** Over 250,000 inhabitants in 1925.

Sources: Silbergleit, *Die Bevölkerungs- und Berufsverhältnisse*, 9*; Heinrich Loewe, "Die Zahl der Juden in Pommern," *ZDSJ* (1911): 18; Loewe, "Die Juden Preussens im Jahre 1817," 46; Schmelz, Territorial Printout.

Trier, and Krefeld. In Baden-Württemberg, most major urban communities continued to grow steadily, although a few such as Ulm peaked in the late nineteenth century and then declined thereafter. In Bavaria, the largest and newest communities showed a steady pattern of growth while many older and medium-sized communities declined. Hesse, too, had both many older communities that contracted after having reached a peak and mainly newer communities that grew steadily as well (Table 9.18).

We have information on the Jewish populations of nearly all 245 German localities that had populations of over 20,000 in 1905 (Table 9.19). Although the largest Jewish communities were generally in the largest towns, there was a broad range in Jewish communities' size in each category of general population, and was often on a regional basis.[19] The most populous Jewish communities in each city-size category were in areas of traditionally heavy Jewish population such as Silesia, Hesse, Baden, Franconia, Posen, and West Prussia. Most of the smallest Jewish communities in each category were in areas of traditionally sparse Jewish population, especially Schleswig-Holstein, Saxony, and Thuringia, as well as newly developing smaller cities in the Ruhr.[20]

---

19 Most of our data on the Jewish communities come from 1900. In a few cases where they were absent, I used 1910 figures.
20 Among towns in the 20,000–25,000 inhabitant category, those with fewer than 100 Jews, were especially common in the Prussian province of Brandenburg (3), the Prussian province of Saxony (5), the Kingdom of Saxony (4), and the Thuringian states (2). There were nine in the Rhineland or Westphalia, four in the south, a few in Pomerania and Mecklenburg (Wismar), and none in Hesse.

Table 9.18. Patterns of Rise and Decline in Selected Urban Jewish Communities in Various Regions of Germany, 1871-1925

City and Region	1871	1880	1890	1900	1910	1925
Upper Silesia						
-Oppeln	688	679	**712**	693	332?	528
-Ratibor	1209	**1331**	1213	957	770	696
Gleiwitz	1890	1838	1767	**2094**	1796	1906
Beuthen	1824	2185	2183	2594	2579	**3263**
Subtotal	5611	6033	5875	6338	5477?	6393
Saxony (Free State)						
**Leipzig	1739	3179	4225	6171	9434	**12594**
**Dresden	1276	2228	2616	3029	3734	**5120**
**Chemnitz	95	294	953	1137	1605	**2796**
*Plauen	10	34	180	208	**749**	623
Subtotal	3120	5735	7974	10545	15522	21133
Rhineland and Westphalia						
**Düsseldorf	919	1008	1401	2131	3985	**5130**
**Essen	832	942	1190	1807	2773	**4209**
*Bochum	370	617	764	1002	992	**1122**
**Dortmund	677	998	1306	1924	2676	**3820**
**Duisburg	253	367	474	786	1554	**2080**
*Elberfeld	626	1104	1378	1664	1919	**2335**
*Krefeld	1085	1532	**1992**	1788	1815	1626
Trier	431	627	**845**	795	734	802
Subtotal	5193	7195	9350	11897	16448	21124
Central Germany						
**Magdeburg	1270	1340	2090	1925	1843	**2356**
*Halle/Saale	464	623	919	1258	**1397**	1236
Frankfurt/Oder	767	**890**	775	747	626	669
Potsdam	476	**551**	535	442	344	399
-Prenzlau	337	382	**423**	342	297	232
-Schwerin (Mecklenburg)	336	**367**	302	299	218	175
Brandenburg	255	209	243	286	283	**469**

From Countryside to City: Urbanization and the Survival of Small-Town Jewish Communities | 417

City and Region	1871	1880	1890	1900	1910	1925
-Halberstadt***	470	595	727	773	759	**937**
Subtotal	4375	4957	6014	6072	5767	6473
Baden and Württemberg						
**Stuttgart	1817	2485	2758	3015	4291	**4548**
*Mannheim	3135	4031	4553	5478	6402	**6972**
*Karlsruhe	1329	1689	2056	2576	3058	**3386**
Ulm	555	**694**	664	609	588	565
Freiburg	333	725	999	1013	1320	**1399**
Heidelberg	651	799	807	882	1242	**1354**
-Heilbronn	610	871	838	815	867	**900**
Subtotal	8430	11294	12675	14388	17768	19124
Bavaria						
Large and new communities						
**Munich	2903	4144	6109	8739	**11083**	10068
**Nuremberg	1831	3032	4307	5956	7815	**8603**
*Augsburg	660	1031	1128	1171	**1217**	1203
Subtotal	5394	8207	11544	15866	20115	19874
Older and medium-sized communities						
Würzburg	1518	2271	2436	**2567**	2514	2261
Regensburg	430	**675**	585	571	493	478
Fürth	3250	**3330**	3175	3017	2826	2504
Bamberg	857	**1269**	1187	1160	1177	972
Subtotal	6055	7545	7383	7315	7010	6215
Bavaria total	11449	15752	18927	23181	27125	26089
Hessian Region						
Steadily growing communities						
**Frankfurt	10009	13856	17426	21974	26228	**29385**
*Kassel	1322	1756	2017	2445	2675	**2750**
*Wiesbaden	893	1202	1537	2109	2844	**3088**
-Fulda***	295	439	525	675	957	**1137**
Subtotal	12519	17253	21505	27203	32704	36360
Older communities that began to decline						
*Mainz	2998	3182	**3231**	3104	2926	2738
-Worms	977	1216	1232	**1298**	1281	1194

City and Region	1871	1880	1890	1900	1910	1925
Darmstadt	906	1275	1438	1689	**1998**	1646
-Hanau	447	554	608	**657**	637	568
Subtotal	5328	6227	6509	6748	6842	6146
Hessian total	17847	23480	28014	33951	39546	42506

*** Orthodox stronghold.

** Over 250,000 inhabitants in 1925.

* 100,000–249,999 inhabitants in 1925.

- = fewer than 50,000 inhabitants in 1925.

The 1910 figure for Oppeln may be a misprint.

Source: Schmelz, Territorial Printout.

Among German Jewry, the share of Jews who lived in towns of 20,000 or fewer declined steadily between 1871 and 1933 from over 70 percent to less than 20 percent (Table 9.20), with an especially sharp drop in the small-town Jewish population between 1910 and 1925. This change was only partly due to migration from small towns to cities; it was also abetted by the postwar ceding of some territories that had large small-town Jewish populations.[21] The loss of 41,828 small-town Jews in these provinces accounts for more than half of the drop in the small-town Jewish population of Germany between 1910 and 1925.[22]

---

21 In Alsace-Lorraine in 1910, there were 19,303 Jews in towns of under 20,000 inhabitants (63.3 percent of all Alsatian and Lorraine Jews). Despite earlier massive losses of Jewish population, the Polish-majority areas in West Prussia and Posen retained many small-town Jews. In 1910, 9,435 (68.0 percent) of 13,954 Jews in West Prussia and 13,090 (49.4 percent) of 26,512 Jews in Posen lived in towns of under 20,000.

22 Small segments of the provinces of West Prussia and Posen remained part of Germany after 1919 as the West Prussia *Regierungsbezirk* of East Prussia and the Grenzmark province of Prussia. Together, these areas had 5,233 Jews in 1925, of whom 4,280 (81.8 percent) lived in towns of under 20,000. Thus, the total Jewish population of the lost territories in towns of under 20,000 was only 37,548. This accounts for 47.8 percent of the loss in small-town Jewry between 1910 and 1925. Many Jews in the areas of Posen and West Prussia, which were ceded to Poland, left the territory, but most migrated to Berlin and other large cities and were no longer small-town Jews.

Table 9.19. Size of Jewish Population by City Size, 1900–1910

Total population (1905)	Jewish population (1900 or 1910)								1900 size of Jewish community	
	Total	Over 10000	2001–10000	1001–2000	501–1000	201–500	101–200	Under 100	Largest	Smallest
Over 500000	5	2	3	0	0	0	0	0	92206 Berlin	3029 Dresden
200000–500000	14	2	8	3	1	0	0	0	21974 Frankfurt	836 Bremen
100000–200000	22	0	9	6	4	3	0	0	5988 Posen	208 Plauen
50000–100000	48	0	6	6	18	13	4	2	3104 Mainz	69 Borbeck
40000–50000	15	0	0	2	7	3	1	1	1298 Worms	47 Buer
30000–40000	43	0	1	2	8	14	8	10	2264 Kattowitz	22 Altenburg
25000–30000	31	0	0	0	2	13	12	6	895 Giessen	26 Naumburg
20000–25000	67	0	0	2	10	11	14	29	1389 Inowrazlaw	8 Merheim

Sources: "Die 525 Gemeinden von mehr als 10,000 Einwohnern nach der Volkszählung vom 1. Dezember 1905," *Statistisches Jahrbuch des Deutschen Reichs* (1907): 16–17; Schmelz, Territorial Printout.

Table 9.20. Subdivisions of Small-Town Jewry, 1925

Subdivision	Total population:	Up to 499	500–999	1000–1999	2000–4999	5,000–19999	All
Hesse-Darmstadt	Number of Jews:	362	1861	2860	x	x	20401
	Percent of total	1.8	9.1	14.0	16.6	17.9	
Unterfranken*	Number of Jews:	482	1946	1262	1587	1074	9879
	Percent of total	5.0	20.1	13.1	16.4	11.1	

* Jewish population of 1925 based on total town size in 1933.

x: Schmelz gives only percentages and not absolute figures for the 2000–2999 and 5000–19999 categories.

Sources: Schmelz, *Hessen*, 54–56; *Pinkas ha-Kehillot, Germania, Bavaria*, 13, 379–580.

Migration and Urbanization

The urbanization of German Jewry involved both local and long-distance migration. Areas that had higher rural population percentages in Germany tended to lose Jewish population while more urbanized regions gained. Within each region, including those that remained relatively rural, the percentage of Jews who lived in larger towns gained at the expense of smaller towns.

Migration to large cities had three main sources—short-distance migration from nearby smaller communities, medium- and long-distance migration from non-contiguous provinces within Germany, and immigration from other countries. Although a combination of all three factors was present in all growing communities, the balance between them varied widely. In southern Germany, urban communities often depended heavily on migration from nearby towns and villages. There was a similar phenomenon in some East German communities, where migrants came from outlying towns in the province as well as from the nearby "reserve" of Posen and West Prussia. In the south, such short-distance migration was important in cities such as Frankfurt, Nuremberg, Würzburg, Stuttgart, and Mannheim and in the east in Stettin, Breslau, Beuthen, and Gleiwitz. It played a role, though not as overwhelmingly, in cities like Cologne, Hannover, and Königsberg. Berlin, which had few large Jewish communities in its vicinity, lured Jews from all the eastern provinces, especially Silesia, West Prussia, and Posen.[23] Hamburg, which, like Berlin, had few surrounding small-town Jewish communities, did not attract nearly as many long-distance migrants. In 1933, it had the highest percentage of Jews native to the city of any major Jewish community in Germany (50.8 percent). The growth of the Hamburg Jewish community lagged behind that of most other urban communities.

Many cities that had been historically closed to Jews or expanded rapidly after 1880 attracted heavy contingents of immigrants, mainly from Eastern Europe. This was especially true of the cities of industrial Saxony, Munich, and the Ruhr. By the same token, many immigrants also went to a few industrial cities that had longstanding Jewish communities (notably Altona) (Table 9.21). Cities near each other also sometimes had very different migration characteristics. Although industrial Solingen and Remscheid had very small Jewish communities for their size, in 1933 Solingen had relatively few immigrants (19.4 percent) and Remscheid had many (46.5 percent) (Table 9.22). In the cases of Altona and Hamburg, the high percentage of Jewish immigrants in the former city

---

23 The Jewish population resembled the general population of Berlin in this sense; the latter was also recruited heavily from the eastern provinces of Prussia.

Table 9.21. Types of Communities with High Percent of Jewish Immigrants, 1925, 1933

City	Jewish population 1925	Percent foreign-born plus foreign citizenship, 1933 = *zugewanderte*
Jewish communities, formerly restricted		
Leipzig	12594	73.1
Dresden	5120	60.7
Chemnitz	2796	60.5
Kiel	605	57.1
Plauen	623	53.8
Magdeburg	2356	37.9
Cologne	16093	31.5
Munich	10068	26.7
Rapidly growing industrial cities (mainly in the Ruhr)		
Remscheid	261	46.5
Duisburg	2080	46.2
Ludwigshafen (Palatinate)	1211	45.8
Gelsenkirchen	1441	37.9
Dortmund	3820	36.2
Essen	4209	35.8
Hagen	641	35.0
Bochum	1122	27.0
Oberhausen	513	24.8
Not formerly restricted		
Altona	2409	56.3
Wiesbaden	3088	30.3

Sources: *Statistik des deutschen Reichs* 401 (1930): *Die Bevölkerung des Deutschen Reichs nach den Ergebnissen der Volkszählung 1925*, part 2: *Textliche Darstellung der Ergebnisse*, 620–621; 1933 census, 3/32–33; 5/15.

Table 9.22. Percent Jewish Internal Migrants and Immigrants in Major German Cities, 1933

City	1933			
	Percent born in city	Born outside city elsewhere in Germany (1933 boundaries)	Lost territories	Foreign-born and unknown
Hamburg	50.8	32.3	3.3	13.6
Krefeld-Uerdingen	48.1	[44.9]	[2.1]	[4.9]
Mainz	44.8	42.5	1.1	11.6
Lübeck	43.1	32.4	6.0	18.5
Mülheim an der Ruhr	42.0	[45.3]	[2.1]	[10.6]
Augsburg	41.2	[51.7]	[1.5]	[5.6]
Frankfurt am Main	40.8	43.4	2.5	13.3
Aachen	40.2	[49.3]	[2.1]	[8.4]
Mannheim	39.5	47.4	2.1	11.0
Leipzig	39.4	18.0	2.7	39.9
Breslau	39.0	26.3	26.5	8.2
Berlin	38.0	25.7	15.9	20.4
Munich	37.8	44.4	1.1	16.7
Cologne	37.7	42.5	2.2	17.6
Stuttgart	37.7	48.9	1.8	11.6
Nuremberg	37.7	52.7	1.3	8.3
Dortmund	37.5	37.8	3.2	21.5
Stettin	37.5	36.6	17.1	8.8
Wuppertal	36.9	[47.2]	[2.1]	[13.8]
Kassel	36.7	[49.6]	[2.5]	[11.2]
Karlsruhe	36.6	46.4	2.4	14.6
Mönchengladbach	36.5	[53.3]	[2.1]	[8.1]
Magdeburg	35.6	[24.3]	[16.7]	[23.4]
Duisburg	35.2	[33.1]	[2.1]	[29.6]
Bochum	34.8	[46.2]	[2.9]	[16.1]
Königsberg	34.6	36.7	14.5	14.2
Braunschweig	34.4	[36.7]	[4.1]	[24.8]
Hannover	34.4	43.4	3.6	18.6
Würzburg	34.2	[57.3]	[1.5]	[7.0]

City	1933			
	Percent born in city	Born outside city elsewhere in Germany (1933 boundaries)	Lost territories	Foreign-born and unknown
Gleiwitz	34.1	[26.2]	[31.8]	[7.9]
Beuthen	33.1	20.7	30.0	16.2
Bielefeld	32.9	[59.2]	[2.9]	[5.0]
Gelsenkirchen	32.9	[41.6]	[2.9]	[22.6]
Harburg-Wilhelmsburg	32.7	[33.8]	[4.1]	[29.4]
Hindenburg Oberschlesien	32.7	[24.5]	[31.8]	[11.0]
Oberhausen	32.4	[49.6]	[2.1]	[15.9]
Solingen	31.8	[53.7]	[2.1]	[12.4]
Dresden	31.6	22.4	6.0	40.0
Essen	31.6	42.6	2.9	22.9
Halle/Saale	31.4	[36.4]	[16.7]	[15.5]
Chemnitz	30.8	[28.3]	[3.9]	[37.0]
Plauen	30.3	[32.9]	[3.9]	[32.9]
Münster	29.6	[61.8]	[2.9]	[5.7]
Kiel	29.5	[32.9]	[3.4]	[34.2]
Altona	29.3	[33.6]	[3.4]	[33.7]
Bremen	29.0	51.0	3.8	16.2
Erfurt	28.9	[39.7]	[16.7]	[14.7]
Düsseldorf	27.8	51.4	2.9	17.9
Ludwigshafen	27.5	44.1	2.4	26.0
Hagen	27.0	[49.2]	[2.9]	[20.9]
Wiesbaden	26.9	[53.5]	[2.5]	[17.1]
Remscheid	24.9	[43.2]	[2.1]	[29.8]

Note: Data in square brackets were extrapolated from combined figures for "other large cities" in their province. The data for *zugewanderte* (foreign-born plus native-born without citizenship) for the city were multiplied by the percent of *zugewanderte* who were foreign-born in the "other large cities" category of that province and the combined figure for those born in lost territories for each province. The second column reports the remainder of the city's inhabitants.

Source: based on 1933 census, 5/15, 5/50–53.

(56.3 percent) may be explained by the stricter regulations of the city-state of neighboring Hamburg (18.4 percent). The higher concentration of foreign Jews in Offenbach than in nearby Frankfurt also seems to have been the result of difference in anti-immigrant policies.

The degree of the general population's urbanization correlated closely, generally speaking, with the degree of the Jewish population's urbanization in the same district. Jews were usually much more urbanized than non-Jews, though less markedly in western and southern Germany than in the east and central Germany (Table 9.23). The areas that were most urbanized in 1925 were also those with the greatest gains in Jewish population between 1871 and

Table 9.23. Percent of Population Living in Cities of over 50,000 (1925), by Region

Region	Eastern and central Germany			Western and southern Germany	
	General	Jewish		General	Jewish
Lübeck	94.4	100.0			
Hamburg	93.6	99.1			
Bremen	87.1	88.1			
Brandenburg	64.5	96.4			
			Middle Franconia	46.7	80.6
			Rhineland	46.6	68.3
			Upper Bavaria	40.4	93.3
Saxony (*Land*)	36.5	92.5			
			Westphalia	33.8	50.4
			Hesse-Nassau	30.9	66.8
Schleswig-Holstein	30.5	74.1			
Braunschweig	29.5	53.6			
			Baden	27.5	58.7
			Hannover	22.4	47.9
			Hesse-Darmstadt	20.6	29.7
Anhalt	20.3	35.0			
			Bavarian Swabia	19.3	42.5

Silesia	19.1	74.5			
Prussian Saxony	19.0	54.1			
East Prussia	17.5	45.2	Rhenish Palatinate	17.3	24.9
			Württemberg	15.5	47.2
Pomerania	13.5	33.7			
			Upper Palatinate	12.3	40.5
			Lower Franconia	11.8	22.9
Mecklenburg	9.9	19.8			
Oldenburg	9.7	20.9			
Thuringia	8.3	21.8			
			Oberfranken	6.6	38.2

Source: Calculated from Schmelz, Territorial Printout,

1925, while the most rural areas tended to lose Jewish population (Table 9.24). Even in relatively rural parts of Germany, however, Jews tended to regroup in the larger towns and move out of the smallest villages. This was evident in the Bavarian province of Lower Franconia, one of the classic centers of rural Jewry. Migration from the smallest villages (fewer than 1,000 inhabitants) was already noticeable before the unification of Germany, whereas Jewish communities in small towns and cities (2,000–9,999) continued to grow until about 1900 and then declined.[24] Similar conditions were found in Hesse, an area somewhat more urbanized than Lower Franconia (Tables 9.25 A and B).[25]

Not all communities followed the simple linear patterns of gains in larger villages at the expense of smaller villages, smaller cities at the expense of larger villages, and larger cities at the expense of smaller ones. Characteristics other than large size also sometimes induced Jews to migrate to a town. County seats

---

[24] Based on records in *Pinkas ha-Kehillot, Germania, Bavaria*. The towns included in the above data do not include all known Jewish inhabitants of Lower Franconia. They are most incomplete for the earliest years. The sum of all data for each year listed equals the following percentages of the known Jewish population of Lower Franconia: 1816—72.8 percent (1818), 1867—84.8 percent, 1900—93.0 percent, 1910—92.3 percent, 1925—96.0 percent, 1933—100 percent.

[25] Schmelz, *Hessen*, 387–388. The main reason for the greater urbanization of this area was the presence of the large community of Frankfurt.

Table 9.24. Increase or Decrease of Jewish Population by Degree of Urbanization

District	Percent of general population in towns over 50,000 (1925)	Increase or decrease in Jewish population, 1871–1925
Lübeck	94.4	+11.3
Hamburg	93.6	+44.3
Bremen	87.1	+224.3
Brandenburg	64.5	+281.4
Mittelfranken	46.7	+26.7
Rhineland	46.6	+50.2
Oberbayern	40.4	+255.8
Saxony (*Land*)	36.5	+592.6
Westphalia	33.8	+25.2
Hesse-Nassau	30.9	+44.4
Schleswig-Holstein	30.5	+10.9
Braunschweig	29.5	+50.0
Baden	27.5	-6.4
Hannover	22.4	+16.5
Hesse-Darmstadt	20.6	-19.6
Anhalt	20.3	-39.9
Bavarian Swabia	19.3	-35.1
Silesia	19.1	+10.8*
Prussian Saxony	19.0	+40.0
East Prussia	17.5	-21.4
Rhenisch Palatinate	17.3	-37.0
Württemberg	15.5	-11.6
Pommern	13.5	-40.5
Upper Palatinate	12.3	-3.3
Mecklenburg	9.9	-59.0
Lower Franconia	9.7	-32.2
Thuringia	8.3	+8.9
Upper Franconia	6.6	-37.1
Lippe	0	-43.2
Lower Bavaria	0	+213.5

* Adjusted for lost territories.

Sources: Calculated from Schmelz, Territorial Printout.

Table 9.25. Redistribution of Jewish Population among Small Towns of Various Sizes

A) Lower Franconia

Year	1816	1867	1900	1910	1925	1933	1925 as percent of 1816
Town population							
Under 500	1827 (16)	1433 (21)	908 (20)	730 (20)	476 (20)	387 (21)	26.1%
500–999	5518 (51)	4691 (54)	3581 (52)	2620 (51)	1896 (50)	1683 (51)	34.3
1000–1499	2466 (22)	2536 (26)	1741 (24)	1040 (15)	824 (16)	744 (16)	33.4
1500–1999	383 (5)	409 (6)	532 (6)	424 (7)	438 (9)	387 (9)	114.4
2000–9999	1384 (13)	1842 (16)	2750 (17)	2139 (22)	2197 (23)	1859 (24)	156.8
Over 10000	310 (2)	1303 (2)	3170 (2)	4049 (4)	3739 (4)	3459 (4)	1206.1

Numbers in parentheses denote the number of communities in the category.

Source: Calculated from *Pinkas ha-Kehillot, Germania, Bavaria*, 379–580.

B) Hessian Area (percentages)

Year	Under 500	500–999	1,000–1,999	2,000–4,999	5,000–9,999	10,000–19,999	20,000+
1861	6.2	24.9	23.5	16.2	4.5	4.4	20.3
1925	1.7	6.6	9.8	10.3	4.4	4.0	63.2

Source: Schmelz, *Hessen*, 361.

often gained Jewish population even if they had fewer than 3,000 inhabitants, especially if they had formerly had few Jewish inhabitants or none at all (Table 9.26). South German resort towns like Kissingen, Neustadt an der Saale, Brückenau, Mergentheim, and Schwalbach, although small in population, also attracted Jewish migrants. Several relatively small cities, notably Halberstadt and Fulda, had growing Jewish communities because they were centers of Orthodoxy.[26]

Regional Patterns of Rural Jewish Survival

Despite the overall urbanization of German Jewry, its extent varied immensely from region to region and important pockets of small-town and rural Jewry survived into the Weimar era. In 1925, when only 20.8 percent of German Jews lived in towns of under 20,000, the small-town population exceeded 30 percent in all South German states as well as in the Prussian provinces of East Prussia, Pomerania, and Grenzmark in the east and Hesse-Nassau, Westphalia, and Hanover in the west (Table 9.27). Few small-town Jewish communities in heavily urbanized central Germany endured.[27] Much of this region had a sparse Jewish population until the nineteenth century, and almost all Jews who settled there later moved to the largest cities. The same is true of southern Germany areas such as Upper and Lower Bavaria, which excluded Jews until the nineteenth century. Thus, even as more than 10,000 Jews lived in Munich in 1925, only 759 Jews dwelled in towns of under 20,000 in Upper and Lower Bavaria. The eastern Prussian provinces of Pomerania and East Prussia were exceptions to the rule that new Jewish settlers chose mainly urban locations. Many Jews who settled in this once sparsely Jewish area in the early and mid-nineteenth century chose to live in relatively small towns.[28]

---

26 The city of Halberstadt in the Prussian province of Saxony was located in an area of generally sparse Jewish population. In 1871, its overall population was 25,419 and its Jewish population was 470. By 1925, both populations had doubled to 48,184 and 937, respectively. Fulda was in a Catholic area that had a lower Jewish density than the rest of heavily Jewish Hesse-Nassau. In 1871, the city had 9,470 inhabitants, of whom 295 were Jews. By 1925, the city had almost tripled in size, to 26,057, but the Jewish population increased even more rapidly—from 3.12 percent of the total population in 1871 to to 1,137 or 4.36 percent in 1925.
27 In Brandenburg in 1925, there were only 5,192 Jews in towns of under 20,000 in a total Jewish population of 181,114 (mostly in Berlin); in the Land of Saxony, Jews in towns under 20,000 numbered only 1,210 of 23,252.
28 Maurer, "Problemskizze," 217–247.

Table 9.26. Growth of Jewish Population in Small-Town County Seats in Unterfranken

County seat	Jewish population			General population
	1814–1816	1867	1925	1925
Alzenau		63	97	2481
Bad Neustadt an der Saale	37	147	162	2391
Bad Kissingen	181	314	504	9517
Brückenau		19	128	2393
Gemünden	15	23	74	2374
Gerolzhofen	39	58	115	2806
Hassfurt	22	48	93	3088
Hofheim		7	54	1087
Königshofen	27	50	108	1839
Mellrichstadt	45	81	151	2178

Source: *Pinkas ha-Kehillot, Germania, Bavaria*, 402, 415–416, 419, 431, 442, 445, 455, 458, 522, 560.

The *Handbuch der jüdischen Gemeindeverwaltung*, published in 1911, lists all Jewish communities in Germany along with their populations alongside the general populations of the towns in which they were located.[29] Although the listings are unofficial and sometimes based on estimates, they give us a basic idea of the geographic variations in small-town communities. It is remarkable to see how the nineteenth-century patterns were still in evidence in 1911. In the eastern sections of Germany,[30] relatively few Jews lived in villages of under 2,000 inhabitants but many dwelled in towns of 2,000–10,000. In southern Germany, especially in the area around the River Main,[31] in contrast, Jews in villages of

---

29 A comparison with other data shows that some of the listed populations are either overestimates or refer to a decade or so earlier than the publication date.
30 Taking together the figures for the formerly Polish areas of eastern Germany (Posen, West Prussia and Upper Silesia) with figures for Pomerania, Lower Silesia, and East Prussia as well as Brandenburg and Prussian Saxony, we find 30,948 Jews recorded as living in towns of 2,000–9,999 inhabitants as against only 3,417 in towns of under 2,000 inhabitants (and 10,286 in towns of 10,000–19,999). In Brandenburg-Saxony, most Jews lived in big cities.
31 Taking together the southern Rhineland, Hesse (excluding *Regierungsbezirk* Wiesbaden), Alsace-Lorraine, and Rheinpfalz-Unterfranken-Schwaben, we find 37,385 Jews in villages

Table 9.27. Jews in Towns of under 10,000 (absolute numbers and percentages of provincial Jewish population)

Region	1880		1925 under 20,000		1925 under 10,000		1933	
East Prussia	10780	59.3%	5081	44.8%	3822		2888	32.7%
Brandenburg and Berlin	8612	12.6	4536	2.5	3505		3175	2.0
West Prussia	20385	76.8	—	—			—	
Posen	40738	72.0	—	—			—	
Grenzmark		83.0	2851	83.0	2611		2051	73.9
Pomerania	8612	62.0	3760	48.5	2694		2010	31.8
Silesia	19681	37.4	6154	15.4	3813		2654	7.7
Saxony Province	2536	37.9	1637	19.6	880		675	9.5
Schleswig-Holstein	711	20.2	854	20.6	384		237	7.6
Independent Saxony	455	7.0	1210	5.2	663	2.9	448	2.2
Thuringia	2550	59.7	1565	43.4	1020		817	28.3
Hamburg	4009	25.0	110		37		40	0.2
Mecklenburg	2218	73.0	905	64.3	496		272	27.1
Oldenburg	1458	88.2	903		720		582	46.9

Region	1880		1925 under 20,000		1925 under 10,000		1933	
Braunschweig	749	54.0	814		335		237	20.2
Bremen	81	10.6	57		57		37	2.6
Anhalt	637	36.4	290	25.4	182		107	11.9
Lübeck	10	10	1.8	0	0		0	0
Northern and Eastern Germany	124222	30727					16230	5.9
Lippe	1030	100	787		273		247	48.4
Schaumburg-Lippe	295	100	180		180		187	100
Hannover	8119	54.9	5963	40.0	4613		3559	28.2
Westphalia	12833	68.2	7439	34.5	5262		4471	23.8
Rhine Province	27120	62.1	14214	24.6	11366		9942	19.0
Western Germany	49397		28583				18406	21.7
Waldeck	851	100						
Hesse-Nassau	22942	55.5	16143	30.0	13187	32.2	12404	26.5
Hohenzollern	771	100	335	100	335	100	301	100
Bavaria	33422	62.4	16952	34.5	14967	35.0	11911	28.4

Region	1880		1925 under 20,000		1925 under 10,000		1933	
Württemberg	8060	60.4	3878	35.8	3657	33.8	2994	29.9
Baden	18556	68.0	9095	37.8	7444	30.9	5640	27.3
Hesse	17212	64.4	12124	59.4	10775	52.8	9282	51.9
Southern Germany	101814		58527		50365		42532	30.9
Total Germany	303980 (275433)		117388 (117837)		97127		77168 (77986)	15.5
Percent north and east	40.9		26.2				21.3	
Percent west	16.3		24.4				24.1	
Percent south	33.5		49.9		51.9		54.7	

Sources: Bosse, *Die Verbreitung der Juden*, 1–127; "Die Juden im Deutschen Reich 1816–1933," *Wirtschaft und Statistik* 15, no. 4 (1935): 150; Schmelz, handwritten tables, "Juden Ortsgrössenklassen"; 1933 census, 5/11; Lothar Bauer, "Schicksal in Zahlen: Die Juden in der Volkszählung 1933," *Der Morgen* 10, no. 9 (1934–1935): 408, gives somewhat discrepant numbers for 1933.

under 2,000 far outnumbered those in towns of 2,000–10,000 (Table 9.28). In 1925, village Jewry also made up a substantial proportion of towns under 20,000's Jewish population of in these areas of southern Germany. Jews were especially numerous in larger villages of 1,000–2,000 inhabitants.

The areas in which the most small-town Jews remained had usually had substantial numbers of Jewish residents in the pre-Emancipation era. Rural Jewry survived in especially large numbers near the River Main, which crossed the northern edge of southern Germany. The Bavarian provinces of Lower Franconia and Rhine Palatinate, the state of Hesse-(Darmstadt), the Prussian *Regierungsbezirk* of Kassel, the southern Rhineland *Regierungsbezirke* of Trier and Koblenz, and the states of Baden and Württemberg all continued to host vibrant rural Jewish life (Table 9.29). In 1925, this area was home to only 17.3 percent of all Jews in Germany but accounted for 45.5 percent of all German Jews in towns with fewer than 20,000 inhabitants. The 1933 census carefully delineated the boundaries of a very specific area in the Main-Rhine region where the Jewish population in towns of fewer than 10,000 inhabitants made up a substantial part of the small-town population. In this area, there were 39,794 Jews out of 4,813,682 inhabitants, just over half of the 77,177 Jews who lived in towns of that size in all of Germany (Map 9/1).[32] Another much smaller area where small-town Jewry predominated was Grenzmark, the remnant of Posen-West Prussia that had not been assigned to Poland after World War I.

Variations in the Urbanization Process

A detailed analysis of Jewish migration from small towns and villages shows that sometimes two towns seemingly identical in every respect had completely different patterns. Württemberg, for instance, had at least eleven small-town

---

of under 2,000 as against only 13,410 in towns of 2,000–9,999, and 7,165 in towns of 10,000–19,999. In other south-German territories such as Baden-Württemberg, Middle Franconia and *Regierungsbezirk* Wiesbaden, villages and small towns were more evenly balanced with 10,440 Jews in villages of under 2,000 inhabitants and 10,644 Jews in towns in the 2,000–9,999 class.

32 *Statistik des deutschen Reichs* 451, no. 5 (1936): *Die Glaubensjuden im Deutschen Reich*, 12. The statisticians went out of their way to include only counties with the largest percentages of rural Jews to make the picture of a region of small-town Jews particularly clear. The area includes sections of southeastern Westphalia, *Regierungsbezirk* Wiesbaden, and *Regierungsbezirk* Aachen not included in the area described in the previous sentences, and excludes all but the northernmost part of Baden and Württemberg and the eastern parts of the Rhine Palatinate.

Table 9.28. Number of Jews in Towns of Various Size by Region, 1911 (towns with at least 20 Jews)

City	Over 20000	10000–19999	5000–9999	2000–4999	1000–1999	Under 1000
Polish-speaking areas						
Posen	9996	2806	7603	5247	1726	283
Marienwerder	1950	1086	2084	3393	338	90
Oppeln	12319	1842	1356	1223	114	30
Total	24265	5734	11043	9863	2178	403
Percent	45.4	10.7	20.7	18.4	4.1	0.8
Other eastern Germany						
Danzig	2946	783	370	275	—	—
Breslau	22483	746	486	498	92	31
Liegnitz	2570	497	53	20	—	—
Pomerania	4806	882	1967	770	68	33
East Prussia	7071	603	1395	1256	389	64
Total	39876	3511	4271	2819	549	128
Percent	78.1	6.9	8.4	5.5	1.1	0.1
Central Germany						
Brandenburg	149283	375	1967	530	20	—
Prussian Saxony	6418	591	222	233	26	—
Saxony (*Land*)	15602	75	—	—	—	177
Total	171303	1041	2189	763	46	177
Percent	97.6	0.6	1.3	0.4	0.02	0.1

City	Over 20000	10000-19999	5000-9999	2000-4999	1000-1999	Under 1000
Central Germany II						
Mecklenburg	574*	317	172	333	34	—
Thuringian Principalities	1939*	753	342	207	321	351
Anhalt	1080*	88	67	59	30	—
Total	3593	1158	581	599	385	351
Percent	53.9	17.4	8.7	9.0	5.8	5.3
Northwestern Germany						
Schleswig-Holstein	2428	229	56	70	—	—
Oldenburg (Nord)	402*	—	338	58	—	—
Braunschweig	720*	321	447	90	—	—
Hamburg	19292*					
Bremen	1137*					
Lübeck		623*				
Hannover	9430	755	1261	1423	781	656
Schaumburg-Lippe	—	—	150	—	—	—
Lippe	—	250	286	112	59	32
Waldeck	—	—	—	252	168	22
Total	34032	1555	2538	2005	1008	710
Percent	82.3	3.7	6.1	4.8	2.4	1.7

City	Over 20000	10000–19999	5000–9999	2000–4999	1000–1999	Under 1000
Western Germany						
Ruhr and Northern Rhineland						
Düsseldorf	15727	1129	769	637	80	438
Cologne	13781	717	352	937	254	237
Arnsberg	4848	1675	381	546	368	42
Aachen	2220	88	180	408	82	353
Total	36576	3609	1682	2528	784	1070
Percent	79.1	7.8	3.6	5.5	1.7	2.3
Northern Westphalia						
Münster	1750	344	785	282	143	—
Minden	1862	65	684	1072	369	114
Total	3612	409	1469	1354	512	114
Percent	48.4	5.5	19.7	18.2	6.9	1.5
Southern Rhineland						
Koblenz	1770	519	500	875	958	1110
Trier	1900	400	869	806	838	2063
Birkenfeld	20*	99	56	60	228	76
Total	3690	1018	1425	1741	2024	3249
Percent	28.1	7.7	10.8	13.2	15.4	24.7
Hesse						

City	Over 20000	10000–19999	5000–9999	2000–4999	1000–1999	Under 1000
Wiesbaden	27786	1052	470	1698	770	465
Pecent	86.2	3.3	1.5	5.3	2.4	1.4
Kassel	4972	641	1004	2812	4123	3480
Starkenberg	4359	40	1652	1932	1228	408
Upper Hesse	1035	400	203	1032	1907	1566
Rhine Hesse	4207	650	521	1088	892	304
Total	14573	1731	3380	6864	8150	5758
Percent	36.0	4.3	8.4	17.0	20.2	14.2
South Germany						
Baden	12007	2054	1153	4093	3122	1835
Württemberg	6700	131	1032	1122	1319	1135
Hohenzollern	—	—	—	138	270	—
Total	18707	2185	2185	5353	4711	2988
Percent	51.8	6.1	6.1	14.8	13.0	8.3
Alsace-Lorraine	11180	2762	2282	5215	5242	4451
Percent	35.9	8.9	7.3	16.8	16.8	14.3
Upper Bavaria	10583	—	—	—	—	—
Lower Bavaria	161	47	—	—	—	—
Total	10744	47	—	—	—	—
Percent	99.6	0.4	—	—	—	—

City	Over 20000	10000–19999	5000–9999	2000–4999	1000–1999	Under 1000
Upper Palatinate	659	150	200	128	—	167
Upper Franconia	1647	42	309	—	221	558
Total	2306	192	509	128	221	725
Percent	56.5	4.7	12.5	3.1	5.4	17.8
Middle Franconia	9961	344	296	642	626	880
Percent	78.1	2.7	2.3	5.0	4.9	6.9
Rhenish Palatinate	2700	1454	700	1448	1661	890
Lower Franconia	3780	—	450	2383	1930	3379
Swabia	1171	200	400	815	305	346
Total	7651	1654	1550	4646	3896	4615
Percent	31.9	6.9	6.5	19.4	16.6	19.2
All Germany	419855	28002	35870	46218	31102	26020
Percent	71.5	4.8	6.1	7.9	5.3	4.4

Source: *Handbuch der jüdischen Gemeindeverwaltung* (1911).
* Supplemented by Schmelz, Territorial Printout, 1910.

Table 9.29. Proportion of Jewish Population in Small Towns in Selected Areas near River Main, 1925

Region	Total Jewish population	Jews in towns under 20,000	Percent
Koblenz	6674 [6171]	[5965] 4523	89.4
Trier	3023	2221	73.5
Kassel	[15021] 15498	10673	68.9
Lower Franconia	9879	6561	66.4
Hesse-Darmstadt	20401	12124	59.4
Rhenish Palatinate	7850	4326	55.1
Baden	24064	9095	37.8
Württemberg	10827	3878	35.8
Total	97713	53401	54.7%

Source: based on Schmelz, Territorial Printout. Alternative figures are given by Silbergleit, *Die Bevölkerungs- und Berufsverhältnisse*, 27*, 32*–33*.

communities with 250 or more Jews in 1828.[33] By 1886, only three of these towns (Laupheim, Buttenhausen, and Rexingen) retained Jewish populations of over 250 and two others (Oberdorf and Buchau) had 200–249. Of the remainder, two had 100–120 Jewish inhabitants, two had 50–100, and information on the other two is unavailable. Once a very substantial community, all the Jews of Jebenhausen left the village before 1900, some to America and others to the industrial town of Göppingen just a few miles away.[34] In a few cases, village Jewish communities were swallowed up by the geographical expansion of nearby cities.[35] Between 1886 and 1925, the eleven Württtemberg towns that had once had over 250 Jewish inhabitants continued to develop in contrasting directions.

---

33 Laupheim 556, Buchau 532, Oberdorf (and Bopfingen) 453, Mühringen 417, Jebenhausen 410, Freudenthal (and Zaberfeld, Bietigheim, and Mühlacker) 348, Rexingen 337, Affaltrach (and Eschenau) 310, Aufhausen 265, Nordstetten 265, and Buttenhausen 263.
34 Several other Jewish communities located just outside larger towns that had formerly excluded Jews showed similar patterns. When a larger town or city was opened to Jews, those in nearby villages quickly moved there. Examples are the migrations of Jews from Steinheim to Schwäbisch Hall; from Horkheim, Talheim, and Sontheim to Heilbronn; from Dreissigacker and Waldorf to Meiningen; from Kriegshaber, Pfersee, and Steppach to Augsburg; from Fellheim to Memmingen; and from Moisling to Lübeck.
35 Bockenheim and Bornheim near Frankfurt, Biebrich near Wiesbaden, and Heidingsfeld near Würzburg, not to speak of the suburban communities around Berlin (Charlottenburg, Schöneberg, Wilmersdorf, Neukölln, and Spandau).

In three of them, the Jewish population fell to below fifteen, much too few for a viable community. Three survived as small communities with 30–99 Jews while five maintained substantial Jewish populations of over 100.[36] Two communities that retained substantial Jewish populations—Buchau and Laupheim—were small cities relatively far from any other Jewish collective. The largest surviving community, however, was in Rexingen, a small village of under 1,000 inhabitants in Horb County. Only a few miles from Rexingen, the community of Nordstetten dwindled from 265 in 1828 to eleven in 1925, that of Mühlen sank from 106 to ten, and the former seat of the county rabbinate, Mühringen, declined from 417 to fifty-nine. Apart from the new community of 109 in the county seat, Baisingen was the only other community in Horb County that remained relatively large. It retained 104 Jews in 1925 as against the 210 who had lived there in 1828. Why the different communities in the same isolated Black Forest County met such different fates awaits further analysis. Altogether, Horb County, which was the only county in the entire Schwarzwaldkreis that had a substantial Jewish population, lost about 57.75 percent its Jewish population between 1828 and 1925 (from about 1,420 to about 600). The population decline left only four viable Jewish communities in 1925 instead of the six that had existed a century earlier. Similar thinning processes (the disappearance of some communities and the survival of others) took place in other parts of southern and western Germany as well. Like the largest rural Jewish communities, smaller ones also had different patterns of survival or disappearance. Having begun the process with smaller numbers, however, they had a greater chance of disappearance than the large communities (Table 9.30).

Although most surviving small-town Jewish communities in and after 1925 were remarkably small, several large communities in this class countered the general trend and were well known as exceptions to the rule in early twentieth-century Germany. Approximately ten percent of Jews in towns of under 10,000 inhabitants lived in such communities; most of the rest were scattered among small communities of 30–100 souls (Table 9.31).

Just as urbanization had uneven effects on the loss or shrinkage of rural Jewish communities, those in large cities grew at widely differing rates. Although German Jewry was disproportionately urban by the turn of the twentieth century, the size of urban communities did not necessarily correlate with that of the city itself. Berlin was both the largest city in Germany and the home of the largest Jewish community. In many ways, its position was much

---

36 Rexingen 307, Laupheim 255, Buchau 240, Oberdorf-Bopfingen 137, Buttenhausen 133, Freudenthal 73, Mühringen 59, Affaltrach 30, Nordstetten 11, Aufhausen 9, and Jebenhausen 5.

Table 9.30. Patterns of Population Loss among Village Jewish Communities in Württemberg, 1828–1925*

Population Size	Size in 1828	Size in 1925				
		0–19	20–49	50–99	100–149	150+
Over 250	10	3	1	2	2	3
150–249	10	4	2	2	2	—
100–149	18	9	4	3	—	2
50–99	15	10	3	2	—	—
20–50	12	10	1	1	—	—

* Communities in cities of over 20,000 inhabitants are excluded.

Source: "Die Statistik der jüdischen Geminden Württembergs 1831–1931," *Gemeindezeitung für die israelitischen Gemeinden Württembergs* (December 1, 1931): 194–195.

mightier among Jewish communities than among German cities as a whole. In 1925, its 172,672 Jews were 30.6 percent of all German Jews in Germany and 44.2 percent of all German Jews in cities of over 100,000 inhabitants, while the city's general population was only 6.5 percent of the population of Germany and 21.4 percent of all inhabitants of cities over 100,000.[37] German cities that ranked from second to tenth in overall population showed large discrepancies between their Jewish and general populations. Frankfurt am Main, which was ninth in population among German cities (540,115), ranked second among Jews (29,658) and had the highest percentage of Jews of any major German city (5.5 percent). The Ruhr cities of Essen and Dortmund, which ranked sixth and tenth among German cities, had relatively small Jewish populations (4,504 and 4,424, respectively). Breslau, which was eighth in general population, had more Jews than Hamburg, the country's second-largest city overall. The Jewish density of cities with more than 100,000 inhabitants ranged from 0.2 percent in Solingen to 5.5 percent in Frankfurt.

Jewish migration to cities was not primarily motivated by the size of the city, but rather by the types of opportunities that it offered. Jews were more likely to move to old cities than to new ones; they were particularly sparse in the newer industrial cities of the Ruhr basin that had grown from villages in the late

---

[37] Although historians often emphasize the predominance of the Berlin Jewish community in twentieth-century Germany, it was not nearly as overwhelming as the concentration of Jews in a single major city in Great Britain (London), France (Paris), the Netherlands (Amsterdam), or even the United States (New York City).

Table 9.31. Small-Town Communities (under 10,000) with Jewish Populations Exceeding 150 in 1911 (not including Alsace-Lorraine)

Province	1911 Combined Jewish population		1925 Combined Jewish population	
Posen*	(36 towns)	9745	(1 town) (32 towns no longer in Germany)	403
Bavaria	(15 towns east of Rhine)	3998	(9 towns)	2122
Rhine Palatinate	(5 towns)	1026	(2 towns)	404
West Prussia*	(17 towns)	4544	(3 towns) (11 towns no longer in Germany)	706
Hesse-Nassau	(22 towns) (including Waldeck)	4187	(8 towns)	1589
Baden	(16 towns)	3867	(7 towns)	1655
Württemberg	(11 towns)	2693	(7? towns)	1452
Hesse-Darmstadt	(10 towns)	1953	(5 towns)	1079
Rhineland	(9 towns)	1780	(2 towns) (3 towns no longer in Germany: Saar)	431
Silesia	(8 towns)	1450		
Hannover	(4 towns)	969	(2 towns)	629

Province	1911		1925	
	Combined Jewish population		Combined Jewish population	
Pomerania	627	(3 towns)		
Westphalia	557	(3 towns)	150	(1 town)
East Prussia	490	(3 towns)	195	(1 town)
Prussian Saxony	326	(2 towns)		
One town each:				
Braunschweig	274			
Hohenzollern	270		213	
Oldenburg	250			
Brandenburg	167			
Lippe	150			
Total	39323	(169 towns)	11028	(60 towns)

Source: based on *Handbuch der jüdischen Gemeindeverwaltung und Wohlfahrtspflege* (1911); and ibid. (1924/1925).

Table 9.32. Jewish Population of Cities in Regierungsbezirke Arnsberg and Düsseldorf

Old cities (with over 20,000 inhabitants in 1852)			New cities (less than 20,000 in 1852)		
	1925	1933		1925	1933
Düsseldorf	5130 (1.1%)	[5053]	Essen	4209 (0.9%)	[4506]
Dortmund	3820 (1.2%)	[4108]	Duisburg	2080 (0.8%)	[2560]
Wuppertal* 3056	(0.9%)	[2471]	Gelsenkirchen	1441 (0.7%)	[1615]
Krefeld*	1626 (1.2%)	[1481]	Bochum	1122 (0.5%)	[1069]
Total	13632 (1.1%)	[13112]	Mönchen-Gladbach	951 (0.8%)	[907]
			Mülheim an der Ruhr	626 (0.5%)	[517]
			Hagen	580 (0.6%)	[508]
			Oberhausen	513 (0.5%)	[525]
			Remscheid*	229 (0.3%)	[273]
			Solingen	210 (0.2%)	[217]
			Total	11961 (0.7%)	[12697]

Sources: 1925 data is from Silbergleit, *Die Bevölkerungs- und Berufsverhältnisse*, 31*–32*; 1933 data is from 1933 census, 3/32–33. The 1933 census also has comparative figures for 1925, which all differ from and are usually a little higher than the Silbergleit figures, presumably because the cities annexed territories between 1925 and 1933. The 1925 census figures in *Statistik des deutschen Reichs* 401 (1930): *Die Bevölkerung des Deutschen Reichs nach den Ergebnissen der Volkszählung 1925*, part 2: *Textliche Darstellung der Ergebnisse*, 620–621, agree with Silbergleit.

nineteenth and early twentieth centuries (Table 9.32). Jews were particularly numerous in towns that had had traditionally large Jewish communities before the mid-nineteenth century, such as Frankfurt am Main, Breslau, Hamburg, Mannheim, Altona, and Mainz (Table 9.33). Despite all the migrations of the nineteenth and twentieth centuries, the forces of inertia and tradition made many cities with a long Jewish past remain attractive to Jewish migrants. There were, however, some exceptional large Jewish communities in cities that had severely limited Jewish settlement before the Emancipation, including Leipzig, Munich, Cologne, Nuremberg, Stuttgart, and Würzburg. Many of these cities were commercial and banking centers that also had universities; some were administrative capitals as well. Several of these large new communities, such as those in Nuremberg, Stuttgart, and Würzburg, had had densely populated hinterlands of small-town Jewish communities. Those that lacked such hinterlands often became important magnets for East European immigration (Tables 9.34 and 9.35)

Table 9.33. Jewish Population of Cities with Traditionally Large Jewish Populations—1925

City	Jewish Population
Frankfurt/Main	29,658 (5.5%)
Breslau	23,452 (3.9%)
Hamburg	19,794 (1.8%)
Mannheim	6,985 (2.7%)
Mainz	2,835 (2.2%)
Altona	2,650 (1.2%)

Source: 1933 census, 3/32–33.

Table 9.34. Large Jewish Communities in Formerly Restricted Cities—1925

City	Jewish population 1925	(1871)	1925/1871	Jewish density	Percent of Jewish foreign-born or with foreign citizenship (1933)
Leipzig	12594	(1739)	7.24	1.8%	73.1%
Cologne	16093	(3172)	5.07	2.3	31.5
Munich	10068	(2903)	3.47	1.5	26.7
Stuttgart	4548	(1817)	2.50	1.2	18.2
Nuremberg	8603	(1831)	4.70	2.2	13.9
Würzburg	2261	(1518)	1.49	2.5	10.3

Sources: Schmelz, Territorial Printout; *Statistik des deutscher. Reichs* 401 (1930): *Die Bevölkerung des Deutschen Reichs nach den Ergebnissen der Volkszählung 1925*, part 2: *Textliche Darstellung der Ergebnisse*, 620–621; 1933 census, 5/10, 15; *Pinkas ha-Kehillot, Germania, Bavaria*, 8, 474. The 1933 census 3/32–33 gives slightly higher figures for 1925 probably as the result of territorial growth of some cities between 1925 and 1933.

Table 9.35. Jews in Various Districts in Towns of under 10,000 Inhabitants—1939 Census (*Glaubensjuden*)

Region	All Jews by religion	Jews in towns of under 10,000	Percent of Jews in towns of under 10,000
East Prussia	3004	630	21.0%
Berlin	77850	0	0
Brandenburg	3586	1522	42.4
Pomerania	3254	1080	33.2
Silesia	16336	1043	6.4
(Prussian) Saxony	2420	355	14.7
Schleswig-Holstein	586	104	17.8
Braunschweig	409	128	31.2
Oldenburg	330	108	32.7
Bremen	625	2	0.3
Anhalt	346	37	10.7
Saxony (State)	6920	149	2.2
Thuringia	1714	350	20.4
Hamburg	8359	0	0
Mecklenburg	270	62	23.0
Northern and eastern Germany	126009	5570	4.4
Hannover	5413	1738	32.1
Westphalia	7534	2189	29.1
Rhine Province	23611	4199	17.8
Lippe	224	115	51.3
Schaumburg-Lippe	116	116	100
Northwestern and western Germany	36898	8357	22.7
Hesse-Nassau	20554	3206	15.6
RB Kassel	4292	2081	48.5
RB Wiesbaden	16262	1125	6.9
Hohenzollern	184	184	100
Bavaria	16231	3685	22.2
Upper Bavaria	4823	104	2.2

Region	All Jews by religion	Jews in towns of under 10,000	Percent of Jews in towns of under 10,000
Lower Bavaria and Upper Palatinate	535	108	20.2
Rhenish Palatinate	1723	884	51.3
Upper Franconia and Middle Franconia	4413	351	8.0
Lower Franconia	3417	1680	49.2
Swabia	1320	558	42.3
Württemberg	**4447**	**1272**	**28.6**
Baden	**8886**	**2377**	**26.8**
Konstanz	559	343	61.4
Freiburg	1508	783	51.9
Karlsruhe	2403	374	15.6
Mannheim	4416	877	19.9
Hesse	**5801**	**1879**	**32.4**
Rhenish Hesse	2334	296	12.7
Starkenburg	2150	715	33.3
Upper Hesse	1315	937	71.3
Southern Germany	**56103**	**12603**	**22.5**
Entire *Altreich*	**213789**	**26530**	**12.4**
Percent of total in northern and eastern Germany	58.9	21.0	
In northwestern and western Germany	17.3	31.5	
In southern Germany	26.2	47.5	

Source: *Statistik des Deutschen Reichs* 552, no. 4 (1944): 10–35.

10

Jewish Residential Concentration in German Cities

German Jews tended to live near each other within each major city and in many smaller towns as well. While Jewish residential concentration had been required by law in certain places, it was also clearly noticeable in cities that lacked legal restrictions and persisted in formerly ghettoized cities long after the abolition of the legal ghetto or *Judengasse* itself. Walled ghettos seem to have been most common along the middle Rhine in cities like Frankfurt, Koblenz, Mainz, Worms, and Bonn. In other cities, Jews were restricted to certain streets or excluded from certain neighborhoods in the absence of a walled ghetto and total residential segregation. Still other major cities, notably Berlin and Mannheim, do not seem to have had any official restrictions on where Jews could live.

In some small towns and villages, Jews lived scattered among the other inhabitants with little concentration. In others, Jews were barred from certain streets (as in Ichenhausen) or confined to a separate Jewish quarter (as in Jebenhausen, Hechingen, and Fellheim). Sometimes they were even restricted to parts of old castles or to other buildings belonging to minor noblemen, as in the Württemberg villages of Talheim and Sontheim and the Lower Franconian village of Gaukönigshofen. In some south German villages, Jewish families inhabited multiple dwellings that could hold up to fourteen families.[1] The attenuation of Jewish segregation in villages and overcrowding in the course of the nineteenth century followed two main patterns. In the first, which was found mainly in villages that retained a substantial proportion of their Jewish populations, Jews bought houses from Christians or built new ones in areas outside the traditional Jewish quarters. The second pattern was in communities in which most Jews left the village. Here Jews rarely bought houses from Christians, although some built new homes in the "Jewish quarter." Christians gradually moved into Jewish dwellings as the Jewish population declined.[2]

Although legally restricted ghettos disappeared in most of Germany by 1815, Jews did not automatically leave their old Jewish quarters. In the few cities for which we have accurate data from the early nineteenth century, Jewish residential concentration remained extremely high. In Frankfurt, where the ghetto was damaged in the French attack of 1796 and the last restrictions on Jewish residence in parts of the city were abolished in 1824, 84.7 percent of the Jews still lived in the immediate vicinity of the ghetto in 1823. In 1817, the index of dissimilarity between the Jewish and general population was .651, indicating that 65.1 percent of the Jewish population would have to move for the Jewish and general distribution within the city to be identical. The index fell to .417 in 1858, which was still rather high. Newcomers to the city (*Fremde*) were more likely to live in or near the old ghetto than were more longstanding residents[3] (Table 10.1).

While Berlin never had a ghetto *de jure*, Berlin Jews in the pre-Emancipation period were highly segregated *de facto*. In 1777, 3,000–3,500 Berlin Jews lived in the Alt Berlin section among a total civil population of about 22,000. In 1812, 286 (81.7 percent) of the 350 Jewish taxpayers in the city lived in districts 1–4, which roughly corresponded to the Alt Berlin area of the city's twenty-four police districts. The dissimilarity index in Berlin (.643 in 1809) was almost identical to that in Frankfurt.[4] In Mannheim, which also had never imposed segregation *de*

---

1 Steven M. Lowenstein, "Changing Housing Conditions in the Nineteenth-Century German Rural Ghetto," in *Jüdische Welten: Juden in Deutschland vom 18. Jahrhundert bis in die Gegenwart*, ed. Marion Kaplan and Beate Meyer (Göttingen: Wallstein, 2005), 33–36.
2 Lowenstein, "Changing Housing Conditions," 38–40.
3 Lowenstein, *Mechanics*, 157–159.
4 Lowenstein, *Berlin Jewish Community*, 12–13, 16, 19, 199, note 8, 202, note 37, quoting Friedrich Nicolai, *Beschreibung der königlichen Residenzstädte Berlin und Potsdam* (Berlin: Nicolai, 1786), 232, 240. Nicolai reports 122,667 inhabitants in the city of Berlin in 1764. In 1777, the (Alt) Berlin section of the city was listed as having 22,017 civilian inhabitants. In 1809, 78 percent of the 288 Jews registering for citizenship there lived in Alt Berlin, where only about 18 percent of the overall population of Berlin dwelled.

Table 10.1. Changing Jewish Neighborhood Patterns in Frankfurt, 1817–1858

Neighborhood	1817		1823		1858	
	Number	Percent of district population	Number	Percent of district population	Number	Percent of district population
A	2199 (621)	48.3	2297 (677)	47.9	1740 (834)	32.6
B	1745 (591)	30.7	1542 (394)	26.5	749 (296)	12.4
Judenquartier					875 (494)	47.8
C	116	3.6	126 (36)	3.8	395 (153)	7.4
D	15	0.5	4 (2)	0.1	311 (92)	6.8
E	2	0.0	6 (1)	0.1	116 (50)	1.8
F	0	—	0	—	50 (29)	1.9
G	38	1.8	45 (11)	2.1	173 (70)	6.7
H	144	7.3	301 (102)	15.0	417 (145)	18.2
I	7 (2)	0.2	17 (5)	0.5	35 (16)	0.9
K	64 (24)	3.3	66 (18)	3.8	126 (41)	6.4
L	68	3.4	94 (30)	4.2	123 (58)	4.7
M	4	0.2	18 (6)	1.0	51 (39)	1.9
N and O (Sachsenhausen)	0	—	2 (1)	0.0	1 (1)	0.0

Frankfurter Gemarkung					566 (180)	7.9
Sachsenhäuser Gemarkung				2	(1)	0.2
Gemarkungen combined	9	0.8	11 (4)	0.7	568 (181)	9.0
All Frankfurt	4411 (1238)	10.6	4530 (1288)	10.3	5730 (2490)	9.0
Percent of all Frankfurt Jews living in:						
A, B, and Judenquartier	89.4	(98.1)	84.8	(82.4)	58.7	(65.2)
In Gemarkung	0.2		0.2	(0.3)	9.9	(7.3)

In parentheses: number of *Fremde* (foreigners) among the Jews.

The censuses of 1817, 1823, and 1858 divided Frankfurt into fourteen districts, each assigned a letter. In addition, the *Gemarkung* (the region beyond the Neustadt) was counted with separate numbers for the Frankfurt (north bank of the Main) and Sachsenhausen (south bank) *Gemarkungen*. In the 1858 census, the old Judengasse was counted separately as the *Judenquartier*. Districts A and B bordered on the Judengasse on the west and east, respectively.

Sources: *Beiträge zur Statistik der Freien Stadt Frankfurt* 1, no. 1 (1858): 4–5; ibid. 1, no. 3 (1861): XXXI–XXXIII.

jure, an 1836 list of all Jews in the city showed that two-thirds lived in three of the city's twenty rows of blocks (*Quadrate* E, F, and G) not far from the main synagogue. There were clear differences among Jewish social classes; those of the upper classes were more likely than poorer Jews to live in the Oberstadt near the ducal palace and outside the chief Jewish quarter[5] (Table 10.2).

It is possible to trace the changes in Jewish population distribution within major cities in detail beginning around the time of the German unification in 1871. From then until the 1930s, data are available from a growing number of cities—mainly Frankfurt, Berlin, and Hamburg at first, but also Munich, Leipzig, Cologne, and others later on. There were three main patterns of Jewish distribution as cities and their Jewish populations expanded. In the first, the Jewish area of concentration moved almost entirely from the older center in the inner city to a new Jewish neighborhood in newer and more prosperous parts of the city. This pattern is most conspicuous in cities that had small immigrant populations and a relatively large number of Jewish residents born in the city, most prominently in Hamburg. The second and probably most common pattern among large cities involved the bifurcation of the Jewish population. A Jewish neighborhood in or near the historical Jewish population center survived while a new Jewish agglomeration developed in a more prosperous area that was usually farther from the city center. This was the pattern in Berlin, Frankfurt, and other cities. The longer-established part of the Jewish population usually moved to the new neighborhood while newcomers, including immigrants from Eastern Europe, settled in the older Jewish area. In some cases,[6] following a special type of the "two neighborhoods" pattern (discussed at the end of this chapter), a nearby smaller city became the center of a more proletarian immigrant Jewish population while the main city housed more prosperous

TABLE 10.2. Difference in Jewish Geographical Location by Class—Mannheim, 1836

Location	Upper class	Upper-middle	Lower-middle	Lower class
Oberstadt	52.0%	27.9%	13.9%	8.2%
Unterstadt	48.0	72.1	86.1	91.8

Source: Bayer, *Minderheit im städtischen Raum*, 48–52.

---

5 Tilde Bayer, *Minderheit im städtischen Raum. Sozialgeschichte der Juden in Mannheim während der 1. Hälfte des 19. Jahrhunderts* (Stuttgart: Thorbecke, 2001), 48–52.
6 For instance, Altona and Hamburg, Ludwigshafen and Mannheim, Offenbach and Frankfurt.

Jewish inhabitants. There was sometimes a third pattern in Jewish communities that had a very heavy immigrant presence, in which the old Jewish area remained the main Jewish neighborhood, and Jewish settlement elsewhere in the city was sparser. The best example of this type of settlement pattern was in Leipzig. In each city, of course, matters developed somewhat differently due to factors peculiar to the city. Some communities displayed features that lay between the main three patterns. Except in relatively small cities like Heidelberg, there were few examples in which Jewish residential concentration was not substantially greater than that of Christian religious minorities (Catholics in Protestant cities and vice versa).

Pattern I: Abandonment of the Old Neighborhood

Hamburg

In eighteenth-century Hamburg, Jews were legally restricted to thirteen streets and a marketplace in the Neustadt along with three streets in the Altstadt. While none of these streets had an exclusively Jewish population, Jews were not permitted to live anywhere else in the city.[7]

The Hamburg Jewish community grew much slower than the overall population of the city, and the Jewish percentage of the Hamburg population declined. Around the time of German unification, the vast majority of Hamburg Jews still lived in the Neustadt, where they had concentrated for over a century. The 1866 census showed that Jews were 21.5 percent of the population in the fifth tax district (probably a section of the Neustadt) as against 4.5 percent in the city at large (Table 10.3). The 1871 census found that 8,323 (60.3 percent) of the 13,796 Jews in the city lived in the Neustadt, 5,462 of them in the northern half of the district, where they accounted for 11.9 percent of the population. In 1871, outside of the Neustadt area, Jews were moving west into St. Pauli (1,522 or 3.8 percent of the population), which bordered Altona, and north to the wealthy area west of the Alster (1,533 or 7.4 percent).[8] The Jewish population of Neustadt Nord actually increased to 6,100 in 1880 but then began a slow

---

7 Jürgen Ellermeyer, "Schranken der Freien Reichsstadt: Gegen Grundeigentum und Wohnungswahl der Hamburger Juden bis ins Zeitalter der Aufklärung," in *Die Hamburger Juden in der Emanzipationsphase (1780–1870)*, ed. Peter Freimark and Arno Herzig (Hamburg: H. Christians, 1989), 174, 194.
8 This already represented some change from the 1866 census, which unfortunately was based on a different division of the city. That year, only 1,196 Jews lived in the *Vorstädte* (possibly

Table 10.3. Neighborhood Patterns in Hamburg, 1866

District	General	Jewish (German and Portuguese)		Catholic	
Tax Districts					
Innere Stadt					
1	25069	376	(1.5%)	547	(2.2%)
2	28424	399	(1.4)	551	(1.9)
3	21862	1593	(7.3)	416	(1.9)
4	25675	541	(2.1)	538	(2.1)
5	20881	4488	(21.5)	607	(2.9)
6	33462	2760	(8.3)	974	(2.9)
Vorstädte					
7	30379	297	(1.0)	533	(1.8)
8	29141	899	(3.1)	612	(2.1)
Geestlande	41035	1122	(2.7)	544	(1.3)
Marschlande	20016	11	(0.05)	78	(0.4)
Ritzebüttel	6112	64	(1.1)	13	(0.2)
Total	282056	12550	(4.5)	5413	(1.9)

Dissimilarity index, percent

General/Jewish	General/Catholic	Catholic/Jewish
43.2	13.1	34.3

Source: *Ergebnisse der Volkszählung vom 3ten December 1866: Stand der Bevölkerung* (Hamburg, 1867): 166–173.

decline to 5,173 in 1890 and a faster descent to 3,363 in 1900, by which time it was home to only 18.7 percent of the city's Jewish population and had a Jewish density of 6.9 percent. The Jewish population of the other central parts of the city (Neustadt Süd and Altstadt) fell even more rapidly between 1871 and 1900, from 4,417 to 1,855. When Jews left the Jewish neighborhood, they tended to move west or north. The Jewish population of St. Pauli peaked in 1890 (2,605) and then declined to 1,973 by 1900. In the Rotherbaum neighborhood just north

the later St. Georg and St. Pauli) and only 1,122 in the Geest areas outside of the main city (possibly the area north of the old city).

of Neustadt beyond the Dammtor, the Jewish population rose steadily from 1,763 (12.3 percent of the total) in 1880 to 5,115 in 1900. Jews moving north spilled into areas beyond Rotherbaum such as Harvestehude, Eppendorf, and Eimsbüttel (Table 10.4). East of the Altstadt in St. Georg, the Jewish population increased between 1871 and 1890 from 492 to 896, only to drop back to 777 by 1900. This was parallel to Jewish population developments in St. Pauli. Few Jews lived in any other part of the city, with only 1,006 of 17,949 in 1900 (Map 10/1).

These patterns continued in the twentieth century as well. The Jewish population of the old Jewish neighborhood of Neustadt Nord shrunk rapidly to 1,612 in 1910 and then to 812 in 1925. The other central neighborhoods retained only 921 Jews in 1910; 1,933 remained in St. Georg and St. Pauli combined (as against 2,750 in 1900). The Jewish population of Rotherbaum reached its peak in percentage in 1905 (18.6 percent) and in absolute numbers in 1910 (5,603). The neighborhoods farther north (Harvestehude and Eppendorf) increased even faster, from 2,853 in 1900 to 5,693 in 1910. By 1925, the Jewish density of Harvestehude exceeded that of Rotherbaum. The Jewish population of Eimsbüttel stagnated. In the rest of the city, the Jewish population increased from 1,006 in 1900 to 2,189 in 1910 but its share of the total population remained low (0.5 percent). Nearly all Jews in the old Jewish neighborhood moved to wealthier areas in the north, where they recreated something akin to the dense Jewish concentration that had existed in the old neighborhood. Paradoxically, Hamburg, which had the largest percentage of Jews born in the city and one of the highest intermarriage rates of any major German city, also had a higher degree of neighborhood segregation among Jews than most other cities.

Pattern II: The Two-Neighborhood Model

Frankfurt

Frankfurt's original ghetto was located on the border of the Altstadt and the Neustadt at the eastern end of the historic medieval city. The 1858 Frankfurt census still showed more than half of the Jewish population concentrated in the areas immediately bordering the old *Judengasse*, but later censuses reported an increasing spread from the area, leading eventually to a new concentration in the prestigious Westend[9] (Map 10/2, Tables 10.5 A and B). In 1895, the Ostend of

---

9   Unfortunately, most Frankfurt censuses between 1858 and 1895 did not give precise data on Jewish population in the various neighborhoods. The sparse details available showed only a

Table 10.4. Jewish Population in Hamburg Neighborhoods, 1871–1933

Neighborhood	1871	1880	1885	1890	1895	1900	1905	1910	1925	1933
Altstadt Nord	**816**	794	630	579	458	382	282	137	81	57
		1.9%				1.0	0.8	0.7	0.7	0.8
Altstadt Süd	**734**	626	497	338	179	141	121	60	38	30
		1.8				1.1	1.1	0.7	0.5	0.4
Neustadt Nord	**5,492**	**6,100**	5,764	5,173	4,057	3,363	2,479	1,612	812	527
		11.8				6.9	5.3	3.9	2.3	1.7
Neustadt Süd	**2,870**	2,501	2,320	1,856	1,474	1,332	1,120	724	522	408
		6.0				3.2	3.1	2.3	1.7	1.5
Inner City	9,912	**10,021**	9,211	7,946	6,168	5,218	4,002	2,533	1,453	1,022
St. Pauli (west of Neustadt)	1,522	2,144	2,414	**2,605**	2,332	1,973	1,539	1,232	814	597
		3.8				2.6		1.6		0.9
St. Georg (east of Altstadt)	492	720	764	**896**	849	777	882	761	618	407
		1.2				0.8		0.7		0.4
St. Georg and St. Pauli	2,014	2,864	3,178	**3,501**	3,181	2,750	2,421	1,993	1,432	1,004
Rotherbaum (north of Neustadt)		1,763	2,768	3,190	4,178	5,115	5,463	**5,603**	4,759	3,586
		12.3				17.7	18.6	17.9	15.2	12.1
Harvestehude		482	834	1,347	1,884	2,512	3,266	3,950	**4,681**	3,722

Jewish Residential Concentration in German Cities | 459

Area									
(north of Rotherbaum)				8.4	13.9	15.6	15.7	15.9	12.9
Eppendorf	19	47	125	144	341	931	1,743	**3,044**	2,691
(north of Harvestehude)	0.4				2.4	1.9	2.4	3.6	3.2
Eimsbüttel	392	538	878	763	855	1,189	1,281	**1,334**	1,221
(west of Rotherbaum)	2.4				1.3	1.5	1.1	1.0	1.0
Northern areas	2,656	4,187	5,540	6,969	8,823	10,849	12,577	**13,818**	11,220
Rest of city				798	1,006	2,153	2,189	3,091	**3,639**
Total	11,954	12,915	17,785	17,797	19,425	19,292	19,794	**19,794**	16,885
					2.4	1.5	2.1	1.7	1.5

Rotherbaum, Harvestehude and Eppendorf were wealthy neighborhoods. Harvestehude was the wealthiest area in the city, and Eimsbüttel was relatively poor.

Sources: *Statistik des Hamburgischen Staats* (1873): 32, (1880): 149, (1887): 92–99, (1894): 124–125, (1900): 51, (1902): 56–57, (1919): 56–57; Weigert, "Bevölkerung," 76–77; Helga Krohn, *Die Juden in Hamburg 1848–1918*, 81.

Table 10.5.

A) Jewish Population Distribution in Frankfurt, by Major Division, 1871–1880

District	1871	1875	1880
Altstadt	1827 (7.3%)	1734 (6.8%)	1647 (6.8%)
Neustadt	4535 (14.3)	4762 (14.9)	4355 (13.2)
Sachsenhausen	12 (0.1)	17 (0.2)	10 (0.1)
Bornheim	237 (1.5)		
Frankfurter Gemarkung	3622 (16.5)	5358 (17.7)	7594 (17.0)
Sachsenhäuser Gemarkung	13 (0.4)	16 (0.3)	13 (0.2)
Frankurt Total	10,009 (11.0)	11,887 (11.5)	13,856 (10.1)

Sources: *Beiträge zur Statistik der Stadt Frankfurt am Main* 2, no. 5 (1866–1874): 278; ibid. 3, no. 2 (1876–1880): 72; ibid. 4, no. 1 (1882–1885): 61.

B) Jewish Population Distribution in Frankfurt by Police District, 1890

Police District	Total population	Jewish Population	Percent Jewish
1	14,689	3028	20.6
2	15,530	1685	10.9
3	17,166	553	3.2
4	15,453	653	4.2
Total Inner City	62,838	5919	9.4
5 West and Northwest	15,821	2530	16.1
6 North	23,081	2646	11.4
7 East	19,027	4848	25.5
8 Sachsenhausen	24,401	60	0.2
9 Bornheim	23,145	522	2.3
10 Southwest	9,567	881	9.4
Military, etc.	2,140	20	1.0
Total Frankfurt	180,020	17,426	9.7

Source: *Beiträge zur Statistik der Stadt Frankfurt am Main* (1895): 132.

Frankfurt, the middle-class area immediately east of the old ghetto,[10] was home to 7,285 Jews, which represented 24.5 percent of the 29,766 inhabitants of that part of the city. Certain sections of the Ostend had particularly high Jewish concentrations (44.4 percent in District 14, 32.3 percent in District 8). By 1895, the Westend was just beginning to develop as a rival to the Ostend; its combined Jewish population that year[11] was 3,712 (17.0 percent of the neighborhood's total population). The highest concentration among the Westend districts was 22.0 percent in District 11. Together, the Ostend and Westend were home to 56.4 percent of Frankfurt's Jews and 22.5 percent of the total population of the city. There were 5,666 Jews (9.2 percent of the total population there)[12] in the northern and northeastern sections of the city between the Ostend and Westend.[13] In the rest of Frankfurt, which was home to half of the city's population, there were only 2,825 Jews (less than 15 percent of all Jews in Frankfurt). The 1900 census showed little change except a slow drift to more outlying districts (Table 10.6).[14] In 1925, the Ostend and Westend remained the chief areas of Jewish settlement in Frankfurt. The Westend grew somewhat faster than the Ostend, and within the Ostend there was a tendency to move to areas farther from the city center. Despite the shift toward the Westend, more Jews remained in the older Jewish neighborhood in the Ostend in absolute numbers than were in the the Westend in 1925. There was little increase in Jews' tendency to scatter throughout the city (Table 10.7).

There were significant social differences between the two main Jewish neighborhoods. The Ostend was a middle-class area that boasted several important Orthodox synagogues, schools, and other institutions. Although the immigrant Jewish population in Frankfurt was not very large (5,753 out of 29,385 in 1925, or 19.6 percent), many institutions that served East European immigrants were also located in the Ostend. The Westend, by contrast, was the wealthiest part of Frankfurt. It contained a large Liberal temple but few Orthodox institutions.[15]

---

steady move of Jews from the inner districts (especially the Neustadt) toward more outlying areas.
10 Östliche Neustadt and Östliche Aussenstadt: districts 7, 8, 14, 25, and 26.
11 Westliche and Nordwestliche Aussenstadt: districts 10, 11, 17, 18, and 19.
12 Excluding the far northern and northeastern areas of the city and including only the more centrally located districts 6, 12, and 13 (those closest to both the Ostend and Westend), we are left with 4,392 Jews out of a total population of 25,251 (17.4 percent of the total).
13 Districts 6, 12, 13, 20, 21, 22, 23, and 24.
14 The total Jewish population of Frankfurt increased by about 2,000, with upturns of 519 and 570 in the Westend and Ostend, respectively.
15 There was one small Orthodox house of worship in the Westend inside a building on the Unterlindaustrasse.

Table 10.6. Jewish Population of Frankfurt by District, 1890–1900

District	1890 (households)			1895 (individuals)			1900 (individuals)		
	Total	Jews	Percent Jewish	Total	Jews	Percent Jewish	Total	Jews	Percent Jewish
Altstadt									
1	2029	28	1.4	8540	103	1.2	8711	79	0.9
2	2100	101	4.8	9003	423	4.7	9734	482	5.0
3	1758	144	8.2	7635	593	7.8	8247	615	7.5
Total	5887	273	4.6	25178	1119	4.4	26692	1176	4.4
Westliche Neustadt									
4	736	60	8.2	3862	246	6.4	3976	225	5.7
5	1509	81	5.4	6119	333	5.4	6497	411	6.3
Total	2245	141	6.3	9981	579	5.8	10473	636	6.1
Nördliche Neustadt									
6	1991	184	9.2	8730	739	8.5	8424	689	8.2
Östliche Neustadt									
7	1566	216	13.8	8236	1370	16.6	8944	1658	18.5
8	1052	351	33.4	5517	1779	32.3	5817	1889	32.5
Total	2612	567	21.7	13753	3149	22.9	14761	3547	24.0

District	1890 (households)			1895 (individuals)			1900 (individuals)		
	Total	Jews	Percent Jewish	Total	Jews	Percent Jewish	Total	Jews	Percent Jewish
Westliche Aussenstadt									
10	1002	270	27.0	5371	805	15.0	5653	771	13.6
17	236	54	22.9	1896	317	16.7	3101	651	21.0
Total	1238	324	26.2	7267	1122	15.4	8754	1422	16.2
Nordwestliche Aussenstadt									
11	796	228	28.6	4072	894	22.0	4177	950	22.7
18	1028	246	23.9	6655	1313	15.4	6769	1467	21.7
19	662	56	8.5	3820	383	10.0	4140	389	9.4
Total	2486	530	21.3	14547	2590	17.8	15086	2806	18.6
Nördliche Aussenstadt									
12	1581	378	23.9	8172	1436	17.6	8828	1583	17.9
20	1581	111	7.0	8641	523	6.1	9008	467	5.2
21	1097	21	1.9	9336	101	1.1	11121	123	1.1
Total	4259	510	12.0	26149	2060	7.9	28957	2173	7.5
Nordöstliche Aussenstadt									
13	1642	443	27.0	8352	2217	26.5	8842	2514	28.4
22	87	0	0	1491	27	1.8	7424	196	2.6

District	1890 (households)			1895 (individuals)				1900 (individuals)		
	Total	Jews	Percent Jewish	Total	Jews	Percent Jewish		Total	Jews	Percent Jewish
23	2080	128	6.0	12261	601	4.9		12911	590	4.6
24	985	4	0.4	4932	22	0.5		5686	40	0.7
Total	4794	575	12.0	27036	2867	10.6		34863	3340	9.6
Östliche Aussenstadt										
14	1260	627	49.8	7786	3470	44.6		8287	3443	41.6
25	1184	67	5.7	6637	477	7.2		7246	647	8.9
26	211	34	16.1	1552	189	12.2		1825	224	12.3
Total	2655	728	27.4	15975	4136	25.9		17358	4314	24.9
Südwestliche Aussenstadt										
9	436	83	19.0	6994	531	7.6		10779	985	9.1
15	603	4	0.7	11325	82	0.7		17259	192	1.1
16	97	1	1.0	765	4	0.5		1722	10	0.6
Total	1136	88	7.7	19084	617	3.2		29760	1187	4.0
All other (27–39)										
27	1355	6	0.4	5858	20	0.3		6154	23	0.4
28	726	2	0.3	4171	12	0.3		4836	12	0.3
29	264	0	0	1046	0	0		1204	0	0

District	1890 (households)			1895 (individuals)			1900 (individuals)		
	Total	Jews	Percent Jewish	Total	Jews	Percent Jewish	Total	Jews	Percent Jewish
30	1126	1	0.1	4858	12	0.3	5125	9	0.2
31	1437	5	0.4	6674	15	0.2	6857	28	0.4
32	1434	7	0.5	10165	34	0.3	13615	81	0.6
33	1333	4	0.3	7681	12	0.2	10436	61	0.6
34				4585	98	2.1	6816	101	1.5
35				10673	218	2.0	11488	233	2.0
36				5713	89	1.6	6711	100	1.5
37							8877	7	0.1
38							8407	29	0.3
39							3098	0	0
Ships	165	0	0	237	0	0			
Total	7675	25	0.3	52562	510	1.0	93861	594	0.6

Source: *Beiträge zur Statistik der Stadt Frankfurt am Main*, neue Folge 1, no. 2 (1895): xxxii.

Table 10.7. Distribution of Jewish Population in Frankfurt—1895, 1900, and 1925

District	1895 Number (percent) Jewish	Change 1895–1900	1900 Number (percent) Jewish	1925 Number (percent) Jewish	Change 1900–1925
Östliche Neustadt	3149 (22.9)	+398	3547 (24.0)	2804 (19.6)	−743
Östliche Aussenstadt	4136 (25.8)	+178	4314 (24.9)	6384 (16.7)	+2070
Ostend combined	7285	+576	7861 (24.5)	9188 (17.5)	+1327
Westliche Aussenstadt	1122 (15.4)	+300	1422 (16.2)	2921 (21.9)	+1499
Nordwestliche Aussenstadt	2590 (17.8)	+216	2806 (18.6)	4410 (22.9)	+1604
Westend combined	3712	+516	4228 (17.7)	7331 (22.5)	+3103
Nördliche Neustadt	739 (8.5)	−50	689 (8.2)	521 (8.7)	−168
Nordöstliche Aussenstadt	2867 (10.6)	+473	3340 (9.6)	3671 (7.9)	+331
Nördliche Aussenstadt	2060 (7.9)	+113	2173 (7.5)	3723 (9.1)	+1550
North and Northeast (between Ostend and Westend)	5666	+536	6202 (8.6)	7915 (7.0)	+1713
Altstadt	1119 (4.4)	+57	1176 (4.4)	619 (2.7)	−557
Westliche Neustadt	579 (5.8)	+57	636 (6.1)	408 (4.7)	−228
Südwestliche Neustadt	617 (3.2)	+570	1187 (4.0)	1184 (1.9)	−3
Bornheim	32 (0.3)	+3	35 (0.3)	420 (1.6)	+385
Inneres Sachsenhausen	27 (0.2)	+10	37 (0.3)	99 (0.9)	+62
Äusseres Sachsenhausen	46 (0.3)	+96	142 (0.6)	870 (2.1)	+728
Bockenheim	405 (2.0)	+29	434 (1.7)	814 (1.8)	+380
Other areas	36 (0.1)	+501	537 (0.7)		
All other parts of Frankfurt	2825	+858	3683 (2.3)	4951 (1.7)	+1268
Frankfurt total	19,488 (8.5)	+2486	21,974 (7.6)	29,385 (6.3)	+7411

Sources: *Statistisches Jahrbuch der Stadt Frankfurt am Main 2: Statistik der Jahre 1906/07 bis 1926/27* (1928): 68–69.

Berlin

In Berlin, too, remnants of the pre-Emancipation neighborhood pattern endured, but toward the end of the nineteenth century it began to be replaced by a second neighborhood. The old patterns persisted in the 1860s and 1870s even though the the Berlin community's numerical growth exceeded that of the Jewish population of any other major German city (Map 10/3). In 1812, over 80 percent of the 3,500 or so Berlin Jews dwelled in the Alt Berlin neighborhood north of the Spree in the city center; elsewhere there were smaller clusters of Jews just to the northwest and to the south on the island of Kölln. In 1871, following the vigorous growth of the Jewish population, the Alt Berlin neighborhood had 5,941 Jewish inhabitants, about one-sixth of all Jews in the city and 18.5 percent of the neighborhood's population. As Berlin's Jewish population grew rapidly, the Jewish neighborhood expanded to the northwest (Spandauer Viertel) and the northeast (the nearest sections of Königstadt and Stralauer Viertel). The Spandauer Viertel, centered around Oranienburgerstrasse, already had more Jews (8,882) in 1871 than did Alt Berlin, albeit with a lower Jewish density (12.3 percent of the population). Another 6,697 Jews lived in Königstadt and Stralauer Viertel West in 1871. Concentration of Jews was somewhat lower (3,826 or about six percent of the total population) in central Berlin neighborhoods to the immediate south, southwest, and southeast of Alt Berlin (Alt Kölln, Friedrichswerder, Dorotheenstadt, and Neukölln).[16] Areas of the city farther west accommodated only 5,000 Jews, with a density of about 3 percent. In the southeast, a Jewish neighborhood began forming in the westernmost part of Luisenstadt, where 2,805 Jews had settled by 1871. Few Jews lived in the outermost areas of the northwest, south, southeast, and northeast of the city.

With the development of public transportation during the *Kaiserreich* period, Berlin expanded in all directions and the population in the city center began to decline. Thus, the total population of the central neighborhoods of Alt Berlin, Alt Kölln, Friedrichswerder, and Dorotheenstadt decreased from 78,374 in 1871 to 40,793 in 1905 and the Jewish population dropped by an even larger margin from 9,219 to 3,299. In the Spandauer Viertel, where the general population remained steady, the Jewish population doubled to 14,145 in 1890 and then continued to increase slowly to 15,228 in 1905. The Spandauer Viertel was now Berlin's chief Jewish neighborhood, with a Jewish density of 21.0 percent. Areas immediately abutting the Spandauer Viertel to the north, northeast, and east (Rosenthaler Viertel Süd, Königsviertel, and Stralauer Viertel West)

---

16 Not to be confused with the later district of Neukölln, which was then called Rixdorf.

also became densely Jewish as the population spilled beyond the Spandauer Viertel's borders. The combined Jewish populations in these quarters grew from approximately 7,250 in 1871 to 32,606 in 1905, bringing the Jewish density to 9.2 percent. Although the Jewish area in north-central Berlin[17] grew in absolute numbers throughout the *Kaiserreich* era, it did not keep pace with the overall growth of Berlin Jewry, and sank from almost 60 percent of all Berlin Jews in 1871 to about 40 percent in 1905.

Berlin began to develop a second major center of Jewish population in its western sector during the *Kaiserreich* era. The massive move to the west that brought this about this expansion was hardly evident in 1871. That year, areas just south and west of the central city had a much larger Jewish population than the neighborhoods on the western border of the city near the Tiergarten. The Friedrichstadt area, south of Unter den Linden in the "near west," experienced a decline in general population but an increase in Jewish population between 1871 and 1890 (from 3,277 to 6,254). Thereafter, its Jewish population receded at about the same rate as the general population, to 4,836 in 1905. Areas farthest west, however, showed more explosive growth, increasing from 1,719 Jews in 1871 to 8,774 (8.6 percent) in 1890, and continued to grow rapidly thereafter to 13,232 (17.9 percent) in 1905. Jewish density was high in the area south of the Tiergarten (Friedrich und Schöneberger Vorstadt) but not as spectacularly so as in the Hansaviertel (Tiergarten Vorstadt) northwest of the park. In that small area, where only 359 Jews had lived in 1880, the Jewish population jumped to 1,208 (11.7 percent) in 1890, 3,138 in 1895 (17.3 percent), and 4,581 (21.2 percent) in 1905 (Table 10.8). As Berlin grew, its Jewish population spilled over the western borders of the city into the suburbs outside of the city boundaries (Charlottenburg, Schöneberg, and Wilmersdorf). By the early twentieth century, these suburbs had become completely contiguous to the city proper and in 1920 they were incorporated into Greater Berlin. In 1890, Charlottenburg had 1,475 Jews and Schöneberg 611; Wilmersdorf, still a small village, had few Jews. By 1905, the combined Jewish population of the three suburbs had increased to 26,830 (6.0 percent of their total population.

Data from the 1905 census (excluding the suburbs), which was broken down by 394 small Stadtbezirke,[18] yield a more detailed picture of Jewish

---

17 Alt Berlin, Spandauer, Königstadt, and Stralauer West.
18 "Die Bevölkerung in Berlin: I Die anwesende Bevölkerung nach dem Geschlecht in den einzelnen Stadtbezirken und Polizeirevieren," *Die Wohnungs- und die Bevölkerung-Aufnahme vom 1. Dezember 1905 in der Stadt Berlin und 29 benachbarten Gemeinden* (Berlin: Puttkammer & Mühlbrecht, 1910), 1–5. For the Spandauer Viertel and Rosenthaler Viertel Süd it was necessary to use the data from 1900.

Table 10.8. Jewish Population of Berlin by Districts, 1867–1905

District	1867	1871	1875	1880	1885	1890	1895	1900	1905
(Alt)Berlin	5331	5941	5448	4835	4043	4144	3512	2597	1919
Percent Jewish	17.8	18.5	18.0	19.0	16.8	17.6	17.3	15.2	13.6
Kölln	996	1169	1051	941	758	686	516	495	390
Percent Jewish	6.5	7.1	6.9	6.8	5.5	5.5	4.6	5.1	4.4
Friedrichswerder	676	635	627	565	445	335	290	202	159
Percent Jewish	7.4	6.4	7.0	6.9	6.2	5.9	6.3	5.0	4.4
Old Center	7003	7745	7126	6341	5246	5165	4318	3294	2468
Percent Jewish	12.9	13.5	13.1	13.4	11.6	12.4	12.0	10.7	9.3
Spandauer Viertel	7843	8822	9473	10827	12256	14154	14466	14538	15228
Percent Jewish	11.7	12.3	13.7	16.1	16.8	17.9	19.5	19.0	21.0
Center and Spandauer Viertel	14846	16608	16599	17168	17502	19319	18784	17832	17696
Percent Jewish	12.2		13.4	15.0	14.8	16.0	17.1	16.6	17.8
Spandauer Viertel Outside of Berlin	557								
Percent Jewish	0.6								

District	1867	1871	1875	1880	1885	1890	1895	1900	1905
Rosenthaler Vorstadt		851	2394	4383	S4906	6100	6955	8937	9725
Percent Jewish	1.8	3.2	3.9		5.5	6.5	8.0	7.8	8.8
					N647	1331	2712	2286	NW1182
Percent Jewish					1.3	1.6	2.1	1.7	1.4
									NO2197
Percent Jewish									2.6
Oranienburger Vorstadt		505	907	1386	1839	2532	2546	2613	2762
Percent Jewish		0.7	1.2	1.6	1.8	2.1	2.0	1.9	2.0
									Innere 4607
Percent Jewish									18.4
Königsviertel	2957	3945	4590	5148	6884	8752	9220	10878	
Percent Jewish	7.1	8.0	8.0	8.1	9.0	9.6	9.6	8.3	
									Äussere 9748
Percent Jewish									8.6

District	1867	1871	1875	1880	1885	1890	1895	1900	1905
Petersburger Strasse									527
Percent Jewish		2752							1.2
						7348	8559	8837	9725
Percent Jewish					West5707	6.8	8.0	7.9	8.1
Stralauer Vorstadt	1785		4386	5005	5.6				NO897
Percent Jewish	2.2	439(?)	3.8	3.5 Ost	397	653	607	1319	1.3 SO1046
Percent Jewish		0.6	0.8	0.6	1.0	0.9	0	1.0	0.9
North and northeast	5299	8492	12277	15922	20380	26716	30599	34870	42416
Percent Jewish	2.5	3.2	3.8	3.9	4.2	4.6	4.8	4.5	4.7
Dorotheenstadt	1335	1474	1409	1396	1283	1155	872	843	831
Percent Jewish	6.3	7.1	7.7	7.9	7.5	7.1	6.1	6.4	5.8
Friedrichstadt	2420	3277	4068	4963	5790	6254	5722	5216	4836
Percent Jewish	3.3	4.3	5.7	7.1	8.4	9.2	9.2	9.1	9.3
Königsplatz			280						
Percent Jewish			10.4						
Inner west	3755	5031	5477	6359	7073	7409	6594	6059	5667

District	1867	1871	1875	1880	1885	1890	1895	1900	1905
Percent Jewish	4.0	5.2	5.9	7.3	8.2	8.8	8.6	8.6	8.5
Friedrichstadt (Vorstadt) oberhalb			514	914			1038		
Percent Jewish			3.2	5.3			6.6		
Outside of Berlin	821	1251							
Percent Jewish	3.3	Unterhalb 1570	1643				2261		
Percent Jewish		14.2	14.9				15.1		
Friedrichstädter and Schöneberger Vorstadt					5889	7566		9007	8651
Percent Jewish					6.7	7.5		8.9	8.9
Schöneberger Vorstadt		468	1178	2166					6236
Percent Jewish			3.4	3.9					7.4
	285								
Percent Jewish	0.7								

Jewish Residential Concentration in German Cities

District	1867	1871	1875	1880	1885	1890	1895	1900	1905
Percent Jewish Tempelhofer Vorstadt		143	272	754		O	1622	1958	1892
Percent Jewish			0.6	1.0			1.5	1.6	2.1
Percent Jewish Friedrichstädter and Tempelhofer Vorstadt					2425	3372		W	1256
Percent Jewish					2.1	2.1			2.9
Obere Friedrichstädter and Tempelhofer West								2659	2806
Percent Jewish								4.2	2.9
Tiergarten (Hansaviertel)				359	606	1208	3138	4293	4581
% Jewish				9.6	11.0	11.7	17.2	20.0	21.2

District	1867	1871	1875	1880	1885	1890	1895	1900	1905
Outer west	1106	1862	3534	5836	8920	12146	15551	17917	17930
Percent Jewish	1.7		3.3	3.7	4.2	4.5	5.4	5.8	5.9
Neukölln	428	548	650	744	660	753	720	528	488
Percent Jewish	6.0		9.6	11.2	10.4	11.7	13.2	11.0	11.3
	diesseits der Kanal	2805	4702	5724	6981	8280	8287	8604	8110
Percent Jewish			4.0	4.8	5.6	6.7	7.2	7.4	7.4
Luisenstadt	1714								
Percent Jewish	1.1								
	jenseits der Kanal	294	706	1053	W1093	1385	1498	1551	1435
Percent Jewish			0.7	0.9	1.1	1.3	1.5	1.5	1.5
					O119	272	268	362	381
Percent Jewish					0.3	0.4	0.3	0.4	0.4
Southeast	2142	3647	6058	7521	8853	10690	10773	11045	10414
Percent Jewish	1.4		2.7	3.0	3.2	3.5	3.6	3.5	3.5
Friedrich	325	570	740	690	865	1005	975	890	788
Wilhelm-Stadt									
Percent Jewish		1.8	3.9	3.9	4.4	4.9	5.1	4.8	4.5

District	1867	1871	1875	1880	1885	1890	1895	1900	1905
Percent Jewish							O1319	1579	1892
Moabit	17	39	62	145	418	1304	3.2	3.5	4.3
Percent Jewish	0.1	0.3	0.3	0.5	0.9	1.4			
Percent Jewish							W668	917	1780
Gesundbrunnen							0.8	0.8	1.2
Percent Jewish									766
Wedding	75	100	235	275	344	700	889	1097	0.8
Percent Jewish	0.4	0.4	0.5	0.5	0.5	0.7	0.8	0.8	743
(Far) northwest	417	709	1037	1110	1627	3009	3851	4483	0.8
Percent Jewish	0.9		1.2	1.1	1.2	1.4	1.5	1.4	5959
									1.5

Sources: Schwabe, *Die Resultate der Berliner Volkszählung vom. 3. December 1867*, LVIII–LIX, 30–31; Schwabe, *Die Königliche Haupt- und Residenzstadt Berlin in ihren Bevölkerungs-, Berufs- und Wohnungsverhältnissen*, 68*–71*; Richard Böckh, *Die Bevölkerungs-, Gewerbe-, und Wohnungsaufnahme vom 1. December 1875* (Berlin, 1878), vol. 3, 52.; R. Böckh, *Die Bevölkerungs und Wohnungsaufnahme vom 1. December 1880 in der Stadt Berlin* (Berlin, 1883), vol. 2, 40–41; R. Böckh, *Die Bevölkerungs und Wohnungsaufnahme vom 1. December 1885 in der Stadt Berlin* (Berlin, 1890), vol. 2, 38; R. Böckh, *Die Bevölkerungs und Wohnungsaufnahme vom 1. Dezember 1890 in der Stadt Berlin* (Berlin, 1893), vol. 1, 46, and vol. 2, 46; R. Böckh, *Die Bevölkerungs- und Wohnungsaufnahme vom 2. December 1895 in der Stadt Berlin* (Berlin, 1900–1901), 1–3; *Die Grundstücks-Aufnahme Ende Oktober 1900 sowie die Wohnungs- und die Bevölkerungsaufnahme vom 1. Dezember 1900 in der Stadt Berlin* (Berlin, 1904), part 2, 1–4; *Die Grundstücks-Aufnahme Ende Oktober 1905 sowie die Wohnungs- und die Bevölkerungsaufnahme vom 1. Dezember 1905 in der Stadt Berlin und 29 benachbarten Gemeinden* (Berlin, 1910–1911), part 2, 1–5.

concentration. Eleven districts had populations that were more than 25 percent Jewish; in twelve others, there were proportions of 20–25 percent. Except for the Hansaviertel, virtually all these districts were in north-central Berlin. More than 55 percent of Berlin Jews lived in the seventy-six districts that were at least ten percent Jewish. In contrast, the 100 districts that had Jewish densities of under one percent were home to fewer than 3.5 percent of Berlin's Jews.

By 1910, Jewish migration westward from Berlin had become so great that the number of Jews within the political borders of the city actually decreased from 98,893 in 1905 to 90,013 in 1910. The Jewish population of the Spandauer Viertel in the heart of north-central Berlin began to decline (from 15,228 in 1905 to 11,343 in 1910), whereas Jewish populations in the areas to the immediate north continued to increase. The tally of Jews in the three western suburbs increased from 26,830 to 43,847 (7.5 percent of the total) between 1905 and 1910. The Jewish population of Charlottenburg, the oldest of the western suburbs, was thickest in the eastern districts bordering immediately on Berlin proper, which effectively fused Jewry in the western suburbs and western Berlin into a single agglomeration (Table 10.9). In 1910, 57,584 Jews lived in far-west Berlin and the three western suburbs as against 45,962 in the older Jewish neighborhood in north central Berlin.[19] As time passed, there was an ever-increasing social gap between the mostly wealthy, native, and liberal Jews of western Berlin and the poorer, more traditional, and often immigrant Jews of north-central Berlin (Table 10.10).

Despite some continuing changes, the overall pattern of two main Jewish neighborhoods in Berlin—north-central and western—persisted after World War I (Table 10.11). Between 1910 and 1933, Jews tended to move increasingly farther from the city center, especially towards the west (Map 10/3B). The Jewish population in most of the older parts of Berlin continued to decline after 1910, often at rates somewhat greater than the general decline in the general population there. This was most evident in Kreuzberg, an area outside the main Jewish neighborhood of central Berlin, and in the central-west district of Tiergarten.[20] The decline in the Tiergarten district was most likely the result of migration farther west into Charlottenburg, Schöneberg, and Wilmersdorf, all of which gained Jewish population, at least until 1925. The most central area

---

19 Far-western Berlin included Untere Friedrich Vorstadt, Schöneberger Vorstadt, Friedrich Wilhelm Stadt, Tiergarten Vorstadt, and Moabit Ost. North-central Berlin comprised Alt Berlin, Kölln, Friedrichswerder, Spandauer Viertel, Stralauer Viertel West, Königsviertel, and Rosenthaler Viertel Süd.
20 Not to be confused with the pre-1920 district of Tiergarten (Hansaviertel), which was only a small part of the post-1920 Tiergarten district.

Table 10.9. Jewish Density in Different Neighborhoods of Charlottenburg, 1905

Neighborhood	Total population	Jewish population	Percent
Westend	4599	80	1.7
Spandauer Berg	1452	5	0.3
Schlossviertel	42793	237	0.6
Lietzensee	15512	1182	7.6
Kalowswerder	3409	7	0.2
Nonnendamm	203	0	0
Königsdamm	764	1	0.1
Martinikenfelde	6025	29	0.5
Halbinsel	2419	164	6.8
Lützow	18691	446	2.4
InnereStadt	59890	1934	3.2
Hochschulviertel	29162	2487	8.6
Kurfürstendamm	19597	3529	18.0
Ostviertel	34188	5780	16.9
Charlottenburg total	238704	15881	6.7

Source: *Charlottenburger Statistik* 20 (1907): 9.

of Berlin (Mitte) showed a slow decline in Jewish population, which at first was slower than the decline in the general population there. Just to the north, the growth in Jewish population in Prenzlauer Berg before 1925 indicates that at least some of those leaving the Mitte district were simply moving to another part of the same neighborhood. Jewish density in Prenzlauer Berg District was much higher in the southern sections bordering on Mitte than elsewhere.[21] The western suburbs gained steadily until 1925, after which the trend reversed direction in the suburbs closest to central Berlin (Charlottenburg and Schöneberg). Wilmersdorf, the westernmost district in the neighborhood,

---

21 Michael Kreutzer, "Über konzentrierte jüdische Nachbarschaften in Prenzlauer Berg 1886–1931: Eine historisch-statistische Beschreibung anhand von Adreßbüchern und Adressenverzeichnissen," in *Leben mit der Erinnerung: Jüdische Geschichte in Prenzlauer Berg* (Berlin: Hentrich, 1997), 353–380, gives details on Jewish density in various parts of the district (Table 10.11). In the areas south of Danzigerstrasse there were 5,047 Jews (10.9 percent) out of 46,190 individuals listed in the address books, while north of that thoroughfare 1,597 Jews (2.9 percent) were listed out of a total of 55,207.

Table 10.10. Birthplaces of Jews in Berlin and Selected Suburbs, 1910

Birthplace	Berlin				Western suburbs			Other suburbs			
	Central	North	East	South	West	Southwest	Charlottenburg	Schöneberg	Wilmersdorf	Neukölln	Lichtenberg
b. Berlin or Berlin suburbs	4834	6112	7323	3272	6186	1657	7706	3764	3245	658	350
Percent	28.0	34.8	33.1	32.0	**36.1**	29.4	34.2	32.3	33.5	31.6	31.7
Other Prussia	7091	7409	11338	4846	7997	2689	10357	5752	4461	899	510
Percent	41.1	42.1	**51.2**	47.4	46.6	47.7	45.9	49.4	46.0	43.2	46.2
Other Germany	625	433	605	449	1082	481	1447	865	714	119	23
Percent	3.6	2.5	2.7	4.4	6.3	**8.5**	6.4	7.4	7.4	5.7	2.1
Abroad	4689	3629	2862	1649	1883	812	2996	1260	1278	404	221
Percent	**27.2**	20.6	12.9	16.1	11.0	14.4	13.3	10.8	13.2	19.4	20.0
Unknown	30	4	3	6	3	4					
Total	17269	17587	22131	10222	17151	5643	22506	11641	9698	2080	1103(?)

Red = lowest row percent; bold = highest row percent.

Sources: Blau, *Entwicklung*, 101, 107–113; Segall, "Juden in Gross-Berlin," 124–125.

Table 10.11. Relative Jewish Density in Parts of Prenzlauer Berg District of Berlin, 1931–1932

South of Danzigerstrasse		North of Danzigerstrasse	
	South of S-Bahn		North of S-Bahn
Teutoburger Platz	10%	Falkplatz	3%
Kollwitzplatz	10	Helmholtzplatz	3
Winsstrasse	13	District 8 (between	9
Bötzowstrasse	10	Greifwalderstrasse and	
Mendelssohnstrasse	17	Kniproderstrasse)	
		(North of district 8)	
(Southeasternmost area)		East of Kniproderstrasse	1

		District 10	2%
		District 11	3
		District 12	2
		District 13	6
		District 14	0

Within the districts south of the Danzigerstrasse, Jewish concentration was greatest on streets in the southern half of each district. District numbers are found in *Leben mit der Erinnerung: Jüdische Geschichte in Prenzlauer Berg* (Berlin: Hentrich, 1997).

Source: Kreutzer, "Über konzentrierte jüdische Nachbarschaften," esp. 358, 360–361.

continued to grow in Jewish population. Zehlendorf, the wealthy district to the southwest that included the villa districts of Grunewald, Nicolassee, and Wannsee, grew in Jewish density and numbers, although the overall numbers were not very large (Tables 10.12 A and B).

Despite these changes, the broader pattern of Jewish concentration in six of the city's twenty districts continued throughout the Weimar and early Nazi periods. More than three quarters of Berlin's Jewish population lived in these six districts throughout the 1910–1939 period. Berlin Jewry outside the six districts increased in number and in percentage during the Weimar era between 1925 and 1933 as well. In the first six years of Nazi rule, however, the Jewish population's mild tendency to scatter was completely reversed. The Jewish population in outlying areas declined and instead began to concentrate in the most Jewish districts, especially Schöneberg and Wilmersdorf. Although a ghetto was not created, Jews were more inclined to cluster. Decreases were especially sizable in wealthy villa districts such as Zehlendorf (Table 10.13).

Pattern III: Multiple Neighborhoods with Strong Central-City Concentrations

Munich

Unlike the cities discussed above, Munich had a relatively small Jewish population until the middle of the nineteenth century[22] (Map 10/4). By 1871, however, there were almost 3,000 Jews in the city who were concentrated very heavily in the central area (the Altstadt). In 1875, 2,174 (62.6 percent) of the city's 3,475 Jews dwelled in the four districts (1–4) that made up the Altstadt, as against only 24.9 percent of the city's overall population (Table 10.14). Jews accounted for 4.4 percent of central Munich's overall population but only 1.8 percent of the city as a whole. The district that had the highest concentration of Jews by far was in the northwestern section of the central city (district 4), where the city's main synagogue was built in 1887. Between 1875 and 1885, the distribution of Munich's Jewish inhabitants changed little. Twenty years later, some noticeable shifts were evident. The Jewish population grew at

---

22 Munich's Jewish population was 451 in 1814, 1,423 in 1840, 1,208 in 1852, 1,400 in 1861, and 2,903 in 1871. Its percentage in the total city population was 1.13, 1.08, 1.71, 1.80, and 1.74 in the respective years. The figures for 1840 and 1852 (and perhaps all pre-1871 figures) count "non-Christian population," most but perhaps not all of whom were Jews.

Table 10.12.

A) Greater Berlin Jewish Population by District

District	1910	1925	1933	1939	1933–1939 decline
*Mitte	33,262 (9.8%)	30,977 (10.5%)	24,425 (9.2%)	13,821 (5.3%)	43.4%
*Tiergarten	16,493 (5.5%)	15,943 (5.5%)	12,286 (4.9%)	5,312 (2.5%)	56.8
Wedding	2,775 (0.8%)	3,695 (1.1%)	3,500 (1.1%)	1,961 (0.6%)	44.0
*Prenzlauer Berg	19,081 (6.3%)	20,419 (6.3%)	18,051 (5.8%)	9,577 (3.2%)	46.9
Friedrichshain	8,423 (2.3%)	8,061 (2.4%)	6,437 (2.1%)	3,563 (1.0%)	44.7
Kreuzberg	10,012 (2.4%)	8,167 (2.2%)	6,096 (1.8%)	2,652 (0.8%)	56.5
*Charlottenburg	22,657 (7.3%)	30,553 (8.9%)	27,013 (7.9%)	11,393 (3.8%)	57.8
Spandau	316 (0.4%)	514 (0.5%)	725 (0.5%)	205 (0.1%)	71.7
*Wilmersdorf	10,160 (8.3%)	22,704 (13.0%)	26,607 (13.5%)	13,810 (6.7%)	48.1
Zehlendorf	373 (1.5%)	1,513 (3.4%)	2,331 (3.5%)	411 (0.5%)	82.4
*Schöneberg	12,511 (6.0%)	17,785 (7.7%)	16,261 (7.4%)	10,056 (3.6%)	38.2
Steglitz	1,185 (1.0%)	2,475 (1.5%)	3,184 (1.6%)	1,226 (0.6%)	61.5
Tempelhof	247 (0.6%)	921 (1.4%)	2,322 (2.0%)	455 (0.4%)	80.4
Neukölln	2,104 (0.8%)	2,832 (1.0%)	2,941 (0.9%)	1,129 (0.4%)	61.6

District	1910	1925	1933	1939	1933–1939 decline
Treptow	438 (0.6%)	661 (0.7%)	1,006 (0.8%)	232 (0.2%)	76.9
Köpenick	263 (0.5%)	494 (0.8%)	609 (0.7%)	284 (0.2%)	53.4
Lichtenberg	1,384 (0.8%)	1,918 (1.0%)	2,208 (0.9%)	563 (0.3%)	74.5
Weissensee	669 (1.3%)	920 (1.6%)	1,336 (1.6%)	590 (0.7%)	55.8
Pankow	1,335 (1.8%)	1,566 (1.6%)	2,079 (1.5%)	1,080 (0.7%)	48.1
Reinickendorf	355 (0.5%)	554 (0.5%)	1,115 (0.7%)	363 (0.2%)	67.4
TOTAL	144,043	172,672	160,564	78,713	51.0

* Six heavily Jewish districts.

The highest statistic for each district is in bold.

Sources: *Statistisches Jahrbuch der Stadt Berlin* (1924): 3, (1927): 6–7; *Berlin in Zahlen* (Berlin, 1945), 68; H. G. Sellenthin, *Geschichte der Juden in Berlin und des Gebäudes Fasanenstrasse 79/80* (Berlin, 1959), 72.

B) Estimated Distribution of Berlin Jewish Population before 1910 (by post-1920 districts)

District	1867	1871	1875	1880	1885	1890	1895	1900	1905
Mitte	20696	24963	27408	30283	33409	38224	38076	38353	39478
Tiergarten	838	1341	2748	4313	6913	10078	13622	15796	16904
Wedding	75	353	777	922	1173	1988	2642	2630	3612
Prenzlauer Berg	1972	3397	5216	5879	7477	9776	11437	13250	16808
Friedrichshain	1191	2274	3274	2884	4200	5554	6316	7213	8430
Kreuzberg	2353	4363	6662	9021	11188	13679	14070	14877	14341
Total	27125	36691	46085	53302	64360	79299	86163	92119	99573
Charlottenburg		142		287	478	1475	4687	9701	15604
Spandau	149	165	307	344					
Wilmersdorf		8			14	26	354	989	4297
Schöneberg		35			159	611	1399	2994	6929
Steglitz						149		145	
Neukölln					22	118	220	450	1176
Köpenick				59				112	
Lichtenberg		6			41	113	185	316	471
Weissensee								360	
Pankow						189		423	

Source: Estimates by author based on sources in Table 10.8.

Table 10.13. Distribution of Berlin Jews in Various Sections of Town, 1910-1939

Location	1910	1925	1933	1939
Three inner Jewish districts (Mitte, Tiergarten, Prenzlauer Berg)	68,836 (47.5%)	67,339 (39.0)	54,762 (34.1)	28,710 (36.5)
Three outer Jewish districts (Charlottenburg, Schöneberg, Wilmersdorf)	45,328 (31.5)	71,042 (41.1)	69,881 (43.5)	35,259 (44.8)
All other districts	29,879 (20.7)	34,291 (19.9)	35,921 (22.4)	14,744 (18.7)

Distribution of Jews outside the six main Jewish districts:

A) By geographical direction

Geographical Direction	1910	1925	1933	1939
NW (Wedding, Spandau, Pankow, Reinickendorf)	4781 (16.0)	6329 (18.5)	7419 (20.7)	3609 (24.5)
SW (Zehlendorf, Steglitz, Tempelhof)	1805 (6.0)	4909 (14.3)	7837 (21.8)	2092 (14.2)
NE (Friedrichshain, Lichtenberg, Weissensee)	10476 (35.1)	10899 (31.8)	9981 (27.8)	4716 (32.1)
SE (Kreuzberg, Neukölln, Treptow, Köpenick)	12817 (42.9)	12153 (35.4)	10652 (29.7)	4297 (29.2)

B) Inner vs. outer districts

District Location	1910	1925	1933	1939
Inner districts (Wedding, Friedrichshain, Kreuzberg)	21210 (71.0)	19231 (57.2)	16033 (44.7)	8176 (55.7)
Outer districts (Spandau, Zehlendorf, Steglitz, Tempelhof, Neukölln, Treptow, Köpenick, Lichtenberg, Weissensee, Pankow, Reinickendorf)	8669 (29.0)	14368 (42.8)	19856 (55.3)	6508 (44.3)

Sources: based on sources in Table 10.11 B.

Table 10.14. Munich—General, Jewish, and Protestant Population by District

A) Absolute Numbers

District	General population					Jewish population					Protestant population	
	1875	1880	1885	1905	1910	1875	1880	1885	1905	1910	1875	1910
I	14047	13761	14454	10643	10667	518	432	509	290	304	1335	1438
II	12682	12907	13402	12610	13230	375	472	491	625	614	1136	1373
III	11808	11767	11626	9702	10018	316	386	392	376	382	1169	1223
IV	10875	10210	10106	7268	6591	965	1001	897	569	448	1422	1093
V	19237	19556	21261	26293	26270	157	206	216	548	488	2664	6216
VI	16861	23159	26214	23940	28696	273	288	406	614	597	3185	4697
VII	5024	7369	9232	31552	29493	4	8	27	411	343	356	6042
VIII	11010	11753	13723	31552	24446	39	48	101	411	272	1322	3469
IX	20147	23024	26214	28964	28696	207	292	479	1792	2021	3437	5367
X	5818	9644	11964	29485	30453	17	27	39	393	564	552	4071
XI	4920	9088	12047	29295	32213	30	98	151	1056	1143	458	4168
XII	15502	20093	22339	19222	19659	475	774	944	896	925	1829	2540
XIII	10083	10121	11476	20716	22217	67	78	116	1042	1123	1011	4073
XIV	9321	9923	10824	28103	32037	0	9	12	128	170	366	3806
XV	5702	8280	10999	33085	26601	15	10	14	99	105	275	2920
XVI	5073	5061	5172	7870	22624	6	6	5	30	121	187	1978
XVII	7618	8312	9558	15864	24730	3	8	37	159	33	239	1783

District	General population					Jewish population					Protestant population	
	1875	1880	1885	1905	1910	1875	1880	1885	1905	1910	1875	1910
XVIII	7296	8390	10203	29857	21609	0	0	8	67	118	240	1692
XIX	5805	7605	10074	14783	20410	8		10	23	44	423	2737
XX				37983	22733				67	81		1572
XXI				39552	33307				139	101		5237
XXII				40652	24801				479	431		5452
XXIII				10752	24733				31	82		4068
XXIV				7300	9532				9	11		1256
XXV					23459					49		2025
XXVI					31343					453		8457

B) Percent of District Population

District	Jewish					Protestant	
	1875	1880	1885	1905	1910	1875	1910
I	3.7	3.1	3.5	2.7	2.9	9.5	13.5
II	3.0	3.7	3.7	5.0	4.6	9.0	10.3
III	2.7	3.3	3.4	3.9	3.8	9.9	12.2
IV	8.9	9.8	8.9	7.8	6.8	13.1	16.6
V	0.9	1.0	1.0	2.2	1.9	13.9	23.7
VI	1.6	1.2	1.5	2.6	2.4	18.9	16.4

VII	0.1	0.1	0.3	1.3	1.2	7.1	20.5
VIII	0.4	0.4	0.7	0.9	1.1	12.0	14.2
IX	1.0	1.3	1.8	6.2	7.0	17.1	18.7
X	0.3	0.3	0.3	1.3	1.9	9.5	13.4
XI	0.6	1.1	1.3	3.6	3.6	9.3	12.9
XII	3.1	3.9	4.2	4.7	4.7	11.8	12.9
XIII	0.7	0.8	1.0	5.0	5.1	10.0	18.3
XIV	0	0.1	0.1	0.5	0.5	3.9	11.9
XV	0.3	0.1	0.1	0.3	0.4	4.8	11.0
XVI	0.1	0.1	0.1	0.4	0.5	3.7	8.7
XVII	0	0.1	0.4	1.0	0.1	3.1	7.2
XVIII	0	0	0.1	0.2	0.6	3.3	7.8
XIX	0.1		0.1	0.2	0.2	7.3	13.4
XX				0.2	0.4		6.9
XXI				0.4	0.3		15.7
XXII				1.2	1.7		22.0
XXIII				0.3	0.3		16.5
XXIV				0.1	0.1		13.2
XXV					0.2		8.6
XXVI					1.5		27.0

Sources: von Tyszka, "Die jüdische Bevölkerung Münchens," 91, *Mitteilungen des Statistischen Amtes der Stadt München* 24 (1912–1913): 25.

about the same pace as that of the city as a whole and surpassed 11,000 souls by 1910. Here, as in most German cities, the center began to lose population and become mainly a commercial area. District 4, where the concentration of Jews was greatest, experienced the largest population decline as it became the city's business core. Although the city center retained a substantial Jewish presence, the Jewish population of the Ludwigsstadt, which ringed the central city from the southwest to the southeast and east, grew considerably. Within the Ludwigsstadt there was variance among subdistricts. West of the central city, the Theresienwiese district (district 9)—a wealthy residential area with many villas—had by far the largest number of Jews (2,021 individuals) by 1910 and a Jewish density of more than seven percent. East of the city center, district 13, which bordered the Englischer Garten, also had a substantial Jewish population. To the southeast, the districts that had large Jewish populations (11–12) seem to have been less wealthy. The main synagogue that served East European Jews was built in this neighborhood in 1931. Relatively few Jews inhabited the more distant and mainly poorer sections of the city to the south (Westend and Ostend). In the Maxstadt north of the central city, Jewish population density approximated the city average. Farther north, the artist and intellectual quarter of Schwabing experienced an influx of Jews that was, to some observers' surprise, rather limited. Therefore, in 1910 there were fewer than 900 Jews in the two districts (22 and 26) that made up Schwabing, making Jews barely one inhabitant in sixty. The overall pattern indicated a move from the central city mainly into nearby and often prosperous areas that were most contiguous to the center but stretched a fair distance across the city.[23]

Cologne

In many ways, the demographic history of the Jews of Cologne resembles that of Munich. Cologne had no Jews before the 1790s and relatively few until the middle of the nineteenth century.[24] By 1871, however, there were over 3,000 Jews in the city and the number grew rapidly to a peak of over 16,000 in 1925.

---

23 Unfortunately, I did not have access to information on Jewish population distribution in the 1925 and 1933 censuses.

24 Jewish population of Cologne:

1817	1837	1843	1852	1861	1871
124	454	784	1,531	2,322	3,172

1.51 percent in 1852, 1.93 percent in 1861, and 2.45 percent in 1871.

Unfortunately, the only information available on Jewish population distribution in the city before 1925 dates to the middle of the nineteenth century. In 1844, the Jews tended to live in three of the city's six districts, especially the central ones, halfway between the north and south. Jews' tendency to concentrate in the Altstadt Mitte district (approximately districts 2 and 5) more than in the northern and southern districts continued into the twentieth century (Table 10.15). Until 1881, all of Cologne was located inside the original fortifications, in what would later be called the Altstadt. From 1881 on, the area between these fortifications and a second ring of fortifications was built up and called the Neustadt. A series of annexations outside the second ring created a large urban area that included many formerly independent cities and villages (Map 10/5).

The 1925 census showed a Jewish population with a large concentration in the central city (Altstadt and Neustadt) as well as several smaller concentrations in parts of town far from the center. The 11,991 Jews in the Altstadt and Neustadt constituted 75.9 percent of all Jews in Cologne as against 40.8 percent of the total urban population. The main synagogues were located there as well. East European Jewish immigrants congregated along a compact group of streets in the center of the Altstadt.[25] Jewish concentration was especially high in the Altstadt-Mitte (3,255 Jews, 5.6 percent of the population there) and Neustadt-Mitte (3,597 Jews, 8.4 percent Jewish) districts (Table 10.16). Alexander Pinthus's analysis of Jewish housing conditions in Cologne[26] stresses the acute housing density that typified the main agglomeration of Jewish population in central Cologne. The Altstadt and, to a lesser extent, the Neustadt were areas of small apartments in

Table 10.15. Jewish Population in Cologne Districts, 1844

District	Population
1	24
2	114
3	138
4	82
5	278
6	94

Source: Magnus, *Jewish Emancipation in a German City*.

---

25 Zvi Asaria, *Die Juden in Köln: Von den alten Zeiten bis zur Gegenwart* (Cologne: Bachem, 1959), 288.
26 Alexander Pinthus, "Die Wohnverhältnisse der Juden in Köln," *ZDSJ* (1927): 108–114.

Table 10.16. Cologne—General, Jewish, and Protestant Populations, 1925, 1933

District	1925			1933		
	General	Jewish		General	Jewish	Protestant
Altstadt-Süd	55936	1384 (2.5%)		52403	1256 (2.4%)	8509 (16.2%)
Altstadt-Mitte	58786	3255 (5.6)		55415	2537 (4.6)	9472 (17.1)
Altstadt-Nord	34833	426 (1.2)		31237	334 (1.1)	5124 (16.4)
Altstadt	149555	5065 (3.4)		139055	4127 (3.0)	23105 (16.6)
Neustadt-Süd	49323	1715 (3.5)		46151	1333 (2.9)	9984 (21.6)
Neustadt-Mitte	42998	3597 (8.4)		40314	3126 (7.8)	8203 (20.4)
Neustadt-Nord	44751	1614 (3.0)		41852	1144 (2.7)	9260 (22.1)
Neustadt	137072	6926 (5.1)		128318	5603 (4.4)	27447 (21.4)
Marienburg	2649	233 (8.8)		2999	253 (8.4)	1052 (35.1)
Bayenthal				7062	88 (1.3)	1443 (20.4)
Arnoldshöhe				2401	16 (0.7)	457 (19.0)
Mannsfeld				1187	5 (0.4)	263 (22.2)
Raderberg				2117	20 (0.9)	379 (17.9)
Raderthal				2442	18 (0.7)	447 (18.3)
Bayenthal	13068	105 (0.8)		18208	400 (2.2)	4041 (22.2)
Zollstock				16356	57 (0.4)	3630 (22.2)
Sülz	42618	548 (1.3)		46868	1054 (2.3)	11321 (24.2)

District	1925			1933		
	General	Jewish		General	Jewish	Protestant
Lindenthal	27579	971 (3.5)		22626	760 (3.4)	5550 (24.5)
Melaten				2053	42 (2.1)	348 (17.0)
Braunsfeld				5269	472 (9.0)	1267 (24.1)
Lindenthal				29948	1274 (4.3)	7165 (23.9)
Ehrenfeld				50065	815 (1.6)	8609 (17.2)
Bickendorf				26805	146 (0.5)	4577 (17.1)
Ossendorf				9559	7 (0.1)	1291 (13.5)
Müngersdorf				5305	195 (3.7)	1220 (23.0)
Bocklemünd				1064	4 (0.4)	56 (5.3)
Mengenich				395	0	14 (3.5)
Ehrenfeld	73423	802 (2.0)		93193	1167 (1.3)	15767 (16.9)
Nippes				45959	254 (0.6)	8727 (19.0)
Riehl				14018	111 (0.8)	3624 (25.9)
Mauenheim				6401	13 (0.2)	1402 (21.9)
Merheim (lft)				8214	45 (0.6)	1645 (20.0)
Niehl				4263	6 (0.1)	343 (8.1)
Longerich				3421	2 (0.1)	347 (10.1)

District	1925			1933		
	General	Jewish	General	Jewish	Protestant
Volkhoven			1045	1 (0.1)	112 (10.7)
Nippes	46997	308 (0.7)	83321	432 (0.5)	16200 (19.4)
Worringen			944	3 (0)	466 (4.9)
Deutz			22913	182 (0.8)	4899 (21.4)
Humboldtkolonie			13039	7 (0.1)	2263 (17.4)
Poll			5478	21 (0.4)	733 (13.4)
Deutz	21723	159 (0.7)	41430	210 (0.5)	7895 (19.1)
Kalk			29857	137 (0.5)	5733 (19.2)
Gremberg			2228	2 (0.1)	351 (15.8)
Vingst			7932	10 (0.1)	1238 (15.6)
Höhenberg			7009	17 (0.2)	1572 (22.4)
Kalk	29975	171 (0.6)	47026	166 (0.4)	8894 (18.9)
Buchforst			8795	37 (0.4)	2150 (24.5)
Mülheim	54971	238 (0.4)	52294	236 (0.5)	11488 (22.0)
Mülheim			61089	273 (0.5)	13638 (22.3)
Rath			3132	20 (0.6)	533 (17.0)
Brück			2970	1 (0.03)	490 (16.5)

District	1925			1933		
	General	Jewish	General	Jewish	Protestant
Merheim(rt)			2503	5 (0.2)	439 (17.5)
Ostheim			2121	0	417 (19.7)
Holweide			7206	8 (0.1)	1163 (16.1)
Dellbrück			11065	13 (0.1)	2467 (22.3)
Höhenhaus			4774	1 (0.02)	1002 (21.0)
Dünnwald			4405	4 (0.1)	543 (12.3)
Stammheim			2113	0	188 (8.9)
Flittard			2699	1 (0.04)	428 (15.9)
Merheim			42988	53 (0.1)	7670 (17.5)
All	702252	15807 (2.3)	757240	14819 (2.0)	147239 (19.4)

Sources: Pinthus, "Die Wohnverhältnisse der Juden in Köln," 108; "Einige Ergebnisse der Volkszählung in Köln am 16.6. 1933," *Statistisches Jahrbuch der Stadt Köln, Berichtsjahr 1932* (1933): 1–4, Tables 1–3.

multiple dwellings. Certain streets within census districts had extremely high Jewish concentrations; fifteen streets in the central Altstadt contained nine percent of the entire Jewish population of Cologne. The Altstadt was also home to 60 percent of families aided by the Jewish community welfare bureau.

There were also much smaller areas with high percentages of Jews in specific, mainly prosperous, sections of the outer city. These were chiefly to the south and west of the central city, especially in the Bayenthal and Lindenthal areas. Within Bayenthal, the tiny wealthy villa district of Marienburg numbered 233 Jews among its 2,649 inhabitants and had the highest Jewish density in Cologne (8.8 percent). The social status of the Jews in these outer enclaves contrasted sharply to the poverty that prevailed in some inner-city Jewish areas.

The 1933 census, which gave much more detail about the various districts, showed essentially the same patterns as 1925 except for Jews' moderate tendency to move from central areas to outlying districts. Instead of 11,991 Jews in the Altstadt and the Neustadt in 1925, the census found 9,730 (65.7 percent of all Jews in the city) in 1933 and a decline in the city's total Jewish population. Still, substantial growth in several outlying districts, especially those in the Sülz and Lindenthal areas, meant that Cologne's total Jewish population outside of Altstadt and Neustadt rose from 3,535 in 1925 to 5,089 in 1933. There were several small areas of heavy Jewish concentration in the outer western and southern districts, few of them contiguous to each other. They included the *Villenkolonien* of Marienburg (a mile south of the inner city near the Rhine), Braunsfeld (slightly more than a mile due west of the inner city), and Müngersdorf (west of Braunsfeld). These three villa districts had only 920 Jews combined. Jewish population was very sparse in most of the outlying districts, especially north of the city and on the right bank of the Rhine. A separate calculation of Cologne's Jewish population on the basis of Catholic parishes (*Kirchspiele*) in 1933 showed six parishes with more than five percent Jews,[27] sixteen with 2–5 percent, fourteen with 1–2 percent, thirteen with 0.5–1 percent, twenty-nine with under 0.5 percent, and eight with no Jewish inhabitants.

As in Berlin, during the early Nazi period the Jewish population of Cologne reversed its earlier tendency toward scattering. The 1939 census showed 71.2 percent of Cologne Jews in the Altstadt or the Neustadt. Nearly all of the remaining 28.8 percent lived in the Sülz, Lindenthal, and Ehrenfeld sections.[28]

---

27 St. Mauritius—Altstadt Mitte, St. Peter—Altstadt-Mitte, St. Michael—Neustadt-Mitte, St. Joseph—Braunsfeld, Herz Jesu—Neustadt-Mitte, and St. Marien—Marienburg.
28 "Einige Zählungsergebnisse 1939," *Statistisches Jahrbuch der Hansestadt Köln, Berichtsjahr 1939* (1941): VI.

Leipzig—Continued Concentration in the Central City

Unlike most German cities, Leipzig had a Jewish population made up mostly of non-citizens. Recent immigrants in Leipzig, as in other German cities, tended to settle and remain in the central parts of the city near the main railway station. Leipzig, like many other German cities, was built in concentric circles with an inner city dating back to the Middle Ages, inner and outer suburbs, and a large outer area (Neu Leipzig) composed of annexed but once-independent cities and towns. The Jews in Leipzig concentrated heavily in the inner city and the inner suburbs, especially those in the north and the west (Table 10.17). Although the Innere Stadt lost much of its overall population between 1880 and 1905, its Jewish population doubled as more and more East European Jews settled in the city. The Jewish population more than doubled in the Innere Westvorstadt and increased by 60 percent in the Innere Nordvorstadt where the overall population was stagnant and attained by far the highest Jewish densities in town. In the recently incorporated areas of Neu Leipzig, the Jewish population remained sparse.

Statistics from 1925 and 1935, while not easily comparable with those of the period before 1905, showed some scattering of the Jewish population and considerable migration to the inner northern suburbs. Otherwise, Jewish concentration remained near the city center. The 1925 census material, organized on the basis of Protestant parishes rather than by districts (Table 10.18), showed 6,576 Jews (52.2 percent of all Leipzig Jews) residing in just two of the city's thirty-six parishes. The two parish churches, St. Matthew's and St. Michael's, were located in the northwestern section of the Innere Stadt and in the Äussere Nordvorstadt, respectively. In 1900, the same parishes had had 2,489 Jewish inhabitants (40.3 percent of all Jews in Leipzig). Two other parishes, both in the Innere Stadt, had Jewish densities of just over five percent. The next most-densely Jewish parishes, at only 1.5–2.0 percent, were mostly in southern and western Leipzig near the inner city. Jewish settlement in the parts of Leipzig that were incorporated in the 1890s remained sparse in 1925.

The 1935 card file of the Leipzig Jewish community showed continued strong concentration in the areas immediately west and north of the inner city (Table 10.19). The Innere Stadt declined both in overall numbers and in Jewish density between 1905 and 1935. In contrast, the inner-west and inner-north areas bordering the inner city showed major increases in Jewish population relative to 1905, and were the main Jewish neighborhoods of Leipzig. These two neighborhoods, although adjacent, were considerably different in their social indicators. The Innere Nordvorstadt, near the main railroad station,

Table 10.17. Jewish Population Distribution in Leipzig by District

District	Overall population			Jewish population			Percent Jewish		
	1880	1900	1905	1880	1900	1905	1880	1900	1905
Innere Stadt	24,185	16,938	14,632	706	1500	1550	2.9	8.9	10.6
Nordostvorstadt		17,445	15,767		703	634		4.0	4.0
Südostvorstadt	40946	26,497	26,116	541	234	302	1.3	0.9	1.2
Innere Südvorstadt	27534	33587	31262	202	275	290	0.7	0.8	0.9
Äussere Südvorstadt	9913	29531	34699	8	105	186	0.1	0.4	0.5
Innere Westvorstadt	26265	29751	34507	699	932	1510	2.7	3.1	4.4
Äussere Westvorstadt	5243	10471	9933	21	173	184	0.4	1.7	1.9
Innere Nordvorstadt	10383	10586	10155	814	1059	1304	7.8	10.2	12.8
Äussere Nordvorstadt	4612	12410	11669	188	513	776	4.1	4.1	6.7
Alt Leipzig	149081	191834	188740	3179	5504(?)	6736	2.1	2.9	3.6
Neu Leipzig		264025	314896		669	940		0.3	0.3
Total	455859	503637			6171	7676		1.4	1.5

Sources: "Die Bewohner der einzelnen Stadtbezirken nach ihren Haupteigenschaften am 1. Dezember 1900," in *Die Ergebnisse der Volkszählung vom 1. Dezember 1900 in der Stadt Leipzig*, part 1 (Leipzig, 1901), 55–60; "Die Juden im Stadtbezirk Leipzig," *ZDSJ* (1907): 14–15.

Table 10.18. General and Jewish Population in Leipzig by Parish, 1880, 1900, 1925

Parish	1880			1900				1925		
	General	Jewish	Percent	General	Jewish	Percent		General	Jewish	Percent
St. Thoma	40265	573	1.4	25149	495	2.0		19471	1002	5.2
St. Nicolai	33993	888	2.6	26287	1814	6.9		19190	1091	5.7
St. Mathäi	33680	1503	4.5	32733	1966	6.0		29235	4514	15.4
St. Petri	41143	215	0.5	37114	331	0.9		34130	648	1.9
St. Andrea				29085	103	0.4		27334	232	0.9
Luther				16373	185	1.1		14884	295	2.0
St. Johannis				12353	85	0.7		16153	130	0.8
Nord Parochie				13007	523	4.0	Michaelis	15481	2062	13.3
Bethlehem				16945	348	2.1				
St. Marcus				40545	130	0.3		27413	242	0.9
St. Lucä				23616	37	0.2		22244	68	0.3
Kreuz Parochie				19150	161	0.8		20358	317	1.6
St. Trinitatis				15767	16	0.1		24258	86	0.4
Emmaus Kirche				12017	6	0.1		23398	30	0.1
Erlöser Kirche				8553	7	0.1		23066	49	0.2
Connewitz				15030	13	0.1		28600	88	0.3
Klein Zschocher				25777	45	0.2	Tabor	29717	106	0.4
Plagwitz				17085	58	0.3	Heiland	12661	102	0.8

Parish	1880			1900				1925		
	General	Jewish	Percent	General	Jewish	Percent		General	Jewish	Percent
Lindenau				43789	105	0.2	Nathanael	38473	139	0.4
Phillipus								24321	65	0.3
Gohlis				30114	70	0.2	Friedens	29013	472	1.6
Versöhnung								20171	101	0.5
Eutritzsch				11962	21	0.2	Christus	18434	126	0.7
Gethsemane								4881	0	0
Stephanus								10765	1	0.0
Auferstehung								17924	55	0.3
Paunsdorf								5945	1	0.0
Immanuel								5845	27	0.5
Bethanien								16788	76	0.5
Gedächtnis								21288	47	0.2
Marien								21840	57	0.3
Garnison								2007	1	0.1

Sources: "Die Bewohner der Kirchspiele nach Stadtbezirken am 1. Dezember 1900," *Die Ergebnisse der Volkszählung vom 1. Dezember in der Stadt Leipzig*, (Leipzig, 1901), 65–68; "Die Wohnbevölkerung der Kirchspiele nach der Zugehörigkeit zu den verschiedenen Religionsgesellschaften am 16 Juni 1925," in *Statistisches Jahrbuch der Stadt Leipzig 6 (1919–1926)* (Leipzig, 1928), 18–19.

Table 10.19. Jewish Population Distribution in Leipzig by District, 1935

District	General population	Jewish population	Percent Jewish	Percent of Jews non-citizens
Innere Nordvorstadt	8,512	2,696	31.7	73
Waldstrassenviertel		2,170		57
Gottschedstrasse etc.		1,158		57
Innere Westvorstadt	32,276	3,328	10.3	57
Vordergohlis		981		45
Äussere Nordvorstadt		430		73
Outer north total	16,626	1,411	8.5	
Zentrum	8,087	426	5.4	68
Nordostvorstadt	14,123	600	4.2	60
Äussere Südvorstadt		501		28
Südvorstadt		192		51
Musikviertel		303		24
Outer south total	71,042	996	1.4	
Südostvorstadt	22,066	230	1.0	57
Leipzig-Neustadt, Leipzig-Neu-Schönfeld, and Leipzig-Volkmarsdorf	36,670	334	0.9	60

District	General population	Jewish population	Percent Jewish	Percent of Jews non-citizens
Gohlis		275		52
Krochsiedlung		199		29
Leipzig-Gohlis total	54,580	474	0.9	
Lindenau		78		63
Plagwitz		65		54
Schleussig		47		28
Eutrisch		71		20
Leipzig-Schönefeld		33		39
Total northern and western suburbs		294		
Total Leipzig		10,799		58
Address unknown		1,488		

Source: Grubel and Mecklenburg, "Leipzig: Portrait of a Jewish Community," 168, 169, 171.

was the neighborhood most favored by East European immigrants. Despite its declining general population, the number of Jewish inhabitants doubled since 1905 and attained a remarkable Jewish density of 31.7 percent in 1935. Most of the small East European synagogues were located in this lower middle-class and proletarian area. Only 27 percent of the Jewish inhabitants there were German nationals. About a mile to the west, a numerically slightly larger but less densely concentrated group of Jews lived in the solidly middle class Waldstrassenviertel and Gottschedstrasse area, of whom 43 percent were German nationals. The city's two large communal synagogues (one Liberal and the other Orthodox) were located there as well. Both areas had far higher Jewish densities in 1935 than at the turn of the century. Well over half of all Leipzig Jews lived in either the Innere Westvorstadt or the Innere Nordvorstadt; many of the others dwelled in nearby areas to the north or east of the two districts. Fewer than ten percent of Leipzig Jews lived in the prosperous areas south and southwest of the city center. In these more outlying areas, the percentage of foreign Jews was much lower than in the denser Jewish neighborhoods.[29]

Neighboring Cities that Functioned like Separate Neighborhoods

Sometimes an analysis of Jewish neighborhood patterns must look beyond the political boundaries of a city. Fairly often, neighboring cities with Jewish populations had sharply different residential patterns. Some of these cities eventually merged while others remain independent to this day. In several such cases—both Altona and Hamburg and Ludwigshafen and Mannheim—the neighboring cities were in different German states. Even where political divisions endured, however, commuter transportation and close economic ties often connected the cities.

Neighboring cities often differed both in relative Jewish densities and in widely varying percentages of East European immigrants in their Jewish populations. Adjacent cities that remained politically separate at least until after 1933 included Hamburg and Altona, Nuremberg and Fürth, Frankfurt and Offenbach, and Mannheim and Ludwigshafen. Hamburg and Altona (along with the much smaller Wandsbeck) had a united Jewish community until 1803. Altona was under Danish rule until 1864 and thereafter became part of Prussia while Hamburg remained a separate city-state. Although

---

29 Grubel and Mecklenburg, "Leipzig: Portrait of a Jewish Community," 168–172.

Altona was a substantial city with a sizable Jewish population, it remained in the shadow of the more rapidly growing Hamburg. By the twentieth century, Hamburg had almost ten times as many Jews as Altona. As previously discussed, most Hamburg Jews were native-born, prosperous, and lived in the city's better neighborhoods. The more proletarian Altona, in contrast, had a much larger percentage of Jews with foreign citizenship, partly due to stricter regulations against foreigners in Hamburg, especially during the Weimar era (Table 10.20). Frankfurt overshadowed its neighbor Offenbach across the Main River, much as Hamburg overshadowed Altona. Prussia annexed the former Free City of Frankfurt in 1866 while Offenbach remained part of the

Table 10.20. Comparison of Makeup of Jewish Populations in Hamburg and Altona

Origin	Hamburg	Altona
1910		
Foreign Jews	3111	643
All Jews	18932	1824
Percent foreign	16.4	35.3
1933		
Born in the city	8571 (50.8)	587 (29.3)
Born elsewhere in Germany	5469 (32.4)	[671*] (33.5)
Born in lost territories	552 (3.3)	[68*] (3.4)
Born abroad	2228 (13.2)	[678*] (33.8)
Unknown	65 (0.4)	0
Citizens	14787 (87.6)	[946*] (47.2)
Non-citizens	2098 (12.4)	[1060*] (52.8)
*Einheimische***	13772 (81.6)	876 (43.7)
*Zugewanderte***	3113 (18.4)	1130 (56.3)
All Jews	16885	2006

[*] Estimated from data on Jews in all large cities in Schleswig-Holstein (Altona and Kiel).

** Nazi-developed categories: *zugewanderte* includes both non-citizens and citizens born abroad, *einheimische* includes all other Jews.

Sources: *Vierteljahrshefte zur Statistik des Deutschen Reichs—Ergänzungsheft zu 1916* 4 (1918): *Die Deutschen im Ausland und die Ausländer im Deutschen Reiche,* 86; 1933 census, 5/15, 50–52.

Grand Duchy of Hesse(-Darmstadt). Offenbach, a center of leather industry, attracted a very large Russian-Jewish population in the years before World War I while Frankfurt's stricter anti-foreigner regulations kept the Jewish immigrant population low (Table 10.21). Mannheim, a major city founded in the seventeenth century, had an old and substantial Jewish population. Ludwigshafen, which was across the Rhine in the Bavarian Palatinate, developed rapidly from a village of 2,296 in 1852 to a city of 28,768 in 1890, and 101,869 in 1925. Industrial and growing rapidly, Ludwigshafen attracted a much higher percentage of East European Jews than did the larger and more diversified Mannheim (Table 10.22). The Jewish community of Fürth was much older than its counterpart in much larger Nuremberg, which excluded Jews until the 1860s. By 1933, however, the latter community was almost four times as large as the former (Table 10.23).

In many other cases, independent cities merged or larger cities absorbed surrounding cities and towns. The Greater Berlin law of 1920 expanded the city to twice its former population and more than doubled its former area. In the outlying districts, Jews were present in higher percentages in the three western

Table 10.21. Comparison of Makeup of Jewish Populations in Frankfurt am Main and Offenbach

Origin	Frankfurt/Main	Offenbach
1910		
Foreign Jews	3541	1131
All Jews	26228	2361
Percent foreign	13.5	47.9
1933		
Born in the city	10680 (40.8)	
Born elsewhere in Germany	11324 (43.3)	
Born in lost territories	665 (2.5)	
Born abroad	3475 (13.3)	
Unknown	14 (0.1)	
Citizens	20881 (79.8)	
Non-citizens	5277 (20.2)	
All Jews	26158	1435

Sources: *Vierteljahrshefte zur Statistik des Deutschen Reichs—Ergänzungsheft zu 1916* 4 (1918): *Die Deutschen im Ausland und die Ausländer im Deutschen Reiche*, 86; 1933 census, 5/50.

Table 10.22. Comparison of Makeup of Jewish Populations in Mannheim and Ludwigshafen

Origin	Mannheim	Ludwigshafen
1880		
Jewish population	4031	210
1933		
Born in the city	2527 (39.5%)	294 (27.5%)
Born elsewhere in Germany	3033 (47.4%)	472 (44.1%)
Born in lost territories	136 (2.1%)	26 (2.4%)
Born abroad	706 (11.0%)	278 (26.0%)
Citizens	5507 (86.0%)	593 (55.4%)
Non-citizens	895 (14.0%)	477 (44.6%)
Total	6402	1070

This is an exception to the usual rule that East European Jews preferred to settle in older central-city locations more than did native Jews.

Sources: Bosse, *Die Verbreitung der Juden*, 71, 104; 1933 census, 5/15, 51.

Table 10.23. Jewish Populations of Nuremberg and Fürth

City	1852	1871	1880	1890	1900	1910	1925	1933
Nuremberg	87	1831	3032	4307	5956	7815	8603	7502
Fürth	2651	3250	3330	3175	3017	2826	2504	1990

Sources: *Pinkas ha-Kehillot, Germania, Bavaria*, 8, 320, 342; Schmelz, Territorial Printout.

suburbs of Charlottenburg, Schöneberg, and Wilmersdorf than in the city itself but were found in sparser numbers in other incorporated suburban towns. Many Jews moved from Berlin proper to the western suburbs before 1920. In most other cities that annexed surrounding towns, Jewish densities were much higher in the original city than in the annexed areas. Thus, Duisburg had a much higher Jewish density than neighboring Hamborn and other industrial cities that it eventually incorporated. Between 1910 and 1925, however, the Jewish population of Hamborn increased rapidly, mainly due to the immigration of a large East European Jewish workforce. Duisburg had a high percentage of foreign Jews but Hamborn's was much higher; it was one of the few German cities where most Jews did not hold citizenship (Table 10.24). Similar distinctions occurred in other cities in the Ruhr district that merged (Tables 10.25 A–D).

Table 10.24. Difference in Makeup of Jewish Population in Cities that Merged into Duisburg

Population Composition	Duisburg	Hamborn	Meiderich	Beeck
1880				
City population	41242			
Jewish population	367			
1900				
City population	92730	32597	33690	20456
Jewish population	786	123	65	34
Percent Jewish	0.9	0.4	0.2	0.2
1910				
City population	229483	101703		
Foreigners	18311	16724		
Foreign Jews	309	59		
Jewish population	1554	345		
Percent of Jewish population foreign	19.9	17.1		
Percent of population Jewish	0.7	0.3		
1925				
City population	272798	126618		
Jewish population	2080	818		
Percent of population Jewish	0.8	0.7		
Foreign Jews	807	476		
Percent of Jewish population foreign	38.8	58.2		

Sources: Bosse, *Die Verbreitung der Juden*, 38; *Vierteljahrshefte zur Statistik des Deutschen Reichs—Ergänzungsheft zu 1916* 4 (1918): *Die Deutschen im Ausland und die Ausländer im Deutschen Reiche*, 86; Silbergleit, *Die Bevölkerungs- und Berufsverhältnisse*, 36*, 80, 93; Schmelz, Territorial Printout.

Table 10.25. Difference in Makeup of Jewish Communities in Ruhr Cities that Merged

A) Oberhausen, Osterfeld, and Sterkrade

Population	Oberhausen	Osterfeld	Sterkrade
1910			
General population	89900	26527	34518
Jewish population	403	28	73
Percent Jewish	0.5	0.1	0.2
1925			
General population	105436	32592	50757
Jewish population	513	48	130
Percent Jewish	0.5	0.2	0.3

B) Dortmund and Hörde

Population	Dortmund	Hörde
1900		
General population	142733	25126
Jewish population	1924	347
Percent Jewish	1.4	1.4
1910		
General population	214226	32791
Jewish population	2676	285
Percent Jewish	1.3	0.9
1925		
General population	321743	34694
Jewish population	3820	238
Percent Jewish	1.9	0.7

C) Gelsenkirchen and Buer

Population	Gelsenkirchen	Schalke	Ückendorf	Bismarck	Buer	Horst
1900						
General population	36935	26077	21937	21169	28521	
Jewish population	811	83	47	71	47	
Percent Jewish	2.2	0.3	0.2	0.3	0.2	
1910						
General population	169513				61510	20978
Jewish population	1251				117	47
Percent Jewish	0.7				0.2	0.2
1925						
General population	208512				99058	24663
Jewish population	1441				171	113
Percent Jewish	0.7				0.2	0.5

D) Essen

Essen	1890	1900	1910	1925	1933
General population	78706	118862	294653	470524	654461
Jewish population	1190	1807	2773	4209	4506
Percent Jewish	1.5	1.5	0.1	0.9	0.7
Altendorf	1890	1900	1910	1925	1933
General population	31892	63238			
Jewish population	17	63			
Percent Jewish	0.1	0.1			
Borbeck	1890	1900	1910	1925	1933
General population	28707	47217	71106		
Jewish population	42	69	142		
Percent Jewish	0.2	0.2	0.2		
Altenessen	1890	1900	1910	1925	1933
General population		28668	40644		
Jewish population		25	34		
Percent Jewish		0.1	0.1		
Steele	1890	1900	1910	1925	1933
General population					33823
Jewish population					157
Percent Jewish					0.5

Kray	1890	1900	1910	1925	1933
General population					25405
Jewish population					7
Percent Jewish					0
Katernberg	1890	1900	1910	1925	1933
General population			22381		
Jewish population			45		
Percent Jewish			0.2		

Sources: Schmelz, Territorial Printout, Silbergleit, *Die Bevölkerungs- und Berufsverhältnisse*, 31*–32*.

When two cities of approximately equal size merged, there was often a great difference in Jewish density between the two, which then translated into neighborhood differentiation in the new large city. Thus, in the city that eventually became Wuppertal, Jewish presence was much denser in Elberfeld than in neighboring Barmen. At first, the percentage of foreign Jews was also higher in Elberfeld than in Barmen, but it fell into balance by the 1925 census (Table 10.26). In Saarbrücken, which was created in 1909 by the merger of the three cities of Saarbrücken, St. Johann, and Malstatt-Burbach, Jews were far more numerous in middle-class St. Johann than in either of the other two cities that merged with it (Table 10.27).

Measuring Jewish Residential Concentration

Overall, it seems clear that urban Jewish residential concentration decreased considerably between the early nineteenth century and unification in 1871. Thereafter, Jewish segregation continued at an intensity that, while lessened, remained much greater than that of Christian urban religious minorities. The degree of Jewish residential segregation can be calculated through the index of dissimilarity, a standard demographic measure of segregation that calculates the percentage of one population that would have to move in order to duplicate the pattern of the other population.[30] Although the index helps us to compare the general degree of Jewish segregation in various cities, the exact figures are not always directly comparable due to internal differences in Jewish densities by subdistrict within each district analyzed.[31] By and large, Jews within major German cities displayed a level of segregation similar to those of white ethnic groups in the first half of twentieth century in the United States, which was lower than that of American racial minorities but much higher than that of Christian religious minorities in German cities.

---

30 The dissimilarity index is calculated by taking the percentage of the city total, in a particular district, of each of the populations being compared. The sum of the differences of the percentages for each district is then divided by two to create the index.

31 The smaller the size of the census areas enumerated (that is, the more detailed the geographical analysis), the higher the level of the index appears. For Berlin in 1905, for instance, dividing the city into its twenty-nine main districts yields a dissimilarity index of 39.8 percent. A more detailed analysis using the city's 394 *Stadtbezirke* yields the substantially higher figure of 46.4 percent. When the same divisions are used over a period of time, however, the increases and decreases in Jewish segregation become rather clear. For this reason, all reports of dissimilarity indices in this volume specify the number of districts into which the data divide the city.

Table 10.26. Difference in Makeup of Jewish Communities in Cities that Merged to Form Wuppertal

Barmen	1880	1890	1900	1910	1925
City population	95941	116144	141944	169214	187099
Jewish population	239	416	592	643	721
Percent Jewish	0.3	0.3	0.4	0.4	0.4
Total foreigners				1392	
Foreign Jews				69	120
Percent of Jewish population foreign				10.7	16.6
Elberfeld	1880	1890	1900	1910	1925
City population	93538	125899	156966	170192	167577
Jewish population	1104	1378	1664	1919	2335
Percent Jewish	1.2	1.1	1.1	1.1	1.4
Total foreigners				2559	
Foreign Jews				289	387
Percent of Jewish population foreign				15.1	16.6

Sources: Schmelz, Territorial Printout; Blau, *Entwicklung*, 284; Silbergleit, *Die Bevölkerungs- und Berufsverhältnisse*, 24*, 59*; Bosse, *Die Verbreitung der Juden*, 39; *Vierteljahrshefte zur Statistik des Deutschen Reichs—Ergänzungsheft zu 1916* 4 (1918): *Die Deutschen im Ausland und die Ausländer im Deutschen Reiche*, 86.

In Berlin and Frankfurt, the Jewish population displayed similar dissimilarity indices in the early nineteenth century—64.3 percent and 65.1 percent, respectively. By the 1850s and 1860s, these levels sank to the 40 percent range for both cities, approximating the index for Hamburg in the same period.[32] For most of the period after 1870, most major Jewish communities for which

---

32 Dissimilarity indices: Frankfurt (1858): 41.7 percent; Berlin (1867): 43.5 percent; Hamburg (1866): 43.4 percent.

Table 10.27. Difference in Makeup of Jewish Communities in Cities that Merged to Form Saarbrücken

Saarbrücken	1880	1890	1900	1910
General population	9514	13812	23237	105089
Jewish population	37	61	98	1081
Percent Jewish	0.4	0.4	0.4	1.0
St. Johann	1880	1890	1900	1910
General population	12346		21266	
Jewish population	254		567	
Percent Jewish	2.1		2.7	
Malstatt/Burbach	1880	1890	1900	1910
General population	13158		31195	49112
Jewish population	23		92	100
Percent Jewish	0.2		0.3	0.2

Source: Schmelz, Territorial Printout; Bosse, *Die Verbreitung der Juden*, 42.

we have data had dissimilarity indices in the 35–45 percent range, albeit with some significant deviations. In cities where substantial portions of the Jewish population left old Jewish neighborhoods in the central city for new and more outlying districts, Jewish concentration levels continued to decline until the 1880s. During this period of the late nineteenth century, migrants from old neighborhood often settled in many different neighborhoods before they began to reassemble in a new Jewish neighborhood at around the turn of the century (especially in Berlin and Hamburg). From the 1880s and 1890s to the Nazi period, Jewish concentration increased slightly in cities where a two-neighborhood pattern evolved, such as Berlin, Frankfurt, Munich, and Cologne, but jumped more sharply in cities that followed a one-neighborhood pattern. In Hamburg, the dissimilarity index exceeded 50 percent in 1900 and declined only slightly in the years before 1933. Leipzig, in contrast to the other major cities, experienced a sharp and rising increase in dissimilarity. By 1935, Jewish segregation in Leipzig attained the level of early nineteenth-century Berlin and Frankfurt. The unusually acute segregation in Leipzig seems directly tied to both the high percentage of immigrants among Leipzig Jewry and their tendency to remain concentrated in the central parts of the city.[33] In the relatively small city

---

33 In 1880, when the Jewish population of Leipzig consisted mostly of recently arrived German Jews, Jewish segregation was lower there than in other cities. Between 1889 and 1892, Leipzig

of Heidelberg, Jewish segregation was substantially weaker than in larger cities (Tables 10.28 and 10.29).[34]

Notwithstanding the historically large difference in distribution between Catholics and Protestants in various regions of Germany, there was little evidence of such segregation within urban German neighborhoods. Members of the minority Christian denomination in a particular city had much lower indices of dissimilarity than those of Jews, ranging from a low of approximately five percent for Catholics in Frankfurt and Berlin and Protestants in Cologne, to highs of 13–17 percent among Catholics in Hamburg and Protestants in Munich. Evidently, this reflected the smaller socioeconomic differences between

Table 10.28. Jewish Neighborhood Distribution in Heidelberg, 1933

Neighborhood	General population	Jewish population	Percent Jewish
Schlierbach	1763	5	0.3
Östliche Altstadt	9937	130	1.3
Westliche Altstadt	8762	287	3.3
Weststadt	21829	346	1.6
Neuenheim	10489	186	1.8
Handschuhsheim	10248	103	1.0
Pfaffengrund	2686	1	0
Wieblingen	5007	0	0
Kirchheim	7926	5	0.1
Rohrbach	5994	39	0.7
Total	84641	1102	1.3

Source: Arno Weckbecker, *Die Judenverfolgung in Heidelberg 1933–1945* (Heidelberg: Müller Juristischer Verlag, 1985), 31.

---

annexed a large area of formerly independent towns, creating what came to be known as Neu Leipzig. Both during and after that same period, immigrants from Eastern Europe arrived in large numbers and soon became the majority of the Jewish community; almost all of them settled in the central city. Excluding Neu Leipzig, where Jews were scarce throughout the late nineteenth and early twentieth centuries, Jewish concentration becomes much less extraordinary.

34 Table 10.28 shows that Jewish segregation remained in the 35–45 percent range in most cities with "two-neighborhood" patterns between 1867 and 1933 but was higher in cities with one-neighborhood patterns, such as Hamburg and Leipzig. The difference in results as a function of the number of districts used in the analysis also shows how increasing the number of districts inflates the results slightly.

Table 10.29. Indices of Dissimilarity between Jews and General Population

Berlin

	1809	1867	1875	1880	1885	1890	1895	1900	1905	1910	1925	1933	1939	Total
	64.3	43.5	34.2	34.4	34.4	37.2	41.3	40.1	39.8	36.7	38.9	40.1	45.4	46.4
		(16)	(21)	(21)	(22)	(22)	(26)	(24)	(29)	(20)	(20)	(20)	(20)	(394)

Cologne

	1925	1933	1939
	40.4 (17)	43.1 (87)	44.3 (16)
(Catholic parishes)		38.4 (32)	
(Protestant parishes)		39.7 (50)	
		36.2 (13)	

Munich

	1875	1880	1885	1905	1910
	43.6 (19)	44.1 (19)	39.0 (19)	40.7 (24)	40.5 (26)
	37.7 (5)	34.9 (5)	31.8 (5)	38.9 (5)	38.9 (sic) (5)

Leipzig

	1880	1900	1925
By Protestant parishes	29.8 (4)	56.4 (20)	[54.0 (32)]

	1880	1900	1905	1935
By districts	31.7 (8)	54.7 (25)	58.4 (10)	66.4 (10)
Alt Leipzig only	38.8 (7)	41.9 (7)	43.4 (7)	

Dresden

By Protestant parishes	1925
	45.9 (38)

Frankfurt/Main

1817	1858	1890	1895	1900	1925
65.1 (14)	41.7 (14)		36.8 (14)	**38.9 (15)**	**43.7 (15)**

Hamburg

1866	1871	1880	1885	1900	1910	1925	1933
43.4 (11)	50.3 (13)	**42.4 (16)**	33.5 (20)	52.4 (15)	49.1 (13)	49.6 (27)	47.0 (13)

Heidelberg

1933
25.9

Data in bold are between 35 percent and 45 percent. Figures in parentheses denote the number of districts in the analysis.

Protestants and Catholics than those between Jews and Christians. Persons with no recorded religion seem to have been somewhat more segregated than Christian minorities. There was a slight tendency for Christian denominations' degree of separateness to decrease over time. In the 1925 and 1933 censuses, which were the only ones in which those without religion were represented in large numbers, the unchurched seem to have been most common in working-class districts, where the influence of left-wing parties was strong. The Jewish and the "no denomination" populations were often more dissimilar than the Jewish and overall populations were. This was an indication that few "non-denominational" inhabitants were Jews in disguise. There seems to have been no overall correlation between the neighborhood distributions of Jewish and Christian minority populations (Tables 10.30 and 10.31).

The above analysis shows clearly that Jews retained a much higher degree of residential segregation than did members of minority non-Jewish denominations. While Jewish segregation did wane considerably between the early nineteenth century and the 1860s and 1870s, it remained obvious in most large cities. This seems to indicate that Jews in Germany acted more like an American ethnic group than did German Protestants or Catholics when they were urban minorities themselves. There were three common patterns of Jewish distribution. The first was the migration of most of the population to a new prosperous neighborhood in cities with few East European immigrants (as in Hamburg). The second was a two-neighborhood pattern (in most cities, especially Berlin and Frankfurt) with substantial but not overwhelming numbers of immigrants. Finally, in Leipzig we see continued concentration in the central city, presumably because immigrants were in the majority. There is little evidence of marked changes in the degree of Jewish segregation during the early twentieth century, although Jews in many places tended to drift away from the city center. The early Nazi period between 1933 and 1939 was marked by a moderate degree of largely voluntary increased Jewish concentration. In the final stages of German-Jewish life before deportation to extermination camps, involuntary Jewish concentration either in *Judenhäuser* in various parts of cities where Jews had previously lived or in specially constructed "settlements" became part of government policy.[35]

---

35 Examples of forced Jewish "settlements" were the camps set up in the outlying districts of Milbertshofen and Berg am Laim in Munich in 1941. See *Pinkas ha-Kehillot, Germania, Bavaria*, 127–128.

Table 10.30. Index of Dissimilarity between Non-Jewish Populations and General Population in Leading German Cities

City	Year	Non-Jewish minority	Dissimilarity index	Number of districts
Hamburg	1866	Catholics	13.1	
Berlin	1875	Catholics	5.3	20
	1905	Catholics	9.2	394
	1939	Catholics	6.7	20
	1939	No religion	10.2	
Munich	1875	Protestants	17.1	19
	1910	Protestants	14.7	26
Cologne	1933	Protestants	6.0	13
	1933	Protestants	7.0	32
	1933	Protestants	7.4	50
	1933	No religion	12.1	32
Leipzig	1900	Catholics	13.4	20
	1925	Catholics	11.5	32
Frankfurt	1895	Catholics	4.6	
	1925	Catholics	5.0	21
	1925	No religion	6.3	21

Table 10.31. Index of Dissimilarity between Jews and Non-Jewish Minority Communities

City	Year	Jews versus:	Index of dissimilarity	Number of districts
Berlin	1875	Catholics	33.6	
Munich	1875	Protestants	44.3	19
	1910	Protestants	40.1	26
Cologne	1933	Protestants	35.1	13
	1933	Protestants	38.1	32
	1933	Protestants	37.6	50
	1933	No religion	43.2	32
Leipzig	1900	Catholics	52.3	20
	1925	Catholics	52.3	32
Frankfurt	1895	Catholics	39.2	15

Source unknown.

REGIONAL SECTION

11

The Eastern Provinces

The final section of this volume is devoted to the five major geographical regions of Germany—the eastern provinces in chapter 11, the central and northwestern sections in chapter 12 (Map 1, the western areas in chapter 13, and the south in chapter 14.

According to their Jewish population distribution, the eastern provinces of Germany may be divided into three main subregions: 1) the formerly Polish provinces of Posen and West Prussia, 2) the provinces of East Prussia and Pomerania, and 3) Silesia. In some ways, *Regierungsbezirk* Danzig was distinctive from the rest of the first-mentioned subregion and Upper Silesia shared some characteristics with it. The three subregions had different histories and their Jewish populations developed quite differently. In 1815, when the entire region was united under Prussian rule, *Regierungsbezirk* Posen and the West Prussian *Regierungsbezirk* Marienwerder had 71–72 percent of all Jewish inhabitants of eastern Germany combined,[1] leaving Silesia with 17–18 percent and East Prussia plus Pomerania with only about 5.8 percent.

---

1   In 1816, the three *Regierungsbezirke* of Posen, Bromberg and Marienwerder were home to a total of 60,792 Jews, as against 4,976 in Pomerania and East Prussia and 15,079 in Silesia. In 1817, the census showed 66,322, 5,365 and 16,476 in the three subregions, respectively. Danzig District had 3,796 Jews in 1816 and 3,854 in 1817. The total Jewish population of the entire region was 84,643 in 1816 and 92,017 in 1817.

The Formerly Polish Provinces

In the eighteenth century, the Commonwealth of Poland had a much denser Jewish population than did the Prussian districts to its west. When various Polish districts fell to Prussia as did most of West Prussia and Netze District in 1772, and most of Posen in 1793, their Jewish populations differed in density.[2] In West Prussia, Jews were heavily concentrated in the Notec (Netze) River valley whereas their presence in the more northerly areas was relatively sparse. When the Netze District fell to Prussia in 1772, the anti-Jewish Prussian King Frederick II attempted to reduce the Jewish population, which was met with only modest success. In Posen, which fell to Prussia after the king's death, the Jewish population was allowed to remain at the high level it had reached under Polish rule. The results of the different histories of the formerly Polish areas were a relatively low Jewish density in the north that increased as one moved south[3] (Table 11.1). In the sparsely Jewish Danzig District, the Jews were concentrated in the port city of Danzig itself (2,148 of the 3,854 Jews in 1817). In Marienwerder District, Jews were especially numerous in the southwest, where four communities had over 500 Jews and two (Zempelburg and Märkisch Friedland) had Jewish majorities. Large shtetl-like settlements of this type were even more common in Posen province, where there were eleven Jewish communities of over 500 persons in Bromberg District and nineteen in the Posen *Regierungsbezirk*. Three of these towns had Jewish majorities and twenty-one were over 25 percent Jewish. Jews in communities of over 500 made up 66 percent of the Jewish population of Posen province.

In the first three decades of renewed Prussian rule, the Jewish population of the former Polish districts continued to grow. While almost all of this in Danzig District traced to an excess of births over deaths, the other three districts showed evidence of modest in-migration. Before 1840, only a few Posen cities lost Jewish population; most were either in the northern half of the province near West Prussia or in the south near Silesia (Table 11.2). In 1843, there were 109 Jewish communities with over 100 individuals in Posen province and forty-eight in West Prussia. In Posen, 93.4 percent of Jewish inhabitants lived in communities of at least 100 Jews and 70.9 percent dwelled in communities of at least 500 (Table 11.3).

---

2 This chapter will not deal with the large areas of Poland that were under Prussian control after 1793 but were assigned to the Russian-ruled Kingdom of Poland in 1815.
3 The former Polish *Regierungsbezirke*, from north to south, were: Danzig, Marienwerder, Bromberg, and Posen. The former Netze District was divided between the Marienwerder and Bromberg *Regierungsbezirke*.

Table 11.1. Jewish Population of Formerly Polish Districts

District	1803			1816		1817
Marienwerdersches Kammerdepartment	4500	0.8%	Danzig	3,796	1.6%	3,854
Netzedistrikt	13600	6.0	Marienwerder	8,833	2.7	8,778
Posensches Kammerdepartment	36600	6.0	Bromberg	14,184	5.8	15,021
			Posen	37,772	6.6	37,547

Source: Silbergleit, *Die Bevölkerungs- und Berufsverhältnisse*, 5*, 7*, 11*.

Table 11.2. Towns in Posen Province that Lost Jewish Population before 1840 (only towns with over 300 Jews at any time)

Town	1817	Highest Jewish population (year)	1840
Lissa	3644	3719 (1823)	3466
Murowana Goslin		548 (1831)	488
Kurnik	774	1213 (1831)	1170
Fraustadt	648		558
Kempen	2406	3830 (1831)	3577
Filehne	1231	1525 (1834)	1467
Schönlanke	756	904 (1831)	791
Labischin	608	901 (1823)	690 (1837)
Schokken		445 (1823)	346
Margonin		456 (1823)	438

Sources: Blau, Entwicklung, 33–34; Breslauer, *Abwanderung*, Table A.

By the 1840s, the migration patterns in the formerly Polish districts were transitioning from net in-migration to out-migration. After cresting in 1846, the Jewish population of *Regierungsbezirk* Posen began to decline, at first slowly but then with increasing rapidity. The absolute decline in Jewish population in the three other districts began somewhat later. In Bromberg District, the downturn was slight until after 1861 while in Marienwerder and Danzig, it proceeded slowly until after 1880 (Table 11.4).

Between 1840 and 1860, by far the fastest declines in Jewish population in Posen province occurred in the westernmost counties, especially those in

Table 11.3. Jewish Communities of over 1,000 in Posen Province, 1843

Regierungsbezirk Bromberg		*Regierungsbezirk* Posen	
Inowraclaw	2120	Posen	7359
Gnesen	1794	Kempen	3528
Fordon	1378	Lissa	3261
Filehne	1328	Krotoschin	2214
Wittkowo	1128	Rawicz	1878
Czarnikau	1101	Rogasen	1727
Chodziesen	1040	Schwerin/Warthe	1622
		Grätz	1548
		Schwersenz	1511
		Ostrowo	1498
		Wreschen	1453
		Meseritz	1078
		Kurnik	1077
		Schrimm	1014

Jewish Communities with over 500 in West Prussia, 1843

Regierungsbezirk Danzig		*Regierungsbezirk* Marienwerder	
Danzig	2434	Zempelburg	1688
Preussisch Stargard	608	Tuchel	715
		Gollub	665
		Krojanke	665
		Märkisch Friedland	609
		Deutsch Krone	566
		Strassburg	559
		Flatow	535
		Jastrow	509
		Lau[t]enburg	508

Source: Bleich, *Die erste vereinigte Landtag*, 322–324.

Table 11.4. Changes in Jewish Population of Formerly Polish Districts, 1843–1910

District	1843	1849	1852	1858	1861	1867	1871	1880	1890	1900	1910	1843–1871	1871–1910
Danzig	5402	5566	5893	6386	6716	6349	6782	6567	5928	5504	4653	+25.5%	-31.4%
Marienwerder	15939	17409	18493	19513	20014	20368	19850	19980	15822	12722	9301	+24.5	-53.1
Bromberg	24788	24528	24098	24291	24223	23055	21758	20039	15915	13024	9548	-12.2	-56.1
Posen	54787	52486	50155	47907	49949	42453	40224	36570	28431	22303	16964	-26.6	-57.8

Sources: Silbergleit, *Die Bevölkerungs- und Berufsverhältnisse*, 18*–19*, Blau, *Entwicklung*, 69.

Regierungsbezirk Posen, where German speakers were the majority (Map 11/2). In towns like Meseritz, Schwerin an der Warthe, and Birnbaum, which were not far from the Brandenburg frontier, Jewish migration westward, probably mainly to Berlin, began early and reduced a larger proportion of the population than it did farther east in the province. Areas bordering on Russian-ruled Poland were more likely to gain in Jewish population rather than lose it because they were much farther from Berlin and also likely due to migration across the Russian-Prussian frontier. In many parts of *Regierungsbezirk* Bromberg, the Jewish population declined little or did not change at all before 1860 even in most areas that had German-speaking majorities. This was possibly because of growing Jewish communities in cities like Bromberg, Gnesen, and Inowraclaw (Table 11.5).

After 1880, Jewish migration from Posen and West Prussia accelerated. Except in Danzig District, where Jewish density had always been much lower, the Jewish population in these provinces dropped by more than one-half between 1880 and 1910. The decline was never as steep in Danzig District as in the other three districts mainly because the port city of Danzig, where half of the Jews in the district lived, lost only 12.65 percent of its Jewish population from 1871 to 1910. Until 1871, the western counties of *Regierungsbezirk* Posen continued to have much higher out-migration than did other sections of the province; thereafter, however, the differences between regions diminished steadily. After around 1880, other regions of Posen province made up much of the difference and began losing Jewish population even faster than did the western counties.

Out-migration was greatest in the smaller towns of Posen and West Prussia and slightest in the larger cities. Although even in 1910 many communities remained large by the standards of other parts of Germany, most towns that were over 25 percent Jewish experienced large drops in Jewish population. While most large Jewish communities in Posen province had already shrunk considerably by 1880, most of those in West Prussia remained near their 1843 levels in 1880 and began their sharp decline only afterwards (Table 11.6).

Several communities in larger and medium-size cities (even in Posen province) either retained much of their 1843 Jewish populations or even gained in numbers (Table 11.7). By 1905, however, the greatest density of Jews in any town, which was in Kempen, a town that had once had a Jewish majority, had fallen to fifteen percent.

By the 1910 census, the Jewish population of Posen province had fallen to 26,512 (1.26 percent of the total), about one-third of its highest point in 1846. The Jewish population of West Prussia at that time was 13,954 (0.82 percent), slightly above half of its peak in 1861. The Jewish populations of both provinces

Table 11.5. Changes in Urban Jewish Population in Various Sections of Posen Province, 1840–1860

Regierungsbezirk Posen	1840	1860	Percent change	Percent German-speaking in 1860
Western counties				
Birnbaum	2750	2026	-26.3%	76.2
Meseritz	2147	1546	-28.0	85.9
Bomst	1878	1294	-31.1	58.8
Fraustadt	4442	3279	-26.2	77.4
Subtotal	11217	8145	-27.4	
Southeastern counties				
Kröben	2886	2464	-14.6	41.1
Krotoschin	4291	3870	-9.8	35.0
Adelnau	1781	2167	+21.7	17.5
Schildberg	4238	3962	-6.5	22.3
Pleschen	1814	1998	+10.1	18.9
Subtotal	15010	14461	-3.7	
Northeastern counties				
Wreschen	2327	1920	-17.5	14.0
Schroda	1236	1271	+2.8	19.2
Schrimm	2794	2667	-4.5	26.1
Subtotal	6357	5858	-7.8	
North-central counties				
Posen	8490	8988	+5.9	45.7
Obornik	2812	2346	-16.6	54.5
Samter	2992	3161	+5.6	37.1
Subtotal	14294	14495	+1.4	
Central counties				
Kosten	860	920	+7.0	18.8
Buk	2753	2171	-21.1	42.8
Subtotal	3613	3091	-14.5	
Total, *Regierungsbezirk* Posen	50491	46050	-8.8	40.7

Regierungsbezirk Bromberg	1840	1860	Percent change	Percent German-speaking in 1860
Northwest				
Czarnikau	3339	2707	-18.9	76.5
Chodziesen	2752 (1837)	3169	+15.2	81.4
Wirsitz	1936 (1837)	2319	+34.2	56.7
Subtotal	8017	8195	+2.2	
All other				
Bromberg	2178 (1843)	3846	+76.6	67.7
Schubin	2579 (1837)	2405	-6.7	45.1
Inowraclaw	2495	2640	+5.8	34.3
Mogilno	955	1161	+21.6	31.9
Gnesen	3354	2927	-12.7	22.5
Wongrowitz	1355	1830	+35.1	26.5
Subtotal	12916	14809	+14.7	
Total, *Regierungsbezirk* Bromberg	20933	23004	+9.9	50.6
Total, Posen province	71424	69054	-3.3	44.2

Counties with German speakers	1840	1860	Change
Counties with under 30% German speakers	19759	19662	-0.5%
30%–50% German speakers	27441	26860	-2.1
50%–70% German speakers	8804	9805	+11.4
Over 70% German speakers	15430	12727	-17.5

Sources: Karl Heink Streiter, *Die Nationale Beziehungen im Grossherzogtum Posen (1815–1848)* (Bern and New York: Peter Lang, 1986), Table IV. 1840 figures are based on Heppner and Herzberg, *Aus Vergangenheit und Gegenwart*, recalculated to fit the same county boundaries.

Table 11.6. Decline in Jewish Population of Towns in Posen Province with over 1,000 Jews in 1843

Town	1843	1880	1905
Posen	7,359	7,063	5,761
Kempen	3,528	2,193	804
Lissa	3,261	1,833	996
Krotoschin	2,214	1,192	525
Inowrazlaw (Hohensalza)	2,120	1,615	1,157
Rawicz	1,878	1,123	428
Gnesen	1,794	1,543	980
Rogasen	1,727	1,318	591
Schwerin/Warthe	1,622	473	161
Grätz	1,548	656	250
Schwersenz	1,511	611	208
Ostrowo	1,498	1,496	744
Wreschen	1,453	917	382
Fordon	1,378	427	204
Filehne	1,328	718	378
Wittkowo	1,128	395	111
Czarnikau	1,101	896	479
Meseritz	1,078	377	170
Kurnik	1,077	350	111
Chodziesen (Kolmar)	1,040	665	298
Schrimm	1,014	989	396

Sources: Bleich, *Die erste vereinigte Landtag*, 323; Bosse, *Die Verbreitung der Juden*, 24–29; Breslauer, *Abwanderung*, Table A.

continued to decline between 1910 and the outbreak of World War I as well as during the war itself, although no figures for this period are available. At the end of the war, most both provinces' territory was assigned to the new Republic of Poland; a rump remained under German rule and the city of Danzig received the status of an independent Free City. The large majority of Jews who still lived in the areas assigned to Poland at the end of World War I left these territories by the early 1920s and were replaced, in part, by Jewish migrants from farther east in Poland. Most postwar migrants from Posen and West Prussia followed the pattern of earlier out-migrants and settled chiefly in Berlin, in which those from

Table 11.7. Declines in Jewish Population in Cities in Posen Province with over 10,000 Total Inhabitants

City	Jewish population				General population
	1843	1880	1905	1910	1905
Posen	7359	7063	5761	5605	117033
Bromberg	482	1889	1513	1349	52504
Inowraclaw (Hohensalza)	2120	1615	1157	951	26114
Gnesen	1794	1543	980	778	21693
Schneidemühl	859	805	653	582	19655
Lissa	3261	1833	996	804	14263
Krotoschin	2214	1192	525	411	12373
Ostrowo	1498	1496	744	714	11800
Rawitsch	1878	1123	428	363	11741
Total, cities over 10,000	21465	18559	12757	11557	
All other Posen province	58110	38050		14955	

Sources: Bleich, *Die erste vereinigte Landtag*, 323–324; Bosse, *Die Verbreitung der Juden*, 24–29; Breslauer, *Abwanderung*, Tables A and B; "Die 525 Gemeinden von mehr als 10,000 Einwohnern nach der Volkszählung vom 1. Dezember 1905," *Statistisches Jahrbuch für das Deutsche Reich* (1907): 10–11.

several specific towns established *landsmanshaftn*. A smaller number settled in Silesia, especially in Breslau.[4] By contrast, most of Danzig's Jews remained in the city after it was separated from Germany and were joined by increasing numbers of migrants from Poland.[5]

The areas that Germany retained were assigned either to a new Prussian province—Grenzmark Posen and West Prussia—or to a new West Prussian District in East Prussia province. In the 1925 census, the former had a Jewish

---

4 The 1933 census, 5/49, 50, counted a total of 46,550 Jews born in "the lost territories." Of these, 25,524 lived in Berlin, 5,362 in Breslau, and 3,990 in other places in Silesia.
5 The Jewish population of Danzig was 2,717 in 1910, 7,282 in 1923, and 9,239 in 1924. In 1923, only 2,500 Jews held Danzig citizenship. n.a., "Die jüdische Bevölkerung des Freistaates und der Stadt Danzig," *ZDSJ* 4, 7-8 (1927): 126–127.

Table 11.8. Jewish Population in Posen and West Prussian Districts that Remained in Germany

District	1910	1925
West Prussian District of East Prussia	1398	1358 (0.5%)
Grenzmark	3835	3437 (1.0%)

Source: Silbergleit, *Die Bevölkerungs- und Berufsverhältnisse*, 18*–19*.

population of 3,437 and the latter had 1,358 Jewish inhabitants, represesnting a decline of about 400 in Grenzmark and approximately forty in the new district since 1910 (Table 11.8). By 1933, the Jewish population of Grenzmark fell by another 662 to 2,775. Almost all remaining Jews in the district held German citizenship. *Regierungsbezirk* West Prussia, in turn, had only 1,075 Jews left, 367 of them in the city of Elbing.

Pomerania and East Prussia

At the time of the 1812 Emancipation decree, the Prussian provinces of Pomerania and East Prussia had sparse Jewish populations. An 1803 estimate counted 1,350 Jews in Pomerania and 1,030 in East Prussia.[6] Most of both provinces had been part of the Prussian kingdom for some time, but Stralsund District in the extreme west of Pomerania had been under Swedish rule—and therefore off-limits to Jewish residence—until 1815.[7] Prussia did not acquire the area of Warmia in East Prussia from Poland until 1772; unlike the rest of the province, its population was overwhelmingly Catholic. While the Jewish populations of Pomerania and East Prussia more than doubled between 1803 and 1817, they still remained rather low (Table 11.9). In 1817, Jewish density in the various districts ranged from a low of 0.08 percent in Gumbinnen District and 0.09 percent in Stralsund District to a high of 0.65 percent in Köslin District and 0.38 percent in the districts of Königsberg and Stettin. In East Prussia, a large percentage of the Jews lived in the capital city of Königsberg (1,027 of 2,389 or 42.9 percent in 1817). In Pomerania, in contrast, the largest Jewish community in 1816 was in Stargard and numbered only 172 individuals.[8] Only five communities in all of Pomerania had at least 100 Jews.

---

6 Silbergleit, *Die Bevölkerungs- und Berufsverhältnisse*, 5*.
7 A much larger portion of western Pomerania had belonged to Sweden prior to 1713.
8 Loewe, "Die Zahl der Juden in Pommern," 146–149.

Table 11.9. Jewish Population of East Prussia and Pomerania, 1803–1817

District	1803	1816	1817
Königsberg	970	1903	2098
Gumbinnen (Littauisches Department)	60	264	291
East Prussia total	1030	2167	2389
Köslin		1468	1585
Stettin		1218	1269
Stralsund		123	122
Pommern Total	1350	2809	2976

Source: Silbergleit, Die Bevölkerungs- und Berufsverhältnisse, 5*, 7*, 11*.

The Jewish populations of both Pomerania and East Prussia grew rapidly between 1817 and 1880. From 1817 to 1843, the number of Jews at least doubled in every Regierungsbezirk of the region except Stralsund and tripled in Stettin District. Growth was particularly spectacular in the eastern half of East Prussia where it increased five-fold in Gumbinnen District. Although one could credit these huge increases to massive influxes from the nearby Russian Empire, this was not the case even in Gumbinnen District, which lay directly on the Russian border. With the exception of Stralsund, the number of Jews without citizenship in 1843 was negligible in all Pomeranian and East Prussian districts.[9] The influx of Jews generally came from areas that had been part of Prussia at the time of the 1812 Emancipation decree. All evidence points to migration from West Prussia, the heavily Jewish province between Pomerania and East Prussia (Table 11.10).

A study of the growth of Jewish population in East Prussia shows indications of the influx from West Prussia.[10] This was particularly the case in the area around the Netze (Noteć) River, in which Prussian policy had tried to eliminate Jewish village residence and Jewish participation in crafts from 1772 onward. Among Jews residing in West Prussian towns like Flatow, many adult men spent most of the year in East Prussia on business. After the decree of 1812, many of these men acquired official residency there.[11] Of thirty-seven Jewish individuals

---

9 Stralsund District was not part of Prussia at the time of the Emancipation decree and its Jewish residents did not acquire citizenship by this means. The number of non-citizens in the other four Regierungsbezirke in 1843 was eighty-nine in Königsberg, thirty-three in Gumbinnen, forty in Stettin, and twenty-four in Köslin.
10 Maurer, "Problemskizze," 217–247.
11 See Jacob Adam, Zeit zur Abreise: Lebensbericht eines judischen Handlers aus der Emanzipationszeit (Hildesheim: Olms, 1993).

Table 11.10. Changing Jewish Population of Pomerania and East Prussia by *Regierungsbezirk*

Regierungsbezirk	1817	1825	1834	1843	1852	1861	1871	1880	1890	1900	1910	1925	1933
Königsberg	2098	2934	3611	4730	6101	7975	10588	12427	9780	9187	7138	5503	4306
Allenstein											2734	2275	1756
Gumbinnen	291	547	950	1467	2082	2930	3837	5791	4631	4690	3155	2201	1701
West Prussia												1358	1075
East Prussia	2389	3481	4561	6197	8383	10905	14425	18218	14411	13877	13027	11337	8838
Köslin	1585	2036	2686	3781	4822	5823	6189	6465	5343	4300	3374	2862	2174
Stettin	1269	1971	2743	3779	5361	6387	6501	7014	6527	6292	5217	4577	3866
Stralsund	122	169	184	156	210	278	347	407	376	288	271	322	277
Pomerania	2976	4176	5613	7716	10393	12488	13037	13886	12246	10880	8862	7761	6317
Percent change from previous period	1817	1825	1834	1843	1852	1861	1871	1880	1890	1900	1910	1925	1933
Königsberg		+39.9	+23.1	+31.0	+29.0	+30.7	+32.8	+17.65	-21.3	-9.1		-22.9	-21.8
Allenstein												-16.8	-22.8
Gumbinnen		+88.0	+73.7	+54.4	+41.9	+40.7	+31.0	+50.9	-20.0	+1.3		-30.2	-22.7
West Prussia													-20.8
East Prussia		+45.7	+31.0	+35.9	+32.05	+33.3	+32.3	+26.3	-20.9	-3.7	-6.1	-13.0	-22.0
Köslin		+28.5	+31.9	+28.6	+27.5	+20.8	+6.3	+4.5	-17.4	-19.5	-21.5	-15.2	-24.0
Stettin		+55.3	+39.2	+37.8	+41.9	+19.1	+1.8	+7.9	-6.9	-4.1	-16.7	-12.3	-15.5
Stralsund		+38.5	+8.9	-15.2	+34.6	+32.8	+24.82	+17.3	-7.6	-23.4	-5.9	+18.8	-14.0
Pomerania		+40.3	+34.4	+37.5	+34.7	+20.2	+4.4	+6.5	-11.8	-11.2	-18.6	-12.4	-18.6

Sources: Silbergleit, *Die Bevölkerungs- und Berufsverhältnisse*, 11*, 18–19*; Schmelz, Territorial Printout; 1933 census, 5/11.

and families that settled in the East Prussian Gumbinnen district between 1817 and 1819, twenty-five had originally resided in West Prussia. The first Jews in Mohrungen, East Prussia, came from Flatow and Krojanke in the Netze section of West Prussia. The growth of several cities on the Russian border was often spectacular. Although many of the new arrivals came from Russian territory, quite a few originated in more distant Westp Prusia.[12] In Tilsit, for instance, the Jewish population increased from thirteen in 1811 to 265 in 1843 and 515 in 1871.[13]

In Pomerania, in-migration was strongest in Stettin District, which had formerly had a sparse Jewish population. This new wave established many new communities and greatly expanded old ones. The increase was most considerable in the city of Stettin, in which the first Jews settled in 1812. Thereafter, the city's Jewish population grew to 250 in 1831, 519 in 1843, and 1,438 in 1861. Even as the city itself grew rapidly and developed into one of Germany's major ports, its Jewish population did so with greater celerity—from 0.91 percent of the city population in 1831 to 2.46 percent in 1861. By 1861, there were sixteen Jewish communities of over 100 souls in *Regierungsbezirk* Stettin and nineteen in *Regierungsbezirk* Köslin (Table 11.11). Aside from Stettin, only four towns in Stettin District and seven in Köslin District had 250 or more Jewish residents. Among the eight cities in Pomerania province that had populations of over 10,000 in 1861, all but Greifswald and Stralsund had over 100 Jewish inhabitants.

In East Prussia, the Jewish population grew rapidly both in the cities and the countryside. In the province's largest city of Königsberg, it climbed steadily from 1817 to 1880, and increased twice as quickly as the overall population

Table 11.11. Jewish Population Growth in Major Pomeranian Communities

Community	1816	1843	1861
Stettin district			
Anklam	33	200	299
Garz	2	44	114
Gollnow	24	146	145
Greifenberg	35	132	134
Greifenhagen	100	118	205

---

12 Maurer, "Problemskizze," 227–229.
13 Ibid., 228.

Community	1816	1843	1861
Stettin district			
Kammin	28	57	112
Labes	62	100	167
Naugard	33	60	103
Pasewalk	20	226	284
Pyritz	80	203	299
Regenwalde	47	102	148
Stargard	172	260	436
Stettin	74	519	1438
Treptow an der Rega	51	161	181
Wangerin	53	72	126
Wollin	22	98	106
Köslin district			
Bärwalde	59	129	180
Belgard	56	97	179
Bublitz	77	139	189
Bütow	126	239	343
Dramburg	49	121	186
Falkenburg	50	86	100
Kallies	92	164	119
Körlin	55	95	148
Köslin	60	210	278
Kolberg	40	135	202
Lauenburg	65	262	259
Neustettin	11?	163	348
Polzin	106	248	215
Rügenwalde	48	67	117
Rummelsburg	106	123	147
Schivelbein	78	142	253
Schlawe	87	208	250
Stolp	135	391	757
Tempelburg	60	194	168
Stralsund district			

(Stralsund district: No community larger than 100)

Source: Loewe, "Die Zahl der Juden in Pommern," 147–148; Bleich, *Die erste vereinigte Landtag*, 324.

(Table 11.12). In 1843, only twelve Jewish communities in East Prussia had more than 100 members and only Tilsit and Königsberg had more than 250. By 1880, there were thirty communities of over 100 Jews, twenty of them in Königsberg District and ten in Gumbinnen District (Table 11.13). Of these thirty communities, sixteen were in market towns of 3,500–7,000 inhabitants.

An important and unusual Jewish community evolved in the port city of Memel, which was at the northern end of East Prussia on the border with the Russian Empire. The Jewish population of the city increased from thirty-five in 1815 to 289 in 1855, and then to 887 in 1867. The vast majority of newcomers came from the Russian Empire; in 1871, 631 of the 1,043 Jews in the city (60.5 percent) were born outside Germany. For decades, there were separate German and Russian Jewish communities in the town. In 1880, 6.2 percent of the city's population was Jewish. Due to expulsions of Jewish foreigners in 1885, the Jewish population of Memel declined from 1,214 in 1880 to 861 in 1890 and remained below 900 until Lithuania annexed the city (which was thence known as Klaipeda) in 1923.[14]

After 1880, both Pomerania and East Prussia lost much of their Jewish populations. This was partly due to the expulsion of foreign Jews from Prussia's eastern provinces in the late 1880s and in other part because of migration to Berlin, Breslau, and other areas farther west. Since Jewish population growth before 1880 had been more vigorous in East Prussia than in Pomerania, Jewish density remained considerably higher in the former province than in the latter. Within Pomerania, the sharpest declines occurred in Köslin District near the West Prussian border, where the Jewish population fell by almost one-half between 1880 and 1910. In Stettin District, the decline in the same period was only about 25 percent, which was mainly due to the relative stability of the large Jewish community in the city of Stettin (Table 11.14). Whereas Jews in the city of Stettin were only 17.2 percent of those in Pomerania in 1880, 33.7 percent of all Pomeranian Jews lived there by 1925. In many rural parts of the province, Jewish out-migration was overwhelming. In several counties, especially in the southern and southeastern part of the province, Jewish populations declined by more than 70 percent.

East Prussia province, unlike Pomerania, was heavily affected by the territorial changes that followed World War I; the new Polish Corridor separated East Prussia from the rest of Germany. The northernmost parts of East Prussia, including the province's second-largest Jewish community (Memel), were

---

14 Joseph Rosin, "Klaipeda (Memel)," trans. Sarah and Mordechai Kopfstein, https://kehilalinks.jewishgen.org/memel/oldmemel/memel.html (link no longer available).

Table 11.12. Jewish and General Population of the City of Königsberg

Populatin	1817	1843	1871	1880	1890	1900	1910	1925	1933
Jewish population	1027	1688	3836	**5082**	4008	3975	4565	4049	3170
General population	63239		112082	140909	161666	189483	245994	279926	315794
Percent Jewish	1.6%		3.4	**3.6**	2.5	2.1	1.9	1.5	1.0

Source: Schmelz, Territorial Printout; Bleich, *Die erste vereinigte Landtag*, 324; Silbergleit, *Die Bevölkerungs- und Berufsverhältnisse*, 9*, 28*; 1933 census, 5/15.

Table 11.13. Communities with over 100 Jewish Inhabitants in East Prussia, 1880

Regierungsbezirk Königsberg			Regierungsbezirk Gumbinnen		
City	General population	Jews	City	General population	Jews
Königsberg	140,909	5,082	Tilsit	21,400	608
Memel	19,660	1,214	Insterburg	18,745	363
Allenstein	7,610	331	Lyk	6,846	250
Osterode	6,468	222	Johannisburg	2,973	186
Neidenburg	4,351	221	Sensburg	3,611	155
Guttstadt	4,487	213	Schirwindt	1,420	145
Soldau	3,062	183	Lötzen	4,514	134
Preussisch Holland	4,773	175	Stallupönnen	3,997	132
Braunsberg	11,542	169	Gumbinnen	9,530	124
Wormditt	4,720	149	Marggrabowa	4,847	103
Ortelsburg	2,146	152	Total		2,200
Rastenburg	6,534	141			
Rössel	3,590	133			
Bischofsburg	4,071	133			
Labiau	4,683	131			
Heilsberg	5,874	127			
Gilgenburg	1,859	119			
Hohenstein	2,467	111			
Wartenburg	4,499	111			
Liebstadt	2,441	110			
Total		9,227			

Source: Bosse, *Die Verbreitung der Juden*, 29–33.

separated and eventually annexed by Lithuania, while some counties that had formerly belonged to West Prussia were incorporated into East Prussia. Both the losses and gains caused by these territorial changes generally offset their respective effects (Table 11.15). Due to the Prussian expulsion of foreign Jews, the Jewish population of Königsberg declined sharply between 1880 and 1890 (from 5,082 to 4,008), recovered to 4,565 between 1900 and 1910, and then declined sharply again after World War I to 3,170 in 1933. With the exception of a spike between 1900 and 1910, the percentage of East Prussian Jews who

Table 11.14. Decline in Jewish Population in Counties of Pomerania and East Prussia, 1880-1925 (not including former West Prussian counties)

Regierungsbezirk Köslin				Regierungsbezirk Stettin				Regierungsbezirk Stralsund			
City	1880	1925	Change	City	1880	1925	Change	City	1880	1925	Change
++Lauenburg	471	343	-27.2	++Stettin (city)	2388	2615	+9.5	Rügen	14	39	+178.6
+Kolberg-Körlin	519	342	-34.1	+Usedom-Wollin	280	246	-12.1	Franzburg	28	38	+35.7
++Schivelbein	385	230	-40.3	++Saatzig	868	445	-48.7	Stralsund	140	116	-16.6
++Belgard	561	254	-54.7	+Randow	562	260	-53.7	Grimmen	36	24	-33.3
++Stolp	1168	527	-54.9	Kammin	202	91	-55.0	Greifswald	189	105	-44.4
+Köslin	409	182	-55.5	++Greifenberg	381	164	-57.0	Total	407	322	-20.9
++Bütow	399	166	-58.4	++Ueckermünde	357	152	-57.4				
+Bublitz	185	69	-62.7	+Anklam	196	82	-58.2				
++Schlawe	537	196	-63.5	+Regenwalde	408	159	-61.0				
++Dramburg	437	159	-63.6	+Naugard	421	148	-64.9				
++Neustettin	1062	301	-71.7	Demmin	135	34	-74.8				
+Rummelsburg	332	93	-72.0	+Pyritz	431	98	-77.3				
Total	6465	2862	-55.7	+Greifenhagen	385	83	-78.4				
				Total	7014	4577	-34.7				

Regierungsbezirk Königsberg				Regierungsbezirk Gumbinnen			
City	1880	1925	Change	City	1880	1925	Change
++Memel	1432	—		+Heydekrug	382	—	
+Allenstein	481	676 A	+40.5	Gumbinnen	203	208	+2.5
Fischhausen	135	140	+3.7	+Insterburg	454	357	-21.4
++Königsberg (city)	5082	4049	-20.3	+Johannisburg	286	210 A	-25.6
Rastenburg	179	142	-20.7	Angerburg	132	96	-27.3
Wehlau	183	135	-26.2	+Sensburg	288	174 A	-39.6
Friedland	216	139	-35.7	Goldap	167	99	-40.7
Heiligenbeil	130	66	-49.2	+Niederung	339	191	-43.7
+Osterode	644	326 A	-49.5	+Lötzen	271	144 A	-46.9
Königsberg (rural)	106	53	-50.0	++Tilsit	975	797	-46.9
Eylau	183	79	-56.8	+Ragnit	527		
+Mohrungen	348	149	-57.2	++Lyk	552	273 A	-50.5
+Heilsberg	375	146	-61.1	+Oletzko	260	113	-56.5
+Ortelsburg	533	206 A	-61.4	++Stallupönen	526	199	-62.2
+Labiau	311	112	-64.0	+Pillkalen	286	96	-66.4
+Preussisch Holland	310	104	-66.5	Darkehmen	143	45	-68.5
Gerdauen	168	54	-67.9				
+Braunsberg	452	135	-70.1				
+Rössel	461	132 A	-71.4				
++Neidenburg	697	134 A	-80.8				

+ = over 0.5% Jewish in 1880.
++ = over 1% Jewish in 1880.
A = *Regierungsbezirk* Allenstein in 1925.
Sources: Bosse, *Die Verbreitung der Juden*, 20–24, 29–33; Silbergleit, *Die Bevölkerungs- und Berufsverhältnisse*, 28*–29*.

Table 11.15. Gains and Losses in the Jewish Population of East Prussia Caused by World War I Boundary Changes

Regierungsbezirk	1910			1925
	Old boundaries	Within new boundaries		Within new boundaries
RB Königsberg	7138	6258		5503
RB Allenstein	2734	2385		2275
RB Gumbinnen	3155	2674		2201
Total East Prussia	13027	11317	Losses: 1710	9979
West Prussia		1398	Gains: 1398	1358
		12715	Balance: -312	11337

Source: Silbergleit, *Die Bevölkerungs- und Berufsverhältnisse*, 19* (including notes), 27*.

lived in Königsberg fluctuated within a narrow range.[15] In 1925, there were only five communities with over 250 Jews in East Prussia and an equal number in Pomerania (Table 11.16). In both provinces, slightly over half of the Jews lived in these larger communities.

Silesia

Silesia was part of the Austro-Hungarian Empire until 1740 and had a rather restrictive policy on Jewish settlement. When Prussia acquired the province, initially it continued to limit Jewish settlement to three cities—Glogau, Breslau, and Zülz—but later allowed Jews to settle in additional communities. In 1812, the Jews of the province benefited from the Prussian Emancipation, which gave them complete freedom of settlement throughout the province.

Prussian Silesia was divided into three *Regierungsbezirke*,[16] each with a different type of settlement pattern. In the northwest was Liegnitz District, where

---

15 Percent of Jews in East Prussia who lived in Königsberg:

1880	1890	1900	1910 (old boundaries)	1910 (new boundaries)	1925	1933
27.9	27.8	28.6	35.0	35.9	35.7	35.9

16 Until 1820, there was a fourth *Regierungsbezirk* called Reichenbach in south-central Silesia, bordering on Bohemia-Moravia. Reichenbach later merged

Table 11.16 Communities of over 250 Jews in Pomerania and East Prussia, 1925

East Prussia		Pomerania	
Königsberg	4049	Stettin	2615
Tilsit	644	Stolp	469
Allenstein	612	Stargard	297
Elbing	434	Lauenburg	293
Insterburg	338	Kolberg	290
Total	6077	Total	3964
Percent of Jews in province	53.6	Percent of Jews in province	51.1

Source: Silbergleit, *Die Bevölkerungs- und Berufsverhältnisse*, 36*.

Jewish settlement had always been sparser than elsewhere in Silesia. In 1817, the district had 1,649 Jewish inhabitants (0.33 percent of the total), of whom 1,238 lived in Glogau, where they were 12.1 percent of the total population. Elsewhere in the district, there were only 411 Jews. In the central Silesian district of Breslau, there were 6,771 Jews (1.32 percent of the total), of whom 4,409 lived in the major city of Breslau where they accounted for 5.7 percent of the total population. The short-lived district of Reichenbach (see note 403) had only 448 Jews, which were 0.10 percent of the total. The situation in the easternmost district of Oppeln was different in several respects. Unlike the other parts of Silesia, this Upper Silesian district had a large Polish-speaking population and many social conditions similar to those in Poland. Jews there were much more likely than elsewhere in Silesia to engage in estate management, inn keeping, and liquor manufacturing. Oppeln District was also an area of coal mining (and, later, steel manufacturing) and Jews eventually became quite active in heavy industry, which was rare in other parts of Germany. Oppeln District had 7,608 Jews in 1817 (1.47 percent of the total) of which 3,161 (41.5 percent) lived in villages (Table 11.17). Elsewhere in Silesia, in contrast, 7,879 Jews dwelled in towns legally designated as cities and only 989 lived in villages.

The differences among the three Silesian districts persisted throughout the nineteenth and early twentieth centuries. Liegnitz District continued to have the lowest percentage of Jews of these districts. While the old ghettoized community of Glogau declined somewhat in size, several important new communities

into the other Lower Silesian districts (mainly *Regierungsbezirk* Breslau) and had only a small Jewish population.

Table 11.17. Jewish Population in Silesian *Regierungsbezirke*

Regierungsbezirk	1817	1843	1861	1871	1880	1890	1900	1910	1925	1933
Liegnitz	1649	2670	4201	4664	**5158**	4624	4031	3556	3508	2712
Breslau	6771	10376	15860	19189	23176	22232	23285	23161	**26445**	22433
Oppeln (including territories lost after World War I)	7608	15560	20795	22766	**24348**	21147	20270	18268		
Oppeln (excluding territories lost after World War I)								9700	10069	9228
Reichenbach	448	—								
Total	16476	28606	40856	46619	**52682**	48003	47586	44985	40022	34373

Data in bold = highest Jewish population figure for the district.

Source: Silbergleit, *Die Bevölkerungs- und Berufsverhältnisse*, 11*, 18–19*, 27*; Blau, Entwicklung, 69; Schmelz, Territorial Printout.

arose, all of which were in substantial cities. By 1843, there were three Jewish communities of over 250 individuals in the district (Glogau 978, Liegnitz 332, and Grünberg 265), which accommodated 59 percent of the Jewish population of the *Regierungsbezirk* combined. In 1880, the Jewish population of the district reached its highest point of 5,158 persons totaling 0.50 percent of the total population. Jews also spread to several additional cities in the district but still rarely lived in the countryside; there were eleven communities with over 100 Jews,[17] all but three in cities of over 10,000 inhabitants. Scattered fairly evenly around the district, together they were home to 81.85 percent of all Jews in the district. In both 1880 and 1925, the five largest cities in the district had about 65 percent of the total Jewish population. The slow decline in the district's Jewish population after 1880 was evidenced generally equally in larger and smaller cities.

Most Jews in Breslau District were concentrated in the city of Breslau itself. This concentration increased over time, surpassing 90 percent after World War I (Table 11.18). The relatively few Jews in the district's small towns were concentrated in four northeastern counties bordering on Posen and Upper Silesia.[18] In 1880, seventeen communities in the district had over 100 Jews but only four of them exceeded 300.[19] Thirteen of these communities were in county seats and eleven were in towns of under 10,000 inhabitants.

Regierungsbezirk Oppeln (Upper Silesia) had a much denser and more widely scattered Jewish population than the other two Silesian districts. In 1817, only 13.8 percent of Jews in the district lived in the largest Upper Silesian community of Zülz. Unlike Glogau or Breslau, Zülz was a "shtetl," with 1,070 Jews out of a total of 2,423 inhabitants. Once they attained freedom of movement, Jews moved out of Zülz rather rapidly, lowering the town's Jewish population to 709 in 1843 and then to 129 in 1880. Many other parts of Upper Silesia, however, experienced a considerable influx of Jews, both increasing the size of existing communities and founding new ones. As in other parts of Silesia, Jewish density was greatest in the northern and eastern part of the district, an indication of migration from nearby Posen and perhaps from Galicia as well. Upper Silesia

---

17 Glogau 1,010, Liegnitz 970, Görlitz 683, Hirschberg 386, Grünberg 264, Bunzlau 194, Landeshut 177, Sagan 170, Hainau 134, Jauer 128, and Lüben 106.
18 In 1880, 1,892 of the 5,663 Jews outside of the city of Breslau lived in the four northern counties of Namslau, Wartenberg, Oels, and Militsch, where they constituted 0.9 percent of the population. In the other non-metropolitan counties of the district, Jews were only 0.4 percent of the population.
19 Brieg 422, Schweidnitz 339, Oels 330, Waldenburg 300, Glatz 251, Namslau 223, Bernstadt 211, Ohlau 203, Militsch 178, Strehlen 163, Reichenbach 155, Frankenstein 147, Striegau 140, Münsterberg 117, Trachenberg 116, Polnisch Wartenberg 108, and Steinau 105.

Table 11.18. Jewish Population in *Regierungsbezirk* Breslau

Location	1817	1843	1861	1871	1880	1890	1900	1910	1925	1933
City of Breslau	4409	6339	10483	13916	17543	17754	19743	20212	**23240**	20202
Other communities	2262	4037	5457	5273	**5633**	4478	3542	2949	3205	2231
Total	6771	10376	15940	19189	23176	22232	23285	23161	**26445**	22433
Percent in city of Breslau	65.1	61.1	66.1	72.5	75.7	79.9	84.8	87.3	91.3	90.1

Source: Silbergleit, *Die Bevölkerungs- und Berufsverhältnisse*, 9*, 11*, 18*–19*, 24*; Bleich, *Die erste vereinigte Landtag*, 344; 1933 census, 5/10; Schmelz, Territorial Printout.

was one of the few parts of Germany that saw considerable Jewish migration to the countryside in the nineteenth century. As the *Allgemeine Zeitung des Judentums* reported in 1858, "There is hardly any village or hamlet where you cannot find a few families of our tribe by now. In many villages, they already pray with a *minyan* [quorum composed of at least ten males aged thirteen or over]."[20] The number of Jews outside officially recognized cities increased steadily until 1858, although not as rapidly as the number of Jews in the cities. After 1858, the rural Jewish population declined slowly until 1880, and then more quickly afterward (Table 11.19).

In 1843, Upper Silesia had twenty-eight Jewish communities with over 100 members, including fourteen with more than over 250 (Table 11.20), This communities were more substantial than in the rest of Silesia combined. No single community dominated the district in the way that Glogau and Breslau dominated theirs. In 1880, with industrialization in Upper Silesia well underway, the province had thirty communities with over 100 members, including eighteen with over 250 and five with more than 1,000 (Table 11.21). Of these substantial communities, twenty-one were in towns of under 10,000, six in towns of 10,000–20,000, and only three in towns of 20,000 or more. At least ten of the communities were in Polish-speaking towns in areas that were later assigned to Poland in 1921–1922.

After the end of World War I, Poland and Germany struggled for control of the heavily industrialized coal and steel region of Upper Silesia. The Polish population was concentrated in the most heavily industrialized section of the district. In 1922, the district was definitively partitioned into a Polish eastern section and a western German area. The area that went to Poland had a total population of 918,785 and a Jewish population of 8,565 (0.93 percent). About 53.1 percent of Jews in the district lived in areas that remained German. Many who dwelled in the newly Polish territories moved elsewhere in Silesia, although not necessarily within Upper Silesia. The Jewish population of those Upper Silesian areas that remained in German hands increased by only 369 between 1910 and 1925. In the 1933 census, 2,642 (28.6 percent) of the 9,228 Jewish inhabitants of Upper Silesia were born in the "lost territories."[21] Presumably, most of them came from the Upper Silesian territories that were ceded to

---

20 Arno Herzig, "Landjuden—Stadtjuden: Die Entwicklung in den preussischen Provinzen Westfalen und Schlesien im 18. und 19. Jahrhundert," in *Jüdisches Leben auf dem Lande*, ed. Monika Richarz and Reinhard Rürup (Tübingen: Mohr Siebeck, 1997), 101, quoting Toury, *Soziale und politische Geschichte*, 39.

21 Lower Silesia (RB Liegnitz plus RB Breslau) was home to 6,710 Jews who had been born in the lost territories (26.69 percent of the total Jewish population).

Table 11.19. Rural and Urban Jewish Settlement in *Regierungsbezirk* Oppeln (Upper Silesia)[22]

Location	1817	1849	1858	1867	1871	1880	1895	1905	1910	1925
Stadt	4447	10547	12170	14785	15697	16842	14828	14460	13768	6609
Land	3161	6115	7859	7368	7069	7506	5867	4979	4500	3460
Percent *Land*	41.5	36.7	39.2	33.3	31.1	30.8	28.35	25.6	24.6	34.4

Source: Silbergleit, *Die Bevölkerungs- und Berufsverhältnisse*, 11*, 29*; Blau, *Entwicklung*, 69.

---

22 Blau, *Entwicklung*, 69 and Herzig, "Landjuden—Stadtjuden," 102 report quite different urban/rural figures (especially for 1905), showing urban Jews making up 70.2 percent of the district Jewish population in 1871, 72 percent in 1895, and 88.5 percent in 1905.

Table 11.20. Jewish Communities in Upper Silesia with over 100 Members in 1843

City	Number of Jews	City	Number of Jews	City	Number of Jews
Beuthen	826	Rosenberg	285	Kosel	160
Ratibor	761	Neisse	261	Ujest	156
Gleiwitz	760	Peiskretscham	261	Neustadt O/S	154
Zülz	709	Pless	250	Gross Strehlitz	150
Sorau	508	Hultschin	248	Leobschütz	139
Oppeln	496	Guttentag	244	Oberglogau	135
Nicolai	406	Tarnowitz	232	Kotschen	132
Lublinitz	381	Tost	214	Landsberg O/S	112
Rybnik	365	Kreuzburg	195	Pitschen	101
Loslau	290				

Source: Bleich, *Die erste vereinigte Landtag*, 324–325.

Table 11.21. Largest Upper Silesian Jewish Communities in 1880

City	Number of Jews	City	Number of Jews	City	Number of Jews	City	Number of Jews
Beuthen	2185	Gross-Strehlitz	509	Loslau	290	Neustadt O/S	184
Gleiwitz	1838	Leobschütz	441	Kreuzburg	289	Katscher	179
Kattowitz	**1597**	Neisse	422	Rosenberg	241	Oberglogau	170
Ratibor	1331	**Nicolai**	**396**	Kosel	236	Tost	163
Königshütte	**1020**	**Rybnik**	**371**	Guttentag	232	Landsberg	155
Myslowitz	**816**	**Sohrau**	**371**	Peiskretscham	217	Zülz	129
Oppeln	679	**Pless**	**354**	Konstadt	213	**Hultschin**	**123**
Tarnowitz	**603**	Lublinitz	336				

Towns in bold were in the eastern Silesian area that was ceded to Poland in 1921–1922; Hultschin was ceded to Czechoslovakia.

Source: Bosse, *Die Verbreitung der Juden*, 35–37.

Poland, although some could have come from Posen or other "lost" areas while others could have moved well before World War I. In 1925, 73.7 percent of Jews in the parts of Upper Silesia that remained German lived in just five cities (Table 11.22). In 1933, 66.45 percent of the Jews in Upper Silesia lived in the three cities of over 100,000 inhabitants.

Overall, the Jewish population of Silesia more than tripled between 1817 and 1880. Between 1880 and 1910, it declined by about fifteen percent, which was still 2.7 times its 1817 level. Perhaps because it was the closest district to the great magnet of Berlin, the drop was greatest (32 percent) in Liegnitz District and was absent in Breslau District. The Jewish community of the city of Breslau, which had always dominated the Jewish population of Silesia, increased from 26.8 percent of all Silesian Jews in 1817 to 33.3 percent in 1880, and 58.1 percent in 1925. The decline in Jewish population in Upper Silesia between 1880 and 1910 was just under 25 percent. Much of the decrease in 1910–1925 traced to the loss of territory to Poland as opposed to a decline in the Jewish population of territories that remained German.

In sum, the distribution of Jewish population in the eastern parts of Germany underwent a mammoth shift between the early nineteenth century and 1933. During the 1817–1880 period, the greatest gains were in East Prussia and Pomerania. Thereafter, these two provinces lost Jewish population much more quickly than did Silesia. Concurrently, the formerly Polish provinces of Posen and West Prussia, which were home to the overwhelming majority of East German Jews in the early nineteenth century, became the home of an ever-shrinking remnant (Table 11.23).

Table 11.22. Towns with over 250 Jews in German Upper Silesia, 1925

City			
Beuthen	3263	62543	5.2%
Gleiwitz	1906	81888	2.3
Hindenburg	1027	73123	1.4
Ratibor	696	40959	1.7
Oppeln	528	41507	1.3

Source: Silbergleit, *Die Bevölkerungs- und Berufsverhältnisse*, 36*.

Table 11.23. Distribution of Jewish Population in Eastern Germany

Region	1817	1843	1880	1910	1933
Posen	52568 (**60.4%**)	79575 (55.5)	56609 (33.7)	26512 (24.7)	2775* (5.3)
West Prussia	12632 (14.5)	21341 (14.9)	26547 (**15.8**)	13954 (13.0)	—
East Prussia	2389 (2.7)	6197 (4.3)	18218 (10.8)	13027 (12.1)	8838 (**16.9**)
Pomerania	2976 (3.4)	7716 (5.4)	13886 (8.3)	8862 (8.3)	6317 (**12.1**)
Silesia	16476 (18.9)	28606 (19.9)	52682 (31.4)	44985 (41.9)	34373 (**65.7**)
All eastern Germany	87041 (100)	143435 (100)	167942 (100)	107340 (100)	52303 (100)

* Grenzmark Posen/West Prussia.

Source: Silbergleit, *Die Bevölkerungs- und Berufsverhältnisse*, 11*, 18*–19*; 1933 census, 5/11.

12

Central and Northwestern Germany—from Sparse Jewish Density to an Urban and Immigrant Center

For almost any period between 1815 and 1939, the map of Jewish population distribution in Germany showed a swath of very small Jewish communities on both sides of the Elbe all the way across the northwestern and central parts of the country.[1] These contiguous areas, notwithstanding their different political histories and economic characteristics, were all unattractive (and inhospitable) to Jewish inhabitants, although this changed in Saxony and Berlin in the course of the nineteenth century. Apart from a few scattered urban communities in the region (some of them very significant), only a small number of Jews dwelled outside these few cities. While the region's urban Jewish population grew considerably, the small town and rural Jewish population in most of the region remained extremely small throughout these 124 years.

The historic scarcity of Jewish population in much of northwestern and central Germany was due to economic, religious, and political reasons. Most states in the area were overwhelmingly Protestant, often with Catholic populations barely larger than Jewish ones (Table 12.1). Many, but not all,

---

1   The area of low Jewish density actually extended farther east than the region covered in this chapter. The density of Jewish population in RBs Stettin and Köslin in Pomerania, as well as in RB Liegnitz in Silesia, were also very low at the beginning of the nineteenth century. In the case of RB Liegnitz, many counties still had tiny Jewish populations as late as 1880.

Table 12.1. Percent of Protestants in Various Northwestern and Central German States and Provinces, 1871

State or Province	Percent	State or Province	Percent
Sachsen-Altenburg	99.8	RB Gumbinnen	97.7
Reuss Junior Line	99.7	Anhalt	97.4
Schwarzberg-Rudolstadt	99.7	Schaumburg-Lippe	97.4
Reuss Elder Line	99.6	Dresden district (Saxony)	97.3
Schwarzburg-Sondershausen	99.4	RB Frankfurt an der Oder	97.3
Mecklenburg-Strelitz	99.3	Duchy of Braunschweig	97.2
Mecklenburg-Schwerin	99.2	Sachsen-Meiningen	96.8
Sachsen-Coburg-Gotha	99.1	Lippe	96.7
Zwickau district (Saxony)	99.1	Bremen	96.5
RB Merseburg	99.0	Sachsen-Weimar	96.3
Schleswig-Holstein	98.9	RB Magdeburg	95.9
RB Stralsund	98.9	Ostfriesland	95.3
RB Stade	98.8	RB Hannover	95.3
Leipzig district (Saxony)	98.7	RB Bautzen (Saxony)	91.6
RB Lüneburg	98.6	Hamburg	90.4
Lübeck	97.9	Berlin	88.6
RB Potsdam	97.9	RB Hildesheim	84.1
RB Stettin	97.8	Oldenburg	76.7
		RB Erfurt	74.9
		RB Osnabrück	44.9

Source: *Vierteljahrshefte zur Statistik des Deutschen Reichs* 1 (1873): 144–145.

parts of northern Germany were heavily agrarian and had small populations overall. Government policies also had much influence on the size of the Jewish population. The Swedes who ruled *Regierungsbezirk* Stralsund until 1815 allowed no Jews in their territory; neither did the rulers of the small Thuringian principalities of Reuss, Sachsen-Gotha, Sachsen-Coburg, Sachsen-Altenburg, and the free city of Bremen. The Kingdom of Saxony, which in the eighteenth century also controlled large areas of what became the Prussian provinces of Saxony and Brandenburg, allowed Jews only in Dresden and Leipzig. In the Danish-ruled areas of Schleswig-Holstein, Jews were allowed in certain commercial cities like Altona and Glückstadt but were absent in most other places. While Brandenburg-Prussia admitted Jews after 1671, it severely limited their numbers. Other small principalities such as Mecklenburg-Schwerin, Mecklenburg-Strelitz, Ostfriesland, Hohenstein, Bentheim, and Anhalt were much more favorable to Jewish inhabitants than most of the other states. Territories ruled over by bishops and archbishops of the Catholic Church, such as the bishoprics of Osnabrück, Münster, and Hildesheim, varied considerably in their treatment of Jews.

Although northwestern and north-central Germany had a generally sparse Jewish population at the end of the Napoleonic Wars, there were pockets of heavier Jewish density within the region. Much of the Jewish population there was concentrated along the western and southern edges of the region (hereinafter: Area A, Map 12/1). Many Jews lived in the areas closest to the Dutch border, especially in Ostfriesland and in a chain of counties stretching southward along the frontier. Jews were also present in fairly large numbers in the southern Hannover *Landdrosteien* of Hannover and Hildesheim. Here they were primarily in the principalities of Braunschweig, Lippe, and Schaumburg Lippe, and, somewhat farther east, in the principalities of Anhalt as well. In most of these regions, the Jewish density was close to the average for Germany as a whole. The districts of Hannover, Braunschweig, and parts of Osnabrück showed growth in Jewish population while many of the other areas, especially those on the southwestern and southeastern periphery, lost considerably during the Empire and Weimar periods (Area A, Table 12.2).

In much of the rest of northern Germany, particularly near the Elbe River, Jewish populations were extremely sparse. This was especially the case outside the large cities, with a few anomalous areas of larger Jewish population interspersed as well. Historically and in terms of later industrial development, areas of sparse Jewish population can be divided into a northern region (hereinafter: Area B) and the more southerly Saxon areas (hereinafter: Area C), which later became heavily industrialized. The northern area (B) included Schleswig-Holstein, northeastern Hannover, Oldenburg, Mecklenburg, and formerly Swedish Pomerania (*Regierungsbezirk* Stralsund). Within Area B, the cities of Hamburg and Altona (and later Bremen as well) stood out for their large Jewish populations. Much of the area, however, remained agrarian until well into the twentieth century. Except for the notable urban areas, far northern Germany was generally unattractive to Jewish migrants, and most provinces there lost rather than gained Jewish population after 1880 (Area B, Table 12.3).

The more southerly area near the Elbe (Area C) can be divided further into the Prussian province of Saxony, the Kingdom of Saxony, and the tiny

Table 12.2. Area A—Northwest German Districts with Relatively Large Jewish Populations

District	Earliest data	1871	1880	1910	1925	1933	Change, 1871–1925
Landdrostei Hannover	1848: 3099	4221	5656	7093	7063	6255	+67.3%
Percent		0.9%	1.0%	1.2%	0.9%	0.7%	
Braunschweig	1834: 1124	1171	1388	1757	1753	1174	+49.7
Percent		0.44	0.38	0.40	0.36	0.35	
Ostfriesland (*Landdrostei* Aurich)	1848: 2254	2511	2671	2787	2456	2048	-2.2
Percent		1.29	1.33	1.26	0.9	0.7	
Landdrostei Hildesheim	1848: 3147	2765	2847	2541	2240	1811	-19.0
Percent		0.9	0.68	0.66	0.4	0.3	
Counties in Osnabrück district on Dutch border*	1848: c. 368		817		765		
Percent			0.7		0.5		
Anhalt	1864: 2302	1,896	1752	1383	1140	901	-38.9
Percent		1.2	0.9	0.8	0.4	0.3	
Lippe	1842/1844: 1017	1,035	1030	780	607	510	-41.4
Percent		0.93	0.86	0.5			

District	Earliest data	1871	1880	1910	1925	1933	Change, 1871–1925
Schaumburg-Lippe	1842/1844: 309	351	295	230	180	187	-48.7
Percent		1.0	0.8	0.5			
Total Population	c. 13634	13950+	16456	16571+	16204	12886+	
Percent in RB Hannover and Braunschweig		38.7	42.8	53.4	54.4	57.7	

*The counties of Meppen and Lingen, their subdivisions in 1880, and Aschendorf, Bentheim, Hümmling, Lingen, and Meppen in 1925.

Sources: "Die allgemeine Volkszählung vom 3. December 1852 im Königreich Hannover," *Zur Statistik des Königreichs Hannover* 4 (1855): 36–39; *Statistisch-topographisches Handbuch des Herzogthums Braunschweig* (Braunschweig, 1851), 35–36; "Die Ergebnisse der Volkszählung im Herzogtum Anhalt vom 3. December 1867," *Mitteilungen des herzoglich Anhaltischen Statistischen Bureaus* (1868): 10; *Vierteljahrshefte zur Statistik des Deutschen Reichs* 1 (1874): 188 b–d; Bosse, *Die Verbreitung der Juden*, 6–15, 118, 122, 126; *Statistik des Deutschen Reichs* 240 (1915): 210; Toury, *Soziale und Politische Geschichte*, 19; Silbergleit, *Die Bevölkerungs- und Berufsverhältnisse*, 18*–19*, 31*; 1933 census, 5/16; Schmelz, Territorial Printout.

Table 12.3. Area B—Northern Areas Near the Elbe River with Sparse Populations outside Largest Cities

Area	Earliest data	1871	1880	1910	1925	Change, 1871–1925
Landdrostei Stade	1848: 1130	1165	1137	786	712	-38.9%
Percent		0.38%	0.35%	0.18%	0.16%	
Landdrostei Lüneburg	1848: 918	1065	1092	959	934	-12.3
Percent		0.28	0.27	0.18	0.16	
Landdrostei Osnabrück, not near Dutch border*	1848: c. 257		570		725	
Percent			0.33		0.28	
Oldenburg (minus Birkenfeld)	1822: 746	842	977		1059	+25.8
Percent		0.30	0.33			
Mecklenburg-Schwerin	1825: 3050	2945	2580	1413	1407	-52.2
Percent	0.7	0.53	0.45	0.22	0.18	
Mecklenburg-Strelitz		485	458	254		
Percent		0.5	0.46	0.2		
Regierungsbezirk Stralsund	1817: 122	347	407	271	322	-7.2
Percent		0.17	0.19	0.12	0.13	
Schleswig-Holstein	1835: 3674	3729	3522	3311	4152	+11.3
Percent	0.5	0.4	0.3	0.2	0.3	
Altona	1835: 2014	2233	1929	1824	2409	

Area	Earliest data	1871	1880	1910	1925	Change, 1871–1925
other Schleswig-Holstein	1835: 1660	1496	1593	1487	1743	+43.5
Hamburg (urban)	1811: 6,300	13796	16024	19472	19904	+224.3
Percent		4.1	3.5	1.9	1.7	
Bremen		465	766	1843	1508	+11.3
Percent		0.4	0.5	0.6	0.5	
Lübeck	1840: 478	565	560	623	629	
Percent		1.0	0.9	0.53	0.49	
Total		25404+	28093	29364+	29458+	+16.0
Three city-states plus Altona		17059	19279	24194	24340	+42.7
Minus the three city-states and city of Altona		8345+	8814	5170+	5118+	−38.7

* Comprising the counties of Bersenbrück, Osnabrück, and Melle and their subdivisions in 1880 as well as Bersenbrück, Iburg, Melle, Osnabrück, and Wittlage in 1925.

Sources: "Die allgemeine Volkszählung vom 3. December 1852 im Königreich Hannover," in *Zur Statistik des Königreichs Hannover* (Hannover, 1855), 36–39; *Tabelle über die . . . in den Herzogthümern Schleswig und Holstein am ersten Februar 1835 vorgenommene Volkszählung* (Kopenhagen, 1836), 63–64; *Bevölkerung des Gebiets der freien Hansestadt Lübeck im Jahre 1840* (Lübeck, 1841), Table 1; Bosse, *Die Verbreitung der Juden*, 10–15, 60, 111–112, 115, 116, 127; Silbergleit, *Die Bevölkerungs- und Berufsverhältnisse*, 11*, 19*, 31*; Schmelz, Territorial Printout.

principalities that later merged to form Thuringia. Except the southwesternmost parts of Thuringia (Sachsen-Meiningen and the Eisenach section of Sachsen-Weimar), all of these Saxon provinces had very small Jewish populations. Unlike the area farther north, the cities in the Saxon and Thuringian provinces attracted sizable urban Jewish populations in the twentieth century, among which were many immigrants from Eastern Europe (Area C, Table 12.4).

Area D, which centered around Berlin, was a somewhat special case. Although starting with a relatively small Jewish population, the province of Brandenburg (and especially Berlin and its suburbs) lured Jewish migration from all over eastern Germany and Eastern Europe. It was also a transitional area between central Germany's thin Jewish population and the much more densely Jewish eastern provinces, especially Posen and Silesia. Berlin's Jewish population increased both explosively and steadily. The Potsdam *Regierungsbezirk* to its west experienced massive growth between 1890 and 1910 as Jews flooded into the western suburbs of Berlin. After 1920, these areas were removed from the Potsdam district and added to the city of Berlin. In the district of Frankfurt an der Oder farther to the east, the Jewish population embarked on a slow and steady decline beginning around 1861 (Area D, Table 12.5).

Each of the four main areas showed distinctive dynamics. Area A, located on the southern and western edge of the larger northwest and central region, was initially the only part of the region in which the Jewish population was not noticeably sparse. As the area had only a few major cities (Hannover and Braunschweig)[2] and was mainly agrarian, after 1880 its Jewish population tended to either fall or stagnate (Table 12.6). Despite the growing importance of the two largest cities, much of the Jewish population remained in small towns. The small-town population's rate of decline varied greatly from one province to another. In the extreme northwest, the district of Ostfriesland showed a remarkably stable population; there were no large cities nearby[3] to attract migration from the region. Jewish cattle dealing and meat cutting continued to be lucrative livelihoods in this dairy farming region. The Jewish population remained largely Orthodox and resembled the rural Jewish population of eastern Holland, which was just across the border, as much as it resembled the Jewish communities of the rest of northern Germany. Relatively small cities such as Emden and Aurich retained substantial Jewish communities into the

---

2 In 1933, these were the only cities in the area that had over 100,000 inhabitants.
3 The one exception, Bremen, does not seem to have drawn many migrants from Ostfriesland.

Table 12.4. Area C—Saxon and Thuringian Areas with Originally Sparse Jewish Populations

Area	Earliest data	1871	1880	1910	1925
Regierungsbezirk Magdeburg	1817: 2142	3372	3568	3670	4255
Percent	(0.5)	(0.39)	(0.38)		
Regierungsbezirk Merseburg	1817: 189	1008	1332	2208	2236
Percent	(0.04)	(0.11)	(0.14)		
Regierungsbezirk Erfurt	1817: 911	1537	1800	1955	1850
Percent	(0.38)	(0.41)	(0.45)		
Bautzen (Saxony)	1834: 4	83	187	304	316
Percent	(0.001)	(0.03)	(0.05)		
Leipzig (Saxony)	1834: 152	1793	3372	9874	13047
Percent	(0.04)	(0.3)	(0.45)		
Dresden (Saxony)	1834: 684	1319	2370	4255	5491
Percent	(0.17)	(0.19)	(0.3)		
Zwickau (Saxony)	1834: 10	162	587	3154	4398
Percent	(0.001)	(0.02)	(0.05)		
Thuringia:		[3309]:	3784	[3816]	3603 without Coburg
Sachsen-Weimar-Eisenach	1834: 1427	1120	1248	1323	
Percent	(0.6)	(0.39)	(0.40)		
Sachsen-Meiningen	1833: 1524	1625	1627	1137	
Percent	(1.08)	(0.9)	(0.8)		

Central and Northwestern Germany—from Sparse Jewish Density to an Urban and Immigrant Center | 561

Sachsen-Altenburg	1864: 1	10	33	194
Percent	(0.001)	(0.01)	(0.02)	
Sachsen-Koburg-Gotha	1864: 80	210	490	783
Percent	(0.05)	(0.12)	(0.2)	
Reuss Elder Line	1864: 16	19	60	44
Percent	(0.02)	(0.04)	(0.1)	
Reuss Junior Line	1864: 16	20	69	375
Percent	(0.02)	(0.02)	(0.07)	
Schwarzburg-Rudolstadt	1864: 153	119	45	78
Percent	(0.21)	(0.16)	(0.1)	
Schwarzburg-Sondershausen	1864: 174	186	212	215
Percent	(0.26)	(0.28)	(0.30)	
Total	7482	12583	17000	29236	35196
Minus Magdeburg and two southwestern Thuringian principalities	2389	6466	10557	23106	

Sources: Silbergleit, *Die Bevölkerungs- und Berufsverhältnisse*, 11*, 18*–19*, *Statistische Mittheilungen aus dem Königreich Sachsen* (Dresden, 1851), Table VII; Hildebrand, *Statistik Thüringens*, 220–221; *Vierteljahrshefte zur Statistik des Deutschen Reichs* 1 (1874): 188 b–d; Bosse, *Die Verbreitung der Juden*, 44–48, 83–88, 113–114, 119–121, 123, 125; Schmelz, Territorial Printout.

Table 12.5. Area D—Brandenburg Province

Area	1817	1843	1861	1871	1880	1890	1900	1910	1925
Berlin	3700	8348	18859	36015	53949	79286	92206	90013	172672
Percent	(1.9)			(4.4)	(4.9)			(4.4)	(4.3)
RB Potsdam	1933	3211	4660	4548	5423	7831	20780	57289	4311
Percent	(0.4)			(0.45)	(0.47)			(2.0)	(0.3)
RB Frankfurt/ Oder	2865	4642	7175	6921	6873	5944	4986	4054	4131
Percent	(0.5)			(0.7)	(0.6)			(0.33)	(0.32)
Total	8498	16201	30694	47484	66245	93061	117972	151356	181114

Sources: Based on Silbergleit, *Die Bevölkerungs- und Berufsverhältnisse*, 11*, 18*–19*.

Table 12.6. Area A—Urban and Non-Urban Jewish Population

Area	1880	1890	1900	1910	1925	1933	1880–1925
Hannover	3450	3933	4540	5155	5521	4839	+60.0%
Braunschweig	506	650	861	720	939	682	+85.6%
Combined Area A—non-urban Jewish population	3956	4583	5401	5875	6460	5521	+63.3%
Other RB Hannover	2206	2117	2035	1887	1542	1416	-30.1%
Other Herzogtum Braunschweig	882	985	963	1037	814	492	-7.7%
RB Hildesheim	2847	2761	2697	2541	2240	1811	-21.3%
RB Aurich	2671	2713	2755	2787	2456	2048	-8.0%
Anhalt	1752	1580	1605	1383	1140	901	-34.9%
Lippe	1030	989	879	780	607	510	-41.1%
Schaumburg-Lippe	295	366	257	230	180	187	-39.0%
Counties in Osnabrück	817				765		-6.4%
Total	11683+	11511+	11191+	10645+	8979+	7365+	-23.1%
Percent in two cities	25.3	28.5	32.65	35.6	41.8	42.8	

Sources: Silbergleit, *Die Bevölkerungs- und Berufsverhältnisse*, 18*–19*, 30*–31*; Bosse, *Die Verbreitung der Juden*, 6–10, 13–15, 118, 122, 126; *Vierteljahrshefte zur Statistik des Deutschen Reichs* 1, no 3 (1892): 30–31; *Statistik des Deutschen Reichs* 150 (1903): 108, 240 (1915): 210, 401, no. 2 (1930): 609; 1933 census, 5/16; Schmelz, Territorial Printout.

early twentieth century.[4] The western counties of the neighboring Osnabrück District had a similar structure and retained a similarly large a percentage of their Jewish population (Map 12/2).

Far to the east, there were highly different developments in the duchy of Anhalt. Its Jewish population declined steadily from at least 1864 onward. Once an important hub of Jewish life in central Germany and home to the important community of Dessau, Anhalt was subject to conditions opposite of those in Ostfriesland, that is, the nearby cities of Leipzig and Berlin lured Jewish migrants away from the region. The tiny duchies of Lippe and Schaumburg-Lippe, about halfway between Ostfriesland and Anhalt, lost even more of their Jewish population than did Anhalt. The two southern Hannoverian *Regierungsbezirke* of Hannover (except for the city of Hannover itself) and Hildesheim lost only slightly less of their Jewish populations by percent than did Anhalt and Lippe (Table 12.7).

Areas B and C, which straddled the Elbe River, not only had small total Jewish populations in the early nineteenth century, but also had counties that had almost no Jews at all. In the north, this was most evident in Schleswig-Holstein and the Hannoverian districts of Stade and Lüneburg. In Schleswig-Holstein in 1880, the 3,522 Jews were concentrated in the Hamburg suburbs, especially in Altona, where 56.6 percent of Jews in the province lived. Another 514 Jews (14.6 percent) lived adjacent to Hamburg in the Stomarn and Pinneberg counties. Of the remaining 1,013 Jews, almost 80 percent lived in only five counties. None of the other twelve counties in Schleswig-Holstein had a Jewish density of over 0.15 percent and only one had more than twenty Jewish inhabitants. The situation in the two Hanoverian districts was similar. Of the eight counties in Stade District in 1880, the three on the Weser River closest to Bremen held 68.6 percent of the Jewish population; all the other districts had Jewish densities of 0.21 percent or less. In the seven counties that comprised the Lüneburg District, 71.6 percent of the Jewish population lived in Celle, Lüneburg, and Harburg combined. Two of these three counties were close to Hamburg. The remaining four had a total of 310 Jews and Jewish densities of 0.20 percent or lower (Table 12.8).

In the thirteen counties of Oldenburg in 1880, including the Oldenburg district of Lübeck but excluding Birkenfeld District in the Rhineland, there were six counties with Jewish densities greater than 0.40 percent, six that ranged from 0.03 to 0.21 percent, and one with no Jews at all. Only two counties, Jever and Oldenburg, had over 100 Jews.

---

4 In 1925, Emden had 688 Jews out of a population of 27,770 (2.48 percent) and Aurich had 398 out of 6,136 (6.49 percent).

Table 12.7. Density of Jewish Population in Area A Counties

A) Jewish Density by County, 1880—Number of Counties in Each Category (total Jewish population in parentheses, counties over 1.0 percent listed)

Percent	RB Hannover	RB Hildesheim	RB Aurich	Osnabrück West	Anhalt
Above 1.0%	1 (3450)	2 (1580)	1 (1204)	0	1 (540)
Percent	Hannover city	Hildesheim, Göttingen	Emden		Dessau
0.5%–0.99%	5 (1995)	1 (650)	2 (1467)	2 (819)	3 (1109)
0.2%–0.49%	1 (211)	3 (495)	0	0	1 (103)
0.1%–0.19%	0	0	0	0	0
Below 0.1%	0	1 (22)	0	0	0

Towns with over 100 Jews, 1880

RB Hannover		RB Hildesheim		RB Aurich		Osnabrück West		Anhalt	
Hannover	3450	Hildesheim	513	Emden	697	Lingen	102	Dessau	420
Linden	190	Göttingen	490	Aurich	377			Bernburg	344
Hameln	131	Einbeck	139	Leer	290			Köthen	270
Stolzenau	101	Münden	134	Norden	273				
Nienburg	100	Peine	101	Weener	209				

Source: Bosse, *Die Verbreitung der Juden*, 6–10, 14, 15, 122.

B) Jewish Density in Counties in Area A that were Part of Prussia, by Counties, 1925

Percent	RB Hannover	RB Hildesheim	RB Aurich	Osnabrück West
Above 1.0%	1 (5521) Hannover city	1 (535) Göttingen	3 (1341) Emden Norden-Weener	0
0.5%–0.99%	3 (637)	4 (970)	3 (897)	
0.2%–0.49%	8 (870)	5 (460)	1 (166)	3 (490)
0.1%–0.19%	1 (35)	4 (211)	1 (52)	
below 0.1%	0	4 (64)	0	

Source: based on Silbergleit, *Die Bevölkerungs- und Berufsverhältnisse*, 30*–31*.

Table 12.8. Density of Jewish Population in Area B—Low Jewish Density in Northern Germany (Mecklenburg not divided into counties)

A) By County, 1880

Percent	Lüneburg	Stade	Osnabrück East	Schleswig-Holstein	Braunschweig	Oldenburg	City-states
Over 1.0%	0	0	0	1 (1995)	0	0	1 (16024)
Percent				Altona			Hamburg
0.5%–0.99%	0	3 (890)	1 (417)	1 (373)	2 (626)	2 (342)	1 (560)
0.2%–0.49%	3 (782)	0	1 (102)	4 (781)	2 (659)	5 (497)	1 (766)
0.1%–0.19%	3 (261)	4 (210)	1 (51)	2 (159)	1 (81)	3 (125)	
Below 0.1%	1 (49)	2 (37)	0	13 (214)	1 (22)	3 (23)	

Cities with over 100 Jews, 1880

Lüneburg	Stade	Osnabrück East	Schleswig-Holstein	Braunschweig	Oldenburg	City-states
Harburg 227	Verden 118	Osnabrück 379	Altona 1929	Braunschweig 506	Jever 219	Hamburg 12885
Lüneburg 149			Wandsbek 299	Seesen 194	Oldenburg 196	Bremen 602
Burgdorf 133			Kiel 242	Wolfenbüttel 133		Lübeck 550
Celle 113			Friedrichstadt 152	Holzminden 122		
			Rendsburg 136			
			Elmshorn 129			

Source: Bosse, *Die Verbreitung der Juden*, 10–15, 57–60, 116, 118, 127.

B) By County, 1925 (Prussia Only)

Percent	Lüneburg	Stade	Osnabrück-East	Schleswig-Holstein
Over 1.0%	0	0	0	1 (2409) Altona
Percent 0.5%–0.99%	0	0	1 (454)	0
0.2%–0.49%	4 (680)	3 (392)	1 (184)	3 (1189)
0.1%–0.19%	0	4 (218)	1 (54)	4 (243)
Below 0.1%	12 (254)	8 (102)	3 (23)	15 (311)

Source: based on Silbergleit, *Die Bevölkerungs- und Berufsverhältnisse*, 30*–31*.

In most cases, counties that had highly sparse Jewish populations in 1880 continued to have low numbers of Jews in 1925 as well. In Mecklenburg, where the original Jewish density was considerably higher than elsewhere in the region, the Jewish population went into a sharp decline after 1845. The number of Jews in Mecklenburg-Schwerin sank from 3,318 in 1845 to 2,945 in 1871, and to 1,413 in 1910. Mecklenburg was a mainly agricultural area and was near two major cities (Berlin and Hamburg) that attracted migrants away from the province. In the early and mid-nineteenth century, Jews were scattered over a considerable number of settlements in most parts of the region. In 1845, the largest Jewish community was in the capital city of Schwerin (303 Jews), and nine other communities had over 100 members. Most of the medium-sized communities shrank acutely in the second half of the nineteenth century. Two new communities developed in the port cities of Rostock and Wismar. By 1910, there were only three communities with at least 100 members: Güstrow (115), Rostock (317), and Schwerin (218). Together, these accounted for more than 45 percent of the remaining Jews in the duchy.

The Jewish population remained small throughout the northwestern parts of the Duchy of Oldenburg.[5] Even though the percentage of Jews was generally much higher in major port cities (Hamburg, Bremen, Lübeck, Kiel) and their environs (Altona, Harburg) than elsewhere in the region, the absolute number of Jews in these cities generally stagnated. Only Bremen and Kiel, which initially had tiny Jewish populations, grew rapidly (Table 12.9).

With the exception of southwestern Thuringia, the Saxon and Thuringian districts all began with very few Jews. Although politically part of central Germany, this area southwest of the Thüringerwald hills was culturally and economically much more like Bavarian Franconia. In southwestern Thuringia, the duchy of Sachsen-Meiningen-Hildburghausen was home to 1,524 Jews (1.06 percent) of the population in 1833. All but ten of these lived in the three southern counties of Meiningen, Römhild, and Hildburghausen. In Meiningen County, Jews were over four percent of the population. In the neighboring duchy of Sachsen-Weimar-Eisenach, there were 1,427 Jews in 1834 (0.60 percent of the population). Almost all of these Jews lived in the Eisenach *Kreis*, which bordered on Hesse-Nassau, where they were 1.79 percent of the population in 1834. A similar situation prevailed in two detached Prussian enclaves in the same part of Thuringia-Schmalkalden in Hesse-Nassau and in Schleusingen in Erfurt District. In 1861 there were 335 Jews in the fomer region (1.21

---

5 Excluding the Rhineland enclave of Birkenfeld, which had a much denser Jewish population.

Table 12.9. Changes in Jewish Population of Large Cities in Northwestern Germany (Area B only)

City	1871	1880	1890	1900	1910	1925	1933
Hamburg	11954	12915	17785	17797	19292	19794	16885
Altona	2233	1929	2109	2006	1824	2409	2006
Bremen	321	570	734	836	985	1328	1314
Harburg	201	227	295	312	329	358	315*
Lübeck	525	550	645	660	610	629	497
Kiel	187	242	350	383	526	605	522
Total	15421	16433	21918	21994	23566	25123	21539

* Harburg-Wilhelmsburg.

Sources: Based on Blau, Entwicklung, 284; Bosse, Die Verbreitung der Juden, 12, 59–60, 127; Schmelz, Territorial Printout.

percent of the total population)[6] and in 1880 there were 234 in the latter (0.54 percent). The Prussian *Regierungsbezirk* of Magdeburg was the only other part of the Saxon region that had a significant Jewish population at the beginning of the nineteenth century (with the exception of Anhalt, discussed together with Area A above). Within the district, Jews were concentrated heavily in the cities of Magdeburg and Halberstadt. In the neighboring Erfurt District, a high percentage of the Jewish population was concentrated in a few counties on either the Hesse-Nassau or Hannover border. Everywhere else, the Jewish presence was extremely sparse. In the Kingdom of Saxony, Jewish populations were harshly limited up to and including the beginning of the review period. Outside of the communities of Dresden (683 Jews) and Leipzig (152), there were only fifteen Jews in the whole kingdom in 1834. Most of the *Regierungsbezirk* of Merseburg and several counties in the Potsdam, Frankfurt an der Oder, and Liegnitz districts had been part of the Saxon kingdom before 1815. Their Jewish populations, first counted in the Prussian census of 1817, were extremely small (189 in the entire *Regierungsbezirk* Merseburg). In Thuringia, there were several principalities that had excluded Jews (Reuss, Sachsen-Altenburg), and others that had very limited Jewish populations. As late as 1864, the six Thuringian states outside the two southwestern principalities had a total of only 424 Jews (0.08 percent of the population).

---

6 Schmelz, *Hessen*, 353.

Much of Saxony and Thuringia became heavily industrialized in the late nineteenth century. The urban parts of these areas attracted many Jewish migrants, including a very large percentage of East European immigrants. The rural sector, on the other hand, remained as free of Jews in the early twentieth century as it had been a century earlier. Until the unification of Germany, almost all Jewish in-migration in the region was to the Prussian province of Saxony and remained within rather limited bounds. By 1871, however, the Jewish population of the province's three *Regierungsbezirke* had grown considerably (Table 12.10). The biggest increases were the cities of Magdeburg, Halle an der Saale, and Erfurt, where the combined Jewish population grew from 476 in 1817 to 941 in 1843, and to 2,067 in 1871. Smaller cities such as Halberstadt and Nordhausen also had substantial communities with much longer histories (566 combined in 1843).

After German unification and its attendant removal of all restrictions on Jewish rights of settlement throughout Germany, Jews began to move into the Kingdom of Saxony in large numbers as well as to cities in Prussian Saxony and Thuringia where there had been no prior Jewish community. The especially rapid increase in the Kingdom of Saxony after 1880 was fueled mainly by immigration from Eastern Europe. The kingdom's Jewish population grew from 3,357 in 1871 to 6,518 in 1880, 17,587 in 1910, and to 23,252 in 1925. The greatest increase occurred in Leipzig, where Jewish presence eventually outstripped that in Dresden by far. In 1885, 24.5 percent of Leipzig Jews were born in the city and 49.9 percent were born elsewhere in Germany (but hardly any in the Kingdom of Saxony). Only 931 of the 3,640 Jews in the city were born abroad, mostly in Austria-Hungary.[7] The percentage of Leipzig Jews born abroad increased from 25.6 percent of the total in 1885 to 31.4 percent in 1890, and 43.0 percent by 1900. The number of Jews in Leipzig who did not hold German citizenship was even higher than that of Jews born abroad. Most of the 1,929 German-Jewish

Table 12.10. Growth of Jewish Population in Prussian Saxony

City	1817	1843	1871	Change in absolute numbers	Percent change
Magdeburg	2142	2612	3372	+1230	+57.4
Merseburg	189	458	1049	+860	+455.0
Erfurt	911	1452	1537	+626	+68.7

Source: Silbergleit, *Die Bevölkerungs- und Berufsverhältnisse*, 11*, 18*–19*.

---

7   Segall, "Die Juden im Königreich Sachsen," 42.

migrants to Leipzig in 1900 were born in Posen (345), Prussian Saxony (211), Silesia (198), Berlin (143), Anhalt (117), and Hesse-Nassau (102).[8] By 1910, 6,396 (67.8 percent) of the 9,434 Jews in Leipzig lacked German citizenship. The situation was a little less extreme in Dresden, where citizens were still 46.9 percent of the Jewish population in 1910. The Dresden figures show an upturn in the non-citizen population of the Jewish community, which increased from 766 in 1895 to 1,983 in 1910, while the number of Jews who were German citizens stagnated (1,792 in 1895 and 1,749 in 1910). Overall, by 1910 only 43.0 percent of Jews in the Kingdom of Saxony were citizens. Nearly all Jews in Saxony settled in the largest cities. In 1910, almost 75 percent of the 17,587 Jews in the kingdom lived in either Dresden or Leipzig, and only 2,065 lived outside cities of at least 100,000 inhabitants.

No other part of the region had as many Jewish foreigners or as rapid an increase in Jewish population as the Kingdom (later Free State) of Saxony, but both Prussian Saxony and Thuringia displayed smaller versions of the same phenomenon. In Prussian Saxony, the Jewish population increased from 5,958 in 1871 to 8,341 in 1925. Although the Jewish population of *Regierungsbezirk* Merseburg remained minuscule—many counties had almost no Jews—its percentage growth was greater there than elsewhere in Prussian Saxony (from 1,049 in 1871 to 2,236 in 1925). Almost all of this growth occurred in cities; by 1925, more than half of the province's Jews lived in the cities of Magdeburg, Halle, or Erfurt. While the percentage of foreign Jews was higher in Prussian Saxony than in most other Prussian provinces, it was lower than in the Kingdom of Saxony and Berlin (Table 12.11).

While the Jewish population of the Thuringian principalities declined or stagnated in the southwestern principalities, it increased steeply in the other six states (Table 12.12). In the Thuringian principalities, the percentage of foreigners was especially large in areas that had previously excluded Jews (Table 12.13).

In Brandenburg, Jewish population's growth in Berlin and its closest suburbs was the main development in the regrion. In 1817, the city of Berlin was home to 43.54 percent of the province's Jewish population. This increased to 81.44 percent by 1880 and to 95.34 percent by 1925. In Potsdam District, which surrounded the city, there were originally a considerable number of small and medium-sized communities, mostly in cities and larger towns. In 1843, the largest of them were in Prenzlau (361 Jews), Potsdam (182), and Brandenburg (140). In 1880, *Regierungsbezirk* Potsdam had nineteen Jewish communities

---

8 n.a., "Die Zahl der Juden in Leipzig," ZDSJ 2, 7 (1906), 111.

Table 12.11. Foreign Jews in Prussian Saxony by Citizenship

Status	1910	1925	1933 (Prussian Saxony and Anhalt)
Total Jewish population	7833	8341	8047
Foreign Jews	1070	1849	1929
Percent foreign	13.66%	22.17%	23.97%

Sources: *Vierteljahrshefte zur Statistik des Deutschen Reichs—Ergänzungsheft zu 1916* 4 (1918): *Die Deutschen im Ausland und die Ausländer im Deutschen Reiche*, 53; Silbergleit, *Die Bevölkerungs- und Berufsverhältnisse*, 19*, 44*; 1933 census, 5/50.

Table 12.12. Jewish Population Change in Various Parts of Thuringia

Principlaity	1871	1890	1910
Sachsen-Meiningen	1625	1560	1137
Sachsen-Weimar-Eisenach	1120	1252	1323
Other six principalities	564	1102	1689

Sources: *Vierteljahrshefte zur Statistik des Deutschen Reichs* 1 (1873): 188d; 1, no. 3 (1892): 31; *Statistik des Deutschen Reichs* 240 (1915): 210.

with at least fifty Jewish inhabitants,[9] not counting the later suburbs of Berlin. Jewish density was greatest north and east of Berlin and lowest in the southern and formerly Saxon counties (Table 12.14). The Jewish population of *Regierungsbezirk* Potsdam increased rapidly after 1890, but this was almost completely attributable to the growing Jewish communities in the western Berlin suburbs. There was stagnation outside the areas that were later incorporated into Berlin in 1920. In the area that remained part of the *Regierungsbezirk* after the Berlin suburbs were incorporated into Greater Berlin, the cities of Potsdam (399), Brandenburg (469), Eberswalde (270), and Prenzlau (232) had the largest Jewish populations in 1925 (Table 12.15).

In the eastern half of the province (*Regierungsbezirk* Frankfurt an der Oder), the Jewish population was initially greatest in the east and northeast. It dropped off to the south and west, especially in the formerly Saxon areas of

---

9 Potsdam 551, Prenzlau 382, Schwedt 235, Brandenburg 209, Eberswalde 171, Neuruppin 146, Angermünde 135, Wriezen 114, Perleberg 109, Zehdenick 82, Freienwalde 82, Beeskow 73, Nauen 70, Rathenow 68, Wittstock 64, Oranienburg 61, Luckenwalde 61, Storkow 60, and Strausberg 55.

Table 12.13. Foreign Jews in Thuringian Principalities, 1910

Status	Sachsen-Altenburg	Sachsen-Coburg-Gotha	Schwarzberg-Sondershausen	Schwarzberg-Rudolstadt
Total Jewish population	194	783	215	78
Foreign Jewish citizens	100	186	24	18
Percent foreign	51.5	23.8	11.2	23.1

Status	Reuss Elder Line	Reuss Junior Line	all six northeastern principalities	
Total Jewish population	44	375	1689	
Foreign Jewish citizens	28	198	554	
Percent foreign	63.6	52.8	32.8	

Status	Sachsen-Meiningen-Hildburghausen	Sachsen-Weimar-Eisenach	total southwestern principalities	
Total Jewish population	1137	1323	2460	
Foreign Jewish citizens	62	129	191	
Percent foreign	5.5	9.8	7.8	

Sources: *Vierteljahrshefte zur Statistik des Deutschen Reichs—Ergänzungsheft zu 19164 (1918): Die Deutschen im Ausland und die Ausländer im Deutschen Reiche*, 53; *Statistik des Deutschen Reichs* 240 (1915): 210.

Jewish population in Thuringia, 1933

Total Jewish population	Foreign Jewish citizens	Percent foreign
2882	658	22.8

Source: 1933 census, 5/51.

Table 12.14. Jewish Population Density in Counties of *Regierungsbezirk* Potsdam, 1880 (from north to south)

North and east of Berlin			North and west of Berlin			South of Berlin		
Prenzlau	490	0.9%	Westpriegnitz	237	0.3%	Teltow	596	0.4
Templin	166	0.4	Ostpriegnitz	160	0.2	Beeskow-Storkow	229	0.5
Angermünde	542	0.8	Ruppin	265	0.3	Jüterbog-Luckenwalde	76	0.1
Oberbarnim	533	0.7	Charlottenburg	287	0.9	Zauch-Belzig	92	0.1
Niederbarnim	557	0.4	Potsdam	551	1.1			
			Osthavelland	317	0.4			
			Brandenburg	209	1.0			
			Westhavelland	116	0.2			
Total	2288	0.6	Total	2142	0.5	Total	993	0.3

Source: Bosse, *Die Verbreitung der Juden*, 1–3.

Table 12.15. *Regierungsbezirk Potsdam*

Location	1880	1890	1895	1900	1905	1910
Total Jewish population	5423	7831	20780	20780		
Three western suburbs of Berlin	2112	2112	6440	13684	26830	43919
Other areas incorporated into Berlin in 1920	990	990	(405)	2255	(1647)	6307
Rest of district	4729	4729	7473	4841		7063

Three western suburbs = Charlottenburg, Schöneberg, Wilmersdorf.

Other areas include Neukölln, Spandau, Köpenick, Steglitz, Pankow, Weissensee, Reinickendorf, Rummelsberg, Treptow, Friedenau, Tempelhof, Oberschönweide, and Lichtenberg. The figures for 1895 and 1905 only include Neukölln and Lichtenberg.

Sources: Silbergleit, *Die Bevölkerungs- und Berufsverhältnisse*, 19*; Blau, *Entwicklung*, 99; Schmelz, Territorial Printout.

Lusatia (Lausitz) south of Berlin. Throughout much of the nineteenth century, the counties east of the Elbe had the densest Jewish populations, especially in the northeastern areas (Neumark). In 1843, there were important Jewish communities in northeastern Brandenburg, especially in Landsberg an der Warthe (395), Schermeisel (206), Friedeberg (177), Königsberg in der Neumark (137), and Soldin (126). Of these five, only Landsberg was more than a country town. The areas north of the Warthe and east of the Elbe also saw the steepest declines in Jewish population after 1880 (Table 12.16).

A substantial shift in Jewish settlement patterns took place during the late nineteenth and early twentieth centuries in the area of northwestern and central Germany that began the review period with sparse Jewish populations. Although the rural Jewish population declined substantially or remained as sparse as it had been before in most areas, many urban regions saw strong Jewish in-migration. Altogether, the share of these formerly scantily Jewish regions among all German Jews grew from fewer than twenty percent in 1871 to almost half in 1925. Berlin and its suburbs (Area D) transitioned from having a sparse Jewish population to posessing the greatest concentration of Jews in all of Germany. The cities of Saxony (Area C) also attracted large numbers of Jews, mainly East European immigrants. Areas A and B, on the other hand, had stagnant Jewish populations from 1880 to 1925 (Table 12.17).

Almost all of the increase in Jewish population in northwestern and central Germany occurred in just five cities—Hannover, Hamburg, Berlin, Leipzig, and Dresden. Elsewhere in that part of the country, the total Jewish population hardly changed[10] (Table 12.18). Even outside the five largest cities, most Jews in these regions were urban dwellers, often living in cities of over 100,000 inhabitants (Table 12.19).

In most areas, rural Jewish populations dwindled almost to the point of disappearance. The only area where small-town Jewry remained significant was Area A in northwestern Germany. This area resembled neighboring eastern Holland and western Germany, both of which were home to many rural Jews. With fewer than 6.5 percent of all Jews in the region, Area A accommodated 33.7 percent of Jews in towns smaller than 10,000 in 1933. The 1925 census shows that almost half of small-town Jews in Area A were either in Ostfriesland or in the western counties of RB Osnabrück on the Dutch border.

In contrast to its small, vestigial rural population in the northwest, the region characterized by an originally sparse Jewish population was the main center of

---

10 The seeming increase in 1910 was the result of huge population growth in suburbs of Berlin that were annexed to the city in 1920.

Table 12.16. Counties in *Regierungsbezirk* Frankfurt an der Oder, 1880–1925

West of the Oder-Neisse						East of the Oder-Neisse, north of the Warthe					
County	1880			1925		County	1880			1925	
Lebus	407	0.43%		315	0.31%	Königsberg/Neumark	745	0.76%		253	0.26%
Frankfurt/Oder	890	1.74%		669	0.94%	Soldin	386	0.79%		182	0.37%
Guben (both sides)	281	0.41%		272	0.32%	Arnswalde	531	1.21%		189	0.42%
Lübben	95	0.27%		46	0.14%	Friedeberg	704	1.21%		253	0.46%
Luckau	52	0.08%		32	0.04%	Landsberg	840	0.97%		563	0.57%
Kalau	22	0.04%		85	0.08%	Total	3206	0.96%		1440	0.42%
Cottbus	385	0.51%		404	0.39%	Decline: 55.1%					
Spremberg	37	0.15%		20	0.05%						
						East of the Oder-Neisse, south of the Warthe					
						County	1880			1925	
						Weststernberg	178	0.39%		91	0.20%
						Oststernberg	424	0.83%		125	0.29%
						Züllichau-Schwiebus	270	0.54%		180	0.35%
						Krossen	353	0.57%		128	0.21%
						Sorau (both sides of Neisse)	273	0.28%		324	0.26%
						Total	1498	0.49%		848	0.29%
						Decline: 43.4%					
						Total for areas north and south of the Warthe	4704			2288	0.36%
						Decline: 51.4%					
Total	2169	0.47%		1843	0.30%						
Decline: 15.0%											

Sources: Bosse, *Die Verbreitung der Juden*, 3–6; Silbergleit, *Die Bevölkerungs- und Berufsverhältnisse*, 28*.

Table 12.17. Changing Distribution of Jewish Population in Northwestern and Central Germany

Area	Early nineteenth century (est.)	1871	1880	1910	1925	Change 1871–1925
A	13634	13950+	16456	**16571+**	16204	+16.2%
B	c. 16500	25404+	28093	29364+	29458+	+16.0%
C	7482	12382	17000	29236	35196	+184.3%
D	8498 (1817)	47484	66245	151356	181114	+281.4%
Total	46114	99220+	127794	226527+	261972+	

Percent of all German Jews living in northwestern and central Germany

| | c. 16.3% | 19.4% | 22.75% | 36.8% | 46.4% | |

Percent of Jews of northwestern and central Germany in each area

A	29.6%	14.1%	12.9	7.3	6.2	
B	35.8	25.6	22.0	13.0	11.2	
C	16.2	12.5	13.3	12.9	13.4	
D	18.4	47.9	51.8	66.8	69.1	

Table 12.18. Jewish Population in Regions of Northwestern and Central Germany in and outside the Five Main Cities

Area	1871	1880	1910	1925
Area A	13950+	16456	16571+	16204
City of Hannover	3450	4540	5155	5521
Remainder of Area A	10500+	11916	11416+	10983
Area B	25404+	28093	29364+	29458+
State of Hamburg	13796	16024	19904	19794
Remainder of Area B	11608+	12069	9460+	9664+
Area C	12382	17000	29236	35196
City of Leipzig	1739	3179	9434	12594
City of Dresden	1276	2228	3734	5120
Remainder of Area C	9367	11593	16068	17482
Area D	47484	66245	151356	181114
City of Berlin	36015	53949	90013	172672
Remainder of Area D (mainly Berlin suburbs)	11469	12296	61343	8442

Percent of Jews in Northwestern and Central Germany outside the Five Main Cities in the Various Subregions

Area	1871	1880	1910	1925
A	10500+ (24.45)	11916 (24.89)	11416 (11.61)	10983 (23.58)
B	11608+ (27.03)	12069 (25.21)	9460 (9.62)	9664 (20.75)
C	9367 (21.81)	11593 (24.22)	16068 (16.34)	17482 (37.54)
D	11469 (26.71)	12296 (25.68)	61343 (62.41)	8442 (18.13)
Total	42941	47874	98287	46571

Table 12.19. Jewish Population of Northwestern and Central Germany by Size of Town

Population size per area	1880		1933	
	Jewish population	Percent of general population	Jewish population	Percent of general population
A (Hannover)	3450		4839	
Other over 100,000 (Braunschweig)			682	
Total over 100,000	3450	21.0	5521	41.1
10,000–100,000	4103	24.9	4352	32.4
Under 10,000	8903	54.1	3554	26.5
Total A	16456		13427	
B (Hamburg)	12885		16885	
Other over 100,000 ([Altona,] Bremen, [Harburg, Kiel, Lübeck])	602		4654	
Total over 100,000	13487	50.2%	21539	82.8
10,000–100,000	5198	19.4	2599	10.0
Under 10,000	8156	30.4	1874	7.2
Total B	26841		26012	

	1880		1933	
Population size per area	Jewish population	Percent of general population	Jewish population	Percent of general population
C (Leipzig, Dresden)	5407		15961	
Other over 100,000 (Chemnitz, Erfurt, Halle an der Saale, Magdeburg, Plauen)			6796	
Total over 100,000	5407	31.8%	22757	74.3
10,000–100,000	6276	36.9	5915	19.3
Under 10,000	5317	31.3	1940	6.3
Total C	17000		30612	
D over 100,000 (Berlin)	53949	81.4%	160564	95.5
10,000–100,000	4812	7.3	4441	2.6
Under 10,000	7484	11.3	3175	1.9
Total D	66245		168180	
Total, all four regions				
Over 100,000	77,162	60.6%	210,381	88.8
10,000–100,000	20,389	16.0	16,041	6.8
Under 10,000	29,860	23.4	10,543	4.4
Total	127,411		236,965	

Sources: Bosse, *Die Verbreitung der Juden*, 1–15, 44–49, 83–88, 111–127; 1933 census, 5/10, 11, 15, 31–41.

foreign Jews in Germany. In 1933, the area discussed in this chapter was home to slightly under half of all German Jews and almost two-thirds of Jews of foreign birth or citizenship (*zugewanderte*). In proportional terms, foreign Jews were roughly twice as numerous in central and northwestern Germany as they were in all other parts of the country. The vast majority of the foreign Jews in this region lived in Berlin or Saxony (Table 12.20).

Table 12.20. Foreign Jews in Central and Northwestern Germany, 1933

Area or Region	Total	*Zugewanderte*	Percent
RBs Hannover, Hildesheim, Aurich, and half of Osnabrück	10700	2111 (est.)	19.7
Braunschweig	1174	286	24.4
Lippe	510	18	3.5
Schaumburg-Lippe	187	6	3.2
Anhalt	901	204	22.6
Area A	13472	2625	19.5
RBs Stade, Lüneburg, and half of Osnabrück	1911	290 (est.)	15.3
Schleswig-Holstein	3117	1530	49.1
Hamburg	16973	3124	18.4
Bremen	1438	357	24.8
Lübeck	497	153	30.8
Oldenburg	1240	211	17.0
Mecklenburg	1003	250	24.9
Area B	26179	5915	22.6
Prussian Saxony	7146	2009	28.1
Saxony	20584	13716	66.6
Thuringia	2882	722	25.0
Area C	30612	16447	53.7
Berlin	160564	48075	29.9
Brandenburg	7616	1200	15.8
Area D	168180	49275	29.3
A and B	39651	8540	21.5
C and D	198792	65722	33.1
Total central and northwestern Germany	238443	74262	31.1
Percent of all Germany	47.7	64.6	
All rest of Germany	261239	40743	15.6

Source: based on 1933 census, 5/16.

13

Western Germany

After 1815, nearly all of western Germany was incorporated into the two Prussian provinces of the Rhine and Westphalia, which left a few additional small enclaves in the hands of non-Prussian states. Thus, the Grand Duchy of Oldenburg controlled a small enclave (Birkenfeld) in the southern part of Rhine Province west of the Rhine. The Principality of Lichtenberg, next to the Birkenfeld pocket, was incorporated into the Prussian Rhine Province in 1834. Next to Lichtenberg, the Meisenheim District belonged to the territory of Hesse-Homburg and was incorporated into the Prussian Rhine Province in 1866. The unification of the bulk of western Germany under Prussian control marked a major departure from the pre-1815 history of the region, which had been divided into numerous duchies, principalities, independent bishoprics, and other Church territories, some of them very small.[1]

The Prussian province of Westphalia was divided into three districts (*Regierungsbezirke*): Münster, Minden, and Arnsberg. The Rhine Province was

---

1 Among territories later incorporated into the Prussian provinces of the Rhine and Westphalia were the duchies of Jülich, Berg, Kleve-Geldern, Westphalia, and Rietburg; the counties (*Grafschaften*) of Mark, Wied, Sayn, and Wittgenstein; the principality of Blankenheim; the archbishoprics of Cologne and Trier, the bishoprics of Münster and Paderborn; the Abbey of Prüm; parts of the Austrian Duchy of Luxembourg; the Duchy of Pfalz-Zweibrücken; the Bishopric of Liege; and numerous other smaller territories.

originally divided into the six districts of Kleve, Düsseldorf, Cologne, Aachen, Koblenz, and Trier, which were then reduced to five in 1822 when Kleve was incorporated into Düsseldorf District. In 1817, all the districts in the two provinces had substantial Jewish populations, their densities averaging about one percent of the total population (Table 13.1). The districts farthest to the northwestern and the west—Münster and Aachen, respectively—had Jewish densities substantially below the average for the region. The district farthest to the southeast, Koblenz, exceeded the average density considerably. A substantially higher percentage of Jews in these districts lived in villages rather than cities than in the rest of Prussia. In general, the share of those living in villages increased as one moved southward (Table 13.2).

Table 13.1. Jewish Population in Various Districts of Western Germany, 1817

Province	Regierungsbezirk	General population	Jewish population	Percent Jewish
Westphalia	Münster	353283	2304	0.7
Westphalia	Minden	340614	3930	1.2
Westphalia	Arnsberg	380182	3489	0.9
Rhine	Kleve	216731	1833	0.9
Rhine	Düsseldorf	379902	3190	0.8
Rhine	Cologne	338416	3349	1.0
Rhine	Aachen	310619	1621	0.5
Rhine	Koblenz	359204	5791	1.6
Rhine	Trier	302901	3057	1.0
Total		2981852	28564	1.0

Source: Silbergleit, *Die Bevölkerungs- und Berufsverhältnisse*, 11*.

Table 13.2. Percent of Jews Living in the Countryside (*Land*), 1817 (districts from north to south)

District	Percent
Münster	22.1
Minden	37.2
Kleve	16.5
Düsseldorf	52.8
Arnsberg	41.7
Cologne	53.7
Aachen	68.2
Trier	68.5
Koblenz	66.5

Source: Silbergleit, *Die Bevölkerungs- und Berufsverhältnisse*, 11*.

Jewish density within each district varied substantially. Two areas in western Germany had very sparse Jewish populations: one west of the Rhine and one to its east. For the western area, the available data, which began with the French census of 1808 and continued into the twentieth century, show a consistent pattern with very little change over time. In 1808, the area of the Eiffel Mountains west of the Rhine and north of the Mosel River had almost no Jewish population. This region runs from about ten kilometers north of the Mosel to about 25 kilometers south of the Bonn–Aachen line. Throughout this territory, Jewish communities were located only within about 25 kilometers of the Rhine. The rest of the area, which lacked a Jewish population, measured about 75 kilometers from east to west and 60–110 kilometers from north to south and was divided among the districts of Trier, Koblenz, and Aachen. A group of seven adjacent counties had a combined Jewish population of only 134 in 1871; this itself was more than twice as many as in 1837. In 1880, the Jewish population of these counties reached 233 (0.11 percent of the total population). Among the seven counties, only Bitburg County near the city of Trier and the Luxembourg border showed substantial growth in its Jewish population in the course of the nineteenth and early twentieth centuries. Even during the Weimar Republic era the other six counties still had only about 140 Jews (Table 13.3). The second area of very low Jewish density, which was east of the Rhine on the border between the Westphalian district of Arnsberg and the Rhineland district of Cologne, spilled over into the southeastern sections of Düsseldorf District and neighboring Dillkreis in the Hesse-Nassau district of Wiesbaden. It stretched from the industrial region along the Wupper just south of the Ruhr to the northwestern sections of the Westerwald, east of Bonn. The Jewish population in the more rural parts of this area was tiny (343 out of a total of 204,012 inhabitants in 1871). While Jews were more prevalent in the industrial part of the region south of the Ruhr, even there Jewish density was a mere 0.30 percent in 1871 (Table 13.4).

Some parts of western Germany had much denser Jewish populations. This was especially the case in the heavily rural areas in eastern Westphalia and the southeastern Rhine Province that bordered on the more densely Jewish areas of Hesse and the Palatinate. In the districts of Minden and Arnsberg in eastern Westphalia, six counties had Jewish densities ranging from 1.81 percent to 3.37 percent in 1871. Most of the eight heavily Jewish counties in the southeast were near the Rhine and either south of or only slightly north of the Mosel River, mainly in Koblenz district. In the same region, the Oldenburg enclave of Birkenfeld also had a relatively dense Jewish population (Table 13.5). In general, Jews who lived south of Bonn in the Rhineland were concentrated

Table 13.3. Counties in or near Eiffel Mountains with Very Small Jewish Populations, 1871, 1880, and 1925

District	County	General population			Jewish population				Percent Jewish		
		1871	1880	1925	1837	1871	1880	1925	1871	1880	1925
Koblenz	Adenau	20965	21772	25153	13	15	11	5	0.05	0.05	0.02
Trier	Daum	26692	27475	34034	0	1	30	75	0.004	0.11	0.22
Trier	Prüm	34911	35485	37603	8	13	18	31	0.04	0.05	0.08
Trier	Bitburg	44543	44585	49454	15	90	147	221	0.2	0.33	0.45
Aachen	Monschau	18276	18176	20192	0	2	2	5	0.01	0.01	0.02
Aachen	Eupen	25299	25888	*	0	5	10	*	0.02	0.04	*
Aachen	Malmedy	30171	30974	*	0	8	15	*	0.03	0.05	*
Total		200857	204355	166436	36	134	233	337*	0.02	0.11	0.20

*The territories surrendered by Germany to Belgium after World War I (Eupen and Malmedy counties) had a Jewish population of 23 (0.04 percent) of a general population of 60,003 in 1910 (Silbergleit, *Die Bevölkerungs- und Berufsverhältnisse*, 23*).

Sources: *AZJ* 109, no. 2 (1838): 442; Hoffmann "Neueste Nachrichten von der Bevölkerung des Preußischen Staates," *Allgemeine Preussische Staatszeitung* 229 (1838); "Confessionelle Verschiedenheiten der Ortsanwesenden am 1. Dezember 1871: Die Ergebnisse der Volkszählungen und Volksbeschreibung im Preussischen Staate von 1. December 1871," *Preussische Statistik* 3 (1875): 95–102; Bosse, *Die Verbreitung der Juden*, 37, 41, 43; Silbergleit, *Die Bevölkerungs- und Berufsverhältnisse*, 32*–33*.

Table 13.4. Areas of Sparse Jewish population on the Arnsberg/Cologne Border, 1871–1925

District	County	General population			Jewish population					Percent Jewish		
		1871	1880	1925	1837	1871	1880	1925		1871	1880	1925
Cologne	Wipperfürth	27592	28289	29341	0	2	0	1		0.01	0	0
Cologne	Gummersbach	29107	30783	52764		57	73	34		0.2	0.2	0.1
Arnsberg	Olpe	30947	34142	59946	47	70	86	71		0.2	0.3	0.1
Arnsberg	Siegen	59779	71425	98298	19	94	206	97		0.2	0.3	0.1
Wiesbaden	Dillkreis	35044	38008	57803		68	119	157		0.2	0.3	0.3
Cologne	Waldbröl	21543	22895	30212	23	52	75	55		0.2	0.3	0.2
Total, rural districts		204012	225542	328364		343	559	415		0.2	0.3	0.1
Düsseldorf	Lennep-Remscheid	82123	94351	162547	24	56	68	286		0.1	0.1	0.2
Düsseldorf	Barmen (city)	74449	95941	187099		143	239	721		0.2	0.3	0.4
Düsseldorf	Solingen	92484	107365	232743		188	387	481		0.2	0.4	0.2
Arnsberg	Hagen	109215	125182	187256		440	524	667		0.4	0.4	0.4
Düsseldorf	Mettmann	54037	63332	125310		232	214	180		0.4	0.4	0.1
Arnsberg	Altena	54984	66129	94460		252	265	155		0.5	0.4	0.2
Total, industrial area south of Ruhr		467292	552300	989325		1311	1697	2490		0.3	0.3	0.3
Total		692580	834726	1403722		1871	2561	3165		0.3	0.3	0.2

The city of Elberfeld (626 Jews in 1871) was the only island of relatively heavy Jewish population in an industrial area that otherwise accommodated few Jews.

Sources: as in Table 13.3.

Scattered counties with low Jewish density:

County	Territory	General population		Jewish population		Percent Jewish	
		1871	1880	1871	1880	1871	1880
Münster	Warendorf	28102	28246	134	132	0.5	0.5
Düsseldorf	Geldern	49812	52774	234	231	0.5	0.4
Münster	Recklinghausen	52897	64699	230	207	0.4	0.3
Münster	Münster (*Land*)	45469	37572	152	162	0.3	0.4
Trier	Saarbrücken	87744	111489	333	428	0.4	0.4
Düsseldorf	Essen (*Land*)	83523	117904	304	384	0.4	0.3
Cologne	Mülheim/Rhein	57821	69629	182	245	0.3	0.4
Minden	Bielefeld (*Land*)	37334	40123	83	73	0.2	0.2
Total		442702	522436	1652	1862	0.4	0.4

Sources: "Ergebnisse 1871" *Preussische Statistik* 30 (1875): 95–102; Bosse, *Die Verbreitung der Juden*, 38, 40, 42, 60–62.

Table 13.5. Jewish Density in Birkenfeld

Population	1871	1880	1885	1890	1900	1910	1925
Total population	36128	38685	39693	41242	43406	50496	55649
Jewish population	640	677	678	583	524	560	454
Percent Jewish	1.8	1.8	1.7	1.4	1.2	1.1	0.9

Sources: *Vierteljahreshefte zur Statistik des Deutschen Reichs für das Jahre* 1 (1873): 188 d; neue Folge 1 (1892): III, 30–31; *Statistik des Deutschen Reichs* 57 (1883): 250; neue Folge 32 (1888): 242–243.

both in the valleys of the Rhine and its tributaries—the Mosel, Ahr, Nahe, and Glan—and along the Saar, a tributary of the Mosel. Many of these valleys were in wine producing regions. Fewer Jews lived in the highlands between the rivers. There was a third area of relatively heavy Jewish density: a fairly compact zone west of the Rhine about halfway between Cologne and Aachen in the districts of Aachen, Cologne, and Düsseldorf (Table 13.6). Much of this area had once been part of the Duchy of Jülich. Also heavy in Jewish density, although not contiguous with the other areas, was the county of Bonn.

In much of the rest of western Germany, Jews accounted for 0.5–1.5 percent of the total population. Of the fifty-three counties that fell into this range in 1871, thirty-four had Jewish densities of 0.80–1.18 percent, seven had lower densities, and the other twelve had higher ones (Table 13.7). In Münster District, there was a slight tendency for counties in the northwest near the Dutch border to have somewhat higher densities than the rest of the district.

Most Jews in the Rhineland and Westphalia lived in relatively small communities. In 1808, only eleven of 443 towns west of the Rhine, which was then a part of Napoleonic France, had 100 or more Jewish inhabitants. Four of these relatively large communities (all in the area south of the Mosel) were small towns; the others were cities of various sizes. The mean community size (excluding groupings of nine or fewer Jews) was 37.8, slightly higher in the more northern French *département* of Roer and slightly lower farther south (Table 13.8). Many major cities in western Germany, including Cologne, Aachen, Münster, and Dortmund (but not the smaller cities farther south in the Rhineland and farther northeast in Westphalia) had not permitted any Jewish residency in most of the eighteenth century. Although these cities did allow Jewish communities to take shape starting in the 1790s, their Jewish populations remained relatively small as late as 1843 (Table 13.9). The cities in what later became the industrial area of the Ruhr valley had relatively few Jewish inhabitants in the early nineteenth century. In 1843, there were only five or six[2] communities in the Ruhr with more than 100 Jewish inhabitants, bringing the total Jewish population to 940 or 1,092, respectively. By 1880, there were either sixteen or eighteen such towns, with a total Jewish population of 5,821 or 6,195. This was still low as against the 14,513 or 14,858 Jews who later inhabited communities of 100 or above in 1910. The largest community in the Ruhr numbered 269 in 1843, 998 in 1880, and 2,773 in 1910 (Table 13.10).

---

2 The difference depends on how one defines the exact geographical boundaries of Ruhr District.

Table 13.6. Areas of Heavy Jewish Density in Rhine Province and Westphalia, 1871–1925

District	County	General population				Jewish population				Percent Jewish		
		1871	1880	1925	1837	1871	1880	1925	1871	1880	1925
Mainly rural eastern Westphalia:												
Minden	Warburg	31061	31075	36215	1265	1046	925	382	3.4	3.0	1.0
Minden	Höxter	49022	50836	62168	1181	1259	1163	623	2.6	2.3	1.0
Arnsberg	Lippstadt	34757	37199	54188	551	764	721	329	2.2	1.9	0.6
Arnsberg	Brilon	38105	37866	47068	706	727	735	431	1.9	2.0	0.9
Arnsberg	Wittgenstein	19789	20352	27493		372	380	250	1.9	1.9	0.9
Minden	Büren	35441	35878	40670	580	653	598	247	1.8	1.7	0.6
Subtotal		208175	213206	267802		4821	4522	2262	2.3	2.1	0.8
Southeastern Rhineland:												
Koblenz	Meisenheim	13530	13777	13534		377	342	131	2.8	2.5	1.0
Koblenz	Kreuznach	60771	67115	86111	1506	1584	1781	1270	2.6	2.7	1.5
Trier	Bernkastel	44138	44820	50453	825	867	883	481	2.0	2.0	1.0
Koblenz	Neuwied	69194	73448	100116	1076	1349	1325	870	2.0	1.8	1.3
Koblenz	Mayen	58879	58879	82680	765	976	1048	751	1.8	1.8	0.9
Koblenz	Koblenz	74802	83162	126779	1119*	1209	1382	1294	1.6	1.7	1.0
Koblenz	Wetzlar	44913	48867	70464		702	875	503	1.66	1.8	0.7
Koblenz	Simmern	35621	36124	36970	626	552	547	429	1.6	1.5	1.2
Subtotal			426192	566927		7616	8183	5729		1.9	1.0
West of the Rhine:												
Düsseldorf	Grevenbroich	38756	40676	53632		819	875	480	2.1	2.2	0.9
Cologne	Euskirchen	37070	39989	55957		786	819	653	2.1	2.1	1.2

Cologne	Rheinbach	31299	32629	36755		625	674	358	2.0	2.1	1.0
Aachen	Jülich	41432	42007	49465		693	635	328	1.7	1.5	0.7
Cologne	Bergheim	39940	41154	64286		630	586	384	1.6	1.4	0.6
Subtotal		188497	196455	260095		3553	3589	2203	1.9	1.8	0.9
Cologne	Bonn (*Land*)	43618	49822	81324		796	851	502	1.8	1.7	0.6
Total			885675	1176148		16786	17145	10696		1.9	0.9
non-urban											
Major cities:											
Cologne	Cologne	129233	144772	700222	454	3172	4523	16093	2.5	3.1	2.3
Cologne	Bonn	26030	31514	90249	495	536	572	1167	2.1	1.8	1.3
Minden	Bielefeld	21834	30679	86062	266	436	653	865	2.0	2.1	1.0
Trier	Trier	31869	37431	58140	293	633	885	802	2.0	2.4	1.4
Düsseldorf	Krefeld	57105	73872	131098		1085	1532	1626	1.9	2.1	1.2
Arnsberg	Bochum	21192	33440	211249		370	617	1122	1.8	1.9	0.5
Düsseldorf	Essen	51513	56944	470524		832	942	4209	1.6	1.7	0.9
Arnsberg	Dortmund	44420	66544	321743		677	998	3820	1.5	1.5	1.2
Total (cities)		383196	475196	2069287		7171	10722	29704	1.9	2.3	1.4
Total			1360871	3245435		23957	27867	40400		2.0	1.2

* Koblenz city and rural areas.

Sources as in Table 13.3.

Warburg and Höxter counties had even larger Jewish populations earlier in the century. The share of Jews in their total populations in 1821 was four percent and 2.5 percent, respectively. Herzig, "Landjuden—Stadtjuden," 94.

Table 13.7. Jewish Densities in Counties and Cities of Western Germany, 1880 and 1925

Year	Regierungsbezirk	Number of cities or counties in each category					
		Over 2.0%	1.5%–1.99%	1.0%–1.49%	0.75%–0.99%	0.5%–0.74%	0.2%–0.49%	Below 0.2%
1880	Münster	0	0	3	3	2	3	0
	Minden	3	1	1	2	3	0	1
	Arnsberg	0	4	3	3	3	4	0
	Düsseldorf	2	1	4	6	1	5	0
	Cologne	3	1	1	2	0	2	1
	Aachen	0	1	2	0	3	1	3
	Koblenz	2	5	4	0	1	0	1
	Trier	1	1	6	1	0	2	2
1925	Münster	0	0	0	1	3	8	5
	Minden	0	0	4	0	2	6	1
	Arnsberg	0	0	1	3	8	12	6
	Düsseldorf	0	0	3	4	4	15	4
	Cologne	1	0	2	1	2	2	4
	Aachen	0	0	0	1	3	4	1
	Koblenz	0	0	3	5	4	1	1
	Trier	0	0	1	3	1	3	2

Sources: Based on Bosse, *Die Verbreitung der Juden*, 36–43, 60–65; Silbergleit, *Die Bevölkerungs- und Berufsverhältnisse*, 31*–33*.

Table 13.8. Community Size in Rhineland (West of the Rhine, From South to North), 1808

A) French Département

Number of communities in each category

Département	1–9	10–49	50–99	100 or above	Total	Mean community size	Mean not counting 1–9
Sarre	26 (136)	79 (1,691)	15 (1,071)	5 (642)	125 (3,540)	28.3	34.4
Rhin et Moselle	57 (321)	94 (2,246)	9 (556)	3 (937)	163 (4,060)	24.9	35.3
Roer	35 (177)	80 (2,211)	37 (2,526)	3 (404)	155 (5,318)	34.3	42.8
Total	118 (634)	253 (6,148)	61 (4,153)	11 (1,983)	443 (12,918)	29.2	37.8

In parentheses: number of Jewish residents in each category.

Includes Birkenfeld but excludes towns later in the Netherlands.

B) Towns with over 100 Jews, 1808 (* = total population over 10,000 in 1880)

Town	Jewish Population
Koblenz*	342
Bonn*	309
Kreuznach*	286
Trier*	198
Krefeld*	160
Cologne*	124
Kleve*	120
Hottenbach	116
Steinbach	116
Saarwellingen	108
Meisenheim	104

Source: "Übersicht der Zahl der Juden in den linksrheinischen Departements in den Jahren 1806–1808," in *Zur Geschichte und Kultur der Juden im Rheinland*, ed. Falk Wiesemann (Düsseldorf: Schwann, 1985), 90–97.

Table 13.9.

A) Large Jewish Communities in Southern Rheinland

City	1808	1843
Bonn	309	498
Kreuznach	286	404
Koblenz	342	349
Trier	198	232

B) Large Jewish Communities in Eastern Westphalia

City	1808	1843
Paderborn		332
Minden		202

C) Jewish Populations in Cities that Banned Jews in the Eighteenth Century

City	1808	1843
Cologne	124	784
Aachen	60	274
Münster		183
Dortmund		153

Sources: "Übersicht der Zahl der Juden in den linksrheinischen Departements"; Bleich, *Die erste vereinigte Landtag*, appendix A, 325–326.

Table 13.10. Towns that Had over 100 Jews in Rhineland and Westphalia[1]

Ruhr Towns	1843	1871	1880	1910	1925
Essen	269	832	942	2773	4209
Mülheim/Ruhr	242	319	431	664	626
Bochum*	165	370	617	992	1122
Dortmund*	153	677	998	2676	3820
Hagen*	111	224	322	513	580
Witten*		264	378	354	311
Duisburg*		253	367	1554	2080
Hörde			322	285	238
Gelsenkirchen*		96	321	1251	1441
Hamm*		174	221	384	401
Ruhrort			181	520H	
Steele			165	224H	157
Wattenscheid		130	148	285(185H)	192
Hattingen			147	162(150)H	
Schwerte			142	109(60)H	
Oberhausen*		91	119	403	513
Hamborn				345	818
Herne				319	474
Recklinghausen			72	368	451
Gladbeck				97	264
Wanne-Eickel				332	316
Kamen			108	111(126)H	
Iserlohn*	152	223	266	234	211
Total Ruhr	940(6)	3653(12)	6267(19)	14955(23)	18224(19)

---

1 Not including the Duchy of Birkenfeld.

Other Rhineland Towns (Urban)	1808	1837	1843	1871	1880	1910	1925
Düsseldorf*		409	412	919	1,008	3,985	5,130
Krefeld*	160	293	404	1,085	1,532	1,815	1,626
Kleve*	120		140		185	165(210)H	158
Elberfeld*		125		626	1,104	1,919	2,335
M-Gladbach*				356	504	840	951
Neuss*				264	310	225	236
Barmen*		38		143	239	643	721
Rheydt*				177	228	279	288
Solingen*				182	194	266	210
Viersen*				109	158	141	157
Remscheid				1	8	167	229
Wesel*		208	187	206	205	235	184
RB Dusseldorf	280(2)	1073(5)	1143(4)	4068(11)	5675(12)	10680(12)	12225(12)
Cologne*	124	454	784	3,172	4,523	12,156	16,093
Deutz*		258	240		206		
Ehrenfeld*					250		
Mülheim/Rhein					172	229	

Bonn*	309	495	498	536	572	1,228	1,167
RB Cologne	433(2)	1207(3)	1522(3)	3708(2)	5723(5)	13613(3)	17260(2)
Kreuznach*	286	443	490	470	601	603	600
Koblenz*	342	257	349	468	558	677	709
RB Koblenz	628(2)	700(2)	839(2)	938(2)	1,159(2)	1280(2)	1309(2)
Aachen*	60	190	274	825	1,091	1,565	1,420
Eschweiler*				141	148	156	114
RB Aachen				966	1239	1721	1534
Trier*	198	266	232	431	627	734	802
Saarbrücken					37	1,081	
St. Johann*					254		
RB Trier					918	1815	

Western Germany | 599

Rhineland (smaller cities)	1808	1837	1843	1871	1880	1910	1925
Goch	94		194		153	132(100)H	
Rees			121		97	49H	
Emmerich					158	122	
Geldern					120	97	
Kempen					110		
Dinslaken			134		167	196H	239
Dülken			100		83	104H	
RB Dusseldorf	94		549(4)		888(7)	590(6)	239
Siegburg			185		331	311H	255
Zülpich					113	84(80)H	
Euskirchen					170	248H	259
Münstereifel					119	77(90)H	
RB Cologne			185	136	733(4)	729(4)	514(2)
Düren					252	304	330
Geilenkirchen					153	167(200)H	
Linnich					134	117H	
Jülich					108	137(125)H	
RB Aachen				136	647(4)	725(4)	330

Neuwied		276	305	379	366	417	339
Simmern	74		170		82	94(87)H
Mayen	56		161		289	307H	253
Bendorf			117		117	99(275)H
Vallendar			113		196	151(167)H
Linz			109		134	96(88)
Sobernheim	64		108		122	109H
Wetzlar					210	181H
Braunfels					105	
Boppard					101	108(130)H
Kochem					110	67(100)H
Kirchberg					108	84(90)H
RB Koblenz	194	276	1083(7)	379	1940(12)	1685(11)	592(2)
Saarlouis			208		134	307(315)H
Merzig	83		182		223	275H
Ottweiler	92		170		99	52(47)H
Wittlich	54		110		214	229(258)H
RB Trier	229		670(4)		670(4)	863
Steuss			139			

Westphalia outside Ruhr (urban)	1808	1837	1843	1871	1880	1910	1925
Paderborn*		253	332	371	391	389	304
Minden*			202	249	267	173	233
Herford*			146	175	226	267	228
Bielefeld*				436	653	847	865
RB Minden		253	680(3)	1231(4)	1537(4)	1676(4)	1630(4)
Münster*		180	183	366	491	637(1000)	580
						H	
Soest*			121		322	201H	192
Siegen*					111	126	130
RB Arnsberg			121		433	327	322

Westphalia outside Ruhr (rural)	1808	1837	1843	1871	1880	1910	1925
(Burg) Steinfurt			179		208	155(165)H	
Lengerich			139		76	50H	
Bocholt			136		152	298	250
Coesfeld			104		74	81(50)H	
Ibbenbüren			103		79	69	
Rheine					103		
Ahlen					101	81(90)H	
Dülmen					100	77(73)H	
RB Münster			661(5)		893(8)	950(8)	
Beverungen			201		120	105	250
Brakel			174		146		131(115)H
Warburg			166		294		106(122)H
Salzkotten			135		141		232(240)H
							83(97)H

Vlotho	131	77	78(84)H
Bünde	126	135	112(104)H
Lübbecke	117	80	62H
Nieheim	110	151	93(100)H
Lügde	109	44	22(18)H
Höxter	106	186	126(120)H
Steinheim		165	94H
RB Minden	1375(10)	1539(11)	1139(11)
Marsberg	157	145 (Ndr Marsberg)	105(110)H
Gesecke	157	163	72(75)H
Berleburg	122	106	64(65)H
Laasphe	112	152	112H
Lippstadt		245	192(200)H
Brilon		135	81H
Arnsberg		117	69H
Unna		172	190(121)H
(Hohen) Limburg	120	150	108(150)H
Werl		116	83H
RB Arnsberg	668(5)	1501(10)	1076(10)

* Total population over 10,000 in 1880.

H = *Handbuch der jüdischen Gemeindeverwaltung* (1911).

Sources: "Übersicht der Zahl der Juden in den linksrheinischen Departements"; *Allgemeine Zeitung des Judentums* 108, no. 2 (September 11, 1838); Bleich, *Die erste vereinigte Landtag*, 325–326; Bosse, *Die Verbreitung der Juden*, 36–43, 60–65; *Handbuch der jüdischen Gemeindeverwaltung* (1911).

Between 1817 and 1880, the Jewish populations in the various sections of the Rhineland and Westphalia changed at significantly different rates (Table 13.11). The Jewish densities of Aachen and Cologne Districts grew substantially as the Jewish population increased much more rapidly than the rest of the population. Much like Aachen, Münster District began with a relatively thin Jewish presence and also increased in percentage, although less so than Aachen and Cologne. Most other districts, including those that eventually became the center of the most industrialized parts of the region, showed relatively little change in density.

The rapid growth in the Jewish population of Cologne District is attributable mainly to the meteoric rise of the Jewish presence in the city of Cologne itself. The first Jew to live in Cologne in the modern era arrived in 1798. The Jewish population of the city then grew to 124 in 1808, 354 in 1823, 784 in 1843, 1,286 in 1849, and 3,172 in 1871. The Jewish presence in the rest of the district increased much slower from about 3,000 in 1817 to 4,435 in 1843, and 5,366 in 1871. In Aachen District, just west of Cologne, the eponymous city's Jewish community's growth, while certainly substantial—rising from sixty in 1808 to 274 in 1843, and to 825 in 1871—accounted for a smaller proportion of gains than in Cologne District. The city of Münster played an even smaller role in the growth of the Jewish population in the district that bore its name.

Between 1817 and 1843, the Jewish population of western Germany grew at approximately the same pace in all districts except for the northwesternmost and southeasternmost districts of Münster and Koblenz, respectively, where it was somewhat slower. Between 1843 and 1880, in contrast, the difference among these districts widened greatly. The two northern districts of Westphalia saw hardly any increase in Jewish population throughout the period, and lost Jews in absolute terms after 1861. The rate of increase in the heavily rural southern-Rhineland districts of Trier and Koblenz exceeded that of northern Westphalia but fell far short of that in both the northern Rhineland and the Arnsberg district of Westphalia.

After 1880, the internal differences between various parts of the Rhine province and Westphalia widened further, with some regions industrializing and urbanizing rapidly and others remaining more rural. The three areas of rapid growth were the city of Cologne, the Ruhr industrial district, and the iron and coal region of the Saar (Table 13.12). Several more rural districts such as Minden in the northeast and Koblenz and Aachen in the south saw their Jewish populations decline. Cologne District had the highest percentage of Jewish population growth of any district in western Germany both before and after 1880. The city of Cologne figured overwhelmingly in this growth; its share in the Jewish population of the district surged from 43.6 percent in 1871 to 79.0

Table 13.11. Changes in Jewish Population and Density of West German Districts, 1817–1880

District	1817	Percent Jewish	1825	1834	1843	Percent increase 1817–1843	1852	1861	1871	1880	Percent Jewish	Percent increase 1843–1880
Münster	2304	0.7	2611	2884	3215	39.54	3364	3535	3403	3466	0.7	7.8
Minden	3930	1.2	4667	5320	5782	47.12	6126	6164	5949	5849	1.2	1.2
Kleve	1833	0.9										
Düsseldorf	3190	0.8	5679	6298	7102	41.39	8087	9556	11419	13211	0.8	86.0
Arnsberg	3489	0.9	3864	4685	5408	55.00	5987	6932	7893	9495	0.9	75.6
Cologne	3349	1.0	3559	4416	5219	55.84	6127	7288	8538	10370	1.5	98.7
Aachen	1621	0.5	1881	2196	2522	55.58	2819	3141	3769	4235	0.8	67.9
Trier	3057	1.0	3437	4237*	4762	55.77	5047	5554	5985	6566	1.0	37.9
Koblenz	5791	1.6	6480	7205	7965	37.54	6436	8709	8713	9312	1.5	16.9
Birkenfeld					684		739	722	640	677	1.8	

Sources: Silbergleit, *Die Bevölkerungs- und Berufsverhältnisse*, 11*, 18–19*; Blau, *Entwicklung*, 69; *Vierteljahreshefte zur Statistik des Deutschen Reichs* 1 (1873): 188 d; *Statistik des Deutschen Reichs* 57 (1883): 250; *Statistische Nachrichten über das Grossherzogthum Oldenburg* 7 (1857): 30; 6 (1863): 79.

Table 13.12. Changes in Jewish Population in Various Parts of Western Germany, 1880–1925

City	1880	1890	1900	1910	1925	Percent change 1880–1925
Münster	3466	3593	3743	4040	4315	+24.5
Minden	5849	5402	5095	4609	3890	-33.5
Düsseldorf	13211	15151	17664	21276	24494*	+85.4
Arnsberg	9495	10177	11802	12387	13390*	+41.0
Cologne	10370	12043	14950	17041	20361	+96.3
Aachen	4235	4387	4325	4211	3671*	-13.3
Trier	6566	6562	6773	6849	3023**	**
Koblenz	9312	9091	8539	7910	6674	-28.3
Birkenfeld	677	583			454	-32.9

* Minor territorial changes disregarded.
** Not counting territory lost to Saarland after World War I.

Sources: Silbergleit, *Die Bevölkerungs- und Berufsverhältnisse*, 19*; *Vierteljahreshefte zur Statistik des Deutschen Reichs*, neue Folge 1 (1892): III, 30–31; *Statistik des Deutschen Reichs* 57 (1883): 250.

percent in 1925. Elsewhere in the Cologne district, the Jewish population actually contracted from 5,847 in 1880 to 4,268 in 1925. While the number of Jews in Cologne rose rapidly, the percentage increase could not keep up with the city's rapid growth in both geographic and demographic terms. Cologne's Jewish population declined from 3.12 percent of the total in 1880 to 2.30 percent in 1925.

Neither the Ruhr District nor the Saar District fit exactly into the administrative districts or counties into which the Rhineland and Westphalia were divided. In both areas, the absolute number of Jews grew rapidly but not nearly as fast as the general population and the Jewish percentage of the population fell more steeply in these two areas than in Cologne District.

The Ruhr District contained a large number of originally independent cities and villages that grew rapidly and often merged with each other. By the twentieth century, many cities in this area had annexed smaller neighboring cities to become contiguous. Some areas that remained "rural" (that is, lacking an independent city status outside a county administration) were as industrialized as the larger cities. Within the approximate boundaries of the Ruhr basin, the urban Jewish population almost doubled between 1880 and 1900, and nearly doubled again between 1900 and 1925. The general population of the industrial cities in this area, however, grew much more rapidly than the Jewish one, which in turn reduced Jewish density in these localities from 1.53 percent of the population to 0.66 percent between 1880 and 1925. The Jewish population increased only slightly between 1880 and 1925 in the areas of the Ruhr basin that were still administered as rural counties, and its percentage in the total fell to half of what it was in 1880 (Table 13.13). South of the Ruhr there was another industrial area that had only two large Jewish communities in 1880—Düsseldorf and Elberfeld—and a sparse Jewish population everywhere else. Although the Jewish population outside the main cities remained minuscule, that in the urban parts of this region grew by 238 percent between 1880 and 1925—more rapidly than in the Ruhr proper and even faster than the general population (Table 13.14). The rest of Düsseldorf District, most of which was west of the Rhine, was less urbanized than the areas east of the Rhine. This district had several significant urban communities, in some of which the absolute number of Jews peaked before World War I. The urban Jewish population in this part of the district increased by 22.61 percent between 1880 and 1890 and then leveled off thereafter. The rural population declined by 36 percent between 1880 and 1925 (Table 13.15). Outside the Ruhr (mainly to its east and south) in Arnsberg District there were relatively few major cities and even there the Jewish population was not large. In the more rural areas, the Jewish population

Table 13.13. Jewish Population in the Ruhr Basin (absolute number followed by percent Jewish)

Area	1880		1890		1900		1910		1925		1933	
Cities												
Bochum	617	1.9	764	1.5	1002	1.5	992	0.7	1122	0.5	1069	0.3
Dortmund	998	1.5	1306	1.5	1924	1.4	2676	1.3	3820	1.2	4108	0.8
Hoerde (Dortmund)	322	2.6			347	1.4	285	0.9	238	0.7		
Duisburg	367	0.9	474	0.8	786	0.9	1554	0.7	2080	0.8	2560	0.6
Hamborn (Duisburg)					123	0.4	345	0.3	818	0.7		
Ruhrort (Duisburg)	181	2.0										
Essen	942	1.7	1190	1.5	1807	1.5	2773	0.9	4209	0.9	4506	0.7
Mülheim/Ruhr	431	2.0	493	1.8	643	1.7	664	0.6	626	0.5	517	0.4
Oberhausen	119	0.7	147	0.6	302	0.7	403	0.5	513	0.5	525	0.3
Sterkrade (Oberhausen)							73	0.1	130	0.3		
Gelsenkirchen	321	2.2	561	2.0	811	2.2	1251	0.8	1441	0.7	1615	0.5
Buer (Gelsenkirchen)					47	0.2	117	0.2	171	0.2		
Recklinghausen	72	1.0	120	0.9	220	0.7	368	0.7	451	0.5	411	0.5
Gladbeck* (Recklinghausen)							97	0.3	264	0.4	224	0.4
Bottrop					58	0.2	70	0.2	207	0.3	194	0.2
Herne					272	1.0	319	0.6	474	0.7	467	0.5

Location												
Hamm	221	1.0	280	1.1	293	1.0	384	0.9	401	0.8	393	0.7
Hattingen	147	2.3										
Wanne-Eickel									316	0.4	196	0.2
Wattenscheid	148	1.7	173	1.3	124	0.3	332	0.5	192	0.3	148	0.2
Witten	378	1.8	335	1.3	198	1.0	285	1.0	311	0.7	297	0.4
Total	5586	1.5			9849		13855		18364	0.7	17738	
Rural areas												
Dinslaken*	377	0.4							259	0.4		
Essen (*Land*)	384	0.3							328	0.2		
Dortmund (*Land*)	815	0.8							595	0.3		
Bochum (*Land*)	438	0.3							156	0.2		
Hagen (*Land*)	202	0.2							87	0.1		
Schwelm (Hagen)									109	0.1		
Recklinghausen (*Land*)	135	0.2							357	0.2		
Hamm (*Land*)	326	0.7							343	0.3		
Hattingen (*Land*)									210	0.3		
Hoerde (*Land*)									285	0.2		
Total	2677	0.5							2729	0.2		

Sources: Bosse, *Die Verbreitung der Juden*, 38–40, 61, 63–65; Silbergleit, *Die Bevölkerungs- und Berufsverhältnisse*, 31*–32*; 1933 census, 5/15; Schmelz, Territorial Printout.

Table 13.14. Jewish Population in Düsseldorf District East of the Rhine and South of Ruhr Area (absolute number followed by percent Jewish)

Area	1880		1890		1900		1910		1925		1933	
Cities												
Düsseldorf	1008	1.0%	1401	0.8%	2131	1.0%	3985	1.1%	5130	1.2%	5053	1.0%
Remscheid	8	0.03	66	0.2	136	0.2	167	0.2	229	0.3	273	0.3
Solingen	194	1.1	257	0.7	301	0.7	266	0.5	210	0.4	217	0.2
Elberfeld	1104	1.1	1378	1.1	1664	1.0	1919	1.1	2335	1.4		
Barmen	239	0.3	416	0.4	592	0.4	643	0.4	721	0.4		
Wuppertal											2471	0.6
Total	2553	0.8	3518		4824		6980		8625	0.9	8014	
Rural areas												
Düsseldorf (*Land*)	299	0.6							249	0.2		
Lennep	60								57	0.1		
Mettmann	214	0.3							180	0.1		
Solingen	193								271	0.2		
Total	766	0.2							757	0.2		

Sources: Silbergleit, *Die Bevölkerungs- und Berufsverhältnisse*, 32*; Bosse, *Die Verbreitung der Juden*, 38–40; Schmelz, Territorial Printout.

Table 13.15. Jewish Population in Düsseldorf District West of the Rhine

Area	1880		1890		1900		1910		1925		1933	
Cities												
Krefeld	1532	2.1%	1992	1.9%	1788	1.7%	1815	1.4%	1626	1.2%	1481	0.9%
M-Gladbach	504	1.4	631	1.3	741	1.3	840	1.3	951	0.8	907	0.7
Neuss	310	1.8	316	1.4	245	0.9	225	0.6	236	0.5	227	0.4
Rheydt	228	1.2	217	0.8	313	0.9	279	0.6	288	0.6	351	0.5
Total	2574	1.7	3156		3087		3159		3101	0.9	2966	
Rural areas												
Cleve	491	0.1							374	0.4		
Geldern	231	0.4							161	0.3		
Gladbach	772	0.9							328	0.4		
Grevenbroich	875	2.2							480	0.9		
Kempen	701	0.8							497	0.5		
Krefeld	270	0.9							151	0.3		
Mörs	499	0.8							494	0.3		
Neuss	290	0.9							156	0.4		
Total	4129	0.9							2641	0.4		

Jewish Population in Düsseldorf District East of the Rhine and North of the Ruhr Area

Town	1880		1925	
Rees	616	1.0%	407	0.5%

Sources: Bosse, *Die Verbreitung der Juden*, 38–40; Silbergleit, *Die Bevölkerungs- und Berufsverhältnisse*, 32*; Schmelz, Territorial Printout.

declined considerably in both absolute and relative terms and fell most of all in areas that formerly had large numbers of Jews. Nevertheless, the counties in eastern Arnsberg District retained much higher Jewish densities than those in the southwest (Table 13.16).

Both the Ruhr industrial region and the city of Cologne attracted a rapidly growing population of East European Jewish immigrants. After Berlin, Saxony, and the city of Munich, the northern Rhineland and Ruhr District were the most important centers for Jewish immigrants in Germany. In both the Rhine province and in Westphalia, the number of foreign Jews more than doubled between 1910 and 1925, even as the overall Jewish population of these provinces hardly changed. The percentage of non-citizens in the Jewish population varied from city to city but was highest in Cologne and the Ruhr and lower by far in the rest of these two provinces. In Cologne, 3,908 non-citizen Jews made up 24.28 percent of the total Jewish population in 1925. In eight major cities in the Ruhr, 4,434 Jews with this status accounted for 30.3 percent of all Jews that year (Table 13.17), and in five cities in Düsseldorf District outside the Ruhr, 16.04 percent—1,726 individuals—of the Jewish population in 1925 did not hold German citizenship. In three major cities south of Cologne or northwest of the Ruhr in Westphalia, in contrast, only 289 Jews (8.36 percent of the Jewish population) were not citizens in 1925. Outside the major cities in the Rhineland and Westphalia provinces, there were 3,048 foreign Jews equaling 8.31 percent of the total Jewish population of 36,697 in 1925.

The Saar District's Jewish population grew later and less rapidly than did that of the Ruhr. After World War I, this district was placed under French administration and its population was not calculated in either the 1925 or 1933 German census. In contrast, the parts of Trier District that were not administered by France showed virtually no change in Jewish population[3].

The two northern Westphalian districts of Münster and Minden and the three southern Rhineland districts of Aachen, Trier, and Koblenz had several similar characteristics. This was especially the case when the sections of the districts that were in the Ruhr and Saar basins are filtered out.[4] All had a larger percentage of Jews in rural areas and a much smaller percentage of foreign Jews

---

3 Silbergleit, *Die Bevölkerungs- und Berufsverhältnisse*, 19*, shows a population of 3377 for the 1910 Jewish population of the area in RB Trier that remained in Germany after the war. This left 3472 in the part that became the Saar territory under Franch control. In 1925, there were 3023 Jews in the part that remained in Germany. The entire RB Trier had an increase of only 76 Jews between 1900 and 1910.
4 A small section of Münster District, for instance, was in the industrial Ruhr.

Table 13.16. Jewish Population in Arnsberg District outside Ruhr

Area	1880		1925		Change 1880–1925
Cities					
Iserlohn	266	1.4%	211	0.7%	
Lüdenscheid	59	0.5	114	0.4	
Siegen	111	0.7	130	0.4	
Total	436	1.0	455	0.5	+4.4%
Rural areas					
Brilon	735	2.0	431	0.9	
Lippstadt	721	1.9	329	0.6	
Wittgenstein	380	1.9	250	0.9	
High density	1836	1.9	1010	0.8	−44.9
Soest	577	1.1	326	0.5	
Iserlohn	392	0.9	204	0.3	
Arnsberg	386	1.0	231	0.3	
Meschede	226	0.6	161	0.4	
Medium density	1581	0.9	922	0.3	−41.7
Altena	206	0.4	155	0.2	
Siegen	95	0.2	97	0.1	
Olpe	86	0.3	71	0.1	
Low density	387	0.3	323	0.1	−16.5
Total	4240		2710		

Sources: Based on Bosse, *Die Verbreitung der Juden*, 63–65; Silbergleit, *Die Bevölkerungs- und Berufsverhältnisse*, 31*–32*.

Table 13.17. Foreign Jews in Western Germany (in Order of Percent Foreign in 1925, by Province)

City	1910			1925			1900–1925		1933
	Jewish population	Foreign Jews	Percent of Jews without German citizenship	Jewish population	Foreign Jews	Percent of Jews without German citizenship	Percent change in Jewish population	Foreign and foreign-born Jews	Percent zugewanderte
Westphalian cities									
*Dortmund	2,676	391	14.6	3,820	1,200	31.4	+98.6	1,489	36.2
*Hagen							+22.6	178	35.0
*Bochum	992	81	8.2	1,122	268	23.9	+11.2	289	27.0
*Gelsenkirchen	1,251	229	18.3	1,441	326	22.6	+77.7	612	37.9
Münster				580	23	4.0	+15.5	53	9.5
Bielefeld				865			+9.1	66	8.3
Total cities	4,919	701	14.3	6,963	1,817	26.1		2,687	
Other Westphalia	16,117	973	6.0	14,632	1,622	11.1		1,274	
Westphalia	21,036	1674	8.0	21,595	3,439	15.9	+4.6	3,961	
Rheinprovinz cities									
*Hamborn	345	59	17.1	818	476	58.2	+565.0		
Remscheid							+68.4	127	46.5
*Duisburg	1,554	309	19.9	2,080	807	38.8	+164.6	1,184	46.2

*Essen	2,773	445	16.1	4,209	1,173	27.9	+132.9	1,615	35.8
Cologne	12,156	1672	13.8	16,093	3,908	24.3	+65.2	4,664	31.5
Düsseldorf	3,985	569	14.3	5,130	1,054	20.6	+140.7	1,371	27.1
*Oberhausen				513	98	19.1	+69.9	130	24.8
Barmen	643	69	10.7	721	120	16.6	+21.8		
Elberfeld	1,919	289	15.1	2,335	387	16.6	+40.3		
Wuppertal								531	21.5
Solingen							-30.2	42	19.4
*Mülheim/Ruhr		54		626	86	13.7	-2.6	86	16.6
Bonn				1,167	127	10.9	+33.1		
Aachen	1,565	131	8.4	1,420	139	9.8	-10.1	176	13.1
M-Gladbach				951	85	8.9	+28.3	114	12.6
Saarbrücken	1,081	146	13.5						
Krefeld	1,815	97	3.8	1,626	80	4.9	-9.1	112	7.6
Total	27,836	3353	12.0	36,158	8,274	22.9		10,152	
Other Rheinland	29,451	1490	5.1	22,065	1,426	6.5		1,136	
Rheinland	57,287	4843	8.5	58,223	9,700	16.7	+10.5	11,288	21.5

* City in the Ruhr basin.

Sources: *Vierteljahrshefte zur Statistik des Deutschen Reichs—Ergänzungsheft zu 1916 4 (1918): Die Deutschen im Ausland und die Ausländer im Deutschen Reiche*, 86; Silbergleit, *Die Bevölkerungs- und Berufsverhältnisse*, 31*–33*, 58*–61*, 67, 346; 1933 census, 5/15, 16; Schmelz, Territorial Printout.

than did the rest of western Germany. The southern Rhineland in particular had had relatively high Jewish density before 1880. After that year, all these areas lost much of their Jewish populations, although some sections nevertheless retained a rather large number of small-town Jews well into the twentieth century.

In the southern Rhineland, the steepest declines occurred in areas that had originally had the densest Jewish populations. Except in the vicinity of Koblenz and the areas to the south and east of that city, this decline was particularly evident the Mosel valley. In Aachen District, the declines were greater in the northern half than in the southern half (Tables 13.18–13.22).

The general population underwent grew vigorously in Western Germany in the nineteenth and early twentieth century, especially in the industrial Ruhr District. There were many large cities in a small area but no single dominant metropolis in the Ruhr. Over time, an increasing proportion of both the general and Jewish populations of western Germany moved from the more rural areas in the northwest and southeast towards the industrial sections of the region—the vicinity of Cologne, the Ruhr basin, the wider industrialized region of RBs Düsseldorf and Arnsberg, and the Saar. The main difference between the Jews and the general population was the much larger proportion of the former that was attracted to the city and district of Cologne. Both Jews and non-Jews migrated in large numbers to the Düsseldorf-Arnsberg area, but the scale of migration was somewhat larger among Gentiles than among Jews. The percentage of Jews in the other less industrialized sections of Rhineland and Westphalia dropped sharply. The absolute number of Jews in these less industrialized districts declined after 1880 while that of the rest of the population grew sharply (Table 13.23).

Table 13.18. Changes in Jewish Population of Münster District, 1880–1925

Jewish Presence	1880		1890		1900		1910		1925		Change 1880–1925
Jews in entire district	3466	0.7%	3593	0.7%	3743	0.5%	4040	0.4%	4315	0.3%	+24.5
Jews in Ruhr area*	207	0.3							1141		+451.2
Rest of district	3259	0.8							2817	0.4	-13.6

* Including Recklinghausen County and city in 1880.

Including cities of Bottrop, Buer, Gladbeck, Osterfeld and Recklinghausen, and Recklinghausen County in 1925.

Ruhr Cities	1880		1925	
Bottrop			207	0.3%
Buer			171	0.2
Gladbeck			264	0.4
Osterfeld (Oberhausen)			48	0.2
Recklinghausen	72	1.0%	451	0.5
Recklinghausen County	135	0.2	357	0.2
Total	207		1141	

	1880		1925		Change
Non-Ruhr					
Cities (non-Ruhr)					
Bocholt	152	1.8%	250	0.8%	+64.5%
Münster	491	1.2	580	0.6	+18.1
Total	643		830		+29.1
Counties (non-Ruhr)					
Steinfurt	503	1.0	413	0.4	-17.9
Ahaus	329	0.9	300	0.5	-8.8
Borken	310	0.9	265	0.5	-14.5
Coesfeld	344	0.8	242	0.4	-29.7
Beckum	331	0.8	313	0.4	-5.4
Lüdinghausen	266	0.7	166	0.2	-37.6
Tecklenburg	239	0.5	136	0.2	-43.1
Warendorf	132	0.5	84	0.2	-36.4
Münster	162	0.4	68	0.1	-58.0
Total	2616		1987		-25.0
Percent cities					30.7

Sources: Bosse, *Die Verbreitung der Juden*, 60–61; Silbergleit, *Die Bevölkerungs- und Berufsverhältnisse*, 19*, 31*.

Table 13.19. Changes in Jewish Population of Minden District, 1880–1933

Population	1880		1890		1900		1910		1925		1933		Change 1880–1925
District population	5849	1.2%	5402	1.0%	5095	0.8%	4609	0.6%	3890	0.5%	3441	0.4%	-33.5%

City or County	1880		1900		1910		1925		Change 1880–1925
Cities									
Bielefeld	653	2.1%			865			1.0%	+32.5%
Herford	226	1.7			228			0.6	+0.9
Total	879	2.0			1093			0.9	+24.4
Counties (minus city population)									
Warburg	925	3.0			382			1.1	-58.7
Höxter	1163	2.3			623			1.0	-46.4
Büren	598	1.7			247			0.6	-58.7
Paderborn	466	1.1			362			0.5	-22.3
Wiedenbrück	379	0.9			260			0.4	-31.4
Minden	621	0.8			455			0.4	-26.7
Halle	177	0.6			81			0.3	-54.2
Lübbecke	287	0.6			141			0.3	-50.9
Herford	281	0.5			198			0.2	-29.5
Bielefeld (*Land*)	73	0.2			48			0.1	-34.5
Total	4970				2979				-43.7
Percent cities	15.02%				28.1				

Sources: Bosse, *Die Verbreitung der Juden*, 62–63; Silbergleit, *Die Bevölkerungs- und Berufsverhältnisse*, 19*, 31*; Schmelz, Territorial Printout.

Table 13.20.

A) Changes in Jewish Population of Aachen District, 1880–1933

Populaiton	1880		1890		1900		1910		1910 postwar boundaries		1925		1933		Change 1880–1925
District population	4235	0.8%	4387	0.8%	4325	0.7%	4211	0.6%	4188	0.7%	3671	0.5%	3482	0.5%	-13.3%

City or County	1880		1925		Change
Cities					
Aachen	1091	1.3%	1420	0.9%	+30.2%
Counties					
North					
Jülich	635	1.5	328	0.7	-48.4
Geilenkirchen	281	1.1	175	0.5	-37.7
Heinsberg	224	0.6	109	0.2	-51.3
Erkelenz	191	0.5	104	0.2	-45.6
Total	1331		716		-46.2
South					
Düren	876	1.2	771	0.7	-12.0
Schleiden	327	0.7	284	0.6	-13.1
Aachen	583	0.6	475	0.3	-18.5
Malmedy	15	0.1	in Belgium		
Eupen	10	0.04	in Belgium		
Monschau	2	0.01%	5	0.3	+150
Total	1813		1530		-15.6
Percent cities	25.8		38.7		

Sources: Bosse, *Die Verbreitung der Juden*, 42–43; Silbergleit, *Die Bevölkerungs- und Berufsverhältnisse*, 19*, 33*; Schmelz, Territorial Printout.

B) Changes in Jewish Population of Trier District, 1880–1933

Population	1871	1880	1890	1900	1910	1925	1933	Percent change 1871–1910
Total Jewish population	5985	6566	6562	6773	6849			
Saar Region								
General population	241200				572112			+137.2
Jewish population	2600	2700			3472			+33.5
Percent Jewish	1.1				0.6[1]			
Outside Saar region								
General population	350362				437022			+24.7
Jewish population	3385	3862			3377	3023	2743	-0.2
Percent Jewish	1.0				0.8			

Sources: Bosse, Die Verbreitung der Juden, 41–42; Silbergleit, Die Bevölkerungs- und Berufsverhältnisse, 19*; Schmelz, Territorial Printout.

1 Jewish distribution in Saar District, 1910 (based on Handbuch [Berlin, 1913]).

City or County	1880	Percent Jewish	1925	Percent Jewish	Percent change, 1880–1925
City					
Trier	627	2.6	802	1.4	+27.9
Counties					
Daun	30	0.1	75	0.2	+150
Prüm	18	0.1	31	0.1	+72.2
Bitburg	147	0.3	221	0.5	+50.3
Wittlich	503	1.3	370	0.8	-26.4
Bernkastel	883	2.0	481	1.0	-45.5
Trier (*Land*)	1089	1.4	625	0.6	-42.6
Saarburg	346	1.1	285	0.8	-17.6
Merzig	336	0.9	[8	0.03]	rest in Saarland
Saarlouis	931	1.4			in Saarland
Saarbrücken	428	0.4			in Saarland
Ottweiler	758	1.2			in Saarland
St. Wendel	470	1.0	[125	0.4]	rest in Saarland

Source: Bosse, *Die Verbreitung der Juden*, 41–42; Silbergleit, *Die Bevölkerungs- und Berufsverhältnisse*, 33*.

Table 13.21. Changes in Jewish Population of Koblenz District, 1880–1933 (absolute numbers followed by percent Jewish)

Population	1880		1890		1900		1910		1910, changed borders		1925		1933		Change 1880–1925
District population	9312	1.5%	9091	1.4%	8539	1.3%	7910	1.0%	7287	1.1%	6171	0.9%	5406	0.7%	-33.7%

City or County	1880		1900		1925		Change 1880–1925
Cities							
Koblenz	558			1.7%	709	1.2%	+27.1%
Counties							
Kreuznach	1781			2.7	1270	1.5	-28.7
Meisenheim	342			2.5	131	1.0	-61.7
Neuwied	1325			1.8	870	0.9	-34.4
Wetzlar	875			1.8	503	0.7	-42.5
Mayen	1048			1.8	751	0.9	-28.3
Koblenz (*Land*)	824			1.7	585	0.9	-29.0
Simmern	547			1.5	429	1.2	-21.6
Kochem	500			1.3	295	0.7	-41.0
Ahrweiler	437			1.2	382	0.8	-12.6
St. Goar	450			1.1	310	0.7	-31.1
Zell	309			1.0	174	0.5	-43.7
Altenkirchen	305			0.5	260	0.3	-14.8
Adenau	11			0.1	5	0.02	-54.6
Percent cities	5.99				11.34		

Sources: Bosse, *Die Verbreitung der Juden*, 36–37; Silbergleit, *Die Bevölkerungs- und Berufsverhältnisse*, 19, 32*; Schmelz, Territorial Printout.

Table 13.22. Differences within Koblenz and Trier Districts, 1880–1925

County	1880		1925		Change 1880–1925
Counties directly on Mosel River					
Bernkastel	883	2.0	481	1.0	-45.5
Kochem	500	1.3	295	0.7	-41.0
Zell	309	1.0	174	0.5	-43.7
Trier (*Land*)	1089	1.4	625	0.6	-42.6
Trier (*Stadt*)	627	2.6	802	1.4	+27.9
Total	3408	1.6	2377	0.8	-31.4
Koblenz	558	1.7	709	1.2	+27.1
Koblenz (*Land*)	824	1.7	585	0.9	-29.0
Total	1382	1.7	1294	1.0	-6.4
North and west of Mosel River					
High density					
Mayen	1048	1.8	751	0.9	-28.3
Ahrweiler	437	1.2	382	0.8	-12.6
Wittlich	503	1.3	370	0.8	-26.4
Subotal	1988	1.5	1503	0.9	-24.4
Low density					
Daun	30	0.1	75	0.2	+150

Prüm	18	0.1	31	0.1	+72.2
Bitburg	147	0.3	221	0.5	+50.3
Adenau	11	0.1	5	0.2	-54.6
Subtotal	206	0.2	332	0.2	+61.2
Total	2194	0.8	1835	0.6	-16.4
South and east of Mosel River (excluding Saarland)					
Saarburg	346	1.1	285	0.8	-17.6
Kreuznach	1781	2.7	1270	1.5	-28.7
Meisenheim	342	2.5	131	1.0	-61.7
Simmern	547	1.5	429	1.2	-21.6
St. Goar	450	1.1	310	0.7	-31.1
Total	3466		2425		-30.0
East of the Rhine					
Neuwied	1325	1.8	870	0.9	-34.3
Wetzlar	875	1.8	503	0.7	-42.5
Altenkirchen	305	0.5	260	0.3	-14.8
Total	2505		1633		-34.8

Sources: Bosse, *Die Verbreitung der Juden*, 36–37, 41–42; Silbergleit, *Die Bevölkerungs- und Berufsverhältnisse*, 32*–33*.

Table 13.23. Overall Changes in Rhineland and Westphalia, 1817–1925

District	1817	1880	1900	1910	1925
General population					
All Rhineland and Westphalia	2981852	6117442	8947575	11246136	12068197
RB Cologne	338416	702934	827074	1249540	1434827
RB Düsseldorf (and Cleve)	596633	1591369	2599806	3433735	3866119
RB Arnsberg	380182	1068141	1851319	2214964	2721367
All other districts	1666621	2848508	3669376	3715805	4045884
Jewish population					
All Rhineland and Westphalia	28564	62504	72891	78323	79818
RB Cologne	3349	10370	14950	17041	20361
RB Düsseldorf (and Cleve)	5023	13211	17664	21276	24494
RB Arnsberg	3489	9495	11802	12387	13390
All other districts	16703	29428	28475	27619	21573
(Ruhr in strict sense)		8263			21093
(Other Düsseldorf-Arnsberg)		14443			16791

Percent of total western Germany					
General population					
RB Cologne	11.4	10.0	9.2	11.8	11.9
RB Düsseldorf (and Cleve)	20.0	26.0	29.0	32.4	32.0
RB Arnsberg	12.8	17.5	20.7	20.9	22.6
All other districts	55.9	46.6	41.0	35.0	33.5
Jewish population					
RB Cologne	11.7	16.6	20.5	21.8	25.5
RB Düsseldorf (and Cleve)	17.6	21.1	24.2	27.2	30.7
RB Arnsberg	12.2	15.2	16.2	15.8	16.8
All other districts	58.9	47.1	39.1	35.3	27.0
Percent of population Jewish					
All Rhineland and Westphalia	1.0	1.0	0.8	0.7	0.7
RB Cologne	1.0	1.7	1.8	1.4	1.4
RB Düsseldorf (and Cleve)	0.8	0.8	0.7	0.6	0.6
RB Arnsberg	0.9	0.9	0.6	0.6	0.5
All other districts	1.0	1.0	0.8	0.7	0.5

Sources: Silbergleit, *Die Bevölkerungs- und Berufsverhältnisse*, 11*, 19*, 27*, 31*–33*; Bosse, *Die Verbreitung der Juden*, 36–43, 60–65; *Statistik des Deutschen Reichs* 150 (1903): 185; 240 (1915): 210; Schmelz, Territorial Printout.

14

Southern Germany

Geographic Distribution of Jews in the Early Nineteenth Century

After 1867, the southern regions of Germany were comprised of the Grand Duchy of Hesse(-Darmstadt), the Grand Duchy of Baden, the kingdoms of Württemberg and Bavaria, and the Prussian provinces of Hesse-Nassau and Hohenzollern. These areas were the classic centers of rural Jewry in Germany. With the exception of the extreme southern and eastern part of the region (which had been Bavarian before 1800), most of this area had substantial Jewish populations that were often scattered in relatively small rural communities. Jewish density, but not the average size of Jewish communities, tended to be highest in the northern and western sections of southern Germany, especially in the areas along the Middle Rhine and both north and south of its chief tributary, the Main River.

The territories with the densest Jewish populations in the late eighteenth century were often in tiny noble enclaves (*Ritterschaften*) or in either the bishoprics or archbishoprics of Mainz, Würzburg, and Bamberg. The Kingdom of Bavaria and the Grand Duchy (later Kingdom) of Württemberg were just beginning to admit small numbers of Jews at this time. When the kingdoms expanded north into the Franconian territories, they acquired dense Jewish populations.

In the early nineteenth century, the territories in southern Germany exhibited one of three main patterns: a dense network of small rural communities, a looser spread of larger communities, or almost no Jews at all. This last-mentioned pattern was exhibited in southernmost and easternmost Bavaria. In the southern half of Baden and Württemberg, in Bavarian Swabia, and in Prussian Hohenzollern, there were mainly widely scattered large communities. Jewish communities were numerous, relatively small, and close to each other in most areas north and south of the Main River, west of Bamberg in a wide band up to 100 kilometers north and south of the river, as well as in the Hessian areas. Jewish population was sparser in the westernmost parts of Hesse than it was further east, especially in the Duchy of Nassau.

In the newly expanded Kingdom of Bavaria, a rather sharp border separated the Jewish-populated areas from the rest. There were large Jewish populations throughout the northwestern district of Lower Franconia, parts of Middle Franconia that were west of Nuremberg and north of Pappenheim, the sections of Upper Franconia west of Bayreuth, and the Swabian areas north of Memmingen. Southeast of this line, there were only a few isolated Jewish communities. In 1818, there were 489 non-Christians in Upper Bavaria, almost all of whom were Jews, only five in Lower Bavaria, and 991 in the Upper Palatinate (Oberpfalz). By 1840, the Jewish population of Upper Bavaria had grown to 1,528, with all but ninety-seven living in Munich.[1] Of the 1,062 Jews in the Upper Palatinate in 1840, 122 lived in the city of Regensburg and almost all the others dwelled in three counties—Neumarkt, Neustadt an der Waldnaab, and Sulzbach—that were not Bavarian territory in the eighteenth century. Of the 6,568 Jews in Upper Franconia, all but thirteen lived either in Bamberg or Bayreuth or in fourteen of thirty-one counties (*Landgerichte*) and two of five manor districts (*Herrschaftsgerichte*), most of which were in the western half of the district. In Middle Franconia, Jews lived in three of the eight cities and twenty-six of the thirty-six counties and manor districts. There were hardly any Jews in the extreme south and east of Middle Franconia. In Swabia, the vast majority of Jews lived in just eleven of the forty-five counties and manor districts, all of which were in the northwestern part of the district. In Lower Franconia, in contrast, only seven cities, counties, and manor districts had fewer than fifty Jews. Jewish density increased in Bavaria as one moved north and west.[2]

---

1 And almost all of the ninety-seven lived in counties immediately bordering the city of Munich.
2 *Beiträge zur Statistik des Königreichs Bayern. I Bevölkerung aus amtlichen Quellen*, ed. F. V. W. von Herrmann (Munich, 1850).

West of Bavaria in Württemberg, there were widely scattered but large Jewish communities in the southern area and numerous small communities in the northern fringe bordering Baden and Bavaria while the central area had almost no Jews. In 1821, the Jagstkreis in the northeast had a Jewish density of 1.14 percent and accommodated 42 percent of Jews in the kingdom. Each of the other three districts had a Jewish density of under 0.50 percent. These proportions remained the same twenty years later in 1841. Of eighty-one towns that had Jewish populations in 1821, forty were in the Jagstkreis and only six were in the Donaukreis. Communities in the south were much larger on average than those in the north (Table 14.1). In 1858, 1,468 of the 1,742 Jews in the Schwarzwaldkreis lived in the county of Horb, where they were 6.60 percent of the population. This county, which was previously divided among various rulers—including the Habsburgs—was just across the northern border of the Hohenzollern principalities that Prussia had annexed in 1849. In the northern half of Hohenzollern District, there was a substantial Jewish population in the towns of Hechingen, Haigerloch, and Dettensee. In 1852, Hohenzollern District had a Jewish population of 1,052 (1.60 percent of the total), which declined steadily thereafter.[3]

Like the Jewish population of Württemberg, Jewish settlement in the Grand Duchy of Baden exhibited a sharp north–south differentiation. Overall Jewish density increased as one moved north and was much higher in the northernmost quarter of the country (Unterrheinkreis) than in the other sections. The southern communities, although more scattered, were often much larger than those in the north. In the southernmost area along Lake Constance (Seekreis) in 1845, all but twenty-three Jews lived in four large communities in the county of Radolfzell. The largest of these communities was Gailingen, which had 596 Jewish inhabitants in 1825, comprising nearly half of the local population. In Baden's southwestern district (Oberrrheinkreis), all but nineteen of the 4,007 Jews lived in six of the eighteen counties. In 1835, the largest community in this area (Breisach) had 572 Jews while the next-largest (Schmieheim) had 325 in 1825. In contrast, every county in the northernmost section of Baden had Jewish inhabitants and only four of twenty-two counties had fewer than 100. Only three village communities in the Unterrrheinkreis had 200 or more Jewish inhabitants.[4]

---

3 Considering that the two largest Jewish communities in Hohenzollern had 809 and 332 members respectively in 1843 and 1844, the Jewish population of Hohenzollern must have been even larger in the 1840s.

4 They were Hoffenheim, Merchingen, and Neidenstein. *Pinkas ha-Kehillot, Germania, Württemberg-Hohenzollern-Baden*, 305, 409, 416.

Table 14.1. Number and Size of Jewish Communities in Various Parts of Württemberg, 1821

North	Neckarkreis	Jagstkreis
Number of Jews	2023	3761
Number of communities	25	40
Average community size	80.9	94.0
South	Schwarzwaldkreis	Donaukreis
Number of Jews	1466	1643
Number of communities	10	6
Average community size	146.6	273.9

Source: "Vergleichende Uebersicht der Bevölkerung Württembergs."

The various Hessian states had patterns similar to those of the northern parts of Bavaria, Baden, and Württemberg, with many small village communities and high overall Jewish density. While few of the large cities in the other three southern states had large Jewish communities, there were important Jewish populations in almost all of Hesse's main cities. All major sections of the Hessian area had substantial Jewish densities, but these were greater both in Frankfurt and farther south than in the northernmost areas. In 1828, only two of eighteen counties in the Grand Duchy of Hesse(-Darmstadt) had Jewish populations smaller than two percent of the total. The northeastern Upper Hesse county of Lauterbach had a very scanty Jewish presence (Table 14.2). In Kurhessen to the north and east of Frankfurt, Jewish density was highest first in the southernmost and then in the northernmost province. The enclaves of Schmalkalden (in Thuringia to the east) and Rinteln (in Hanover to the north) had much lower Jewish densities than the rest of Kurhessen. The east-central province of Fulda had both the highest and the lowest Jewish densities by county (Table 14.3). In the Duchy of Nassau to the northwest of Frankfurt, Jewish density varied considerably from county to county and was lowest in the northern parts of the Westerwald bordering on the Rhineland and Westphalia (Table 14.4).

After 1815, Bavaria ruled the Rhine Palatinate, a territory that was west of the Rhine and south of Rhenish Hesse and the Prussian Rhineland, and far to the west of the rest of the Bavarian Kingdom. The demographic patterns in this territory, which, like many others elsewhere in the region, was formerly divided into many small independent states, resembled those of Hesse in numerous ways. The overall Jewish density was high, reaching 2.70 percent in 1840.

TABLE 14.2. Jewish Population of Grand Duchy of Hesse by County, 1828 (from densest to least dense)

County	Number of Jews	Percent of population Jewish	Hessian province
Offenbach	1688	4.8	Starkenberg
Worms	1901	4.3	Rhenish Hesse
Bingen	1047	4.1	Rhenish Hesse
Mainz	2113	4.1	Rhenish Hesse
Gross-Gerau	968	3.8	Starkenberg
Alzey	1255	3.7	Rhenish Hesse
Friedberg	1780	3.5	Upper Hesse
Oppenheim	1323	3.5	Rhenish Hesse
Dieburg	1420	3.1	Starkenberg
Büdingen	1176	3.1	Upper Hesse
Darmstadt	1234	2.9	Starkenberg
Giessen	1476	2.8	Upper Hesse
Schotten	728	2.5	Upper Hesse
Alsfeld	899	2.3	Upper Hesse
Bensheim	831	2.3	Starkenberg
Erbach	881	2.3	Starkenberg
Heppenheim	480	1.5	Starkenberg
Lauterbach	36	0.1	Upper Hesse

Source: Schmelz, Hessen, 346–34.

TABLE 14.3. Jewish Population of Kurhessen by Province and County

By province (from densest to least dense), 1861

Province	Number of Jews	Percent of population Jewish
Hanau	4230	3.4
Lower Hesse	8531	2.7
Upper Hesse	2696	2.3
Fulda	2003	1.8
Schmalkalden	335	1.2
Rinteln	391	1.1

By county (from densest to least dense), 1861

County	Number of Jews	Percent of population Jewish	Hessian province
Hünfeld	1322	5.0	Fulda
Eschwege	1662	4.0	Lower Hesse
Schlüchtern	1208	4.0	Hanau
Fritzlar	1064	3.9	Lower Hesse
Gelnhausen	1108	3.5	Hanau
Rotenburg	1100	3.4	Lower Hesse
Kirchhain	873	3.3	Upper Hesse
Melsungen	963	3.3	Lower Hesse
Wolfhagen	791	3.1	Lower Hesse
Hanau	1914	3.1	Hanau
Ziegenhain	1017	3.0	Upper Hesse
Hofgeismar	829	2.2	Lower Hesse
Homberg	478	2.1	Lower Hesse
Kassel	1217	1.6	Lower Hesse
Frankenberg	304	1.5	Upper Hesse
Witzenhausen	427	1.3	Lower Hesse
Marburg	502	1.3	Upper Hesse
Schmalkalden	335	1.2	Schmalkalden
Rinteln	391	1.1	Rinteln
Hersfeld	311	0.9	Fulda
Fulda	370	0.8	Fulda

Source: Schmelz, Hessen, 352–353.

Table 14.4. Jewish Populations of Counties of Nassau, 1842 (from densest to sparsest)

County	Number of Jews	General population	Percent of population Jewish
Höchst	666	17,081	3.9
Runkel	519	13,795	3.8
Wiesbaden (*Land*)	372	11,672	3.2
Langenschwalbach	348	11,417	3.1
Hochheim	403	13,324	3.0

County	Number of Jews	General population	Percent of population Jewish
Selters	469	16,198	2.9
Nassau	301	12,760	2.4
Braubach	244	11,157	2.2
Diez	336	15,619	2.2
Wiesbaden (*Stadt*)	247	12,269	2.0
Nastätten	226	11,963	1.9
Königstein	283	15,800	1.8
Hachenburg	202	11,754	1.7
Wehen	160	10,223	1.6
Limburg	235	15,494	1.5
Hadamar	257	18,127	1.4
Rennerod	198	14,436	1.4
Idstein	235	17,541	1.3
Usingen	242	21,287	1.1
Weilburg	201	18,433	1.1
St. Goarshausen	98	11,290	0.9
Rüdesheim	95	12,611	0.8
Eltville	82	12,167	0.7
Wallmerod	61	14,488	0.4
Montabaur	71	17,566	0.4
Herborn	41	15,691	0.3
Dillenburg	1	16,900	0.005
Marienburg	0	9,092	0
Reichelheim	0	1,468	0

Source: C. D. Vogel, *Beschreibung des Herzogthums Nassau* (1843, reprint: Niederwalluf bei Wiesbaden, 1971), 428–429.

Only three of twelve counties (*Land Commisariate*), all of which were in the westernmost part of the province bordering the Prussian Rhine province, had Jewish populations that fell short of two percent of the total (Table 14.5).

Throughout southern Germany, most Jews lived in villages of 2,000 or fewer inhabitants. Except in the Hessian regions, Jews had been excluded by law from most major South German cities until the nineteenth century. In the early nineteenth century, there were Jewish communities in all twelve cities

Table 14.5. Population of Various Counties in Rhine Palatinate, 1840

County	Jewish population	General population	Percent Jewish
Frankenthal	2302	41367	5.6
Landau	2109	64683	3.3
Kirchheimbolanden	1678	51837	3.2
Bergzabern	1386	42966	3.2
Kaiserslautern	1458	47674	3.1
Neustadt/Hardt	1597	61624	2.6
Pirmasens	1017	41002	2.5
Speyer	1036	42946	2.4
Germersheim	1087	50780	2.1
Cusel	606	38498	1.5
Homburg	625	45168	1.4
Zweibrücken	495	50575	1.0

Source: von Hermann, *Beiträge zur Statistik des Königreichs Bayern*, vol. 1, 42–43.

in what later became Hesse-Darmstadt and Hesse-Nassau and that had at least 10,000 inhabitants by 1880. Only one of these communities (Marburg) numbered fewer than 100; one other (Giessen) had fewer than 200. Elsewhere in southern Germany, the admission of Jews to cities that had once excluded them generally came in two waves. Some cities began to admit Jews between 1750 and 1815 while others did not do so until the 1860s. Outside Hesse, the only major urban Jewish communities in southern Germany before 1800 were those in Mannheim, Karlsruhe, Fürth, Bayreuth, Bamberg, Landau, Heidelberg, Speyer, and Ansbach. In Hesse, Frankfurt am Main, Mainz, Kassel, Darmstadt, Hanau, and Wiesbaden had sizable communities (Table 14.6). Major South German cities that began to admit Jews between around 1750 and 1850 were Munich, Würzburg, Regensburg, Stuttgart, Augsburg, and Ulm. Nuremberg, Freiburg, Heilbronn, and Konstanz largely did not open up to Jews until the 1860s (Table 14.7).

The largest number of communities with the smallest average size were in the areas of southern Germany nearest the Main River. South and west of these areas, there were smaller numbers of much larger communities. In 1900, there were Jews in 3,451 (4.48 percent) of the 76,959 towns and villages in Germany. The average size of these communities was 162.4 Jews. In several southern states, the average community was much smaller but there was a much higher

Table 14.6. Major Older Urban Jewish Communities in Southern Germany and Their Populations in the Early Nineteenth Century

Location	Cities over 10000	Jewish population	Date	Total population in the early nineteenth century	Percent Jewish
Outside Hesse	Fürth	2535 (1809: 2499)	1840	13989	18.1
	Mannheim	1465	1825	20306	7.1
	Karlsruhe	893	1825	22909	3.9
	Bayreuth	504	1840	16660	3.0
	Bamberg	423 (1811/12: 469) (1811: 287)	1840	20863	2.0
	Landau	379	1840	11818	3.2
	Heidelberg	349	1825	17458	2.0
	Speyer	301	1840	11147	2.7
	Ansbach	250	1840	11939	2.1
Hessian area	Frankfurt am Main	4530 (1809/10: 385)	1823	43918	10.3
	Mainz	1620	1828	30566	5.3
	Kassel	946	1861	38930	2.4
	Darmstadt	556	1828	23240	2.4
	Hanau	379	1861	16582	2.3
	Wiesbaden	247	1842		

Location	Cities 5000–9999	Jewish population	Date	Total population in the early nineteenth century	Percent Jewish
Outside Hesse	Dürkheim	277	1840	5050	5.5
	Schwabach	211	1840	6981	3.0
	Aschaffenburg	207	1840	9273	2.2
	Kaiserslautern	197	1840	8250	2.4
	Bruchsal	178	1825	6853	2.6
	Pirmasens	174	1840	6410	2.7
	Edenkoben	161	1840	5064	3.2
Hessian area	Offenbach	848	1828	7466	11.3
	Worms	773	1828	9568	8.1
	Eschwege	470	1861	6969	6.7
	Alzey	351	1861	5245	6.7
	Fulda	284	1861	9339	3.0
	Giessen	197	1828	7251	2.7

v: Schmelz, Hessen, 50–51, 343; Pinkas ha-Kehillot, Germania, Bavaria, 205, 223, 268, 342; von Hermann, Beiträge zur Statistik des Königreichs Bayern, vol. 1, 54–55, 60–61, 66–67, 90–91; Pinkas ha-Kehillot, Germania, Württemberg-Hohenzollern-Baden, 175, 209, 373, 444.

Table 14.7. Growth of Jewish Communities in Cities Opening up to Jewish Settlement after c. 1750

Cities opening up to Jewish settlement between 1750 and 1850

Size	City	Approximate earliest date of settlement	Jewish population in:				
			1815	1840	1867	1871	
Cities over 10,000	Munich	c. 1750	20 (1750)	451 (1814)	1423	2097	2884
	Würzburg	1805		138 (1816)	425	1099	1518
	Regensburg	1694	70 (1694)	121 (1809/10)	122	359	430
	Stuttgart		200 (1820)				2074
	Augsburg	1751		102 (1811/12)	97	449	660
	Ulm		13 (1823)				694 (1880)
	Cannstatt		13 (1831)				256
Cities 5,000–9999	Schwäbisch Hall				24 (1824)		137
	Marburg				40	166 (1861)	333 (1880)

Cities opening up to Jewish settlement in the 1860s

Size	City	Approximate earliest date of settlement	Jewish population in:			
			1855	1867	1871	Later date
Cities over 10,000	Heilbronn	1861	65		600	994 (1885)
	Schwäbisch Gmünd	1845		22	97 (1890)	271 (1875)
	Konstanz	1825	15 (1825)		164	559 (1875)
	Freiburg	1860			333 (1871)	175 (1880)
	Erlangen	c. 1852	219 (1858)	54	63	3032 (1880)
	Nuremberg		2 (1811/12)	1254	1831	60 (1880)
	Ingolstadt			21	34	
Cities 5,000–9999	Baden-Baden	1862	4	18 (1865)		73 (1880)
	Lahr	1852	1 (1852)			59 (1880)
	Offenburg	1862	37 (1863)	223		387 (1880)
	Schweinfurt		27 (1852)	200 (1867)	223	490 (1880)
	Memmingen	1862	1 (1814)	36	54	144 (1880)
	Rothenburg	1870		10		86 (1880)
	Kitzingen	1863		57	97	337 (1880)
	Nördlingen	1860		61	176	347 (1880)
	Öhringen	1864	8	57		158 (1880)

Sources: *Pinkas ha-Kehillot, Germania, Bavaria,* 8, 103, 105, 178, 184, 276, 320, 359, 474, 545, 572, 583, 620, 629; *Pinkas ha-Kehillot, Germania, Württemberg-Hohenzollern-Baden,* 34, 79, 138, 141, 163, 254, 361, 434, 463; von Herrmann, *Beiträge zur Statistik des Königreichs Bayern,* vol. 1, 30–31, 48–49; 1933 census, 5/10.

percentage of towns that had communities. Hesse-Darmstadt and Kurhessen had especially dense networks of small Jewish settlements. In 1900, there were Jews in 307 (30.9 percent) of the 994 settlements in Hesse-Darmstadt and the average community size was 78.3 individuals. Jews lived in 5.35 percent of towns in Bavaria, 4.4 percent of those in Württemberg, and 10.1 percent of those in Baden (Table 14.8).

Changes in South German Jewry in the Mid- and Late Nineteenth Century

Southern Germany was most likely the first part of the country to experience large-scale Jewish emigration. It first started in Bavaria east of the Rhine, spread to Württemberg, and finally encompassed the whole region. Urbanization was part of another significant set of changes that began later than emigration, especially as the last cities that were closed to Jews opened up after the middle of the nineteenth century. Although several large Jewish communities formed in South German cities, village and small-town communities survived longer in southern Germany than they did in the rest of the country.

Jewish emigration and migration from the region, especially to the United States, became especially noticeable after 1840. Although there is evidence that the Jewish population in parts of Bavaria emigrated in considerable numbers even before 1840, most other regions of southern Germany showed increases in population before that year. Within Bavaria, the greatest early losses were in the provinces of Swabia and Upper Franconia on the southern and eastern fringes of the area of dense Jewish settlement. In Swabia, the Jewish population declined by 7.43 percent between 1840 and 1852 and by 31.31 percent between 1852 and 1871. Comparable figures for Upper Franconia were 17.21 percent and 25.62 percent, respectively (Table 14.9). Much of the decline took place in towns with large and crowded Jewish populations (Table 14.10). Similar sharp drops in Jewish population were registered in the contiguous districts of both the Schwarzwaldkreis of Württemberg and the Prussian territory of Hohenzollern. These areas, which were relatively isolated from other areas of Jewish concentration, were characterized by large Jewish communities in small towns.[5] Two other provinces that lost an important part of their

---

5 The territory of Hohenzollern lost 327 (31.50 percent) of its 1,038 Jewish inhabitants between 1852 and 1871. Although overall figures for the territory are lacking, we have evidence that the two largest communities there, Haigerloch and Hechingen, had a combined Jewish

Table 14.8. Percent of All Communities with Jewish Inhabitants and Average Community Size in Various Parts of Southern Germany

Region	Total number of towns	Number with Jews	Percent with Jewish inhabitants	Total number of Jews	Average size of Jewish community
Baden 1825	1550	173	11.2		
Baden 1875	1555	334	21.5		
Baden 1900	1555	236	15.2		
Baden 1925	1555	242	15.6		
Württemberg 1821					
Jagstkreis	388	40	10.3	3761	94.0
Neckarkreis	395	25	6.3	2023	80.9
Schwarzwaldkreis	517	10	1.9	1466	146.6
Donaukreis	535	6	1.1	1643	273.7
Total Württemberg	1838	81	4.4	8893	109.8
Kurhessen 1861					
Lower Hesse	525	130	24.8	8531	65.6
Upper Hesse	259	67	25.9	2696	40.2
Fulda	276	27	9.8	2003	74.2
Hanau	169	67	39.7	4230	63.1
Schmalkalden	38	3	7.9	335	111.7
Rinteln	94	13	13.8	391	30.1
Total Kurhessen	1361	307	22.6	18186	59.2
Hesse-Darmstadt 1861					
Starkenburg	382	136	35.6	10021	73.7
Upper Hesse	529	175	33.1	9232	52.8
Rhenish Hesse	185	112	60.5	9747	87.0
Total Hesse-Darmstadt	1096	427	39.0	29000	67.9

Sources: "Vergleichende Uebersicht der Bevölkerung Württembergs"; Alice Goldstein, "The Urbanization of Jews in Baden, Germany 1825–1925," *Papers in Jewish Demography* (1981): 74, Table 1; Schmelz, *Hessen*, 348–349, 352–353.

Table 14.9. Jewish Population of South German Regions, 1818–1925

Region	1818	1840	1852	1871	1880	1890	1900	1910	1925
Upper Bavaria	489	1528	1252	3033	4343	6291	9076	11652	10790
Lower Bavaria	5	15	15	111	134	182	294	468	348
Upper Palatinate	991	1062	916	1221	1522	1487	1472	1395	1181
Swabia	6514	6891	6379	4369	4436	4323	3904	3462	2834
Middle Franconia	11816	11377	10674	10830	11689	12294	13111	14219	13719
Upper Franconia	6286	6568	5438	4045	4148	3664	3322	2946	2544
Lower Franconia	16637	16451	15848	14573	15256	14646	13641	11925	9879
Palatinate	10470	15396	15636	12466	11998	10998	10108	8998	7850
Total Bavaria	53208	59288	56158	50662	53526	53885	54928	55065	49145

Region	1821	1841	1858	1871	1880	1890	1900	1910	1925
Jagstkreis	3761	4827	4838	4024	3911	3494	2990	2412	1745
Neckarkreis	2023	2609	2820	4227	5288	5463	5544	6276	6378
Schwarzwaldkreis	1466	1849	1742	1328	1505	1432	1296	1359	1010
Donaukreis	1643	2299	2806	2666	2627	2250	2086	1935	1694
Total Württemberg	8893	11584	12206	12245	13331	12639	11916	11982	10827

Region	1845	1852	1858	1871	1880	1890	1900	1910	1925
Seekreis*	1483	1644		1926	2015	2025	1872	1669	1833
Oberrheinkreis*	4007	4098		6003	6385	6243	5063	4341	4835
Mittelrheinkreis*	6725	7084		5299	5948	6196	6858	6904	4763
Unterrheinkreis*	1043	10873		12475	12930	12271	12306	11538	11986
Total Baden	**23258**	**23699**		**25703**	**27278**	**26735**	**26132**	**25896**	**25896**

Region	1828	1843	1861	1871	1880	1890	1900	1910	1925
Rhenish Hesse	7639		9747	9138	9452	8963	8601	7769	6675
Starkenburg	7502		10021	9207	9700	9166	9070	9740	7994
Upper Hesse	6095		9232	7028	7594	7402	6815	6554	5732
Hesse-(Darmstadt) (old)	**22306**	**28325**	**29000***	**25373**	**26746**	**25531**	**24486**	**24063**	**20401**
Hesse-(Darmstadt) (new)	21236	27255	27930						
RB Kassel (Kurhessen)	13100 (1817)	18623 (1852)	18186 (1861)	18030	19142	18468	17483	17072	15021
RB Wiesbaden				18360	22174	26075	30622	34709	37736
Minus Frankfurt				8351	8318	8649	8648	8481	8351
Nassau		6639 (1842)	6988 (1859)						
Frankfurt am Main	4530 (1823)	4737 (1847)	5730 (1858)	10009	13856	17426	21974	26228	29385
Hesse-Homburg			1138 (1863/64)						
Hesse-Nassau				**36390**	**41316**	**44543**	**48105**	**51781**	**52757**

Region	1852	1871	1880	1890	1900	1910	1925
Hohenzollern	1038	721	771	661	532	405	335
Total southern Germany		151084	162968	163994	166100	169192	157529

* The four *Kreise* of Baden (Seekreis, Oberrheinkreis, Mittelrheinkreis and Unterrheinkreis) were replaced in 1864 by eleven districts, which are used in the 1871 and 1880 censuses. I have considered Konstanz, Villingen, and Waldshut as equivalent to Seekreis; Freiburg, Lörrach, and Offenburg as equivalent to Oberrheinkreis; Baden-Baden and Karlsruhe as equivalent to Mittelrheinkreis and Mannheim, and Heidelberg and Mosbach as equivalent to Unterrheinkreis. The statistics from 1890 once again use four districts approximately corresponding to the original ones and called Konstanz, Freiburg, Karlsruhe, and Mannheim

Sources: Schmelz, *Hessen*, 45, 46, 48–49, 346, 348–349; Silbergleit, *Die Bevölkerungs- und Berufsverhältnisse*, 18*–19*; *Vierteljahrshefte zur Statistik des Deutschen Reichs* 1 (1873): 188 b–d; (1892): III, 28–31; *Statistik des Deutschen Reichs* 67 (1883): 248–250; 150 (1903): 108*; 240 (1915): 210; Toury, *Soziale und Politische Geschichte*, 18; *Pinkas ha-Kehillot, Germania, Bavaria*, 9, 13; *Pinkas ha-Kehillot, Germania, Württemberg-Hohenzollern-Baden*, 5; *Pinkas ha-Kehillot, Germania, Hessen-Hessen-Nassau-Frankfurt* (Jerusalem: Yad Vashem, 1992), 599; *Die politischen, Kirchen- und Schulgemeinden des Grossherzogthums Baden 1845* (Karlsruhe, 1847), 94–98; *Beiträge zur Statistik der inneren Verwaltung des Grossherzogthums Baden* (Karlsruhe, 1855), 214–215; Schmelz, Territorial Printout.

Table 14.10. Declines in Large Village Communities in Upper Franconia and Swabia

Villages by Region	1837	1840	1852	1867
Upper Franconia				
Adelsdorf	265			115
Altenkunstadt	400			184
Burgkunstadt	420		479	282
Zeckendorf	166			79
Swabia				
Harburg	360 (1834)		300	171
Illereichen	403 (1834)		284	215
Öttingen	430	351	396	248
Hürben	576 (1839)			342 (1871)
Wallerstein		276	236	78

Sources: *Pinkas ha-Kehillot, Germania, Bavaria*, 197, 200, 221, 246, 595, 605, 612, 616, 637; *Beiträge zur Statistik des Königreichs Bayern* (Munich, 1850), 102–103; *Beiträge zur Statistik des Königreichs Bayern* (Munich, 1855), 126–127, 180–181, 186–187, 192–193.

Jewish population in the pre-unification decades were Upper Hesse in the Grand Duchy of Hesse and the Bavarian-ruled Rhine Palatinate. There was considerable growth in Jewish population in both of these areas in the period leading up to 1852. The vast majority of those who left the rural territories of southern Germany before 1871, and especially those who did so before 1860, emigrated abroad, particularly to the United States; relatively few migrated to cities within Germany. This pattern changed in later decades. In most of the rest of southern Germany, the Jewish population continued to grow. In some areas it did so slowly, but grew more rapidly in urbanizing areas that originally had small Jewish populations such as Upper Bavaria and the Neckarkreis of Württemberg, as well as to Frankfurt, which had long had a dense Jewish presence.

In the decade between German unification in 1871 and 1880, nearly all South German districts gained Jewish population.[6] After 1880, Jewish numbers in most

---

population of 1,131 in 1842–1843 and the remaining community, Dettensee had 173 Jews in 1830 (*Pinkas ha-Kehillot, Germania, Württemberg-Hohenzollern-Baden*, 168–171). Almost all Jews in the Schwarzwaldkreis lived in Horb County immediately bordering Hohenzollern.

6 The exceptions were the Rhine Palatinate (down 3.75 percent), the Jagstkreis of northeastern Württemberg (down 2.81 percent), the Donaukreis of southeastern Württemberg (down 1.46

rural sections of southern Germany began to decline steadily, and those in most of the more urbanized districts rose. The total Jewish population of the South German states therefore remained virtually unchanged from 1880 to 1910. Most of those who left village communities moved to cities that were mainly in southern Germany. Consequently, the share of the southern German-Jewish population that lived in Frankfurt am Main, Munich, Nuremberg, and Stuttgart increased from 14.42 percent (23,504 Jews) in 1880 to 29.21 percent (49,417) in 1910. More than half of these urban Jews lived in Frankfurt am Main.

During the *Kaiserreich* period, the South German Jewish population slowly shifted from Franconia, Palatinate, and Upper Hesse areas toward Hesse-Nassau and Frankfurt (Tables 14.11, 14.12). The steepest declines were in the Jagstkreis of Württemberg (58.3 percent between 1871 and 1925) and Hohenzollern (55.3 percent). Due to the growing community in Stuttgart, the Neckarkreis steadily gained Jewish population. The Jewish presence in Württemberg's Donaukreis and Schwarzwaldkreis lost much ground (27.3 percent and 38.6 percent, respectively, between 1871 and 1925) but not as much as did the Jagstkreis. In Bavaria, after some districts' severe declines in the 1850s and 1860s, the contraction of Jewish population in most districts slowed for a while after 1880 and then picked up speed in the rural districts of Schwaben, Upper Franconia, Lower Franconia, and the Rhenish Palatinate. In Lower Franconia, where there was small early out-migration, the Jewish population declined more than twice as fast between 1900 and 1925 than it did between 1880 and 1900. Due to growth of the urban communities in Nuremberg and Munich, the Jewish populations of Upper Bavaria and Middle Franconia rose steadily until World War I. Declines in Jewish population in Baden did not begin until 1880, and even then did not affect Karlsruhe District. They remained relatively modest except in the southern parts of Baden after 1890. In the Grand Duchy of Hesse, there were steady but fairly moderate losses of Jewish population in all three districts from 1880 to 1910, and a sharper decline after World War I. In Hesse-Nassau, the Jewish population increased due to the Frankfurt community's growth. Outside of Frankfurt, losses were minimal in Wiesbaden District and moderate in Kassel District.

There was a noticeable shift of population from rural to urban areas after 1860 within each district. Jews migrated to southern Germany cities in several waves. In 1840, eleven of the twenty-three Bavarian cities that had over 10,000 inhabitants (as enumerated in 1880) had fewer than 100 Jewish residents and nine had fewer than ten. Three of the cities that had more than 100 Jews—Munich,

---

percent), and *Regierungsbezirk* Wiesbaden outside of Frankfurt (down 0.24 percent).

Table 14.11. Percent Distribution of All South German Jews in Various Districts, 1871–1925

District	1871	1880	1890	1900	1910	1925
Upper Bavaria	2.0%	2.7	3.8	5.5	6.9	6.9
Lower Bavaria	0.1	0.1	0.1	0.2	0.3	0.2
Upper Palatinate	0.8	0.9	0.9	0.9	0.8	0.8
Swabia	2.9	2.7	2.6	2.4	2.1	1.8
Middle Franconia	7.2	7.2	7.5	7.9	8.4	8.7
Upper Franconia	2.7	2.5	2.5	2.0	1.7	1.6
Lower Franconia	9.7	9.4	9.3	8.2	7.1	6.3
Rhenish Palatinate	8.3	7.4	6.7	6.1	5.3	5.0
Bavaria	33.5	32.8	32.9	33.1	32.66	31.2
Jagstkreis	2.7	2.4	2.1	1.8	1.4	1.1
Neckarkreis	2.8	3.2	3.3	3.3	3.7	4.1
Schwarzwaldkreis	0.9	0.9	0.9	0.8	0.8	0.6
Donaukraus	1.8	1.6	1.4	1.3	1.1	1.1
Württemberg	8.1	8.2	7.7	7.2	7.1	6.9
Konstanz	1.3	1.2	1.2	1.1	1.0	0.8
Freiburg	4.0	3.9	3.8	3.3	3.0	2.8
Karlsruhe	3.5	3.7	3.8	4.0	4.0	4.4
Mannheim	8.3	7.9	7.5	7.3	7.3	7.3
Baden	17.0	16.8	16.3	15.7	15.3	15.3
Rhenish Hesse	6.1	5.8	5.5	5.2	4.6	4.2
Starkenburg	6.1	6.0	5.6	5.5	5.8	5.1
Upper Hesse	4.7	4.7	4.5	4.1	3.9	3.6
Hesse(-Darmstadt)	16.8	16.4	15.6	14.7	14.2	13.0
RB Kassel	11.9	11.8	11.3	10.7	10.1	9.5
RB Wiesbaden minus Frankfurt am Main	5.5	5.1	5.3	5.2	5.0	5.3
Frankfurt am Main	6.6	8.5	10.6	13.2	15.5	18.7
Hesse-Nassau	24.1	25.4	27.2	29.0	30.6	33.5
Hohenzollern	0.5	0.5	0.4	0.3	0.2	0.2

Table 14.12. Change in Number of Jews in Various Sections of Southern Germany, 1840–1925

Bavaria	1840–1852	1852–1871	1871–1880	1880–1890	1890–1900	1900–1910	1910–1925
Upper Bavaria	-276	+1781	+1310	+1948	+2785	+2576	-862
Percent	-18.1	+142.3	+43.2	+44.9	+44.3	+28.4	-7.4
Upper Palatinate	-146	+305	+301	-35	-15	-77	-214
Percent	-13.8	+33.3	+24.7	-2.3	-1.0	-5.2	-15.3
Swabia	-512	-2010	+67	-113	-419	-442	-628
Percent	-7.4	-31.4%	+1.5	-2.6	-9.7	-11.3	-18.2
Middle Franconia	-703	+156	+859	+605	+817	+1108	-500
Percent	-6.2	+1.5	+7.9	+5.2	+6.7	+8.5	-3.5
Upper Franconia	-1130	-1393	+103	-484	-342	-376	-402
Percent	-17.2	-25.6	+2.6	-11.7	-9.3	-11.3	-13.7
Lower Franconia	-603	-1275	+683	-610	-1005	-1716	-2046
Percent	-8.1	+4.7	-4.0	-6.9	-6.9	-12.6	-17.2
Rhenish Palatinate	+240	-3170	-468	-1000	-890	-1110	-1148
Percent	+1.6	-20.3	-3.8	-8.3	-8.1	-10.9	-12.8

Württemberg	1841–1858	1858–1871	1871–1880	1880–1890	1890–1900	1900–1910	1910–1925
Jagstkreis	+11	-814	-113	-417	-504	-578	-667
Percent	+0.2	-16.9	-2.8	-10.7	-14.4	-19.3	-27.7
Neckarkreis	+211	+1407	+1061	+175	+81	+732	+102
Percent	+8.0	+49.9	+25.1	+3.3	+1.5	+13.2	+1.6
Schwarzwaldkreis	107	-414	+177	-73	-136	+63	-349
Percent	-5.8	-23.9	+13.3	-4.9	-9.5	+4.9	-25.7
Donaukreis	+507	-140	-39	-377	-164	-151	-241
Percent	+22.1	-5.0	-1.5	-14.4	-7.3	-7.2	-12.5

Baden	1845–1852	1852–1871	1871–1880	1880–1890	1890–1900	1900–1910	1910–1925
Konstanz	+159	+93	+89	+10	-153	-203	-388
Percent	+9.5	+5.1	+4.6	+1.0	-7.6	-10.8	-23.3
Freiburg	+182	+986	+382	-142	-732	-448	-722
Percent	+3.8	+19.7	+6.4	-2.2	-11.7	-8.3	-14.3
Karlsruhe	+94	+442	+649	+248	+365	+297	+46
Percent	+2.0	+9.1	+12.3	+4.2	+5.9	4.5	+0.7
Mannheim	+6	+483	+455	-659	-83	+118	-768
Percent	+0.1	+4.0	+3.7	-5.1	-0.7	+1.0	-6.2

Hesse(-Darmstadt)	1828–1861	1861–1871	1871–1880	1880–1890	1890–1900	1900–1910	1910–1925
Rhenish Hesse	+2108	-609	+314	-489	-362	-832	-1092
Percent	+27.6	-6.2	+3.4	-5.2	-4.0	-9.7	-14.1
Starkenburg	+2519	-814	+493	-534	-96	+670	-1746
Percent	+33.6	-8.1	+5.4	-5.5	-1.1	+7.4	-17.9
Upper Hesse	+3137	-2204	+566	-192	-587	-261	-822
Percent	+51.5	-23.9	+8.1	-2.5	-7.9	-3.8	-12.5
Hesse-Nassau	1828–1861	1861–1871	1871–1880	1880–1890	1890–1900	1900–1910	1910–1925
RB Kassel	+5086	-156	+1112	-673	-985	-411	-2051
Percent	+38.8	-0.9	+6.2	-3.5	-5.3	-2.4	-11.9
RB Wiesbaden			+3814	+3901	+4547	+4087	+3027
Less Frankfurt am Main			-20	+318	-1	-167	-130
Percent			-0.2	+3.82%	-0.01	-1.9	-1.5
Frankfurt am Main	+1200	+4279	+3834	+3583	+4548	+4254	+3157
Percent	+26.5	+74.7	+38.3	+25.9	+26.1	19.4	+12.0
Hohenzollern	1828–1861	1861–1871	1871–1880	1880–1890	1890–1900	1900–1910	1910–1925
Hohenzollern		-327	+60	-110	-129	-127	-70
Percent		-31.5	+8.4	-14.3	-19.5	-23.9	-17.3

Italics = decline of over 10%, italics and bold = decline of over 20%.
Sources: same as Table 14.9.

Würzburg, and Regensburg—recently began admitting Jews and four others were in the Rhine Palatinate, where Jewish settlement history was different than in the rest of Bavaria. In eighteenth-century Munich, only a few court Jews and bankers were permitted to settle in the city, and Jews without residence permits were periodically expelled. In 1781, fifty-three Jews were counted in the city; their numbers increased to 263 in 1801 and 451 in 1814. Thereafter, the Jewish population grew at a rate slightly higher than that of the city as a whole, reaching 2,097 in 1867 (1.2 percent of the city population). Munich was far from any other Jewish community and migration to the city naturally came from a fairly long distance. Würzburg, in contrast, was surrounded by numerous village communities but had no Jewish residents of its own until 1805 when the Hirsch family (ancestors of the Barons de Hirsch) moved there. Thereafter, the number of Jews in the city grew to 138 in 1816, 425 in 1840, and 496 (1.66 percent of the total) in 1852. In Regensburg, the first Jews were readmitted in small numbers in 1669; by 1694, seventy Jewish individuals lived there. Their numbers increased to 121 in 1809/1810 and remained stable at 122 in 1840.[7] The only city in Bavaria that had a large longstanding Jewish population was Fürth, just outside of Nuremberg, where 2,499 of the 12,438 inhabitants in 1809 were Jewish. Smaller longstanding urban communities existed in Bamberg (287 in 1811), Bayreuth (469 in 1811/1812), Ansbach (385 in 1809/1810), and Aschaffenburg (172 in 1814/1815), as well as the Rhine Palatinate cities of Kaiserslautern, Pirmasens, Speyer, and Zweibrücken. Other major Bavarian cities remained either partly or completely closed to Jews in the early nineteenth century. In Augsburg, the number of Jews hovered around 100 between 1809 and 1840 and grew to only 128 in 1852. This was because Jews from the large Jewish communities just outside the city gates in Pfersee, Kriegshaber, and Steppach were legally restricted from moving to the city. The Augsburg community grew rapidly in the following period, reaching 449 in 1867 and 1,031 (1.7 percent of the city population) by 1880. The development of the Nuremberg community occurred later and even more rapidly than in Augsburg. In 1840 there were only six Jews in this city of over 50,000 inhabitants; their numbers increased to eighty-seven in 1852 and to 219 in 1858. The city truly opened up to Jews in the 1860s, and as a result, the city's Jewish population grew to 1,254 in 1867, 1,831 in 1871, and 3,032 in 1880. As the Fürth Jewish population did not decline during the rapid migration into Nuremberg, it is unlikely that most of these new inhabitants came from the large community of Fürth, despite it being less than ten miles away. The Jewish presence in Fürth increased from 2,651 in 1852 to 3,116 in

---

7   *Pinkas ha-Kehillot, Germania, Bavaria*, 105–106, 474, 478.

1867 and leveled off at just over 3,000 in the rest of the nineteenth century. It is more likely that many of Nuremberg's new Jewish residents came from large village communities in the Nuremberg area, such as Ottensoos, Hüttenbach, Schnaittach, and Baiersdorf (Table 14.13).[8]

Relatively small Bavarian cities also experienced rapid Jewish growth in the 1860s. The city of Nördlingen, in Swabia province, had only one Jewish family in 1860. This minute presence expanded rapidly to sixty-one Jews in 1867, 176 in 1871, 347 in 1880, and 469 in 1890 in a city with a total of 8,004 townspeople. As in Nuremberg, many of the new settlers in Nördlingen, came from surrounding rural Jewish communities such as Harburg, Kleinerdlingen, Wallerstein, Öttingen, and Mönchsdeggingen (Table 14.14). The long-established urban Jewish communities in Bavaria (Ansbach, Aschaffenburg,

Table 14.13. Jewish Population of Villages near Nuremberg, 1837–1880

Village	1837	1867	1871	1880
Ottensoos	133	112		80 (1890)
Hüttenbach	378 (1823)	208	164	134
Schnaittach	262	175	140	110
Baiersdorf	440	153	128	86
Total	1213	648		410

Source: *Pinkas ha-Kehillot, Germania, Bavaria*, 259, 295, 372, 281.

Table 14.14. Jewish Population of Villages near Nördlingen, 1837–1880

Village	1837	1867	1871	1880
Harburg	360 (1834)	171	142	94
Kleinerdlingen	235 (1811/12)			18 (1899)
Wallerstein	276 (1840)	78	57	56
Öttingen	430	248	205	185
Mönchsdeggingen	226 (1811/12)	139		3
Total	1517	636+		338

Sources: *Pinkas ha-Kehillot, Germania, Bavaria*, 595, 612–613, 616, 627.

---

8 Arnd Müller, *Geschichte der Juden in Nürnberg 1146–1945* (Nuremberg, 1968), 158 states that four times as many Jews came to Nuremberg before 1871 from Fürth than from any single other place but then he mentions six other places that contributed large numbers, including five villages (Ottensoos, Adelsdorf, Baiersdorf, Burghaslach and Schnaittach). These alone must have contributed more migrants than did Fürth.

Bamberg, Bayreuth, Kaiserrlautern, Primasens, Speyer, and Zweibrücken) grew at very different paces. The old centers of Ansbach and Bayreuth actually lost Jewish population even as Bamberg recorded rapid growth. Bamberg's Jewish population almost tripled between 1852 and 1880, making it the fifth-largest Jewish community in Bavaria with a Jewish density of 4.3 percent (Table 14.15). The communities that began growing in the early nineteenth century (Munich, Würzburg, Regensburg) increased much more rapidly between 1852 and 1880, with all three more than tripling their Jewish populations during this period (Table 14.16).

None of the major cities in Württemberg had many Jewish inhabitants in the early nineteenth century. Thereafter, there was extremely rapid Jewish population growth in the three largest cities of Stuttgart, Heilbronn, and Ulm. Stuttgart, the capital of Württemberg, had only ninety-two Jewish residents in 1807. Its Jewish population quadrupled between 1828 and 1858 to 512, gained another 335 in the next three years, and grew by 322 between 1861 and 1864. Thus, the Jewish population of Stuttgart more than doubled in six years. It doubled again between 1864 and 1880, by which point almost one in every four Jews in Württemberg lived in the capital. The Jewish population in the Stuttgart suburb of Bad Cannstatt also grew rapidly from thirty-three in 1858 to 256 in 1871, and 375 in 1880. In Heilbronn, there were almost no Jewish inhabitants until the early 1860s. The Jewish population there almost tripled in the three years between 1861 to 1864, rising from 137 to 369, and then grew almost as quickly again from 1864 to 1880. In doing so it became the second-largest Jewish community in Württemberg. The community in Ulm grew somewhat earlier than that in Heilbronn and was about twenty percent smaller at its peak. In 1864, the eleven other Württemberg towns with over 5,000 inhabitants had Jewish populations ranging from one in Biberach to 144 in Esslingen (Table 14.17). Laupheim was the largest town in Württemberg that had a traditionally large Jewish community, where 768 of the 3,836 inhabitants in 1864 were Jewish. Several Württemberg towns in the 2,000–10,000 population class, especially in the northern half of the kingdom, originally had no Jews but developed fair-sized communities in the late nineteenth century. This was the case in Oehringen, Künzelsau, Schwäbisch Gmünd, and Schwäbisch Hall. The small central Württemberg textile city of Göppingen was a case unto itself, with much of its Jewish population having migrated from the nearby village community of Jebenhausen. Farther south, the cities of Rottweil, Tübingen, and Reutlingen developed fairly small Jewish communities after the mid-nineteenth century (Table 14.18).

Even though Jews were almost totally excluded from most cities in the southern half of Baden, such as Freiburg, Konstanz, Baden-Baden, and Lahr, there were important Jewish communities in the main northern cities of

Table 14.15. Jewish Population of Long-Established Urban Jewish Communities in Bavaria, 1840–1880

City	Jewish population					Percent change	General population		Percent Change
	1840	1852	1867	1871	1880		1840	1880	
Ansbach	250	171	239		220	−12.0	11939	14195	+18.9
Aschaffenburg	207	231	204	286	493	+138.2	9273	12152	+31.1
Bamberg	423	455	708	851	1269	+200.0	20863	29587	+41.8
	333*					[+381.1]			
Bayreuth	504	309	336	362	357	−29.2	16660	22072	+32.5
Kaiserslautern	197	191	519	616	716	+263.5	8250	26323	+219.1
	116*					[+517.2]			
Pirmasens	174	212	202	200	234	+34.5	6410	12039	+87.8
Speyer	301	315			539	+79.1	11147	15589	+40.0
Zweibrücken	167	151			265	+58.7	7578	10382	+37.0
Total		2052			4093	+99.6			

Source: *Beiträge zur Statistik des Königreichs Bayern* (1850): 54–55, 60–61, 66–67, 90–91; (1855): 84–85, 90–91, 108–109, 132–133, 150–151; *Pinkas ha-Kehillot, Germania, Bavaria*, 8, 205, 223, 268,409; Bosse, *Die Verbreitung der Juden*, 70–71, 73, 76, 78.

* *Pinkas ha-Kehillot* (the other figure is from *Beiträge*).

Table 14.16. Jewish Population in Newer Urban Communities in Bavaria, 1840–1880

City	Jewish population					Percent change	General population
	1840	1852	1867	1871	1880		1880
Munich	1423	1208	2097	2884	4144	+191.2	230,023
Würzburg	425	496	1099	1518	2271	+434.4	51,014
Regensburg	122	137	359	430	675	+453.3	34,516
Augsburg	97		449	660	1031	+962.9	75,629

Sources: *Pinkas ha-Kehillot, Germania, Bavaria*, 8, 583; Bosse, *Die Verbreitung der Juden*, 67, 71, 78; *Beiträge zur Statistik des Königreichs Bayern* (Munich, 1855), 48–49, 90–91, 150–151.

Table 14.17. Growth of Newer Urban Jewish Communities in Württemberg, 1828–1880

City	1828	1843	1858	1861	1864	1871	1880
Stuttgart	124	230	512	847	1169	1817	2485
Ulm	12	19	57 (1854)	327	373	555	694
Heilbronn	0		65 (1855)	137	369	610	871
Esslingen	96	115	118 (1854)	184	144		166
Ludwigsburg	64	70		70	72		199

Sources: "Die Statistik der jüdischen Gemeinden Württembergs 1831–1931," *Gemeindezeitung für die Israelitischen Gemeinden Württembergs* III (December 1, 1931): 194–195; *Württemberger Jahrbücher zur Statistik und Landeskunde* (1864): 124–125; Bosse, *Die Verbreitung der Juden*, 89–97; Schmelz, Territorial Printout; *Pinkas ha-Kehillot, Germania, Württemberg-Hohenzollern-Baden*, 34, 79, 141. The last source gives the 1871 Jewish population of Stuttgart as 2074, most likely because it includes the Jewish population of the suburb of Cannstatt.

Table 14.18. Jewish Population of Medium-Sized Cities with Growing Jewish Populations in Württemberg

City	1828	1861	1864	1871	1880	1925
Schwäbisch Gmünd	0	2 families	9		49	77
Schwäbisch Hall	0	81	72	137	263	132
Oehringen	0	0	2		158	159
Künzelsau	0	20	33		119	78
Göppingen*	0	112	130	174 [194] (1867)	242	351
(Jebenhausen	410)					5)
Tübingen	0	16	20	34 (1869)	123	82
Reutlingen	0	5	21	19 (1875)	44	84
Rottweil	34	94	105		136	97

Göppingen was settled mainly by Jews from the neighboring village of Jebenhausen.

Schwäbisch Hall, like Göppingen, was settled to a considerable extent by Jews from neighboring villages (Steinbach and Unterdeufstetten).

Sources: "Die Statistik der jüdischen Gemeinden Württembergs 1831–1931," *Gemeindezeitung für die Israelitischen Geminden Württembergs* III (December 1, 1931): 194–195; *Württemberger Jahrbücher zur Statistik und Landeskunde* (1864): 124–125; Bosse, *Die Verbreitung der Juden*, 89–97; *Pinkas ha-Kehillot, Germania, Württemberg-Hohenzollern-Baden*, 48, 71, 94–95, 98, 120, 127, 134, 138.

Mannheim, Heidelberg, Pforzheim, Bruchsal, and Karlsruhe in the early nineteenth century. The boundary between these two regions ran through the middle of the Mittelrheinkreis, just south of Karlsruhe and Pforzheim. The southern Baden cities generally opened to Jews in the early 1860s. Jewish in-migration was especially rapid in the university town of Freiburg, where the Jewish population expanded from thirteen in 1852 to 333 in 1871, and more than doubled again by 1880. Growth in Konstanz, which was on the Swiss border in an area that had several large Jewish village communities, was also quite rapid. After the first Jew reached this city in 1845, the Jewish population grew to 164 in 1871 and 332 in 1880. Smaller southern and south-central Baden cities such as Lahr, Baden-Baden, and Offenburg also developed Jewish communities at the same time. Those in Lahr and Baden-Baden generally remained below 150 in number. The Jewish communities in Mannheim and Karlsruhe, which were already substantial in the early nineteenth century, grew steadily but less rapidly than the new southern urban communities. Due to faster population growth in Mannheim at large, the Jewish community there grew much more quickly than it did in Karlsruhe. The Jewish population in the university city of Heidelberg leaped from 386 in1861 to 651 in 1871. Bruchsal's Jewish community did much the same between 1862 and 1875, increasing from 325 to 609 (Table 14.19).

Unlike the rest of southern Germany, most cities in the Hessian areas already had substantial Jewish populations in the early nineteenth century. In the Grand Duchy of Hesse(-Darmstadt), the Jewish population's growth in most main cities was much faster between 1828 and1861 than it was between 1861 and 1880. In contrast, in the Prussian province of Hesse-Nassau—especially in Frankfurt—urban Jewish population growth was relatively slow between 1828 and 1861 and much faster thereafter (Table 14.20). Once Frankfurt no longer limited Jewish settlement starting in 1866, much migration to other cities in the Hessian region shifted to Frankfurt. Curiously, although both Marburg and Giessen registered large gains in the 1870s, these two university towns had smaller Jewish densities than other cities in the Hessian region.

Outside the major towns, the Jewish population generally declined, but did so at uneven rates. Jews often moved from villages of under 2,000 to towns of 2,000–10,000 and then to larger cities. Village communities of fewer than 1,000 inhabitants lost larger percentages of their Jewish populations than did towns with 1,000–2,000 residents.

Even though urbanization played a major role in South German Jewry after 1860, the region remained the chief center of rural Jewry in Germany. Inasmuch as Jews in other areas urbanized much more rapidly, the percentage of small-town German Jewry living in the south increased. Thus, the share of Jews living in towns of under 10,000 inhabitants who also lived in the southern states of Bavaria, Württemberg, Baden, and Hesse-Darmstadt climbed from 26.1 percent in 1880 to 37.9 percent in 1925 and 38.4 percent in 1933. Including the Prussian provinces of Hesse-Nassau and Hohenzollern, the proportions were 51.85 percent in 1925 and 54.7 percent in 1933. In the latter year, 31 percent of South German Jews still lived in towns of under 10,000 residents as against only 15.45 percent in Germany as a whole (Table 9.27). Where existing data break down the small-town population into more precise subgroups, it is evident that a large proportion of the Jews in this category were still living in villages of under 2,000 (Table 14.21).

Many large village communities shrank during the nineteenth century and either became small communities or disappeared altogether. Nevertheless, several large communities in towns of under 10,000 inhabitants survived in

Table 14.19. Growth of Urban Jewish Communities in Baden, 1825–1895

City	1825	1845	1852	1871	1880	1895
Mannheim	1465	1578	1670	3135	4031	4768
Karlsruhe	893	1163	1073	1329	1689	2169
Freiburg	15	18	13	333	725	989
Heidelberg	349		365 [445]	651	799	800
Pforzheim	128		220	215	343	435
Konstanz	0			164	332	528
Baden-Baden	0			84 (1875)	73	156
Rastatt	61	100	158 (1865)	230 (1875)	212	197 [218]
Bruchsal	178	256 (1842)	325 (1862)	609 (1875)	730	743
Lahr	0		22	48 (1875)	59	117

Sources: *Pinkas ha-Kehillot, Germania, Württemberg-Hohenzollern-Baden*, 254, 274, 309, 361, 373, 425, 434, 444, 462, 490; *Die politischen, Kirchen- und Schulgemeinden des Grossherzogthums Baden 1845* (Karlsruhe, 1847), 94–98; *Beiträge zur Statistik der inneren Verwaltung des Grossherzogthums Baden* (Karlsruhe, 1855), 206–215; "Ortsanwesende Bevölkerung am 2. Dezember 1895 mit Unterscheidung nach der Religion. In den Städten mit mehr als 3000 . . .", 66; Schmelz, Territorial Printout.

Table 14.20. Growth of Urban Jewish Communities in Hesse

City	Absolute numbers				Percent growth		
	1828	1861	1871	1880	1828–1861	1861–1871	1871–1880
Hesse-Nassau							
Frankfurt/Main	4530 (1823)	5730 (1858)	10009	13843	+26.5	+74.7	+38.3
Kassel	827 (1827)	946	1322	1756	+14.4	+39.8	+32.8
Hanau	540 (1822)	379	447	554	−29.8	+17.9	+23.9
Fulda	324 (1827)	284	295	439	−13.3	+5.0	+48.8
Wiesbaden	237 (1840)	693 (1867)	893	1202	+192.4	+28.9	+34.6
Marburg	80 (1827)	40	166	295	−7.5	+124.3	+77.7
Total	6538	8072	13132	18089	+23.9	+62.1	+37.8
Less Frankfurt	2008	2342	3123	4216	+18.2	+31.6	+35.0
Hesse-Darmstadt							
Mainz	1620	2665	2998	3182	+64.5	+12.5	+6.1
Offenbach	848	1078	1003	987	+30.2	−7.0	−1.6
Worms	773	944	977	1216	+51.3	−0.8	+24.5
Darmstadt	556	641	906	1275	+20.5	+41.3	+40.7
Giessen	197	336	458	612	+70.6	+14.3	+59.4
Total	3994	5664	6342	7272	+49.0	+9.9	+16.0

Sources: Schmelz, *Hessen*, 50–51; Bosse, *Die Verbreitung der Juden*, 15–20, 107–110; *Pinkas ha-Kehillot, Germania, Hessen-Hessen-Nassau-Frankfurt*, 427, 467, 498, 527, 556, 599. There are some discrepancies in the 1861 numbers between Schmelz, *Hessen*, and *Pinkas ha-Kehillot, Germania, Hessen-Hessen-Nassau-Frankfurt*.

Table 14.21. Jews in Small Towns in Southern Germany, by Subgroup

Bavaria Population	1871	1880	1885	1900	1910	1925	1933
Under 5000	34419	30858	28790	22537	17191		
5,000–10000		2564					
Under 10000		33422				14967	11911
10000–20000		3253				1985	1494
5000–20000	4780	5817	6106	6173	5955		
Total under 20000	39199	36675	34896	28710	23146	16952	13405

Population size	Hesse-Darmstadt		Hesse-Nassau
	1861	1925	1925
Under 1000	7292	2223	3807
1000–1999	8305	2860	4296
2000–4999	5088	3384	4157
5000–10000	1501	2308	927
Subtotal	22186	10775	13187
10000–19999	2022	1349	1576
Total under 20000	24208	12124	14763

Source: *Pinkas ha-Kehillot, Germania, Bavaria*, 8, 10; Schmelz, *Hessen*, 360; 1933 census, 5/11; Schmelz, handwritten tables "Ortsgrössenklassen."

southern Germany during the Weimar Republic era. Those in Gailingen, Rhina, Rexingen, and Ichenhausen, for example, maintained lively Jewish life in the 1920s and early 1930s. Most of these surviving communities were marked by the continuation of traditional Jewish religious practice, active Jewish organizations, and significant Jewish influence on the town's overall life. Approximately thirty communities in southern Germany, which were generally evenly divided among villages of under 2,000, small towns of 2,000–5,000, and larger towns of 5,000–10,000 inhabitants, still had 150 or more Jewish inhabitants in 1933 (Table 14.22).

Just as some important small-town Jewish communities survived German Jewry's sweeping urbanization, not all larger cities developed substantial communities. This was especially true in areas that had virtually no Jewish population in the early nineteenth century. Thus, while cities originally without Jews and near traditional village communities often gained substantial Jewish populations as was the case in Ulm, Heilbronn, Nördlingen, and Memmingen, this rarely happened in Upper Bavaria, Lower Bavaria, the southern part of Bavarian Swabia, and the eastern part of Upper Franconia. Most cities in the 10,000–30,000 class in these regions had fewer than 100 Jews at their peak (Table 14.23).

Although southern Germany is rarely considered a center for foreign Jews, several cities did attract significant numbers of East European Jewish immigrants. In 1910, Jews lacking German citizenship made up more than one-fifth of the Jewish populations in Wiesbaden and Offenbach near Frankfurt, Munich in Bavaria, and Karlsruhe in Baden. Munich had the largest concentration of foreign Jews in southern Germany (3,857) while the leather-working industrial city of Offenbach had the highest percentage of foreign Jews. In most rural districts, in contrast, the percentage of the Jewish population that was foreign was very small, often under five percent (Table 14.24). During World War I, many East European Jews were recruited, and sometimes forced, into German industry, although this happened mainly outside southern Germany. After the war, there was a ferocious anti-Eastern Jewish campaign, especially in Bavaria. In the Nazis' early center of Munich, the foreign Jewish population declined sharply from 3,457 non-citizens in 1910 to 2,041 in 1933. Largely due to the departure of Russian-Jewish leather workers, the Jewish population of Offenbach also plummeted from 2,361 in 1910 to 1,682 in 1925 and to 1,435 in 1933. While the foreign Jewish population in much of Bavaria and in Offenbach declined between 1910 and 1933, it rose in many other southern cities, notably in Frankfurt, Wiesbaden, and rapidly growing Ludwigshafen in the Rhine Palatinate. Overall, the share of foreign Jews in Germany who lived in the southern areas fell from 23.1 percent in 1910 to 16.1 percent in 1933.

Table 14.22. Large Jewish Communities in South German Towns of under 10,000 Inhabitants, 1933

Under 2,000 inhabitants		2,000–4,999		5,000–9,999	
Gailingen	314	Schlüchtern	316	Bad Kissingen	344
Rexingen	262	Ichenhausen	309	Emmendingen	296
Haigerloch	213*	Breisach	231	Laupheim	231
Rhina	225*	Gelnhausen	218	Langenselbold	226
Königsbach	162*	Kirchhain	189*	Alsfeld	198
Guxhagen	158	Öhringen	163	Bad Nauheim	198
Thüngen	152	Bad Buchau	162	Alzey	197
Burghaun	152*	Mosbach	159*	Bad Mergentheim	196
Schenklengsfeld	149*	Neustadt an der Saale	158	Nördlingen	186
Kippenheim	144			Gunzenhausen	184
Gross Krotzenburg	137*			Crailsheim	160
Schmieheim	121				

* 1925 figures.

Sources: Schmelz, Hessen, 382, 385; Pinkas ha-Kehillot, Germania, Bavaria, 49–51, 288, 416, 419, 598, 629; Pinkas ha-Kehillot, Germania, Hessen-Hessen-Nassau-Frankfurt, 70, 72, 84, 393, 405, 409, 415, 492, 567, 583, 590, 595; Pinkas ha-Kehillot, Germania, Württemberg-Hohenzollern-Baden, 48, 51, 55, 100, 124, 130, 168, 244, 231, 399 476, 484, 506.

Haigerloch had 213 Jews in 1925 and 186 in 1933; Mosbach had 159 in 1925 and 139 in 1933.

Table 14.23. South German Cities of over 10,000 Inhabitants with Small Jewish Populations, 1925 (in ascending order by percent Jewish)

City	Jewish	Total	Percent Jewish	Province where located
Ebingen	2	12128		Schwarzwaldkreis (Württemberg)
Aalen	7	12171		Jagstkreis (Württemberg)
Tuttlingen	16	16281	0.1	Schwarzwaldkreis (Württemberg)
Freising	17	14974	0.1	Upper Bavaria (Bavaria)
Heidenheim/Brenz	25	21903	0.1	Donaukreis (Württemberg)
Lindau	18	13582	0.1	Southern Schwaben (Bavaria)
Ravensburg	28	17012	0.2	Donaukreis (Württemberg)
Landshut	45	26105	0.2	Lower Bavaria (Bavaria)
Hof	80	41377	0.2	Eastern Upper Bavaria (Bavaria)
Passau	48	24428	0.2	Lower Bavaria (Bavaria)
Rosenheim	39	17998	0.2	Upper Bavaria (Bavaria)
Amberg	63	26330	0.2	Upper Palatinate (Bavaria)
Kempten	56	21874	0.3	Southern Swabia (Bavaria)
Reutlingen	84	30501	0.3	Schwarzwaldkreis (Württemberg)
Durlach	60	18016	0.3	Karlsruhe (Baden)
Kulmbach (1933)	41	12476	0.3	Upper Franconia (Bavaria)
Schw Gmünd	77	20406	0.4	Jagstkreis (Württemberg)
Ingolstadt	103	26630	0.4	Upper Bavaria (Bavaria)
Tübingen	82	20276	0.4	Schwarzwaldkreis (Württemberg)
Straubing	115	23593	0.5	Lower Bavaria (Bavaria)

Sources: *Pinkas ha-Kehillot, Germania, Bavaria*, 103, 134, 141, 145, 146, 153, 232, 252, 619, 636; *Pinkas ha-Kehillot, Germania, Württemberg-Hohenzollern-Baden*, 59, 95, 98, 133, 134, 136, 301.

In 1933, the Jewish populations of the cities in Württemberg were Ebingen 21, Aalen 8, Tuttlingen 24, Heidenheim 35, Ravensburg 28, Reutlingen 65, Schwäbisch Gmünd 90, and Tübingen 90. Sauer, *Die jüdischen Gemeinden*, 159, 177, 178, 194–195.

Table 14.24. Jewish Non-Citizens in Southern Germany

City or Region	1910			1933				Change in non-citizens
	Non-citizens	All Jews	Percent foreign	Foreign-born	Non-citizens	All Jews	Percent non-citizens	
Hesse-Nassau	4835	51781	9.3	4498	6909	46923	14.7	+2074
Frankfurt am Main	3541	26228	13.5	3475	5277	26158	20.2	+1736
Wiesbaden	750	2844	26.4	724	1168	5014	23.3	+161
Kassel	257	2675	9.6					
Other Hesse-Nassau	287	20034	1.4	299	464	15751	2.9	+177
Hohenzollern	5	405	1.2					
Upper Bavaria	3966	11652	34.0					
Munich	3857	11083	34.8	1506	2041	9005	22.7	-1816
Other Upper Bavaria	109	569	19.2					
Lower Bavaria	83	468	17.7					
Pfalz	402	8998	4.5	414	719	6487	11.1	+317
Ludwigshafen				278	477	1070	44.6	
Other Palatinate				136	242	5417	4.5	

City or Region	1910			1933				Change in non-citizens
	Non-citizens	All Jews	Percent foreign	Foreign-born	Non-citizens	All Jews	Percent non-citizens	
Upper Palatinate	181	1395	13.0					
Upper Franconia	209	2946	7.1					
Middle Franconia	1803	14219	12.7					
Nuremberg	1226	7815	15.7	624	850	7502	11.3	-376
Other Middle Franconia	577	6404	9.0					
Lower Franconia	398	11925	3.5					
Swabia	278	3462	8.0					
Augsburg	155	1217	12.7					
Other Swabia	123	2245	5.5					
Bavaria	7320	55065	13.3	3466	4640	41939	11.1	-2680
Outside 3 main Bavarian cities	2082	34950	6.0	1058	1272	24362	5.2	-810
Württemberg	1156	11982	9.6	745	957	10324**	9.3	-199
Stuttgart	836	4291	19.5	520	680	4490	15.1	-156
Other Württemberg	320	7691	4.2	225	277	5834	4.8	-43
Baden	2620	25896	10.1	1797	2205	20617	10.7	-415

City or Region	1910			1933					Change in non-citizens
	Non-citizens	All Jews	Percent foreign	All Jews	Percent foreign	Foreign-born	Non-citizens	All Jews	Percent non-citizens	
Mannheim	887	6425	13.8			706	895	6402	14.0	+8
Karlsruhe	654	3058	21.4			456	689	3119	22.1	+35
All other Baden	1079	16413	6.6			635	621	11096	5.6	-458
Hesse	2494	24063	10.4			969	1194	17888	6.7	-1300
Mainz	373	2926	12.7			302	298	2609	11.4	-75
Other Hesse	2121	21137	10.0			667	896	15279	5.9	-1225
Darmstadt	512	1998	25.6							
Offenbach	1131	2361	47.9							
All other Hesse	479	16778	2.9							
All southern Germany	18430	169192	10.9			11475	15905	137691	11.6	-2525
All other Germany	61216	445829	13.7			62218	82842	361991	22.9	+21626

* Or birthplace unknown.
** Including Hohenzollern.

Sources: *Vierteljahrshefte zur Statistik des Deutschen Reichs—Ergänzungsheft zu 19164 (1918): Die Deutschen im Ausland und die Ausländer im Deutschen Reiche*, 53, 86; *Statistik des Deutschen Reichs* 240 (1915): 210; 1933 census, 5/10, 50–51; Schmelz, *Hessen*, 49, 50–51; Schmelz, Territorial Printout; *Pinkas ha-Kehillot, Germania, Bavaria*, 13.

Changes in South German Jewry under Weimar and Nazi Rule

Until 1910, rural southern Germany still had a substantial Jewish population. In the four southern states of Bavaria, Württemberg, Baden, and Hesse(Darmstadt), 47.4 percent of all Jews lived in towns of under 20,000 inhabitants. After 1910, the Jewish population of southern Germany, especially the rural population, declined substantially (Table 14.25). Thus, between 1910 and 1933, the Jewish population of southern Germany decreased by 18.6 percent even as German Jewry (not counting the territories that Germany lost after World War I) contracted by only 6.6 percent overall. In the four southern states, the number of Jews in towns of under 20,000 inhabitants fell by 20,822—37.5 percent—between 1910 and 1933. While the percentage decline of small-town Jewish populations in the rest of Germany was greater, this was partly due to the loss of the provinces of Posen, West Prussia, and Alsace-Lorraine, and their sizable populations of small-town Jews.

The degree to which the Jewish population of southern Germany remained rural varied sharply among subregions, partly depending on the respective extent of urbanization. In the former Grand Duchy of Hesse, most of the Jewish population dwelled in towns of under 20,000 in 1933, but the share of rural Jews among those in neighboring Hesse-Nassau was much lower due to Frankfurt's huge Jewish population. In Bavaria, almost all Jews in Upper Bavaria were urban and residents of Munich. In Lower Franconia, Swabia, and the Rhine Palatinate, in contrast, a large percentage of the Jewish population still lived in small towns during the Weimar Republic years (Table 14.26). In Middle Franconia, several important small-town communities survived the Weimar period but were increasingly overshadowed by the agglomeration of Jews in Fürth and Nuremberg. Various sections of Baden and Württemberg also differed in their degree of Jewish urbanization. In the latter state, nearly all Jews in the Jagstkreis were rural, while a large share of Jews in the Neckarkreis were urban.

The demographic decline of South German Jewry varied considerably from region to region (Table 14.27). Developments before 1933 often differed radically from those thereafter, partly because of the influence of different Nazi governors (Gauleiters). In Hohenzollern, the decrease was the sharpest among southern subregions before 1933 but the slowest under the Nazis. Before 1933, the Jewish population's decline was rather strong in all parts of the mainly rural state of Hesse(Darmstadt). After the Nazi accession to power in 1933, Jewish emigration was greatest in the most antisemitic and rural district (Upper Hesse) and somewhat less extreme in the more urbanized district of Rhine-Hesse. In

Table 14.25. Decline in Small-Town Jewish Population in Southern Germany

Regions with towns under 20,000	1910	Percent of all Jews	1925	Percent of all Jews	1933	Percent of all Jews	Percent change
Bavaria	23,146	42.0	16,952	34.5	13,405	32.0	-42.1
Württemberg	5,665	47.3	3878	35.2	3346	33.4	-40.9
	(5394)	(45.0)			(3344)	(33.4)	
Baden	12,232	47.2	9095	37.8	7383	35.8	-39.6
Hesse	14,462	60.1	12124	59.4	10549	59.0	-27.1
					(10546)	(59.0)	
Total	55,505	47.4	42049	40.3	34683	38.3	-37.5
Hesse-Nassau			14763	28.0			
Total plus Hesse-Nassau			56812				
All Germany	195,907	31.9	117388	20.8	94,610	18.9	-51.7

Sources: Schmelz, handwritten table "Juden Ortsgrössenklassen"; Schmelz, *Hessen*, 360.

Table 14.26. Rural and Urban Jewish Populations in Various Parts of Bavaria by Overall Population

Region	Cities of over 50,000		
	1910	1925	1933
Upper Bavaria	11083	10068	9005
Percent	95.1 (Munich)	93.3	94.6
Lower Bavaria	0	0	0
Upper Palatinate	493	478	427
Percent	35.3 (Regensburg)	40.5	42.5
Upper Franconia	0	972	812
Percent		38.2 (Bamberg)	38.1
Middle Franconia	10641	11107	9492
Percent	74.8 (Nuremberg, Fürth)	81.0	81.7
Lower Franconia	2514	2261	2145
Percent	21.1 (Würzburg)	22.9	25.2
Swabia	1217	1203	1030
Percent	35.2 (Augsburg)	42.5	43.7
Rhenish Palatinate	1474	1955	1718
Percent	16.9 (Ludwigshafen, Kaiserslautern)	24.9	26.5

Region	Cities 20,000–50,000		
	1910	1925	1933
Upper Bavaria	102	103	100
Percent	0.9 (Ingolstadt)	1.0	1.0
Lower Bavaria	274	208	198
Percent	58.6 (Straubing, Landshut Passau)	59.7	67.6
Upper Palatinate	88	63	232
Percent	6.3 (Amberg)	5.3	23.1 (Weiden)
Upper Franconia	1953	700	590
Percent	59.6 (including Bamberg in 1910) (Hof, Coburg, Bayreuth)	27.5	26.9
Middle Franconia	224	393	327
Percent	1.6 (Erlangen)	2.9 (plus Ansbach)	2.8

Region	Cities 20,000–50,000		
	1910	1925	1933
Lower Franconia	1098	1057	954
Percent	9.2 (Aschaffenburg, Schweinfurt)	10.7	11.2
Swabia	91	56	50
Percent	2.6 (Kempten)	2.0	2.1
Rhenish Palatinate	980	1569	1470
Percent	11.2 (Pirmasens, Speyer)	20.0 (plus Neustadt, Frankenthal)	22.7 (plus Zweibrücken)

Region	Cities under 20,000			Cities under 10,000
	1910	1925	1933	1933
Upper Bavaria	467	619	417	348
Percent	4.0	5.74	4.38	3.6%
Lower Bavaria	194	140	95	
Percent	41.4	40.3	32.4	440
Upper Palatinate	814	640	345	33.9
Percent	58.4	54.2	34.4	
Upper Franconia	1326	872	731	
Percent	40.4	34.3	35.0	2399
Middle Franconia	3354	2219	1802	17.4
Percent	23.6	16.2	15.5	
Lower Franconia	8313	6561	5421	5061
Percent	69.7	66.4	63.6	59.4
Swabia	2154	1575	1279	1062
Percent	62.2	55.6	54.2	45.0
Rhenish Palatinate	6267	4326	3299	2601
Percent	71.9	55.1	50.9	40.1

Sources: 1933 census, 5/11; *Pinkas ha-Kehilllot, Germania, Bavaria,* 12–13, 14–16, 49–51, 52, 103, 141, 145, 146, 153, 156, 268, 276, 409, 572, 583. For the Rhenish Palatinate, also Schmelz, Territorial Printout.

The general population of Bamberg passed the 50,000 mark between 1910 and 1925. The general populations of Weiden and Zweibrücken passed the 20,000 mark in 1933. The general populations of Ansbach, Neustadt an der Haardt, and Frankenthal, passed 20,000 in 1925.

Table 14.27. Decline in South German Jewish Population, 1910–1939

District and Region	1910	1925	Percent change	1933	Percent change	1939 (Glaubensjuden)	Percent change
Hesse-Nassau	51781 (52371)	52757 (53737)	+1.9	46923	-11.1	20554	-56.2
RB Kassel	17603	15498	-12.0	13589	-12.3	4292	-68.4
RB Wiesbaden	34709	37736	-2.8	33334	-19.0	2511	-65.0
Minus Frankfurt	8481	8351	-2.8	7176	-19.0	2511	-65.0
Frankfurt am Main	26228	29385	+12.0	26158	-11.0	13751	-47.4
Hohenzollern	405	335	-17.3	301	-10.2	184	-38.9
Upper Bavaria	11652	10790	-7.4	9522	-11.8	4823	-49.4
Lower Bavaria	468	348	-25.6	1297	-15.2	535	-58.8
Upper Palatinate	1395	1181					
Palatinate	8998	7850	-12.8	6487	-17.4	1723	-73.4
Upper Franconia	2946*	2544	-13.7	13754	-15.4	4413	-67.9
Lower Franconia	14219	13719	-3.5				
Nuremberg	7815	8603	+10.1	7502	-12.8	2589	-65.5
Fürth	2826	2504	-11.4	1990	-20.5	800	-59.8
Other Middle Franconia and Upper Franconia	3578	2612	-27.0	4262		1024	-76.0
Lower Franconia	11925	9879	-17.2	8520	-13.8	3417	-59.9

Southern Germany | 671

District and Region	1910	1925	Percent change	1933	Percent change	1939 (Glaubensjuden)	Percent change
Swabia	3462	2834	-18.1	2359	-16.8	1320	-44.0
Bavaria	55065 [55117]	49145	-10.8	41939	-14.7	16231	-61.3
Württemberg	11982	10827	-9.6	10023	-7.4	4447	-55.6
Jagstkreis	2412	1745	-27.7	1513	-13.3	757	-50.1
Neckarkreis	6276	6378	+1.6	6090	-4.5	2942	-51.7
Stuttgart	4291	4548	+6.0	4490	-1.3	2198	-51.1
Other Neckarkreis	1985	1830	-7.8	1600	-12.6	744	-53.5
Schwarzwaldkreis	1359	1010	-25.7	882	-12.7	347	-60.7
Donaukreis	1935	1694	-12.5	1538	-9.2	641	-58.3
Baden	25896	24064	-7.1	20617	-14.3	8886	-56.9
RB Konstanz	1669	1281	-23.3	1108	-13.5	559	-49.6
Freiburg	5063	4341	-14.3	3575	-17.7	1508	-57.8
Karlsruhe	6858	6904	+0.7	5806	-15.9	2403	-58.6
Karlsruhe city	3058	3386	+10.7	3119	-7.9	1368	-56.1
Other Karlsruhe District	3800	3518	-7.4	2687	-23.6	1035	-61.5
Mannheim	12306	11538	-6.2	10128	-12.2	4416	-56.4
Mannheim city	6402	6972	+8.9	6402	-8.2	2962	-53.7

District and Region	1910	1925	Percent change	1933	Percent change	1939 (Glaubensjuden)	Percent change
Other Mannheim District	5904	4566	-22.7	3723	-18.5	1454	-61.0
Hesse	24063	20401	-15.2	17888	-12.3	5801	-67.6
Starkenburg	9740	7994	-17.9	7003	-12.4	2150	-69.3
Rhenish Hesse	7769	6675	-14.1	5830	-12.7	2336	-59.9
Upper Hesse	6554	5732	-12.5	5055	-11.8	1314	-74.0
All southern Germany	169162	157529	-6.9	137691	-12.6	56103	-59.3
All Germany	615021	564379	-8.2	499682	-11.5	219020 Altreich	-56.2
Percent southern Germany	27.5	27.9		27.6		25.6	
Germany in 1910 boundaries	535152				+5.5%		
Percent southern Germany		31.6					

Sources: Schmelz, Hessen, 41, 49; Pinkas ha-Kehillot, Germania, Bavaria, 49, 50; 1933 census, 5/11, 15; Statistik des Deutschen Reichs 552 no. 4 (1944): 20–34; Schmelz, Territorial Printout.

Note: the 1910 Upper Franconia figure does not include the 313 Jews in the Coburg district, which was transferred to Upper Franconia after World War I.

Württemberg and Baden, Jewish population in the chief cities of Mannheim, Karlsruhe, and Stuttgart continued to grow until 1925 and declined only slightly before 1933. Population losses in the more rural parts of both states were much greater before 1933 than after. Next to Hesse-Darmstadt, the steepest contraction of Jewish population took place in Bavaria, caused at least in part by this state's role as the first center of the Nazi movement. Nazi strength in Munich was a precipitant of the decline in this city's Jewish (especially foreign Jewish) population between the early 1920s and 1933. In Nuremberg-Fürth, agitation by Julius Streicher and other vicious local antisemites led to the severe depletion of Jewish numbers after 1925. Significant declines occurred in all Bavarian areas where the Jewish population was largely rural, most notably Bavarian Swabia, which dropped 31.9 percent from 1910 to 1933. Due to the the Frankfurt community's continued growth until 1925, Jewish numbers declined less in Hesse-Nassau than anywhere else in southern Germany.

During the early years of Nazi rule, there was much Jewish migration within Germany as well as emigration to countries abroad. The emigration rate between 1933 and 1939 was somewhat higher in southern Germany than elsewhere. This was partly because Nazi persecution may have been more severe there, but was also due to the greater likelihood of South German Jews (especially those in Bavaria) having American relatives who could sponsor their immigration to America. The pattern of internal migration in the south was complicated. New migrants leaving the more exposed countryside for the relative safety of the large cities often replaced long-term inhabitants of the latter localities who left Germany. Consequently, urban Jewish populations, especially in Frankfurt and Stuttgart, declined much less than did South German Jewry at large. Only the neighboring cities of Nuremberg and Fürth experienced a decline that exceeded the average for southern Germany (Table 14.28). A special case was Middle Franconia District, where Streicher was the Gauleiter. The Jewish population of this district's small towns was decimated by expulsion orders in late 1938. Of 2,129 Jews who were counted in Middle Franconia outside Nuremberg and Fürth in 1933, only seventy-five Jews by religion were still there according to the May 1939 census. Elsewhere in southern Germany, especially in Lower Franconia, Swabia, Rhenish Palatinate, and the Prussian district of Kassel, a substantial Jewish population remained in small towns at the time of the 1939 census. Although only 23.8 percent of Jews in the *Altreich* lived in southern Germany in 1939, 47.5 percent of Jews in towns of under 10,000 lived in this region at that time (Table 9.35). Among the South German Jews who were deported to extermination camps between 1941 and 1943, several thousand came from the region's villages.

Table 14.28. Percent of South German Jewish Population in Largest Cities

City	1933	Percent of south German Jewish population	1939	Percent change	Percent of south German Jewish population
Frankfurt am Main	26158	19.0	13751	-47.4	24.5
Munich	9005	6.5	4535	-49.6	8.1
Place name is absent		25.5			32.6
Stuttgart	4490	3.3	2198	-51.1	3.9
Mannheim	6402	4.67	2962	-53.7	5.3
Karlsruhe	3119	2.3	1368	-56.1	2.4
Place name is absent		35.7			44.3
Fürth	1990	1.5	800	-59.8	1.4
Nuremberg	7502	5.5	2589	-65.5	4.6
Place name is absent	58666	42.6	28203	-51.8	50.3

Sources: 1933 census: 5/15; *Pinkas ha-Kehillot, Germania, Bavaria*, 342; *Statistik des Deutschen Reiches* 552 (1944): 4/21, 26, 29, 31.

Conclusions

The plethora of available statistics concerning the demographic characteristics of German Jewry offers us a bewildering richness of information on diverse trends that are difficult to summarize. The categories of data collected by government officials sometimes do not align with questions that scholars would like to ask and the statistics lack vital information that may never come to light. Additional information is still hidden in local records of statistics that require minute dissection through the use of family reconstruction methods. Despite these shortcomings, the amount of information available is remarkable and its relative accuracy is impressive. Though more thoroughgoing studies in the future will surely modify them, we may nevertheless draw some general conclusions about the German Jewish population's development from 1815 to 1939.

The overall trends in German Jewish demography in the nineteenth and early twentieth centuries reveal two seemingly opposite main characteristics. First, German Jews began the period with several specific traits that distinguished them from the rest of the German population. The changes that ensued over the following 125 years built on this historic foundation and, in many ways, retained the influence of the earlier formative period of German Jewry. Second, however, there is often the impression that the chief characteristic of German-Jewish demography was constant and thoroughgoing change. German Jews' principal traits in the twentieth century differ quite strikingly from those of the early nineteenth century. A summary of the main attributes of German-Jewish population history will clarify this seemingly contradictory picture of concurrent continuity and profound change.

German Jewry possessed certain characteristics in 1815 that seem to influence all later developments. Historically, German Jewry consisted of two separate geographic centers; one of which was a heavy population in the formerly Polish territories of West Prussia and Posen that spilled over into bordering East German provinces, especially Silesia. Living mainly in cities and market towns, Jews here were often concentrated in large communities of at least 500 Jewish inhabitants and sometimes even made up the majority of their town's population. The other center was in southern and western Germany, especially in the valleys of the Main and the middle Rhine. With a few notable exceptions, the major cities of southern and western Germany excluded Jews in to the nineteenth century. This meant that most Jews in these regions lived in villages and small towns, often in rather small communities. Between the two centers of German-Jewish concentration there was a large area on both sides of the Elbe River where the Jewish population consisted of large urban agglomerations that were widely scattered over regions that had few Jewish inhabitants. Given this large geographical gap in the center of Germany, Jewish customs and folk culture in northeastern Germany and southwestern Germany differed in many crucial details. This is best exemplified by the liturgical difference between the use of *Minhag Ashkenaz* (the Ashkenazi or German rite) west of the Elbe and that of *Minhag Polin* (the Polish rite) to the east.

The central region, where Jewish population was initially very sparse, was also the location of many of Germany's major cities such as Berlin, Hamburg, Leipzig, and Dresden, which eventually became large centers of Jewish life. In contrast to the vigorous growth of these urban Jewish communities, the central German countryside remained largely devoid of Jews. Small-town Jewry, often a pillar of Jewish tradition, remained concentrated in the southwest and the northeast.

German Jewry in 1815 had additional characteristics that carried over into the following century. Jewish families stood out from the rest of the German population in at least three ways. First, Jews had strikingly lower rates of illegitimacy and infant mortality than did their Christian neighbors. This was due either to the influence of Jewish religious traditions or to the bourgeois occupational and social structure of the Jewish community. Both of these remained noticeable characteristics throughout modern German-Jewish history. Late marriage was another trait of early nineteenth-century German Jews that appears to have endured despite later changes. German Jews tended to marry even later than the rest of the German population, which itself shared the West European pattern of marrying late. A third stable characteristic of German Jewry from Emancipation onward was differential residential density within major cities. Jews' degree of concentration in specific neighborhoods remained consistently higher than the urban concentration of adherents to other faiths in Germany.

In contrast to these elements of continuity in German-Jewish life, its demography was characterized by overwhelming change in many ways. In 1815, German Jews lived primarily in small towns and villages; fewer than fifteen percent dwelled in cities with over 20,000 inhabitants. In the mid-nineteenth century, however, German Jewry began urbanizing rapidly. The percentage of German Jews in cities over 20,000 increased from 29.6 percent in 1871 to 59.3 percent in 1900, and to 79.2 percent in 1925. A much larger percentage of the general German population remained in villages and small towns. Concurrently, German Jewry made a "demographic transition" to modernity decades ahead of the rest of the population. The transition was characterized by a sharp decline in fertility, a substantial decline in mortality—especially infant mortality—and the emergence of the "one- and two-child system" of family size. By using birth control and the tools of modern medicine, German Jews were pioneers in bringing the natural processes of birth and death under rational control. After World War I, German Jews showed signs of going through the "second demographic transition" that did not hit most of the rest of the West European population until the very end of the twentieth century. Here the Jewish population became noticeably more aged and much less prolific than before, with deaths far outnumbering births. Indeed, by the last years of the Weimar Republic, German Jews were no longer having enough children to compensate for deaths in the community. This prompted many Jewish observers to fear that German Jewry might disappear as a result of insufficient fertility. Other considerable changes in German Jewry included a heavy wave of emigration, mainly to the United States between 1840 and 1880, and a wave of immigration from Eastern Europe from 1880 to the 1920s. Though the latter process involved smaller numbers than the earlier emigration, it had a greater impact both Jewish and non-Jewish observers' consciousness and aroused far more opposition.

Both the characteristics of massive change and those that showed remarkable continuity revealed considerable similarities and differences between German Jews and German. Jews resembled non-Jews by starting the nineteenth century as an overwhelmingly small-town and village population as well as by marrying no earlier than their late twenties. Although they shared urbanization and fertility decline with Germany's general population, they underwent these processes much earlier, with greater geographical uniformity, and more extensively. Their consistently lower rates of out-of-wedlock births and infant mortality suggest different traditions concerning child raising and premarital sex. The main period of Jewish emigration to America also coincided with the largest surge of Christian emigration; even the regional origins of most emigrants changed in parallel patterns among both the minority and the majority groups. Jews, however, were heavily overrepresented among the emigrants and were even more so among both immigrants to Germany and resident non-citizens in the period from 1880 to 1933.

Many of German Jews' demographic characteristics made them pioneers within the German population in a similar manner to their seemingly greater modernity in economic development, education, and cultural innovation. While some demographic characteristics like low illegitimacy may be linked to the strength of Jewish cultural traditions, others such as birth control and late marriage clashed with Jewish religious heritage. The extent to which Jewish demographic traits can be attributed either to Jewish heritage or to greater secularization requires further inquiry and analysis. Under the new post-Emancipation conditions, some characteristics of Jewish life prior to Emancipation gave Jews a head start on the road to modernity as defined by the majority society. These include concentration in commercial occupations, a more urban lifestyle, lack of an agrarian tradition, and a strong emphasis on formal learning (at least for men). In contrast to these traditional elements, adjusting to citizenship requirements, integrating into German cultural life, as well as the opportunities offered by the Industrial Revolution each drove German Jews to break with the Jewish traditional way of life to a greater extent than they impelled non-Jews to dispense with Christian traditions. Thus, German Jewry's demographic distinctiveness during this period was the result of a combination of traditional tendencies, secularization, and the peculiar position of Jews in German society.

Although government policies and changing political conditions influenced German demographic traits at large,[1] German-Jewish demographic behavior

---

1 Knodel, *Decline*, 57–58, 71, 76, 249. Here Knodel discusses restrictions on marriage for the general population of Germany before the 1870s and its effect on marriage rates and illegitimacy. See also John Knodel, *Demographic Behavior in the Past: A Study of Fourteen German Village Populations in the Eighteenth and Nineteenth Centuries* (Cambridge: Cambridge University Press, 1988), 124–125, 195; and John Knodel, "Law, Marriage and Illegitimacy in Nineteenth-Century Germany," *Population Studies* 20 (March 1967): 279–294. Many other writers make passing mention of legal marriage restricions but not all agree they were the main cause of illegitimacy in South German states.

was even more susceptible to the influence of changing political conditions. The geographic distribution of Jewish residence in Germany in the first half of the nineteenth century was largely the result of multiple German states' widely differing eighteenth-century policies on allowing, limiting, or forbidding Jewish residence. Changing government positions toward Jews also influenced some migration patterns in the middle of the nineteenth century. Pressure from early nineteenth-century governments to turn from commerce toward crafts and political restrictions that lingered into the 1860s were the two main factors that induced Jews to emigrate from Germany in larger numbers than their proportion in the population warranted. The concurrent repeal of residence restrictions and the acceleration of the Industrial Revolution triggered a disproportionate Jewish rush to the cities between 1840 and 1914. Both the persecution of Jews in Eastern Europe and the pressures of a changing economy generated a huge wave of westward migration that carried some of its participants to Germany, especially after 1880. As this occurred, both governmental and popular opposition to the immigration of these so-called *Ostjuden* limited the numbers of immigrants to Germany, led to the expulsion of some, and kept immigrants from Russia a minority within the Jewish immigrant community. Government crackdowns in the late nineteenth century prevented the number of immigrants residing in the eastern provinces of Prussia from growing beyond a small minority. Antisemitic hostility to immigrants in Bavaria after World War I also led to a steep decrease in their numbers in that state between the 1910 and 1933 censuses.

The Jewish poulation's extraordinary sensitivity to political changes was also evident in familial behavior. The number of Jewish marriages fluctuated much more sharply than German marriages at large after 1914. This variation in Jewish marriage patterns was characterized by a steeper decrease at the outbreak of the First World War, a more powerful marriage boom after the war, and a much greater decline in both marriages and births among Jews than among the overall German population after 1923. The downturn in marriages may have been related to the devastating effects that Weimar-era hyperinflation had on Jewish dowry funds. The even sharper decrease in births may be attributed in part to a reluctance to bring children into a world of increased antisemitism and decreased economic opportunity in the late 1920s and early 1930s. The overwhelming wave of Jewish emigration from Germany that began in 1933 was, of course, the most obvious instance of political change precipitating demographic change.

During the period under consideration, Germany was a country of extraordinary economic, cultural, and demographic diversity. Significant differences existed among regions and between the urban and rural sectors within both its Jewish and non-Jewish populations. However, German Jews exhibited less internal geographical differentiation than did Germans as a whole, and the extent of these differences weakened over time. This is best illustrated by the spread of birth control among the Jewish and the general population. In the general population, urbanites almost always preceded rural inhabitants in restricting births and showed consistently lower fertility rates. Although urban birth rates tended to decline among Jews earlier and more rapidly as well, the differences were far smaller and generally decreased as the transition proceeded. This phenomenon is even clearer when considering regional differences. Whereas changes in fertility rates widened among the German population and the first noticeable declines varied by more than three decades,[2] among Jews, almost all regions declined at approximately the same time (the late 1870s through the late 1880s) and interregional differences lessened. There was also a similar tendency toward regional uniformity in the decline of infant mortality. While regional differences in intermarriage rates remained noticeable from the 1870s to the 1920s, they did narrow over time. The sharp fluctuations in Jewish marriage and birth rates in the 1920s appear to have been fairly uniform across the various German regions. Despite perceptible regional differences in degree, urbanization was stronger among Jews than among non-Jews almost everywhere in Germany.

Demographic developments within German Jewry often took place under the anxious scrutiny of both Jewish and non-Jewish publics. Many German governments's policies on Jews in the eighteenth century, as well as some in the nineteenth, were based on fears of an increase in Jewish population. Frederick II (1740–1786) of Prussia severely restricted Jews' right to marry, allowed some categories of Jews to settle only one or two children, and forbade other classes of Jews to marry off and settle any of their children in Prussia. Prussia, as well as many other German states, carefully maintained lists of Jewish families and struggled, often unsuccessfully, to prevent an increase in the number of families living in their cities. The Bavarian regulations of 1813–1861 essentially imposed the same policies as in Prusisa. As the prospect of the repeal of anti-Jewish restrictions loomed in the early nineteenth century, many non-Jewish officials and writers expressed their fear of a Jewish population explosion that would eventually leave non-Jews outnumbered, at least at the local level.[3] Although

---

2 Knodel, *Decline*, 62, gives the years in which the marital fertility index (Ig) declined by ten percent from its high point in the various regions of Germany. The dates range from 1879 in Bremen to 1912 in Oppeln District, with 1895 for Germany on average.
3 One example is given by Jeggle, *Judendörfer in Württemberg*, 82–86.

Jewish emigration and declining birth rates disproved this particular fear, new ones developed in its place. Non-Jews' concern about Jewish immigration from Eastern Europe was disproportionate considering the actual relatively modest scale of such immigration.[4]

The rising rate of intermarriage between Jews and non-Jews in Germany after 1870 sparked a new set of fears. In this case, the trend was equally upsetting to both many Gentiles and many Jews. Jewish analysts worried about Jewish population decline through what they saw as defections from Judaism: intermarriage, conversion, and withdrawal from the Jewish community. Many right-wing Germans, on the other hand, saw intermarriage and conversion as vehicles for tainting German society with Semitic blood and the corruption of its so-called "Aryan" purity. Among both Jewish leaders and German antisemites, these fears led to an exaggerated view of intermarriage and conversion's influence. Conversion to Christianity, though not intermarriage or formal withdrawal from the Jewish community, actually declined in the 1920s. The steep decrease in Jewish births in the late 1920s was almost just as effective in reducing the number of German Jews as were conversions to Christianity or intermarriages.[5]

---

4 Expressions of fears of the "invasion" of Jewish immigrants from Eastern Europe to Germany were especially marked in the 1880s and from the end of World War I through much of the 1920s. The actual numbers of Jewish immigrants from Eastern Europe, at least as shown by official figures, was always much lower than those feared by antisemites, who also did not take into account Jewish emigration from Germany and the decreasing proportion of the German population that was Jewish. Schmelz's calculation of Jewish migration in Prussia between 1871 and 1933 (from his handwritten table labelled Folder 8, "Migration balances") shows a net out-migration of 74,769 Jews between 1871 and 1895. Excluding the provinces lost after World War I there were 20,313 and then a net in-migration of 35,640 within the postwar boundaries from 1896 to 1925, and a renewed out-migration of 40,710 between 1925 and 1933. Silbergleit looked at a longer period of time and calculated a net Jewish in-migration of 10,092 between 1819 and 1840, a net out-migration of 21,606 between 1840 and 1864, a continued out-migration of 28,940 between 1875 and 1895, and a net in-migration of 16,545 in 1895–1910 (Silbergleit, *Die Bevölkerungs- und Berufsverhältnisse*, 15*). During the 1880s, there was much published debate about the extent of Jewish immigrant especially between Neumann and Treitschke. We do not know if there were in fact many more uncounted Jewish immigrants in Germany in the years immediately after World War I, but if there were, they mostly left the country before the first postwar census of Jews in 1925. In 1933, there were only 73,693 Jews in Germany who were either born abroad or in an unknown place. This constituted barely one in every 1,000 residents of Germany (1933 census, 5/50). Even artificially inflating the figures by including the German-born non-citizen children of immigrants, as did the census of 1933, still left only 115,005 *zugewanderte*, hardly an overwhelming proportion of the German population. *Zugewanderte* Jews never made up more than 1.2 percent of the total city population in any German major city, and only in Leipzig, Berlin and Frankfurt were they more than one percent of the population.

5 If we look at date from Prussia between 1925 and 1932, we find 11,019 fewer Jewish births than would have been expected had the number of births remained at the 1925 level. In the

The actual percentage of "Aryan" Germans who diluted German "racial purity" by marrying Jews never exceeded 0.15 percent of all Germans who married.[6] Many Nazis who had expected the number of persons of mixed ancestry to exceed the number of Jews by religion were surprised when the "racial" census of May 1939 counted only 71,126 "half-Jews" and 41,456 "quarter-Jews" in Greater Germany as against 330,539 "Jews by race," of whom 297,407 were also Jews by religion.[7]

Whereas some Jewish criticism of intermarriage, conversion, illegitimacy, birth control, divorce, and other unwelcome demographic trends had a moralistic or religious tone in the nineteenth century, twentieth-century Jewish sociologists such as Theilhaber and Ruppin saw them in more "scientific" or biological terms. For them, children born out of wedlock to Jewish women were an addition to the Jewish people whereas intermarriage was harmful to Jewish survival due to the low fertility rate among those who intermarried.

The demographic trends among German Jews after World War I often seem to foreshadow aspects of the European "second demographic transition" in the late twentieth century. German Jewry's low fertility, rapid aging, and rising mortality in the 1920s and early 1930s was highly alarming for many Jewish analysts. American Jews developed somewhat similar fears of Jewish demographic disaster in the 1990s. One cannot tell, however, if the worrisome demographic developments of the late Weimar-Republic era would have persisted afterward, dooming German Jewry to contraction by natural means. Nazi policies, which first led to mass emigration, and then the extermination of those who remained later on, did not just halt the natural German-Jewish demographic developments; they brought them to a violent end. How they would have continued without this tragic denouement will never be known.

---

same period there were 11,926 Jewish-Gentile intermarriages in all of Germany and around 1,600 conversions of Jews to Protestantism and 1,118 conversions in Prussia alone. Between 1901 and 1909, intermarriages in Prussia were about 75 percent of all intermarriages in Germany. Accordingly, there were approximately 8,950 intermarriages in Prussia between 1925 and 1932 and the conversion plus intermarriage numbers about equaled the shortfall in Jewish births.

6   See the discussion at the end of chapter 6 including footnote 214 and the sources given.
7   The terminology used in the census was *Jüdische Mischlinge 1. Grades* for "half-Jews," *Jüdische Mischlinge 2. Grades* for "quarter-Jews," *Juden* for "Jews by race," and *Glaubensjuden* for Jews by religion. Many historians question the low figures for "half-Jews" and "quarter-Jews" in the census, but there are many reasons to accept them as relatively accurate.

Bibliography

Primary Literature

Allgemeine Zeitung des Judenthums 2/97. August 14, 1838.
"Austritt vom und Uebertritte zum Judentum im Jahre 1904." *ZDSJ* (1906): 176.
Bauer, Lothar. "Schicksal in Zahlen: Die Juden in der Volkszählung 1933." *Der Morgen* 10, no. 9 (1934–1935): 403–409.
Bericht über die finanziellen Verhältnissen der Deutsch-Israelitischen Gemeinde in Hamburg. Hamburg, 1849.
"Die Bewegung der Geburten im Königreich Bayern 1908 und 1909 mit Rückblick bis 1875." *ZDSJ* (1911): 152.
Bleich, Eduard, ed. "Uebersicht sämmtlicher Städte des Preussischen Staates in welchen nach der Zählung zu ende 1843 einhundert Juden und darüber wohnen." In *Der erste vereinigte Landtag in Berlin 1847*, vol. 1, 323–326.
Bosse, Friedrich. *Die Verbreitung der Juden im deutschen Reiche auf Grundlage der Volkszählung vom 1. Dezember 1880.* Berlin, 1885.
Brämer, K. "Das neue deutsche Reichsland Elsass mit Deutsch-Lothringen," *Zeitschrift des königlich Preussischen Statistischen Bureaus* 11, nos. 1–2 (1871): 23–24.

Cohen, Arthur. "Die jüdischen Bevölkerung in München im Jahre 1910 mit besonderer Berücksichtigung der Gebürtigkeit." *ZDSJ* (1919): 121–130.

de le Roi, Johannes Friedrich Alexander. *Judentaufen im 19. Jahrhundert: Ein statistischer Versuch*. Leipzig, 1899.

"Eheschliessungen im Jahre 1903." *ZDSJ* 1, no. 1 (1905).

"Eheschliessungen im Jahre 1904." *ZDSJ* 2 (1906).

"Die Eheschliessungen, Geburten und Sterbefälle im Deutschen Reich im Jahre 1887." *Monatshefte zur Statistik des Deutschen Reichs* 12 (December 1888): 2–20.

Eschelbacher, Klara. "Die ostjüdische Einwanderungsbevölkerung der Stadt Berlin." *ZDSJ* (1920): 1–24.

"Die Fremdbürtigen im preussischen Staate." *Zeitschrift des Königlichen Preussischen Statistischen Bureaus* 20 (1880).

"Die Gestaltung der jüdischen Sterblichkeit im Staate Hamburg 1923/27." *ZDSJ* (1930).

Goldscheider, Anton. "Die Entwicklung der jüdischen Bevölkerung in Preussen im 19. Jahrhundert mit besonderer Berücksichtigung der Zeit von 1816 bis 1875." *ZDSJ* 3 (1907): 70–75.

Hanauer, Wilhelm. "Zur Mortalitätsstatistik der Juden." *ZDSJ* (1919): 16–17.

Handbuch der jüdischen Gemeindeverwaltung (1911)

Heppner, Aron, and Isak Herzberg. *Aus Vergangenheit und Gegenwart der Juden und der jüdischen Gemeinden in den Posener Landen*. Koschmin-Bromberg, 1909.

Hoffmann, Johann Gottfried. "Neueste Nachrichten von der Bevölkerung des preußischen Staates." *Allgemeine Preußische Staatszeitung* 229 (1838).

———. "Übersicht der Anzahl und Vertheilung der Juden im Preussischen Staate nach einer Vergleichung der Zählungen zu Ende der Jahre 1840 und 1822." *Allgemeine Preussische Staatszeitung* 141 (1842).

"Die jüdische Bevölkerung des Freistaates und der Stadt Danzig." *ZDSJ* (1927).

Knöpfel, Ludwig. "Stand und Bewegung der jüdischen Bevölkerung im Grossherzogtum Hessen während des 19. Jahrhunderts." *ZDSJ* (1906).

———. "Die gegenwärtige Sterblichkeit der jüdischen und christlichen Bevölkerung des Grossherzogtums Hessen nach Gechlecht, Alter und Todesursache." *ZDSJ* (1914).

———. "Geburten und Sterbefälle im Grossherzogum Hessen im Jahre 1910 mit Rückblick." *ZDSJ* (1912).

———. "Die jüdische Bevölkerung vom Grossherzogtum Hessen nach den Ergebnissen der Volkszählung vom 1. Dezember 1910." *ZDSJ* (1912).
Loewe, Heinrich. "Die Zahl der Juden in Pommern." *ZDSJ* (1911).
———. "Die Juden Preussens im Jahre 1817." *ZDSJ* (1911).
Nathanson, Hugo. "Die unehelichen Geburten bei den Juden." *ZDSJ* (1910).
Neumann, Salomon. *Die Fabel von der jüdischen Masseneinwanderung. Ein Kapitel aus der preussischen Statistik*. Berlin, 1881.
———. *Zur Statistik der Juden in Preussen von 1816 bis 1880*. 2nd ed. Berlin, 1884.
Nicolai, Friedrich. *Beschreibung der königlichen Residenzstädte Berlin und Potsdam*. Berlin, 1786.
Philippsthal, Herbert. "Die Bewegung der Juden in Deutschland." *ZDSJ* (1924).
———. "Die jüdische Bevölkerung in Leipzig." *Gemeindeblatt der Israelitischen Religionsgemeinde zu Leipzig* 7, nos. 2–3 (1931).
Pinthus, Alexander. "Die Wohnverhältnisse der Juden in Köln." *ZDSJ* (1927).
Ruppin, Arthur. *Die Juden der Gegenwart: Eine sozialwissensschaftliche Studie*. Cologne and Leipzig: Jüdischer Verlag, 1911.
———. *Die Soziologie der Juden*. Berlin: Jüdischer Verlag, 1930.
———. "Der Verlust des Judentums durch Taufe und Austritt." *ZDSJ* (1930).
Samter, Nathan. *Judentaufen im neunzehnten Jahrhundert mit besonderer Berücksichtigung Preussens*. Berlin, 1906.
Schwarz, Ph. "Nachwuchsverhältnisse der jüdischen Familien in Bayern." *Bayerische Israelitische Gemeindezeitung* (April 1, 1930).
Segall, Jacob. "Die Entwicklung der jüdischen Bevölkerung in Württemberg von 1820 bis 1910." *ZDSJ* (1913).
———. "Die Juden im Königreich Sachsen von 1832 bis 1910." *ZDSJ* (1914).
———. "Die Juden in Gross-Berlin." *ZDSJ* (1914).
———. *Die Entwicklung der jüdischen Bevölkerung in München 1875–1905: Ein Beitrag zur Kommunalstatistik*. Berlin: Bureau für Statistik der Juden, 1910.
Silbergleit, Heinrich. *Die Bevölkerungs- und Berufverhältnisse der Juden im Deutschen Reich*. Vol. 1: *Freistaat Preussen*. Berlin, 1930.
Theilhaber, Felix. "Deutsche Juden im Ausland und ausländische Juden im Deutschen Reich." *ZDSJ* (December 1905).
———. *Der Untergang der deutschen Juden: Eine volkswirtschaftliche Studie*. Munich, 1911.
———. "Bevölkerungsvorgänge bei der Berliner Juden." *ZDSJ* (1926).
Thon, J. "Die Bewegung der jüdischen Bevökerung in Bayern seit dem Jahre 1876." *ZDSJ* (August 1905).

von Tyszka, Carl. "Die jüdischen Bevölkerung von München nach dem Stande vom 1. Dezember 1905." *ZDSJ* (1907).

———. "Alter und Familienstand der Juden und Christen in München im Jahre 1900." *ZDSJ* (1907).

"Uebersicht über die jüdische Bevölkerung in Württembergs Städten mit mehr als 2000 Einwohner nach der Aufnahme vom 3. Dez. 1864." *Württ. Jahrbücher für Statistik und Landeskunde* (1864).

"Uebertritte der Juden zur evangelischen Landeskirche von 1901 bis 1918." *ZDSJ* (1924).

"Uebertritte von Juden zur evangelischen Landeskirche 1919–1924." *ZDSJ* (1927).

Unna, Josef. "Statistik der Frankfurter Juden bis zum Jahre 1866: Ein Versuch historischer Bevölkerungsstatistik." *ZDSJ* 1–3 (1926).

Weigart, Dora. "Die jüdische Bevölkerung in Hamburg." *ZDSJ* (1919).

"Die Zahl der Juden in Leipzig." *ZDSJ* 2 (1906).

Secondary Literature

Adam, Jacob. *Zeit zur Abreise: Lebensbericht eines judischen Handlers aus der Emanzipationszeit.* Edited by Jorg H. Fehrs und Margret Heitmann. Hildesheim and New York: Olms, 1993.

Asaria, Zvi. *Die Juden in Köln. Von den alten Zeiten bis zur Gegenwart.* Cologne: J. P. Bachem, 1959.

Barkai, Avraham. *Branching Out: German-Jewish Immigration to the United States 1820–1914.* New York: Holmes and Meier, 1994.

———. "German Jewish Migrations in the Nineteenth Century, 1830–1910." *YLBI* 30 (1985): 301–318.

Bayer, Tilde. *Minderheit im städtischen Raum. Sozialgeschichte der Juden in Mannheim während der 1. Hälfte des 19.Jahrhunderts.* Stuttgart: Jan Thorbecke, 2001.

Behr, Stefan. *Der Bevölkerungsrückgang der deutschen Juden.* Frankfurt, 1932.

Biale, David. *Eros and the Jews. From Biblical Israel to Contemporary America.* Berkeley and Los Angeles: University of California Press, 1997.

Blau, Bruno. *Die Entwicklung der jüdischen Bevölkerung in Deutschland von 1800 bis 1945.* Manuscript in Leo Baeck Institute archives, New York.

Brinkmann, Tobias. *Von der Gemeinde zur "Community": Jüdische Einwanderer in Chicago 1840–1900.* Osnabrück: Rasch, 2002.

Brown, John C., and Timothy W. Guinnane. "The Fertility Transition in Bavaria." Economic Growth Center Discussion Paper 821, April 2001.

Cahnman, Werner J. "The Decline of the Munich Jewish Community, 1933–38." *Jewish Social Studies* 3 (1941): 285–300.

Carlebach, Elisheva. *Divided Souls: Converts from Judaism in Germany, 1500–1750.* New Haven and London: Yale University Press, 2001.

Caron, Vicki. "The Social and Religious Transformation of Alsace-Lorraine Jewry, 1871–1914." *YLBI* 30 (1985): 319–336.

Doebke, Matthias. "Child Mortality and Fertility Decline: Does the Barro-Becker Model Fit the Facts?" *Journal of Population Economics* 18 (2005): 337–366.

Ellermeyer, Jürgen. "Schranken der Freien Reichsstadt. Gegen Grundeigentum und Wohnungswahl der Hamburger Juden bis ins Zeitalter der Aufklärung." In *Die Hamburger Juden in der Emanzipationsphase (1780–1870)*, edited by Peter Freimark and Arno Herzig. Hamburg: Wallstein, 1989.

Engelman, Uriah Zevi. "Intermarriage among Jews in Germany, U.S.S.R., and Switzerland." *Jewish Social Studies* 2 (1940): 157–178.

Freimark, Peter. *Juden in Preussen, Juden in Hamburg.* Hamburg: Institut für die Geschichte der deutschen Juden, 1983.

Friedrich, Martin. *Zwischen Abwehr und Bekehrung: Die Stellung der deutschen evangelischen Theologie zum Judentum im 17. Jahrhundert.* Tübingen: J. C. B. Mohr, 1988.

Gabor, Oded. "The Demographic Transition and the Emergence of Sustained Economic Growth." *Journal of the European Economic Association* 3 (2005): 494–504.

Galloway, Patrick R., E. A. Hammel, and R. D. Lee. "Final Report on the Project: Economic and Cultural factors in Demographic Behavior." R01 HD25841, unpublished manuscript.

Goldstein, Alice. "Village Jews in Germany: Nonnenweier 1800–1931." In *Modern Jewish Fertility*, edited by Paul Ritterband. Leiden: Brill, 1981.

———. "Aspects of Change in a Nineteenth-Century German Village." *Journal of Family History* 9 (Summer 1984).

———. "The Urbanization of Jews in Baden, Germany 1825–1925." *Papers in Jewish Demography* (1981). Reprinted in *Social Science History* 8, no. 1 (Winter 1984): 43–66.

Grossman, Abraham. "Nisuei Boser be-Hevrah ha-Yehudit bi-Yemei ha-Benayim ad ha-Meah ha-Shlosh-Esre." *Peamim* 45 (1990): 108–125.

Grubel, Fred, and Frank Mecklenburg. "Leipzig: Portrait of a Jewish Community during the First Years of Nazi Germany." *YLBI* 42 (1997): 157–188.

Hajnal, John. "The European Marriage Pattern in Historical Perspective." In *Population in History*, edited by D. V. Glass and D. E. C. Eversley. Chicago: Aldine, 1965.

Harris, James F. *The People Speak! Anti-Semitism and Emancipation in Nineteenth-Century Bavaria*. Ann Arbor: University of Michigan Press, 1994.

Hertz, Deborah. "The Troubling Dialectic between Reform and Conversion in Biedermeier Berlin." In *Towards Normality? Acculturation and Modern German Jewry*, edited by Rainer Liedtke and David Rechter. Tübingen: Mohr Siebeck, 2003.

Herzig, Arno. "Landjuden—Stadtjuden: Die Entwicklung in den preussischen Provinzen Westfalen und Schlesien im 18. und 19. Jahrhundert." In *Jüdisches Leben auf dem Lande: Studien zur deutsch-jüdischen Geschichte*, edited by Monika Richarz and Reinhard Rürup. Tübingen: Mohr Siebeck, 1997.

Hohorst, Gerd, Jürgen Kocka, and Gerhard Albert Ritter. *Sozialgeschichtliches Arbeitsbuch. Vol. 2: Materialen zur Statistik des Kaiserreichs 1870–1914*. Munich: Beck, 1978.

Homeyer, Friedel. *Gestern und Heute: Juden im Landkreis Hannover*. Hannover: Landkreis Hannover, 1984.

Honigmann, Peter. *Die Austritte aus der jüdischen Gemeinde Berlin 1873–1941: Statistische Auswertung und Historische Interpretation*. Frankfurt: Peter Lang, 1988.

Hubbard, William H. *Familiengeschichte: Materialen zur deutschen Famillie seit dem Ende des 18. Jahrhunderts*. Munich: Beck, 1983.

Hyman, Paula. "Jewish Fertility in 19th-Century France." In *Modern Jewish Fertility*, edited by Paul Ritterband. Leiden: Brill, 1981.

Jakob, Reinhard. *Die jüdische Gemeinde in Harburg (1671–1871)*. Nördlingen: Steinmeier, 1988.

Jacobson, Jacob. *Die Judenbürgerbücher der Stadt Berlin 1809–1851*. Berlin: de Gruyter, 1962.

———. *Jüdische Trauungen in Berlin 1759–1813*. Berlin, 1968.

Jeggle, Utz. *Judendörfer in Württemberg*. Tübingen: Tübinger Vereinigung f. Volkskunde e. V., 1969.

Kaplan, Marion, ed. *Geschichte des judischen Alltags in Deutschland: Vom 17. Jahrhundert bis 1945* Munich: Beck, 2003.

Kilian, Hendrikje. *Die jüdische Gemeinde in München 1813–1871.* Munich: Utz, 1989.

Knodel, John. *The Decline of Fertility in Germany 1871–1939.* Princeton: Princeton University Press, 1974.

———. "Law, Marriage and Illegitimacy in Nineteenth-Century Germany." *Population Studies* 20 (March 1967): 279–294.

———. *Demographic Behavior in the Past: A Study of Fourteen German Village Populations in the Eighteenth and Nineteenth Centuries.* Cambridge: Cambridge University Press, 1988.

Kreutzer, Michael. "Über konzentrierte jüdische Nachbarschaften in Prenzlauer Berg 1886–1931: Eine historisch-statistische Beschreibung anhand von Adreßbüchern und Adressenverzeichnissen." In *Leben mit der Erinnerung: Jüdische Geschichte in Prenzlauer Berg.* Berlin: Hentrich, 1997.

Laessig, Simone. *Jüdische Wege ins Bürgertum. Kulturelles Kapital und sozialer Aufstieg im 19. Jahrhundert.* Göttingen: Vandenhoeck & Ruprecht, 2004.

Lowenstein, Steven M. *The Berlin Jewish Community: Enlightenment, Family and Crisis 1770–1830.* New York and Oxford: Oxford University Press, 1994.

———. *The Mechanics of Change: Essays in the Social History of German Jewry.* Atlanta: Scholars Press, 1992.

———. "The Rural Community and the Urbanization of German Jewry." *Central European History* 13 (1980): 218–236.

———. "Changing Housing Conditions in the Nineteenth-Century German Rural Ghetto." In *Jüdische Welten: Juden in Deutschland vom 18. Jahrhundert bis in die Gegenwart,* edited by Marion Kaplan and Beate Meyer. Göttingen: Wallstein, 2005.

———. "Ashkenazic Jewry and the European Marriage Pattern: A Preliminary Study of Jewish marriage Age." *Jewish History* 8, nos. 1–2 (1994) 155–175.

———. "Voluntary and Involuntary Limitation of Fertility in Nineteenth-Century Bavarian Jewry." In *Modern Jewish Fertility,* edited by Paul Ritterband. Leiden: Brill, 1981.

———. "Jewish Intermarriage and Conversion." *Modern Judaism* 25 (2005): 23–61.

Magnus, Shulamit S. *Jewish Emancipation in a German City: Cologne 1798–1871.* Stanford: Stanford University Press, 1997.

Marschalck, Peter. *Deutsche* Überseewanderung *im 19. Jahrhundert: Ein Beitrag zur soziologischen Theorie der Bevölkerung*. Stuttgart: Ernst Klett Verlag, 1973.

Maurer, Trude. *Ostjuden in Deutschland 1918–1933*. Hamburg: H. Christians, 1986.

———. "Migration von Juden—Eine Problemskizze." In *Probleme der Migration und Integration im Preussenland vom Mittelalter bis zum Anfang des 20. Jahrhunderts*, edited by Klaus Militzer. Marburg: Elwert, 2005.

Menes, Abraham. "The Conversion Movement in Prussia during the First Half of the 19th Century." *YIVO Annual of Social Science* 6 (1951): 187–205.

Mostov, Stephen G. "A Sociological Portrait of German Jewish Immigrants in Boston: 1845–1861." *AJS Review* 3 (1978): 121–152.

———. "A 'Jerusalem on the Ohio': The Social and Economic History of Cincinnati's Jewish Community." PhD diss., Brandeis University, Waltham, 1981.

Neubach, Helmut. *Die Ausweisungen von Polen und Juden aus Preussen 1885/86*. Wiesbaden: Harrassowitz, 1967.

Pinkas ha-Kehillot, Germania, Bavaria. Jerusalem: Yad Vashem, 1973.

Pinkas ha-Kehillot, Germania, Hessen-Hessen-Nassau-Frankfurt. Jerusalem: Yad Vashem, 1992.

Pinkas ha-Kehillot, Germania, Württemberg-Hohenzollern-Baden. Jerusalem: Yad Vashem, 1986.

Raphael, Marc Lee. *Jews and Judaism in a Midwestern Community: Columbus, Ohio, 1840–1875*. Columbus: Columbus, Ohio, Historical Society, 1979.

Ritterband, Paul, ed. *Modern Jewish Fertility*. Leiden: Brill, 1981.

Rohrbacher, Stefan. "From Württemberg to America." *American Jewish Archives* 41 (1989): 142–171.

Rosenwaike, Ira. "Characteristics of Baltimore's Jewish Population in a Nineteenth-Century Census." *American Jewish History* 82 (1994): 123–140.

Sauer, Paul. *Die jüdischen Gemeinden in Württemberg und Hohenzollern: Denkmale, Geschichte, Schicksale*. Stuttgart: Kohlhammer, 1966.

Schmelz, Usiel Oskar. *Die jüdische Bevölkerung Hessens von der Mitte des 19. Jahrhunderts bis 1933*. Tübingen: Mohr Siebeck, 1996.

Statistisches Bundesamt. *Bevölkerung und Wirtschaft 1872–1972*. Stuttgart: Kohlhammer, 1972.

Weckbecker, Arno. *Die Judenverfolgung in Heidelberg 1933–1945*. Heidelberg: Müller Juristischer Verlag, 1985.

Wertheimer, Jack. *Unwelcome Strangers: East European Jews in Imperial Germany.* New York and Oxford: Oxford University Press, 1987.

Journals

Allgemeines Kirchenblatt für das evangelische Deutschland (1900–1933).
Beiträge zur Statistik der Freien Stadt Frankfurt 1, no. 1 (1858): 4–5; 1, no. 3 (1861): 31–33.
Beiträge zur Statistik der Stadt Frankfurt am Main (1895).
Charlottenburger Statistik 20 (1907).
"Einige Ergebnisse der Volkszählung in Köln am 16.6. 1933." *Statistisches Jahrbuch der Stadt Köln, Berichtsjahr 1932* (1933): 1–4, Tables 1–3.
Ergebnisse der Volkszählung vom 3ten December 1866: Stand der Bevölkerung (Hamburg, 1867).
Mitteilungen des Statistischen Amtes der Stadt München 24 (1912–1913).
Statistisches Jahrbuch für den Preussischen Staat (1905).
Statistisches Jahrbuch für das Deutsche Reich 1 (1880).
Statistik des deutschen Reichs 401 (1930): *Die Bevölkerung des Deutschen Reichs nach den Ergebnissen der Volkszählung 1925.* Part 2: *Textliche Darstellung der Ergebnisse.*
Statistik des deutschen Reichs 451, no. 5 (1936): *Die Glaubensjuden im Deutschen Reich.*
Statistik der Israelitischen Religionsgemeinschaft Württembergs.
Statistik des Hamburgischen Staats (1873): 32; (1880): 149; (1887, 1894, 1900, 1902).
Statistisches Jahrbuch für das Deutsche Reich (SJDR, 1903): 11–14.
Statistisches Jahrbuch für den Freistaat Preussen (1933).
Vierteljahrshefte zur Statistik des deutschen Reichs 1 (1873).
Vierteljahrshefte zur Statistik des Deutschen Reichs—Ergänzungsheft zu 1916 4 (1918): *Die Deutschen im Ausland und Die Ausländer im Deutschen Reiche.*
"Die Volkszählung vom 1. Dezember 1871." *Beiträge zur Statistik der inneren Verwaltung des Grossherzogthums Baden* (1874).
Zeitschrift für Demographie und Statistik der Juden (ZDSJ).

Schmelz Archival Documents

1. Territorial Printout (in the possession of the author). BENJAMB, GRMPR3, 90/06/06, 12.14.22.
2. Live Births (*"Lebendgeborene Preussen Staat"*), 1840–1933, by individual years and by five-year intervals, for Prussia in general and by Prussian province, distinguishing between in-married and intermarried parents and out-of-wedlock births, also by individual cities and by all cities combined.
3. Deaths (*"Sterbefälle Preussen Staat"*), 1840–1932, handwritten tables for Prussia by individual years and by five-year intervals, for each Prussian province, also divided by the age of death over or under fifteen, and by place of residence, city or countryside).
4. Migration Balances (*Wanderungssaldo*), from Folder 8.
    II 4a7: Absolute Numbers of Jewish Migrants, 1871–1933: JD (*Jahresdurchschnitt*, difference between censuses), NBB (*Natürliche Bevölkerungsbewegung*, natural population movement),WB (*Wanderungsbewegung*, migration movement).
    II 4b7: Migration Balances, 1871–1933 (different areas between censuses).
    II 4b7: Migration Balances, 1849–1871 (different areas by three-year intervals).
5. Size Categories of Jews (*Juden Ortsgrössenklassen*), from Large Folder 6.

Geographic Names in German and English (Alphabetized in German)

Bayern	Bavaria
Braunschweig	Brunswick
Hannover	Hanover
Hessen (Hessen-Darmstadt, Grossherzogtum Hessen, Kurhessen)	Hesse (Hesse-Darmstadt, Grand Duchy of Hesse, Electorate of Hesse)
Hessen-Nassau	Hesse-Nassau
Köln	Cologne
Mittelfranken	Middle Franconia
Mühlhausen	Mulhouse
München	Munich
Niederbayern	Lower Bavaria
Nürnberg	Nuremberg
Oberbayern	Upper Bavaria
Oberfranken	Upper Franconia
Oberpfalz	Upper Palatinate
Oberschlesien	Upper Silesia
Ostpreussen	East Prussia
Pfalz	Palatinate
Pommern	Pomerania

Preussen	Prussia
Rheinprovinz or Rheinland	Rhine Province or Rhineland
Sachsen	Saxony
Schlesien	Silesia
Schwaben	Swabia
Strassburg	Strasbourg
Thüringen	Thuringia
Unterfranken	Lower Franconia
Westfalen	Westphalia
Westpreussen	West Prussia

Throughout this volume I have distinguished between the larger administrative subdivisions, which I have translated as "districts," and the smaller subdivisions, which I translate as "counties." There were approximately 100 districts in Germany, and many more counties. In Prussia in 1925 there were 35 districts (*Regierungsbezirke*) and 539 counties (*Kreise*, divided between 117 city counties, *Stadtkreise*, and 422 *Landkreise*) (Silbergleit, Die Bevölkerungs- und Berufsverhältnisse, 28*–33*).

The German names of districts and counties differed between German states as well as over time. The boundaries of the various counties also changed in a number of German states. The following were the main German official terms for:

District
- Bezirk (Alsace-Lorraine)
- Kreis (Baden, Württemberg)
- Kreisdirektionsbezirk (Kingdom of Saxony)
- Kreishauptmannschaft (Kingdom of Saxony)
- Landdrostei (Kingdom of Hanover)
- Landeskommissärbezirk (Baden)
- Provinz (Hesse-Darmstadt)
- Regierungsbezirk (Prussia, Bavaria)

County
- Amt (Kingdom of Hanover)
- Amtsbezirk (Baden)
- Bezirksamt (Bavaria)
- Kreis (Prussia, Hesse-Darmstadt)
- Landgericht (Bavaria)
- Oberamt (Württemberg)

A Note on Discrepancies

German bureaucracies' reputation as accurate, even pedantic, keepers of statistics and other records was mainly well-deserved. The published censuses, statistical yearbooks, and other statistical materials issues by German central, state and municipal governments can generally be considered accurate and reliable. This was especially true after around the mid-nineteenth century.

Despite this general accuracy, anyone who collects and compares the various reports, censuses, analyses, and scholarly publications soon notices discrepancies between some of the figures presented. Most of these discrepancies are relatively minor, but in a few cases they are substantial. In this volume I have tried to remain aware of and to report discrepancies between the various sources.

In a few cases the original documents contain misprints. This was the case when Bleich, *Die erste vereinigte Landtag*, 322, transposed numbers in the Jewish population for Danzig in 1843 and wrote 4234 when the correct number was almost certainly 2434. Similarly, Silbergleit, *Die Bevölkerungs- und Berufsverhältnisse*, 15*, gave the annual increase in the Jewish population of Prussia from 1831–1834 as 2,043 and from 1834–1837 as 3,373 when the correct figures were 3,043 and 2,373. Schmelz, *Hessen*, 148–150, described two discrepant statistical tables on Jewish gender and age distribution for the year 1925 from the Hesse-Darmstadt archives. He attributed them to different hand counts of the census returns but was unable to decide which of the two was more accurate.

Besides simple errors, there are many reasons for discrepancies between different statistical counts. In records of municipal populations, some took later changes in city territory (annexations) into account, while others did not. Some birth statistics included only live births, while others included stillbirths as well. The same is true of death statistics, which may or may not include the stillborn. Some counts only included the civilian populations, while others included soldiers in garrisons as well.

There were also changes in which individuals were included within the population counted. Some earlier counts included only those with the legal right of residence. Later it became usual to count the *Ortsanwesende Bevölkerung* (population present in the town on the day of the census). Still later, the common practice was to count the *Wohnbevölkerung* (resident population). In this latest method, which may have been closer to the earlier legal resident count, people were counted in the place they regularly resided rather in the places they happened to find themselves on the day of the census. For the Jewish population, which was particularly mobile, this could make a considerable difference for merchants away on business or for emigrants at the harbor waiting to embark on ships for America.

Finally, there was always a certain proportion of the population that evaded the official counts because they were in the country illegally, because they distrusted government officials, or because the government was not well organized enough to count in every corner of the country. This missed population seemed to be especially large in the early post-Napoleonic years when many Jews did not have legal rights. Although logic would lead us to believe that some Jews evaded the census during the years of Nazi persecution, there is internal evidence that their numbers were not very large.

All of these considerations lead us to the conclusion that we are dealing with relatively accurate approximations of the actual demographic facts, rather than a complete presentation of "what actually happened." The statistics that form the basis of this work were certainly more accurate than those of some other countries and certainly closer than the approximations in countries like the United States where there are no official statistics, but we should understand them as having some limitations that we can never overcome.

MAPS

MAP 1/1: Jews as percentage of overall population, 1817

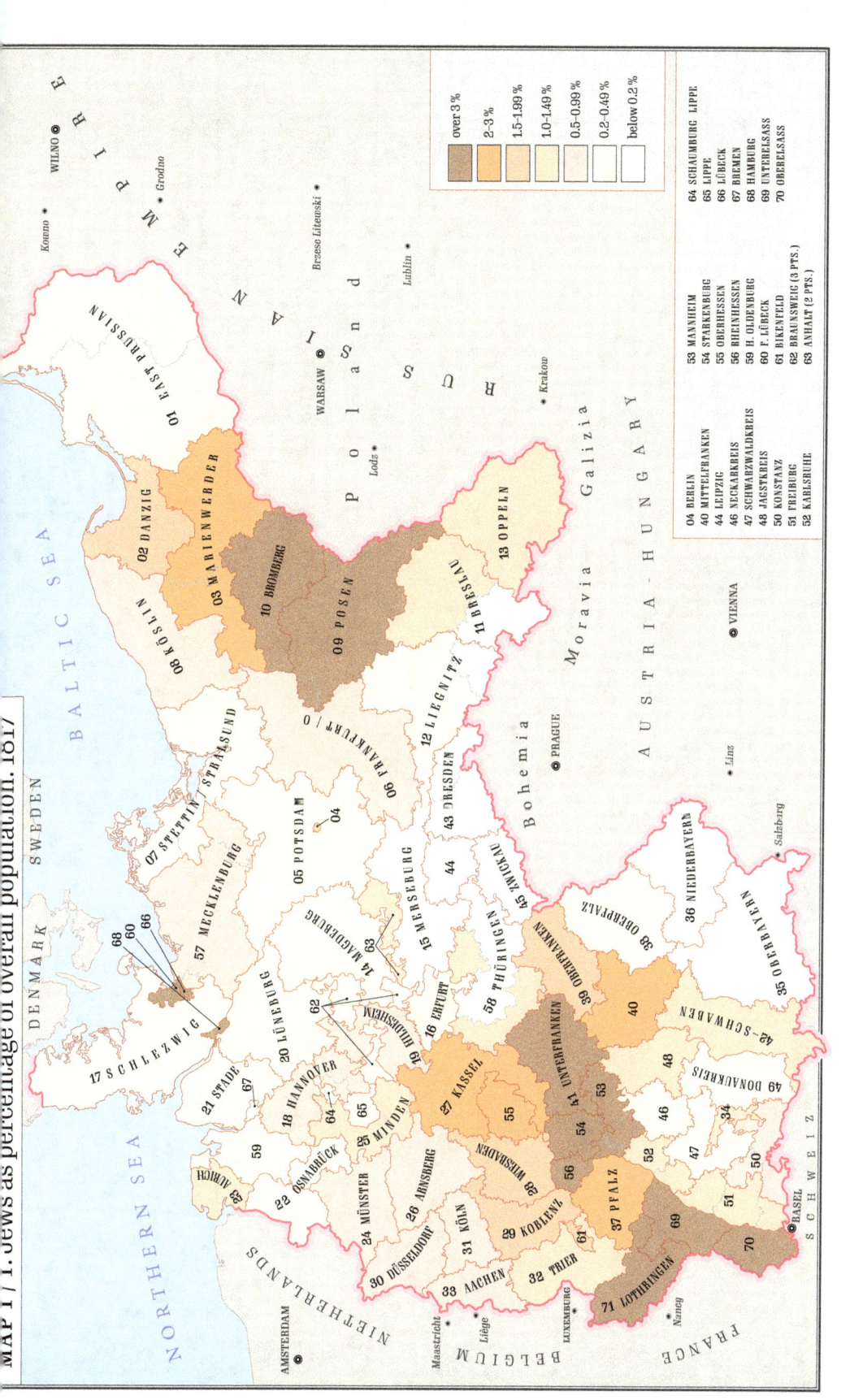

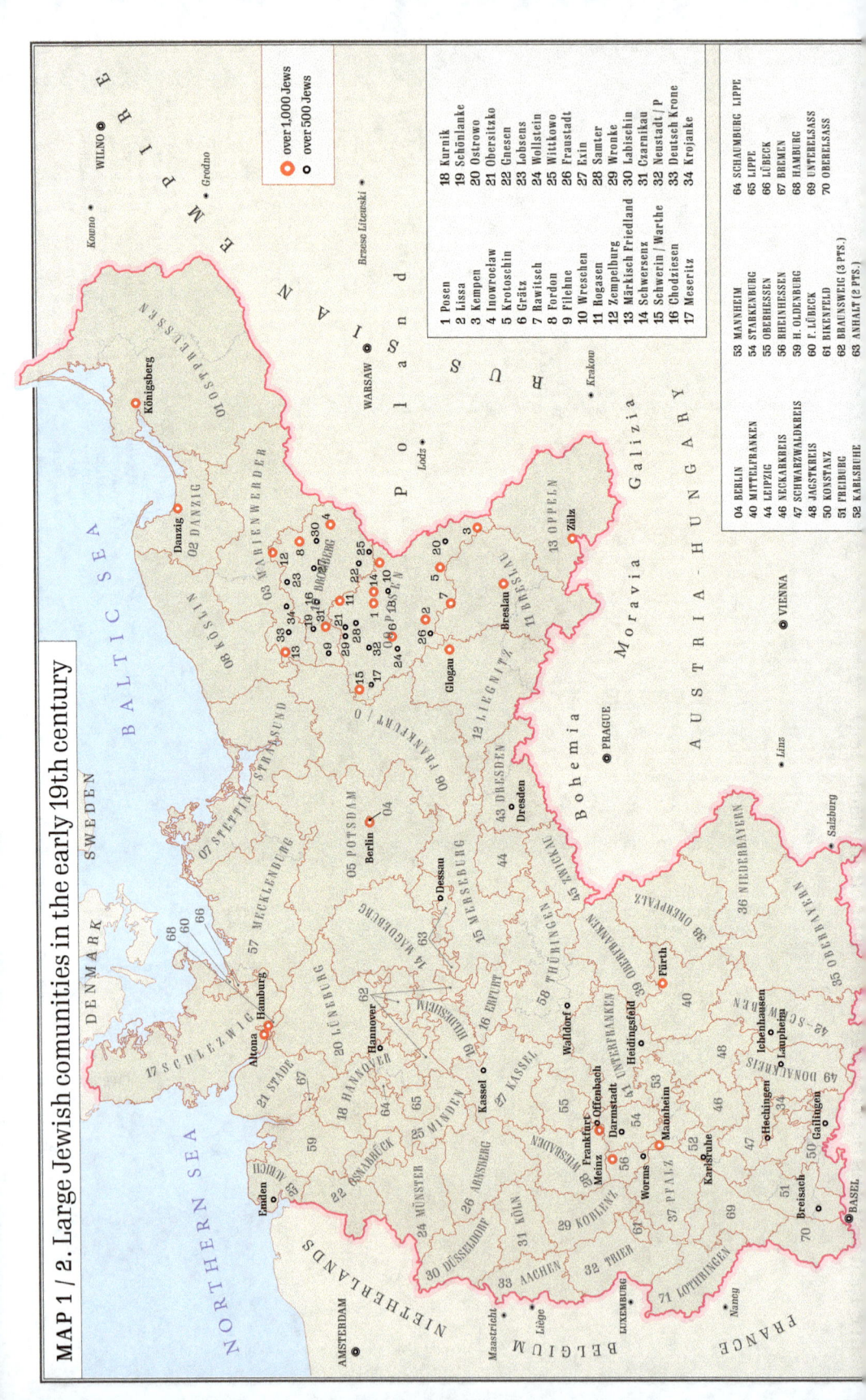

MAP 1 / 2. Large Jewish communities in the early 19th century

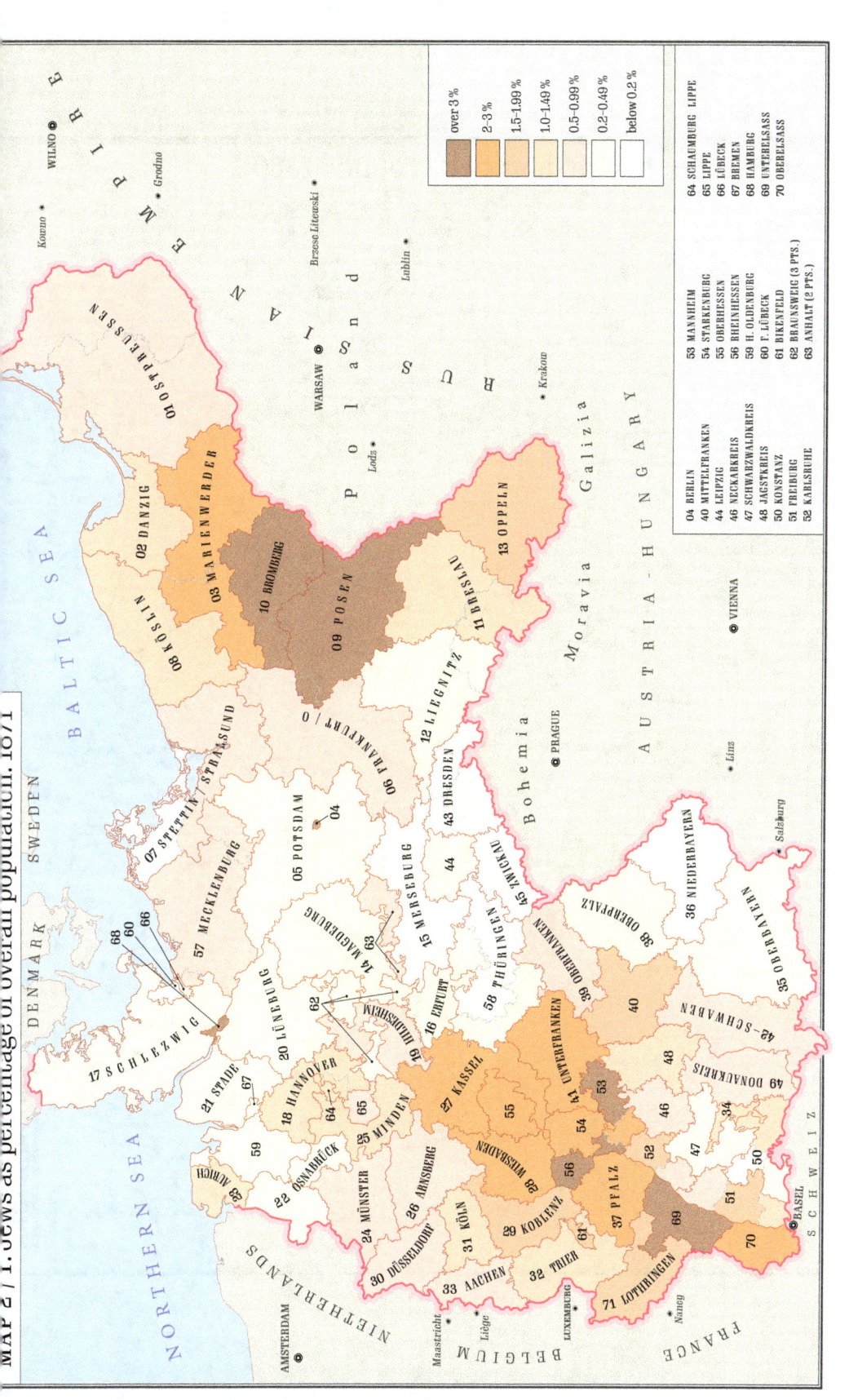

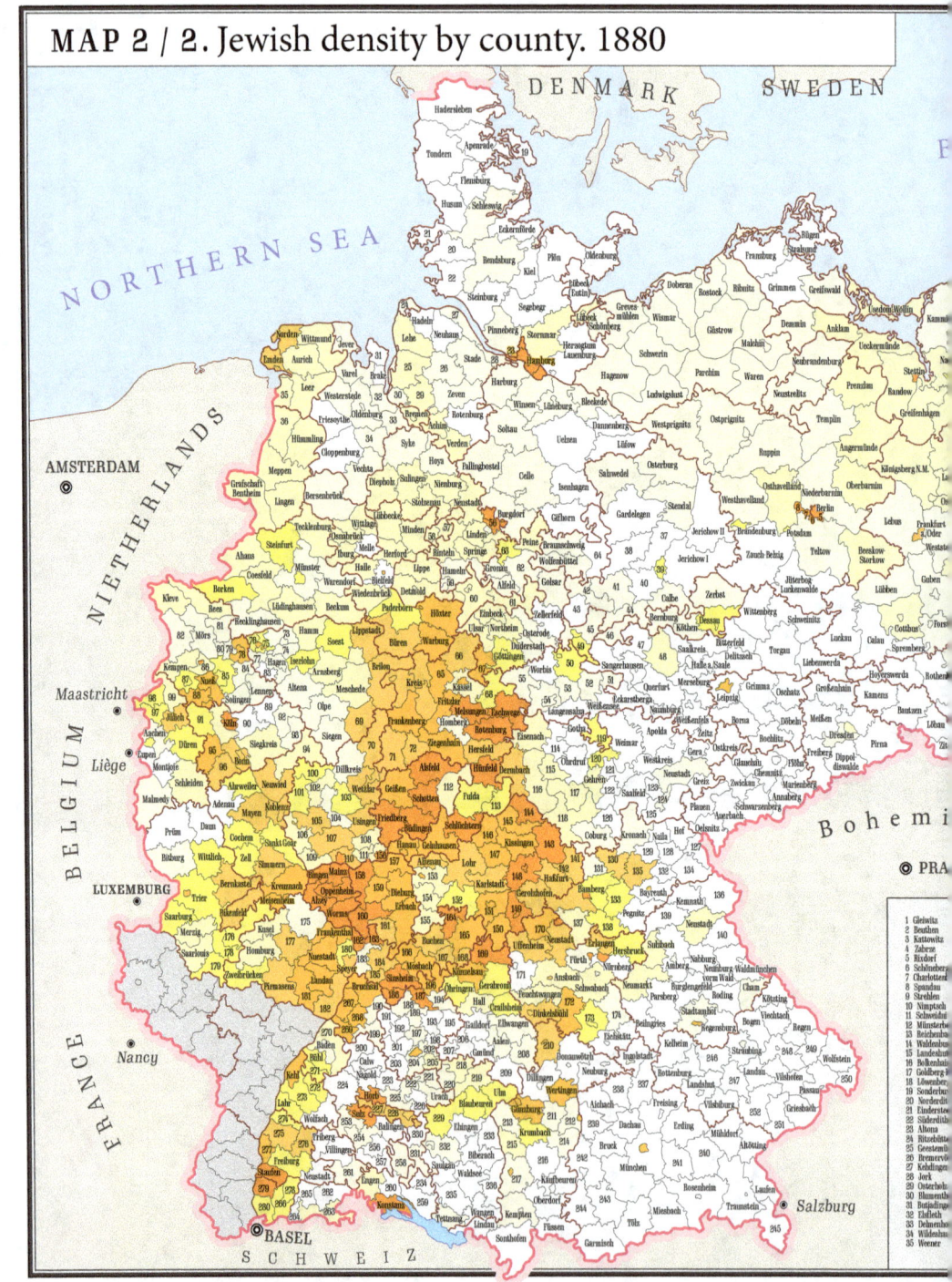

MAP 2 / 2. Jewish density by county. 1880

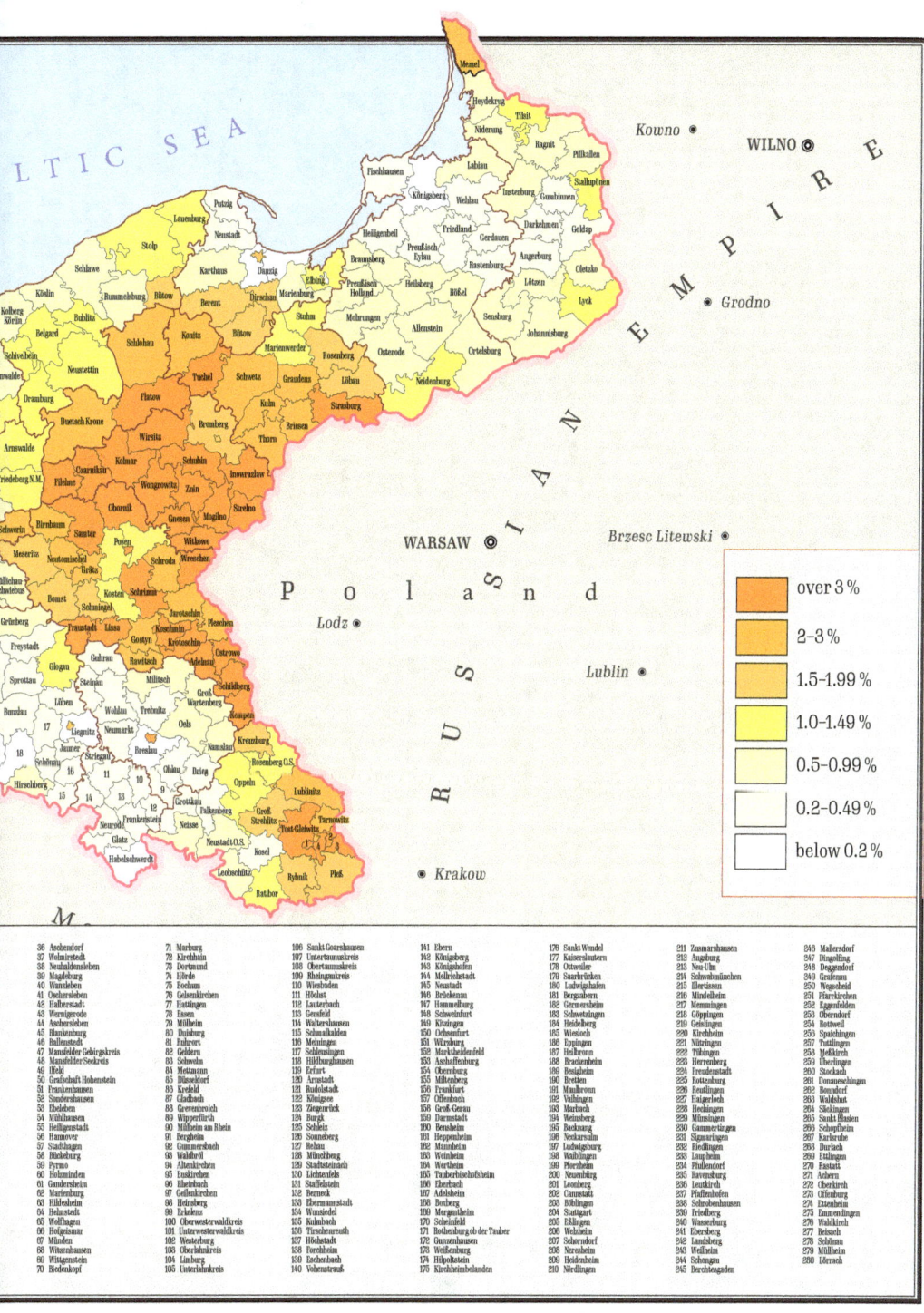

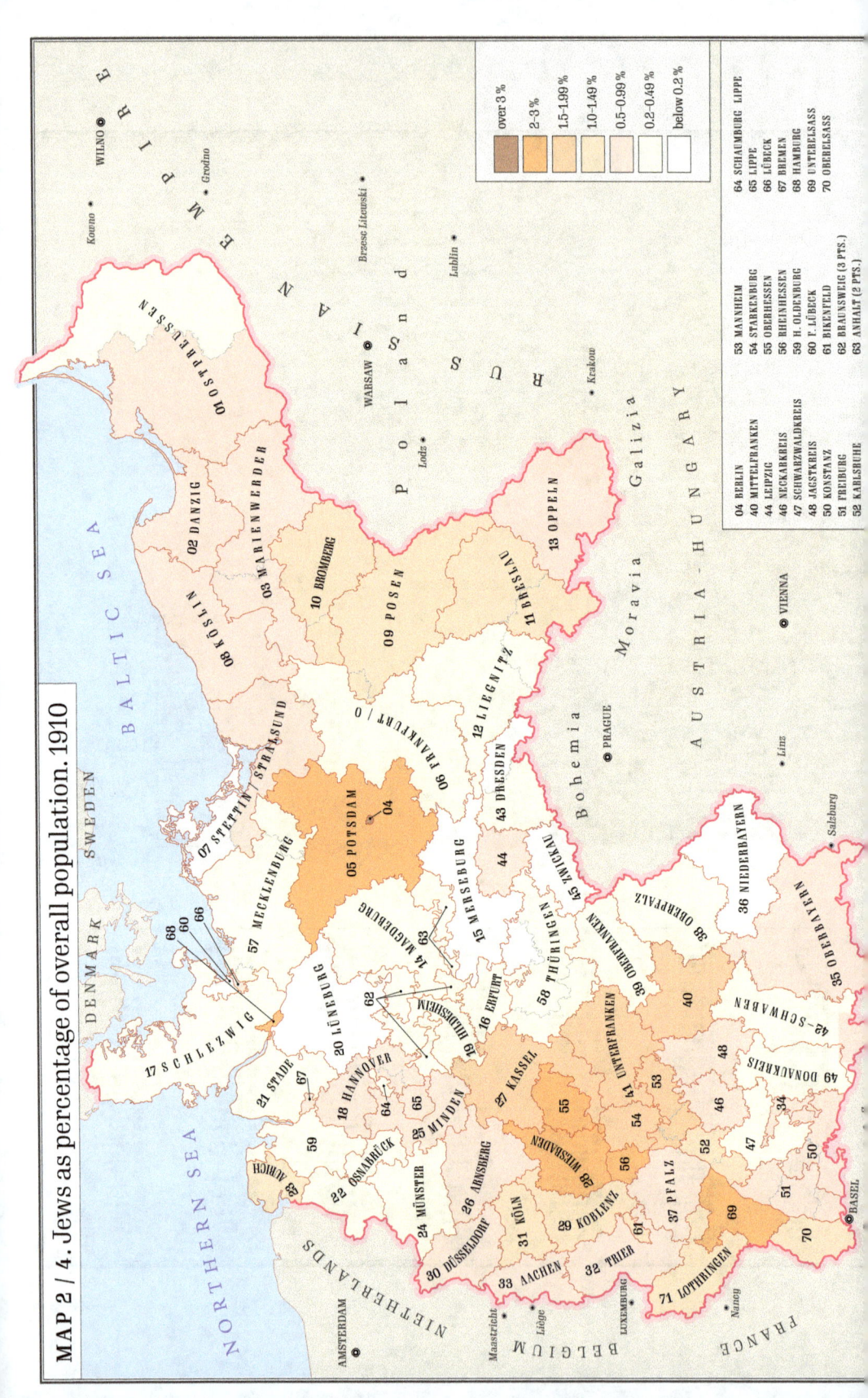

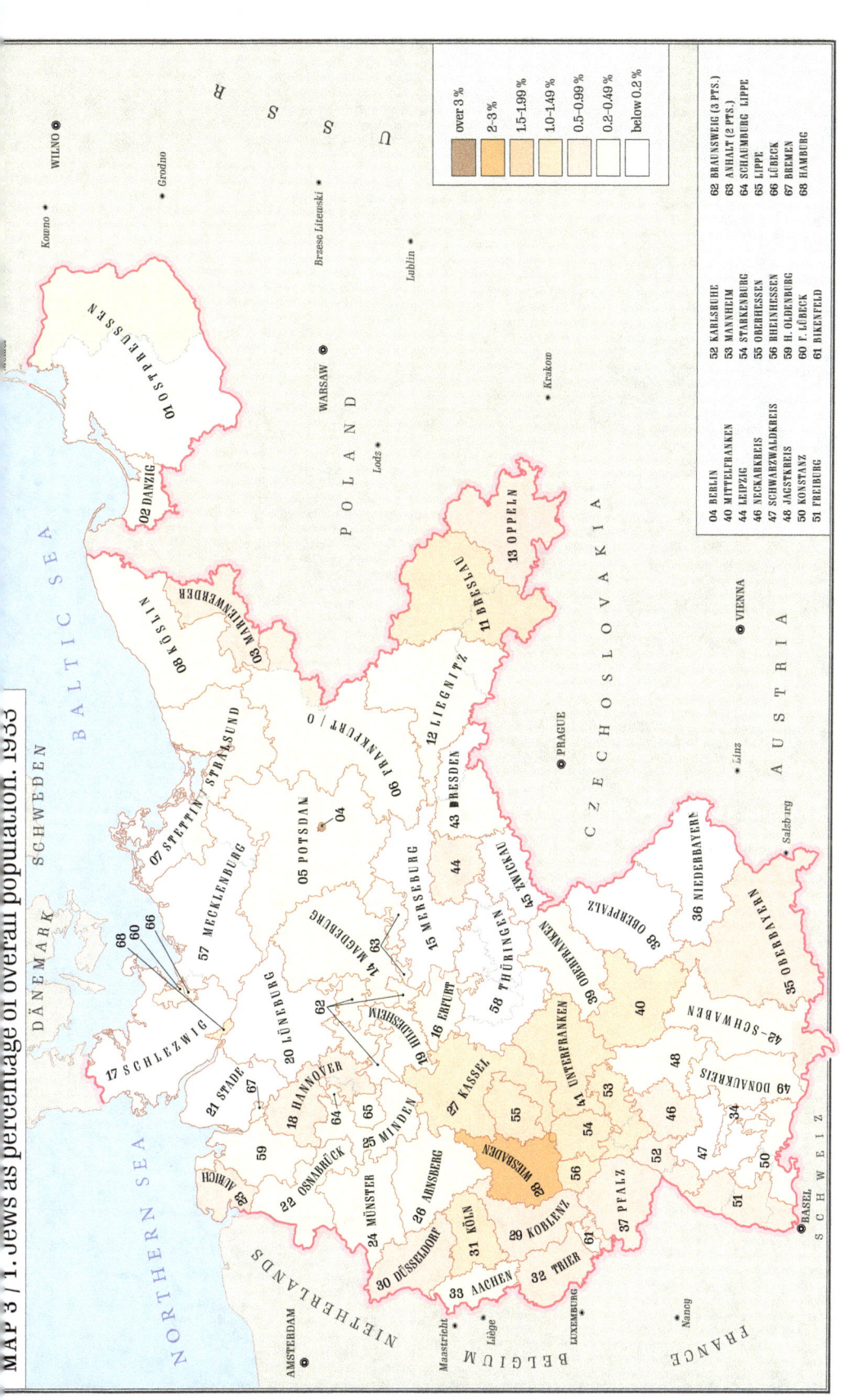

MAP 3 / 1. Jews as percentage of overall population, 1933

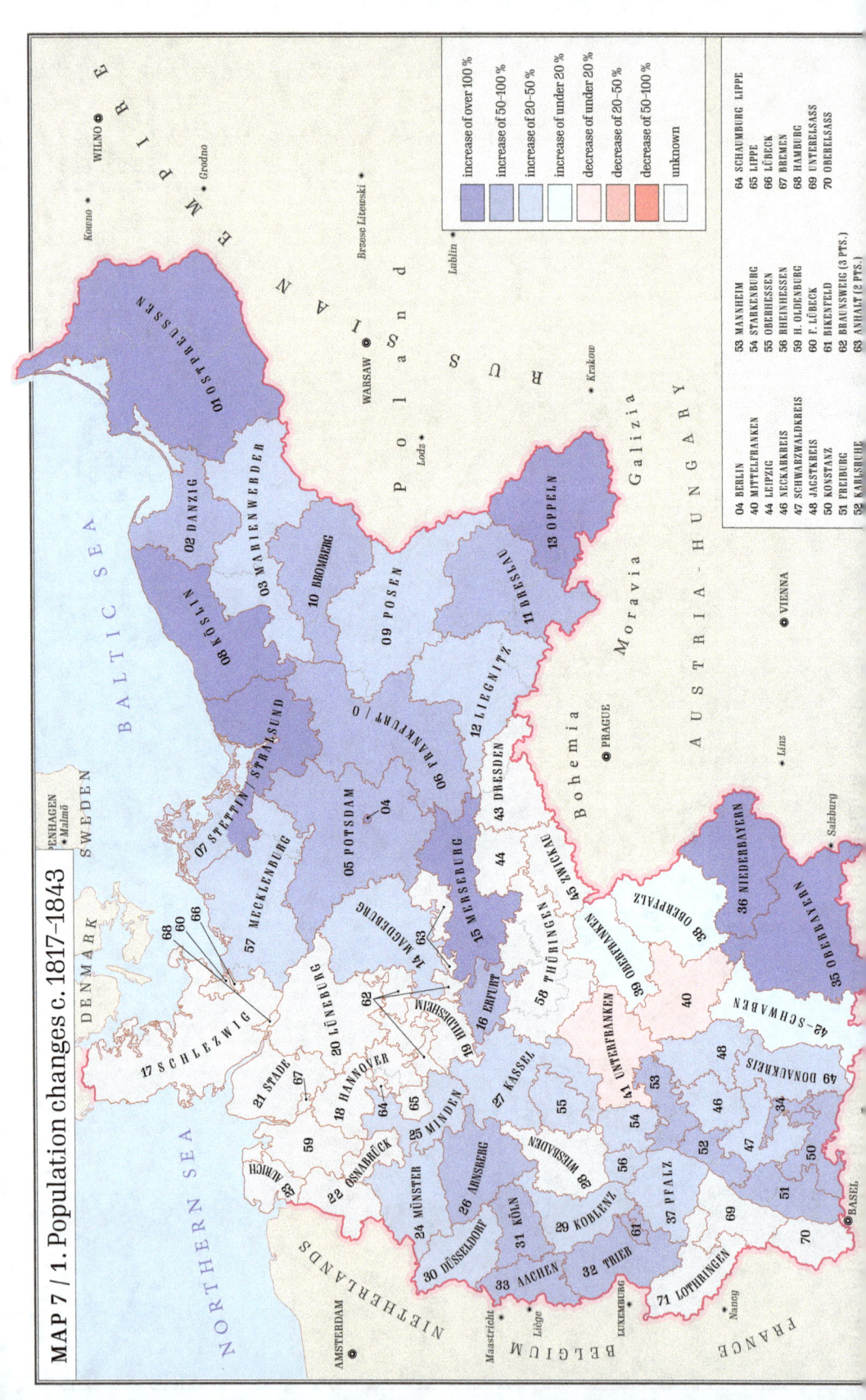
MAP 7 / 1. Population changes c. 1817–1843

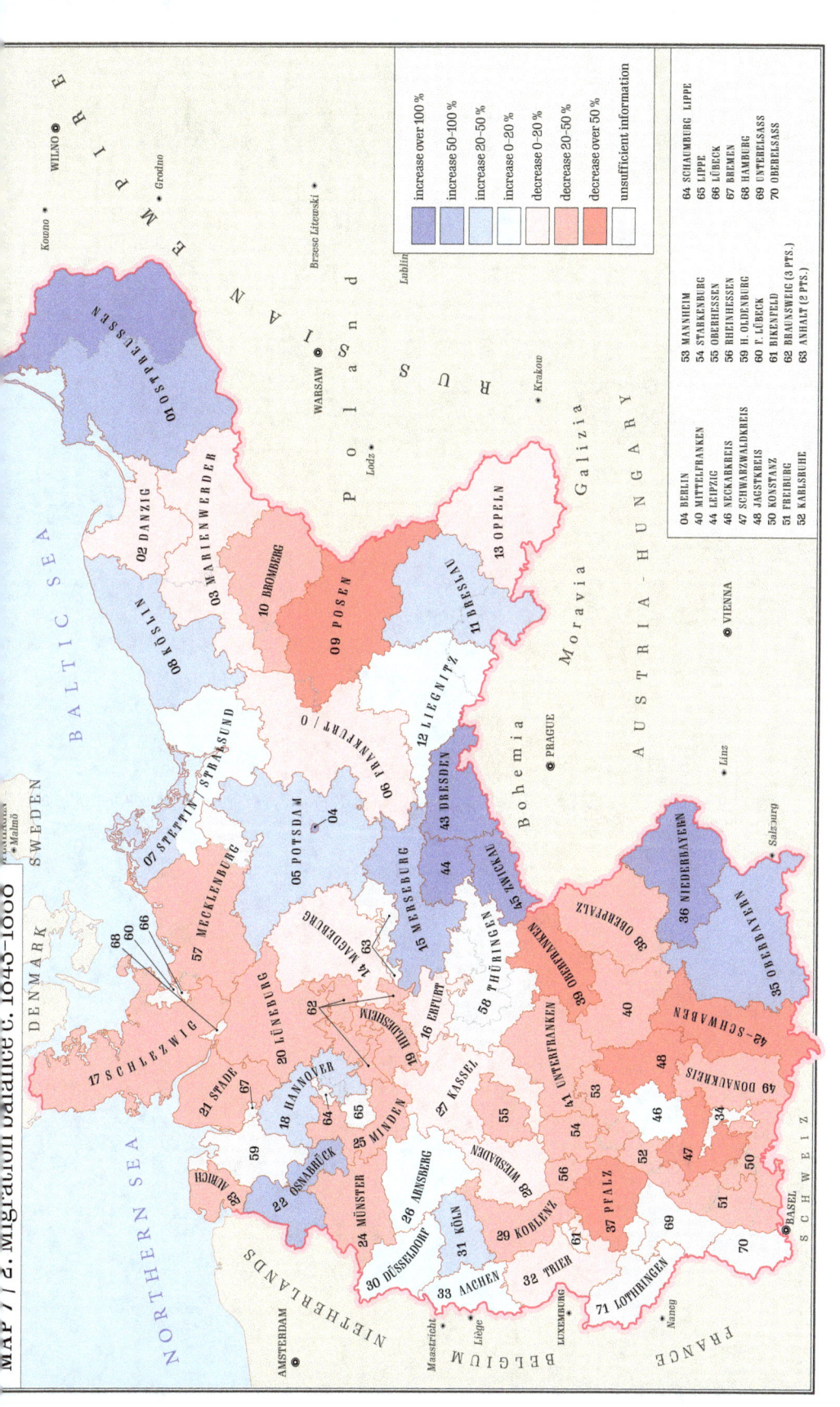

MAP 7 / 2. Migration balance c. 1845-1866

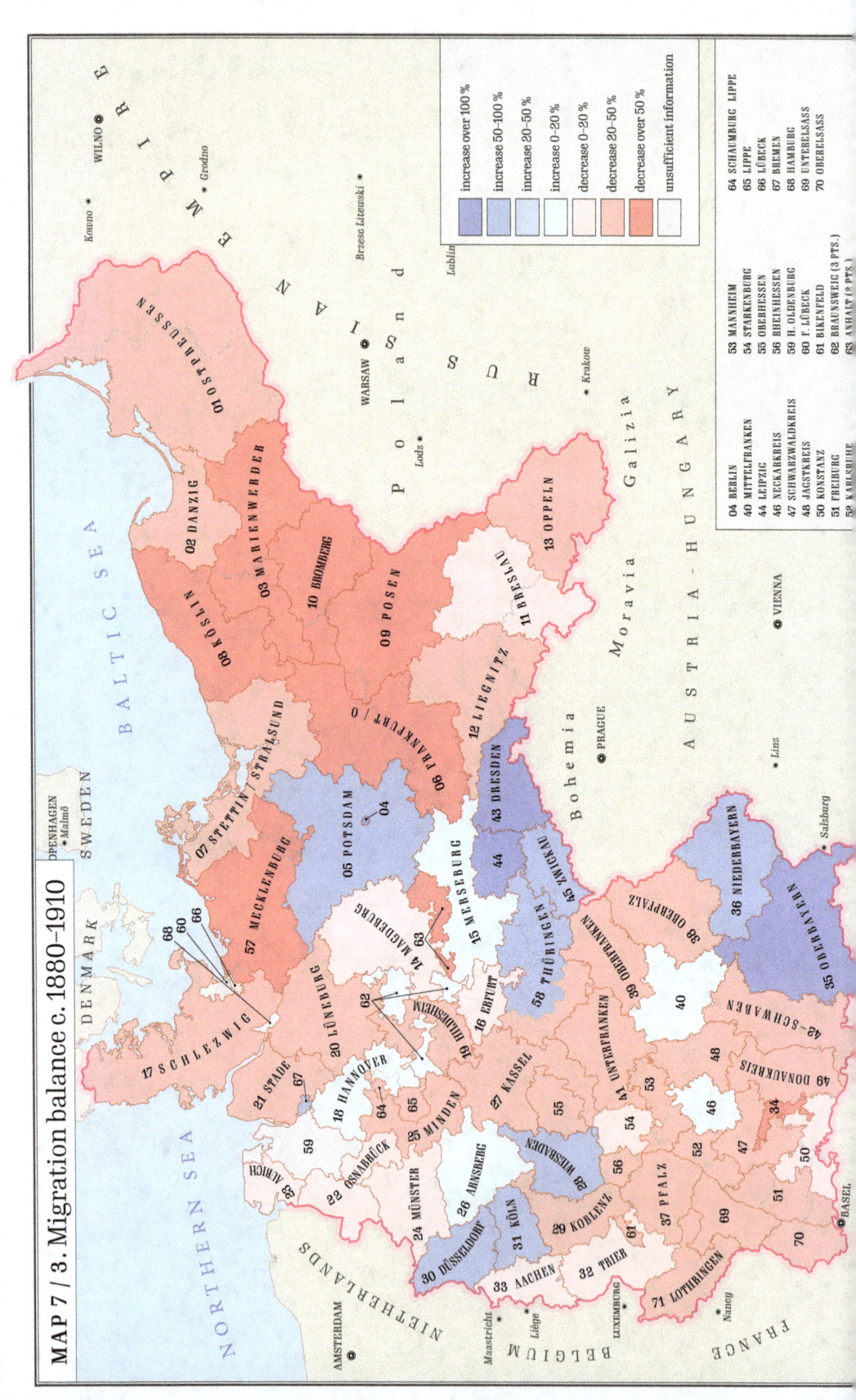

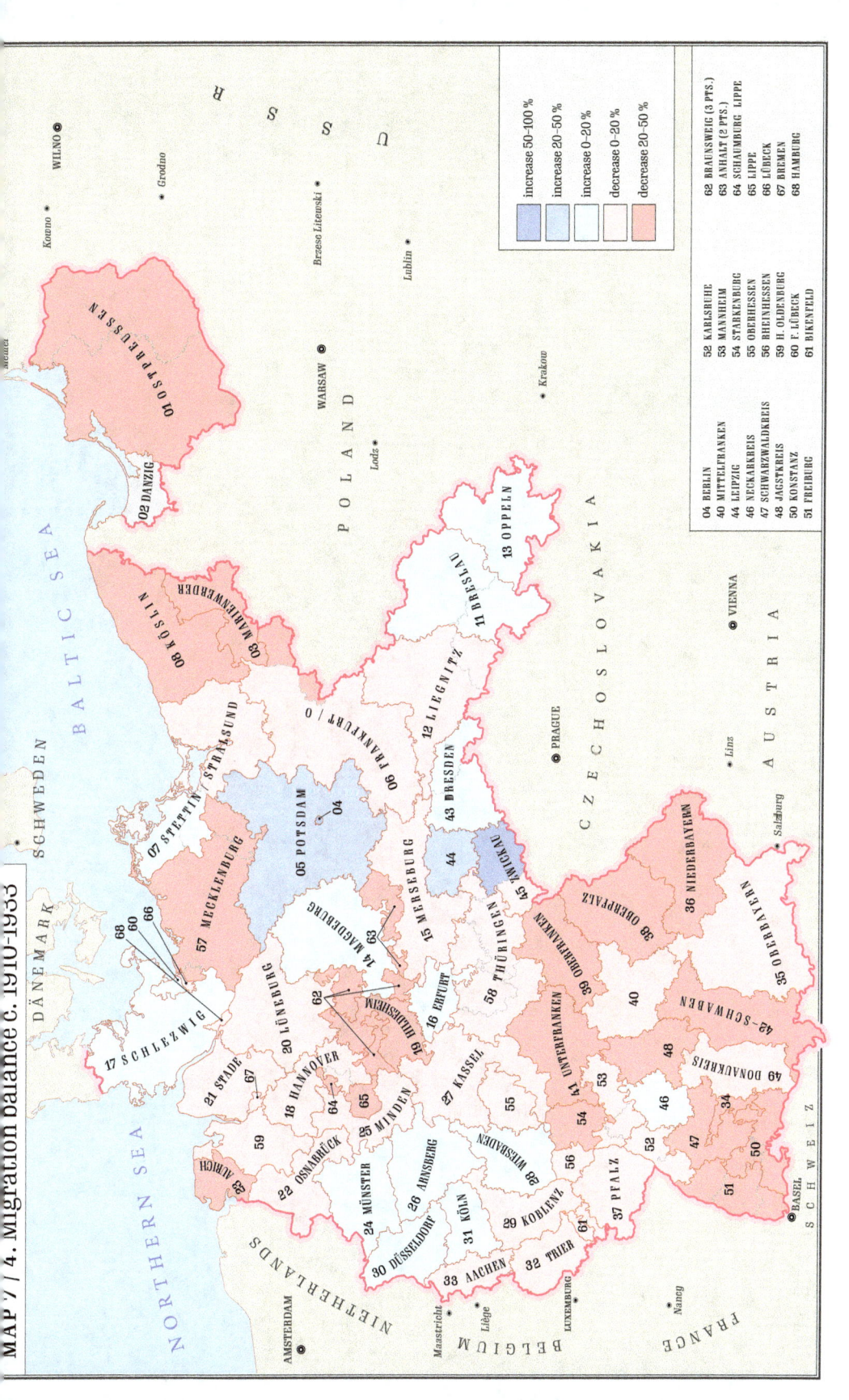
MAP 7 / 4. Migration balance c. 1910-1933

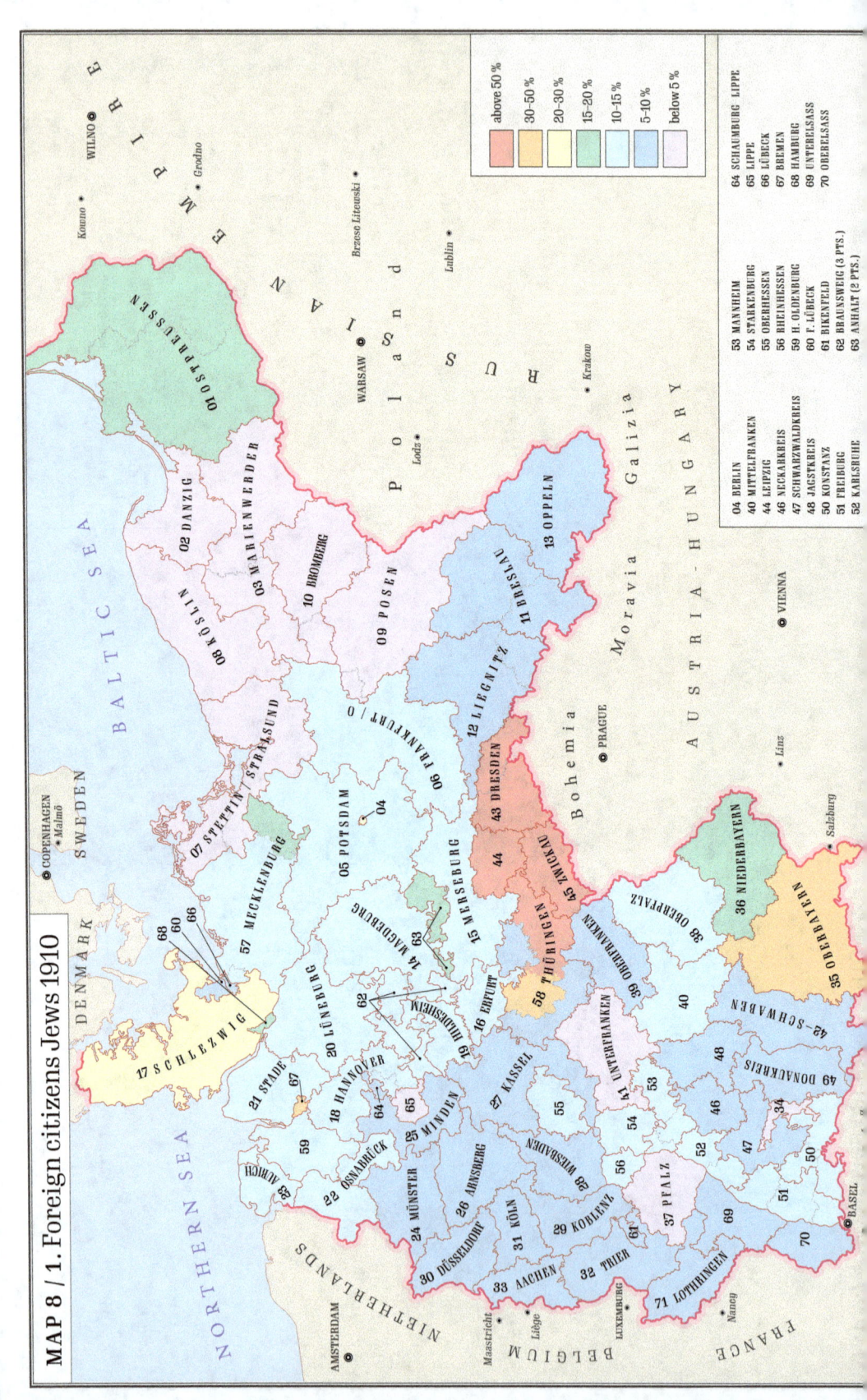

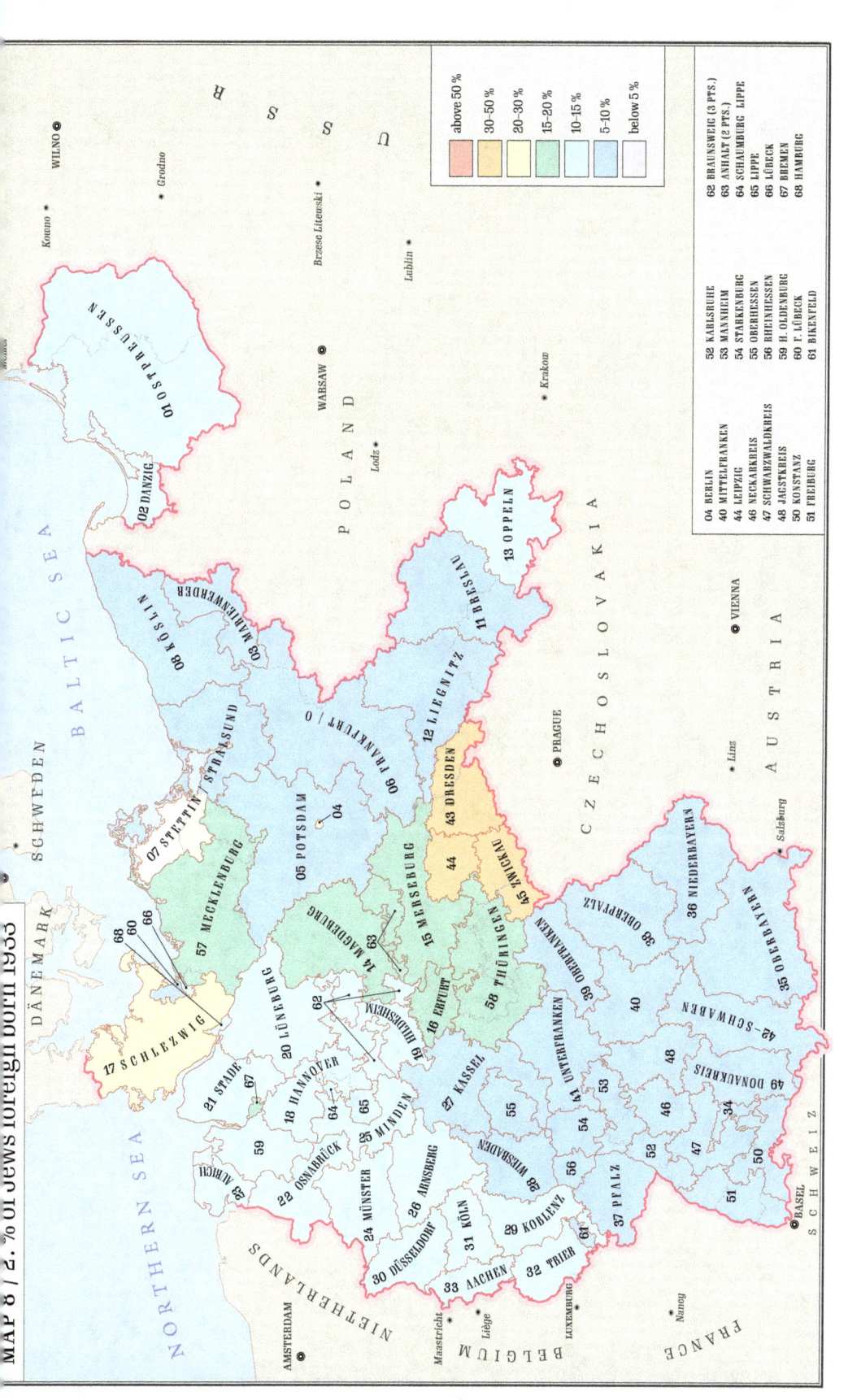

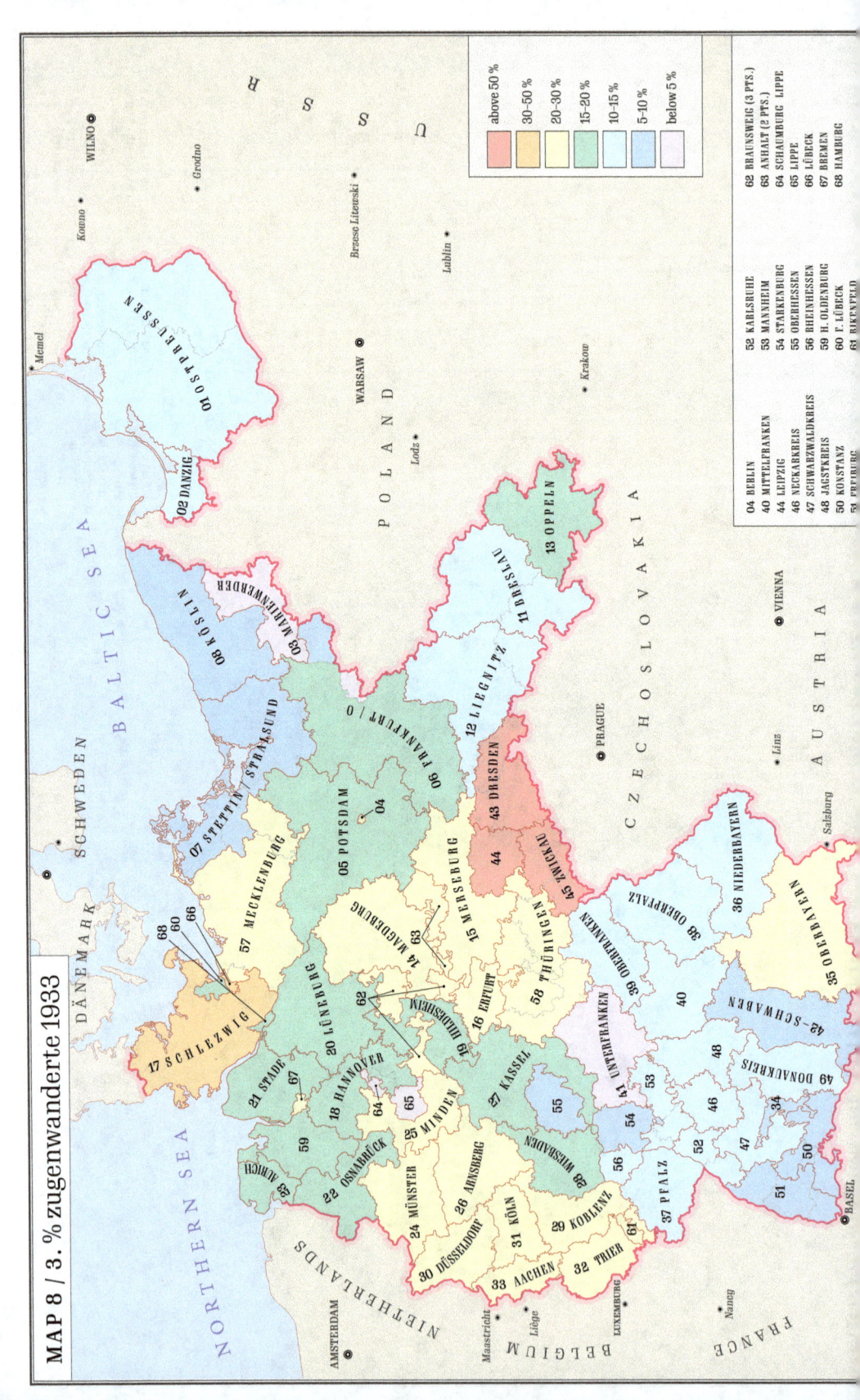

MAP 8 / 3. % zugewanderte 1933

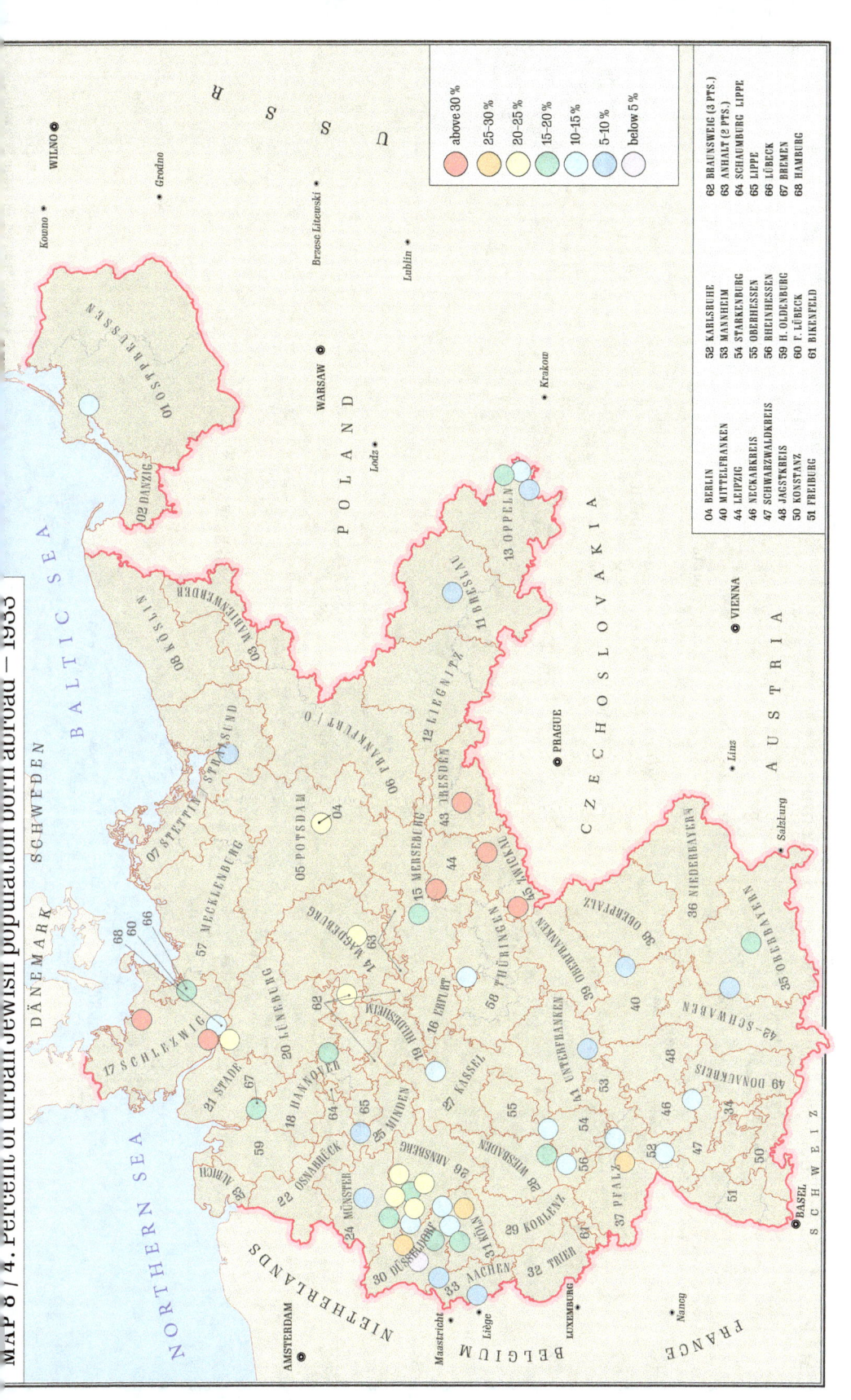

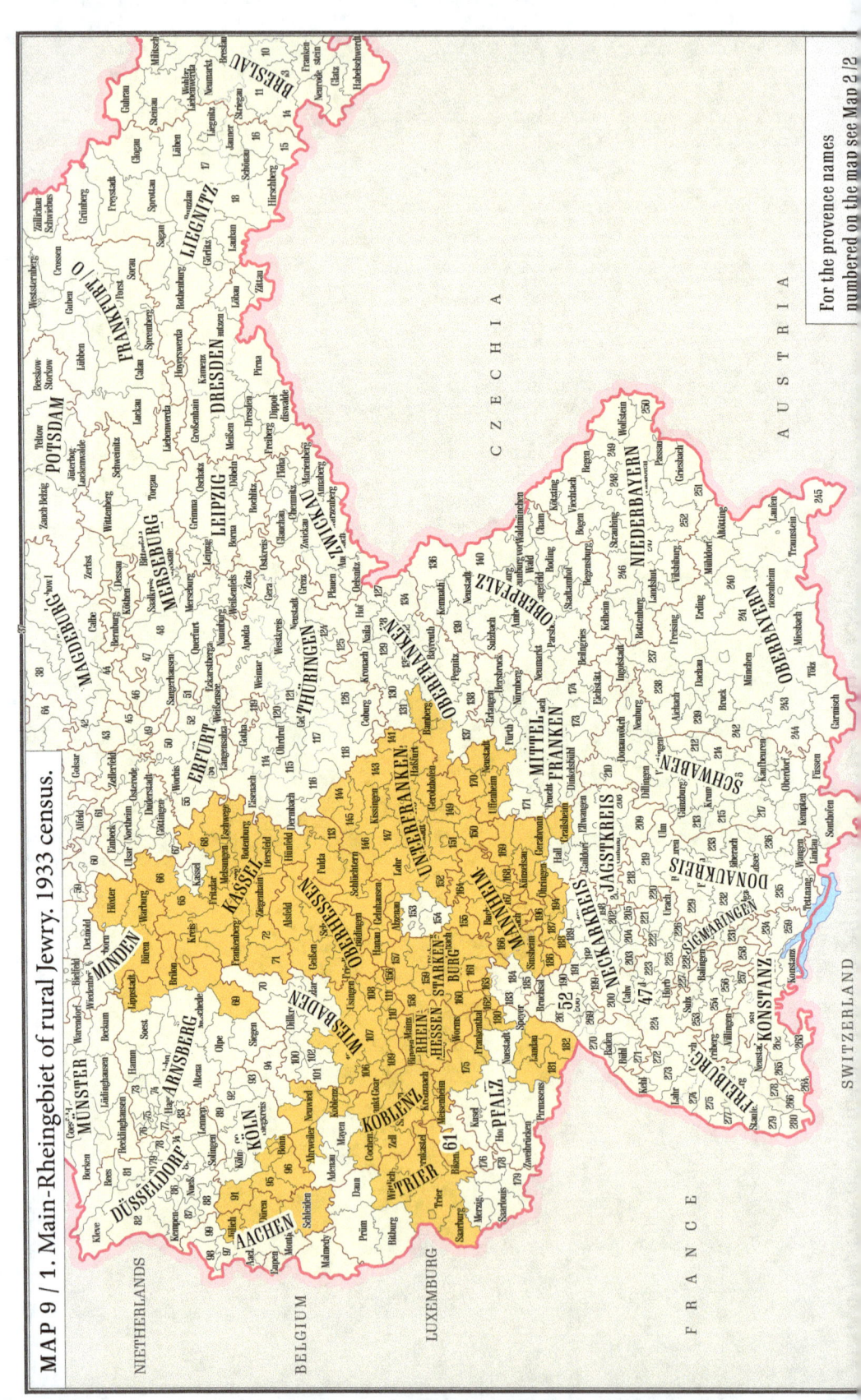

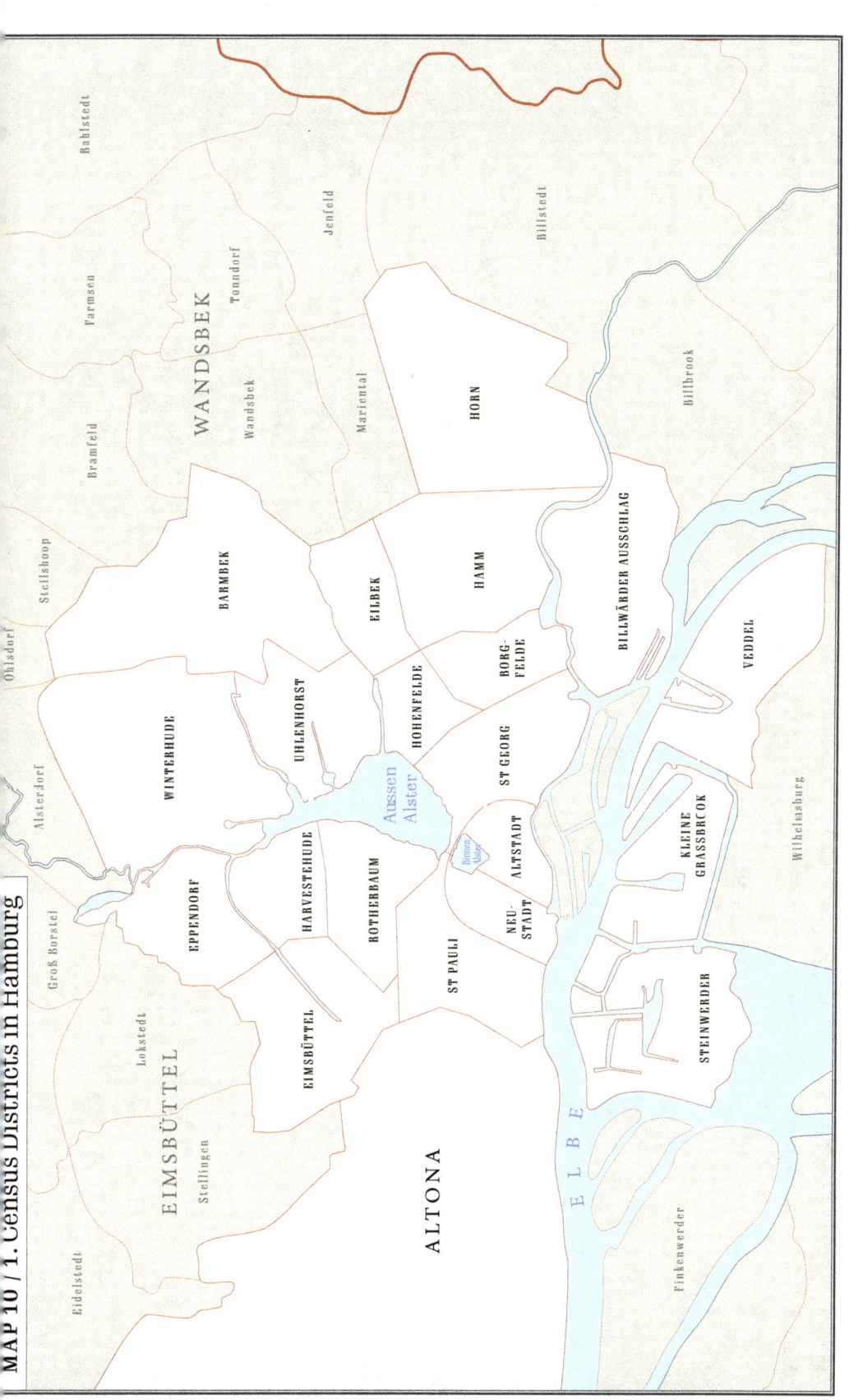

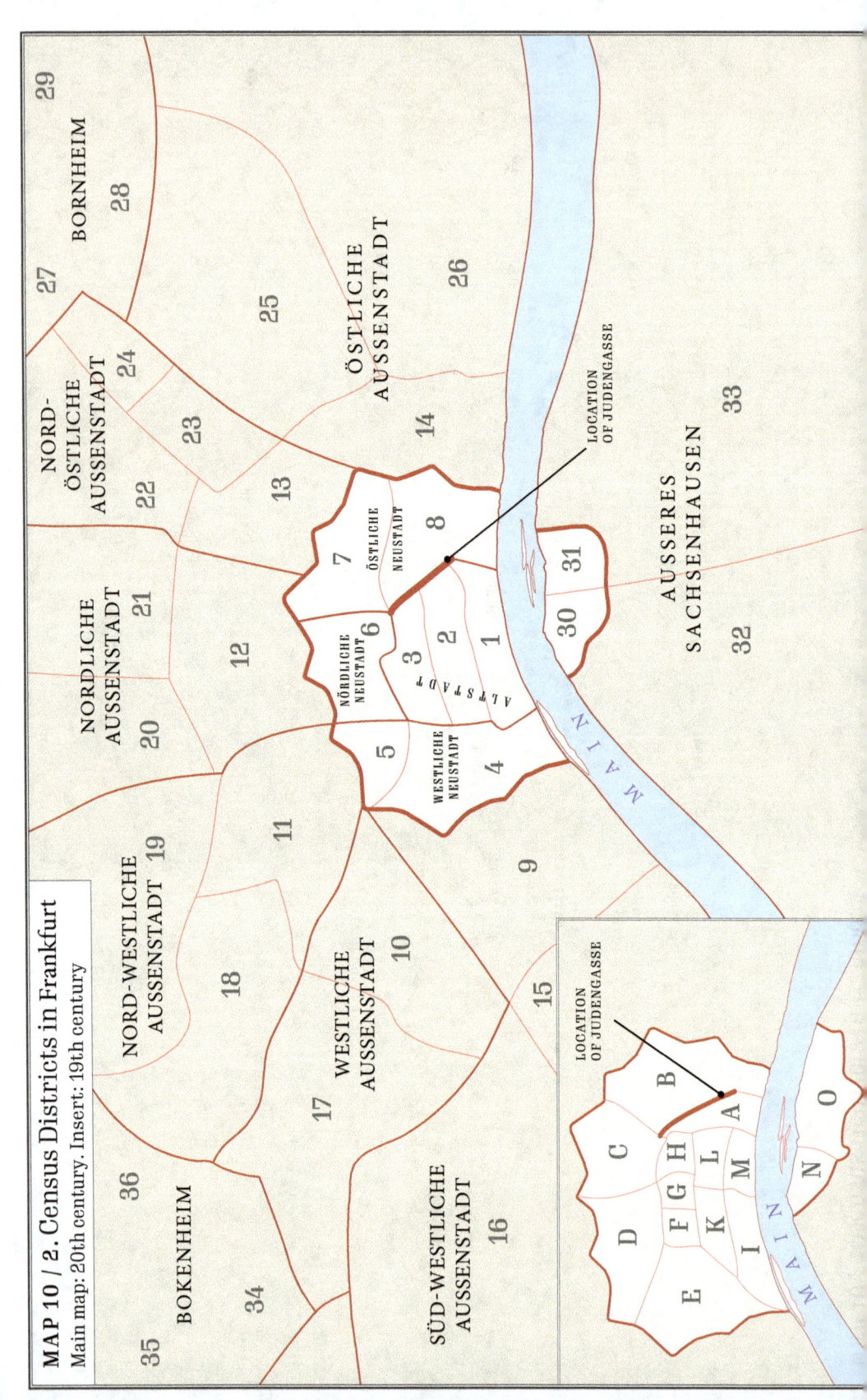

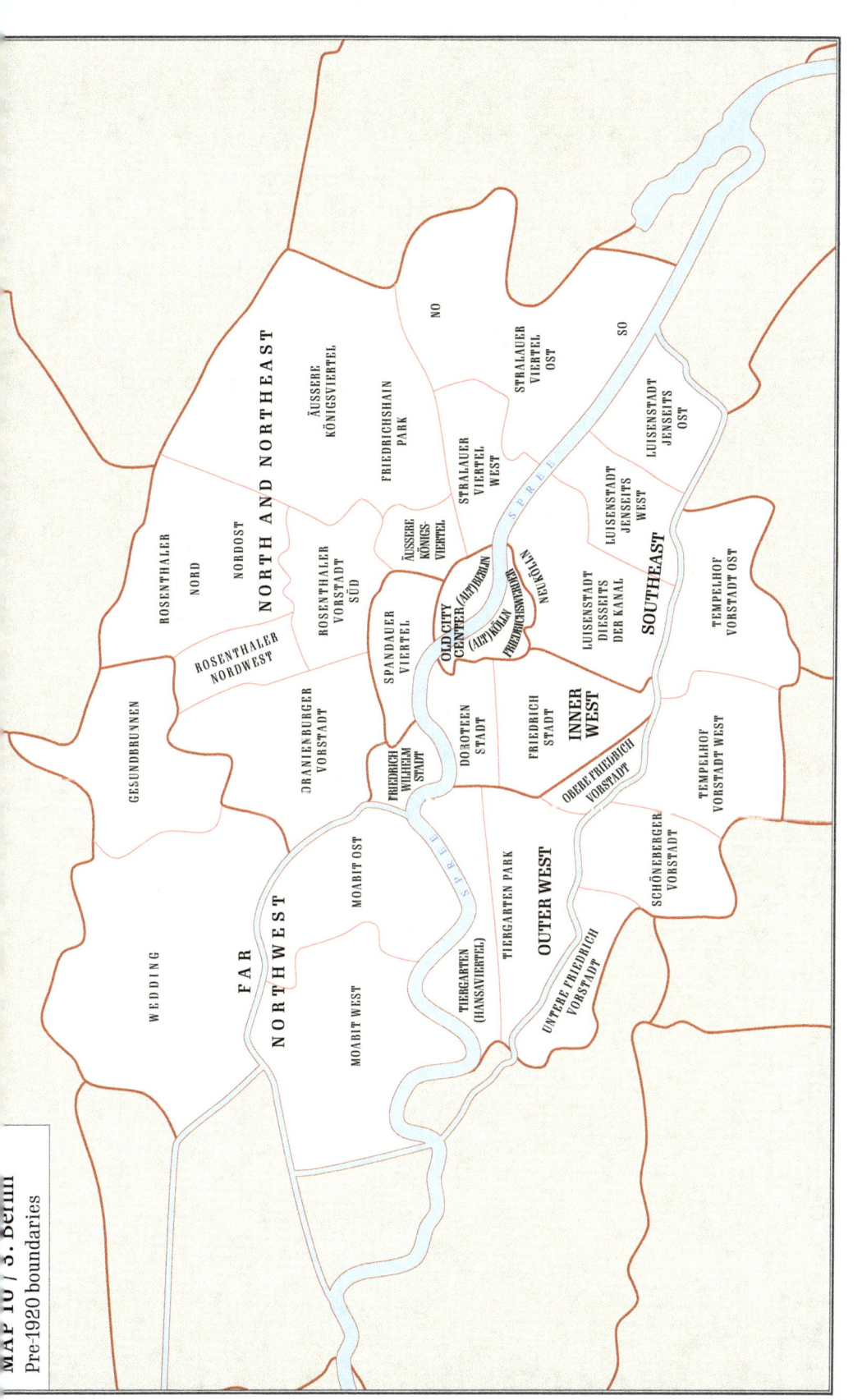

MAP 10 / 3. Berlin
Pre-1920 boundaries

MAP 10 / 3B. Greater Berlin Districts
1920–1938

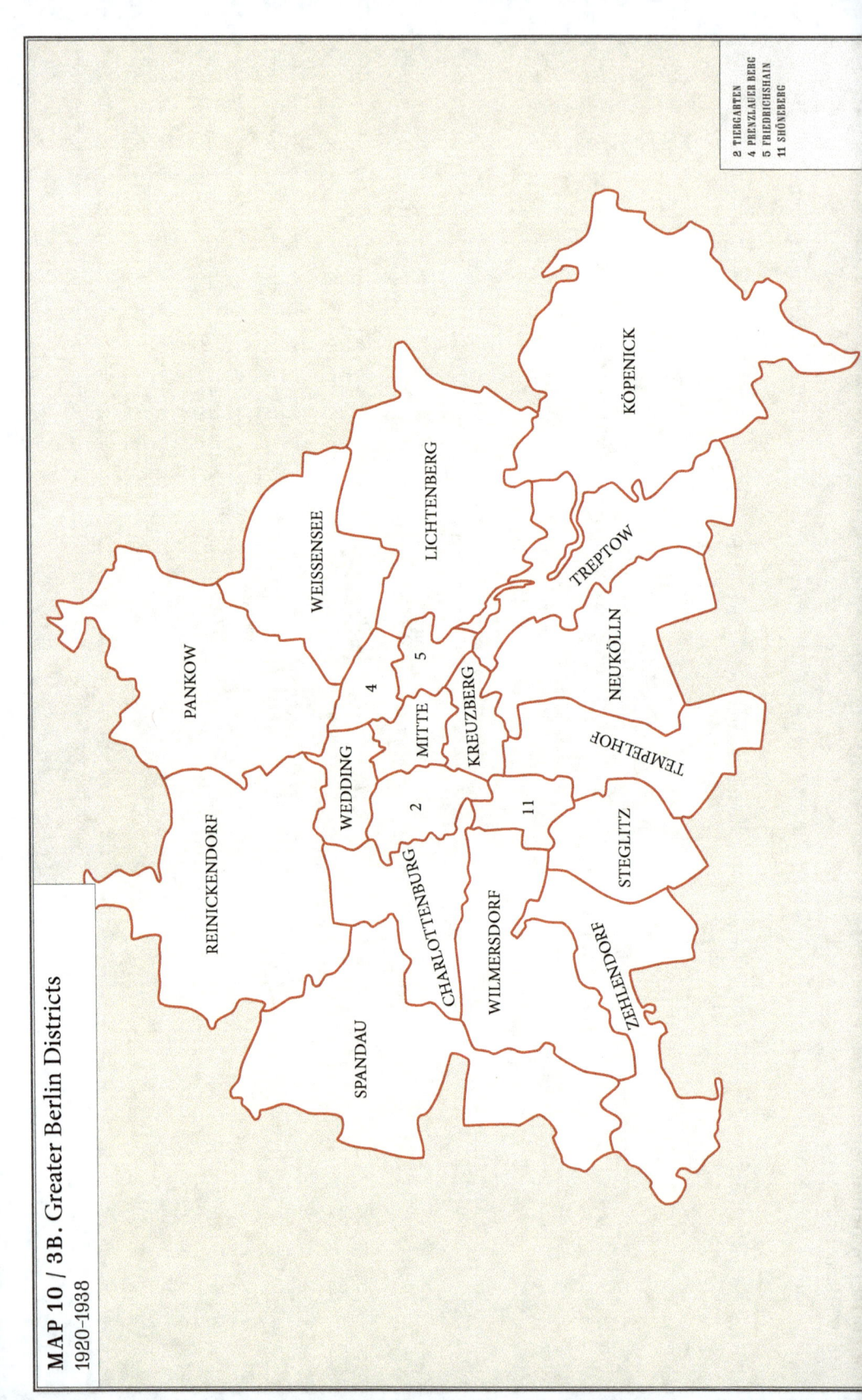

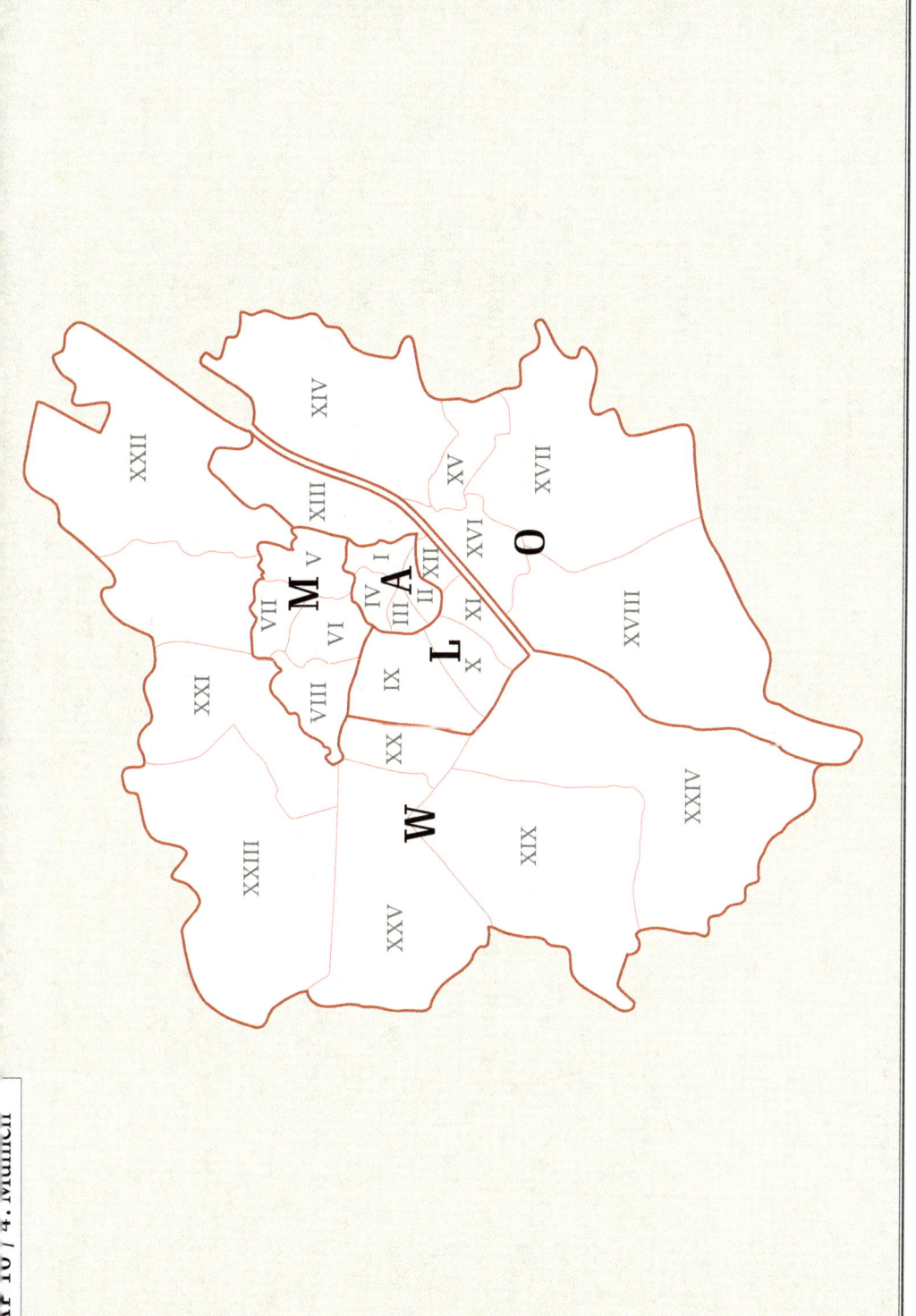

MAP 10 / 4. Cologne. 1933

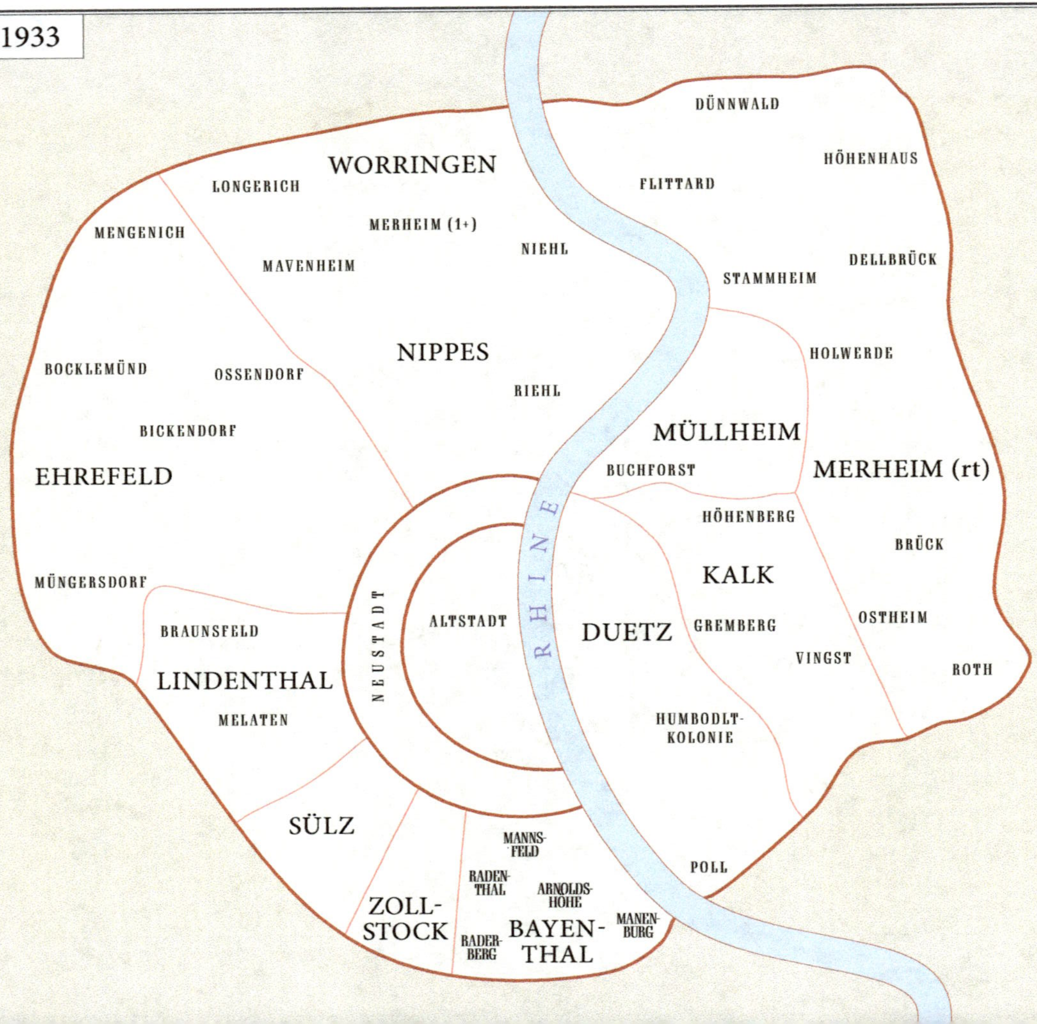

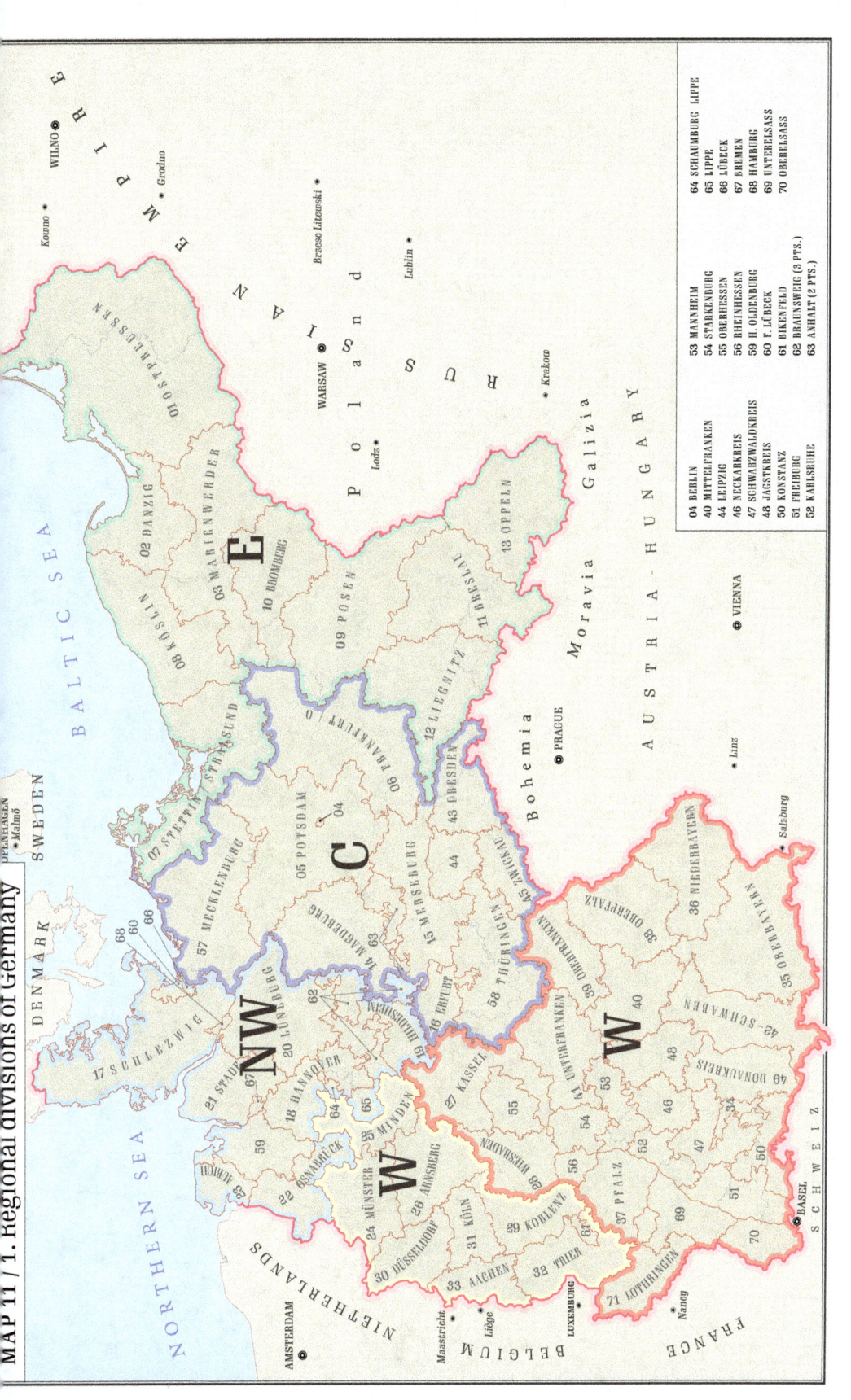

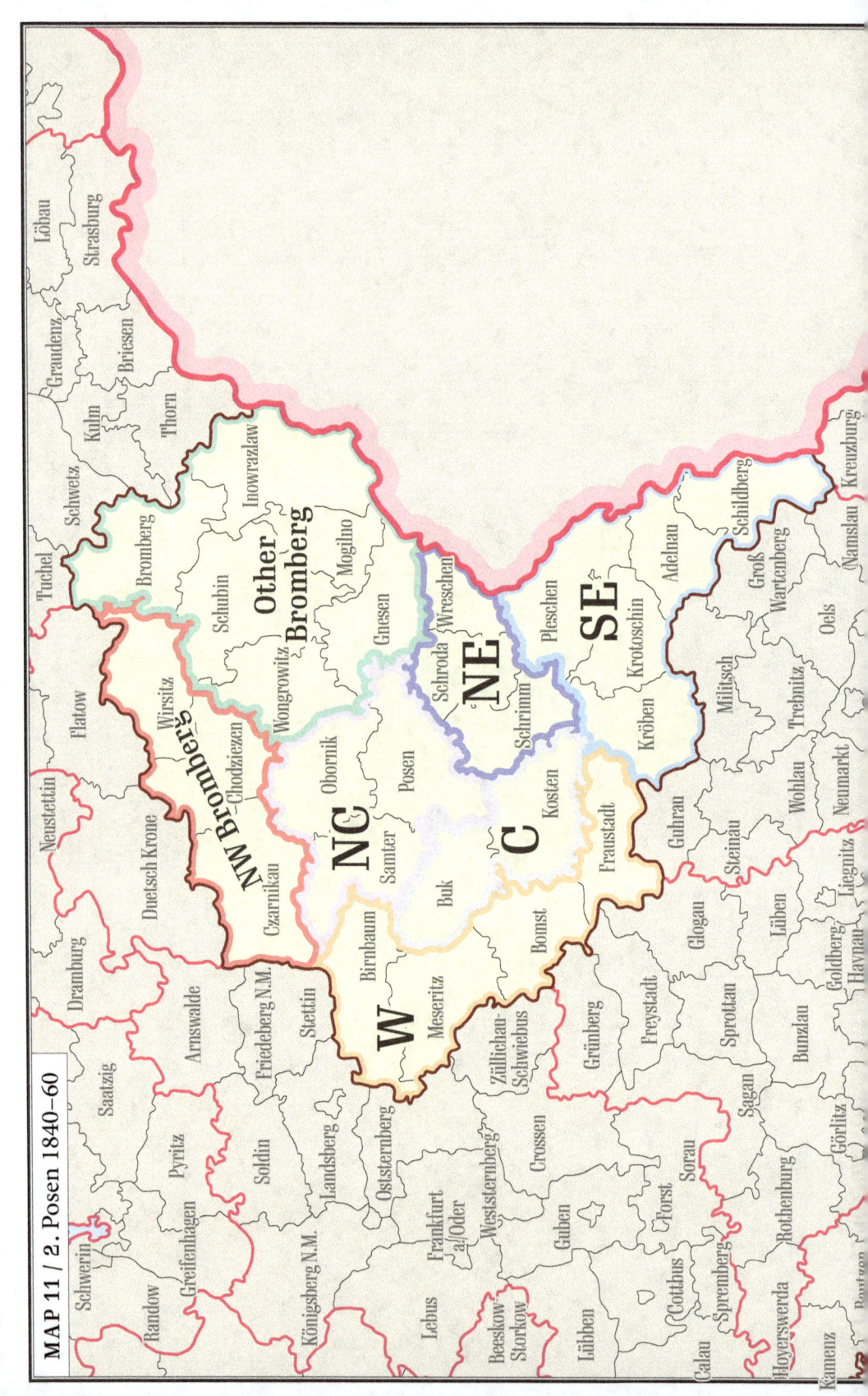

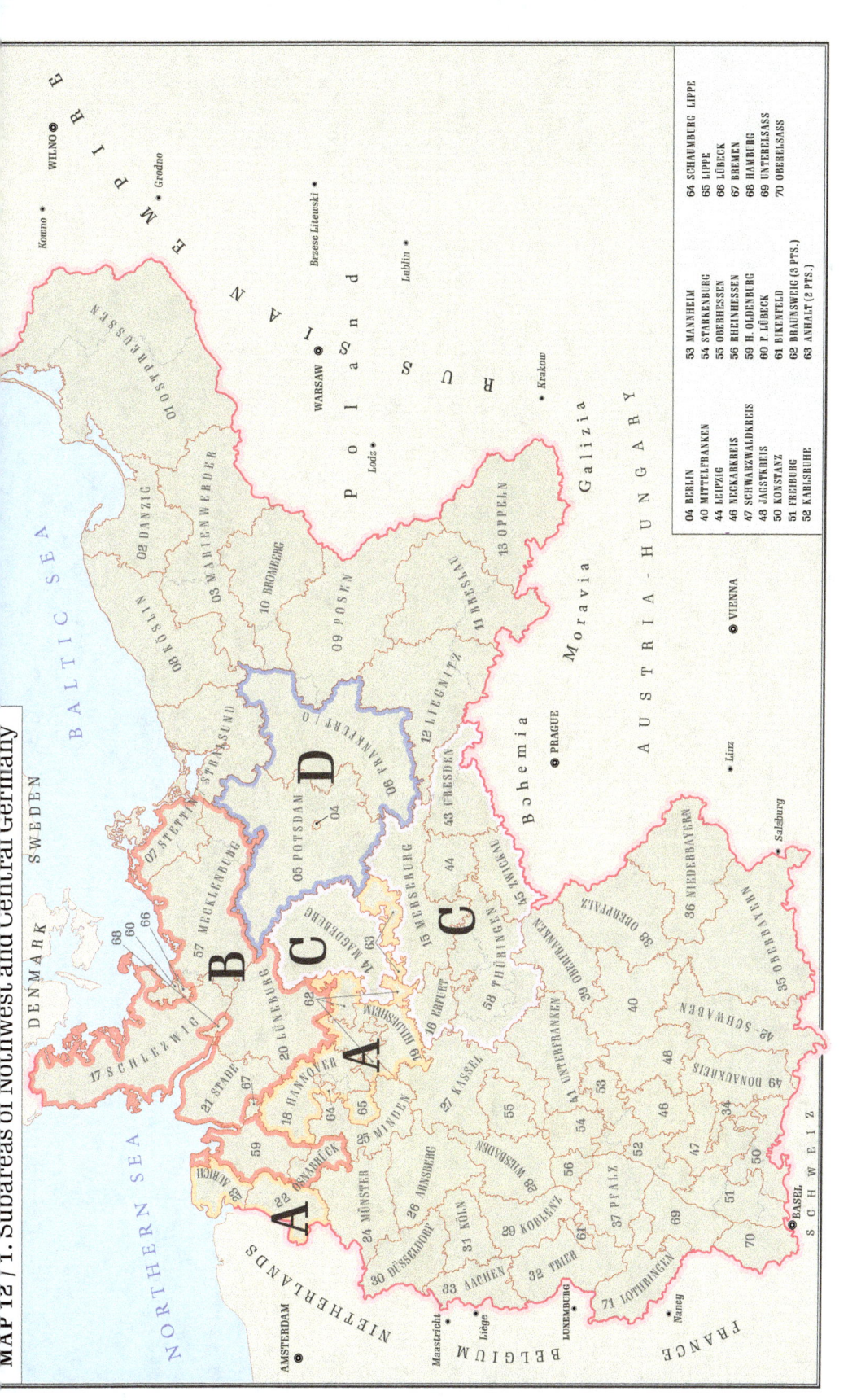

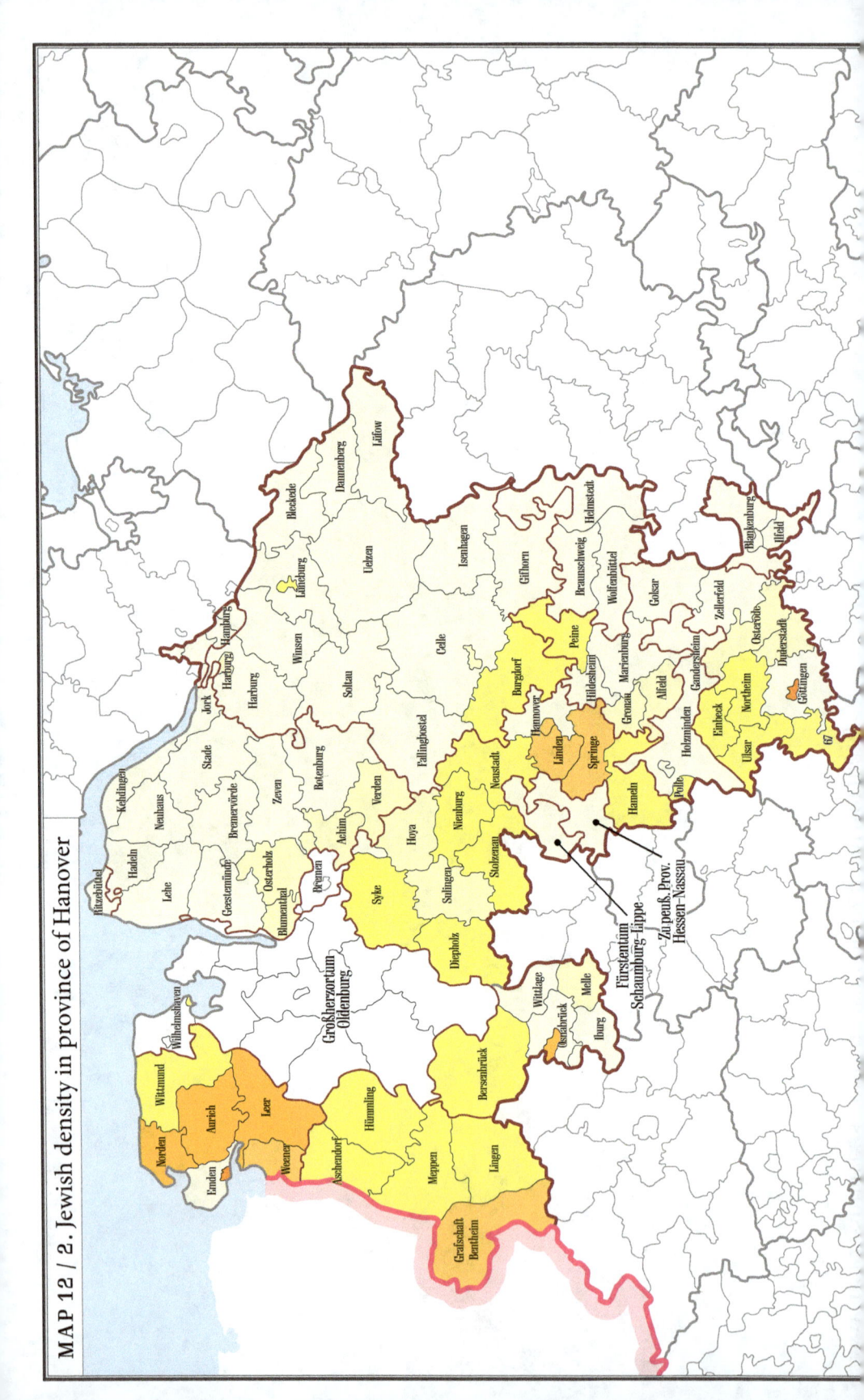

www.ingramcontent.com/pod-product-compliance
Lightning Source LLC
Chambersburg PA
CBHW070752300426
44111CB00014B/2383